THE STANDARD BOOK OF

American Antique Furniture

THE STANDARD BOOK OF

American

Antique Furniture

ABRIDGED FROM THE TWO-VOLUME EDITION
OF "AMERICAN ANTIQUE FURNITURE"

BY EDGAR G. MILLER, JR.

GREYSTONE PRESS   NEW YORK, N. Y.

This encyclopedic volume represents a lifetime of devotion to the study of antiques by its author, Edgar G. Miller, Jr. Mr. Miller was famous as a jurist, scholar, and writer, besides being a noted collector of antiques. His primary purpose in writing this book was to provide a helpful guide for everyone interested in antiques, particularly the beginner. How well he has succeeded is readily apparent on every page.

THE PUBLISHERS

CONTENTS

THE STANDARD BOOK OF
American Antique Furniture

Chapter I

CONCERNING THIS BOOK

Section 1.   A book for everyone
Section 2.   The text and the notes
Section 3.   The illustrations
Section 4.   Methods of treating the subject

Section 1. A book for everyone.—So many books have been written on the subject of American antique furniture that it is proper in this first chapter to mention the particular features of this volume; and the writer hopes that this chapter will be fully examined in order that the reader may understand the plan and scope of the book and have pleasure in reading it.

As appears in the preface, and as suggested by the name of this section, this book is meant for those who wish to know the important features of the subject, without going into details in which they are not interested, and yet will prove of equal value to persons who already have a solid background in antiques.

With this in view, technical words[1] of the cabinet maker are not used to any greater extent than is absolutely necessary. The amateur reader or collector is not often familiar with technical words and does not care to burden his mind

---

1.   Certain non-technical words often used in connection with antique furniture may be mentioned. The subject of antiques seems to excite in some writers an ambition to use unusual words.

A.   The word "Colonial" is often used erroneously. The true meaning is, of course, "pertaining or belonging to a colony; specifically, in American history, relating to the thirteen British colonies which became the United States of America, or to their period." Thus "Colonial architecture" means "the style of architecture prevalent in the American colonies just before and at the time of the Revolution"; Century Dictionary. But the word "Colonial" is often mistakenly applied to the heavy Empire style of furniture made over half a century after the colonies ceased to be colonies and became the United States. A misnamed "Colonial" sofa—one of the most massive pieces of the American Empire style furniture—would never have been tolerated by the builders of the fine "Colonial" mansions of Maryland and other States.

B.   At present there is a fad for using the words "exotic" and "provenance" in regard to furniture, instead of the simpler words, "foreign" and "place of origin."

C.   The Latin word "circa," sometimes abbreviated "c." is also popular at present, instead of the word "about"; thus, a chair is said to have been made "circa 1780," instead of "about 1780."

D.   A word frequently used in an erroneous, or perhaps an enlarged, sense is "Replica." See Webster's New International Dictionary and the synonyms under "Duplicate." The Century Dictionary defines "Replica" as "a work of art made in exact likeness of another and by the same artist, differing from a copy in that it is held to have the same right as the first made to be considered an original work." If Chippendale himself made an exact duplicate of one of his chairs, the second chair would be a replica of the first; but nowadays, especially in catalogues, a recent copy of a Chippendale style chair may be given the learned name of "replica" instead of the commonplace name of "copy." However, the dictionaries also define the word as meaning merely a copy; so that there seems to be no word meaning solely a copy or duplicate made by the original artist. (*Note 1 continued on page 8*) with them. Whenever it is necessary to use such words they are explained at least once, generally in connection with an illustration so that they may be well understood by looking at the illustration. They are often in quotation marks as an indication of their technical character and are listed in the Index, so that they may easily be found when desired.

Moreover it is presumed that the amateur collector desires the elementary matters to be stated as well as the more advanced matters; therefore certain things are mentioned which may seem, to persons already familiar with the subject, to be self–evident and obvious, and not worth while to be stated. But the aim of this book is to provide an answer to almost every question which an amateur collector may wish to ask; excepting, however, questions as to the money value of specific articles, which is an ever–changing matter and beyond the scope of this book.

(Note 1, *continued*)

E.   A much overworked word is "sophisticated." Webster's New International Dictionary defines this word as "experienced in, or pertaining to, the more artificial phases of life; worldly–wise"; and "sophistication" is defined as the "state of being involved or subtle; especially, state of being without directness, simplicity or naturalness; artificiality."

F.   The word "prototype" is defined in the Century Dictionary as "a primitive form; an original or model after which anything is formed." Thus it may be said that a certain early chair in the Chippendale style is the "prototype" of later chairs of the same type. This is a favorite word in the magazines, and is often used loosely.

G.   A word occasionally used is "mobiliary." In the great English "Murray's Dictionary," and in the supplement to the Century Dictionary, this word is defined as "of, or pertaining to, household furniture." It is connected with the word "mobile," the principal definition of which is "movable; not fixed or stationary," and is thus applicable to furniture. The French word "mobilier" means "a set of furniture."

H.   Almost all of the usual adjectives and words of praise having been exhausted, or rendered commonplace by constant usage, other words and expressions are now often applied to articles of antique furniture. For example, a portion of a piece has been called "daring," and even "dramatic." "Honesty" of design is noticed in some pieces, and others are "naïve." A leg is a "triumph." A certain desk shows "raciness." A fine piece of mahogany is "suave." Another object shows much "subtlety." When these words become overworked, others of an even more meaningless character will no doubt be found or invented.

I.   The words "beauty" and "beautiful" are so vague in meaning that they, and also the word "pretty," are not used in this book in connection with articles of antique furniture, except in quotations. Whether an article has "beauty" or is "beautiful" or "pretty" depends upon one's personal taste, which may be based upon nothing or upon study and contemplation of the best. In some cases even the adjectives in the preceding paragraph may be more appropriate.

J.   In some books there is a "glossary," that is, a collection of explanations of words not in general use, as those of an art or science. In this book there is no need for a glossary because the definitions of the few technical words are given when those words are first used, and in the Index the pages on which the technical words first appear are cited. In some of the glossaries many technical words are defined by other technical words equally unknown to the amateur.

K.   Some years ago, before modern styles of certain garments were in vogue, the use of the word "legs" was thought not quite elegant in polite society, even with reference to a chair or table. A story is told of an artistic but modest young man of Baltimore who was calling upon a witty and somewhat worldly-wise young lady. In the drawing-room the young man admired a handsome chair in the Chippendale style, with finely carved legs, and remarked to the young lady: "That chair has lovely . . (pause) . . limbs." The young lady replied, "Oh, Mr. B., how shocking to use that word in my presence—you should say 'members.'"

The selection of articles for illustration in this book should be referred to at this point, and is also mentioned in section 3. The connoisseur is familiar with all of the articles which are commonly seen, and is generally interested only in rare and valuable examples.[2] The amateur collector, however, is mainly interested in antique furniture of a more usual kind; he is not apt to be concerned with articles which are seldom seen outside of a museum,[3] and which he will probably never have the opportunity of purchasing. The familiar and home-like furniture of our forefathers is the most interesting and attractive to most of us; and moreover not all of our ancestors were able to purchase and leave to their descendants many handsome and expensive pieces. For these reasons not much attention is given to very rare and unusual articles; for example, but little of the furniture of the Pilgrim Century, (1600 to 1700), appears in the illustrations.[4] The aim is to present mainly such articles as may be seen in our homes, and which are prized for their design and workmanship and because of their association with former generations of our own people; always, however, favoring the best pieces and not merely the old ones.

In many of the comments and notes on articles shown in this book there are "cross-references" to other articles having similar or the same features. For example, the cane chair No. 35 has the characteristic spiral parts of the period of about 1650-1700, and in the notes on that chair are references to other articles of the same period in which similar spirals are seen, such as the table No. 1279, which

2. In his book on "Antique Furniture," American edition published by G. P. Putnam's Sons, Mr. Fred. W. Burgess makes the following remarks on page 174: "The advanced connoisseur is apt to become somewhat narrow in his views, in that as he gradually discards first one piece and then another in favor of finer specimens, he loses interest in the pieces that delight a less advanced collector. In that way he gets out of the common work, and eventually seeks pleasure only in extravagant expositions of style, or in the specimens of which there are few, and probably never were many, examples."

And on pages 146-147 the same writer says that "it is an unfortunate fact that when writing on furniture, or describing so-called typical pieces of well-known makers, the examples quoted and referred to, and even illustrated, are exceptionally fine specimens. Some of the illustrations in this book have been chosen because they are typical of the actual furniture used in (English) middle class homes throughout the eighteenth century, rather than for their exceptional grandeur and suitability as show pieces in a museum."

One book on American antique furniture begins with a photograph of a Flemish cabinet of the sixteenth century; and in other books are illustrations of huge and magnificent English bedsteads of a very early period. Such articles are of course important and valuable, but are of little interest to the amateur collector, as they are seldom seen and perhaps never offered for sale.

3. "Museum piece." In antique shops this expression is generally used to convey the idea that the piece is worthy of being exhibited in a museum of some kind; this is of course a vague expression, depending upon the standard of excellence in a particular museum.

A "museum piece" has been humorously defined as "any object that has been presented by a donor whom it is thought injudicious to offend"; "Antiques," October, 1930, page 299. Another such definition is "an undesirable piece accepted in hopes of a nice legacy from the same giver."

An article entitled "The Museum and the Collector. What is a museum piece?", by Mr. Charles Over Cornelius, of the Metropolitan Museum of Art in New York, is in "Antiques," April, 1922, page 180.

4. The volume of Mr. Wallace Nutting, entitled "Furniture of the Pilgrim Century," Revised Edition, 1924, should be consulted with regard to American furniture of this period.

dates from the 1650-1700 period. From these cross-references the reader will observe that this spiral feature is a characteristic of the period and will thus be able to approximate the date of other articles which may have the same spiral design. Another example is in the comments on the desks Nos. 803 and 805 in which attention is called to the inlaid American eagle and stars; in those comments the cross-references refer to other articles of the same period in which the eagle and stars also appear. These cross-references may perhaps be too numerous, but the writer thinks they will be helpful and interesting.

Many advanced collectors, having almost exhausted the study of the styles and dates of American antique furniture, are much interested in discovering the exact place of origin of the finer articles of furniture and the names and history of the men who made them.[5] The place of origin of many articles is now well known, such as the highboys and lowboys of Philadelphia and New England, the block front furniture of Rhode Island, the chairs and tables of Duncan Phyfe in New York, and the elaborately inlaid and painted furniture of Baltimore. The study of these matters, however, is not of much importance to the amateur collector, unless he is particularly interested in the history of American furniture. The distinctive features of various well-known makers are often mere small details of cabinet making, not easily understood by amateurs. The less important local makers and the places of origin of the various articles are therefore not often mentioned in this volume.

Moreover, the purpose of this book is to enable the amateur reader to know what are *not* fine antiques as well as to know what are. With this in view, a number of illustrations are of articles which, although antique to a certain extent, are not now, and never have been, entitled to be called "fine." The principal class of old American articles which are not really antique[6] in the proper sense

5. Those who may become interested in these matters will find much information in numerous articles in the magazines, especially in "Antiques" and "The Antiquarian," many written by scholars of high standing.

      In numerous cases it is possible to state with certainty that a chair or other article is made in a style which prevailed only in a particular city or State. But it does not follow that all articles of a New England style found in Maryland were made in New England. A highboy in the New England style may have been made in any city in which there was a cabinet maker who could make a copy of it. The fact that a chair is exactly the same as an English one does not prove that the chair was made in England.

      An interesting example of the dispersal of a set of chairs in widely different sections of the country, owing to the change of residence of their owners, may be mentioned here. The Senate chamber in the State House of Maryland, at Annapolis, in which George Washington resigned his commission as Commander-in-Chief of the American army on December 27, 1783, is to be refurnished with reproductions of furniture of the period. Later than 1783 the chamber was furnished with chairs in the Hepplewhite style, three of which are in Baltimore, one belonging to the Maryland Historical Society. Dr. Henry J. Berkley, the chairman of the committee in charge of the refurnishing, succeeded in tracing seven others, one of which was in Haverford, Pa., two in Los Angeles, one in Cambridge, Md., two in Cincinnati and one in Annapolis, Md., most of them in the possession of descendants of members of the original maker.

6. See section 5, entitled "When is an article of American furniture an 'antique'?" Suppose we

of the word are those of the late Empire period, about 1830-1840, and the early Victorian period, about 1840-1860; and even if these articles were antique, most of them are not of fine design. Such examples are not generally illustrated in the books on antiques, nor even mentioned; but without such illustrations there seems to be no pictorial information at hand enabling the owners, or prospective purchasers, to know that the articles are not regarded as fine antiques and why they are not. The scope of this book therefore includes a few articles which were made as late as the Victorian period; they are shown here in order that the reader may know what they really are.

Section 2. The text and the notes.—The plan of this book differs from that of others on the subject of American antique furniture, and it seems proper that something should be said about it.

In certain respects the plan is similar to that generally used in law books and other text books. The chapters are divided into numbered sections, and each section treats of one of the articles which are included in the general subject of the chapter. For example, the chapter on chairs is divided into twenty sections, and each section treats of a particular branch of the subject of chairs. In this way, the various kinds of chairs are separately presented to the eye of the reader and are clearly classified in the mind and memory.

The printed matter, as distinguished from the illustrations, consists of two parts; the text is on the upper part of the page, in large type, and the notes to the text are below, in smaller type.[1] The small figures in the text refer to the notes, which are numbered consecutively in each section, and are easily referred to, as, for example, "note 5 in section 1." A note should always begin on the lower part of the page on which it is referred to in the text; and it sometimes extends over upon the next page. Each page is numbered in the usual way at the top, on the outer side; and the number of the section appears on the inner side of each page.

The principal contents appear, of course, in the text;[2] but the notes are almost equally important and sometimes are more interesting. For the purpose of mak-

---

(Note 6, *continued*)

look at the *legal meaning* of the word "Furniture." In many legal cases it has been necessary to decide whether or not the words "furniture," or "household furniture," especially when used in wills, were intended to include certain articles commonly found in homes. These terms have a wide meaning and are said to be incapable of exact definition. The courts in various States, interpreting the word "furniture" in connection with other expressions in a will, have rendered decisions which are apparently not harmonious with other decisions, but are doubtless in accordance with the intentions of the makers of the particular wills. Among the articles which in some cases have, and in other cases have not, been decided to be included in a gift of "furniture" or "household furniture" are the following: books, china, pianos, pictures and portraits on the walls, sewing machines and silverware. A difference of opinion as to the meaning of the words in a will is a frequent cause of family disagreements. The words generally include clocks unless the intention of the testator to exclude them is apparent.

1. A similar method is used in the "Encyclopædia Britannica" and the "Century Dictionary."

2. The comments on the objects illustrated are of course intended to point out the more important features of each object, including in some cases features which are so obvious that it may not be worth

ing the book as useful as possible, many matters appear in the notes which are not generally mentioned in books on antique furniture. For example, numerous references to, or quotations from, other books, and from magazines,[3] are in the notes, due acknowledgment being made in each instance. It may be remarked that it is not customary for writers of books on the subject to refer to other modern books; in fact the rule seems to be to ignore other publications except perhaps by giving a mere list in an appendix. But in the present book the aim is to refer the reader to other publications in which a particular subject may be further studied.

At this point it should be mentioned that the writer frequently refers, by permission, to two books as authoritative; one is "Colonial Furniture in America," by Mr. Luke Vincent Lockwood, in two volumes, third edition, 1926; the other is "English Furniture of the Eighteenth Century," by Mr. Herbert Cescinsky, in three volumes. These are the standard and scholarly works, with many illustrations and full accompanying text.

Many matters stated in the notes are not strictly relevant to the subject, but are of some interest. Even when the information relates to matters which have little direct connection with antique furniture, it is often inserted because the writer found it interesting in his study of the main subject; for example, Note 1 on page 343 digresses from the theme of "American Antique Furniture" to describe the appearance and customs of the people known as "Pennsylvania Dutch." In this case, as in many others, interest in the people increases interest in the furniture which they produced.

The Index at the end of the book is much more detailed than is usual. Whenever the reader desires to find any matter or definition mentioned in the book, he need not hunt through a number of pages, but should examine the index, where it will be, or ought to be, found.

Section 3. The illustrations.—In order that the amateur reader may know and appreciate antique furniture it is necessary that there should be a large number of illustrations.[1] A book with text but without illustrations is difficult to read

(NOTE 2, *continued*)

while to call attention to them. A certain amount of repetition is sometimes unavoidable in cases where there is a group of similar objects, such as a group of Chippendale chairs of a type in which the differences are not very important, or a group of highboys or block–front desks. Often the principal differences are in the decorative treatment, such as the carving on a highboy or the inlay on a bureau; all these points, however, add to or detract from the interest and value of the object.

3. Especially the magazine "Antiques," which is so often referred to throughout this book and is doubtless in the library of many of the readers of this note, and may be found in almost all public libraries. The magazine "The Antiquarian" is also often referred to.

1. A. The number and size of the illustrations largely determine the cost of publishing a book of this kind and the price at which it may be sold. In order to offer the book at a moderate price, probably without financial profit to the writer, many of the illustrations are smaller in size than in some other books; but they are all large and distinct enough to show clearly the form and character of the pieces. In the chapter on chairs, for example, there are four hundred and eighty-two illustrations, generally nine on each page; if there were only four on each page the number of these pages would be more than

and almost impossible to remember; and one with few illustrations gives only a partial view of the subject, leaving the appearance of the furniture which is merely mentioned, not illustrated, to the imagination of the reader. On the other hand, a book with many illustrations but without explanatory text, although valuable as a collection of photographs, does not give the reader a knowledge of the periods and styles of furniture designs which is essential to a full understanding and enjoyment of the subject.

(NOTE 1, *continued*)

doubled and the cost of the book would necessarily be higher; and so also with various other chapters. The writer believes that the reader will prefer to have a great number of small, but fairly good, illustrations at a moderate price rather than a less number of large ones at a higher price. Small illustrations of large articles, however, are seldom as clear and distinct as larger ones would be; as, for example, the illustrations of highboys.

B. The illustrations are necessarily not all on the same scale; one of a very tall highboy, for example, may be of the same size as one of a small highboy. They are all upright on the page and do not require the reader to turn the book sideways. The effort has been made to place the illustrations very close to the description of them in the text, thus avoiding the necessity for hunting for the text when examining the illustrations, or hunting for the illustrations when reading the text; but it is not always possible to do this in a fully illustrated book.

C. Almost all of the photographs, from which the illustrations were made, were taken by the photographer engaged by the writer. These photographs were made in private homes in Maryland, sometimes under difficult circumstances of position or light which prevented the best results.

D. The name of each owner of the more than sixteen hundred and fifty objects illustrated is stated, except when the owner does not wish his name to be used and except when the name of the owner is not known to the writer. In many of the latter examples the illustrations were taken by permission of Mr. Lockwood and Mr. Cescinsky from their books, as mentioned in the preface, and those books are referred to as the source of such illustrations. Many other "anonymous" illustrations are copied from the advertising catalogues of auction sales conducted by the "American Art Association Anderson Galleries," (now the Parke-Bernet Galleries, Inc.—Editor) No. 30 East 57 Street, New York City. It may be mentioned that the catalogues of all the furniture and art sales made by this organization may be obtained for four dollars per season (now seven dollars and fifty cents—Editor), and that these catalogues contain a great number of illustrations and descriptions of interesting objects.

E. All the illustrations in this book are of the kind known as "halftones," or "halftone engravings." The process of engraving cannot be clearly explained by a mere printed description of what is done in making a copper plate engraving from a glossy photograph; but the reader may be interested in knowing that the average cost of making each page of engravings was about $11.00.

F. The writer visited one hundred and forty-eight private houses in order to obtain photographs for this book. With the exception of two, every owner who was approached cheerfully gave permission to photograph his or her antiques for publication; and several gave the use of photographic negatives of articles which they had photographed for their private albums. Nowadays the owners of fine antiques, instead of regarding them as only for their own personal enjoyment, realize that the development of good taste and the appreciation of the best in American homes is based upon the examples of the past; and they gladly extend to others the opportunity of seeing fine antique furniture, either in loan exhibitions or in the pages of a book or magazine. In fact, certain owners allow exact reproductions to be made, just as our museums allow copies to be made of their famous paintings and furnish photographs of all their possessions. The ownership of fine antiques, like the ownership of great wealth, carries with it the duty of using them for the education and enjoyment of our people. It is proper to mention, as the leading instance in our country in connection with antique furniture, the great gift of Mr. and Mrs. Francis P. Garvan, to Yale University, a gift which may be compared to the gift of the superb Wallace Collection, in London, to the British Nation. And it may be noted that the titled owners of great houses in England allow their authentic pieces of Chippendale and others to be photographed for publication.

The best form of book on antique furniture is one having a text explaining the origin, development and changes of furniture styles, and containing a sufficient number of illustrations and explanatory text to make the subject clear to the reader. This is the method adopted in this book, following Mr. Lockwood and Mr. Cescinsky in their volumes mentioned in the previous section. The number of illustrations needed in a book of this kind depends largely upon the extent of detail which the reader desires. In this book it is assumed, as mentioned above, that the reader does not desire many details of cabinet making or cabinet makers, or minute particulars of any kind, but that he does desire as many illustrations as possible of the various articles of furniture in which he may be interested.

Section 4. Methods of treating the subject.—It is worth while to notice that the subject of American antique furniture is treated in different methods in the books.

One method is to divide the book into chapters on the various styles which are named either from a great cabinet maker, as the "Chippendale style," or from a great historical period, as the "Empire style." A chapter is given to each style, for example, the Chippendale style, and in the chapter on that style are illustrated or described all the various articles of furniture, whether large or small, from highboys to knife boxes, all being furniture in the Chippendale style. This method has a certain advantage in presenting in one chapter all the furniture of each style; but a reader desiring to understand a particular article of furniture, such as a chair, will find in the chapter on the Chippendale style only one period of the story of chairs, and he must read the remainder of the story in the chapters on the earlier styles and in the later chapters on the Hepplewhite style, the Sheraton style, the Directory style and the Empire style.[1] The result of this method is that the reader has the difficult task of picking out from six or eight chapters a disconnected mass of information on the subject of chairs and fastening it in his mind in chronological order.

A second method is for each chapter to contain an account of only one of the articles of furniture, and to present a continuous story throughout the various styles, with numerous illustrations. The chapter on chairs, for example, begins with an earlier style than the William and Mary style, and continues the subject through the Queen Anne style, the Chippendale and the later styles. In this way the gradual changes in the styles of chairs will appear in their historical order, and the chapter will be somewhat in the nature of a biography of a chair, from the beginning to the end of its career as an antique. This method gives a clear and logical account of the various articles and is the one used in this book.[2]

1. The leading American books treating the subject in this method are "The Practical Book of Period Furniture," by Eberlein and McClure, published by J. B. Lippincott Co., Philadelphia, 1914; and "American Furniture and Decoration, Colonial and Federal," by Edward Stratton Holloway, also published by J. B. Lippincott Co., 1928.

2. This method is used in the foremost work in our country, mentioned in the preface and in section 2, entitled "Colonial Furniture in America," by Mr. Luke Vincent Lockwood, third edition,

Still another method is to present the subject with reference to the geographical origin or development of the various articles of furniture. This method has little to commend it, for the obvious reason that the styles of chairs and tables and mirrors and other important articles did not each originate in a different part of our country; although some articles may have developed, in different States, certain features of a local character.[3]

A recent type of book is that in which great numbers of illustrations of all the various articles are presented in groups, and to some extent in chronological order, but without a text giving information upon the styles and periods. These books are valuable collections of illustrations, and are not intended as general treatises.[4]

(NOTE 2, *continued*)

1926, in two volumes, published by Charles Scribner's Sons, New York, with 1003 illustrations; also in "Furniture of the Olden Time," by Frances Clary Morse, published by The Macmillan Co., New York, with 428 illustrations; this latter is perhaps the most interesting and useful of the smaller books.

3. This method was adopted in "The Furniture of our Forefathers" by Esther Singleton, first edition, two volumes, 1900, published by Doubleday, Page & Co., New York, in which the subject is divided into "Early Southern," "Early New England," etc. Many inventories of estates of deceased persons are given, showing the articles of the period and the appraised values; also a large number of illustrations. There is also an edition in one volume.

4. "Furniture Treasury," by Wallace Nutting, 1928, published by Old America Co., Framingham, Mass., in two volumes, contains more than 5000 illustrations, of which 931 are of chairs. This is a valuable and interesting work, giving a comprehensive view of all articles of household furniture. Volume 3, published in 1933, contains many drawings, a list of clockmakers in America and much other information.

"Furniture of the Pilgrim Century, (1620-1720)," Revised Edition, by Wallace Nutting, 1924, published by Old America Co., Framingham, Mass., has 1559 illustrations of the furniture of that period, with descriptive comments. This is an excellent volume, with a great amount of information.

"The Collector's Guide to Furniture Design," by Edward Wenham, 1928, published by Collector's Press, Inc., New York, contains 798 photographs, with introductory remarks at the head of each of the chapters, and with brief comments on the articles illustrated.

"The Colonial Furniture of New England" by Dr. Irving Whitall Lyon, published in 1891, is said to be the first American book on the subject. It contains much information, has 113 illustrations and must have been invaluable at the time it was written. More recent volumes, however, have naturally rendered Dr. Lyon's book less important for general use; but acknowledgment is here made to it as the leader in the study of antique furniture in our country. A new edition was published in 1924 by Houghton Mifflin Company, Boston.

"English and American Furniture" by Herbert Cescinsky and George Leland Hunter, published in 1929 by The Dean-Hicks Company, Grand Rapids, Michigan, has 312 pages and more than 400 illustrations. The brief text is written by Mr. Cescinsky whose clear and direct statements are often accompanied by clever comments, several of which are quoted in these pages.

Two large and finely illustrated English books with a great amount of information should be mentioned. "A History of English Furniture," by Percy Macquoid, published 1904-1908, treats the subject in four volumes, which are devoted respectively to the "Age of Oak," the "Age of Walnut," the "Age of Mahogany" and the "Age of Satinwood." The other book is entitled "A Dictionary of English Furniture," by Percy Macquoid and Ralph Edwards, published in America by Charles Scribner's Sons, New York, 1924-1927, in three volumes. These two books are essential to a thorough study of English antique furniture but are not very useful to an American amateur collector. See also section 28, note 1.

CHAPTER II

SEVERAL PRELIMINARY MATTERS

Section 5. When is an article of American furniture an "antique"?—This question, referring to American furniture only, is not connected with foreign furniture imported into our country. Until recently, under an Act of Congress, foreign furniture was admitted without payment of customs duties if made more than one hundred years prior to the date of importation. Partly because of this provision, the period of one hundred years is often popularly regarded as being the age requirement of an "antique," whether foreign or American. A recent Act of Congress[1] now provides that in order to be admitted free of duty, foreign furniture must have been produced "before January 1, 1830." It was not the purpose, under either Act of Congress, to fix the age at which an article becomes "antique."

The collector of American antique furniture, however, is not concerned with the Act of Congress in determining whether a particular article is or is not an "antique." If age were the only thing to be considered, any very old piece of furniture might be called an "antique"; but when "antique" furniture is discussed we refer to furniture made in a style now approved by connoisseurs as a good

---

1.   The Act of Congress of 1930, 71st. Congress, second session, chapter 497, applies to "collections in illustration of the progress of the arts, works in bronze, marble, terra cotta, parian, pottery or porcelain, artistic antiquities and objects of art of ornamental character or educational value." The article must have some artistic character; something more than mere mechanical skill; it must have an esthetic appeal; mere age does not authorize free entry; see "Treasury Decision" No. 44093, June 19, 1930, pages 33-43.

The Treasury Department has defined furniture to be "movable articles of convenience or decoration designed for use in furnishing a house, apartment, place of business or accommodation." Compare the legal meaning of the word "furniture," section 1, note 7.

Certain provisions and penalties of the Act are intended to prevent the importation, free of duty, of fake antiques by dealers. If any article imported for sale is rejected as unauthentic in respect to the antiquity claimed, an extra duty of 25 per cent must be paid.

The Treasury Department regulations may be obtained at a small charge by application to the Superintendent of Documents, Washington, D. C.

Foreign antiques are the subject of section 8.

style, and which was made at a time when that style was in fashion.[2] The last of the styles which are now approved by connoisseurs—the Sheraton style—passed out of fashion in the period from 1825 to 1830, and almost all furniture made for some years after that period was in the style known as the Empire style, which is not now approved. The period mentioned, or approximately the year 1825, is thus generally regarded in our country as the "dead line" dividing the "antique" from the merely "old" furniture.[3]

Section 6. Dating antique furniture.

—To fix with certainty the dates at or about which any particular article of antique furniture was made is a very difficult matter. It is generally possible to determine approximately the date when a certain *style* first began to be used, and how long that style continued to be fashionable; but to ascertain the date of manufacture of an article made between the beginning and the end of the life of that style is a different problem. In the words of Mr. Cescinsky, speaking of English furniture, "to state an exact date of manufacture for any example, in the absence of accredited documentary evidence, is only to make a pretense of superior knowledge."[1]

2.   A piece of furniture made for example in 1790, in the style of that period, may be an antique; but an exact copy of it made some years later, after the style had passed out, would be regarded as a reproduction because it was not made in the period. This sometimes occurred when, for example, one of a set of chairs was damaged beyond repair and an exact copy was made to complete the set. After the lapse of more than one hundred years it is practically impossible to distinguish the copy from the originals of the set. See also section 6, note 5, and section 7, note 6, B.

3.   But in a more popular sense, as used in many antique shops, almost any article of furniture is called an "antique" if it was made within a few years after 1825 and before the Victorian style of furniture became the fashion about the year 1840. In this sense most of our furniture of the Empire style may be regarded as "antique," although many of such articles may, to our eyes, be monstrosities when compared with the fine designs of earlier pieces.

As we travel westward in our country we find that the age requirement is not as strict as in the East. It is said that at the present time the further west we go, the younger the "antiques" become; and that west of the Mississippi River, articles of mahogany, rosewood or walnut, made even as late as the Mid-Victorian period, about 1850 to 1870, are often called "antiques." Such articles may be interesting as the furniture of our grandfathers, but they are not "antiques" in the sense that the word is now used by connoisseurs.

Moreover, the word "antique" as applied to furniture must be distinguished from "old." A dealer may state that a chair, for example, is "old" when one asks him if it is "antique." The word "old" is so indefinite that it is almost meaningless; and in no case does it mean the same as "antique." A chair that is "antique" is necessarily "old"; but a chair that is merely "old" is generally not antique.

Of course not all "antique" pieces are good pieces. In the eighteenth century, as now, many pieces were badly made and were deficient in the three requisites—good materials, good workmanship and good design. Such pieces do not become desirable by lapse of years; but some of them may be "glorified" by expert "fakers"; see section 7.

1.   "English Furniture of the Eighteenth Century," volume 1, page 15. On page 91 it is said that furniture "models were so frequently copied by rival makers—very often those of twenty or thirty years before being chosen for duplication—that to assign any but very approximate dates is merely to pretend to a knowledge not creditable to an author and exceedingly misleading to a reader."

On some early English pieces dates are found; and in France at one time it was required that the cabinet maker should date his pieces. But this method was not used in England in the periods

In this book, a date given to a piece of furniture does not mean the date at which the piece was *made;* the date given is believed to be the date at or about which the *style* of the particular piece was in fashion in the larger cities of our country.

The difficulty of fixing dates of manufacture is apparent when we realize that the styles which prevailed in the cities and larger towns of our country at any given year were not generally adopted in the small towns and the country districts until some years later. This was always the case in England and it is said that the further distant a town was from London the more behind time the furniture style of that town was; and that in the case of pieces made after 1760, the only method of dating is to give the date at which the style was in vogue in London.

One uncertain indication of even the approximate date of manufacture is based upon the kind of wood used in the construction of a particular piece. The "Age of Oak," the "Age of Walnut" and the "Age of Mahogany" are referred to in other sections;[2] and in a general way it may be said that in these "ages" most of the articles of fine furniture were made in the wood of that "age." But these "ages" have no definite beginnings or endings, at least in our country; and even if they had, there was no obligation upon cabinet makers to use, nor upon purchasers to buy, only one particular kind of wood for their household furniture.[3]

(Note 1, *continued*)

in which we are interested; and it is said that in both countries many pieces have been erroneously or fraudulently dated.

Figures on articles of furniture are sometimes thought to be dates if they are between the years of our antiques, about 1625 to 1825, but are more likely to be shop numbers or indications of some other kind. Clocks were occasionally numbered by the makers.

The Pennsylvania Dutch chests illustrated in section 78 are generally dated, and perhaps properly. As a rule, however, such dates are unreliable; they may have been made by a family antiquarian, relying upon family tradition, years after the piece was made; or by some other person, such as a recent owner.

In Mr. Lockwood's "Colonial Furniture in America" many articles are dated by quarters of a century; thus a mirror, figure 316, is dated "first quarter eighteenth century," and a Chippendale style chair, figure 551, is dated "third quarter eighteenth century." This twenty-five year period is sufficiently definite in most cases.

The method adopted by Mr. Cescinsky in "English Furniture," volume 2, page 161, is that of "considering and dating each example from the commencement or inauguration of the particular fashion of which it is a type."

Even if it be possible to fix the date at which articles in a new style *began* to be made it is seldom possible to state the date when they *ceased* to be made.

2. See sections 28 and 29.

3. In Mr. Cescinsky's book volume 2, pages 17-18, it is said that four fashions in English furniture are found in the period from 1714 to 1745 and that it is unsafe to divide the periods into "periods of walnut and mahogany respectively, as examples of each can be found in both woods, walnut persisting in favor, especially with country makers, until about 1760."

In the same volume, page 228, it is said that "mahogany superseded walnut after about the year 1720, yet in the Victoria and Albert Museum are to be seen chairs, apparently of the best period of Chippendale as regards their design, yet made from walnut." In Pennsylvania and other walnut-bearing States walnut was often used for furniture in the Chippendale style. See the chair No. 123.

The abundant or scant supply of a particular kind of wood at a particular time, affecting the cost, and the desires and financial ability of the purchaser, necessarily entered into the choice of wood.

The approved rule for determining the date of a piece of furniture which has characteristic features of more than one style is this: the date of the latest feature determines the date of the piece.[4] The rule is based upon the fact that although any cabinet maker could use in the year 1800, for example, the styles found in articles made at or before that date, no one could use in 1800 a style which was not invented until 1810. An article having features of the styles of 1800 and 1810 must therefore have been made in 1810 or later. It is of course assumed that the piece is a genuine piece, and not a recent fake or reproduction.[5]

Mention should be made of the principal sources of information from which we learn the dates at which the various styles of antique furniture were in vogue. This information is often more definite in England than with us, because, among other reasons, several cabinet makers in that country during the eighteenth century published illustrated and dated books of designs[6] in the nature of catalogues or advertisements, and also because there are several fine houses which are known to have been furnished at certain dates and in which the original furniture is still preserved. In our country many of the English designs were closely followed and became the fashion a few years, perhaps five or six, after they were adopted in England.

Apart from the English dates, there are several important sources of information as to our American furniture. One of the principal sources is the court inventories of the property of deceased persons, which are always dated and often describe the kinds of furniture in terms sufficient to identify them, sometimes referring to them as "old." The date of an inventory was of course often some years after the deceased owner acquired the furniture, and therefore it is thought proper to date the acquisition of the furniture, when it was presumably in style, at about ten years before the death of the owner—an arbitrary estimate, but probably nearly correct on an average.[7]

4. In Mr. Cescinsky's "English Furniture," volume 2, page 45, a walnut chair is illustrated and described which contained nearly all the characteristic designs in vogue from about 1695 to 1730; and it is said that there was no other system of dating possible other than to consider the date of the latest feature as the earliest date of the chair.

5. In Mr. Cescinsky's book, volume 2, page 229, it is said that in the nineteenth century many reproductions of the eighteenth century models of chairs were made by good cabinet makers, "remarkable for fidelity to the originals; and to discriminate between original Chippendale and copies made some forty or fifty years after the master's death, is a nice point, where anything short of omniscience is likely to result in mere ignorant guess-work. The lapse of time would count for a good deal, if every piece were subjected to precisely similar usage; but every one knows how quickly certain furniture will age, for example, with those who possess a large family of healthy children, as compared with other pieces in the houses of their spinster aunts." See also section 5, note 2, and section 7, note 6.

6. In the next chapter reference is made to the books of Chippendale, Hepplewhite and Sheraton.

7. This is the opinion of Mr. Lockwood, as stated in his "Colonial Furniture in America," volume 1, page 61.

Many inventories are quoted in "The Furniture of our Forefathers," by Esther Singleton, mentioned in section 4, note 3.

Other sources of information are the advertisements[8] by cabinet makers and furniture dealers; letters, memoirs and descriptive writings of travelers;[9] paintings and engravings in which furniture appears; and other sources mentioned in the following paragraphs.

An evidence of date is occasionally found in printed matter pasted on an article, such as an original label of a cabinet maker, or other kind of advertisement. If any record of the person whose name is on the label can be found from newspaper advertisements, or in directories, or in court entries of transfers of land or settlement of estates, or by other means, it may be possible to ascertain the approximate date of his business career. In such cases a label is often satisfactory evidence and is entitled to credit. Its presence is sometimes regarded as positive proof of the genuineness of the article, and that the article was made by the person whose name appears; but it should be remembered that the label may not be that of the maker, but of a dealer in furniture or of a repairer; if of a repairer the label was probably pasted on some years after the article was made. Also, a father and son, both cabinet makers, may have had the same name;[10] moreover, a

8. Such as those in the newspapers. Many advertisements are in two books published by the Walpole Society, 1929 and 1932, entitled "The Arts and Crafts in Philadelphia, Maryland and South Carolina." See the Index for references to these books, under "Walpole Society, Arts and Crafts books."

Illustrations of furniture in newspaper advertisements may not have been intended to show the current styles, but merely to indicate the business of the advertiser. Even today many advertisements of auction sales of furniture in country newspapers have illustrations of Victorian furniture.

9. An interesting example of these is on page 154 in "The Homes of our Ancestors," by R. T. H. Halsey and Elizabeth Tower, published by Doubleday, Page and Co., 1925.

10. It seems probable that fine and expensive engraved labels with a blank center were prepared by engravers who would print in the center, as an advertisement, the name and address of the cabinet maker.

As a label generally states the name of the city or town in which the person named resided, it indicates the locality in which the article was made or repaired; this information may be of interest, especially to collectors in that locality.

An illustrated article by Mr. Charles Messer Stow, in which considerable importance, financial and otherwise, is attached to labels, is in "The Antiquarian," February, 1930, page 52.

In the same magazine, April, 1930, page 40, is an illustrated article entitled "French Furniture and the source of the label," by Mr. Alfred M. Frankfurter.

Almost all of the labels which have been found were pasted on at places where they were able to escape the cleansing activities of energetic housewives. Many are of small size, mentioning only the name, address and trade of some person. A large and notable example is the engraved label of Benjamin Randolph, of Philadelphia, which appears in illustration No. 1. In this label some of the furniture designs are taken from "The Director," the book of Chippendale mentioned in section 15. The articles shown are all in the style of Chippendale and include two chairs, three fire-screens, a stool, a sofa, a table, a bedstead, a grandfather clock, a cabinet on a stand, a "Beau Brummel" dressing table with a mirror, and a tall secretary-bookcase. There is an abundance of "C curves," as to which see the Index. An inharmonious feature is the large eagle at the top. In sections 33 and 37 it is said that the American eagle became the national emblem soon after the adoption of the Constitution in 1788. This label is regarded as having been made about 1770. It is owned by the Pennsylvania Museum. In "English and American Furniture," by Cescinsky and Hunter, mentioned in section 4, note 4, it is said, page 22, that this "trade card or advertisement . . was a composite of some seven or eight plates from the 'Director' (as to which see section 15, at note 2), literally copied." Another interesting label is that of John Shaw, cabinet maker of Annapolis, illustrated on page 537. This handsome label, dated 1797, was pasted within the sideboard, which is also illustrated on this page. For further information, see the Index, under the heading of "Labels."

BENJAMIN RANDOLPH'S TRADE CARD

ILLUSTRATION NO. 1. SEE LAST NOTE ON OPPOSITE PAGE.

label may be detached and pasted on another piece; and of course a label is not an indication of excellence. Care should be taken by the amateur collector not to rely too much upon labels, as it is known that they may be successfully faked by using old paper and an old style type; and it is said that in some way the demand for labels will be supplied.

In the first paragraph of this section "accredited documentary evidence" is mentioned as fixing the date of the making of particular pieces of furniture. Evidence of this kind is sometimes found in a dated bill rendered by the cabinet maker, if the articles are sufficiently described to connect the bill with them. A bill of this kind rendered by Chippendale for work done in 1776, and two bills rendered by Duncan Phyfe, are mentioned in the note.[11]

Information as to dates is sometimes derived from inlaid or painted stars, or marks representing stars. The number of stars may indicate the number of States in the Union at the time the article was made, from which the date may be approximated,[12] as in our national flag. These are occasionally seen on desk lids, mirrors, tables, clocks and some other pieces. In some cases stars may have been used merely to fill a vacant space and thus be without significance as to dates.

In seeking the dates of important articles of furniture it is usual to examine closely various details of cabinet making and of ornamental designs; and if several articles are found to have exactly or about the same characteristics, and if the maker of any one of such articles is known, there is a strong tendency to attribute to such maker some or all of the articles, whereby the date of all of the articles may be approximated. This "attribution" is often justified by an exact or close similarity of the pieces; but in many cases it is imaginative and uncertain.[13]

11.   The Chippendale bill is for furniture made for Lord St. Oswald's famous home in Yorkshire, known as Nostell Priory. It appears in part in Mr. Cescinsky's "English Furniture," volume 2, pages 342-343, where a number of items for bedsteads and their furnishings are quoted, showing that the elaborate hangings and equipment cost much more than the bedsteads.

The bill of Duncan Phyfe appears in "Furniture Masterpieces of Duncan Phyfe," by Mr. Charles Over Cornelius, pages 44-45. It is for various articles made for a Mr. Bancker, and is dated January 4, 1816. See section 20, note 3.

In "The Antiquarian," March, 1930, page 37, is an article by Mr. Wm. M. Hornor, Jr., in which is illustrated an original bill of Duncan Phyfe for furniture bought by William Bayard, of New York, dated November 21, 1807.

12.   See section 33, on "Inlay," and the Index, "Stars."

When the stars appear as a series of marks on a streamer held in the eagle's mouth, the number of stars almost always represents the age of the furniture which they decorate.

When there are thirteen stars, the Union of the thirteen original States is generally referred to; they do not necessarily indicate that there were only thirteen States at the time the article of furniture was made. Thirteen stars are occasionally seen on articles made long after the formation of the Union in 1788. The thirteenth State to enter the Union was Rhode Island in 1790 and the fourteenth was Vermont in 1791, and if thirteen stars represented the number of States in the Union at the time the article was made the date would be 1790-1791.

13.   It has been well said that "it is the fate of all the great artists of the past to have had their names attached, by popular rumor or interested artifice, to a multitude of works which they never saw"; Encyclopædia Britannica, eleventh edition, volume 27, page 1032, in an article on "Vernis Martin," which is a French varnish referred to in section 31, entitled "Lacquer," note 2.

Perhaps the most unreliable source of information as to the dates of antique furniture is family tradition, if not supported by written evidence. There seems to be some irresistible tendency in the owners of inherited furniture to regard many family pieces as about two hundred, or at least one hundred and fifty, years of age, especially grandfather clocks. Even Empire furniture of the period of about 1830-1840 is sometimes thought to be of the colonial period of our country, perhaps because the word "colonial" is so often mistakenly applied to furniture of the Empire period.[14] Tactful prudence is needed in discussing such matters with owners who have inherited misinformation with their furniture; for, as has been said, "by the majority of persons any questioning of domestic traditions is viewed as a form of blasphemy."[15]

Fortunately, our enjoyment of a fine piece of antique furniture does not depend upon our knowing exactly when or by whom it was made; a knowledge of its style and approximate date of making is generally sufficient for the amateur collector.

(NOTE 13, *continued*)

In studying a piece of furniture for the purpose of determining whether it can be "attributed" to some well-known cabinet maker, the approved method is not only to compare the obvious similarities of appearance in design and decoration, all of which may have been used by a number of cabinet makers, but also to examine the manner in which the decoration is used in connection with other features, the precise character of the carving and inlay, and all inconspicuous details of cabinet work which might naturally vary in different workshops. These matters of technical niceties are not for the amateur collector; moreover, actual experience in the handling of tools is always desirable and sometimes necessary when dealing with fine woods and delicate designs.

As cabinet makers now unknown or unappreciated are hereafter elevated to high positions in the field of antique furniture, many pieces will no doubt be attributed to them by dealers and in sales catalogues and in articles in newspapers and magazines. The attributions to William Savery, of Philadelphia, during the period of the "Savery vogue," included a great number of fine pieces, until other equally good cabinet makers were discovered. See the remarks in reference to highboys in section 87, note 3.

During the period of the Savery vogue some of the catalogues and other publications contained such statements as this: "the unusually high quality of this important piece of Colonial furniture compels its attribution to the master Philadelphia cabinet maker of the eighteenth century, William Savery." Similar statements have been made in regard to numerous other articles, with merely a change of name from Savery to some other maker whose label on a few pieces gave him prominence. Among these makers are Townsend and Goddard of Newport, Rhode Island, makers of block front furniture. No one knows who will be the next brilliant meteor to shine briefly in the antiquarian sky.

14.   See note 1 in section 1 on certain words used in connection with furniture.

15.   By Mr. Homer Eaton Keyes, the editor of the magazine "Antiques," March, 1931, page 200.

An association of articles of furniture with historical events or personages is often claimed to be an indication of date. Here also family tradition is not reliable. It is no doubt pleasant to believe that George Washington sat in our chairs, wrote at our desks, ate at our tables and slept in our beds, even if our chairs and other pieces are in styles which were not used until years after he died.

Here is one method of calculating the age of antique furniture. The owner says: "that clock of mine belonged to grandfather Brown and he lived to be eighty; then it was my father's and he died at seventy; I am fifty myself; now let me see; 80 and 70 make 150, and add my age, 50, that makes 200; that clock is at least 200 years old."

Section 7. Fakes.—The subject of "fakes"[1] is an unpleasant one, but it must be considered by all collectors, whether connoisseurs or amateurs. In our American books not much attention is given to the subject, but in the English books it is freely discussed.[2] Although books on antique furniture are supposed to treat of

1. The word "fake," in the sense here used, means "a thing not what it is pretended or represented to be"; Webster's International Dictionary; a "faker" is a pretender or swindler; but with one different letter "faker" becomes "fakir," and a "swindler" is changed into a "holy man" of the Hindu or Mohammedan faith.

2. In volume 3, pages 358-363, of his "English Furniture of the Eighteenth Century," Mr. Cescinsky, who mentions, page 363, that he had a "workshop training," writes of several points which would probably not occur to less experienced persons. One point is that in order to detect a forgery "a knowledge of the tools which were used—and also which were not used—by cabinet makers and carvers of the eighteenth century, is a very necessary accomplishment." On page 363 it is said that "the forger of antiques is an artist, of a very high order, in a discreditable way." On page 268 it is said that a "knowledge of woods is one of the most reliable weapons in the armoury of the expert—or the forger." This should especially be borne in mind in the purchase of English antiques, as mentioned in the next section.

"Saw marks" made by a circular saw may indicate a fake, as mentioned in section 44.

An interesting book by Mr. Frederick Litchfield, an English author, is entitled "Antiques, genuine and spurious: an art expert's recollections and cautions." This book treats of porcelain, furniture, enamels and bronzes. Published in New York, by Harcourt, Brace and Howe, 1921.

In trying to decide whether an article is a genuine antique or a clever fake a would-be purchaser may hesitate between contrary opinions. A skillful and observant cabinet maker and repairer who has worked for years with antiques and knows the various kinds of wood, nails, screws, saw marks, tool marks, processes of finishing and other details of antique cabinet work will of course be competent to decide between old manufacture and apparently old. On the other hand, the connoisseur who knows the characteristics of the furniture styles and periods is more competent to decide whether such characteristics properly appear in a given article. Certainly there could be no doubt in cases where both parties agree; but if they differ it may be well for the collector to take the safer course and say "no."

In a book entitled "Old English Walnut and Lacquer Furniture: the present day condition and value, and the methods of the furniture faker in producing spurious pieces," by R. W. Symonds, (American edition published by R. M. McBride & Co., New York, 1923), chapter 3, pages 38-56, is entitled "Spurious walnut furniture." The author begins by stating that "the amazing credulity of that section of the public that sets out to furnish houses with old furniture is the reason for the large production at the present day of spurious examples. It can truthfully be said that not half the furniture sold as antique is genuine." Mention is also made of "the vast quantity of it that has been made during the last quarter of a century."

The author then describes "the way spurious pieces are made and the way they are faked to give them an appearance of age, and how they differ from the genuine examples." Several of the more interesting methods are briefly mentioned in this note. The description of the method of imitating the patina, (as to which see section 10, note 5), is too technical to state here; acids and paint, dirt and dust, gold sizing and wax are used. The surface is dented a little by striking it with a bunch of heavy keys, giving the appearance of dents of different kinds. Old material is used. Surfaces may be bleached in the sun, except where covered by brass escutcheons and other mounts. Signs of shrinkage of veneer may be made by dampening the wood. Runners of drawers are worn down with sand. Gilding is made to look cracked by age by cutting or scratching it. Brass handles are easily imitated. Inlay and carving is used to enrich plain pieces—"glorified." A set of three original chairs may be made into a set of six, each partially antique, by taking the originals apart and making a copy of each part, and using half original and half new parts in each of the six. Marks made by new machine saws or planes may be removed. Mouldings and veneer may be exactly copied. "The commercial faker . . is responsible for most of the fakes that are made. This is an organized trade run on commercial lines."

genuine furniture and not of forgeries, the interest of the amateur collector requires that some general information be given; but it is only by knowledge,
experience and a keen eye that one can learn to detect the false from the true.
Faked furniture is generally made by skillful cabinet makers, using genuine pieces
as models and wood of the proper kind and age; and the makers may be as clever
as the experts who pass upon the articles.

In this book no effort is made to state the various tests which are useful in
detecting fakes of chairs, tables and other articles. The ability to determine
whether pieces of mahogany used in an article of furniture are as old as the
time of Chippendale, or as young as the early days of Queen Victoria, cannot be
acquired from merely reading a printed page and examining the illustrations;
only long experience in the actual handling of antique furniture will be of value
in such a matter. The principal points of importance to the amateur may, however, be fixed in mind by considering the several different kinds of fakes; and it
should be remembered that the business of faking antiques has been carried on in
our country and in England for many years.[3]

One kind of fake is an exact copy of an original antique article in style, size,
kind of wood, finish and all other details, expertly made for the purpose of deceiv-
ing a purchaser into the belief that it is in reality an original antique of the period.
It is of course made of old wood and it looks like an original antique, and is
intended to be sold at the price of an original antique. For example, wood from
parts of damaged tables may be made into another table. This of course is a highly
profitable business, and is said to be carried on extensively in all countries where
antiques, whether furniture or other articles, are appreciated.

A second kind of fake is made from an original antique of its period, but not
of fine character—perhaps a plain article without ornamentation. Such an article
may become a partial fake by the addition of inlay or carving or some other
ornamental feature, so as to make it appear to be one of better character. By this
means the article is said to be "glorified." A favorite device is to carve a sunburst

---

3.   Writing in 1910, Mr. Walter A. Dyer, in his agreeable book, "The Lure of the Antique,"
published by the Century Co., New York, remarks, page 472, that the market is full of fakes and that
"within the past generation at least two men have made fortunes in this country by manufacturing
'antiques,' and many others have made a livelihood. . . ." Chapter 20 in Mr. Dyer's book, pages 467-
488, contains information and advice on the subject. See also section 175.

For the amateur the best practical advice as to the purchase of antiques from a dealer is this:
first, buy only from one known to be truthful and experienced; and, second, ask the dealer whether any
restorations or repairs have been made to the article, and if so, what they are. In Mr. Cescinsky's book
entitled "The Gentle Art of Faking Furniture," his gentle art of clever comment explains the details of
many "detective methods" in questions as to whether certain articles are genuine antiques. On pages
35-36 of that book a question was whether the article was the kind of thing which was made in the
period in which such things were made, and Mr. Cescinsky writes in substance that "if a dealer
possessed Queen Elizabeth's automobile, no one would believe it, even if it were smothered all over with
Tudor roses. There are certain types of furniture which originated at certain definite periods, and are
not found before. Thus a Queen Anne sideboard, or even a fine bedstead without posts and a canopy
was unheard of until the nineteenth century. Upholstery began, and very sparingly, in the reign of
Charles I and did not become general until after 1680. Washstands were as unknown in the eighteenth
century as bathrooms. Baptism must have been the one bathing experience of our Georgian ancestors,
if the testimony of their houses and furniture is to be believed."

or shell upon a plain flat surface of, for example, a highboy or lowboy, or to carve an ornamentation upon the knees of a chair; plain tilt-top tables have been glorified by cutting the rims and thus converting them into pie-crust tables; plain bed posts may be glorified by reeding and carving; and other examples might be mentioned. If the "glorification" consists of adding pieces of wood the pieces added may sometimes be recognized as new under a strong light, or in a photograph, being generally somewhat different in grain from the old wood. Moreover, even new worm holes[5] may be made to assist in giving an antique appearance.

A third kind of fake, not really deserving that unpleasant name unless offered for sale as a genuine antique, is an article of furniture made many years ago as a reproduction.[6] Perhaps one or two chairs of an original set in the Chippendale

5. The addition of worm holes may not be a "glorification"; but real ones are often indicative of age, but not necessarily of great age. Incidentally, these ruinous tunnels through the wood are exit holes, not entrance holes, for the larvae of the furniture beetle.

6. See also section 5, note 2, and section 6, note 5.

A. Not long ago several finely carved mahogany chairs and a china cabinet, all in the style of Chippendale, were exhibited in the Boston Museum of Fine Arts, and attracted much attention. Afterwards they were taken away by the owner because of a question as to whether they were made in the Chippendale period. The chairs followed precisely a drawing in Chippendale's "Director," (as to which book see section 15), so that there was no question as to the correctness of the style. The point was whether they were old or new. The editor of the magazine "Antiques," in the issue of May, 1929, page 371, writes that the controversy was "over the question of their date, and hence, measurably, their source. Their champions assign them to the decade between 1750 and 1760. The opposition insists upon crediting them to the far more recent vintage of 1885-1895, or thereabouts. That they are brand-new imitations, made for purposes of deception, no student has believed or suggested."

B. In the same issue of the magazine "Antiques," pages 383-387, is an article on Chippendale, by Mr. Oliver Brackett, of the Victoria and Albert Museum, London, author of the book "Thomas Chippendale." Mr. Brackett states that "about the middle of the nineteenth century, a Chippendale revival occurred in England, and the work executed at this time has caused a considerable misunderstanding of the character of Chippendale's own. A great deal of furniture produced between 1850-1870, and later, was slavishly copied from the plates in the 'Director,' and although apparently no attempt was made to pass this furniture off as genuine work of the school of Chippendale, the inevitable wear and tear of seventy or eighty years has resulted in giving it an effect of age which is liable to deceive the public."

C. Mr. Wallace Nutting, in his book entitled "The Clock Book," page 21, published by Old American Company, Framingham, Mass., 1924, states that "the aging of new wood has now reached such a degree of success that the best judges may be deceived. Wood may be aged a hundred years in a day by steaming. It may be aged by exposing it to sun and storm for a few months. It may be bleached or stained quickly. So true is this that we can recommend no sure method of detecting fraud" in the wooden case of a clock.

D. Many purchasers only examine the visible parts of upholstered articles, such as wing chairs and sofas—a very dangerous method, as the covered parts may not be original. New wood may also be concealed by paint or stains or clever refinishing.

E. The "planting" of furniture by a dealer generally consists of getting some obliging householder to receive fake articles and to exhibit them to visitors as the householder's inherited family pieces. The dealer mentions to a customer that the householder has some fine old things for sale, but that he, the dealer, cannot afford to pay the prices.

F. The amateur collector always hopes to find good pieces at a moderate price—bargains, in fact; and he is often inclined to believe that an article which he wants, and which is represented to be antique, is in fact antique. An equally bad point of view is to be too suspicious. In either case, if in style were too badly damaged to be repaired or restored, and new ones were made, by order of the owner of the set, to take their place. After years of use and rubbing and cleaning, these chairs may be scarcely distinguishable from the originals of the set; yet they are of course not antique and have only the value of reproductions.

The subject of fakes is also referred to in the next section, entitled "Foreign Antiques." See the Index.

Section 8. Foreign antiques.—What is said in this section applies to foreign furniture, whether bought in Europe or in our country. Moreover, it is not meant to imply that American dealers in foreign antiques are willing to sell as genuine any foreign articles which they have reason to know or suspect to be spurious in whole or in part. The purpose of this section is to refer to facts which are well known to those who have investigated the subject and to those who have suffered from not having investigated it. Naturally, our magazines and newspapers do not often refer to the subject, because by doing so they would to some extent discourage and reduce public interest in the whole subject of antique furniture. The American amateur collector, however, is entitled to know the facts, just as the English collectors are given the facts in the books of English writers, as shown in the previous section. The purpose here is merely to put the amateur collector on his guard in considering the purchase of foreign antiques.

Even if there were no danger of buying a foreign fake instead of a genuine article, it is better to collect American furniture only; first, because American furniture is naturally more interesting and more important to us as Americans, and always will be; and, secondly, because fine American furniture is as fine as European in many respects, although often not so elaborate. But when we consider that warnings are given in the English books, and that European furniture, and especially English, has been sold here in great quantities, and that official warning as to its character has been issued by a consul of the United States in England, the necessity of great caution is very apparent. Of course, it is not intimated that every article offered for sale as a genuine European antique is a fake; but it is certainly true that a great number of pieces offered as genuine European antiques are undoubtedly fakes.

(NOTE 6, *continued*)

doubt, it is well to get the opinion of some reliable cabinet maker who is experienced in the details of antique workmanship.

     G.   Articles of a kind of "freak" furniture, some of which may be called furniture "changelings," may not have been intended to deceive, but were probably made or changed by or for persons who would not object, for example, to a chair composed of remnants of chairs of various styles. An imaginary chair of this kind might have straight legs in the Sheraton style, ball and claw feet in the Chippendale style, a shield shaped back in the Hepplewhite style with an inlaid American eagle holding in its beak a streamer with thirteen stars—a puzzle for the amateur; but not much more so than some of the present day adaptations referred to in section 9. Articles on "Furniture Changelings" are in "Antiques," January, 1928, page 52, and February, 1928, page 36.

The quotations in the note[1] are from a report, entitled "Traffic in Alleged Antiques," written by a consul of the United States and published in the United States "Daily Consular and Trade Reports," November 24, 1909, No. 3644.

One of the reasons for the large business in foreign furniture is that such furniture may be acquired in quantities at any time as desired, but genuine American antiques cannot be found in sufficient numbers. Dealers must have goods to sell, or they must go out of business. The effective slogan of a number of our dealers now is: "American antiques only."[2] While almost all important articles of American furniture originated in the furniture of England, several of our articles are purely American. The most important of the latter are the butterfly tables, seen in section 156; the Philadelphia style highboys and lowboys seen in sections 87 and 92; and the block–front articles seen in sections 114–119. An illustrated article, by Mr. Edward Stratton Holloway, entitled "Furniture Exclusively American" is in "Antiques," May, 1933, pages 182–183.

1. Consul Maxwell Blake, in writing of the frauds which are perpetrated on the inexperienced collectors of old silver and china and period furniture of dealers throughout the United Kingdom and continental Europe says: "The purpose of this article is to state facts, not opinions, and it is not addressed to the experienced collector. A real service, however, may possibly be conferred by warning the inexperienced."

"Just now miniatures and decorated snuff and patchboxes are being extensively collected by Americans. These and other such small articles of vertu are manufactured by dextrous copyists and are readily procurable by the gross."

With reference to china the consul says that "what one may fondly imagine to be a convincing piece, with its refined decoration and simple gilding, bearing the golden anchor, is not a bit of old Chelsea, but a fake made by well-known firms on the Continent. Only the uninitiated now put any reliance in 'Old marks.' They are freely applied to modern copies with open and notorious forgery."

"Difficulties thicken as the subject of old English furniture is approached. Large stakes are here frequently played for, and the cunning of the dealer amounts to sheer genius. . . For instance, in Holland, old chests, cabinets, desks and chairs of little value are collected and, after being veneered with cheaply made marquetry, are sent to Great Britain. Old oak beams from demolished churches or granaries are likewise in constant demand for conversion into Jacobean refectory tables and furniture. Mid-Victorian pedestal sideboards are amputated to specimens of Robert Adam, and conventional inlay suitable for Sheraton furniture is cut out by machinery and supplied in any quantity to those who have skill and inclination to fabricate antiques."

"Those who wish to secure genuine antiques should make up their minds that it will be more satisfactory, and cheaper in the end, to purchase only on expert advice, or of dealers willing to give a written stipulation that all articles sold are guaranteed to be approximately of the period represented; and with respect to English furniture, that no carving, inlay, or repairs not frankly admitted have been added; purchase money to be refunded should any of these statements prove to be untrue."

2. Mr. Wallace Nutting, in his "Furniture Treasury," volume 1, at figure 296, remarks that "a long contemplation of this subject (foreign antiques) leads to the deliberate judgment that the import of really old pieces from Italy is negligible, that it is almost negligible from France, and that much of the English work, like that of the other origins mentioned, is a clever manufacture from old wood."

Several years ago a great number of old Swedish articles of furniture were imported into the United States by dealers. The chairs are said to resemble very closely certain types of plain New England early chairs and other pieces have a similarity to the corresponding furniture of the Pennsylvania Dutch. These had a wide sale as American pieces. Illustrated articles on the subject are in "Antiques," July, 1932, page 16, and August, 1932, page 67.

In the "Saturday Evening Post," May 7, 1927, page 21, Esther S. Fraser writes of the very large number of newly imported articles which she saw in a warehouse in New York. Among

Section 9. Reproductions; adaptations.—There is not enough genuine antique furniture in this country for all of us to get what we want; and there is some consolation in this, for if there were enough for all, it would be so common that we might not want it. But as we cannot all get the real antiques, the question is whether we should get reproductions;[1] and on this point there is a difference of opinion. Many persons who have a number of genuine antiques think that modern reproductions are not much more than counterfeits and will not have such things in their houses. Many other persons, however, who admire the elegant designs of the master cabinet makers of the past, but who cannot secure the original creations, prefer to have good reproductions of fine antique furniture rather than articles in some of the new styles in the shops—styles which will soon be discontinued and will be remembered only as a passing fancy of a factory.

Of course modern reproductions cannot excite the pride of possession which is aroused by genuine antiques. There is something about genuine antiques which makes the owner imagine that his furniture has an elegance and charm not possessed by that of his neighbor who has exact reproductions of the very same articles. Moreover, the owner of such reproductions can never exhibit them with any pride in their pedigree; and yet he may have in his furniture the same fine designs, the same good workmanship, and the same charm and grace that are the delight of his more fortunate neighbor. Naturally they do not have the color—the patina—that comes from the hands of time, as mentioned at the end of the next section; nor did the original antiques have it when they were made.

Looking at the question in a practical way, however, suppose you need a set of chairs for your dining room. There are three kinds of chairs which may be selected; first, a set of the best modern chairs, whether made in New York, London or Paris; secondly, a set of genuine antique chairs, perhaps in the Chippendale style; thirdly, a set of exact reproductions of those genuine antiques. We all know that any present day style of chairs will soon go out of fashion. We also know that to collect a set of genuine antique Chippendale style chairs is almost an impossibility. There remains the set of reproductions, made exactly as the originals were made; not as desirable as the antiques, of course, but the next best, and the only modern ones which will give your room the dignity you wish to have.

(NOTE 2, *continued*)

them were chairs in the Queen Anne style, hanging cupboards, settees and benches, corner cupboards and dressers, gate-leg tables and trestle tables. It is probable that these articles from Norway, Sweden, Holland and Denmark became naturalized in our country very soon after their arrival and as American antiques acquired a new and much increased financial importance.

Articles of foreign furniture which have been in our country for many years are sometimes called "American" on the theory that they have acquired an American nationality by long residence. Another reason may be that a fine American article is generally more valuable than the same article would be if foreign.

1. The reproductions here referred to are of course those made and sold as such, not reproductions offered for sale as genuine antiques, which are referred to in section 7 as "fakes."

It has been suggested that legislation should be passed requiring all reproductions of antique furniture to be marked as such; but thus far this has not been done. An editorial article on this subject is in "The Antiquarian," April, 1930, page 35.

Please notice that in speaking of these desirable reproductions we mean "exact" reproductions. Any reproduction of a fine piece of antique furniture that is not an "exact" reproduction is a bad reproduction, and should not be allowed in your home. Unfortunately many commercial reproducers put into their work some little ideas of their own, which they regard as "improvements"; and they may even add something to, or take something from, the perfect lines of a master-piece of Chippendale. They imagine they can make improvements on the best, and do not hesitate to "paint the lily" and to "gild refined gold."[2]

Of a different class are the objectionable articles of furniture called "adapta-tions"[3] by their designers and makers. A piece of this kind is not made as a repro-duction of an article in a recognized style of antique furniture, but is claimed to be based upon the "spirit" of such a style and to be "inspired" by it, although the resemblance to the antique style may be scarcely visible. Moreover "adaptations" often consist of articles which were not known at the periods when the antique styles were in fashion. For example, we find cabinets for phonographs and radios advertised as being made in the "style of Hepplewhite"—objects which the pur-chaser will wish to cast aside as soon as he acquires a genuine Hepplewhite style piece of almost any kind, or even a good reproduction of one.

Section 10. Restorations; repairs; refinishing.—It is generally better to buy articles of antique furniture "in the rough" rather than to buy them already restored, repaired and refinished.[1] But when you buy an article "in the rough"

2. The writer has seen reproductions of dining room chairs in the Chippendale style decorated with very conspicuous lines of inlay which are never seen on chairs in that style. In Spain one sees Chippendale style chairs with backs covered with gilding; but this is in the Spanish taste.

The quotation is from "King John," act 4, scene 1, line 11.

Cabinet makers who are also dealers in antiques as a rule follow more carefully the exact details of a model in making reproductions than do the designers employed by factories which make reproductions in quantity.

A large department store advertised a few years ago that it had for sale reproductions of gate-leg tables in "fifty-five styles"—many of which were no doubt inventions of the factory which made them.

3. An "adaptation" is defined in Webster's New International Dictionary as "a modification for new uses; a change in form or structure."

1. Of course, the fact that a piece of furniture is found or seen in a bad condition—"in the rough"—is not proof that the piece is a genuine antique; it may have been roughened for the purpose of making it appear older than it really is. The advantage of buying things in the rough is that when they are in that condition it is generally easier to detect any new parts, and to see the history of the piece as shown by the piece itself unaffected by recent restorations, repairs or refinishing.

A book entitled "Knowing, collecting and restoring early American Furniture," by the late Henry Hammond Taylor, published by J. B. Lippincott Co., Philadelphia, 1930, contains informative chapters on restorations, refinishing, brasses and hardware, with a number of illustrations.

The words "repairs" and "restorations" do not have exactly the same meaning when applied to damaged furniture, although they are sometimes used as if they were synonymous.

"Restoration" generally has a larger meaning than "repair." "Restore" means to bring back an object to its former and better state, by the use of substitute parts; as to "restore" a cathedral. "Repairs" generally refers to small matters, such as putting furniture in good condition when broken the question is, how much in the way of restoration, repairs and refinishing should be done, and how much left undone, if you wish the article to keep its character as an antique. For example, a desk in bad condition—"in the rough"—may require so much restoration of ruined or missing parts that when finished it will be more of a new desk than an antique one. A desk may be found without feet, or with feet cut short; with a lid so damaged that it cannot be used; with wooden knobs on the drawers instead of the original brasses; with the front of one drawer entirely gone; and with other injuries. If you put on new feet, a new lid, new brass handles, a new front on the drawer, and fix other matters, is the desk still an antique? And if it is an antique, do you want that kind of an antique?

A few weeks later if you should see in a shop a nice desk, without any defects, apparently a genuine antique, and are told that it is an antique, and that the wood is all old, you may be looking at the wreck above mentioned, restored, repaired and refinished.[2] If it suits you, and you ask what repairs and restorations have been made, and are told the truth, and the whole truth, will you buy it or will you decide to wait until you find one that is more nearly one hundred per cent[3] antique?

The correct answers to these questions are not easily given. Many dealers and some collectors are very liberal in their views as to how much restoration is allowable; but it is better for the amateur collector to be too strict than not strict enough. If that desk is brought to your home, you will often think of those restorations, and will soon tire of it, and will feel obliged to apologize for it to your visitors, and will wish to sell[4] it and get a better one. We are all apt to believe what we want to believe in purchasing antique furniture; we prefer to think well of our purchases, rather than to think badly of them. But in cases like this one's fondness may easily change almost into hatred.

In a general way it may be said that structural defects cannot be cured; minor defects may be cured, but also may often be left uncured without lessening the

or damaged, without substituting new parts to any great extent. To decide in particular cases whether the work should be called a restoration or a repair is not always easy or important. In furniture work a "replacement" means about the same as a "restoration."

If a leg of a chair is missing and a new one is made and put on, the new leg is a restoration rather than a repair; so also a new lid on a desk, or a new glass in a mirror, are restorations. But if a leg of a chair has become loose and needs new glue, the work is a repair; or if the keyhole in the lid of a desk is broken and a new keyhole is made; or if the glass of a mirror has been resilvered—all these are merely repairs.

The word "reconstructed" may mean almost anything, from making a new chair from old wood to converting Howard clocks such as those formerly used in the stations on the Pennsylvania Railroad into Willard banjo clocks. There is not much difference between a "reconstructed" piece and a "fake." It is almost entirely a matter of degree.

2. All of the work may have been so skillfully done, using old wood, that it may not be noticed by an amateur collector, especially if the article is not examined in a strong light and from several points of view.

3. It is said that under the French law an antique article of furniture offered for sale must be at least 90 per cent original. In England and our country there is no legal rule on the subject.

4. It is generally difficult to sell pieces which have been much restored, even at a low price. Few collectors want them.

value of the article; and in all cases repairs and restorations should be kept down to a minimum. Slight but obvious "honorable scars" are to be preferred to obvious new additions and patches. The marks of time and usage constitute one of the charms of antique furniture. These observations may seem simple and reasonable, but the difficulty is to decide what defects are minor and what are major and incurable; what are structural defects and what are mere "honorable scars." A cabinet maker experienced in antique furniture may be a good adviser. But whoever repairs your damaged article, do not let him make it look like new; if the earmarks of age are once lost they can never be regained in your lifetime.

"Refinishing" means removing an existing finish and then finishing the article again. Refinishing may be necessary in many cases, especially where several coats of varnish or paint or stain have been applied to a piece of furniture in past years. It is done by removing the successive coats, either with a "varnish remover," or other liquid preparation, or by scraping the coats off with a tool. In the latter process there is danger of injury if the piece is scraped down to the wood, as the scraping may remove a thin layer of the surface of the wood, and with it any "patina"[5] that time and rubbing may have produced. This patina is described as a lovely and valuable color or appearance, which will be gone forever if the surface of the wood is removed. Refinishing may be necessary even if an antique has a fine patina; but the work should be done only by a cabinet maker experienced in working with antique furniture.

5. This word means "a green film formed on bronze by exposure to the atmosphere, or after burial in the earth, or by treatment with acids, etc. . . A natural patina of fine color has a distinct artistic value. . . By extension (of meaning) it is a film similarly formed on other metals; or the surface–texture or surface–color gained by various materials, as wood, marble, etc., after a long exposure." The above is quoted in part from Webster's New International Dictionary and the Century Dictionary. See also "Oak and Walnut," section 28, note 3.

In his "English Furniture," volume 3, page 337, Mr. Cescinsky states that "much of the so-called 'patina' so prized by collectors and expatiated upon at such great length by many writers on the subject of English furniture, is really the surface of shellac polish which dates from the middle of the nineteenth century." Mr. Wallace Nutting, in his "Furniture Treasury," volume 3, page 318, remarks that "the patter about patina has been much overdone, both by dealers and collectors."

A coat of shiny varnish on an article of antique furniture is a horrible feature of about 1850 in the Victorian era and should not be tolerated.

CHAPTER III

STYLES OF AMERICAN ANTIQUE FURNITURE

Section 11. General remarks on styles and periods.—In this chapter is presented a brief historical account of the various styles of American antique furniture. This may be found to be a somewhat dull subject; and if so, perhaps it may be well to pass it by for the present and come back to it after the later chapters, and the illustrations, are examined.

In the first place it should be realized that almost all of our furniture styles, from the time of the landing of the Pilgrim fathers in the "Mayflower" in the year 1620 until somewhat recently, have been English styles. Our ancestors were English subjects until they declared themselves free and independent in 1776; in fact all the early settlers of our country were English people, except a comparatively small number, such as the Dutch settlers in New York. It was natural therefore that the settlers and their descendants should look to England, rather than to any other country, for their styles of furniture, just as they looked to it in matters of art and literature. Some of the settlers brought English furniture with them, and others imported it; and the cabinet makers who came over at various times, or who learned their trade here, made their furniture in the English style, which was their own and only style. For this reason, what ever is said about the character of English styles applies, in a general way, to American styles also. In later years, however, the cabinet makers in different sections of our country made many changes, or variations, from the then prevailing English styles. In New York, because of the Dutch settlement, the Dutch styles were in vogue for some years.

It should also be remembered that all parts of our country were not settled by the same class of people. The poor Pilgrims, the well-to-do Puritans, the prosperous Dutch of New York, the even more prosperous Quakers of Pennsylvania, and the wealthy settlers of the more southern States, were different types of men, and were not accustomed to exactly the same kinds of household furniture in their native country. This partly accounts for the fact that certain kinds of antique furniture have been found in some portions of our country which have not been found in other parts. An example is mentioned in section 47, note 2.

Moreover it should be noticed that the furniture styles[1] do not begin and end at exact dates. In fact, although the beginning of a style may be approxi-

1. A.   The reasons for the changes in English styles from time to time are in some cases well understood. Thus the Dutch style which is known as the Queen Anne style was made the fashion by the influence of William of Orange, a Dutchman, and Mary, his wife, when they became King and Queen of England in 1689; and this influence was continued by Queen Anne during her reign from 1702 to 1714.

B.   The Empire style of Napoleon is another instance of a style established by royal influence. When Napoleon came into power as Emperor he determined to create a new style of art, including furniture, and the artists employed by him to do this work prepared designs based upon Greek and Roman models. It is sometimes said that the French Empire style was created by order of Napoleon in honor of himself. See section 21, note 2.

C.   In England a change from the style of Chippendale resulted from the influence of Robert Adam, the architect to George III, who designed many great houses for the nobility, and also designed furniture worthy of the buildings, and now known as furniture in the Adam style. See section 16.

D.   In perhaps all cases one underlying reason for the changes in styles was the struggle of cabinet makers for business, and the desire of their customers for some new fashion, that is, something different from the then prevailing style. In this connection the following quotation from Mr. Cescinsky's "English Furniture of the Eighteenth Century," volume 2, page 14, is interesting: "In considering the furniture of this period it must not be forgotten that the fashions of the aristocratic classes were frequently changing. The upper classes separated themselves from the lower by every possible means. It was sufficient for a fashion to be adopted by the latter to be forthwith rejected by the former. Not only in furniture, but in dress, manners, customs and modes of living, this gulf between the poor and rich was always kept as wide as possible. To this is due the ever–changing fashions and the eagerness with which each new foreign innovation was adopted." And it is also said that furniture made for a palace was almost always specially designed to please some noble purchaser and as a rule did not conform closely to the style of the period; and that to include such pieces in a book on English furniture is misleading.

E.   Not only did the styles of various articles of furniture change from time to time, but also the articles of furniture in use in different periods changed. Many articles used in one period passed out of fashion in a later one and were discontinued; and new articles of furniture were made in many cases. For example, highboys and lowboys were seldom made after about 1775 and their place was mainly taken by the low chests of drawers, or bureaus, and by dressing tables respectively. At various periods the making of gate–leg tables, three–legged tables such as pie–crust tables, Windsor chairs and many other articles, altogether ceased and has not been revived, except as reproductions of the antique.

F.   The reader of books on antique furniture occasionally finds a theory advanced that the furniture of a country at a given period to some extent reflects the history of the country and the views and desires of its people; and it has been said, in substance, that the furniture at a given period cannot be understood unless we know the "needs and aspirations" of the people at that period. Without denying altogether the correctness of this theory, it may be said that it is at least somewhat exaggerated. In the seventy years from about 1740 to about 1810, there were in England four different styles of furniture—the Chippendale, Adam, Hepplewhite and Sheraton—each for a time overlapping the following one. If the theory above referred to were literally correct there would have been in England in that space of years at least four great changes in the "needs and aspirations" of the English people. Thus far such changes have not been mentioned by the historians of that country.

mately dated, its ending may not be exactly known. A furniture style is not like the period of the reign of a monarch, as Queen Anne, beginning and ending

(NOTE 1, *continued*)

G. It is sometimes said that the crude and simple style of the furniture of the early settlers in New England was an expression of their strong and rugged character; but another reason why the furniture made and used by them was crude and simple was because the settlers could neither make nor buy the finer articles of their time. They made plain furniture as best they could, no doubt such as they were accustomed to in their former homes. It seems however that on the "Mayflower," there must have been a huge quantity of almost every variety of furniture. This is the celebrated "Mayflower Joke." Dr. Oliver Wendell Holmes wrote of the Pilgrims leaving

"the Dutchman's shore,
With those that in the Mayflower came, a hundred souls or more,
Along with all the furniture to fill their new abodes,
To judge by what is still on hand, at least a hundred loads."

Quoting these lines, Miss Frances Clary Morse, of Worcester, Mass., in her book "_____ ture of the Olden Time," page 1, remarks: "If one were to accept as authentic all the legends _____ various pieces—chairs, tables, desks, spinets and even pianos—Dr. Holmes's estimate wou_____ moderate."

H. Another interesting but irrelevant tradition is that in Albemarle County, Virginia, in which "Monticello," the home of Thomas Jefferson is situated, there is enough "furniture used by Jefferson" to fill the house three or four times. This may be true if it is also true that in addition to his American furniture Jefferson owned at his death the furniture which he had brought with him from Paris, filling eighty-six large cases. All the contents of the house were sold at auction in 1827. In section 62, on Windsor chairs, note 2, it is related that Jefferson, while President, bought four dozen "stick," or Windsor, chairs. Illustrated articles on the furnishings of Monticello are in "Antiques," November, 1927, page 380, and December, 1927, page 482, and in "The Antiquarian," July, 1930, page 38.

I. Several styles which became fully developed in particular periods, for example, the Chippendale and the Empire, actually began earlier than their names would indicate. Certain features of the Chippendale style, for example, made their appearance some years before Chippendale himself made furniture; and some features of the French Empire style are seen in furniture made before the Empire of Napoleon arose. This subject is also mentioned in sections 15 and 21.

J. The eighteenth century included the five great styles of English furniture, that is, the Queen Anne, the Chippendale, the Adam, the Hepplewhite and the Sheraton. It is for this reason termed the "Golden Age" of English cabinet making. No other English styles of that period are known, because no important household furniture in any other styles has been found, except certain special types, such as Windsor chairs and articles made in the French style.

K. In the period in which a particular style, such as the Chippendale style, and a certain kind of wood, such as mahogany, was in fashion, not all articles of furniture were made in that style and of that wood. Fine chairs, for instance, were often, if not usually, made to order, and the cabinet maker was free to make any style of chair and to use any kind of wood which his customer desired; for example, fine chairs in the Chippendale style made of curly maple instead of mahogany have been found near Philadelphia; see section 30, note 2. The customer, or the customer's wife, may have desired maple or any kind of wood, more or less expensive; or a chair like her grandmother's; or with some other departure from the style in fashion at the time; and the cabinet maker would not have been human if he had insisted on making the article in the prevailing style and of mahogany and had declined to do as his customer wished.

L. Many collectors care mainly or only for one style of furniture, such as the Queen Anne style or the Chippendale style, and are not much interested in other styles. Others find more pleasure in collecting furniture of one kind of wood, such as pine or walnut. This concentration upon one style or wood may lead to a somewhat narrow view of the general subject.

on certain dates of certain years; the furniture in the Queen Anne style continued to be made for many years after the end of her reign. While the styles were in the process of changing there was naturally an overlapping of the period of one style into the period of another; for example, in our country the Chippendale style continued to be used for some years after the Hepplewhite style began, and thus two styles were in use at the same time. All the cabinet makers and all the purchasers of furniture could not entirely change their tastes at the same time. The development was gradual and, as remarked by Mr. Cescinsky in "English and American Furniture," page 64, "at no period did a population awake one morning to hail a new manner." The period of the process of gradual change, or transition, from one style to another, is called a "transition" period, and clearly appears in many articles, especially in chairs, as will be seen in the chapter on that subject. This overlapping of styles is a frequent cause of uncertainty as to the age of a piece of furniture; and the uncertainty is increased by the fact that cabinet makers in the country districts who got their styles from the cities were generally several years behind the city styles; and the American cabinet makers who copied the English ones were always several years behind the English.

The names now given to the principal styles[2] of furniture were not used at the time when those styles were in fashion. The names as we now know them were given when the styles were studied and analyzed in recent years. The designation of some of the styles by the names of celebrated cabinet makers and designers, such as the Chippendale style, the Hepplewhite style and the Sheraton style, was not only because of their leadership in the making or designing of fine and distinctive furniture, but also because of the books which they published containing their own designs. By means of these books the changes in styles have been

2. In conversation it is often said that a certain article, for example, a chair, is a "Chippendale chair" or a "Hepplewhite chair"; but, of course, this expression is not intended to mean that the chair was made by Chippendale or Hepplewhite, or under their direction, but merely that it is in the "Chippendale *style*" or the "Hepplewhite *style*." In this book on American antique furniture the expression "a Chippendale *style* chair" is always used for the sake of accuracy; and these words are commended to the reader as the only proper ones. As Adam and Sheraton did not make furniture, the expression "an Adam chair," or "a Sheraton chair," can only imply that the chair is in the *style* of Adam or Sheraton; but for the sake of uniformity, the words "Adam *style*" or "Sheraton *style*" are always used here. The use of the words "Duncan Phyfe" in this connection is referred to in section 20, entitled "The Duncan Phyfe *furniture*," not "The Duncan Phyfe *style*." In fact there is no Duncan Phyfe "style."

A full enjoyment of antique furniture, and a correct understanding of the subject, can only be had by the amateur collector through a knowledge of the *styles* of the pieces in which he is interested. A person may admire a fine antique chair or other article without knowing whether it is in the Chippendale style or the Sheraton style; but this is an ignorant admiration, and is often expressed in two words—"very pretty." The features which distinguish one type of chair from another are unnoticed and unappreciated—the legs, the feet, the back, the inlay, the carving, the whole design of the chair are an unmeaning combination of parts, and the approximate age is unknown. But when the chair is understood, when you know it is in the style of Chippendale or Hepplewhite or Sheraton or Directory or Empire, or is a chair similar to some of those made by Duncan Phyfe, the whole outlook changes; you recognize all the parts as being in one of these styles and you see the fine points and appreciate their design. Apart from any question of value or any connection with one's ancestor's, this is the real enjoyment of antique furniture.

critically studied; and it was natural that the names of the designers of new styles should be given to those styles. These books are referred to more fully in the sections in this chapter on the styles of the three men above mentioned.[3]

Another matter should be realized in regard to the styles of English furniture, and our own, and that is that the various furniture styles were not altogether new and original inventions by Chippendale and other great cabinet makers and designers. The preëminence of those men arose from their skill in producing new designs based upon previous designs. Perhaps every style mentioned in this book was a modification of, or a change in, a previous style, although not always based upon the immediately preceding one. Some were based upon ancient designs, as the Adam style and the French Empire style; these two styles were not inventions of the Adam Brothers or of the artists of Napoleon, but were based upon designs used in ancient Greece and Rome; and Greece and Rome in some cases took their ideas from the still more ancient Egypt, as may be noticed in the great museum at Cairo. Tracing the development of styles in various countries from one period to another, and from one country to another, is an interesting study, but can only be merely mentioned in this book.

Section 12. The Jacobean style.—The Jacobean[1] period, in respect to furniture, is considered as extending through almost the entire seventeenth century— more exactly, the years from 1603, when James I became King of England, to 1688, the year before William of Orange and Mary became King and Queen. History and dates are not so interesting, however, as the fact that the first furniture that was brought over to this country, and the first furniture that was made in this country, was in the style of this period.

Very little American furniture of the earlier part of the Jacobean period is still surviving; but later pieces, from about 1670, are more numerous. The amateur collector, however, may never see any examples of either the earlier or the later dates except in museums; and he will perhaps never have the opportunity of buying a genuine piece.

In the illustrations in later chapters of this book will be seen examples of several articles in the Jacobean style. These illustrations are mainly of wainscot chairs, Nos. 22 and 23; high back cane chairs, Nos. 35 and 36; day bed No. 502;

3. A notable firm of London cabinet makers in the latter part of the eighteenth century was "Seddon, Sons and Shackelton," who had a large business and made much Adam style furniture from the designs of Robert Adam. Mr. Cescinsky, in the book "English and American Furniture," page 265, writes: "but for the accident that they neglected to publish a trade catalogue or book of designs (the two were often synonymous) we might have a 'Seddon style' at the present day, with far greater reason, in actual work realized in wood, than a Chippendale, a Hepplewhite or a Sheraton style; which shows the mistakes which one makes in neglecting to consider posterity." See also section 15, note 2.

1. The Latin name "Jacobus" means "Jacob" or "James"; and the word "Jacobean" means "pertaining to or relating to a person named Jacobus, Jacob or James; specifically to James I, King of England, or to his time; also, in occasional use, to James II"; Century Dictionary.

chests Nos. 595 and 596; press cupboard and court cupboards, seen in section 121; and also a few early tables, especially the gate-leg kind seen in section 155. These illustrations and the comments on them sufficiently indicate the main features of the Jacobean style.[2]

Section 13. The William and Mary style.—We now come to a style which is more interesting, to us at least, than the Jacobean style, because more pieces of fine furniture of this style are to be seen in our country than those in the Jacobean style; and more frequently some of them are offered for sale.

As mentioned in note 1, A, in section 11, William of Orange, a Dutchman, and Mary, his wife, a daughter of James the Second, came over from Holland, and became King and Queen of England in 1689. The result was that the Dutch influence in furniture prevailed at the court and among the upper classes; and this influence continued for some time after the brief reign of fourteen years, 1689-1702. In some respects the William and Mary style was one of transition, leading to the style of Queen Anne.

The new style had in due time a considerable influence in America. Not immediately, of course, for it took several years for a new style to be established in England, and still longer for it to be brought over to our colonies and to become the fashion here.

An important feature of the William and Mary style as a whole was the change from the often heavy and bulky furniture of the Jacobean period to lighter, graceful and more ornamental pieces. Inlay, often called "marquetry" when elaborate, (see section 33), lacquer, (see section 31), painting and gilding, (see section 34), contributed to the decoration of the finer types of furniture. This period is notable also for the introduction of highboys and lowboys, and for the higher bedsteads, some of which reached sixteen feet upward towards a lofty ceiling and whose frames could not be seen because of a covering of satins or silks. Gate-leg tables, also, were favorite articles, so much so that they continued in vogue for more than a hundred years thereafter.

Of the noticeable changes in furniture features, one was in the legs, such as those on highboys and lowboys, with turnings in the shape of inverted cups or in a trumpet shape; see the highboys mentioned below. In this period the "cabriole"

2.   As used in some books on antique furniture the term "Jacobean period," 1603-1688, includes the years, or periods, of James I, 1603-1625; Charles I, 1625-1649; Cromwellian, 1649-1660; Charles II, 1660-1685; James II, 1685-1688; the latter two periods are also known as the Carolean or late Stuart or Restoration period, extending from 1660 to 1688. In other books the Jacobean period is limited to 1649; and the term is also used to mean only the period of James the Second.

Illustrations of articles of Jacobean style furniture are in Mr. Luke Vincent Lockwood's book, "Colonial Furniture in America," in the chapters on chests, cupboards, chairs and tables.

In Mr. Wallace Nutting's book entitled "Furniture of the Pilgrim Century, 1620-1720," published by Old America Company, Framingham, Mass., Revised Edition, 1924, the subject of Jacobean style furniture in our country is considered, with many illustrations, especially of chests.

legs, (see section 24), were probably first used, of which further mention will be made in the next section and in the chapter on chairs. The drop handles, illustrated in section 39, were also a characteristic feature of this style. Walnut was the favorite wood, but other local woods were also used.

A number of pieces in the William and Mary style are shown in the following illustrations: high back chair No. 40; banister back chairs with cresting at the top, Nos. 44-46; highboys Nos. 632-634; lowboys Nos. 669-672; and also tables as shown in the chapter on that subject.

Section 14. The Queen Anne style—and styles until Chippendale.—The term "Queen Anne"[1] period is sometimes followed in furniture histories by the words "and early Georgian," making the name of the combined periods "the Queen Anne and early Georgian."[2] The reason for this is that the addition of the words "Early Georgian" fills in the interval between the death of Queen Anne in 1714, and the beginning of the Chippendale period,[3] about 1745, in which interval no definitely new style began; but as the exact meaning of the words "Early Georgian" is not always clearly recalled by American readers, a title for this section has been adopted which, with this explanation, will make the subject more easily understood. By some writers the Queen Anne style is called the "Dutch[4] style," because during the reign of Queen Anne the Dutch style of furniture, which was introduced in the William and Mary period, continued in fashion, with modifications.

1.   Queen Anne was a sister of Queen Mary, both being daughters of James the Second. Her reign was only twelve years, 1702-1714.

2.   This expression refers to a period of about forty years, (1702-1745), beginning with the reign of Queen Anne and extending through the reign of George the First, (1714-1727), and until about the year 1745 in the reign of George the Second, (1727-1760).

The years of George the Third, (1760-1820), George the Fourth, (1820-1830), and William the Fourth, (1830-1837), include the furniture periods of Chippendale, Adam, Hepplewhite, Sheraton and Empire. These five periods do not have exact beginnings or endings, and the dates are only approximate; and they overlap each other, one style continuing into the period of another. This matter of overlapping is mentioned above in section 11 on page 36, and in several other places in this book; see the Index, "Overlapping."

The term "Georgian," often applied to architecture, includes the reigns of the four "Georges" above mentioned, from 1714 to 1830; a term very indefinite as to dates.

The English "Regency" period is occasionally referred to as having a somewhat characteristic furniture style. In the latter years of the life of George the Third, his son, the Prince of Wales was Regent, 1811-1820, and became George the Fourth on the death of his father in the latter year. The Regency style is not noticed in our furniture. An illustrated article entitled "The revival of English Regency" is in the "International Studio," July, 1930, page 25. A book entitled "Regency Furniture, 1795-1820," by M. Jourdain, is well illustrated.

3.   See the next section, paragraph 3, in which a peculiarity of the term "Chippendale style" is mentioned.

4.   It is said that the museums in Holland do not contain articles of furniture of exactly the style which we call "Dutch" or "Queen Anne." The English cabinet makers made certain changes; and the American styles were based on the English, with further changes.

The principal change of a general character[5] apparent in the Queen Anne style was that the formal lines of the style of William and Mary were abandoned and in their place curved lines of graceful character were used, giving to many articles a more elegant appearance than could be had in the previous rectangular shapes. The extensive use of the "cyma" curve, which the artist Hogarth called "the line of beauty," greatly contributed to the fine character of the period; see section 23, entitled "The cyma curve."

More particularly, three changes are specially noticeable; first, instead of a straight leg, there was a general adoption of the cabriole leg, (see section 24), which was first used in England in the previous period of William and Mary; second, the use of club, and also ball and claw, feet, (see section 25); and, third, the increasing use of mahogany, which however did not displace walnut as the principal wood of the period, (see sections 28 and 29).

It is thought that the full adoption of the English Queen Anne style did not begin in our country until about 1720; see section 50 on Queen Anne style chairs, note 1.

Throughout the period many fine chairs, highboys, lowboys and other pieces were made in our country; and about the end of the period the Windsor chair— said to be the most popular kind of chair ever made—first appeared in England, and later became a favorite in America.

Many illustrations of articles in the Queen Anne style are in the various chapters, among which are: chairs, Nos. 50 to 64; sofa, No. 539; highboys, No. 635 and others; lowboys, No. 675 and others; and many more in the chapters on tables, mirrors and other articles.

5. As mentioned above, no entirely new style arose in the years between the date of the death of Queen Anne in 1714 and the beginning of the Chippendale style, about 1745; but five special types or divisions of the then existing style have been classified by Mr. Herbert Cescinsky, and are illustrated and described in his "English Furniture," volume 2, chapters 2 to 6. On page 16 it is said that "this period of thirty-one years is an exceedingly complicated one in English furniture." Although American examples of all of these types were apparently not made, in any number at least, in our country, it may be well to mention them, as explained in Mr. Cescinsky's book.

From 1714 to 1725. Decorated Queen Anne period. In this period the Queen Anne style pieces had "a tendency to greater elaboration in the carving of arms, legs and backs of settees, chairs and other pieces"; page 17.

From 1720 to 1735. The "lion" period. This period is named from the fashion of decorating the legs of tables, chairs and other articles in the Queen Anne style with carved heads and paws of lions.

From 1720 to 1750. Architects' furniture. This is designed in terms of architecture. Numerous examples in America have fluted flat columns, called "pilasters," as in the secretary-bookcase No. 841 and the much later bookcase No. 870; and the door-heads of houses furnished the idea for the tops of various pieces, such as the secretary-bookcase No. 851. See also the corner cupboards Nos. 912 and 917.

From 1730 to 1740. The "satyr-mask" period. Here the legs are decorated at the top with carved masks of a grotesque appearance.

From 1735 to 1750. The "cabochon and leaf" period. A cabochon is an ornamental oval or round surface, convex or concave, generally surrounded by leaf carving. It was used on the upper part of legs of chairs and tables. The word is also used in connection with precious stones.

Section 15. The Chippendale style.—Having briefly referred to the three English furniture styles bearing the names of kings and queens, we now come to the next style, the first named for a private person—Thomas Chippendale, the most famous of English cabinet makers. Not enough of his life and personality is known to us to make even a short biography of undisputed facts;[1] but "his name has by general consent been attached to the most splendid period of English furniture"; in his day he became "almost the sole arbiter of the furniture fashions of England"; and he "reigned supreme as the fashionable cabinet maker of the metropolis." His skill made the style famous, and his name has become the name of the period.

Chippendale began his London career in 1749, and was soon successful, so much so that he was able to go to the expense of publishing, in 1754, a volume showing his furniture designs, which he termed "The Gentleman and Cabinet-maker's Director," now commonly called the "Director," the title page of which is shown on the next page as No. 2. This book contained one hundred and sixty engraved plates of designs of articles of furniture. It did not advertise these articles as being on hand for sale, but it offered the designs as suggestions to customers who desired to order furniture to be made.[2] It was sold by subscription, and the list of subscribers, many of whom were of the nobility, shows that Chippendale at this time had a large number of customers. Two later editions were published, the last in 1762. One of the advertisements in 1760 of a later edition refers to "Mr. Chippendale's elegant designs of household furniture in the newest and most fashionable taste." These quoted words may explain the fact that some

---

1. Much has been surmised and written about Thomas Chippendale, but as intimated above, not much is definitely known. It is commonly believed that his father, Thomas, or John, Chippendale, was a cabinet maker and wood carver at Worcester, England; and that Thomas, his son, was born in 1718, worked with his father, moved to London, married in 1748, went into business for himself in 1749, and in 1753 moved to St. Martin's Lane, near Trafalgar Square. In 1755 three houses used as his workshops were destroyed by fire, including the chests of twenty-two of his workmen—a number which shows that his business was a large one. In a recent book, "Thomas Chippendale," by Edwin J. Layton, published by John Murray, London, 1928, doubt is cast upon the truth of some of the details mentioned above. Chippendale died in 1779, and his son succeeded to the business. The subject of Chippendale's early life and work is very controversial.

A correct statement and explanation of the "Chippendale style" is not easy, owing to a number of matters which seem difficult to understand because of a lack of authentic information. Several writers have drawn on their imaginations in regard to many things connected with Chippendale and his work. This lack of recorded information is perhaps partly because in the eyes of his contemporaries Chippendale was only and always a tradesman, as other leading cabinet makers were, even though in 1760 he was elected a member of the Society of Arts, indicating the esteem in which he was held.

2. This method of advertising by publishing books of designs was customary at the time, and was used by other cabinet makers. Thus Robert Manwaring, in 1765, published "The Cabinet and Chair Makers' Real Friend and Companion"; notice the two trades here—the "cabinet maker" and the "chair maker"; see the chapter on chairs, section 45. Other publications of the same kind were by Ince and Mayhew, Thomas Shearer, Hepplewhite and Sheraton. See also section 11, note 3.

The main purpose of these books was apparently to offer something new in furniture designs, not to illustrate styles which were already used. This purpose appears in the books and explains why illustrations of existing styles were not more frequently shown.

THE
GENTLEMAN
AND
CABINET-MAKER's
DIRECTOR.

BEING A LARGE
COLLECTION
OF THE MOST
Elegant and Useful Designs of Houshold Furniture
IN THE
GOTHIC, CHINESE and MODERN TASTE:

Including a great VARIETY of

BOOK-CASES for LIBRARIES or Private ROOMS. COMMODES, LIBRARY and WRITING-TABLES, BUROES, BREAKFAST-TABLES, DRESSING and CHINA-TABLES, CHINÆ-CASES, HANGING-SHELVES,	TEA-CHESTS, TRAYS, FIRE-SCREENS, CHAIRS, SETTEES, SOPHA'S, BEDS, PRESSES and CLOATHS-CHESTS, PIER-GLASS SCONCES, SLAB FRAMES, BRACKETS, CANDLE-STANDS, CLOCK-CASES, FRETS,

AND OTHER
ORNAMENTS.

TO WHICH IS PREFIXED,

A Short EXPLANATION of the Five ORDERS of ARCHITECTURE,
and RULES of PERSPECTIVE;
WITH

Proper DIRECTIONS for executing the most difficult Pieces, the Mouldings being exhibited at large, and the Dimensions of each DESIGN specified:

THE WHOLE COMPREHENDED IN

One Hundred and Sixty COPPER-PLATES, neatly Engraved,

Calculated to improve and refine the present TASTE, and suited to the Fancy and Circumstances of Persons in all Degrees of Life.

Dulcique animos novitate tenebo. OVID.
Ludentis speciem dabit & torquebitur. HOR.

BY
THOMAS CHIPPENDALE,
Of St. MARTIN's-LANE, CABINET-MAKER.

LONDON,

Printed for the AUTHOR, and sold at his House in St. MARTIN's-LANE. MDCCLIV.
Also by T. OSBORNE, Bookseller, in Gray's-Inn; H. PIERS, Bookseller, in Holborn; R. SAYER, Print-seller, in Fleetstreet; J. SWAN, near Northumberland-House, in the Strand. At EDINBURGH, by Messrs. HAMILTON and BALFOUR: And at DUBLIN, by Mr. JOHN SMITH, on the Blind-Quay.

ILLUSTRATION No. 2.

of the features which are now known as features of the Chippendale style were not shown in the volume; for example, many fine chairs made at and before the time the book was issued, were supported by ball and claw feet; but not a ball and claw foot is shown in the first or later editions of the volume; the reason probably being that this kind of foot had been in use for some years previously and was not then "in the newest and most fashionable taste."

The preëminence of Chippendale is based upon the fine character of the designs in the "Director" and upon the few pieces of elegant furniture which are definitely known to have been made in his shop. His contemporary standing is shown by the facts that his designs in the "Director" were copied by others, and that he was often employed by Robert Adam to carry out the latter's designs for the furniture to be placed in the great houses of the nobility for whom Adam was the architect. The studies of modern scholars lead to the opinion that the "Chippendale style" took definite shape as the leading English style shortly after the publication of his "Director" in 1754; and that the "Chippendale style" is based upon his book to a greater extent than upon the few known pieces of his furniture.

A peculiarity of the term "Chippendale style" is that it is commonly used to include certain furniture designs which were in fashion at a time before the Chippendale style existed as a definite style.[3] When he began his career certain Queen Anne types were in fashion, and for some years he continued to use these models, making changes which appeared also in his later designs;[4] such pieces may be said to illustrate the beginning of the Chippendale style;[5] and it is thought proper to say that they were of what we now call the "Chippendale school"[6] or the "Chippendale period" or the "Chippendale style."

3. A similar peculiarity is that the Empire style is regarded as having begun before the French Empire came into being; see section 21 and also note 1, I in section 11.

4. It is said, for example, that Chippendale at first worked on existing models of chairs made in the Queen Anne style, and later changed the backs and other parts, and that in the course of a few years the shapes prevailing in the period of Queen Anne gradually disappeared and the Chippendale style designs took their place.

5. In Mr. Cescinsky's "English Furniture of the Eighteenth Century," volume 2, page 161, it is said that "we have the right . . to make the influence of Chippendale . . retrospective, and to class these pieces as being not only the work of the great craftsman and his school, but also as being an integral part of what we now know as his style." And on page 13, it is said that "the first London examples of cabinet work of Chippendale are so purely in the (then) prevailing fashion that it has become customary to style as Chippendale nearly all of the early Georgian models." See the previous section 14, paragraph 1, in regard to the "Early Georgian" period.

6. Some writers refer to various articles of furniture as being in the Chippendale "school" rather than in the Chippendale "style," because similar articles were made also by other contemporary cabinet makers, all of whom, with Chippendale, worked in the same or similar designs, forming thus a "school." There is also a Hepplewhite school and a Sheraton school of cabinet makers.

The term "pre-Director," as applied to the designs of Chippendale style furniture, refers to types which he used in the years before his "Director" was published in 1754. Very few authenticated "pre-Director" specimens of Chippendale's work are known. The term "post-Director" refers to types used after the "Director" was published.

The term "pre-Chippendale" is sometimes used to refer to certain styles which were in vogue shortly before Chippendale became a cabinet maker and which he adopted and improved; some of them are referred to in the previous section, note 5.

It must not be thought that Chippendale originated all of the features which distinguish the "Chippendale style" from other styles. Some writers who quote the familiar saying that "there is nothing new under the sun" are able to convince themselves that the great reputation of Chippendale is ill-founded because almost every fine feature in his furniture designs had previously appeared in England or in other countries. But even if this be true to some extent, Chippendale is entitled to the credit for the style which bears his name because he brought the earlier features to perfection and because he designed new ones of high character and thus produced the finest furniture that had ever been made in England.[7] The fact that Robert Adam, whose style is considered in the next section, drew his inspiration, and in fact made his designs, from ancient Roman models does not detract from his reputation as a great architect and a great designer of furniture.

It is said that it is difficult or impossible to distinguish much of the furniture actually made by Chippendale from similar furniture made by certain other English cabinet makers of the period. In a very few cases the original bills or other documents have definitely proved that certain articles were made in the Chippendale workshop;[8] but the number of such pieces is said to be very small. Other cabinet makers could use the designs shown in his book and could copy the furniture made by him, and many of them did, on both sides of the Atlantic.

During the years in which the Chippendale style prevailed in America, from about 1755 to 1785, practically all of our furniture of the better sort was made in that style; and with us the style continued for some time after it was supplanted in England by the new styles of Adam and Hepplewhite, probably because the Revolutionary War stopped business relations between the two countries for several years, and the American cabinet makers, not having the new styles, continued to use the Chippendale models.

The term "Chippendale style," as applied to his furniture, does not mean that he made all of his chairs or other articles in one style only. Chairs, for

7. In the "Metropolitan Museum Studies," volume 1, part 2, and volume 2, part 1, are several articles entitled "Creators of the Chippendale Style," by Fiske Kimball and Edna Donnell. A review of the first two articles was published in "Country Life," England, September 14, 1929, which was quoted in the "Bulletin of the Metropolitan Museum of Art," October, 1929. The reviewer stated that the articles deal " a hard blow to the reputation of a man deeply versed in all the arts of self-advertisement," meaning Chippendale; and that "the findings . . amount to a verdict that Thomas Chippendale nas masqueraded in borrowed plumes for nearly two centuries"; also that "for the genesis of the Chippendale style, Lock and Copeland were chiefly responsible," they having been Chippendale's draughtsmen; and that the origin of the designs in the "Director" is now settled against Chippendale. It had previously been stated by Mr. Cescinsky in his "English Furniture," volume 2, page 160, that Chippendale was not the sole author of the drawings shown in the "Director."

8. Certain furniture from Chippendale's shop, made for several great houses in England, and authenticated by documents, was made from designs of Robert Adam and is in the Adam style, not in the Chippendale style.

In the magazine "Antiques," May, 1929, page 383, is an article by Mr. Oliver Brackett, of the Victoria and Albert Museum, London, entitled "The Actual Workmanship of Chippendale." Mr. Brackett is the author of a book entitled "Thomas Chippendale: a study of his life, work and influence," Houghton Mifflin Co., 1925; this book is reviewed in "Antiques," November, 1925, page 288.

example, were made by him in several different styles. These include the "Dutch Chippendale style," the "Gothic Chippendale style," the "Chinese Chippendale style" and the "French Chippendale style"; or, as he wrote, chairs "after the Gothick manner" and "after the Chinese manner."[9] Chairs and various other articles were made in two or more of these "sub-styles," each of which has as a basis some Chippendale characteristics.

In his early work Chippendale followed the then prevailing style, which was Dutch in origin, as mentioned above. Some of his chairs and tables were made of walnut, and were more like those of the period following the Queen Anne style than those we now call "Chippendale." This was followed by what is known as the Gothic style, which was suggested by Gothic architectural methods. Then came the Chinese style, which was inspired by a craze for Chinese designs which swept over England and influenced both architects and furniture makers. Both the Gothic and the Chinese styles are illustrated in the "Director." Next, and last, were chairs "in the French taste," suggested by, and some perhaps copied from, the fashionable chairs of the time in France. Each of these four styles continued in vogue to some extent until the Chippendale style itself passed out of fashion.

The styles of the furniture made by Chippendale are sometimes classified in successive periods, as though he made furniture of a particular style only at one time, and of another style only at another time; but after his early period he did not confine himself to one style. Chippendale was in business to make a living, not to establish a furniture style or period, and he naturally made what his customers wanted, so that furniture of any particular style may have been made at any time after that style was adopted.

Furniture known as "Irish Chippendale" is said to be neither Irish nor Chippendale in style. In the book "English and American Furniture," page 196, Mr. Cescinsky remarks that this term reminds him of the "Saturday Evening Post," which "appears on Thursday, is not an evening paper, nor a Post." The style was a fashion in the west of England and applied mainly to tables, the feature being a large and heavily carved "apron," or "skirt." The articles of furniture now called "Irish Chippendale" are found in Ireland, and have acquired their name because it has been supposed that they were made by Irish cabinet makers at a time when the Chippendale style was in vogue; but these pieces are prior to Chippendale.

An illustrated article entitled "Irish Furniture of the Chippendale Period" is in "The Antiquarian," December, 1930, page 69, by Mr. Robert Tasker Evans. See also "Antiques," February, 1932, page 70.

9. An illustrated article entitled "Oriental influences in Chippendale's Designs," by Mr. Robert Tasker Evans, is in "The Antiquarian," September, 1929, page 25.

Section 16. The Adam style.—In our country we know the "Adam style" chiefly through the mirrors and mantelpieces made after the designs of Robert Adam, a Scotsman. His name is given to furniture in a style developed by him, which continued in fashion for about twenty–five years, 1765–1790, during which the styles of Chippendale and Hepplewhite were also successively in vogue. Robert Adam was an architect and twice visited Italy to study classic architecture; and there he absorbed, as stated in his book of architectural designs, published in 1773, "the beautiful spirit of antiquity" from the forms of ancient Rome.[1]

In 1758, after his second return to England, Robert Adam became the leading architect of the time, and he and his brothers[2] who worked with him were employed by the nobility and other wealthy clients. The Adam brothers did not make furniture; but when they designed a house they also designed the furniture in order that it might be in harmony with the style of decoration of the house, the other styles of furniture which were in vogue being unsuitable.[3] From "façade to fire irons, from the chimneys to the carpets," everything pertaining to the house was designed by the four brothers; and they employed leading cabinet makers, including Chippendale and Hepplewhite, to make the furniture according to the Adam drawings. In his Roman studies Robert Adam found many examples of the furniture of the classic period and these were used by him in his furniture designs. As a matter of interest, an illustration, No. 3, is here given of the frontispiece and another page of a large architectural book[4] by Robert Adam, dated 1764.

---

1. In "English Furniture," volume 3, page 10, Mr. Cescinsky remarks that the usual idea that Robert Adam "borrowed his inspiration from French sources is entirely erroneous; the only styles which at all approach his in dignity, the Empire and the Directoire, are of later date. The superficial resemblance which might be thought to exist between the style of Robert Adam and the Louis Sixteenth disappears on examination."

   The Adam style is often called the "Neo–classic" as mentioned in the text of section 21 in connection with illustration No. 5.

   See also section 52 on Adam style chairs.

2. There were four brothers, John, Robert, James and William. Robert was the most distinguished. The four brothers chose as their business name the word "Adelphia," a Greek word meaning "Brothers." The latter part of the word "Philadelphia" is made from the same Greek word. Robert died in 1792 and was buried in Westminster Abbey. Their father, William Adam, was a Scotch architect of distinction. The four sons lived in London.

3. The Adam style was entirely a novelty in England, not connected with any prior English style, and it did not fully develop until some years after it began. Robert Adam was obliged to teach the cabinet makers the real character of his designs, and the cabinet makers in turn influenced him. As stated by Mr. Cescinsky, "English Furniture," volume 3, page 216, "the Adam style was therefore justifiably held to cover much more than the designs of the 'Adelphi' or the work made to their order, and included all the furniture productions exhibiting the influence of the manner of which they were the pioneers."

   A large number of the original Adam architectural and other designs are preserved in the Soane Museum in London.

4. This book is the property of Mrs. Isaac Ridgeway Trimble, of Baltimore. The frontispiece shows the ruins of the palace of the Emperor Diocletian, (A.D. 284–313), at Spalatro, in Venetian Dalmatia. Drawings of the palace were made by Robert Adam and are shown in the book.

For several reasons the Adam style of furniture unfortunately never became important in our country. When the style began in England the Chippendale style was the only one in vogue and as our business relations with that country were suspended during the Revolutionary War our cabinet makers continued to use the Chippendale style and did not adopt the Adam designs. When relations were resumed after 1783 the Adam style was on the decline in England, the Hepplewhite style taking its place as the fashionable one. Our American furniture thus

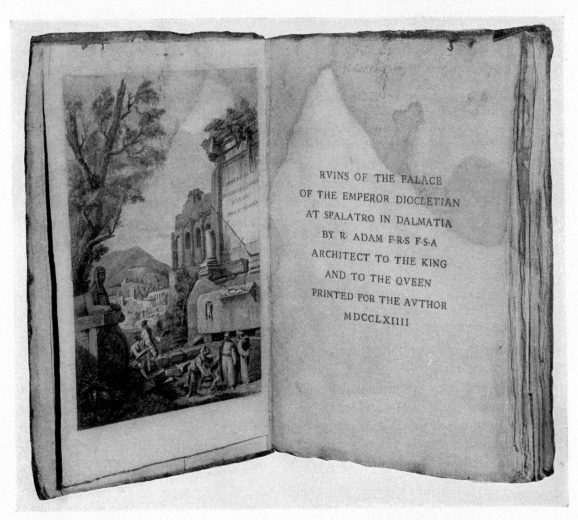

RVINS OF THE PALACE
OF THE EMPEROR DIOCLETIAN
AT SPALATRO IN DALMATIA
BY R· ADAM F·R·S F·S·A
ARCHITECT TO THE KING
AND TO THE QVEEN
PRINTED FOR THE AVTHOR
MDCCLXIIII

ILLUSTRATION No. 3.

changed from the Chippendale style directly to the Hepplewhite style, without the Adam style coming in between as it did in England. Another reason was that the Adam furniture designs were not published in a book, as were Chippendale's, and could not be easily copied by our cabinet makers; and still another reason was that much of the fine furniture made in the Adam style was expensive. Furniture made directly from the designs of Robert Adam is said to be rare in England; and in our country it does not appear that any pieces were made wholly in the Adam style in the Adam period.

But although we may not have any American furniture in the exact Adam style, we have, indirectly, examples of several features of that style. As mentioned above, one of the cabinet makers employed by Robert Adam was George Hepplewhite who thus came into close contact with the Adam designs and naturally was influenced by them, the result being that certain features in articles made in the Hepplewhite style are copies of the designs of Adam; for example, the chair No. 182 is a Hepplewhite style chair with some features of the Adam style, as mentioned in the comment on that chair. The next great furniture designer, Thomas Sheraton, also copied some of the Adam designs, perhaps to a greater extent than Hepplewhite; and it is safe to say that almost all of the classic designs of ancient Rome which appear in our antique furniture prior to the French Empire style came directly or indirectly from the London workshop of Robert Adam and his brothers.

Among the distinctive features of the Adam style is the urn, or vase, which appears on many mirrors and other pieces of furniture. Another favorite design was that of the classic honeysuckle with unopened buds, often called by the Greek name "anthemion," which is also seen on many articles in later styles, as mentioned in section 51, note 48; see also section 171, note 11. Another favorite ornamental feature was a rosette, round or oval, sometimes called a "patera." The legs of almost all articles were straight, not curved; if square, they were often tapered, terminating in spade feet; and whether square or round they were generally fluted or reeded. The mirrors in the Adam style were decorated with graceful and delicate gilded festoons and wreaths, generally made of "composition,"[5] a method which was copied by Hepplewhite. Various other classical features were also used as decorations. Many articles were adorned with paintings, some by Italian artists and by Angelica Kauffman; and plaques made by Wedgwood were often added as a decorative feature. Mahogany was chiefly used, sometimes carved or gilded, and the expensive satinwood (see section 30) was often employed. In general, the principal feature of the design of the Adam furniture was the use of the straight line of classic type instead of the curved line used by Chippendale, although the curved line appears of course in some Adam pieces, as in festoons, half-round tables, oval mirrors, and the characteristic "wheelback" chair with its ornamental spokes.

5. Decorative ornaments made of a kind of plaster composition were much used by Adam. These were also "applied" on ceilings and other parts of a room, and became very hard and could be painted. In appearance they may easily be mistaken for carved wood, as may be noticed in many fine old houses built in our country in the eighteenth century. The molds for the finer work of these American houses were doubtless imported. The plaster molds were sometimes applied on marble mantels; the carved marble mantels were generally imported.

An interesting matter in connection with the Adam brothers is their "Adelphi Lottery." They took a lease of a large lot of ground in London, fronting on the Strand and running back to the Thames, upon which they built, as a speculation, a group of buildings, calling the district "Adelphi." They named the streets after their own names of John, William, Robert and James. The operation was not successful; but they were able to secure a special Act of Parliament authorizing them to hold a public lottery to reimburse them for their expenses, the lottery prizes being for houses, not for money, and also for pictures, furniture and statuary. The sale of the tickets brought the sum of over two hundred and twenty–five thousand pounds. The first prize, valued at fifty thousand pounds, consisted of eleven houses.

Examples of the Adam style

ILLUSTRATION No. 4.

In the chapter on chairs a full page illustration, No. 181, of four English chairs made in the Adam style is given in order to show the style and to enable the reader to see the source from which Hepplewhite and Sheraton derived some of their designs of chairs. In the present section is a full page illustration, No. 4, of six other fine English pieces in the Adam style, as follows: two tables; two mirrors; a mantelpiece; and a pedestal with an urn, one of which was placed at each end of a table in the dining room, making a sideboard; these are more familiar to us than other pieces of furniture in the Adam style. They are all copied, by permission of Mr. Cescinsky, from his "English Furniture of the Eighteenth Century," volume 3, figures 14, 18, 24, 55, 66 and 76. Whenever the reader observes in other pieces of furniture any feature closely resembling any of those here shown it may be assumed that the design is based upon the design of Robert Adam.[6]

Section 17. The Hepplewhite style.

The next style is that of Hepplewhite. In so far as the facts about his life and work are concerned, George Hepplewhite[1] is an almost unknown figure. No details of his family, his training or his business career have been discovered; nor is there a single piece of furniture which is definitely known to have been made by him. It is however clear that he lived in London, that his work became popular about 1780, and that he died in 1786; and that his widow, Alice, in 1788 and twice afterwards, published, under the name of "A. Hepplewhite & Co.," a book or trade catalogue entitled "The Cabinet Maker and Upholsterer's Guide" containing designs of about three hundred articles of furniture. A similar type of book, the "Director" of Chippendale, is mentioned in the second paragraph of the text in section 15. The character of the Hepplewhite style is regarded as fixed by these designs; and the "Guide" is said to be the sole authority upon the subject. The designs in the

6. As the Adam style did not become important in our country, the books on American antique furniture do not always refer to it; but the writer thinks that the reader will be interested in this brief account of its character and in the illustrations of the six articles and of the chairs in No. 181.

In the oval mirror in illustration No. 4, containing six articles, several of the features of the Adam style are seen, that is, the honeysuckle or "anthemion" at the top, the urn or vase below, the festoons of drapery and the "composition" flowers.

An illustrated article on the Adam style is in "The Antiquarian," October, 1929, page 55, entitled "The English Neo–classic style," by Mr. Robert Tasker Evans. In the same magazine, July, 1927, page 31, is an illustrated article by Mr. Henry Branscombe entitled "The Furniture of the Adam Period."

1. The name has sometimes been spelled "Heppelwhite," but the spelling as given above appears in the "Guide," published by his widow; but she was apparently not skilled in spelling, as in a legal paper she signed her name "Aleas," which she afterwards altered to "Alice." Spelling in the eighteenth century and previously was often merely phonetic and incorrect.

An interesting matter in connection with names is that in the eighteenth century a middle name was not often used. Of the fifty–six signatures to the Declaration of Independence only three have a middle name. Most of the courts in our country followed the early English rule that the law recognized only one Christian name and the surname, and that a middle name or initial was not a part of one's name. But in later decisions the courts have given more regard to a middle name or initial. Members of the bar will find the authorities on the subject in 45 Corpus Juris, page 369, and in 19 R. C. L., page 1328.

"Guide" were extensively copied by English and American[2] cabinet makers, the latter using either the book or the pieces of furniture imported from England; the furniture made in the style of these designs is called by his name; and the cabinet makers who made furniture in these designs constituted the "Hepplewhite school."

The Hepplewhite style was in fashion in England from about 1780 to 1792, and in our country it began soon after the close of the Revolutionary War and ended about the year 1800 or later. It seems that before the "Guide" was published in 1788 certain furniture in the Hepplewhite style was imported into America and was advertised in 1785 in our newspapers, not under the name of "Hepplewhite style," but so described that no other kind could have been meant, as appears in section 53, at note 4.

The chief difference between the style of Chippendale and that of Hepplewhite is said to be that the former is of a heavier type, generally with carving and without inlay, the furniture in the Hepplewhite style being lighter,[3] with much inlay but with little carving.

As mentioned in the previous section, Hepplewhite was frequently employed by Robert Adam to make furniture according to the latter's designs, and it was natural that Hepplewhite should use in his own work some of the features of the Adam style.[4] This is especially noticeable in the decorative features of his designs, such as the use of the honeysuckle, called "anthemion," and also fluting, festoons and strings of flowers. Mr. Cescinsky, in his book "English Furniture," volume 3, pages 105–119, has a chapter entitled "Adam–Hepplewhite Furniture."

2. Too much importance should not be attached to the supposed use, by many American cabinet makers, of the books of Chippendale, Hepplewhite and Sheraton. The advertisements in the American newspapers show that much English furniture was imported, and therefore could easily be copied without having the books.

Some of the English chairs called "Hepplewhite style chairs" in the English books are so unlike other chairs of the Hepplewhite style to which we are accustomed that the name seems inappropriate; but if they are in Heppelwhite's book of designs, they are properly called "Heppelwhite style" chairs.

Furniture in the French style was made by Hepplewhite, as also by Chippendale and Sheraton. In Mr. Cescinsky's "English Furniture," volume 3, pages 201–212, are illustrations of this style.

3. It is said that "lightness, delicacy and grace are the distinguishing characteristics of Hepplewhite's work. The massiveness of Chippendale had given place to conceptions, that, especially in regard to chairs—which had become smaller as hoops went out of fashion—depended for their effect more upon inlay than upon carving. . . Elegance was the note of a style which on the whole was more distinctly English than that which preceded or immediately followed it. . . At its best the (Hepplewhite school) taste was so fine and so full of distinction, so simple, modest and sufficient that it amounted to genius." Encyclopædia Britannica, eleventh edition, "Hepplewhite," volume 13, page 305.

4. Mr. Cescinsky in his "English Furniture," volume 3, page 103, states that the work of Hepplewhite falls naturally into three divisions, namely, the Adam, the French and the English. His designs in the French style were copied from the French motives of the period. In his English style his designs and those of Sheraton are often very similar, and are sometimes called "Hepplewhite–Sheraton." See section 18, at note 5.

As to the differences between the Hepplewhite style and that of the next style—that of Sheraton[5]—it will be seen from the illustrations of various pieces, especially of chairs, that Hepplewhite favored the curved line, but that Sheraton generally used the straight line. But there are certain cases where their styles were quite the contrary, as in the straight line glass doors of the Hepplewhite style secretary–bookcases and the curved lines of those in the Sheraton style, as is mentioned in section 110; and as also in the rectangular panels of Hepplewhite and the oval ones of Sheraton. In some of the American furniture the designs are so similar that it is difficult, if not impossible, to determine whether a particular article should be classified as in the style of one or the other. It is said that some articles which we regard as being in the Hepplewhite style are often considered in England as being in the style of Sheraton, especially sideboards, as will appear in section 127.

The principal articles in the Hepplewhite style found in our country are chairs with shield backs, sideboards, bureaus, dining tables in two or more parts, side tables and especially card tables with one leg movable in order to support the hinged top when extended horizontally. More card tables seem to have survived than any other articles in the Hepplewhite style, with the rather easily breakable chairs next in number.

The decoration of American pieces in the Hepplewhite style consisted mainly of inlay and carving. The designs of inlay were generally rectangular forms, festoons and strings of flowers, acanthus leaves and rosettes, all of which will be seen in the illustrations of the various articles in the Hepplewhite style, especially sideboards and tables. Veneering was also an important decorative aid and was done in various woods. Mahogany was generally used, especially where carving was to be done, as on chairs.

Section 18. The Sheraton style.—Thomas Sheraton is generally regarded as second only to Chippendale as a designer of fine furniture. His was the last of the five great styles which made the eighteenth century the "golden age of English furniture"—the Queen Anne style, the Chippendale, the Adam, the Hepplewhite and the Sheraton. He was born in 1750 and went to London in 1790, where he died in 1806. The story of his life is a sad one, ending in poverty and disappointment. His eccentric character and his varied career as Baptist preacher, inventor, author and teacher are almost forgotten;[1] but his skill as a designer of

5. In volume 3, page 119, of his "English Furniture" Mr. Cescinsky mentions that it is "interesting to mark the influence of one designer or craftsman on another. The old–fashioned general classification under hard and fast general headings, such as Adam, Hepplewhite and Sheraton, has long ago proved to be woefully inaccurate in points of detail. Each of these designers occupies a well–merited place in the history of English furniture, and to show how the one was indebted to the other, and all three to the numerous joiners and designers of their time, whose names have been lost, detracts not one whit from their real position."

1. Sheraton was first known as a writer on theological subjects. In 1782 he published a book which he called "A scriptural illustration of the doctrine of regeneration." He was an occasional preacher, and even in his books on furniture designs he sometimes went into religious matters. He was

fine furniture will always have a conspicuous place in our furniture history. Sheraton carried on the business of cabinet making in a very small way, and it is said that only one piece of furniture of his own making is known with certainty.

As with Chippendale and Hepplewhite, the style of Sheraton is based upon a book of designs, which he called "The Cabinet Maker and Upholsterer's Drawing Book." This book[2] was issued in parts, the third of which contains his furniture designs, most of which are dated from 1792 to 1794, probably indicating that any articles made from those designs must have been made after those dates, and suggesting that the Sheraton style did not begin to be popular in our country until about 1795. This book was primarily intended for cabinet makers and was not intended as a catalogue of furniture for sale or to be made by Sheraton on order, in this respect differing from the books of Chippendale and Hepplewhite which were published as advertisements of their business as cabinet makers.

The kind of furniture which is commonly meant in speaking of furniture in the "Sheraton style" is the fine furniture shown or suggested in his "Drawing Book." The designs in his later books, following the change in English styles, showed a great deterioration, and are not in the best "Sheraton style," many being based upon the French Empire style, sometimes with heavy and clumsy features. On account of this change in his designs, and in order to distinguish them, the terms "Early Sheraton style" and "Late Sheraton style" are often used, thus avoiding the inclusion of such different types of furniture in one expression. When the mere term "Sheraton style" is used, without the words "early" or "late," it is generally intended to mean the early and fine Sheraton style, as also in referring to the furniture of Duncan Phyfe as mentioned in section 20 at note 5. In chapter V, on chairs, are three pages of illustrations, Nos. 233, 234, 235, which show the designs of chairs in the "Early Sheraton style," the "Late Sheraton style" and the unlovely "decadent" Sheraton style which was based upon the late French Empire style.[3]

(NOTE 1, *continued*)

first heard of as a designer when he published the first edition of his "Drawing Book," in 1791. In this book he referred to Chippendale and Hepplewhite, stating that the former's designs were "antiquated" and that the latter's had "caught the decline."

2. In addition to the "Drawing Book," of which there were three editions, Sheraton published the "Cabinet Maker's Dictionary" in 1803, and the first part of an "Encyclopædia" which was never finished, in 1804.

Reprints of the books of Chippendale, Hepplewhite and Sheraton may be seen in many public libraries.

An illustrated article entitled "Old English Books of Furniture and Decoration" by Mr. Fiske Kimball, is in "Antiques," September, 1929, page 184.

3. It seems from expressions used by Sheraton in one of his later books that he was unwillingly led into preparing designs based upon the French Empire style. He said that the English public was then "foolishly staring after French fashions."

It is said that "the public, always ready to take its mobiliary fashions from France, demanded Empire furniture, and Sheraton may have been, or have believed himself to be, compelled to give them what they wanted"; Encyclopædia Britannica, eleventh edition, "Sheraton," volume 24, page 842.

See also the remarks on Duncan Phyfe in section 20, at note 5.

As to the special features of the Sheraton style it is said that Sheraton abandoned to a great extent the curved outlines used in the furniture of Chippendale and Hepplewhite, that he was the champion of the straight[4] line, that his style is in general vertical and rectangular and that, like Hepplewhite, he used inlay freely. It is, however, not worth while to try to explain in words the features of Sheraton's designs, as many statements would be subject to exceptions; but an examination of the illustrations of various articles in the Sheraton style in later chapters will in most cases show the prominent characteristics. In considering whether certain pieces should be regarded as being in the Sheraton or Hepplewhite style a difficulty often arises from the fact, mentioned in the previous section and in section 127 on sideboards,[5] that in some articles the styles of Sheraton and Hepplewhite were very similar. Moreover some of our American pieces which we generally regard as being in the Hepplewhite style are often considered in England as being in the Sheraton style, especially sideboards as mentioned in section 17.

Although Sheraton in his book did not acknowledge his obligation to the prior designs of Robert Adam it is evident that he used many of them in his drawings. This may be seen by examining the full page illustration of four chairs in the Adam style, No. 181, in the chapter on chairs, and then observing the full page illustration, No. 234, of thirty designs of chairs said to be in the Sheraton style; from these it will be seen that the legs and feet and lyres of several chairs in the Adam style are used in chairs in the Sheraton style.

Almost all kinds of articles of household furniture in fashion in our country from about 1795 to 1820 were made in the Sheraton style by Duncan Phyfe and others of our cabinet makers working in these years. The pieces most frequently seen are chairs, tables, sewing stands, sideboards, sofas, bureaus and bedsteads, all of which are shown in the illustrations in the appropriate chapters. Many articles of an ingenious character were invented by Sheraton, some of which are occasionally seen.[6]

4. In the four successive styles of Chippendale to Sheraton, inclusive, the use of curved and straight lines alternated as follows: curved in the Chippendale style; straight in the Adam; curved in the Hepplewhite; straight in the Sheraton. Apparently each designer after Chippendale abandoned the lines favored by his predecessor.

5. When sideboards are mentioned, the name of Thomas Shearer should not be omitted. He was a contemporary of Hepplewhite and Sheraton, the author of "The Cabinet Maker's London Book of Prices and Designs," and the man who apparently invented the modern sideboard. Both Hepplewhite and Sheraton adopted his designs. His name and work have been lost sight of in the public eye. The subject of sideboards is treated in sections 126–130.

6. It is said that "his inventive ingenuity led him to devise many of the ingenious pieces which the later eighteenth century loved. Thus a library table would conceal a step–ladder for reaching the top shelves of bookcases. . . His most astonishing fancy was an ottoman with heating irons beneath, that the seat might be kept in a proper temperature in cold weather"; Encyclopædia Britannica, eleventh edition, "Sheraton," volume 24, page 842. Other pieces of this character were folding bedsteads, couches which could be changed into tables, combined bookcases and washstands, small tables with checker boards, sewing stands and work tables with various contrivances—all of which were popular at the time. From this it seems that Sheraton and Thomas Jefferson had similar tastes, judging from some of the latter's clever oddities at Monticello. Jefferson's furniture is mentioned in section 11, note 1, H.

The decorative ornaments were often borrowed from Robert Adam, mentioned in section 16, especially the graceful festoons and the small rosettes, or "patera," either round or oval. Reeding was much used, especially on chairs and sofas and on the legs of tables. Large and graceful inlaid ovals are seen on the doors of bookcases, sideboards and on other surfaces, and small inlaid ovals, often enclosing a shell, are found on many other pieces.

The wood used in the furniture of the Sheraton style, as also in the Hepplewhite style, was chiefly mahogany, and it nowhere shows to better advantage than in the fine veneering of the larger pieces. The brilliant satinwood, so much used in England even for large objects, is not often seen in our country, except in small pieces of veneer or inlay.

Section 19. The American Directory style.

—The period of the French Directory style—often called by the French word "Directoire"[1]—included in France the years from about 1793, when Louis the Sixteenth was executed, to 1804, at which latter date Napoleon became Emperor. In a recent book[2] on American furniture styles a chapter is entitled "The American Directoire style," and it is said that there was a period in America—about 1805 to about 1815—in which furniture of the Directory type was made, and that this type was "one of the simplest, most elegant and loveliest of styles"; and that the style has heretofore been erroneously treated as being in the late Sheraton style or as the beginning of, and a part of, the Empire style, but that in reality it constitutes a style by itself.[3]

1. In this book the English word "Directory" is used instead of the French word "Directoire." There seems to be no reason for using the French word in referring to the furniture style of the "Directory" period, when we use the English word "Directory" in referring to the period itself, that is, the period from October, 1795, to November, 1799, in which the executive power in France was held by a body called in English the "Directory."

An interesting, although irrelevant, matter in regard to the pronunciation of foreign words may be mentioned. It is said that in the debates in the British Parliament referring to countries and cities throughout the world which have names difficult to pronounce in the foreign manner, it is customary to pronounce the names as they would be pronounced if they were English words. We all pronounce the word "France" as it is pronounced in English; but many of us try in vain to pronounce the name of the French city "Rouen" as it is pronounced in France.

2. "American Furniture and Decoration," by Mr. Edward Stratton Holloway, published in 1928 by J. B. Lippincott Co., Philadelphia. On pages 133–152 Mr. Holloway describes the Directory style in France; separates the American furniture of the Directory style from the American Empire style; examines the French illustrated magazines of the period; explains the development in England and in our country of Directory style chairs, sofas, tables and sideboards; and mentions the use of the style by Duncan Phyfe; with many illustrations. The statements in this section are based chiefly upon those in the book of Mr. Holloway.

3. Among the few references to the Directory style in the books are those mentioned below.

Prior to the publication of Mr. Holloway's book, the attention of the public was directed to the Directory style in the book entitled "Furniture Masterpieces of Duncan Phyfe," by Mr. Charles Over Cornelius, published for the Metropolitan Museum of Art, by Doubleday, Page & Company, New York, 1922. In this book a number of chairs and sofas known to have been made by Duncan Phyfe were mentioned as being of the Directory type or as showing Directory influence.

In the book entitled "The Homes of our Ancestors," by R. T. H. Halsey and Elizabeth Tower, printed by Doubleday, Page & Company, New York, 1925, four chairs made by Duncan Phyfe

Many articles of furniture in the Directory style were made by our cabinet makers. The French furniture had been previously copied by English cabinet makers and designers, especially by Sheraton, and his designs, rather than the French models, may have been the principal influence in making the style a popular one in America. Whether the Directory style came to America direct from France or through Sheraton in England is not quite clear at present; perhaps it came from both sources. The style is best seen in chairs, especially in some of those made by Duncan Phyfe, such as Nos. 326 and 327 and those shown in section 55, No. 307 and others. One or more of the features of the style continued to be used in many chairs in the Empire style, appearing even as late as about 1840, as shown in the chairs Nos. 347 to 352. It is also well seen in the curves of many sofas such as Nos. 568, 574 and others.

Section 20. The Duncan Phyfe furniture.—Only a few years ago the name of Duncan Phyfe was almost unknown, but now, largely because of the loan exhibition of his work at the Metropolitan Museum of Art in New York in 1922, his name is more familiar in our country than that of any other cabinet maker. The articles which are definitely traced, by receipted bills and other papers, to his workshop in New York are sufficient in number and quality to entitle him to a very high place among American cabinet makers.[1]

(NOTE 3, *continued*)

are illustrated and they are referred to as showing "Phyfe's interpretation of Directoire designs"; see figures 115–118 and page 155. In the present book see section 56 on the subject of the Duncan Phyfe chairs. Another chair "of Directoire form" in the "Homes of our Ancestors," figure 183, is mentioned on page 232 as "reflecting the Directoire influence of the period." See also section 20, note 4.

In an article in "The House Beautiful," August, 1929, page 198, Mr. Frederick Litchfield, a well known English writer on English furniture, writes: "The Revolutionary Tribunal of the Directorate was established in 1795, and lasted until its deposition some four years later, and although, generally speaking, the term 'Empire furniture' is taken to include that produced during these four years, it is more correct to consider the Directoire style as previous to the time" of the Empire style of Napoleon.

1. Mr. Charles Over Cornelius, in his book "Furniture Masterpieces of Duncan Phyfe," mentioned in the previous section, note 3, presents illustrations of fifty–six articles said to have been made by Phyfe.

Duncan Phyfe was a Scotchman, born in 1768, who came to America about the year 1783. He settled in New York about 1792, retired from business in 1847, and died in 1854. The fine quality of his designs and workmanship soon attracted a large number of customers in New York and other cities, and at one time in the latter part of his career more than one hundred persons were employed in his factory. Mr. Cornelius writes in his "Foreword" that "Duncan Phyfe is the only early American cabinet maker to whom a very large group of furniture may be attributed on documentary grounds," there being almost one hundred pieces.

In the New York Directory for 1792 appears the entry "Duncan Fife, joiner," the latter word meaning "woodworker"; in the Directory for 1794 his name appears as "Duncan Phyfe, cabinet maker." His brother "John Fife," apparently less prosperous, continued his spelling of the family name for several years, but later became a "Phyfe." This information is from an article entitled "Phyfe né Fife," in "Antiques," December, 1929, page 496, by Mr. Thomas Hamilton Ormsbee. In this article it is also said that Duncan Phyfe had a brother "Lachlin."

Through the courtesy of several owners of articles which in most cases have been proven by documentary evidence to have been made by Duncan Phyfe in his good period, a number of illustrations[2] of his best furniture are presented in other chapters. These illustrations give a clear idea of the finest work of Phyfe and will help the reader to discriminate between what is authentic Duncan Phyfe furniture of the best type and what is not.[3]

(NOTE 1, *continued*)

   "Phyfe, Lachlan, cabinet maker, 37 South Gay Street," appears in the Baltimore City Directory for 1807. The address is also that of Robert Fisher, a noted Baltimore cabinet maker, some of whose fine furniture is referred to in connection with the table No. 1528. Whether Lachlan was employed by Fisher or was in business for himself is not known; not even a lively imagination can at present conjure up any theories about him. His name does not appear, whether "Phyfe" or "Fife," in later Baltimore Directories.

   2. These illustrations are mainly of the chairs No. 320 and others; the sofas Nos. 573 and 574; and the tables No. 1547 and others. No articles merely "attributed" to Phyfe are illustrated. As to "attributions" see section 6, note 13.

   3. The furniture of Duncan Phyfe has inspired more fulsome praise than that of any other American cabinet maker. Enthusiastic writers have represented Phyfe as a great genius and as a great originator of a great American style, ignoring the facts that he did not originate a furniture style and that the decorations which he used do not constitute a decorative style. But even though we cannot join in the fanciful eulogies, we may justly say that as a cabinet maker Phyfe stands in the front rank and that his work is one of the great contributions to American furniture. It is to be hoped that further research will elevate to high positions some of the other makers of fine American pieces who are at present "unhonored and unsung." See also section 6, note 13.

   As a result of the widespread publicity given to his authenticated work by magazines, newspaper articles and advertising catalogues, the name "Duncan Phyfe" has often been loosely applied to almost any piece of furniture which is supposed to resemble the fine pieces of Phyfe. Chairs with lyre backs, no matter how crude, tables with sloping and reeded legs, no matter how coarse the reeding may be, sofas with reeding on the rolled arms, legs and seat rail, no matter how inelegant, have all been called "Duncan Phyfe." It should be remembered that the lyre, the reeding, the acanthus leaves and other embellishments indicate merely a style of decoration used by many cabinet makers both before and after the time of Phyfe, and do not point to him or to any other particular cabinet maker. Many owners of such pieces have even been deluded into believing that their furniture was made by Phyfe himself with his own hands. Even the "Mayflower furniture," (see section 11, note 1, G), must yield in number to the supposed creations of Duncan Phyfe. Unfortunately for his posthumous fame, Phyfe did not publish a book of his early designs as so many of the English cabinet makers did.

   Two original bills from Duncan Phyfe may be mentioned. One dated 1816, made out to Mr. Charles N. Bancker, of Philadelphia, appears in the book of Mr. Cornelius, pages 44–45, referred to on opposite page. Another bill, dated 1807, appears in an illustrated article entitled "A new Estimation of Duncan Phyfe," by Mr. W. M. Hornor, Jr., in "The Antiquarian," March, 1930, page 37. This bill is made out to Mr. William Bayard, of New York. In this article Mr. Hornor "laid bare the pretty but utterly false" tradition that Phyfe was aided in his early career, about 1792–1805, by Mrs. Langdon, daughter of John Jacob Astor, by showing that the lady was somewhat young to have been his customer at that time, having been born in the year 1795. See also section 6, note 11

   An interesting article entitled "A Glimpse of Duncan Phyfe" is in "Antiques," April, 1934, page 135. The annotated illustrations "are addressed to the novice, not to the connoisseur. Their purpose is to acquaint the beginning student with a few of the less familiar aspects of Duncan Phyfe's furniture design and, at the same time, to demonstrate how consistently Phyfe impressed his individual manner upon all the earlier products of his shop."

   As a memorial to Mr. H. H. Benkard, a room furnished with furniture made by Duncan Phyfe was recently presented to the Museum of the City of New York by Mrs. Benkard.

(*Note 3 continued on page 58*)

When Duncan Phyfe became prominent in New York, about 1800, the most fashionable furniture style was that of Sheraton,[4] whose book of designs was prob- ably in the hands of the leading American cabinet makers. Many of the features of the Sheraton style are clearly seen in the furniture made by Phyfe from about 1800 to 1825, when his best work was done; and in this period he also made many pieces in the Directory style, which is treated in the previous section. Phyfe's furniture made in those years is regarded as among the very finest of the products of American craftsmen. But in later years when the large and heavy forms of the French Empire style became fashionable it seems that Phyfe followed the French style as a business necessity, and made furniture which he called "butcher furni- ture," and which his admirers do not wish to be associated with his name.[5] The words "early Phyfe" and "late Phyfe" are therefore often used to distinguish the good from the bad.

It cannot be truly said that Duncan Phyfe originated a furniture style in the same sense that Chippendale, Adam, Hepplewhite and Sheraton originated the styles which bear their names. In making his furniture he no doubt followed any of the then prevailing styles, the Sheraton, the Directory or the Empire, as his customers desired. It therefore does not seem proper to speak of a particular chair made by him in the Sheraton style as being a "Duncan Phyfe *style* chair," or even a "Duncan Phyfe *style* chair showing the Sheraton influence," as is sometimes done; it is more accurate[6] to term the chair a "Sheraton *style* chair made by Dun-

(NOTE 3, *continued*)

A collection of about two hundred articles by Duncan Phyfe has been made by Mr. Henry Ford and has been put on display in the museum of the Edison Institute at Dearborn, Michigan. This collection is said to contain examples of all types of Phyfe's furniture, including that of his decadent period.

4. In the above mentioned book of Mr. Cornelius, page 43, it is said that certain of Phyfe's work "which we know was done in 1797 is completely Sheraton and most finished both in design and execution, while many of his details and methods of treatment are so closely allied to Hepplewhite that it seems reasonable to suppose that his very earliest work was based upon Hepplewhite models."

Phyfe apparently did not make much furniture in the Hepplewhite style, which was no doubt becoming old fashioned after 1800. A study of a shield back chair in the Hepplewhite style, attributed to Phyfe, is in "Antiques," April, 1934, pages 129–131.

Phyfe naturally followed the Sheraton style because that was the fashionable style of the time; and the cabinet makers in other cities did the same. But much furniture, wherever made, which resembles to some extent that made by Duncan Phyfe has been popularly called "Duncan Phyfe" furniture, as though the cabinet makers who made it were following Duncan Phyfe rather than Sheraton; but this was certainly not their intention, as they would naturally intend their furniture to be known as following the designs of the celebrated London designer Sheraton, whose book some of them had, rather than the designs of Phyfe, a New York Scotchman who was a rival cabinet maker.

In "The Homes of our Ancestors," referred to in the previous section, note 3, it is said on page 155 that "Phyfe's most distinctive work is that in which certain French influences of the Directory or Early Empire period appear."

5. See also the remarks in reference to Sheraton and the Empire style in section 18, note 3.

6. This is the method adopted by a learned commentator in describing the Duncan Phyfe pieces shown in the catalogue of the "Girl Scouts Loan Exhibition" held in New York in September, 1929; see also section 56, which treats of the Duncan Phyfe chairs.

can Phyfe." The important point is that he made refinements in, and added embellishments to, his furniture in the Sheraton style and impressed upon it a new elegance and grace.

It is not possible to make clear by words alone the fine features of the work of Duncan Phyfe, nor, in fact, of any other cabinet maker. The furniture must be shown to the eye as well as to the mind. His work is distinguished by its gracefulness and fine proportions, as will be seen in the illustrations. The decorative designs in the prevailing style used by him are executed in a delicate manner. We will see the carved acanthus leaf, the festoons, the lion's head, the lion's paw, the lyre, the curved legs and, on so many pieces, the fine lines of reeding; these are characteristic of his work, although of course not original with him, as perhaps all of them appear on pieces in the previous styles of Adam, Hepplewhite or Sheraton; and, in addition to those mentioned, Phyfe used a number of other fine decorative designs which will be particularly noticed on chairs and sofas.[7]

The features which have given to the best furniture of Phyfe a commanding position may perhaps be summarized in this way: he followed fine designs of the Sheraton and Directory styles; he adopted some of the best decorative forms of his predecessors; he used the choicest mahogany; he made most excellent cabinet work in every detail; he added grace and elegance to every form he copied; and he possessed and exercised that talent called "good taste" which appealed to the more cultivated people of his time as it now appeals to us in our time.[8]

Section 21. The American Empire style.—In this section we meet with uncertainties as to what the so-called American Empire style really is, what furniture should be included in it and what dates mark the beginning and the ending of its period. These matters are not usually considered at length in the books, which as mentioned in section 5 generally fix the year 1825 or thereabouts as the "dead line" dividing fine antique furniture from the inferior products of later years. In this section the subject is referred to briefly and with some hesitation, but with the hope of giving to the reader a clear idea of several of the principal matters.[1]

(Note 6, *continued*)

The term "Duncan Phyfe chair" should only be applied to a chair actually made by him; just as, for example, we speak of a "William Savery lowboy," meaning a lowboy made by Savery, a noted cabinet maker in Philadelphia. A chair copied by another cabinet maker from a chair made by Phyfe should be referred to as "a copy of a chair made by Duncan Phyfe." Without accuracy of expression any statement may be misleading.

7. Fine articles of furniture now definitely known to be the work of Duncan Phyfe do not seem to include many of the larger pieces such as secretaries, desks, bookcases, chests of drawers or china closets.

8. Similar remarks have been made in regard to other cabinet makers by their admirers. To a certain extent Phyfe was apparently somewhat of a specialist, because he seems to have made only a limited class of articles and also because his favorite decorative designs were limited in number.

As to "taste" see section 1, note 1, I; and section 22, note 4, D.

1. The answers to various questions which may arise in connection with the furniture of the American Empire style are not attempted here; indeed, the questions may not be important. The chief

The American Empire style was developed from the French and English Empire styles, and it is said that some of its features were seen as early as 1805 and that the style lasted until a few years after 1840, when the Victorian style became the fashion. A vast amount of furniture was made in this long period, beginning with the elegant work in the Sheraton and Directory styles and the fine furniture which Duncan Phyfe made from about 1800 to 1825.

It might be thought that the "French Empire style" began in the period of the first French Empire, which extended from the proclamation of Napoleon as Emperor in 1804, to his abdication after the battle of Waterloo in 1815. But the words "French Empire style," as generally used in connection with furniture, refer back into the reign of Louis the Sixteenth,[2] who was guillotined in 1793, and thus include several years in that reign, and also the periods of the French Revolution, the Directory, the Consulate and the reign of Napoleon.

(NOTE 1, *continued*)

point is to know the changes in the styles after the passing of the style of Sheraton, the last of the great English furniture designers. The names to be given to the later styles, and the dates within which they were in fashion, may be regarded as of little importance at the present time, although in a few years most of the furniture may become really "antique" in point of age. See section 5, entitled "When is an article of American furniture an antique?"

The term "Jeffersonian style" has been suggested as a substitute for the "Empire style"; this is a doubtful compliment to Jefferson, especially as he had no connection with the subject except that he was fond of French furniture and brought a huge amount of it to Monticello; see section 11, note 1, H.

Certain writers divide the styles of American antique furniture into two historical groups. The first group, called the "Colonial styles," consists of the four earlier styles which were in fashion when our country was composed of English "Colonies," namely the Jacobean, the William and Mary, the Queen Anne and the Chippendale. The second group, called the "Federal styles," which were in fashion after our "Federal" government was established in 1789, consists of the styles of Hepplewhite and Sheraton, the Directory and the American Empire. This historical division is interesting, but is of little value in studying the subject.

2. A. The application of the words "French Empire style" to a period before the Napoleonic Empire began is said to be justified by the fact that although the style reached its highest development in the time of Napoleon, it really took its origin from the designs of ancient Rome found chiefly in the excavations at Pompeii, about 1780, in the time of Louis the Sixteenth. Robert Adam had previously drawn his inspiration for classic designs direct from Italy and there was no connection between the Adam style and that of Louis the Sixteenth or the French Empire; see section 16, note 1.

B. Another retrospective application of a style is in the use of the words "Chippendale style," which began before Chippendale himself became a prominent cabinet maker; see section 15, text and notes 3 and 5.

C. The French Empire style was fully developed by artists employed by Napoleon, after he became Emperor in 1804, to create new designs in art, including the art of the cabinet maker. Two of these artists, Percier and Fontaine, published a volume of furniture designs based upon Roman models, in the preface to which they stated that "the style does not belong to us, but entirely to the ancients." Years before, as mentioned above, Robert Adam produced from Roman inspiration the designs of the "Adam style"; see section 16. The French artists, deriving ideas from the same source, produced designs of a different character. The conquest of Egypt by Napoleon, in 1798, also brought in certain elements of the styles of that country; and ancient Egyptian figures, the Sphinx, the lotus flower and the urn appear on the furniture of the period. Not many pieces were apparently made in our

Instead of a mere verbal description of the features of the French Empire style of furniture, much of which was imported in the early part of the nineteenth century, we see some of those features in the illustrations, Nos. 5 and 6, of two alcoves of a group installed in the Metropolitan Museum of Art a few years ago

In No. 5 the furniture is in the French Empire style of the period of about 1804 to 1815, in which the style attained its highest distinction. This style is also known as the "Neo–classic," meaning "New classic," a term which is used to designate the revival of the classic designs of Greece and Rome, and in England is particularly applied to the style introduced by Robert Adam which he called the "antique style"; see section 16 and also note 2, A in this section. Here the decorative "mounts" of brass and ormolu which were so much used in this period are seen, especially on the two very large mirrors, the chair on the right and the small table in the centre. Ormolu is defined and described in section 38, note 2 (page 94).

In No. 6 the style of about 1815 to 1830 is seen. In these years the French Empire style continued in fashion, but in a modified form, showing somewhat of a decline in furniture design. The four chairs, the two Sheraton style tables with lyres, and the French brass clock on the mantel are all of types which will be seen in the illustrations in other chapters of this book. The ungainly secretary on the left is said to be in the Biedermeier style, which is mentioned at the end of the next section; in order to wind the clock on the top the aid of a stepladder is necessary. The small round table in the centre is a French example.

The "English Empire style" was a result of the English custom in fashionable circles of following the French in furniture styles. As previously mentioned, Chippendale, Hepplewhite and Sheraton each designed furniture "in the French taste"; and the latter stated in his last publication that the English people were

(NOTE 2, *continued*)

country strictly in the French Empire style; but articles imported from France during the Empire period, and still in use in American homes, are occasionally found, especially mantel clocks.

D. Whenever the conquest of Egypt by Napoleon is referred to, as above, the writer thinks of the wise men and the asses mentioned in section 64, note 1.

E. The French furniture of the Empire style is often regarded as coarse, heavy and excessively ornamented. Much of this furniture may deserve this condemnation; but many of the early pieces were of high character, made of the best mahogany and ornamented with appropriate and finely designed mounts of brass or ormolu; decoration of this kind may also be seen on the French chairs Nos. 496 and 498, and tables Nos. 1654–1655.

F. An ornamental feature of the French Empire style which became very popular in our country was the round wooden column which we so often see on the fronts of sideboards, wardrobes and other pieces made about 1810 to 1830; also the claw feet of lions or of other real or imaginary animals. Unfortunately, perhaps, the metal mounts, as to which see section 38, with the fine designs and workmanship of the French pieces, were not much used by our cabinet makers, except in the round columns and metal mounts often seen in French mantel clocks.

G. An interesting feature of the Early American Empire style furniture, as distinguished from that of the French, is that it did not use the French decorative designs of sphinxes or military weapons or Roman cupids, but used designs of a character more appropriate to the growing and prosperous Republic, such as horns of plenty, the American eagle, (as to which see section 33), and fruits and flowers.

Above. Illustration No. 5. About 1804–1815.
Below. Illustration No. 6. About 1815–1830.

then "foolishly staring after French fashions," as mentioned in section 18, note 3. The Empire style was not popular in England, however, and passed out of fashion in a few years.

It is said that good American furniture based upon the French or English Empire style was made for some years after the War of 1812, from about 1815 to 1830, during which period the French influence was most pronounced. But after about 1830 the American Empire style declined in character and lost all elegance of form.[3] Heavy and bulky articles of furniture became the fashion, without any redeeming features except fine mahogany and good workmanship. To include all of this good and bad furniture from about 1815 to 1840 in one style, calling some of the best and all of the worst by the same name—"American Empire"—is too confusing for practical use.

In the preceding sections on the styles of Sheraton and Duncan Phyfe we have seen that Sheraton's early and fine designs were followed by his unlovely designs of a later date, and that the terms "early Sheraton" and "late Sheraton" are often used to distinguish such different styles; and that the fine pieces of Duncan Phyfe are commonly referred to as his "early" pieces. These terms—"early" and "late"— are also applicable to the different classes of American furniture made in the Empire style; and therefore it seems proper to designate the early and better work in the Empire style, from about 1815 to 1830, as being in the "American Early Empire style" and the later and bad work of about 1830 to 1840 as being in the "American Late Empire style."

The books on American antique furniture do not discuss fully what is here called the "American Late Empire" style, nor do they present illustrations of articles made in the period. The reasons for this are two; first, because furniture made in this period, from about 1830 to 1840, is not old enough to be considered "antique," as shown in section 5; secondly, and equally important, because most

---

3.   A.   This was the period of the furniture which, unfortunately, by a curious misuse of words, is often called "Colonial" by persons who have forgotten or have never known the elementary facts of American history, as mentioned in section 1, note 1, A. Of course the word "Colonial" in our country means "relating to the thirteen British colonies which became the United States of America, or to their period." Before our separation from England in 1776 our furniture, as well as our government, was "Colonial"; but after that date the colonies ceased to exist as such, and therefore no furniture made in America after the year 1776 may properly be called "Colonial."

B.   This furniture, often massive in size, heavy in weight and unlovely in design, is properly considered to be neither antique nor elegant, especially the tables, sofas and other large pieces; but for some reason the chairs were of a better type and were not so objectionable and in some cases were in fact deserving of praise; all of which will appear in the illustrations in the various chapters. Three chairs in section 60 illustrate this—Nos. 422, 423 and 424. It is strange how such a complete change for the worse could occur in so short a time after about 1825; but the French and English styles had also changed for the worse during the same period; and the desire of our people to follow the foreign styles in furniture, as well as in arts and literature, was doubtless the cause of the change in America. Many of our pieces, however, did not closely resemble the foreign ones.

C.   A revival of the Gothic style, especially with Gothic arches, was attempted about the year 1830, following an English effort in imitation of the Gothic style of Chippendale, but was not popular.

of the furniture made in the style of this period is bad furniture in the eyes of those who have studied the subject and know what is fine and elegant. Hence the subject of "American Late Empire" furniture is ignored, just as the bad furniture made in the late styles of Sheraton and Duncan Phyfe is ignored, as mentioned in previous sections.

In various chapters of the present book, however, many pieces of furniture in the American Late Empire style are illustrated, because the purpose of this book, as stated in the last paragraph of section 1, is not only to show to the amateur collector what *is* fine, but also to show what *is not* fine; and the reader will thus clearly recognize the furniture of the American Late Empire style which is seen in so many shops and private houses, and to distinguish it from fine furniture of the earlier periods. Examples of furniture of this character are illustrated under various headings throughout this book.

Section 22. The Victorian and other styles.—Of course a book on American antique furniture should not include these styles, for the same reason that the American Late Empire style should not have been included, that is, because the styles are not antique; and even if they were antique, much of the furniture in these styles is now so unattractive to our eyes that it should be ignored just as the furniture made in the bad styles of Sheraton and Duncan Phyfe is ignored. However, another year will bring us to the one hundredth anniversary of the coronation of the British Queen and perhaps some of the furniture made in the early part of her reign may then be found more interesting. Moreover, even in a book on antique furniture, it may be allowable, with this apology and explanation, to refer very inadequately and briefly to, and not to completely ignore, almost one hundred years of American furniture history.

The furniture which was in fashion during the reign of Queen Victoria,[1] the longest in English history, 1837–1901, is generally so associated in our minds with

1. The Victorian era is sometimes considered as being in three periods, the Early Victorian from about 1837 to 1850, the Mid–Victorian from about 1850 to 1875 and the Late Victorian from about 1875 to 1901.

B. The furniture of the Early Victorian period is considered as the best from the point of view of those who know antique furniture. In the later periods, especially the Mid–Victorian, the rosewood or mahogany of the early period was superseded by black walnut with coarse carvings. The furniture of the two later Victorian periods are regarded as not worthy of mention.

C. About 1840 there was a revival in France of the style of Louis the Fifteenth, 1715–1774, but of a less elegant character. This revived style, known as that of Louis Philippe, 1830–1848, appears generally in black walnut in many American articles, especially chairs.

D. An illustrated article entitled "Victorian Art and Victorian Taste," by Mr. Fiske Kimball, is in "Antiques," March, 1933, page 103. In the same magazine, November, 1932, pages 170–173, is an illustrated article by Sarah Foster Stovall, entitled "Two Aspects of Victorianism."

E. In his "English Furniture," volume 2, pages 362–363, Mr. Cescinsky expresses his opinion of the Mid–Victorian furniture from about 1850 to 1875. "It is characteristic of this degenerate period that although the cabinet work is usually irreproachable, and the choice and arrangement of figured woods a striking evidence of good taste, . . the artistic side of the trade was in a hopelessly moribund state. When the Victorian designers copied, they imitated merely the faults and ignored the

the furniture and ornamental articles of the worst period of her reign that to call the furniture "Victorian" is equivalent to condemning it with the worst adjectives that may be politely used. From our present point of view this condemnation of the ornaments is no doubt justified; but it does not seem proper to regard all of the furniture in the same light. We can not admire the designs of the furniture, but we should at least acknowledge the fine quality of the materials and workmanship. We judge the furniture of Sheraton and Duncan Phyfe by their best examples, and we ought not to judge the furniture of the Victorian period by its worst examples.

ILLUSTRATION No. 7. ABOUT 1840–1860.

Numerous articles of furniture in the Victorian style are shown in this book, among which are the chair No. 495; the bureaus Nos. 767 and 768; the secretary–bookcase No. 868; the mirror No. 1226; and the tables Nos. 1426, 1622, 1649. In examining these articles and the comments on them it will be seen that features of the previous styles often appear; in some pieces there is a mixture of several styles.

Illustration No. 7 shows an alcove in the Metropolitan Museum of Art, one of the series referred to in the previous section. In this alcove the furniture is

(NOTE 1, continued)

virtues of the eighteenth century work; they included their own grotesque and clumsy details wherever possible. In original creation they were equally incompetent."

F.   A description of an early Victorian home in England is in the book of Mr. Fred. W. Burgess, entitled "English Furniture." On pages 258–260 it is said that the Victorian style furniture chiefly in the early Victorian style of about 1840 to 1860. Here we see a parlor with the type of furniture which is so often found in homes whose elderly owners cling to the "old–fashioned" furniture of their parents or grandparents. On the left is an over–stuffed arm chair, an invention of the period, and the always–present "whatnot,"[2] displaying china and glass and other ornaments. The sofa has a carved and pierced back in three parts, such as the New York cabinet maker John Belter[3] made for his wealthy customers.

Several other styles of furniture are mentioned in the note.[4]

(Note 1, *continued*)

can never command admiration, but that it is homelike; and among those who have inherited it a senti mental attachment exists because of its personal contact with one's family. At the time when the young Queen came to the throne there had been a stagnation in progressive cabinet making for many years. The middle class homes of English people presented a very mixed appearance, containing many pieces of eighteenth century furniture. There might be seen Georgian chests, possibly a highboy, very likely a Queen Anne table and almost certainly a desk with a shell or other typical inlay upon the lid marking it as in the Sheraton style. Pieces made from Chippendale and Hepplewhite models were often in every day use. "The early days of Queen Victoria were rich in antiques, then only in the making. The Georgian furniture had then little or no antiquarian value."

2. An illustrated article by Leah Adkisson Kazmark, entitled "The Lure of the Whatnot" is in "The Antiquarian," August, 1927, page 42. The lower portion was often enclosed as a receptacle for almost anything not too large.

In the rear corner on the left the arm chair has its "tidy" and the chair on the right has a top with a "Gothic arch" of the type referred to in note 3, C, in the previous section. The square piano has abundant carving and enormous legs. On opposite walls grandpa and grandma gaze pleasantly at each other. Nine picture–frame cords are conspicuous on the blue, gray and tan wall paper.

3. From about 1840 to 1860 Belter was a prominent New York cabinet maker, many of whose pieces have survived. His workmanship and his rosewood were of the best. His chairs and sofas are very ornate, with curved and elaborate open fretwork top rails and side rails. In order to avoid shrink-age and to secure strength the wood was built up in several thin layers which were glued together and then cut out. The grain of the wood, in alternate layers, ran in opposite directions. This method is called "lamination," a word meaning "arrangement in layers." His pieces are esteemed in New York as examples of a local style.

4. A. "Biedermeier" furniture. This so-called style of German origin has been much exploited recently in our country. The word "Biedermeier" is said to be a fictitious one coined by a cartoonist in a German humorous magazine to typify an uncultivated but well–to–do middle class man; and as applied to furniture the word means a certain style of furniture which was popular in Germany from about 1825 to 1850. The style seems to be a combination of some of the features of the Sheraton, the Directory and the French Empire styles, without the best features of either. The French Empire style, especially, was followed, but generally without the mounts of ormolu or other fine decorative details. To the writer, there seems to be no reason for the use of furniture of this type in our country. It was always commonplace and it has no connection with America. As a decorative style it may be regarded as a short lived fad. Illustrated articles on the subject are in the magazine "Antiques," March, 1930, page 217, and in "The Antiquarian," July, 1928, page 48, and May, 1932, page 17.

B. "French Provincial" furniture. This is another kind of foreign furniture which has had a certain vogue recently. It is said to show the styles in use in the provincial districts of France for the past two centuries. The usual pieces of domestic furniture are said to follow the Parisian styles in a simple manner; fortunately, the bedsteads are too large for the American home. Reproductions and adaptations, (as to which see section 9), may be found in some shops.

C. The "Eastlake" style prevailed for a few years after about 1868 when a book with furniture designs was published by Charles L. Eastlake, an English architect. It is said that these

(NOTE 4, *continued*)

designs were based upon early English forms of the Jacobean style, which is mentioned in section 12. The style soon degenerated and passed out. To the writer Eastlake's designs seem no better than those he ridicules in his book.

D. Eastlake's book, "Hints on Household Taste in Furniture," etc., contains many interesting remarks which he dared to put in print. We may quote one of these, pages 7–8, on the subject of "that sense of the beautiful, which we call taste," as follows: "The faculty of distinguishing good from bad design in the familiar objects of domestic life is a faculty which most educated people—and women especially—conceive that they possess. How it has been acquired, few would be able to explain. The general impression seems to be that it is the peculiar inheritance of gentle blood and independent of all train ing. . . It is however a lamentable fact that this very quality is commonly deficient, not only among the generally ignorant but also among the most educated classes in this country." Eastlake's remarks include other matters, such as jewelry, women's crinoline, men's beards and black suits, and other features of the Mid–Victorian period.

E. "L'Art Nouveau," or "New Art," is the result of an effort in the latter part of the last century to devise a new style in furniture. It was developed principally by artists who "professed to be free from all old traditions and to seek inspiration from nature alone." A particular feature of the effort was the use of oak. The furniture of the "new art" is said to be an example of the impossibility of creating fine furniture without considering the traditional forms. The "Mission style," based upon the Spanish Missions in California, is said to be one expression of the style. "L'Art Nouveau" had a brief career and disappeared about 1900.

F. Although it may not now seem possible, let us hope that a new style of furniture may arise in our country which will be a worthy successor to the great ones of the past. The inventive and artistic genius of America should lead to the creation of inspiring designs without commercial or mechanical connections. To the writer it seems that the designs of Robert Adam might well be the basis of a new American style.

CHAPTER IV
INTERESTING DETAILS

Section 23. The cyma curve.—This curve, pronounced si–ma, begins this chapter on "Interesting details" because it is the most frequently seen of all ornamental curves, and if we are familiar with it we will generally notice its presence and will thus be better able to enjoy antique furniture. Indeed much of our furniture would be somewhat unlovely without the cyma curve. Its proper form is shown in illustration No. 8, but the variations of it are numerous. This curve was called "the line of beauty" by the celebrated English painter and engraver, William Hogarth,[1] (1697–1764), whose name is sometimes given to certain chairs

1. Hogarth wrote a book entitled "The Analysis of Beauty: written with a view of fixing the fluctuating ideas of taste," which was published in London in 1753. On pages 48–49 it is said that "there is scarce a room in any house whatever where one does not see the waving line employed in some way or other. . . Though all sorts of waving lines are ornamental when properly applied, yet, strictly speaking, there is but one precise line properly to be called the line of beauty"—this line, numbered 4 in figure 49 in his book, being the cyma curve, the distinctive feature of the "cabriole" leg which is the subject of the next section.

in the Queen Anne style having these curves, such as the chair[2] shown here as No. 9.

Through the courtesy of Mr. Luke Vincent Lockwood we are permitted to quote from his "Colonial Furniture in America," volume 1, page 8, as follows, in reference to the use of the cyma curve:

"Two cyma curves placed thus 〕〔

Cyma curve

Hogarth chair

No. 8. Upper. A Cyma Curve; Section 23.
No. 9. Lower. A "Hogarth" Chair; Section 23.

(Note 1, *continued*)

Several series of engravings by Hogarth are well known, the most popular being "Marriage à la mode" which is said to be "an accurate delineation of upper class eighteenth century (English) society," and "a miserable tragedy of an ill-assorted marriage"; Encyclopædia Britannica, eleventh edition, page 568. In some of these engravings the furniture of the period is well seen.

As is seen in illustration No. 8, the cyma curve consists of a continuous double curve, one part being convex and the other part concave. In the drawing, the convex part is above and the concave part is below. When seen on a piece of furniture, if the *convex* part is at the top, as in the drawing, the technical term is "cyma reversa"; if the *concave* part is at the top the term is "cyma recta." These terms are frequently used in the books; and the "cyma recta" may be remembered as concave at the top by noticing that the words "concave" and "cyma recta" each have the letter "c" twice.

The word "ogee" strictly means a cyma curve which is convex at the top and concave below; but "ogee" is frequently used for either or both forms.

2. Eighteen cyma curves, some more exact than others, may be seen on the inner and outer outlines of this chair which is copied, by permission of Mr. Herbert Cescinsky, from his book, "English Furniture," volume 1, figure 93. The two front cabriole legs are in cyma curves; two others of these curves, (one not visible), are at the front and side of the top of each front leg; two more appear on the inner and outer outlines of each of the upright posts of the back; two more are at the centre of the top rail; two others are at the bottom of the central openwork part of the back called the "splat"; and four more are on the outer outlines of the splat. In an arm chair of this type even more cyma curves may be seen.

formed the design of the (Queen Anne style) chair backs. A cyma curve thus

formed the cabriole leg. Two cyma curves placed thus ⌒⌒ formed the scroll top found on highboys, secretaries and cupboards. When placed thus they formed the familiar outline" found in many pieces. Also,

it may be mentioned, two curves in this position form the framework

of the lyre, which was a favorite ornamental design; and in this position they

form a "brace" which is used to connect two or more printed lines.

Section 24. The cabriole leg; and others.

—Of the numerous types of furniture legs, the "cabriole"[1] is the most important and the most graceful. Other types are mentioned in the note.[2] As stated in the previous section, and shown on the

1. The word "cabriole," as applied to furniture seems to be of uncertain origin. Its meaning is about the same as "cyma curve," that is, having an outline consisting of a convex and a concave curve. See the previous section.

The word "bandy" is sometimes used instead of "cabriole." "Bandy" is defined as "having a bend or crook outward; said of legs"; Century Dictionary. The word lacks dignity.

As is the case with the ball and claw foot, the cabriole leg is believed to be of Chinese origin; see the remarks in the next section in regard to the foot.

The upper part of the cabriole leg, where it turns outward is called the "knee"; the lower part, where it turns inward, is called the "ankle."

An illustrated article entitled "Identifying periods by legs and feet," by Mr. George Brobeck, is in "The Antiquarian," June, 1929, page 48.

2. A. For several of the definitions in this note the writer is indebted to Mr. L. V. Lockwood's "The Furniture Collectors' Glossary," a publication of the Walpole Society, 1913. This book is also referred to in the next section, note 1.

B. Turned legs. See also section 35 entitled "Turnings." These legs were in many designs, among which are the "inverted cup" turning, as in highboys Nos. 633 and 634 and lowboys Nos. 669–671; "trumpet" turning, as in lowboy No. 672; "spiral," which is a twisted form resembling a corkscrew, as in the cane chair No. 35 and the table No. 1279. Almost all plain round legs were "turned," not carved. The expression "turned chairs" is explained in section 46, note 11, A. Turned feet are referred to in section 25, note 4, F.

C. Square straight legs. These were used on many chairs in the Chippendale style, to a great extent superseding the cabriole legs. They were less expensive to make than the cabriole legs and by using them the purchaser was enabled to apply much of his money to the chair back, which is the most conspicuous part of a chair. These legs at first sight may seem to be almost the same as the square but tapered legs seen on the chairs in the Hepplewhite style.

D. Tapered legs. These are square or round legs which gradually become narrower toward the bottom. The square tapered leg was a feature in the chairs, tables, sideboards and other articles in the style of Hepplewhite; and both the square and the round ones were used by Sheraton, as will be seen in the illustrations. The "tapering" on legs in the Hepplewhite style was generally on the inside only. See also "Spade foot," figure 17 in illustration No. 11, and the comment.

E. Scroll legs. These are in ornamental curved designs. Several forms of scroll legs have been used, as in the early chairs Nos. 36 and 38 which are known as "Flemish" scrolls. See also "Scroll foot" in the next section, figure 16.

Hogarth chair, No. 9, it is in the form of a cyma curve. Whether the cabriole leg terminates in the "Dutch," or "club," foot in the style of Queen Anne, or in the ball and claw foot of the Chippendale style, both of which are described in the next section, the superiority of the cabriole design is generally acknowledged. It first came into general use in England about the year 1700, in the reign of Queen Anne, and was a conspicuous example of the change from the straight lines of the previous style. In our country the cabriole leg was first used about the year 1705, and it continued in fashion in the styles of Queen Anne and Chippendale until about 1785. It was not used in the styles of Adam, Hepplewhite or Sheraton or in later styles.

Examples of the cabriole leg are best seen on chairs and tables. On chairs it is well seen in the Queen Anne style in illustrations Nos. 9 and 50–67; and in the Chippendale style it is shown in very many chairs, among which are Nos. 118–126; in the chapter on tables it is seen in many illustrations of these two styles, as in the card tables Nos. 1477–1482.

Section 25. The kinds of feet.—In this section mention is made of the principal kinds of feet which are found on articles of American antique furniture;

(NOTE 2, *continued*)

F.   Fretted legs. These were in fretwork designs, either cut on the wood or in forms cut out separately and applied on the leg. Fretwork was used by Chippendale on chairs with square legs, tables and other pieces. See chair No. 141.

G.   Grooved legs. A groove is a channel or hollow cut out of the surface of the wood. Many of the square legs of chairs in the Chippendale style were grooved vertically in order to ornament an otherwise plain leg. In the engravings grooves are more easily seen in the backs of chairs than in the legs; see chairs Nos. 130 and 172.

H.   Splayed, or raked, legs. These are best seen in the six Windsor chairs shown in No. 440. They are not vertical, but are so placed that they slant, the front legs to the sides and the rear legs to the back and sides.

I.   Curule legs. These legs, almost in the shape of a half–circle, were used by Robert Adam as a classical design and were copied by Sheraton and later by Duncan Phyfe and others. They may be seen in figure 30 of the Sheraton style chairs in No. 234. See also note 9 on the curule form in section 52. An early chair having a somewhat similar form of legs is known in England as an "X" chair. See the Index under the word "Curule."

J.   Concave legs. This form was much used in the Sheraton, Directory and Empire styles. As indicated by their name, these legs curved inward in a concave line. Graceful examples are in the pedestal tables in the Sheraton style, copied by Duncan Phyfe and often erroneously attributed to him as the originator; see illustrations of tables Nos. 1322 and 1548 and chairs Nos. 305–310 and 323.

K.   Round legs. These were seldom made in the Chippendale style of furniture but were much used in other styles. They were often reeded or fluted, as to which see section 41. Many illustrations of round legs are seen in the next chapter, on chairs; they were generally "turned," not carved.

L.   Winged lion legs. This was a favorite form on sofas in the Empire period, as may be seen in the chapter on sofas, Nos. 588–592. The idea of combining a wing and the leg of a lion may have come from classic sources, but the design is not pleasing on the legs of a sofa.

M.   Cluster-column legs. This is a leg formed actually or apparently by several columns placed together. Examples are in the chair No. 140; see also the mantel mirror No. 1233.

drawings[1] of many of them appear in the full page illustration No. 11, and definitions of several other kinds not illustrated are in note 4.

Feet are not to be regarded merely as pieces of wood or metal by which articles of furniture are supported; they are important elements of the various styles of furniture, and are often of an ornamental character worthy of the other portions of the object of which they are a part.

It must not be supposed that the use of one style of foot stopped at a particular time and that another style immediately became the fashion. The styles changed gradually; and a particular style of foot often continued in use for some years after a new style began.

Certain kinds of feet were used only or mainly on certain styles of furniture; for example, on furniture in the Queen Anne style with cabriole legs, as to which see the preceding section, the Dutch, or club, foot was generally[2] used, as on the chairs Nos. 50–58 and many others. This Dutch, or club, foot was also used on early pieces in the Chippendale style having cabriole legs. The ball and claw foot was used only on legs of the cabriole form of the Queen Anne and Chippendale styles, never on straight legs; see the illustrations of Chippendale style chairs in section 51, in which section a paragraph is devoted to the legs and feet of the Chippendale style.

Excepting the ball and claw foot, which is the first considered here, the kinds of feet are described in the text in the order of the drawings, figures 2–20, in illustration No. 11, without reference to dates. Most of the feet shown in these drawings are seen in illustrations in this book.

1. Almost all of the drawings shown in illustration No. 11 are copied from "The Furniture Collectors' Glossary," by Mr. L. V. Lockwood, published by the Walpole Society, 1913. For permission to use the illustrations and descriptions in that book the author is much indebted to Mr. Lockwood and the Walpole Society.

An English book entitled "A Glossary of English Furniture of the historic periods," published by R. M. McBride & Co., New York, 1925, is a useful work on this subject, although it has no illustrations.

A large number of feet are shown in volume 3 of Mr. Wallace Nutting's "Furniture Treasury," pages 30–59.

An illustrated article entitled "Identifying periods by legs and feet," by Mr. George Brobeck, is in "The Antiquarian," June, 1929, page 48.

2. A. In a few instances a Dutch, or club, foot is found on a straight leg, as will be seen on a Queen Anne style table No. 1308, which is also illustrated in an article by Dr. Henry J. Berkley in "Antiques," July, 1933, page 12. Several other similar tables are in one of the houses in the reconstructed Williamsburg, Virginia, and illustrations of others are in Mr. Lockwood's "Colonial Furniture," figures 197 and 723. See also the tables Nos. 1286–1289, 1305.

B. Several kinds of feet are called by two or more names; thus the "Dutch" foot is also known as "club" foot or "pad" foot; see figure 10 in illustration No. 11. There are also different forms of a similar type of foot, such as the several kinds of "bracket" feet and "ball" feet shown in the same illustration No. 11.

C. In some sections of our country certain feet are known by local names, especially in New England. These names are generally given because of a similarity of form to some familiar object; thus in a recent advertisement of antiques, certain feet were called "turnip" feet, and others were termed "pumpkin" feet and "bootjack" feet. In one book the name "camel" foot is found. The use of words of this fanciful character is not to be encouraged.

Ball and claw foot. This type of foot, the most interesting and important, is shown in illustration No. 10. It seems to have come from China to Holland and from Holland to England and then to America. In China it represented the three claws of a dragon grasping a pearl. According to the Chinese tradition, the Yellow Dragon was the most honored, "for by him the elements of writing were given to mankind." For several thousand years these emblems have been in use in China; and even at the present day we see Chinese stands made of heavy wood supported by cabriole legs with ball and claw feet.

10. BALL AND CLAW FOOT AND
CABRIOLE LEG.

The ball and claw feet came into general use in England about the year 1730, before the time of Chippendale, and later was made even more important by his skill as a carver. In our country it began to be used about 1735. It is said that in fine pieces the claws appear to hold the ball in a vigorous grasp, and seem to be almost alive, not mere lifeless forms.[3] The ball in some cases is almost round but generally it is somewhat flattened on the bottom, apparently in order that it may sit more firmly on the floor; this will be noticed in many chairs, highboys, lowboys and desks, especially those made in Philadelphia.

(NOTE 2, *continued*)

D. In the "Glossary of English Furniture," above mentioned, it is said, page 165, under the heading "Stump foot," that "the leg of a piece of furniture which is carried down to the floor without the intervention of a foot of any kind, is said to have a 'stump' foot"; and Mr. Cescinsky, in the book "English and American Furniture," page 116, in writing of chairs in the Chippendale style, states that the feature which almost invariably distinguished the American from the English chair is the stump form of back leg which was much used in our country, but not in England. Other kinds of chairs are also without feet, unless the bottom of the leg be regarded as a foot. Thus there are no feet, except the bottom of the legs, on the rounded or rectangular ends of the legs of many chairs in the Hepplewhite, Sheraton, Directory and Empire styles, as will be seen in the illustrations.

E. On many pieces of furniture, as on chairs, only the front legs and feet are ornamented, the rear ones not being conspicuous; but where all parts of an article are easily seen, as on tables made for the centre of a room, all legs and feet are ornamented. In comments on legs and feet of chairs the front ones only are generally referred to.

3. Illustration No. 10 is copied, by permission of Mr. Cescinsky, from one of a table in his book, "English Furniture," volume 2, page 112, figure 108; he remarks that "the cabriole legs, scrolled on the top, and finishing in vigorous claw and ball feet, are finely carved."

Matters in reference to these feet are mentioned in section 15 in connection with the "Director" of Chippendale and in section 36, on "Carving," at note 1; and in the comments on various articles in the Chippendale style in later chapters.

In addition to the term "ball and claw" foot, in which the word "claw" apparently means the claw of the Chinese dragon, there are several other kinds of claws which bear names indicating particular types; thus in figure 2 in illustration No. 11 the name is "animal's" claw; in figure 7 is a "bird's" claw; in figure 14 an "animal's claw" or "paw" is meant; in figure 15 a "rat's" claw is shown.

We now examine the full page illustration No. 11, in which the drawings of other kinds of feet are designated as "figures" 2 to 20; illustration No. 10, showing the ball and claw foot, may be regarded as figure 1.

Figure 2. Animal's ball and claw foot. This is composed of a partially visible ball held by the claws of some kind of animal. An animal's claw foot without a ball, called a "paw" foot, is shown in figure 14.

Figure 3. Ball foot. Three examples of this foot are shown as a group. Their form is spherical or nearly so. This is an early type, seen on several kinds of articles, such as the highboys Nos. 632 and 633, the chest or bureau No. 625, and the desk No. 777. It was also used in later years on wardrobes and other large pieces and on certain types of grandfather clocks. A much flattened form of ball foot, not illustrated, is called a "bun" foot.

Figure 4. Melon ball foot. In this foot the ball is flattened in a form resembling that of a melon of some kind.

Figure 5. Onion ball foot. Here the ball is even more flattened in a form supposed to resemble that of an onion.

Figure 6. Straight bracket foot. A bracket foot is somewhat in the shape of a bracket, such as one hanging on a wall. A "straight" bracket foot is so called because the corner edge is straight as in figure 6, not curved as in figure 9 which is an "ogee" bracket. This type was used on a great number of articles, especially on chests, bureaus, desks and grandfather clocks. In almost all bracket feet, except the French bracket foot, figure 8, the cyma curve may be seen at least once. Three special forms of bracket feet are next mentioned.

Figure 7. Ball and claw bracket foot. This foot is in a different bracket form, with a bird's claw grasping a ball. Examples may be seen on the bureau No. 716 and the desk No. 786.

Figure 8. French bracket foot. This is a slender and graceful bracket foot. The corner edge curves out slightly and the inner edge is in a somewhat long curve. It was much used on furniture in the Hepplewhite style. Examples are in the bureau No. 729 and the desk No. 807. It must not be confused with the "French foot" used by Chippendale and Hepplewhite in their furniture in the French style; see "French foot" below, note 4, C.

Figure 9. Ogee bracket foot. Here the corner edge of a bracket foot is in the shape of a cyma curve with the convex end at the top. This type is generally seen on the better class of furniture. The word "ogee" is defined in section 23, note 1. Examples are on the bureau No. 723 and the desk No. 791.

Figure 10. Dutch, or club, or pad foot. Perhaps this should have been figure 2 because it is next in importance to the ball and claw foot which is the first seen in this section. This foot is in the form of a rounded and thickened disk extending forward from the leg. The term "Dutch" is given to it because it was generally used on the furniture in the Queen Anne style, which was Dutch. The term "club" foot is probably used because of its supposed resemblance to a golf club. As a protection to the foot, as here, another disk is often underneath called a "shoe" or

2. Animal's B & C.   3. Ball   Feet   4. Melon

5. Onion   6. Straight Bracket   7. Ball and Claw Bracket

8. French Bracket   9. Ogee Bracket   10. Dutch or Club

11. Dutch three pointed   12. Dutch elongated   13. Dutch grooved

14. Paw   15. Rat claw   16. Scroll

17. Spade   18. Spanish   19. Stub   20. Snake

ILLUSTRATION No. 11. SEVERAL KINDS OF FEET; FIGURES 2-20.

preferably a "cushion." If the cushion is much higher than the usual one it may be called a "hoof" foot; see the tables Nos. 1288 and 1400. Several modified forms of rounded Dutch feet have been given descriptive names, as below.

Figure 11. Dutch three–pointed or three–toed foot. This is a Dutch or club foot whose sides form points or toes, usually three in number, instead of forming a circle. It is sometimes called a "drake" foot or "web" foot. It has been found mostly in the neighborhood of the Delaware River. Examples are on the chair No. 90, the lowboy No. 692 and the table No. 1401.

Figure 12. Dutch elongated foot. A Dutch foot, the end of which is elongated to a single point. This is sometimes called a "slipper" foot. Examples are on the tables Nos. 1333 and 1365.

Figure 13. Dutch grooved foot; this is a Dutch foot with grooves, like shallow channels, and is well seen in the illustration.

Figure 14. Paw foot. This form, also called a "claw" foot, is seen chiefly on pieces of furniture in the Late Empire style. The animal whose paws are represented is supposed to be a lion. See the bureau No. 761; the sofa No. 589; and the sideboard No. 1013. See also figure 2.

Figure 15. Rat's claw foot. Here a rat's claws grasp a piece of wood which is generally oval or round. This foot was used on many three–legged tables. The legs over these feet are not vertical, as are those with ball and claw feet, but slope gently downward in a concave curve, as also the legs with the "snake" foot, figure 20.

Figure 16. Scroll foot. This is carved in the form of a scroll. A scroll foot may turn forward or backwards; one turning forward is called a Flemish scroll because of its development in Flanders; one turning backward, as here, is called an English scroll. Two other kinds, called "S scroll" feet, and "C scroll" feet, are sufficiently described by their names, although their resemblance to the "S" and "C" is not always obvious; these scroll feet are found on cane chairs such as Nos. 36 and 38, which have front legs in the form of C scrolls. See also "French foot" in note 4, C, "Spanish foot," figure 18, and "Scroll legs" in section 24, note 2, E.

Figure 17. Spade foot. This foot is most frequently seen on chairs and tables. It somewhat resembles a spade in form, tapering downward from its top, at which point it may be somewhat wider than the leg itself. Examples are in Adam style chairs in illustrations Nos. 4 and 181; in the Hepplewhite style chair No. 212; and in the Sheraton style chair No. 245. See also "Tapered legs" in section 24, note 2, D.

Figure 18. Spanish foot. This foot, of which there are several varieties, has vertical grooves in front and turns in a curve backward at the bottom, as in the chair No. 41. The foot was carved out of the solid wood. Sometimes plain legs have been "glorified" by adding these Spanish feet. Occasionally a "cuff" or "bracelet" is seen on the legs just above the feet; see examples in the highboy No. 645 and the lowboys Nos. 673–674.

Figure 19. Stub foot. This is a short tapering foot attached to the body of an article of furniture which has no legs.

Figure 20. Snake foot. This name has been given to a kind of foot because of its supposed resemblance to the head of a snake; in England the term "snake's head" foot is sometimes used. This foot is often seen on three-legged articles such as the graceful tilt-top tables Nos. 1379 and 1394. The legs slope downward in a concave curve.

Several other kinds of feet, not illustrated in this section, are mentioned in the note;[4] and others which require no explanation are mentioned in later chapters, especially in the next chapter, on chairs, in which certain kinds of feet are seen on chairs of certain types.

Section 26. Stretchers.—These familiar parts are seen connecting the legs of many chairs, sofas, tables and other articles. They were primarily made to strengthen the legs by holding them together; but on early chairs and tables the plain kind of stretchers also served the purpose of a foot–rest, especially when cold drafts swept along the floor on the way to the open fireplace.[1]

In the illustrations of chairs many of the different kinds of stretchers appear They vary in design from the highly ornamental ones between the front legs of the cane chairs[2] in the style of about 1690 to the plain and straight stretchers on many chairs in the style of Chippendale. In our country, but not in England, stretchers were often used with cabriole legs on the chairs in the Queen Anne style, as will be seen in illustrations Nos. 50–58. Chairs with cabriole legs in the style of Chip-

4. A. Block foot. This is a short type on square legs somewhat similar to a spade foot but heavier and shorter, square in shape, and not tapering. It is seen on the Chippendale style chairs Nos. 140 and 141, and on the Adam style chair No. 3 in the lower row in the full page illustration No. 181; and also on tables in the same styles. The spade foot was probably developed from it.

B. Brass foot. This kind of foot, generally in an ornamental design, was often used on articles in the Directory and Empire styles. Examples are on the Duncan Phyfe chairs Nos. 320–321, and on the tables Nos. 1540 and 1644.

C. French foot. Chippendale and Hepplewhite made certain kinds of furniture in the French styles of their periods. The feet were on cabriole legs and were scrolled, turning forward. They may be seen on the chairs Nos. 116 and 117. This is not the same foot as the French "bracket foot" mentioned above, figure 8. See also figure 16, "Scroll foot."

D. Stump foot. See note 2, D, in this section.

E. Trestle foot. This early foot consists of a block of wood extending on each side of the leg of a trestle table; see the trestle tables Nos. 1276 and 1300.

F. Turned foot. Turned legs are referred to in section 24, note 2, B, and the general subject of turnings is treated briefly in section 35. Turned feet are seen on the turned legs referred to in those sections, especially on slat–back and banister–back chairs.

1. Stretchers used as foot–rests naturally became somewhat worn, so that a worn stretcher may be an indication of age; but if it is desired to give the appearance of age to a new article the worn condition may be easily produced; see the remarks in note 4 in section 47.

2. See chairs Nos. 36–38.

pendale did not often have stretchers;[3] but when plain square legs were made, Chippendale himself used plain stretchers, even on chairs having elaborately carved backs; and this practice is characteristic of the Chippendale style in both England and America. Whether or not stretchers were used on the chairs in the style of Hepplewhite and Sheraton, and later styles, seems to have depended on the local custom or the taste of the individual chair maker or his customer rather than upon a fixed rule; the same type of chair is found with and without stretchers, as is shown in several illustrations.[4]

Section 27. Casters.—The idea that casters are a modern invention for the purpose of making furniture easily movable is a natural one, because there seems to be something inharmonious in an antique chair or table being fitted with them. But English chairs made as far back as about the year 1700 have been found with casters having leather rollers.[1] Later, chairs and settees in the Chippendale style of about 1750–1765 are seen with metal casters;[2] and from that time they seem to have been continuously used on furniture made in the successive styles from Hepplewhite to the present time, especially on heavy articles.

Casters are occasionally seen on settees, sofas, tables and other articles illustrated in this book. They may not all be the casters originally on the pieces; and in some cases they have been added to articles which did not originally have them, as to chairs whose legs had been shortened. In general it may be said that

3.   In chairs Nos. 152 and 155 four stretchers are seen on Chippendale style chairs having cabriole legs; and in No. 122 there is one stretcher connecting the rear legs only, as in Chippendale's book, the "Director," and as illustrated in Mr. Cescinsky's "English Furniture," volume 1, figure 94, and volume 2, figure 94, and others; see also the Queen Anne style chair No. 65.

4.   Compare the Hepplewhite style chairs Nos. 198 and 199, and the Sheraton style chairs Nos. 245 and 246.

The following are names given to certain kinds of stretchers:

Bulbous; meaning having a bulb or other enlarged and rounded portions; as on chairs Nos. 29–34.

Flat; as on chairs Nos. 53 and 86, on early highboys and lowboys, and on table No. 1600.

Recessed; seen on chairs Nos. 50–54, 108, 187 and very many others. This stretcher does not connect the front legs, but is set back of them, or "recessed," and connects the side stretchers.

H stretchers; three stretchers, one on each side and one "recessed," or set back, when seen from the front form this letter, as in the chairs Nos. 51, 215 and others, and the tables Nos. 1279 and 1282.

Rising; seen on a few tables, as Nos. 1432, 1462 and 1602. Instead of being straight and horizontal, these stretchers "rise" in curves which unite at a central point; also called "domed."

Saltire or "X–shaped"; seen on the lowboy No. 670, and the table No. 1410. The St. Andrew's cross, which resembles an X, is in a saltire shape.

Shaped; meaning any stretcher cut in a shape designed to be ornamental.

1.   In Mr. Cescinsky's "English Furniture," volume 2, pages 21, 64 and 86, these early casters are described, with an illustration of one, figure 79, of the period of 1740–1770, in which the wheel portion is made of hard leather.

2.   As in figures 233, 234, 275 and 295, in the second volume of the above–mentioned book of Mr. Cescinsky.

the presence of casters is not of much value in determining the age of the pieces to which they are now attached.[3]

Section 28. Oak and walnut.—It is said that in England from about 1500 to 1660 oak was almost the only native wood used in the making of fine furniture; and the term "Age of Oak" is often used to indicate that early period.[1] About 1660 the English "Age of Walnut" began. In our country oak was apparently used more than any other wood and later than in England when it was superseded by walnut for the better class of furniture. On the third floor of the American Wing of the Metropolitan Museum of Art, where American furniture made up to about the year 1725 is exhibited, the articles are chiefly of oak. To those particularly concerned with the furniture of this period, sometimes called the "Pilgrim Century," the study of articles made of oak is very interesting; but the amateur collector, for whom this book has been prepared, is not likely to give special attention to oak furniture, which is rarely seen outside of museums and which he has little opportunity of acquiring. Any one desiring to study the subject will find much information and many illustrations in the books mentioned in the note.[2]

In England the "Age of Walnut," meaning the period during which most of the furniture was made of that wood,[3] lasted about sixty-five years, from about 1660 to 1725. In the earlier part of this period walnut and oak were both used; but walnut soon superseded oak and continued to be the fashionable wood until about 1725 when the finely figured mahogany became the favorite wood and was generally used. In our country almost the same dates applied in the cities; but

3. Nor are other fittings which are often broken or are easily detached and attached, such as handles and knobs, as mentioned in section 39, note 4, and section 40.

1. A division of English furniture into four "ages," covering the years 1500 to 1820, is made in the four–volume book entitled "A History of English Furniture," by Mr. Percy Macquoid, as stated in section 4, note 4. This method is perhaps suitable in England, but cannot be applied to our American furniture, for one reason because one of the four "ages," that of satinwood, never existed in our country; and there are objections to the other three ages. As to satinwood, see also section 30.

2. In Mr. Lockwood's "Colonial Furniture," volume 1, pages 22–56, many illustrations of oak furniture from about the years 1650 to 1700 are given.

See also "Furniture of the Pilgrim Century," from 1620 to 1720, revised edition, 1924, by Mr. Wallace Nutting.

Whether a piece of old English oak can be distinguished from one of old American oak is occasionally a matter of earnest argument.

3. A valuable book on this subject is "Old English Walnut and Lacquer Furniture," by Mr. R. W. Symonds, quoted in section 7, note 2. In this volume, pages 18–19, Mr. Symonds refers to the "patina" of old English walnut, which is "the mellow tone and colour of the walnut wood, and the translucent effect which its surface has acquired through the action of time. . . Long exposure to the light causes the varnish to assume a tone which gives a light mellow golden colour. The light also draws out the colour of the stain which was applied to the piece when made and turns the outer skin of the wood to a light tone. . . There is no doubt that this alteration of the original colour of the wood gives a beauty to the piece which it lacked when made."

The "patina" of wood is also described, with comments, in section 10 of this book, note 5.

Two words used in connection with walnut may be mentioned. "Burl," or "burr," means a knot or excrescence in walnut trees and others; the wood of this burl is highly figured and was much just as in furniture styles one style overlapped another,[4] so in the use of woods one kind of wood overlapped another, and the use of walnut continued for many years after 1725 concurrently with mahogany.

It should be understood that all of the dates here given are only approximate and that some are conflicting. Scholars differ in their efforts to establish exact periods; and in fact it is impossible to do so either in England or in our country.[5]

Section 29. Mahogany.—In England the use of mahogany seems to have begun about the year 1725. The brilliance of this wood exceeded that of any other, and its texture made it capable of the most delicate and lasting carving, a feature which contributed greatly to its value.[1] Because of these qualities, mahogany gradually superseded walnut in England for fine furniture and about

(NOTE 3, *continued*)

used for veneer. "Oystering" is a cross–section grain in rings, said to resemble the markings on an oyster shell; it also was used for veneer.

The word "crotch" means "a fork," and as applied to trees it is the fork of a tree, that is the point of separation of the main stem into two parts. See the next section, note 4, paragraph 4, in regard to crotch mahogany.

A kind of walnut much used in the Mid–Victorian period was called "black" walnut in order to distinguish it from the usual kind which had a somewhat reddish color.

It is said that in several States south of New York walnut was very abundant and was often used instead of mahogany in almost all kinds of furniture; but not very much walnut grew in New England and there it was used chiefly for the finer articles.

That Virginia walnut was used in furniture made in England is shown by an advertisement of "Virginia wallnutt–tree chairs" in the "Daily Post" of London, August 30, 1731.

4.   See section 11 at note 1.

5.   See also section 6 at notes 2 and 3.

1.   A.   The wood of the mahogany tree "combines a rich reddish–brown color, beauty of grain and susceptibility of polish with unusual soundness, uniformity, freedom from warping, durability and largeness of dimensions"; Century Dictionary.

B.   It is said that the weight of fine old mahogany from San Domingo and certain other islands in the West Indies is greater than that of the modern wood coming from other places, and is a distinguishing feature of antique mahogany furniture. For example, a chair made of the present day wood is said to be noticeably lighter in weight than a similar chair made of old wood from San Domingo or Cuba. Other countries from which mahogany is now obtained include Mexico and the Central American States and certain coasts of South Africa. The word "mahogany" is also used now as a trade name for certain other woods, not mahogany, as "white mahogany" and "Philippine mahogany," which to a certain extent resemble mahogany. In the eighteenth century the general term "Spanish mahogany" was given to the wood which came from the islands in the West Indies which were owned by Spain.

C.   During the Revolutionary War, when mahogany from the West Indies was not obtainable, a wood called "Bilsted," which was the wood of an American sweet gum tree, was used as a substitute for mahogany, resembling it closely. It is said that this wood is "now commonly mistaken for mahogany."

D.   Both Chippendale and Sheraton, in their books of designs, referred to in sections 15 and 18, expressed their admiration for mahogany. It is said that Thackeray declared that the eighteenth century brought to England three blessings—"Peace, Chippendale and Mahogany."

E.   In spite of its natural fine color mahogany was often artificially reddened in the latter part of the period of the American Empire style, as may be seen on many articles, especially those with large surfaces such as sofas, wardrobes and sideboards.

1725 the use of walnut began to decline and a few years later mahogany was generally used,[2] as mentioned in the preceding section.

In our country it seems that the general use of mahogany for furniture began about 1730 although a few earlier articles made of mahogany have been found. Our "Age of Mahogany" continued in fashion from about 1730 to the early part of the Victorian era, about 1840; after 1730, however, much of our furniture was made of walnut[3] and other woods concurrently with mahogany,[4] as mentioned in the previous section. Nevertheless, throughout the period of Chippendale, when carving was much used, the period of Hepplewhite, when inlay frequently gave the decorative touch, the period of Sheraton, when almost all kinds of decorative woods were used, the period of the French Empire, and the periods of English and American Empire furniture—throughout all of these periods, in all more than one hundred years, 1730 to 1840, mahogany was the "King of Woods."

Section 30. Pine, maple and other woods.—The "Age of Oak," the "Age of Walnut" and the "Age of Mahogany," mentioned in the previous two sections, indicate in a general way the successive periods during which these three woods were in turn chiefly used for fine cabinet work in England and in our country; but it must not be assumed that these woods were at any time the only ones[1] which

2. Walnut was, however, used in England in the mahogany period to some extent; see section 6, note 3; and in our country various other woods were used, as mentioned in section 30.

3. As late as 1767 a Baltimore cabinet maker, Gerrard Hopkins, advertised that he "makes and sells in the newest fashions, in mahogany, *walnut* and cherry, desks, bookcases, tables, chairs," etc. From an article in the "Maryland Historical Magazine," March, 1930, page 11, by Dr. Henry J. Berkley.

4. Two legends of the beginning of the use of mahogany in England are these—both perhaps as near the truth as several other furniture traditions.

One of these is that Sir Walter Raleigh, on one of his cruises, was forced to stop at an island in the West Indies to make repairs to his vessel. The natives supplied mahogany with which he repaired the deck. When he reached England, Queen Elizabeth, in 1595, visited the vessel, and admired the fine color of the deck, and Sir Walter then used some of the wood in making a table for the Queen. This made mahogany known in England. But it was not extensively used until more than a century later.

The other story is that a captain of a vessel brought to England a number of planks of mahogany to be used in constructing certain parts of a house for his brother. The wood was too hard for the workmen to cut into the forms desired and it came into the hands of a cabinet maker who was able to make a bureau of it. The Duchess of Buckingham admired the bureau and ordered one made out of the same wood—and this was the beginning of the use of mahogany, about the year 1724.

"High up in the air, in the trunk of a mahogany tree, a silent but intense struggle takes place among the fibres of wood in the attempt of each to follow its own inclination in determining to which of the great branches overhead it shall pledge its allegiance and support. Consequently the fibres cross, twist and tumble in a swirl that, when manufactured into veneer, produces the most highly figured mahogany of all—the Crotch." From "Stately Mahogany," a pamphlet published by the Mahogany Association, Chicago.

It is said that "there is no such thing as 'mahogany finish.' Ask your dealer the meaning of the term, and, if he is truthful, he will tell you it is merely a trade name which refers to the color of the stain used. He will also tell you that it has nothing to do with mahogany and that it is never used in connection with genuine mahogany." From the pamphlet mentioned above.

1. Thirty-nine kinds of wood used in English furniture of the eighteenth century are described in Mr. Cescinsky's "English Furniture," volume 3, pages 368–377. In Mr. Wallace Nutting's "Furniture Treasury," volume 3, pages 417–426, many kinds of American and other woods are described.

(*Note 1 continued on page 82*)

were used in their respective "Ages." In each of these three periods various other and minor woods were used, from some of which, such as maple and cherry, a handsome article of furniture could be made; but others of these minor woods were more suitable for the inner or rear parts which were not generally seen.

It is impossible for an amateur collector to learn to identify the various kinds of woods by printed descriptions or by illustrations; only by experience in handling woods can their various features be recognized with certainty, and sometimes even experienced cabinet makers may have difficulty in determining their nature at first sight.

Pine. This wood is sometimes regarded as peculiarly an American product, but in England Scotch pine has been used for furniture since about the year 1600. In the time of Chippendale it was used for the frames of mirrors and for other articles which were to be covered with gilding. In our country the settlers found pine in great abundance, both the hard yellow pine and the soft white pine; and the latter being plentiful, cheap and easy to work, soon became the principal wood for the simpler kinds of household furniture. From about the year 1700 to the present time it has probably been used more extensively than any other kind of wood; and a list of the articles of furniture which were and are made of pine, wholly or in part, would include almost every household wooden article with which we are acquainted. In furniture of the better class, made of walnut or mahogany, pine was much used for the parts not generally seen, such as the bottoms and sides of the drawers of bureaus or desks; and furniture of a plainer character, made of pine, was often veneered with a more expensive wood, such as walnut or mahogany. Pine has a very light color when it is new, but when old it is brownish yellow or even yellow.

Maple. At least three kinds of maple wood were used in the making of furniture, commonly known as (1) "maple," (2) "curly" maple and (3) "bird's–eye" maple. The first, merely "maple," is wood having no distinctive markings such as those of the second and third kinds. The words "curly" and "bird's–eye" do not indicate different varieties of maple trees, as both kinds are found in at least one tree, the sugar maple, that noble and useful tree of the northern parts of our country. The appearance of the curly and bird's–eye kinds is given by some accidental arrangement of the fibre of the wood, as is the "burl" wood of walnut or the "crotch" wood of mahogany. The curly maple figure comes from a twisting of the grain of any one of several varieties, particularly the sugar maple. The bird's–eye figure is formed by little spots supposed to resemble birds' eyes, and is found in the wood of the sugar maple.

(NOTE 1, *continued*)

     Pieces of furniture intended to be painted were often made of several kinds of wood; but all of the same parts were generally of the same wood, all the legs being of one kind of wood and all the stretchers of one kind. Windsor chairs are examples of this combination of woods, often intended to be painted green; see "Windsor chairs," section 62.

     An illustrated article entitled "Distinctive features in furniture woods," by Mr. Henry Branscombe, is in "The Antiquarian," November, 1927, page 59.

From an early period in New England, where maple was plentiful, this wood was used for furniture of a middle class character. Not so fine as walnut or mahogany, and not so common as pine, it is sometimes said that maple furniture was generally not intended for the formal room—the "parlor"—of a fine residence, but for the less important rooms.[2] Maple is a very hard wood, and hence was not often used for carving. It was especially favored for use as an inlay. Maple is not shown to advantage in the halftone engravings in this book, as the color and grain do not clearly appear.

Several other woods, less important than those mentioned above, were also much used, both because they were easily obtainable and less expensive, and because some were more suitable for parts of certain articles. But it must not be thought that furniture made of the minor woods was in all cases of a lower degree of style and workmanship than that made of the more expensive woods. There was no reason for the cabinet maker to use inferior designs or to do second-class work merely because he was using a more plentiful wood.

Cherry wood and fruit woods. Many pieces of excellent design and workmanship were made of cherry wood, which was well adapted for general household furniture, although lacking the fine character of some other kinds. Cherry is found in articles made as far back as about 1680 and it continued in use throughout the various furniture styles; so also were the woods which are commonly called "fruit woods," chiefly apple wood and pear wood. Many articles of fine design and workmanship were made of these woods.

Tulip wood, also called poplar, and sometimes known as whitewood, was often used for the interior of drawers of bureaus and other articles. It is light in weight and somewhat soft. As to the names of this wood, see note 4 in section 78, in the chapter on "Chests." Tulip and poplar are not exactly the same woods as the names are understood in New England and the Southern States.

Hickory and ash were much used for certain parts of articles where a strong, but not heavy, wood was required. Hickory, for example, was almost always used for the spindles of Windsor chairs, such as are shown in illustrations Nos. 440 to 467. Birch was also used for legs and spindles as well as for whole pieces of various kinds.

For bright inlay the usual wood was maple, as above mentioned, but for the finest pieces of furniture the favorite was the brilliant and expensive "satinwood,"

2. In Philadelphia, and no doubt in other cities, curly maple was sometimes used for fine furniture. In an article by Mr. W. M. Hornor, Jr., in "Country Life in America," September, 1928, page 49, are illustrations of handsome Chippendale style carved chairs and other pieces made of curly maple. An illustrated article by Mr. Walter A. Dyer is in "The Antiquarian," April, 1930, page 62, entitled "Maple: Craze or Appreciation?"

An advertisement in the "Maryland Gazette," October 14, 1747, mentions "Maple desks lately imported, and to be sold by William Govane at his house near Annapolis by wholesale." This appears in an article by Dr. Henry J. Berkley, in the Maryland Historical Magazine, March, 1930, page 8. Notice that the desks were imported and were to be sold by wholesale.

Several pieces of maple bedroom furniture belonging to one owner are illustrated in No. 644, a highboy; No. 694, a lowboy; No. 1067, a bedstead; comparison will show that the highboy and lowboy are companion pieces.

which came from a tropical tree of Asia and the West Indies. In England satin-wood was used from about 1770 to 1820 not only for inlay, but also for articles as large as tables, desks and bookcases, especially in furniture designed by Robert Adam. A pair of satinwood knife boxes is illustrated in Nos. 1021–1022 in the chapter on sideboards. It is said that satinwood was sometimes used in New Eng-land about 1790 as a veneer on mahogany furniture. The true color of satinwood is a brilliant yellow. Sometimes pieces of inlay made of maple are called satin-wood, possibly by mistake. It is said by Mr. Cescinsky in his "English Furniture," volume 3, page 375, that "modern satinwood is frequently stained with coffee to give the work the appearance of age." See also note 1 in section 28.

Other woods used for inlay were holly and tulip; holly has a fine grain and is almost white; tulip is light in color when new, but becomes yellowish with age.

Rosewood, a tropical wood, was used in England for various articles in the time of Sheraton,[3] and in our country in the Victorian period from about 1845 to 1860. Its name was given because of a faint rose odor which comes from it when freshly cut.

Several woods were used only or chiefly in certain localities, and are not mentioned here.

Section 31. Lacquer.—Although very few articles of lacquered American furniture are found in our homes it may be well to mention the character of the work. The old lacquer was a kind of varnish which was made in China and Japan from the sap of the gum tree growing in those countries, where the art of lacquering has been practiced for many centuries. Much lacquered work was imported into England[1] from about the year 1675 and was copied by the English cabinet makers; and so popular was the style that it continued to be made from time to time until about the year 1800. Many fine examples of this finish are found on the early English grandfather clocks. At one time it became a social fad to practice lacquer-ing as a pastime. The process as employed in England was known as "japanning," and articles were said to be "japanned," these words apparently indicating Japan as the place of origin of the process. The original "japanning" or, as we call it, "lacquering," was generally not made flat on the surface of the article to be decorated; the designs were raised from the surface, somewhat as a cameo is raised from the surface of its base. The raised effect was produced by applying paste or

---

3. Rosewood card tables "by the first workmen of London and of superior style and elegance" were advertised for sale in the "Baltimore American," July 6, 1817.

1. The subject of English lacquer–work is treated at length in Mr. Cescinsky's "English Furni-ture," volume 1, pages 174–226; and also in the same author's book on "English Domestic Clocks," chapter 10.

   The subject is also treated in Mr. Symonds' book, "Old English Walnut and Lacquer Furniture." On page 153 it is said that "it is no exaggeration to say that more than two–thirds of the lacquer furniture sold (in England) as antique, is fraudulent. This, however, refers to the English lacquer, as the Oriental variety with the raised design is not imitated."

   In the eighteenth century the word "lacquer" had a different meaning from its present one, and referred to a coating of varnish put on metals to protect them from tarnishing.

plaster to the surface at the point where the design was desired, which was then colored with paint or gilt. In our country a few "japanned" articles of furniture were made, and "japanning" was mentioned in our newspapers as far back as 1712. The above remarks apply only to the raised kind of "lacquering" or "japanning."

About the year 1790 a new kind of decoration began, having an appearance somewhat similar to that of the "japanning" above mentioned, to which the same word "japanning" was given, although the method was a different one.[2] This process consisted of applying a coat of varnish, resembling lacquer in some respects, on the object to be treated, and painting designs upon the varnish, generally with gilt or other colors. The difference between the earlier work and this work, was that the earlier work was "raised," as above mentioned, but the later work was merely painting on a flat surface, without any raised parts. This latter style of painting was followed by the ordinary painting of the late Sheraton and the Early American Empire styles.

Section 32. Veneer.—This familiar word is well defined as "a thin piece of wood, usually of a choice kind showing a rich grain, laid upon another wood, generally of a plainer kind, so as to give a superior and more valuable appearance to the article so treated." In this definition there is no suggestion of giving a

2. A. Advertisements in Maryland newspapers in 1801 and 1806 referred to "Japanned furniture" and "Japan ware."

B. In "Antiques," May, 1929, pages 398–401, is a handsomely illustrated frontispiece to an article entitled "A pedigreed lacquered highboy," by Esther Stevens Fraser. It seems likely that the highboy was made about 1740 and that the very fine lacquering was done by one of the japanners of Boston, several of whose advertisements, dated from 1713 to 1758, are copied in the article. It is said that the use of pine and maple indicated that the highboy was made in America, but that "the lacquering bore clear evidence of English training." It is not stated that the decoration had any raised figures. Another fine lacquered highboy of somewhat earlier date is shown in Mr. Lockwood's "Colonial Furniture," volume 1, figure 79; this has raised figures.

C. The dry climate and the overheated houses of our country are referred to by Mr. Cescinsky in the book "English and American Furniture," page 75, where it is said that "it is dangerous to introduce the English pieces which in a humid climate have persisted in a perfect state for nearly three hundred years. In America the best European examples fall to pieces in an incredibly short time." Similar results are mentioned in connection with "Boulle" work in section 33, note 1, C.

D. Reference should be made here to a famous kind of French varnish known as "Vernis Martin," meaning literally "Martin's varnish," made by four brothers in Paris, named Martin, the firm being in business from about the year 1725 to 1765. The varnish developed by them had a very fine lustre which compared favorably with the best of the Chinese and Japanese products. The French government granted to the Martins a monopoly for their lacquer work, which they made in their three factories in great quantities, decorating all kinds of articles from snuff boxes and fans to large pieces of furniture and carriages and sedan chairs. Very few authenticated articles treated with "Vernis Martin" are known; but as there were many imitators, there is "an infinite quantity of examples that have been attributed to them"; a similar remark is in section 6, note 13.

E. An illustrated article by Celia Woodward, entitled "Lacquer Furniture in England, 1660–1780," is in "The Antiquarian," May, 1931, page 17. In "Antiques," November, 1932, page 183, is an illustrated article entitled "The Art of Lacquering," by E. L. Price; and in the same magazine, August, 1922, page 65, is an illustrated article entitled "The Art of Japanning" by Mrs. Willoughby Hodgson.

deceptive[1] appearance to the article to which the veneer is attached, the purpose being only to make the article attractive by an approved method of furniture decoration. The use of veneer in England dates from about the reign of William and Mary, (1688–1702), previous to which all furniture was made of solid wood. In our country veneering dates from about the same period, or a little later. Veneer was not often used on furniture made in the Chippendale period, but was much favored on the furniture made in the styles of Hepplewhite and Sheraton, and was extensively used on the larger pieces of the Empire style, such as tables and sideboards. Naturally, veneer is not suitable for carved surfaces.

Certain parts of various woods are more decorative than other parts; and the wood used for veneering was almost always made of the best parts,[2] showing the greatest decorative effect. In the earlier years the veneer was somewhat thicker than in the later, and in the late Empire style furniture it was extremely thin; the thickness of veneer is thus to some extent an indication of its age. Nowadays veneer is made easily by a cutting machine and is sold by the yard in a variety of woods and designs.

Section 33. Inlay; marquetry; eagles; stars, etc.—The use of inlay for decorative purposes is a very ancient one. The artists of Greece and Rome inlaid their chairs and other objects with ivory and precious metals; and in modern

1. The word "veneer" is sometimes used to suggest superficiality or deception, as in the remark that a person has only a "veneer" of culture. But this meaning is not applicable to veneered antique furniture.

2. Especially "burl" walnut, mentioned in section 28, note 3, and "crotch" mahogany, mentioned in section 29, note 3.

An interesting method of veneering is often seen on large surfaces, such as the fronts of bureaus or wardrobes, in which two designs exactly the same appear next to each other, but with the right and left sides reversed. The process of making these, called "matching," is simple. If a piece of wood one–eighth of an inch thick and of a desired size is sawed into two pieces, each one–sixteenth of an inch thick, but of the same size, each of the two new surfaces will be the same in appearance, and when glued reversely on the article will show a "matched" appearance. A somewhat similar effect follows if one places his two hands together, with the palms inside, and then opens his hands as he would open a book; you then see your two palms, which correspond with the two new surfaces of the matched wood. Examples are on the bureau No. 728; and the sideboard No. 991.

Veneered pieces are easily damaged by water standing on them, causing the veneer to swell and crack, or blister, and similar damage may be caused by hot tea pots; for which reason sideboards and serving tables were sometimes made with marble tops which are mentioned in section 44.

"Banding," a word used in veneering and inlay work, may be mentioned here. It consists of a band or strip of wood placed in a wooden surface for decorative effect, and is seen chiefly on the edges of drawers and tables. It gives a contrast either in color or grain between itself and the surface which it decorates. The band or strip is generally from about one half of an inch to two inches in width.

"Herringbone" is a pattern which consists of one or more series of narrow bands of veneer or inlay cut in short diagonal lines, contrasting with another series turned in the opposite direction. This word is also used in architecture and in embroidery.

An illustrated article entitled "Veneers in woodwork," by Mr. Henry Branscombe, is in "The Antiquarian," July, 1928, page 35. In the same magazine, September, 1931, page 15, is an illustrated article entitled "English Walnut Veneers and their preservation," by Mr. Edward Wenham.

times the ornamentation of furniture with inlay equals veneering and carving in widespread use. The meaning of the word "inlay" in connection with furniture may be too generally understood to require its definition here; but for the sake of exactness it may be said that inlay is an ornamentation by which lines or designs are cut out of wood of one color and then inserted into openings cut into wood of another color. The word "marquetry" has a somewhat different meaning, although sometimes used as if synonymous.[1]

Inlay in the decoration of furniture was rarely used in articles made in the Chippendale style, but was particularly favored in the time of Hepplewhite and Sheraton, and is seen in a great variety of objects, in fact in almost all furniture made in the styles of those two masters. The designs of the inlay are varied and numerous, including flowers in festoons and strings, especially bell-flowers, (sometimes called "husks"), stars, shells and large forms, rectangular, oval or round, as will be seen in the illustrations in many chapters of this book. The woods chiefly used for inlay are mentioned in the latter part of section 30.

A favorite patriotic design in the early days of the "United States of America" was the American eagle,[2] which became the national emblem soon after the adoption of the Constitution in 1788. It appeared on the great seal of the United States, on the national flag, on the seals of a number of States, on coins and on

1. A. Marquetry, as used in our antique furniture, is an inlay, in a veneered surface, or ornamental wood, in which shaped pieces of different woods or tints are combined to form a design. Marquetry was much used in England in the decoration of furniture in the period of about 1670–1720. The pattern was usually formed by inlaying light colored woods into a darker background. Marquetry reached a high point of beauty and popularity in the France of Louis XV, and in the England of William and Mary and Queen Anne.

B. In Symonds' "Old English Walnut and Lacquer Furniture," page 94, it is said that "marquetry furniture, unfortunately, is not immune from the attentions of the faker. Not only does he make examples of entirely new construction, but he enhances in value old pieces of plain walnut by the addition of spurious inlay." These remarks are quoted here because of the frequent offerings of English marquetry furniture, especially grandfather clocks, at auctions and otherwise. The subject of marquetry is treated at length in Mr. Cescinsky's "English Furniture," etc., volume 1, pages 86–124. It may be added that the "addition of spurious inlay" is not unknown in our country.

C. "Boulle" work is a form of marquetry brought to perfection by a French cabinet maker of that name, sometimes erroneously spelled "Buhl," (1642–1732); in this work ornamental designs in tortoise shell and brass are attached to a background of wood, the designs fitting each other closely. This "Boulle" work often comes apart because the tortoise shell, the metal and the wood to which they are attached contract and expand unevenly. This may be noticed in many pieces of modern French makers.

D. Lines of brass inlay are often seen on English clocks made about 1800–1810, especially in those known as "lancet" clocks.

2. From the time of Greece and Rome, through the centuries of the Middle Ages, and to the present day, the eagle has been used as an emblem of sovereignty. On foreign furniture the eagle often appears, but not often in inlay, and, of course, not the American bird.

"The wide-spread habitat, the strength and the solitary independence of the eagle have made it of world wide symbolic significance." From an illustrated article by Mr. R. W. Symonds in "Antiques," October, 1930, page 307, entitled "English Eagle and Dolphin Console Tables."

It is said that when the eagle design on the badges of the Society of the Cincinnati was shown to Benjamin Franklin by a friend who mentioned that it resembles a turkey more than an American eagle, Franklin remarked that he wished that it had been a turkey, because the eagle was found in many

many articles of household use, from Lowestoft[3] china to mahogany furniture. On furniture the eagle was used as an inlay on many articles, such as tables and desks, and also as a carved ornament attached to an article, as on a mirror or a clock, as mentioned in section 37.

When used as an inlay, the eagle was generally in an oval medallion, often holding in its mouth a streamer on which appears a series of marks representing stars,[4] the number of which often indicated the number of States then in the Union, just as at the present day the number of stars in our flag indicates the number of States now in our Union. This feature often furnishes a definite date for the piece on which it appears; however, a close resemblance to an American eagle should not be expected in these designs; and, moreover, in some cases the inlaid stars may have been used merely to fill a vacant space. Inlaid single stars, not connected with an eagle, are occasionally seen. Interesting examples of eagle and star designs are to be seen on page 441, Nos. 804 and 806; also on page 644, No. 1160.

Section 34. Painting; gilding; stencil work.

—The decorative painting[1] of various articles of furniture was practiced for several centuries in Europe, but ceased to be used in England about the time the style of Chippendale became the fashionable one; and Chippendale, being a gifted designer of carvings and himself a skillful carver, decorated his furniture with carved designs rather than with painted ones. Throughout this book it will be seen that none of the articles in the Chippendale style are ornamented with painting. In England the next following style, the Adam, used painting on many articles, often by well known artists; but as furniture in the Adam style unfortunately was not made in our country,[2] we have none decorated in that style. Later, however, some of our cabinet makers, especially in Baltimore, following the styles of Hepplewhite and Sheraton, used

(NOTE 2, *continued*)

countries, but the turkey was an original native of our own; from "The Homes of our Ancestors," by R. T. H. Halsey and Elizabeth Tower, page 230, in which the story of eagles as an American patriotic emblem on furniture is interestingly told; see the index of that book, page 292, and also pages 182 and 229-232.

3. See an illustrated article entitled "American Eagle Lowestoft," in "Antiques," June, 1930, page 530, by the editor, Mr. Homer Eaton Keyes. It is here said, page 533, that "eagle forgeries" are common enough on French imitations of Oriental ware. Another article is in the same magazine, November, 1930, page 387, illustrating American eagles on two other pieces of china.

4. Other examples will be seen in later chapters; see especially the desks Nos. 803 and 805. On the subject see also section 6, note 12 and section 37; also the Index under "Stars."

1. By "painting," as used here, is meant decorative painting, consisting of designs of some kind. Furniture painted all over in one color is referred to in the third paragraph of the text.

In "Antiques," are three illustrated articles by Mrs. Esther S. Fraser, entitled "Painted Furniture in America." The first, June, 1924, page 302, discusses "The Sheraton fancy chair. 1790-1817"; the second, September, 1924, page 141, treats of "The period of stenciling. 1817-1835"; the third, January, 1925, page 15, considers "The decadent period. 1835-1845." See also note 5 in this section and the Index under the words "painted furniture" and "stenciling."

2. See the reason for this stated in "The Adam style," section 16.

painting to a limited extent on furniture made in those two styles; and in the Late American Empire style period, from about 1825 to 1840, certain articles, especially chairs, were fully ornamented with painting. Stencil work also was much used on the Empire style furniture, as mentioned and explained below in this section.

In this book a number of painted or stenciled pieces with attractive designs are shown in the illustrations, which however leave the colors largely to the imagination. Among those of special interest are the Sheraton style chairs Nos. 290–295; the Empire style chairs Nos. 328–345; the settees Nos. 515–518; and the tables Nos. 1435 and 1442. Other painted articles include the "Pennsylvania Dutch" chests, four of which are shown in illustrations Nos. 601–604. In all of these pieces the background is painted.

It was the custom at different times in our country to paint the entire surface of various articles, especially chairs, with paint of one color, instead of allowing the natural wood to be seen. These pieces were generally of a plain character, such as would be used in almost every household. For example, early furniture made of pine was often painted, the purchaser selecting the color which he or his wife desired; furniture of maple, which has its own bright color, was also often painted; so also were articles made of cherry. Windsor chairs were generally painted green.

Not only the original coat of paint, put on at the time the article was made, but also several other coats, added from time to time, are frequently found on antique pieces.[3] A person experienced in the work may be able to remove the various coats one by one; but the amateur collector should not try any experiments, as the first coat may have a finely painted design which would probably be ruined by unskillful work.

Gilding. Very little furniture decorated with real gilding, that is, gold leaf or gold dust,[4] was made in our country, with the exception of mirrors. On mirrors the decoration often covers the entire front of the frame; or may be mainly at the top, where scrolls or various ornamental designs were placed, or at the sides where strings of leaves or flowers hang down on the frame. A small object, such as a bird, generally consisted of a wooden form shaped in a design resembling a bird; this form was then covered with a material called "gesso," which is the Italian name for a kind of plaster which becomes very hard, and the gesso was

3.   Paint may cover a multitude of furniture defects, especially new or cracked or broken parts; and recent paint on a piece of furniture said to be antique should naturally excite suspicion as to what is underneath. Where the surface of the wood of an article offered for sale as an antique is painted over, a small part of the paint should be scraped off; if the paint is old, it will be hard and will come off in powder or small particles; but if the paint is new it will be softer and more easily removable. In making this test the kind of wood may also be discovered.

4.   The gilt decorations on many chairs in the Empire style, such as Nos. 337 to 345, were made by gilt paint or stencil and were not "gilded" in the sense above mentioned.

The business of carving and gilding was often carried on by the same person, calling himself "carver and gilder," as appears in the advertisements in the newspapers of the periods; see also section 36, note 1, C.

shaped exactly in the form desired and then gilded; the still smaller ornaments, such as leaves or flowers, were also usually formed of gesso, often supported on a wire.

Stencil work. A stencil is a thin sheet of tin or other metal in which a design is formed by cutting through the sheet. If the sheet thus cut is placed upon a wooden surface and the cut–out part is painted, the design will appear on the underlying wood. Copies of the design may be made with one stencil on as many chairs or other articles as desired. This method of decoration was of course much cheaper than painting or gilding and was therefore used chiefly on the less valuable articles. The subject is mentioned and illustrated in connection with "Painted and stenciled chairs" in the latter part of section 54 in the chapter on chairs; see also the magazine articles cited in note 1 in this section.[5]

Section 35. Turnings.—"Turning" may seem to be too much of a technical detail of cabinet–making to be considered in this volume; but the word is so frequently used in the books and magazines that it is worth while to define[1] it in order that every reader may understand it, even though he or she may never have seen a "lathe." Turning is a simple and inexpensive method of shaping pieces of wood in making articles of furniture; and an object formed by turning is known as a "turning." The forms in which turnings were made at different times and in various styles are numerous; and the character of the turning, if original, is regarded as an indication of the approximate date at which the article on which it appears was made.

Certain portions of several articles of furniture are almost always "turned," especially the legs of chairs; and a good method of conveniently seeing the principal forms of turning is to examine the illustrations in the chapter on chairs,[2] because in chairs we find examples of all of the furniture styles in which we are interested. "Turnings" are generally circular, but may be in oval or some other forms; but square or rectangular legs of chairs were not made by turning, nor were cabriole legs, for the reason that a lathe is not suitable for such forms.

On other articles of furniture various kinds of turnings were used, too numerous to be described here; but some may be referred to. On highboys and low-

5. Other articles on stencils in "Antiques" are "Some Rescued Stencils of Earlier Days," April 1922, page 159, by Mr. Henry Longcope; "The Golden Age of Stenciling," April, 1922, page 162, by Mrs. Esther Stevens Fraser; Editorial, April, 1922, page 154. See also the magazine articles mentioned in note 1 of this section.

1. To "turn" is "to form or fashion (a piece of wood) with a chisel (or other cutting instrument) while the wood is rotated in a lathe; to shape, as wood or other hard substance, especially into round or rounded figures, by means of a lathe; as to 'turn' the legs of a chair or a table"; "turning" is "the art or practice of shaping objects by means of cutting tools while the objects themselves are revolved rapidly on a lathe"; Century Dictionary. See also "Turned legs" in section 24, note 2, B.

To cabinet makers and others familiar with cabinet–making, the word "turning" is as familiar as "sawing." The best way for an amateur collector to understand turning is to see a lathe in operation in the shop of a cabinet maker.

2. Turnings on chairs are mentioned in the chapter on chairs, section 46, note 11.

boys in the William and Mary style, the "inverted cup" turned legs and the "trumpet" turned legs will be seen in the illustrations; see section 24, note 2, B. On tables, especially the gate–leg ones Nos. 1291–1302, various forms of turnings will be noticed. "Spool" turnings, "ball" turnings, "sausage" turnings, "knob" turnings and others are so called, and will be recognized, because of their supposed resemblance in form to the objects whose names they bear. A "spiral" turning is one which is cut in a spiral form resembling a corkscrew, as you may observe in the chair No. 35. "Bulbous" turnings are on the chairs Nos. 29–34. See the Index under the word "Turning."

Section 36. Carving; leaves, shells, etc.—The subject of carving may be briefly considered in two divisions; the first is the carving of designs on the *surface* of the wood of articles of furniture, the subject of this section, comprising carvings of ball and claw feet, leaves such as those of the acanthus plant, shells, sunbursts and others; the second division comprises objects which are not carved on the surface, but separately, and are then attached to the articles but are not necessarily a part of them, which is the subject of the next section, such as eagles and other birds and various other objects.

The *quality* of the carving on furniture varies from the most elegant to the coarse and crude. The artistic character of the work is of course a very important point in valuing the object on which the carving appears; and a knowledge of what is fine carving, and what is not, is necessary in order to form a correct opinion of the work. This knowledge can only be acquired by a close examination of examples of carving of the finer class, learning from them the features of artistic design and skillful workmanship. The good or bad quality of a carving is at once apparent to the trained eye of a connoisseur, but is not often noticed by amateurs.

One of the most interesting of familiar carvings on the surface is that of a ball and claw foot, which is referred to in section 25 at note 3. A good example is in illustration No. 10 in which the claws seem to grasp the ball with vigor and do not merely rest idly upon it.[1] The fact that ball and claw feet or any other

1. A. Carving reached its highest point of excellence in England in the time of Chippendale, who was himself a carver of great skill. The American cabinet makers and carvers followed his designs, and produced the best carving in our country during the years in which the Chippendale style furniture was in fashion here, about 1755 to 1785. Our most highly esteemed carved chairs are those believed to have been made by Benjamin Randolph of Philadelphia, known as the "Sample chairs," three of which are shown in illustrations Nos. 116, 117 and 406. Other important carvers were Townsend and Goddard, of Newport, Rhode Island, whose work is shown in the chapter on block front furniture, sections 114–119. See also section 72 in which Samuel McIntire, of Salem, Mass., is mentioned, with a photograph of one of his beautifully carved sofas, No. 564.

B. It is said that the almost universal use of carving in England and America as a decorative feature in the time of Chippendale was largely due to the introduction of mahogany. This wood supplied all the requirements of the carver, the cabinet maker and the customer. See section 29.

C. Carving and cabinet making were different trades and were usually carried on by different persons in the days of our ancestors; and the same distinction exists now to some extent. The city directories and the newspaper advertisements contained numerous references to "carvers," some of whom

(*Note 1 continued on next page*)

kind of feet are carved on a chair does not make the chair interesting or valuable unless the carving of the feet is well designed and well executed.

A carving very frequently used is that of leaves of the acanthus plant. This plant is a native of Africa and southern Europe, and has large, deeply cut and shining leaves, which for many centuries have been used as a basis of ornamental decoration, especially in Greek and Roman architectural designs. In articles of furniture the leaves have long been a favorite type of carved decoration, in forms not exactly similar to the leaves themselves, but at least suggesting a resemblance, that is, in "conventional"[2] forms. On the chair No. 320, the table No. 1323, the bedstead No. 1063, and on many other pieces of furniture, carvings of acanthus leaves will be found in varieties of form and in different degrees of excellence.[3] See also chairs Nos. 321 and 326.

Another design frequently carved on the surface is that of "shells," which are found on many chairs of the Chippendale style, as in No. 153. Shells were often finely carved on highboys and lowboys; but the highest development of shells was in the "block front" furniture illustrated in sections 115–119. Carved "sunbursts" are supposed to represent the rising sun. Carved "cornucopias" and "wings" are seen on the legs of many sofas of the Empire style; and in addition to those here mentioned there are of course numerous other carvings on the surface, some of which will be seen in the illustrations of the various articles.

Section 37. Carvings; eagles, flames and other finials.—In this section we briefly refer to ornamental pieces which were separately carved and then attached to articles of furniture but are not necessarily a part of them, as mentioned in the preceding section.

(NOTE 1, *continued*)
advertised that they were from London. Frequently the same person was a "carver and gilder." See also the chapter on chairs, section 45, note 5, D, and section 34, note 4.

     D.   Several kinds of carving are here mentioned.

     "Pierced" carving. If the back of a chair or a part of any other article is cut through in a design it is said to be "pierced," as in the chair backs in the Chippendale style; also pedantically called "ajouré," meaning "pierced through" or "showing daylight through."

     "Scratch" carving; meaning scratches on the surface, showing a design.

     "Incised" carving is a pattern cut below the surface.

     Carvings by reeding and fluting are described in section 41.

     2.   The word "conventional" is frequently used in books and magazine articles, sometimes loosely. The meaning in the fine arts, including furniture, is "purposely deviating from natural forms, although properly retaining the principles which underlie them; as, the conventional forms of birds, beasts, flowers, etc." "Conventionality" is defined as "the character of being conventional as opposed to natural; artificiality"; and to "conventionalize" is to represent in a conventional manner either exactly "or in a manner intentionally incomplete and simplified"; Century Dictionary. Many carvings are rescued from reproach by being called "conventional."

     3.   Fine designs of acanthus leaves are seen on some of the articles made by Duncan Phyfe. In "Furniture Masterpieces of Duncan Phyfe," pages 53–54, Mr. Cornelius states that the Phyfe leaf differs from that of classical decoration and partakes much more of the Directory feeling, and that this leaf is the most generally used decorative detail in Phyfe's work. It is always flat, or, as it is said, "in low relief." Examples are on the tables Nos. 1530 and 1548.

The most numerous objects of this kind are the carved wooden ornaments known as "finials," which are placed at the top of a piece of furniture. The finials chiefly used are "flames," which are small upright wooden pieces carved in a manner supposed to represent flames and are seen on the top of many highboys, secretary–bookcases and other high pieces. Other ornaments used as finials are vases, urns, balls, flowers, birds and occasionally a "cartouche" such as is seen on the highboy No. 660 and the mirror No. 1113. At the top of almost all grandfather and certain other clocks are either wooden finials in one of the designs above mentioned, or brass urns or balls.

"Pendants," generally of small size, are carved or turned ornaments pointing downwards, especially seen on the lower portion of many highboys and lowboys, as in Nos. 653 and 675; these were very liable to breakage and many of those now seen are substitutes for the missing originals.

In section 33, on the subject of inlay, mention is made of the American eagle as a national emblem in our country and its use in inlay work on various articles of furniture; another popular form of eagle was the carved and gilded one which was attached as a finial to many objects in the period following the adoption of the Constitution of the United States in 1788, and especially after the War of 1812. This eagle, used as a patriotic ornament, will be seen in the illustrations in the chapters on mirrors;[1] it appears also on clocks[2] and on other subjects. The American eagle was of course not used as our national emblem on any furniture made before the date above mentioned; and it must not be confused with the eagles of other countries nor with the pheasant. The carved eagle as a finial is often regarded as proof that the article to which it is attached is of American make, but this is not always the case.[3]

Section 38. Applied decorations; mounts.

—Another type of decoration, used on many articles of furniture, is "applied" decoration. As is also mentioned in the chapter on highboys, section 87, note 4, the word "applied" means "laid on or put on"; and, in connection with furniture, an "applied" decoration means one of wood or metal which is not carved on the surface of the article but is attached by gluing[1] or by small nails.

1. See the chapter on mirrors, section 142, note 11; also the fretwork mirror No. 1129 and others, and the girandole mirror No. 1245 and others.

2. Many eagles made of brass were imported as ornaments for banjo clocks.

3. In "English Furniture," by Mr. Frederick S. Robinson, London, 1905, it is said that about 1780–1790 mirrors with the American eagle were popular in England. There are certain differences in form between the English and American designs of eagles.

Brass eagles were imported in great numbers, and when an original ornament was lost or broken, a brass eagle was frequently substituted, especially on clocks.

1. It seems remarkable that one piece of wood merely glued to another should remain firmly attached, after undergoing the heat and cold, the moisture and dryness, of more than one hundred years; but we often see various objects which have survived these climatic changes for even longer periods of time.   (*Note 1 continued on page 94*)

The applied decorations most frequently used, but not often particularly noticed by amateur collectors, are the "moldings," which are mentioned in section 41.

Among other applied decorations frequently used are the carved rosettes, generally round or oval, used on many articles, especially on the inner ends of the scrolls on the tops of highboys made in the Philadelphia style, as in Nos. 660 and 668; and on the ends of the seat rails and top rails of chairs, as in Nos. 306 and 307. The graceful streamers on the Philadelphia style highboys and lowboys are also applied, as on Nos. 660 and 712; and on many other articles are applied ornaments, not carved on the surface of the wood.

"Mounts" are defined as pieces of decorative hardware or metal ornaments on furniture; the word includes metal handles, knobs, escutcheons and other hardware necessarily attached, but as these are considered and illustrated in the next two sections, we here refer only to the brass or ormolu[2] decorations.

It has been a matter of regret that our cabinet makers did not more fully avail themselves of the opportunity of using the French brass mounts, with their fine designs and skillful workmanship. These French mounts were used both by Chippendale and Hepplewhite on the furniture made by them in the French style, but in our country this style was not generally followed. The much admired "Boulle work" was apparently invented, and certainly perfected, by Andre Charles Boulle (this name was corrupted in England to "Buhl"). He was born in Paris in 1642 and in 1673 was allotted a room in the Palace of Versailles by Louis XIV as his cabinet maker. "Boulle work" was either an inlay of brass or other metal in a layer of tortoise shell or ivory veneered on a surface, or, reversing the method, an inlay of tortoise shell or ivory in a layer of brass or other metal veneered on the surface.

Section 39. Brass handles.—Handles[1] and their attachments[2] are interesting not only on account of their different designs in the various furniture styles, but also because, if original, they assist in ascertaining the age of the object to which

(NOTE 1, continued)

On many pieces of furniture of the Mid–Victorian period (about 1850–1875) are large applied wood scrolls and other decorations, especially on high pieces such as the secretary–bookcase No. 868.

2. Ormolu is an alloy of copper and zinc, but the word is also used to describe gilded brass or copper. The color is almost that of gold. "The French mounts were usually cast, and then chiselled with extraordinary skill and delicacy"; Encyclopædia Britannica, eleventh edition, volume 20, page 295. In our country ormolu is most frequently seen on French clocks.

3. Examples of ormolu mounts on French furniture are shown on the chairs Nos. 496 and 498; the tables Nos. 1654–1655.

1. "Knobs" of brass, glass and wood are considered in the next section, No. 40.

2. A. For the sake of exactness in the use of words it may be mentioned that the word "handle," strictly speaking, means "that part of a thing which is intended to be grasped by the hand in using it"; Century Dictionary. It is also stated that the handles of many things have distinctive names; for example, the handle of a kettle or bucket is called the "bail."

they were and still are attached. Unfortunately, however, constant usage for many years often resulted in breakage which generally led to the substitution of new handles in place of the old ones. Our forefathers, wishing to have their furniture repaired, and not being interested in antiques, left to the cabinet maker the selection of other handles in the place of the broken ones, and the cabinet maker often put on handles of the then current style; and this process may have occurred several times in the course of a century.[3] The substitution of new things for old probably occurred more frequently in handles than in any other parts of furniture because so many of them were broken, as they were subjected to much strain, especially those on the large lower drawers of highboys, bureaus, desks and other pieces.

Not many pieces of antique furniture now have all of their own original brass handles; but nevertheless all of their handles may be original ones, some being taken from other pieces. It is not likely that any one except an expert in brass can distinguish skillfully made reproductions from genuine antique brass handles; and instead of brass handles of a particular type giving an indication of age to the piece to which they are attached, the handles themselves are often in need of a sponsor to establish their own antiquity.[4] Moreover, if a piece of furniture was made in a country district or small town, it is probable that the handles, as well as the piece itself, were not in the fashion then prevailing in the large cities, but

(NOTE 2, *continued*)

     B. In figures 7, 9–24, 26–48, in illustrations Nos. 12–16, the part "intended to be grasped by the hand" is called the "bail," which is a piece of brass in the form of a half–circle or nearly so. The flat brass piece behind the bail is called the "plate."

     C. The bails, plates and their attachments are often all referred to collectively as the "handles," as in this book; and they are also called the "brasses." For convenience the kinds of handles are distinguished by the name of the part "grasped by the hand" and are therefore commonly called "drop handles," "bail handles," "ring handles" and perhaps other names. The term "pull" is sometimes used to designate the part grasped.

     D. An "escutcheon," in connection with brass handles, is a plate having a keyhole which is placed over a hole cut in the wood to receive the key of a lock. Until about the time of Hepplewhite the escutcheons were generally made in about the same shape as the plates. The word is also applied to the round or oval plates seen in figures 27–29 in illustration No. 14.

     3. Frequently a number of holes bored in the fronts of drawers testify to the fitting of several attachments; for example, there may be two holes for the metal posts which held a brass plate and the handle to the drawer, and also a hole for a screw of a brass or wooden knob.

     The subject of this section is treated in the valuable book of Mr. Henry Hammond Taylor, entitled "Knowing, collecting and restoring early American furniture," published by J. B. Lippincott Co., 1930; and in three articles by him in "Antiques," in the issues of June, July and August, 1927, entitled "Ready reference for furniture hardware." Much of the information presented in this section was obtained from the book mentioned.

     An illustrated article by Mr. R. W. Symonds entitled "An eighteenth–century English Brassfounder's catalogue" is in "Antiques," February, 1931, pages 102–105. In the same magazine, November, 1931, pages 287–289, is an illustrated article by Mr. Samuel Woodhouse, Jr., entitled "English hardware for American cabinet makers."

     4. A. It should be remembered that handles, knobs and other movable parts, including finials of all kinds, are unreliable as indications of the age of the articles to which they are attached, as mentioned also in the next section in regard to wooden knobs and in section 27, note 3, in regard to casters.

(*Note 4 continued on page 96*)

were several years behind the city styles. This difference in styles in vogue in the cities and the country towns is mentioned several times in this book in connection with various articles.

From about the year 1690 until about 1825 brass handles were used on almost all good pieces of American furniture having drawers. These handles, with their attachments and keyhole escutcheons, were generally imported from England, and advertisements in the newspapers offered for sale "imported locks and brasses for desks," etc.[5] In the time of the best work of Duncan Phyfe, about 1800 to 1825, brass handles were still in fashion, but about the latter year they went out of style and knobs began to be used.

The purpose of this section[6] is to enable the reader—the amateur collector—to know what were the various types of brass handles and their attachments, and what were the proper types for the principal furniture styles. With this in view, we now examine the various types which are seen on the furniture made in the successive styles, beginning with the William and Mary style, (1688–1702), which is explained in section 13 in the previous chapter. Not all of the available designs of handles are presented here, but those shown are sufficiently illustrative of the types. They are arranged in periods which cover the years in which they were in style on the better class of furniture; but the dates given are merely approximate and may be conflicting, especially in reference to the handles on furniture made in the Hepplewhite and later styles. For most of the illustrations in this section the writer is indebted to Mr. Israel Sack, now of New York.

Early handles; about 1690–1720. See figures 1–8 in illustration No. 12. The principal brass handles used on the furniture of this period are called "drop handles," sometimes "tear drop" or "pear drop" handles, the two latter terms indicating their form to some extent; see figures 1–5 and a keyhole escutcheon, figure 6. These handles were either solid or hollow, the hollow ones being in the shape of a pear cut lengthwise into two equal parts. The brass plates behind the

(NOTE 4, *continued*)

B. Just how far the presence of good modern reproductions of brass handles lessens the desirability of an article of antique furniture depends somewhat upon the feeling of the owner or purchaser; some persons are more particular in their views on this subject than others. A complete set of suitable antique handles is difficult to secure, and it is not reasonable that an otherwise original article should be considered undesirable because two or three handles are reproductions.

C. If reproductions are used, they should be exact reproductions of originals in every particular. The design should be simple if the piece of furniture is a plain piece, but may be elaborate if the piece is an elegant one. The size of the handle should not be large on a small piece, nor small on a large piece.

5. Among numerous advertisements is the one quoted, which was in the "Maryland Gazette," September 4, 1756; and in the "Maryland Journal" of October 25, 1791, the advertisers state that they "have received from London an assortment of hardware for cabinet makers." These items appear in the "Maryland Historical Magazine" of March, 1930, in an article by Dr. Henry J. Berkley, pages 8 and 16.

6. Perhaps too much attention is given here to brass handles; but the experience of the writer is that a clear knowledge of the subject, somewhat in detail, is interesting and helpful to the amateur collector.

handles were of various shapes and were generally ornamented with designs. A drop handle was not attached to the drawer by metal screws or bolts but by a wire pin, now called a "cotter pin," (a term well known to automobilists), which was passed through the wood to the inside of the drawer and was there bent and driven into the wood, not making a very strong connection. Handles of this type were used on highboys, as in illustrations Nos. 632 and 633; on lowboys, as in Nos. 669 and 670; on chests of drawers, as in No. 608; on desks, as in No. 777; and on other pieces of the period having drawers.

Handles: about 1690-1720

ILLUSTRATION No. 12.

In addition to the "drop" handles, a later form shown in figures 7 and 8 began to be used in this period, having a "bail"[7] and known as a "bail" handle, which is somewhat in the shape of a half-circle, and with a stamped plate and keyhole escutcheon of a different style from the earlier ones. This form of handle was held in place at both ends of the bail by a wire cotter pin fastened inside the drawer. Examples of this early type of bail handles may be seen on the highboy No. 634, and the lowboys Nos. 671 and 672.

Handles from about 1720 to 1780. See figures 9–29 in illustrations Nos. 13 and 14. All of these handles are of the bail type, the "drop" handles having gone out of fashion. The handles in this long period may be arranged for convenience, and to some extent according to their approximate dates, in three types, here marked

7. The word "bail" is defined in note 2. Bail handles in various forms continued to be used until about 1825, but wire fastenings were only used within about the dates mentioned above or somewhat later.

Handles: about 1720 to 1780

ILLUSTRATION No. 13; CONTINUED IN No. 14.

"A," "B" and "C"; the principal difference between these three types is in the designs of the plates.

A. In the first type, figures 9–11 in illustration No. 13, the plates are different in shape from those used with drop handles but are somewhat similar in form to those in figures 7 and 8. They are ornamented with designs stamped on the metal. At first the bails were generally held in place by wires, but in later pieces wires were not used, and the bails were held by bolts or posts which were rounded in front and were fastened by nuts on the inside, as in figure 11. Examples of this type of bail and plate appear on a small scale on the highboys Nos. 635 and 638, and on other articles in the Queen Anne style having drawers.

B. Figures 12–26 illustrate the second type of bail handles within the period of about 1720–1780. In this type the plates were made in many different designs

Handles: about 1720 to 1780, continued.

ILLUSTRATION No. 14.

of the same general character; they are sometimes said to be in the "willow" pattern. They were cut out by hand or were cast in a mold, and the edges were generally beveled. The bails are held in place by bolts, or posts, threaded like a screw, extending through the front of the drawer and fastened on the inside with nuts. These handles, and keyhole escutcheons to match, were used on our highboys, lowboys, chests of drawers, desks and other pieces in the Chippendale style, as illustrated in the chapters on those subjects. Twelve plates, figures 12–23, are in representative designs. Three other plates, figures 24–26 in illustration No. 14, are in pierced or openwork forms of the latter part of this same period of 1720–1780; these were often used on the more elegant pieces of furniture, such as the highboys Nos. 660 and 662, the "block front" chest on chest No. 880 and the desk No. 891.

C. The third type of handles used within the period from about 1720 to 1780 or later is shown in figures 27–29 in illustration No. 14. Here there is a bail without a large plate, thus leaving much of the front of the drawer exposed; but small round or oval ornamental brasses, sometimes called "escutcheons" as men-tioned in note 2, D, and generally known as "plates" or "rosettes," are placed at the ends of the bails. Through these small plates the bolts or posts pass and extend through the wood to the inside where they are made fast with a nut. Two kinds of plates, one round and one oval, are shown on each handle in order to show six plates in a minimum of space. This type, beginning about the year 1750, con-tinued in fashion until about 1780 or later, and was often used on our furniture in the Chippendale and later styles. Examples may be seen on highboys Nos. 649 and 666; lowboys Nos. 694 and 698; and on the drawers of the bureaus Nos. 714 and 720.

Handles from about 1780 to 1820. See figures 30–48 in illustrations Nos. 15–16. Furniture made in this period was mainly in the styles of Hepplewhite and Sheraton and the Early Empire. Separate dates for the handles in these three styles are not given because the exact dates are doubtful and each style overlapped the following style. Moreover, the date 1780 is probably about five years too early for furniture in the Hepplewhite style in America, as intimated in section 17.

On furniture in the Hepplewhite style, about 1785 to 1800 and later, the handles were of the bail type and the plates of thin brass were almost all oval in shape, as seen in figures Nos. 30–41. In some cases handles with small round or oval plates were used instead of the large plates. The plates were not cast or made by hand but were stamped by dies which produced impressions of ornamental designs, among which were the patriotic and always popular eagles and stars,[8] and also cornucopias, acorns, oak leaves, flowers, grapes, animals of several kinds and various other designs, all of which are now highly prized, and some of which are reproduced. This type of handles and plates was also used to some extent on furniture made in the styles of Sheraton and the Early Empire; and many of them will be seen on the bureaus, tables, sideboards and other pieces in later chapters. The keyhole escutcheons were generally oval, but small brass ones, flush with the wood, were also used.

In the Sheraton period, about 1795 to 1820, the handles continued for some years to be mostly of the bail type; and these are found on sideboards and other pieces in the style of Sheraton as they were in the style of Hepplewhite. Other forms of brass handles, figures 42–48 in illustration No. 16, also appear on furni-ture in the Sheraton style, a favorite one being a round or oval ornamental plate with a round or oval handle attached to the top. Another form was a bail suspended from the mouth of a lion, sometimes called a "lion and ring" handle, which was first used in England about 1795; and still another was an eight–sided plate with a bail of the same shape. The plates, like those in the Hepplewhite period, were made of brass stamped by a die, and were held in place by a post, or bolt, which ex-tended to the inside of the drawer where it was fastened with a nut. The orna-mental designs on these plates were often finely made. In this period many pieces of furniture were furnished with a brass knob instead of handles, as mentioned in the next section.

8.   See sections 33 and 37 in which eagles and stars are mentioned.

Handles: about 1780 to 1820

ILLUSTRATION No. 15; CONTINUED IN No. 16.

On the furniture of the Early Empire period, about 1815 to 1830, the handles of the Sheraton style remained in general use. For example, the round, or ring,

Handles: about 1780 to 1820, continued.

ILLUSTRATION No. 16.

handle hanging from the mouth of a lion, figure 48, was used on Early Empire pieces. But the brass "knobs" shown in the next section are more characteristic of this period than the handles of the Sheraton style.

Section 40. Knobs of brass, glass and wood.—On the drawers of tables and on some other pieces in the Sheraton style, about 1795–1820, brass knobs were often

Brass Knobs

ILLUSTRATION No. 17.

used, generally round and projecting about an inch from the surface of the drawer; and similar knobs were popular in the early part of the Empire period, about

1815–1830. They were much used by Duncan Phyfe on his tables and sewing stands in the Sheraton style.[1] These brass knobs were often ornamented with designs of a patriotic character, such as an eagle, or the head of Washington, or with flowers or fanciful forms. Small plain brass knobs were used on the drawers in the interiors of desks of all periods. Many knobs are now well reproduced. In illustration No. 17 four knobs are shown, with different designs.[2]

Glass knobs. These knobs,[3] varying greatly in quality, were in fashion from about 1815 to 1840. Many of them, made of coarsely pressed glass, seem to detract from the appearance of the articles to which they are attached; these are found chiefly on the heavy bureaus, sideboards and tables of the Late Empire style which were made about the years 1830 to 1840, handsomely veneered with brilliantly colored mahogany but badly supplied with knobs. Judging from the quantities and designs found in the antique shops, these pressed glass knobs must have been

ILLUSTRATION No. 18.

made in great numbers by several glass factories, and in many colors, chiefly clear glass, opal or white. They were attached by screws, some of which were of very thick glass and were made as a part of the knob; or by metal rods or screws which were sunk into an opening in the back of the knob and were held in place by plaster of Paris; and in the least desirable class of knobs the screws extend through a hole in the front of the knob, making the head of the screw visible from the front. Almost always some of the knobs have been lost or broken and it is almost impossible to find duplicates.

1. Several authenticated tables made by Duncan Phyfe with brass knobs are illustrated in "Furniture Masterpieces of Duncan Phyfe," by Mr. Charles Over Cornelius, on plates 22, 24, 26.
     Knobs to support mirrors are seen in illustration No. 1254.
     Small ivory or bone knobs were also used, especially on small articles such as sewing stands and dressing glasses.
2. Through the courtesy of Mr. Israel Sack, now of New York.
3. Illustrated articles on glass knobs, by Letitia Hart Alexander, are in "Antiques," May, 1928, pages 393–394, and April, 1929, pages 303–304.

The knobs made of cut glass, however, are more desirable, generally being of better workmanship, design and quality. They are found, naturally, on the better class of furniture and seem to be suitable for their surroundings. The most desirable of the cut glass knobs are the clear glass ones, generally finely cut, which are backed with bright tin–foil, or perhaps silver–foil, and then sunk into a brass cup to which a screw is attached. From whatever point these knobs are viewed they are brilliant and glistening.

In illustration No. 18 the glass knob, figure 1, has a screw showing in front; figure 2 has a glass screw made as a part of the knob; and figure 3 is a cut glass knob backed with tin–foil and sunk in a brass cup.

Wooden knobs. These were not often used on good antique furniture, except on the early chests of the period of about 1700, such as Nos. 596 and 598. Occasionally they were used on bureaus and other pieces in the Late Sheraton[4] and the Late Empire styles. Nowadays they are sometimes found erroneously substituted on drawers in place of the original brass handles which were broken and removed; their substituted presence illustrates the fact that easily removable parts such as handles, knobs and locks, are often unreliable as an indication of the age of the article on which they are found, as mentioned also in section 39, note 4, A. After wooden knobs ceased to be in fashion they were followed, on plain pieces, by wooden or iron handles under which one's fingers could be placed—a convenient but inelegant device. Wooden knobs are not illustrated in this section, but are seen on several articles made in the early Victorian period.[5]

Section 41. Moldings; reeding; fluting.—The word "molding" is an architectural term for the decorative treatment of a building by making outlines in various forms on the exterior or interior surfaces, or edges of parts, of the structure. Familiar types of moldings are on door frames and on the inner sides of window frames. By the use of moldings plain surfaces are made ornamental and the play of light and shade accentuates the designs.

As the word is used in connection with furniture, moldings are of two kinds. One kind is cut on the body of the article, as often seen on the edge of the top of a table or lowboy; the other kind, much more frequently used, is a piece of wood cut in a design, and nailed or glued to the article which it ornaments. A molding projecting beyond the surface of a piece of furniture is almost always applied;[1] a molding receding inward from the surface is almost always cut out of the wood. Applied moldings are found in all the furniture styles in which we are interested; they may be plain pieces of wood or may be carved, reeded, fluted, rounded, or otherwise ornamented. Few persons, other than those interested in cabinet making or architectural forms, realize that the great majority of moldings on articles of

4. Small wooden knobs appear on a sewing stand in the Sheraton style made by Duncan Phyfe, illustrated in plate 25 in "Furniture Masterpieces of Duncan Phyfe," by Mr. Charles Over Cornelius.

5. For example, wooden knobs, generally round and plain, were used on rosewood and walnut furniture in the Early Victorian period of about 1840–1860, as in the bureaus Nos. 767 and 768.

1. As to the word "applied" see the first paragraph in section 38.

furniture are applied;[2] but sometimes the presence of heads of small nails, perhaps inserted by a repairer, or a very slight space between the molding and the other wood will indicate the facts.

The names given to furniture moldings are generally architectural ones, not familiar to amateur collectors; some of the more usual forms are mentioned in the note.[3]

Reeding. If a small cylindrical piece of wood, such as a round lead pencil, is cut lengthwise, making two pieces of equal size which are then laid side by side with the round sides up, we have the design of reeding; and an article of furniture ornamental in this way is said to be "reeded." The design may be cut in the wood or may be made in strips and then glued on. It has the appearance of being raised up from the surface of the wood. Reedings are well seen in the illustrations of very many articles, such as sofas made in the style of Sheraton; and were much used by Duncan Phyfe.

2. The writer confesses that formerly when he admired certain fine moldings, such as the "acorn" moldings, (see note 3, G, below), he regarded them as having been skillfully carved out of the wood behind them; but his admiration moderated when he learned that the moldings were made separately and were merely stuck on with glue.

The designs of moldings changed from time to time and are generally regarded as indicating the approximate dates of the articles; this, however, is somewhat uncertain because a molding may have been used on some objects long after it ceased to be used on other objects. Moldings are not often referred to in the comments in this volume. See the remarks in the chapter on highboys, section 83, at note 5.

3. Several of the definitions below are taken, by permission, from "The Furniture Collectors' Glossary," by Mr. L. V. Lockwood, published by The Walpole Society, 1913.

The first of the following described moldings is cut on the wood; the others are "applied."

A. A "thumb nail" molding slopes down in a concave curve to a narrow edge and is supposed to resemble a thumb nail but does so only remotely. It is often seen on the edges of the tops of tables, lowboys and on some other pieces. See the lowboy No. 712 and the table No. 1289.

B. A "bead" molding is a small convex one, the form of which may be seen if a round lead pencil be cut in half lengthwise, and one of the parts be placed on a surface with the arched side up; this is also called a "half–round" molding, a more descriptive term. The words "cock–beading" means a beading which projects beyond a surface; the words "flush beading" mean a beading which is flush with the surface.

C. The form of a "quarter–round" molding may be seen by cutting a round lead pencil lengthwise into four equal parts, each one of which will have a quarter of the round surface. This is also called an "ovolo."

D. An "ogee" molding is in the design of a cyma curve, which is shown and described in section 23.

E. A "dentil" molding, the word suggesting a row of teeth, consists of a row of small rectangular blocks set at equal distances apart; one may be seen over the drawers at the top of the highboy No. 666.

F. A "torus" molding is a large convex molding. A small torus is called an "astragal." See the bureau No. 765 and the sewing table No. 1579.

G. "Acorn" moldings are so called from the acorns, hanging downward, which are occasionally seen on the upper parts of bookcases, secretary–desks and other tall pieces. It may also be called an arch molding, one arch being between every two acorns. See the secretary–bookcase No. 855 for an excellent example of this acorn molding.

Fluting. A "flute" is a half–round or rectangular groove or furrow cut out of the surface of a piece of wood.[4] It has the appearance of being sunk in, or cut into, the surface. If the musical instrument called a flute, hollow inside, is cut lengthwise in equal parts and the two parts are laid side by side with the round sides down, we have the design of fluting. The grooves should be very close together and should preferably be half–round. This is the reverse of reeding. Flutings were favorites of Robert Adam and are often seen on furniture made in the Adam style, as in the mirrors Nos. 1145 and 1147, and the tables Nos. 1429 and 1647. From Adam, flutes were occasionally copied by the Hepplewhite school as in the arm chair No. 182.

Section 42. Nails; screws; hinges.—A few remarks concerning these pieces of hardware may be of interest. It is sometimes thought that nails were not used on antique furniture and that it was held together mainly by pins or pegs made of wood; but, on the contrary, nails have been used in furniture from early times, and in our country are found in many of the first examples.[1] Before about the year 1790 nails were made only by hand and hence only "hand–made" nails were used on furniture made prior to that date. These nails were of iron and were strong and durable, although somewhat easily bent, and being made by hand separately they were never exactly alike. The heads on these nails were either flat or rounded, each kind showing the marks of the hammer. After about 1790 nails made by machine, and selling for about one–third the former price, displaced the handmade nails.[2] Ornamental nails with large round heads are seen on the upholstery of various pieces, such as the chairs Nos. 139 and 399, and the sofas Nos. 548 and 575. These nails are often so close together that the heads almost touch each other.

4. It is not always easy for the amateur collector to determine whether certain work should be called "reeding" or "fluting." Cabinet makers do not always distinguish the words clearly. See the remarks in section 133 in regard to bed–posts. Reeding and fluting are in reality forms of carving.

1. Perhaps the most important method of holding two pieces of wood together was by the "mortise and tenon" construction which is stronger and somewhat more expensive than other methods. It is difficult to explain in words the several methods, but the reader may probably see them in the shop of a cabinet maker who works in antique furniture. See also the subject of "Mortises and Joints" on pages 386–387 of the third volume of Mr. Wallace Nutting's "Furniture Treasury."

Other important methods are dovetailing, doweling and gluing; in dovetailing, the edges of two pieces of wood are cut into wedge–shaped openings and projections in such a manner that they fit closely into each other and hold tight; in modern doweling, a small cylindrical piece of wood projecting from one of the two pieces is made to fit into a hole (called a mortise) in the other piece, making a strong connection.

Wooden pins were used in some cases where we might expect nails or screws, as to hold the top of a table to the frame, or to hold a stretcher in a leg of a chair. These were made of hard woods in various sizes according to the purposes for which they were intended. The heads of these pins may sometimes be seen projecting a little from the surface of the piece into which they are inserted.

2. It is worth while to examine the modern machines which drive a score or more of nails at a time into the lid of a box with one movement, more quickly than would seem possible.

Screws have been used in cabinet making for several centuries, but not as far back as nails. The screws on most of our antique furniture were made by hand, often somewhat roughly; but about the year 1820, they began to be made by machine with more exactness. The distinguishing feature of these old screws, whether made by hand or by machine, is that they have a flat surface at the lower end, differing from those of the present day which terminate in a sharp point like a gimlet; and, on account of this flat end which could not penetrate the wood easily, it was customary to bore a hole in the wood so as to help the entrance of the screw into the wood.[3]

ILLUSTRATION No. 19. HINGES.

Screws with flat ends, made by hand or machine, continued to be used until about 1850 when they were superseded by the new style machine–made screws which had pointed ends. There are thus three types of screws; those with flat ends made by hand, those with flat ends made by machine, and after 1850 those with pointed ends.

Hinges were not conspicuously seen, unless they were of an ornamental, or at least odd, design. Plain iron hinges, generally rectangular, entirely for service and not at all for decoration, were generally so placed as not to be visible. In illustration No. 19 six ornamental hinges are shown. Hinge No. 6, a "butterfly"[4]

3. It was not good workmanship for the heads of screws to be visible; but in a position where they were not usually seen, as for example, under a table top, it was not improper for the heads to be exposed.

4. The term "dovetail" hinge is more descriptive of this hinge, but the term "butterfly" is more interesting. See also note 1 in section 156 on butterfly tables.

hinge, the earliest of the hinges used in our country, is found chiefly on "butterfly" tables such as Nos. 1303 and 1304, and "gate–leg" tables such as Nos. 1291–1302; Nos. 1 and 2 are the familiar "H" hinge, in the shape of the letter; No. 3 is an "H L" hinge, a variation of the H hinge, so called because its form is a combination of the letter H with the letter L; No. 4 is a rat–tail hinge, which got its name from a supposed resemblance of its lower part to a rat's tail, very different, however, from the "rat–tail" on the back of an antique silver spoon; and No. 5 is a "strap" hinge, which has a pointed or rounded end. All of these hinges, except No. 6, were used on cupboards; No. 5 was used mainly on chests. Reproductions of these and other hinges may be had from dealers.

Section 43. Upholstery; fabrics.—This subject is perhaps beyond the scope of this book, and only a brief mention of some of the more important fabrics can be made.[1]

In the upholstering of American antique furniture of different periods the contemporary types of fabrics made in England were closely followed; and it seems that no purely American style was developed, except perhaps in some of the very plain fabrics made in the household.[2]

From the advertisements in our newspapers and the inventories of the estates of deceased persons it appears that the fine products of the needle and the loom were extensively imported from England and France into our country in the eighteenth century and even before that period. Satins, silks, brocades, damasks, velvets and other materials, such as those mentioned below, appear in the lists.

The principal articles which were upholstered were chairs, especially "wing" chairs, settees, window seats, sofas, cushions, stools and foot–stools; upon these a great variety of fine fabrics were used at various periods. Perhaps the most elegant[3] of all the upholstered articles were those with large surfaces, such as the sofas Nos. 539–553, and the chairs Nos. 391–417.

1.   Upholstery as we now understand it, that is, attached to a piece of furniture and not movable, seems to have appeared first in England in the time of Queen Elizabeth, (1558–1603). Before that time loose cushions were used, which became less important upon the advent of upholstery.

A printed description of upholstery materials is barely intelligible without illustrations large enough to give satisfactory details. The most instructive and agreeable method of understanding our American work is to visit the American Wing of the Metropolitan Museum of Art, and to see the examples there shown, having in your hand the book "The Homes of our Ancestors," by R. T. H. Halsey and Elizabeth Tower, opened at page 301, where the index title "Upholstery and textiles" refers to the various materials appearing on the furniture in the Wing.

2.   At almost every period of English furniture history the women of the household, from the royal palace to the plain dwellings of poor commoners, found occupation in needlework and in weaving fabrics; and in our country the wives and daughters were similarly engaged in the early periods.

3.   In the days when it was the custom for great ladies to hold receptions in their bedrooms, as mentioned in section 133, note 3, the large bedsteads with their elaborate carving were decorated with embroidered velvet hangings and gorgeous silk coverlets. In "Cymbeline," act 2, scene 4, line 69, Shakespeare tells us that Imogen's bedchamber "was hanged with tapestry of silk and silver." Fabrics of great elegance, made in Italy and France, and also in England by French workmen who left their own country because of religious persecution, established a high standard in the homes of the wealthy.

Several fabrics not often described in the books, but much used in the upholstering of furniture and for other purposes, are now mentioned.

Turkey–work. This covering for cushions and the backs and seats of chairs was used in England from about 1660 to 1690. It was made on coarse canvas or sacking on which the pattern was drawn and the worsted was drawn through and knotted in imitation of the Turkish carpets of the period. Very few examples of turkey–work on chairs have survived; a fine original one on a Cromwellian chair is in the American Wing of the Metropolitan Museum of Art.[4]

Chintz. This cotton cloth, printed with flowers or other patterns in different colors, and either glazed or not, was originally made in India, and its name is an Indian word. When first made in England,[5] the silk weavers procured an Act of Parliament prohibiting its manufacture, which however was repealed in 1774. Chintzes of both English and French make were extensively used in our country, and as far back as the year 1712 India chintzes were advertised in the Boston newspapers. The old chintzes are now well reproduced by modern processes.

Toile de Jouy. This is a kind of chintz which was originated at Jouy,[6] a French town near Versailles, by a Frenchman named Oberkampf, and was made from about 1760 to 1814. These toiles de Jouy were used chiefly for hangings on bedsteads, and for curtains and coverings of chairs. The name is often used as merely descriptive of a kind of chintz, not necessarily a chintz made at Jouy.

Horsehair. This kind of cloth, now often regarded as an unpleasant reminder of the Victorian era, was highly favored by Hepplewhite and other cabinet makers of his time.[7] Excellent horsehair fabrics are now made.

4. See the illustration in "The Homes of our Ancestors," figure 15, opposite page 23; the Cromwellian type of chair is referred to in the next chapter, section 46, note 3. The text above is quoted in part from Mr. Lockwood's "Colonial Furniture," volume 2, page 30; in the same volume a sofa is illustrated, No. 653, covered with turkey–work.

5. An illustrated article entitled "Two centuries of English Chintzes" by Mr. Thomas Burrell, is in "Antiques," April, 1929, pages 301–303.

An illustrated article entitled "Chintzes" is in "The Antiquarian," April, 1927, page 39.

6. Another illustrated article by Mr. Burrell, entitled "La Manufacture de Jouy" appears in "Antiques," May, 1927, pages 379–380, in which the process of making the cloth is explained and the rise and fall of the industry is described. It is said that the high point of the business was about the year 1806, when two hundred machines were at work, each capable of printing more than five thousand yards a day. "Toiles de Jouy," so called, were also made in England and on the Continent.

Several fine examples are shown in the catalogue of the "Girl Scouts Loan Exhibition" held in New York in September, 1929, Nos. 911, 913 and others.

In "The Homes of our Ancestors," pages 220–221, figure 171, are illustrations of window curtains of old "toile de Jouy" in the American Wing; and quotations are made from the account book of Thomas Jefferson, while in Paris in 1784, noting the purchase by him of toile de Jouy for curtains.

The covering on the bedstead No. 1054 is regarded as being an original "toile de Jouy."

An illustrated article on the subject, by Marion Thring, is in "The Antiquarian," May, 1931, page 39. Another article is in "Antiques," April, 1930, pages 317–319.

7. Mr. Cescinsky, in his "English Furniture," volume 3, page 171, remarks that the horsehair cloth alluded to by Hepplewhite was made in a wide range of patterns and a large number of colorings— white, red, green, blue and black. "Such are the wearing properties of this material that it is not exceptional to find well-preserved specimens of the chair work of that date with the original coverings intact even at the present day." See also section 53, note 4, D.

"Petit point" and "Gros point." "Petit point" is a fine stitch embroidery, sometimes called a "tent stitch," which is defined as a slanting stitch of silk diagonally over a single thread of coarsely woven canvas. The designs were chiefly of flowers, fruits and rural and classic scenes. "Gros point" was a coarse stitch embroidery, over two threads, of the same general character as petit point. In our country both were used, mainly for upholstering chairs and sofas.

Section 44. Several other matters.—In this section are briefly mentioned several minor matters of some interest which are not often specially referred to in the books. These are (1) marble tops of tables; (2) beveled edge glass; (3) the lyre as an ornament; (4) saw marks and other tool marks; (5) papier maché (6) plastic wood.

1. Marble tops. Marble tops are so often seen on tables, washstands and some other pieces of the Victorian period, and also on hall tables of the French Empire style, and are so seldom seen on earlier American antique furniture, that it is sometimes thought that they are of modern origin. But as far back as the reign of Queen Anne, (1702–1714), fine tables with marble tops were in fashion, and they were also made in the Chippendale style in England about the year 1760. In the "Maryland Gazette," January 9, 1761, a newspaper of Annapolis, an advertisement offered for sale "imported marble top tables." Examples of these tables are illustrated in Nos. 1305 and 1306.

2. Beveled edge glass. This, also, is often thought to be a modern invention, but it was made in England before the year 1700. In the chapter on mirrors several examples are illustrated, Nos. 1088, 1227 and others. The beveling is generally about an inch wide. The angle is not as acute as in the machine-made modern ones, and the bevel can barely be felt by the fingers. In the old mirrors the glass is generally wavy and always thin. The thickness of the glass may be tested if the point of a lead pencil be placed on the glass; the distance between the pencil point and the reflection of it is the thickness of the glass.

3. The lyre as an ornament. Few ornaments on furniture are as graceful as the lyre. The form consists mainly of two cyma curves placed in a certain position, as shown in section 23, with strings added. It is said that the design was brought from Greece and Rome into England by Robert Adam. It was soon copied by Hepplewhite, as in the chair No. 183. Sheraton made much use of it in his drawings, as in the chair, figure 3, in the full page illustration No. 233, and in a later chair, figure 13, in the full page illustration No. 234. Following the style of Sheraton, the lyre was used by Duncan Phyfe, and appears on the chair No. 326, a sofa No. 574, and in the supports of card tables and other tables. In the Late Empire period it was used on the chair No. 349. It also appears on chairs Nos. 305 and 332; also on tables Nos. 1423 and 1425, and on Early Empire dressing table No. 1469. See note 7 in section 171 on the subject of tables; also the Index.

4. Saw marks and other tool marks. We have all heard of the blind man who detected a fake antique table by putting his hand under the top of the table

and feeling there the marks of a kind of saw which was invented long after the alleged date of the table. The old saws were all straight and their teeth made their marks in straight lines, and the modern straight saws do the same, so that straight saw marks may be either old or new. But the modern revolving circular saw makes curved marks, and these could not have been made before the circular saw was invented, which was about 1815, and probably not before it came into general use about 1850. These circular saw marks may of course be cleverly removed, thus destroying their evidence. Other tools whose marks may be seen are the jack planes which made small waves on the wood; and also the straight or curved chisels, the curved ones being used to cut grooves for screws, for example, the screws which hold the top of a card table to the frame. These matters are familiar to cabinet makers experienced in working with antique furniture. See also the remarks on "fakes" in section 7, note 2, first paragraph.

5. The term "papier maché" is a French one meaning "mashed paper." When used for furniture the paper pulp was pressed and molded into forms. This type of work was imported into Europe from Asiatic countries about 1750, chiefly in the form of small boxes and other light articles ornamented in lacquer designs. Papier maché, considering its weight, is strong and durable and not very liable to breakage. It was popular in our country in the Victorian era and is even now used in making various objects. It is not very suitable for furniture, because if it is damaged it is not easily repaired. Forms of wooden furniture were sometimes used as a basis and were covered with papier maché, and these were stronger. A chair with papier maché in the back is illustrated in No. 493. Mother-of-pearl was often used as an inlay. Several magazine articles are mentioned in the note.[1]

6. Plastic wood. This is a modern preparation, said to be made of wood pulp ground very fine and some kind of liquid which holds the pulp together. It is used to fill up cracks or larger openings. It dries quickly and becomes hard enough to be carved; and it may be colored to match the wood surrounding it. Such a useful preparation will doubtless serve bad purposes as well as good ones, and thus one more danger imperils the amateur collector.

1. In "Antiques," March, 1933, pages 86–89, is an article by Louise Karr, entitled "A résumé of Papier–Maché." In the same magazine, March, 1929, page 205, is an illustrated article on the subject by Mr. G. Bernard Hughes. In "International Studio," September, 1929, page 39, is an article entitled "The Re–discovery of Papier Maché." See also section 174, note 7, paragraph 2.

CHAPTER V

CHAIRS

Section 45. General remarks.—We begin our examination of the various articles of American antique furniture with chairs for the reason that chairs are of more importance in our studies than any other article. Chairs were made in every furniture style and period which was in fashion in our country;[1] in chairs the development of furniture styles in chronological order is more clearly seen than in any other articles with the possible exception of tables; and the amateur collector

1.   Several articles of furniture were made only in certain periods and therefore only in certain styles. For example, sideboards and bureaus were not known at the early period when our studies begin, about 1650; and highboys and lowboys were made only in the earlier periods and passed out of style before or about the times of Hepplewhite and Sheraton; but chairs were made continuously in America in each of the styles from the date of our first chairs to the end of the Empire style—the last style which may now be regarded as antique.

In preparing this book the writer purposely examined the subject of chairs before other subjects, realizing that by studying the subject of chairs first he would become familiar with all the furniture styles and periods in chronological order; but if he had studied any other large subject first, except tables, he would not have become acquainted with all of the styles because no articles except chairs and tables were apparently made in all furniture styles. The reader therefore is urged to look over this long chapter on chairs, with its four hundred and eighty–two illustrations, before reading the later chapters.

In connection with each style of chairs it is advisable to read the appropriate section of the chapter on "Styles of American Antique Furniture," sections 12–22.

who knows the styles of chairs knows the styles of almost all other articles. More chairs are seen than any other pieces, having generally been made in sets;[2] and they may easily be examined, all their parts being visible, except in the wing chairs and other fully upholstered ones.

During many centuries the chair was the seat of dignity and authority and was not an article of general use. The chest, the bench and the stool[3] were used as seats for ordinary persons; but the chair was reserved for the head of the family and persons of importance. Similarly the chair was and is an emblem of authority in public meetings; and this idea is represented in such expressions as "the chairman of the meeting," "the chair decides," etc. Even in the time of Christopher Columbus the chair was not in use in the home of the ordinary family; but during the seventeenth century it became a household necessity. The earliest American chairs were almost always made with arms, enclosing the occupant to some extent; and we are even now said to sit "in" an armchair, but to sit "on" a chair without arms.

The approximate date at which a particular chair was probably made may in some cases be fixed with certainty, as where the style[4] was confined to a brief period, or was very distinctive. But as certain types of chairs were made during a

2. Many other pieces were usually made singly. Moreover, chairs were not only made in sets in each of the various period styles, but were also made in various styles of their own, not seen in other articles. Thus the four kinds of early chairs mentioned in section 46, and also the Windsor chairs, slat–back chairs and others exhibit certain styles seen only in chairs. In addition, chairs seem to have aroused the inventive and designing skill of cabinet makers to a greater extent than most other articles.

3. A. Wooden seats known as "joined stools" or "joint stools" or "short forms" were used in our country as chairs about 1650; examples are on display in the "American Wing" of the Metropolitan Museum of Art in New York City.

　　B. Among other uses, these stools or short forms were for persons of minor importance who sat "below the salt." It was the custom, in houses of persons of rank, to place a large silver salt–cellar near the middle of the table. Inferior persons sat "below the salt" and persons of distinction sat "above the salt." The chairs "above the salt" were no doubt in whatever style was fashionable at the time. As to side chairs and arm chairs see section 51, note 1.

4. A. It should also be noted that the cabinet makers, and especially the chair makers, in the country districts, and their customers, did not follow the styles so closely as those in the cities, and often continued the use of a style for years after it had passed out of fashion in the cities. Moreover chair makers felt at liberty to make changes and variations in the established styles, according to their, or their customer's, ideas of utility or taste, thus creating what are called "variants" from the fashion of the time.

　　B. Changes in the form of chairs were sometimes made because of changes in the style of men's and women's clothing. Prior to the time when chairs were in general use, the seat was merely a bench or a stool; but when hooped skirts of great size became the fashion among the higher class, chairs were found necessary; later, when hoops went out of fashion, the chairs became smaller. In his "English Furniture," volume 3, pages 288–290, Mr. Cescinsky remarks that "the hoop skirt was still retained for fashionable functions until about 1796, and at the close of the fashion was of more preposterous size than it had ever been before." In "The Homes of Our Ancestors," by Halsey and Tower, page 153, it is said that the American chair backs were more sturdy than the English ones because in England the strength of the back was not so important, "the fashionable men and women of the period being literally so tightly strapped in by a form of corset, with a board extending down their backs, that a bolt–upright position was obligatory"—and, this being the relevant point here, "the abolition of this form of fashionable torture caused patterns in chair rails to change."

long series of years, such as slat–back chairs and Windsor chairs, it may be difficult or impossible to determine whether a particular chair was made in the earlier or later portion of the period; but generally it is found that the earlier chairs of a given period are heavier and more sturdy than the later ones. Moreover, as with other articles, a chair, on the order of a customer, may have been made to match others in a style long out of fashion. See "Dating Antique Furniture," section 6.

Several other items of interest are in the note.[5]

Section 46. Three–legged, wainscot, Carver and Brewster chairs.—Without attempting to give the exact dates of the chairs which as a group may properly be termed the "earliest" American chairs, or to arrange them in exact chronological order, it may be said that about the year[1] 1650 there were four kinds of chairs in

5. A. Much authentic and interesting information in regard to chair makers and their work in the period 1721–1800 is in the newspaper advertisements and other notices contained in two volumes published by the "Walpole Society" entitled "The Arts and Crafts in Philadelphia, Maryland and South Carolina." These "Gleanings from Newspapers" were collected by the late Alfred Coxe Prime. The first volume, published in 1929, covered the years 1721–1785; the second volume, published in 1932, covers the years 1786–1800. Several items in this book have been taken from and credited to these two volumes. Another book of the Walpole Society is entitled "The Arts and Crafts of New England."

Another valuable compilation, by Dr. Henry J. Berkley, of Baltimore, is in the "Maryland Historical Magazine," published by the Maryland Historical Society, March, 1930. The article is entitled "A Register of the cabinet makers and allied trades in Maryland as shown by the newspapers and directories, 1746 to 1820." Many references to this article are in this book.

B. The business of making chairs, in the larger cities, was often a separate one from the general business of cabinet–making; an advertiser in the newspapers referred to himself as a "chair maker" or "cabinet maker" or "chair maker and cabinet maker." In the country districts, however, the two trades were generally carried on by the same person. The once celebrated cabinet maker William Savery, of Philadelphia, (as to whom see the Index), called himself merely a "chair maker" in 1750; and many others in the large cities did the same.

C. Chair making was divided into several branches. Some chair makers specialized in making Windsor chairs, calling themselves "Windsor chair makers," especially in Philadelphia; others were "Windsor and rush–bottom chair makers." Some made a specialty of "chairs and spinning–wheels." There were also many "fancy–chair" makers. In the Baltimore Directory of 1849–1850 a classified list was entitled "Chair manufacturers, Windsor and Fancy." See "Fancy chairs" in section 54 and "Windsor chairs" in section 62.

D. Carving of chairs and other articles of furniture was advertised to be done by "carvers," as now; and "carving and gilding" was often done by the same person; see section 36, note 1, C. The manufacture of coffins was also carried on by cabinet makers, as now in some country districts; an advertiser in Baltimore in 1792 called himself "Cabinet maker at the sign of the Bureau and Coffin." Cabinet makers began early to do repairs, and to advertise for that business.

E. That the work of a cabinet maker might at times be a dangerous one appears from the following item in the "Maryland Gazette," published in Annapolis, May 6, 1762: "Last Tuesday afternoon as Robert Harsnip, a cabinet–maker, was standing under the Gallows, and giving directions for fixing the Cross Piece, it fell and struck him upon the head, by which he was so much hurt, that he died the next morning." From "The Arts and Crafts," volume 1, page 170.

F. Many cabinet makers and other artisans were "indentured immigrants," brought from abroad and sold in America for a specified time.

1. This date is, of course, a very early one in our furniture history. The first colonists of Virginia came in 1607; the settlement of the Dutch in New York was in 1614; the "Pilgrim Fathers" in the

use in the American colonies. Some of these chairs were imported from England and others were made here, following the English patterns. These chairs are very rare and are seldom seen outside of museums; and although they are of much interest to students and connoisseurs,[2] they are not of special interest to amateurs and are therefore treated very briefly in this book. These four kinds[3] of chairs are illustrated and considered in the following order: three–legged chairs; wainscot chairs; Carver chairs; Brewster chairs. In this section they are all given the merely approximate date of about 1650.

Three–legged chairs. These are said to be the oldest chairs used in our country. The best known chair of this type is the Harvard chair, No. 20, which has been used by the president of Harvard University in conferring degrees for perhaps two centuries. The chair is believed to be of English workmanship.[4] Probably about 1650.

No. 21 is another three–legged chair, but of a different type. From the moldings and the character of the three kinds of wood used in its construction, it is believed that it was made in Connecticut. This chair is in its original condition, without restorations of any kind, a remarkable feature for a chair of its age. Probably about 1650.

It is interesting to know that chairs of this type were regarded as desirable antiques as far back as the year 1765. In a letter written in that year, Horace Walpole, "the prince of collectors," asked a friend to look for certain "ancient wooden triangular" chairs, evidently of the kind here shown, and to purchase them for him.[5]

(NOTE 1, *continued*)

"Mayflower" landed at Plymouth in 1620; the Puritans arrived at Salem in 1630; the ships named the "Ark" and the "Dove" reached Maryland in 1634; Philadelphia was laid out in 1683.

2. The subject is treated at length in Mr. Lockwood's "Colonial Furniture in America," volume 2, pages 3–31; illustrations are also in Mr. Nutting's "Furniture of the Pilgrim Century," Revised edition, page 278, etc., and in the same author's "Furniture Treasury," Nos. 1774–1821.

3. Another kind of chair of about this period, mentioned in the books, is the leather chair, so called from the leather seat and the leather band across the back. This was decorated with tacks having large brass heads. Other chairs of this type were covered with "turkey work." Very few of either of these kinds of chairs have been found. Examples are shown in Mr. Lockwood's "Colonial Furniture," volume 2, figures 442–445, and in Mr. Nutting's "Furniture Treasury," Nos. 1780–1783. This type of chair is sometimes called "Cromwellian." See section 43, note 4, as to "turkey work."

4. Professor S. E. Morison, of Harvard University, has kindly furnished information in regard to this chair. Under date of June 3, 1930, he wrote to the author that all that is known regarding the chair may be found in Quincy's "History of Harvard University," volume 1, page 544, and Pierce's "History of Harvard," page 312; that there is no foundation for the suggestion that it was owned by John Harvard; that it does not appear in the inventories of the early days of the college; and that a portrait of President Edward Holyoke made during his term of office, 1737–1769, shows him seated in the chair. A few years ago a copy of the chair was presented by Harvard graduates to the Johns Hopkins University, Baltimore, and is now used by the president on ceremonial occasions.

5. The author is indebted to Mr. Henry W. Erving, of Hartford, Connecticut, for this item. Horace Walpole's letter was addressed to the Reverend William Cole, and was written on March 9, 1765, at which date he called the chairs "ancient," as quoted in the text.

Wainscot chairs. These heavy oak chairs,[6] made after the English models, are regarded as the finest of the four kinds above mentioned, and are believed to have been made about 1650. Observing No. 22, we see that the back is decorated with carving of somewhat the same character as on some of the chests of the period;[7] and that the under part of the seat rail is also carved. The original seats of these chairs were of wood; but in this chair a leather seat has been inserted, and a portion of the back has a leather panel, both no doubt because the seat and the panel had been damaged and repairs were made with the more comfortable material. This chair has descended to the present owner with the tradition that it came from Virginia. Probably about 1650.

No. 23 also is reputed to have come from Virginia. It is of a plainer type than No. 22, having no carving. This chair is all original except the cresting on the top of the back, the tops of the back legs and the bottoms of the feet. Probably about 1650.

"Carver" and "Brewster" chairs. These two kinds of chairs with turned[8] posts and spindles are called in our country by the names of the two Pilgrim Fathers

(NOTE 5, *continued*)

Horace Walpole, 1717–1797, was an English man of letters—the "best letter writer in the English language"—whose "delightful letters are the crowning glory of his life." Walpole owned a villa called "Strawberry Hill," on the banks of the Thames, in which he accumulated "curiosities of every description." In 1842 the collections which he had spent nearly fifty years in amassing were sold at auction, requiring twenty-four days. In his house he established a printing press upon which many of his writings were printed. From the "Encyclopædia Britannica," eleventh edition, pages 288–290.

Three-legged chairs somewhat resembling those shown here were made about the middle of the Victorian era. They were intended to be used as hall chairs or porch chairs, without pretense of being antique.

6. The word "wainscot" originally meant the best kind of oak wood, of which these chairs were made. The wooden lining or boarding, generally in panels, on the walls of rooms was usually made of this "wainscot" wood, and in the course of time the lining or boarding itself got the name of "wainscot"; Century Dictionary.

Chairs of this kind were no doubt developed from the chairs with high backs which were used in early churches and in the fine houses of the nobility. They illustrate the remarks in section 45 of this chapter in regard to the chair being originally intended as a seat of honor for important persons. Mr. William B. Goodwin, of Hartford, Connecticut, the owner of No. 23, wrote to the author under date of April 30, 1930: "We can attribute almost every one of the seven or eight chairs known here to either governors of States, presidents of colleges, or officials of the colony." Illustrated articles on the subject are in the magazine "Antiques," June, 1930, pages 519–523, by Mr. Luke Vincent Lockwood and Mr. Homer Eaton Keyes. See also an article in the same magazine, May, 1924, page 222, with illustrations of Pennsylvania wainscot chairs, and another article in August, 1934, page 47, in which it is said that twelve of these chairs are now known.

If we imagine the high solid back of the wainscot chair being constructed in such a manner as to permit it being tilted forward and to rest upon the arms of the chair, it will serve as a top of a table. Such a piece is called a "wainscot chair" table. A round or square top was also used. Examples are shown in Mr. Lockwood's "Colonial Furniture," volume 2, figures 439–441.

7. Compare the illustrations of chests Nos. 595 and 596 in section 77, and figure 16 in Mr. Lockwood's "Colonial Furniture," volume 1.

8. To "turn" is "to form or fashion (a piece of wood) with a chisel or other cutting tool while the wood is rotated in a lathe; to shape, as wood or other hard substance, especially into round or rounded

(*Note 8 is continued on page 118.*)

20 (Upper) Harvard University.
23 (Centre) Mr. Wm. B. Goodwin.
26 (Lower) Dr. James Bordley, Jr.

21 (Upper) Mr. Wm. B. Goodwin.
24 (Centre) Pilgrim Hall, Plymouth.
27 (Lower) Hammond-Harwood House.

22 (Upper) Mr. Wm. M. Ellicott.
25 (Centre) Pilgrim Hall, Plymouth
28 (Lower) Hammond-Harwood House.

117

who are supposed to have brought them over in the "Mayflower."[9] No. 24 is the Carver chair and No. 25 is the Brewster chair. The original chairs are in "Pilgrim Hall," at Plymouth, Massachusetts, and through its courtesy are illustrated here.

Many chairs, such as No. 24, made in the style of the Carver[10] chair, have been found. They were used for almost a century, 1621 to about 1700, and were made in this period without much change in form, except that the earlier ones were heavier and with simpler turnings than the later ones. This type of chair generally has in the back three horizontal rails and three[11] vertical spindles. Almost all of these chairs have arms and they generally have rush seats. They seem to have been in use in Holland, as shown in Dutch paintings, and doubtless passed from there to England and thence to America. Probably about 1650.

The Brewster[12] chair shown in illustration No. 25 is more ornamental than the Carver chair and not so many have been found. It had two rows of four vertical

(NOTE 8, *continued*)

figures, by means of a lathe; as to *turn* the legs of a chair or a table"; see Century Dictionary. The "turnings" of a chair or other article are the parts which have been "turned" on a lathe; see also section 35, note 1.

9. In regard to the "Mayflower furniture," see section 11, note 1, G.

10. John Carver was one of the company of about one hundred passengers, men, women and children, who sailed from Plymouth, England, on the "Mayflower," and, after about nine weeks on the ocean, reached what is now Plymouth, Massachusetts, on December 21, 1620. He was one of the leaders of the Pilgrim Fathers and was chosen to be the first Governor of the Colony. More than half of the Colony, including Governor Carver, died during the first winter; but by 1640 the population of the colony was about 3000. The above is not "news" to the reader, but may refresh his recollection of certain events and dates.

11. A. The expression "turned chairs" is sometimes used to designate the particular group of early chairs in which all, or almost all, of the parts are "turned," except the seat. This group includes turned three–legged chairs, as in Nos. 20 and 21; turned spindle back chairs, as in Nos. 24 and 25; and turned slat–back chairs, as in Nos. 26–34. No other chairs, except perhaps the Windsors, consist so largely of turned parts. In very many later chairs one or more of the parts, not the entire chair, were turned. See examples in sections 47, 49 and 62.

B. Several illustrations of turnings on chairs may be referred to. In Nos. 30 and 31 and others, the almost spherical feet are turned in the form known as "ball feet." In Nos. 30 to 33 the front stretchers, (see section 26), are turned in the "bulb and ring" form; in No. 46 and others, the pattern is the "vase, ring and bulb." In No. 35 most of the turnings are "spiral." In the slat–back chair No. 28 the turnings of the supports of the arms are in the "knob" form, and that of the front stretchers is called the "sausage" pattern. In the banister–back chairs Nos. 44–48 the banisters are turned, as described in section 49, note 1.

C. Turned stretchers are on some of the chairs in the Queen Anne style, Nos. 50 and 52 and others; but not often on those in the Chippendale style, (see section 26, note 3); nor on those in the Hepplewhite or the early Sheraton styles. The legs on the chairs in the later Sheraton style were often turned, as in Nos. 284 to 289 and others; and also in the chairs in the Empire style, Nos. 328 to 332 and others. The legs and stretchers of all of the types of Windsor chairs were turned, as appears in Nos. 440 to 467; a special form of turning of the legs of these Windsor chairs was the "bamboo," barely seen in Nos. 457 and 458.

12. William Brewster was the son of an English country gentleman, and was of higher position and education than many others of the passengers on the "Mayflower." He came as their leader and lived until 1644. Besides being the ruling elder of the church, he was a teacher. He preached "both powerfully and profitably to ye great contentment of ye hearers and their comfortable edification."

turned spindles in the back, three rows on each side and two rows in front, making forty spindles in all, some of which are now missing. A few other chairs of this type were even more elaborate. Probably about 1650.

Section 47. Slat–back chairs.—We now examine the turned chairs having horizontal slats in the back, a type with which almost everyone is familiar. Few persons, however, realize that the slat–back chair originated about three hundred years ago, and that some of those seen in museums date from about 1700 to 1725. Even now it is a popular chair and is made by many factories, especially in the form of a rocking chair. It is said that the designs of the fine "ladder–back" chairs of the Chippendale style shown in section 58 were probably based upon these slat–back chairs. The designs and the number of the slats and stretchers, and the variety of the turnings, will be noticed. Apparently slat–back chairs are not connected in origin with certain chairs of another early type, Nos. 44–49, known as "banister–back"[1] chairs, which have vertical spindles instead of horizontal slats.

There are two types of these turned chairs, one of which was made in New England and the other in Pennsylvania; and there are certain minor types also. In the New England chairs, Nos. 26–28, the back vertical posts are ornamented with turned rings or other designs between the slats; in the Pennsylvania chairs, Nos. 30–34, the back posts have no turnings. Another difference is that in the New England chairs the slats are generally cut straight across on the lower edge and are curved on the upper edge, but in the Pennsylvania chairs the slats are curved on both the lower and upper edges.[2] The New England chairs do not often have as many as five slats, but the Pennsylvania chairs frequently have that number and sometimes six. Maple was almost always used in these chairs.

Many slat–back chairs with rockers have been found. Some of these were originally made as rocking chairs, but in others the rockers were added to chairs which had been made without them. The subject of rocking chairs is treated in section 63; see the chairs Nos. 478–480, 486.

1. As to banister–back chairs, see section 49.
2. In Mr. Lockwood's "Colonial Furniture," volume 2, page 16, it is said that the reason for the difference in the slats is "traceable to the section of England from which the colonists came. New England was settled by persons mostly from the east of England, . . while Philadelphia was largely settled by people from (the County of) Surrey, and the same difference in types of slat–back chairs is noticeable there as here." Compare the remarks in paragraphs two and three in section 11.

Illustrated articles on slat–back chairs are in "Antiques" in the following issues and others: March, 1934, pages 104–107, 116, by Mr. Wilson Lynes; December, 1933, page 208, by the same author; October, 1931, page 210, by Dr. Irving Phillips Lyon; May, 1926, page 307, by Mabel C. Powers.

Many slat–back chairs, especially rocking chairs, were made by Shakers. An example is No. 486. The furniture of the Shakers is the subject of three articles in "Antiques," August 1928, April 1929 and January 1933.

A book entitled "The Community Industries of the Shakers," by Dr. Edward D. Andrews, with 322 pages and 65 illustrations, was published in 1933 by the University of the State of New York, Albany.

Remarks on the history and work of the Shakers are in section 63, last note.

Examining first the New England type of slat–back chairs, Nos. 26–28, we see that in each of these three arm chairs the typical New England features appear, namely, the back posts as well as the front ones are ornamented with turnings, and the lower edges of the slats are cut straight across, not curved. The same features are seen on the chairs without arms. The dates of these pieces are thought to be about 1725–1750.

In Nos. 26 and 27, which are very similar but have several minor differences, the shape of the arms is clearly seen, those of No. 27 being somewhat high; the usual turned ornamental finials are on the tops of the back posts; and seven stretchers, two being in the front, hold the legs together. The general form of the lower parts of these chairs may be compared with that of some of the banister–back chairs.[3] In No. 26 the upper portion of the lower front stretcher has been somewhat worn away, presumably by many years of usage as a resting place for feet in heavy shoes.[4]

No. 28 is a good example of an arm chair of the same period, having a "sausage" turning on the two front stretchers, and a "knob" turning on the front posts. About 1725–1750.

No. 29 is an elaborate arm chair with slats of an unusual form, probably made in Canada or in northern parts of New England. A feature which does not appear very distinctly in the illustration is that the supports of the arms extend down through the seat to the upper side stretchers. About 1725–1750.

The Pennsylvania slat–back chairs are shown in the five illustrations Nos. 30–34. Here it will be seen that the back vertical posts have no ornamental turnings between the slats, and are entirely plain except for the decorative finials; and that both the upper and lower edges of the slats are curved. The arms are wide and flat. There are six stretchers, the front one being ornamental with large bulbous or vase–shaped turnings which are referred to in section 26, note 4, and the front legs are finished off with turned feet of various forms; these ornaments give a pleasing appearance to a somewhat plain and stiff type of furniture. About 1725–1750.

In No. 34 the slats are cut in a different form, both the upper and lower edges being cut in the form of two cyma curves. The distances between the slats are graduated, the smallest distance being between the two lower slats. About 1725–1750.

Section 48. Cane chairs.—These chairs are more elegant than any of the chairs thus far shown. They are called "cane chairs" because the seat and a portion of the back were made of cane, this being their distinctive feature; but of equal

---

3. See "Banister–back chairs," Nos. 44–49.

4. It is difficult to see how so much wearing down of the front bottom stretcher could have occurred, as a grown person could not easily put his feet on the stretcher while occupying the chair. Perhaps small children, with short legs, used the chair; or perhaps the effect was recently produced in order to give an appearance of age for the purpose of sale. See also section 26, note 1.

29 (Upper) Mrs. John S. Gibbs, Jr.   30 (Upper) Dr. James Bordley, Jr.   31 (Upper) Mrs. Miles White, Jr.
32 (Centre) Mr. Albert G. Towers.   33 (Centre) Mr. Albert G. Towers.   34 (Centre) Mrs. John S. Gibbs, Jr.
35 (Lower) Lockwood, Col. Furn.,   36 (Lower) Anonymous.   37 (Lower) Mr. John S. McDaniel.
    Figure 448.

interest in the fine[1] specimens is the elaborate carving and turning of many parts of the chair. In most cases the original cane has been broken and new cane or even upholstery or leather has been substituted, as in No. 40; in fact it is very seldom that a chair of this kind is found in its original condition. They came to our country from England about 1690–1700 and some of them were the models from which the American pieces were made. Many of the English types were too elegant and expensive for general use in our colonies; and only the plainer kinds were apparently made here to any extent. They are sometimes called "Charles the Second" chairs because they became the fashion in England in his reign, which was from 1660 to 1685. In our country they appear to have been popular until about 1720.

Following the classification of Mr. Lockwood,[2] cane chairs are considered here in three types.

Examining No. 35, an arm chair of the first type, we see that the top of the back of the chair is ornamented with a carved and pierced cresting[3] which does not extend to the side lines of the chair, but is between the two finials; this is the distinguishing feature of the first type of these chairs. The "stiles," that is, the two upright posts on the sides of the back, as described in note 3 in section 50, are in a turned "spiral"[4] form; so also are the back legs and two of the stretchers, partly. The lower stretcher is "recessed," that is, set back from the front, and connects the

1. In this section, contrary to the usual method in this book, the illustrations are mostly of the finest examples, "museum pieces," which are seldom seen by the amateur collector. The reason for this is that in our country there are very few examples of chairs of the cane variety, except of the plain type of the last one here shown, No. 40. As to "Museum pieces," see section 1, note 3.

The "turned" stretchers and stiles and the "carved" other parts are to be noticed in these chairs. Turning is the subject of section 35, and carving is considered in sections 36–37.

Chairs of this kind, with their high backs, were very effective when standing as ornamental pieces against the wall; but they were not comfortable and were apt to give way when the occupant leaned heavily against the back.

The imported English chairs were generally made of walnut or beech wood. The finer American pieces were usually of some kind of fruit wood; the plainer pieces were often made of maple and were frequently painted black.

2. In his "Colonial Furniture in America," volume 2, pages 32–54, where the subject is fully considered and illustrated.

3. A "cresting" is defined as an ornamental top piece, usually of a chair. It was firmly attached to the connecting parts of the chair. In the finer pieces the cresting and the front stretchers were both carved, generally in the same design. Crestings will also be seen in many other objects.

The feature of the first type is seen in a plainer form in the "banister–back" chairs Nos. 44–48.

4. The spiral column is one of the interesting details in the study of antique furniture. It was a form of turning, not carving, and was a favorite form of ornamentation of cane chairs from about 1660 to 1700. It is also seen on other articles of about the same period, such as the tables Nos. 1279 and 1291 and the tables Nos. 1446, 1472, 1538. Whenever the spiral column is seen, it is an indication that the article on which it appears, if genuine, was of about the period mentioned. This spiral column is not to be confused with the spiral column of a different character seen on articles in the Late Sheraton and the Empire styles, such as the bedstead No. 1070, the sideboard No. 1015, the stand No. 1446 and the small table No. 1615. The cross–references to the older spirals are referred to in the text of section 1. See also the Index under the word "spiral."

side stretchers instead of connecting the front legs.[5] This illustration is copied by permission of Mr. Lockwood from his "Colonial Furniture," volume 2, figure 448. About 1660–1680.

No. 36 is also a chair of the first type, the cresting not extending to the side lines. It is known as the William Penn chair as it is believed that it was brought by Penn from England in 1699 when he made a second voyage to his Pennsylvania. The two "stiles" are "turned" as in No. 35, but not in a spiral form. At the top is the cresting with two scrolls in the form of the letter "C" in a recumbent position, known from their shape as "C–scrolls";[6] six of the same scrolls are on the frame-work around the narrow cane; and two others are on the front stretcher. The front legs and feet are in the form known as "Flemish–scrolled."[7] About 1690–1700.

No. 37 is a plainer chair of the first type, and is of a somewhat later date than the two preceding. The frame holding the large cane work in the back has no carving on the sides, thus making the turned "stiles" more conspicuous than in No. 36. The cresting and the front stretcher are ornamented with carving of the same design. About 1700.

No. 38 is of the second type, of which the distinctive feature is that the cresting extends over the back of the chair to the side lines, that is, over the stiles. This elegant and graceful chair is ornamented with a cresting and front stretcher of the same delicate design; and the carving of C–scrolls and other designs are of a superior character. The front legs are in the Flemish style. The wood is English walnut. About 1680–1700.

In No. 39 we see the third type of cane chairs, in which the feature is that the back posts, or stiles, are molded, not "turned" as they were in the chairs of the first and second types.[8] The cresting extends over the full width of the back, as in No. 38. Here the cane occupies the entire back of the chair and is not enclosed in a separate frame; and we see the "Spanish" feet which are found on other articles of the period and later.[9] The front stretcher is not an elaborately carved one, but a turned one. About 1680–1700.

5.   This type of stretcher is sometimes called an "H stretcher," because it and the two side stretchers to which it is attached are in the form of that letter. See "Stretchers," section 26, note 4.

6.   This C–scroll will also be seen in other articles, especially in mirrors, such as Nos. 1103–1106; see the Index, "C–scroll."

7.   In the Flemish scroll the feet generally turn forward; if they turn backward they are sometimes called "English." Cane chairs with a Flemish scroll foot are sometimes called merely "Flemish chairs." See the comment on figure 16 in illustration No. 11.

        An illustrated article entitled "The evolution of Charles II chairs," by Mr. Ralph Edwards, is in "Antiques," November, 1933, page 168.

8.   Nos. 36 and 39 and two other cane chairs are illustrated and described in "Antiques," April, 1927, pages 274–276, under the title "Four Carolean Chairs." It is there said that these chairs were all made before 1700 and were probably imported; and that the bulbous turnings such as those on the front legs of No. 39 were later modified into the "inverted cups" of the legs of the William and Mary style which are seen in the highboys Nos. 632–634, the lowboys Nos. 669–671, and the table No. 1284.

9.   See "The kinds of feet," section 25; and lowboys Nos. 673–674.

No. 40 is also of the third type, the back posts, or stiles, being molded, not turned; and there is no carved cresting. The small rail at the top of the back and the small rail at the bottom of the back are cut in a similar shape. The entire back and seat were probably filled at one time with cane, which has since been replaced with upholstery.[10] The Spanish feet and the stretchers and legs resemble those of No. 39, except that the turnings of the front legs are different. About 1700.

The next three illustrations, Nos. 41–43, are of chairs in a transition state, that is, they are changing from one style into another.[11] Under the Dutch influence which affected furniture styles in England about 1702, as mentioned in sections 13 and 14, the English cabinet makers began to drop certain features of the cane style, and to take on certain features of the Dutch style; these chairs are thus partly in the English style and partly in the Dutch style. When all the changes were made, the chair was transformed into what we now know as the Dutch, or Queen Anne, style. The splats in these three transition chairs are in the "vase" shape mentioned in section 50 at note 6.

Comparing the transition chair No. 41 with the previous one, No. 40, we see that the principal differences between them are that in No. 41 a solid splat[12] occupies some of the space previously filled by the cane,[13] and the top of the back is curved in a different manner. In other respects the principal features of No. 40 continue in No. 41; in both chairs the part enclosed in the back does not extend down to the seat;[14] the back posts, or stiles, are molded, not turned; the front legs are almost the same; the feet of each chair are of the Spanish type; and the stretchers, unequal in number, are turned in somewhat the same design. The small concave curve in the top rail is a feature of the Queen Anne style chairs. This type of chair is said to be found mostly in New England. About 1710–1720.

In the next example, No. 42, an arm chair, the Spanish feet of previous chairs have been superseded by Dutch feet, as to which see section 50, and the front legs are turned. There is thus little left of the designs of the earlier cane chairs except the turned stiles, or upright posts, and the form of the arms. This type of chair is found mostly in New York. About 1725–1750.

10.   A chair very similar to this one, with the entire back and seat filled with cane, is shown in Symonds' "Old English Walnut and Lacquer Furniture," plate 6; the date given is about 1685.

11.   Several transition chairs of the general type of these three chairs, but with the top rail of the back curved in the Chippendale manner, will be seen in Nos. 82–84 in which the transition is from the style of Queen Anne to the style of Chippendale.

Other transition pieces are cited in the Index under "Transition."

12.   The word "splat" is defined as the "upright wide pieces of wood in the middle of a chair–back"; Morse, "Furniture of the olden time," page 457. "The central vertical member of a chair–back" is also a good definition. The purpose of a splat is of course to provide a support for the back of the sitter without filling the entire frame of the back of the chair.

13.   A cane chair with the cane in the back divided into two parts by a splat like that in No. 42 is shown as figure 488 in Mr. Lockwood's "Colonial Furniture." This seems to show the first important step in the change from the cane style chair to the Queen Anne style chair. Similar chairs are in Mr. Cescinsky's "English Furniture," volume 1, figures 57–59, dated 1700.

14.   A similar method of construction will be seen in the Sheraton style chairs in section 54.

38 (Upper) Anonymous.
41 (Lower) Hammond-Harwood
House.

39 (Upper) Anonymous.
42 (Lower) Mr. Albert G. Towers.

40 (Upper) Mrs. J. W. Williams.
43 (Lower) Mr. & Mrs. J. M.
Matthews.

Another form is shown in No. 43. Here the stiles are turned, and the round front legs are plain. The splat is in the form of a graceful vase. The wood is maple. It is said that these chairs were popular for a very long time, from about 1725 to 1800, and that they were made chiefly in New England.

At this point we approach the next important style in chairs—the Dutch style of Queen Anne. Before taking up that style, however, we must examine the banister back chairs because they are so closely connected with the first type of cane chairs.

Section 49. Banister back chairs.—Banister back chairs seem to have been made in imitation of the plainer cane chairs of the first type shown in the previous section, such as No. 37; and historically they may be considered as a branch of that type. By substituting banisters for the cane back and by using rush instead of cane for the seat, the change from a cane chair to a banister back one was easily made, irrespective of any ornamental carving. The banister back chairs came into general use about 1700–1725. They were generally made of maple and were very popular for many years, especially in the country districts.

In Nos. 44 and 45 we have a front view and a back view of the same chair, in order to show the construction of the banisters. Each banister is one–half of a round banister and for this reason is often called a "split" banister.[1] In most cases the flat side of the banister was placed in front, as it was more comfortable to lean against than the round side. In this chair and in No. 46 we observe the ornamental carved cresting at the top of the back; this may be compared with the crestings on the first type of the cane chairs, Nos. 35–37. The Spanish feet and the turnings of the legs and of the four bulbous stretchers will also be noticed. The seat is made of rush. About 1700–1725.

In No. 46 we see another design of carved cresting. The lower rail of the back, upon which the banisters rest, is cut in curves. Only the front two of the seven stretchers are turned in designs. The front posts are less elaborately turned than those in the previous example, and they terminate in ball feet. About 1700–1725.

The next three chairs, Nos. 47, 48 and 49, are plainer, especially because the carving on the crestings has disappeared. The chair without arms, No. 47, has six stretchers, all of which except the back one are turned with two bulbs, or balls, of unusually large size. The upper cresting and the lower rail of the back are cut in curves. About 1700–1725.

1.   These split banisters were made by taking two pieces of wood and gluing them together temporarily with a strip of paper between to prevent them from getting too firmly united. The turning of the two was then done on a lathe, making a round banister such as those used on stairs. The two pieces were then separated, the glue and paper removed, and the two halves were ready for the chair.

The word "banister" is also spelled "bannister"; both are said in the Century Dictionary to be corrupt forms of the architectural word "baluster" which is the word used in England; see note 19 in section 53.

44 (UPPER) HAMMOND-HARWOOD
    HOUSE.
47 (LOWER) MRS. JOHN S. GIBBS, JR.

45 (UPPER) HAMMOND-HARWOOD
    HOUSE.
48 (LOWER) HAMMOND-HARWOOD
    HOUSE.

46 (UPPER) HAMMOND-HARWOOD
    HOUSE.
49 (LOWER) MRS. JOHN S. GIBBS, JR.

No. 48 has one feature not seen in the other chairs, that is, a round and flat knob at the tops of the two front posts, known as a "mushroom" knob, which was sometimes used on the older slat–back and banister–back chairs. The arms are not quite horizontal, sloping somewhat downwards. The legs have apparently been shortened. About 1700–1725.

In No. 49 the top rail is concave and the banisters are grooved; the other parts of the chair are very similar to the previous ones. About 1740–1750.

Section 50. Queen Anne style chairs.—Brief mention of the origin and general character of the Queen Anne style of furniture was made in section 14, which should be read in connection with this section; it will be recalled that the full title of section 14 is "The Queen Anne style—and styles until Chippendale."

Although the reign of Queen Anne was a short one, from 1702 to 1714, the Queen Anne style continued in fashion for a long period. In our country the style began a few years later than in England, and continued until about 1755–1760 when the style which we call Chippendale became the fashionable one.

Chairs of the Queen Anne style appear to have been made in America from about 1710 to about 1755. During the latter portion of this period it seems that both the chairs of the Queen Anne style and those of the early Chippendale style were made at the same time; and this overlapping of styles continued until the style of Queen Anne lost favor and was no longer used. As stated several times in this book, it must be understood that any *dates of manufacture* which are based entirely upon the *style* of an article are merely approximate, because any particular article may have been made in a certain style long after that style had gone out of fashion.[1] It is proper to say that a particular chair was made in the *style* of certain years, but it is not proper to say that the chair was *made* between those years. The dates in this book are the dates in which it is thought that the *style* was in vogue. With respect to the eighteen chairs in the Queen Anne style illustrated in this section, it may be said that those with four stretchers are generally of the style of about 1710–1725, and that the others are of the later style of about 1725–1755; but this is not an exact classification.

1. See "Dating antique furniture," section 6.

   Scholarly information and opinions in regard to the Queen Anne style of furniture, and especially of chairs, in our country are in an illustrated article by Mr. L. G. Myers, edited by Mr. Homer Eaton Keyes, in "Antiques," December, 1932, pages 213–217. That article is based upon remarks of Mr. Myers in the notable catalogue of the "Girl Scouts Loan Exhibition" in New York in September, 1929, under the heading "American Queen Anne and Chippendale," and upon notes made by Mr. Myers. In that article it is stated that in our country we did not break away from the straight lines of the style prior to that of Queen Anne much before 1720 or even 1725. Many details of interest are illustrated and discussed in this article.

   An illustrated article by Mr. Ralph Edwards entitled "Foreign Influences on Queen Anne Chairs" is in "Antiques," April, 1934, pages 132–134. In the same issue, page 131, is an editorial study of a good chair in the Queen Anne style and on page 150 are illustrations of two New York chairs of the same style.

50 (UPPER) HAMMOND-HARWOOD
    HOUSE.
53 (CENTRE) MR. J. S. McDANIEL.
56 (LOWER) MR. J. S. McDANIEL.

51 (UPPER) DR. M. A. ABRAMS.
54 (CENTRE) MR. J. S. McDANIEL.
57 (LOWER) MRS. HOWARD SILL.

52 (UPPER) MR. ALBERT G. TOWERS.
55 (CENTRE) DR. JAMES BORDLEY, JR.
58 (LOWER) DR. JAMES BORDLEY, JR.

In the last three illustrations in section 48, Nos. 41–43, the chairs are in a transition state, being partly in the previous style of the cane chairs and partly in the Dutch style of Queen Anne. In a short time other changes into the Dutch style were made and finally the transformation became complete.

The special features of an early chair entirely in the Queen Anne style are well seen in No. 50 which is a good example of the style.[2] These features are all different from those seen in the cane chairs of the previous period and are as follows:

1. The back of the chair is curved at the ends of the top and there often is a concave curve in the centre.
2. The splat rests upon the rear rail of the seat, not upon a cross–rail above the seat; see No. 41 and the comment.
3. The front legs are in the curved form known as "cabriole"; see section 24.
4. The front feet are the rounded Dutch, or club, feet; or, on many of the later chairs, ball and claw feet; see section 25.

Certain other features, indicating changes in various details, will be mentioned as we proceed, such as the presence or absence of stretchers; the curved or straight seat; the form of the "stiles";[3] and especially the design of the splat, either solid or pierced.

The most distinctive feature of the Queen Anne style of chairs, however, is the cyma curve, which takes the place of the straight line in the previous styles. This curve is present in almost every part of the chair, and particularly and always in the cabriole form of leg. The cyma curve is illustrated in section 23 in which it is mentioned that the artist Hogarth termed this curve[4] the "line of beauty"; and a "Hogarth chair" is shown as No. 9.

The splats[5] in the chairs of the Queen Anne style are in a variety of forms, many of them graceful, even though simple and plain. The most usual form of splat has a supposed resemblance to the shape of a vase or a fiddle[6] and a chair of

2. In addition to the chairs shown in this section, there were at least two other kinds in the Queen Anne style. One is the "wing" chair which is shown in section 59; the other, not illustrated here, is a chair with a rectangular back and seat, all covered with upholstery except the cabriole legs. Both of these types are dated about 1725–1750.

3. A "stile" and a back leg together form one upright piece of wood. The stile is the part above the leg. Stiles are also known as "uprights," meaning the posts which extend up from the back leg and are braced together at the top by the top rail. They almost disappeared in the chairs of Hepplewhite but are seen again in those of Sheraton and in later styles. For the convenience of readers who may not see this definition, it is repeated in section 51, note 19. See also the Index.

4. Another good example of the use of cyma curves is in the arm chair No. 62. Here we find them in the legs, the arm supports, the stiles and the splat.

5. The word "splat" is explained in section 48, note 12.

6. The outline of a splat often resembles that of a vase but a resemblance to a fiddle is generally imaginary.

A somewhat similar type of solid splat was used in a late Empire style chair of about the year 1840; see section 57, Nos. 346–354.   (Note 6 is continued on page 132.)

59 (Upper) Mr. J. S. McDaniel.
62 (Lower) Mr. A. M. Tyson.

60 (Upper) Dr. M. A. Abrams.
63 (Lower) Mr. A. M. Tyson.

61 (Upper) Dr. M. A. Abrams.
64 (Lower) Mr. A. M. Tyson.

this type is often called a "vase–back" or "fiddle–back" chair. In many Queen Anne style chairs of late date the splats were "pierced," as were most of the splats in the Chippendale style as seen in the next section.

Certain differences have been observed between the Queen Anne and Chippendale style of chairs made in Philadelphia and those made in New England. Most of these differences are details of cabinet making, not interesting to amateurs; one feature, however, may be mentioned here. Looking at the back of a good Philadelphia chair, of about 1750–1785, just above the tops of the rear legs, the ends of the side rails of the seat are often seen extending through the rear posts.[7] This method of construction was used in Philadelphia in the Queen Anne period and until the end of the Chippendale period. It has often been said that the method was not used in chairs made in other States; but this view has been found to be erroneous, as the same method has since been discovered in chairs made in New York and Connecticut. This illustrates the danger of asserting a negative!

The wood of which the New England chairs and other articles in the Queen Anne style were made was generally walnut or other native woods. Walnut was also used in the Pennsylvania chairs until mahogany became the fashion, which was about 1745; after that date mahogany was almost exclusively used in that State in the finer class of chairs. It was recently said that of all the numerous chairs in the Queen Anne style in the American Wing of the Metropolitan Museum of Art only five are of mahogany and they were of about 1750.

Examining the illustrations, we see first a group of five early Queen Anne style chairs, Nos. 50–54. As with the cane chairs of the preceding period, these Queen Anne style chairs are furnished with turned stretchers. The lower stretcher is "recessed," as in the cane chair No. 40, that is, it is set back from the front and is connected with the side stretchers, not with the front legs. The stiles are straight, or almost so, not broken by a curve a few inches above the seat, as in No. 58 and others after about 1725. The splat in each of these five chairs is in a somewhat different design. The legs are in the cabriole form and the feet are of the Dutch, or club, type.

No. 50 is an early form of Queen Anne style chair. The splat is cut in a plain design, more suggestive of a vase than a fiddle. The seat is rounded at the corners and curved on the sides. This kind of chair is often found in New England. The wood is generally walnut or maple. About 1710–1725.

(NOTE 6, *continued from page 130*)

After examining the black splat of a chair with a white background it is often interesting to look at the white background which forms two white silhouettes. In some cases a little imagination may enable the reader to see outlines of an object; thus the head of a parrot may be recognized by the presence of a curved bill, as in Nos. 60, 89 and others.

7. This method is well shown on a Queen Anne style chair, figure 3, illustrated in "Antiques," December, 1932, page 214, in an article by Mr. Louis G. Myers, mentioned in note 1 in this section. See also section 51 at note 12.

Another difference is said to be that turned stretchers, as in Nos. 50, 52–53 and others, are seldom found on Pennsylvania chairs but were used on chairs made in New England. See also section 51, above note 14, sub-title "Stretchers."

In No. 51 the lines of the seat are straight except at the front corners where they are rounded. The three lower stretchers are curved and flat, as also in Nos. 63 and 86, not turned in a round design. The engraving gives a side view of this chair in order to show the profile of the back, the characteristic Queen Anne profile often called a "spoon–shaped curve" or a "spoon–back"; the word "spooning" meaning the shaping of a high–back chair to fit the back of the occupant. In No. 64 the curve is also seen. The Chippendale style chairs Nos. 80 and 81 should be compared with these. The knees at the top of the front legs are carved and the "stiles" are rounded in front, not flat. About 1725.

No. 52 resembles No. 50 in some respects. We notice, however, that the straight seat rail in front is cut in cyma curves and that the stretchers are turned. About 1725.

In No. 53, a maple chair, the back is more ornamental, especially in the form of the splat. As in the preceding chair, the front seat rail is cut in cyma curves. The seat is rectangular, without curved corners. About 1725.

No. 54 is a full–sized arm chair with a large splat in a plain design, not in the vase or fiddle shape. The arms and the stiles are rounded in front. The form of the arms resembles that in the later chair No. 66. About 1725.

The next three chairs, Nos. 55, 56 and 57, are probably a little later in style than those already mentioned. The principal difference is that three of the four stretchers have been omitted; and the remaining one, between the rear legs, was apparently of little value, as it was soon discarded. The seat of No. 55 has straight sides and front, with rounded corners; Nos. 56 and 57 are curved on the sides and front, with carved knees and with small carved knobs on the inner sides of the front legs. The dates are probably about 1725–1745.

In the next four pieces, Nos. 58–61, the straight stiles of the preceding chairs are not used and the stiles curve inward at a point a few inches above the seat.[8] This change began about 1730 and continued until the Queen Anne style passed out; but chairs with straight stiles continued to be made, doubtless because some of the later cabinet makers and their customers preferred the earlier straight pattern.

---

8.   This curved effect was generally obtained, especially in the Pennsylvania chairs, by gluing a small piece of curved wood on the inside of a straight stile at the point needed and cutting away a portion of the outside of the stile.

One or both of Nos. 61–62 might serve in shape, if not in width, as an example of an English "drunkard's chair," a type which was in fashion from the period of Queen Anne until near the end of the Chippendale period. Some of these chairs were about thirty inches in width, wide enough for the comfortable repose of the "hard–drinking nobility of the eighteenth century." These chairs were often sufficiently wide for two persons and therefore they were especially favored by lovers, a use which gave to them the additional name of "lovers' chairs"; the "spooning" mentioned in the comment on chair No. 51 is not connected with these latter chairs.

"Gouty chairs" may be referred to in connection with "drunkard's chairs." Mr. Cescinsky remarks in his "English Furniture," volume 3, page 343, that "gout was a very fashionable complaint in the eighteenth century, and a sure indication of pedigree." A "gouty stool" was a stool with a top which could be adjusted to a height agreeable to a victim of "excessive indulgence in rich wines and highly-seasoned foods," as remarked in "A glossary of English Furniture," page 77.

In No. 58 we see the continued use of four stretchers as in the earlier type, and in No. 59 there are three stretchers, one of which is recessed. In these two chairs the change from the straight line of the stiles of the earlier chairs is slight, but apparently makes a beginning towards the more pronounced curve in the next chairs. In Nos. 60 and 61 the curve is fully developed; the seat is straight on all sides, with curved corners, and the front rail of the seat is cut in curves. The dates of Nos. 58–61 are about 1730.

Nos. 62 and 63, an arm chair and a side chair, were inherited by the present owner from a Philadelphia ancestor. In the arm chair, whose cyma curves are referred to in note 4, we notice the wide splat, the ample rounded seat, the form of the arms[9] and their supports, the carved shell over the splat, the Dutch feet and the carved shells on the knees; in the side chair, No. 63, many of these features will be seen, and also the curved flat stretchers as in No. 51. No. 64 is a side view of No. 62, showing the "profile" or "sweep" of the back of the chair, as mentioned in the comment on No. 51. About 1740–1750.

No. 65 is a handsome side chair with ball and claw feet. The stiles are rounded but not curved. The lower part of the splat is ornamented with two delicate scrolls carved on the sides. The knees and legs are carved in a leaf design. It appears that this chair was made in Baltimore. About 1730–1750.

Two arm chairs of much elegance are shown as Nos. 66–67. Each has ball and claw feet with carved knees, and in each the back is finely crested. In other features, however, these chairs are noticeably different. In No. 66 the splat is solid and is in an unusual design, with carving on the rounded upper portion;[10] the arms are somewhat similar to those in No. 68; each of the stiles is ornamented with two small carved scrolls; and the skirt of the seat is cut in cyma curves, as in Nos. 52 and 60. This chair may be of Dutch origin.

No. 67 is an example of an American chair, in the style of Queen Anne, with ball and claw feet and a pierced splat instead of a solid one. We are so accustomed to associate such feet and a pierced splat with the Chippendale style that it is well to examine this chair closely. This mahogany chair No. 67 has been referred to by a competent critic as "the most remarkable and perhaps the most beautiful chair ever found in this country"; but without fully concurring in this opinion we may admire the proportions, the outlines and the decorative treatment of this Philadelphia product. The arms are of the same type as those in No. 62, and the arm–supports are cut away on the inside surface, a method frequently used by the cabinet makers of Philadelphia. The splat is doubtless the model for those in the Chippendale style chairs Nos. 120–128. About 1740–1755.

9. This form of arm and arm support, and variations, was a favorite one in England and our country throughout the periods of Queen Anne and Chippendale, about 1702–1785, and will be seen on several chairs in the next section. It is said that in our country it is almost infallible evidence of Pennsylvania workmanship. Another approved form is in Nos. 66 and 68.

10. An English chair almost identical with this in form except as to the feet, is No. 80 in volume 1 of Mr. Cescinsky's "English Furniture"; the date given is 1710–1715. An American piece of the same style would be several years later.

65 (UPPER) MRS. MILES WHITE, JR.   66 (UPPER) DR. JAMES BORDLEY, JR.   67 (UPPER) METROPOLITAN MUSEUM.
68 (LOWER) ANONYMOUS.   69 (LOWER) ANONYMOUS.   70 (LOWER) ANONYMOUS.

Nos. 68–70 are three English chairs copied by permission from Mr. Cescinsky's "English Furniture," volume 2, Nos. 31, 25 and 30; and the "Hogarth" chair, No. 9 in section 23, should also be seen with these three. The purpose in illustrating these chairs is to impress upon the reader that pierced splats and ball and claw feet were not originated by Chippendale but were in common use before he became a cabinet maker. In Nos. 68 and 70 the form of the top rail is changing and the back is almost square.

No. 68 is said by Mr. Cescinsky to be a transition chair between the Queen Anne and Chippendale styles. The arms and the feet are in the Dutch, or club, style. The rail at the top is in a flat form approaching the "cupid's–bow" rail of the true Chippendale style chair. The chair No. 165 has a pierced splat of a similar type. About 1725–1730.

In No. 69 the top is curved in the Queen Anne style and the feet are in the usual Dutch, or club, form. The pierced splat is perhaps the model for the splats in the Chippendale style chairs Nos. 118 and 119. About 1725–1730.

No. 70, also a transition chair, has ball and claw feet and a flat top somewhat similar to that in No. 68. The pierced splat is in an elongated vase form which is not seen on other chairs in this section. About 1725–1730.

The "Hogarth" chair, shown as No. 9 in section 23, has a pierced splat, ball and claw feet and many cyma curves, as mentioned in note 2 in section 23. It is dated about 1710 by Mr. Cescinsky.

The transition style chairs Nos. 82–84 in the next section are between the Queen Anne style and the Chippendale style;[11] after which the next transition is from the Chippendale style to the Hepplewhite style, which is treated at the end of the next section.

Section 51. Chippendale style chairs.—The term "Chippendale style chairs" includes, of course, all kinds of chairs made in the Chippendale style; but certain chairs of special types made in the Chippendale style, such as "ladder–back" chairs, "wing" chairs and others, are generally referred to by their special names, and in this chapter on "chairs" are treated in separate sections. In the present section the illustrations are of the side[1] chairs and arm chairs which are generally known

11.   The two chairs Nos. 68 and 70 are forerunners of the Chippendale style and represent forms which Chippendale and his school used and improved.

It may seem strange to refer to any chairs made before the time of Chippendale as chairs in the Chippendale style; the reason is that the designs which we now call Chippendale, although not all originated by him, were perfected and made famous by him. His name is not used as the inventor of the style but as the foremost designer and developer of a style which had previously been originated in part by others. See also section 11, note 1, I; section 15, notes 3, 5; section 21 at note 2.

1.   The meaning of the word "side" in connection with chairs has been the subject of discussion. A "side chair" is understood to mean a chair without arms; but why should the word "side" indicate an absence of "arms"? By some it is thought that as chairs without arms, when not in use, especially in a dining room, were placed against the sides of the room they were properly called "side chairs"; but arm chairs as well as side chairs were placed against the sides of a room. If the word has any connection with a

simply as "Chippendale style chairs"—the chairs which are perhaps most highly esteemed[2] of all the antique chairs of England or America. It is suggested that section 15, entitled "The Chippendale style," be examined in connection with this section.

In our country it is probable that the Chippendale style was first adopted about the year 1755, certainly so in Philadelphia where it was most closely followed and most highly developed; and it continued in vogue in that city and elsewhere until about 1785. Within these approximate dates it seems that all of the types of our chairs in the Chippendale style were probably made, unless positive evidence, not mere family tradition,[3] is found to the contrary. These dates, 1755–1785, appear to be sufficiently accurate for most purposes; and it does not seem necessary to attempt to fix more precise dates for each individual chair.[4]

At this point attention is called to the illustrations of six chairs, Nos. 71–76, in which four[5] principal styles are seen in chronological order, namely, the Queen Anne, the Chippendale, the Hepplewhite and the Sheraton. These illustrations give a preliminary idea of the principal styles. In almost all styles of chairs including the Chippendale style, the distinctive feature which determines the style is the form of the back; and in the backs of the Chippendale style chairs the distinctive feature is the form of the rail across the top, called the "top rail."

No. 71 shows the Queen Anne, or Dutch, style back, which has already been seen in No. 50. The top rail and the two side upright posts, or "stiles," as to which see note 19 in this section, are separate pieces of wood but appear to be one piece bent into the shape. The splat in these chairs is usually, but not always, solid, not pierced.

(NOTE 1, *continued*)

dining room it would well apply to chairs without arms which were placed at the "sides" of the table instead of the head of the table where the head of the house sat in an arm chair; but some may say— "where Macgregor sits, there is the head of the table."

Frequently in this chapter both a side chair and an arm chair of the same set are shown. Although the design of a side chair is duplicated in the arm chair the illustrations of the arms are desirable because in many cases the arms indicate the period and are finely designed. Occasionally arms have been added to side chairs in recent years and in some cases such additions are unworthy of the other parts of the chairs.

See the ancient Egyptian arm chair No. 487.

2. Financially speaking, the most highly esteemed American chair is a "wing" chair in the Chippendale style believed to have been made about 1770 by Benjamin Randolph, of Philadelphia, which was sold for $33,000 at the Reifsnyder auction sale in April, 1929. The illustration of this chair is No. 406. It is one of the famous "Sample" chairs, including Nos. 116 and 117 shown on page 153.

Because of the importance of the Chippendale style chairs, more space is given to them in this book than to any other type of chair.

3. As to "family tradition" see section 6 at note 15.

4. In his "Colonial Furniture," Volume 2, Mr. Lockwood dates very many of the side and arm chairs in the Chippendale style shown by him, figures 538–584, merely "third quarter eighteenth century," 1750–1775.

5. The Adam style, as to which see section 16, is not included here because furniture in that style was apparently not made in our country; but in order that the Adam influence on chairs made by Hepplewhite and Sheraton may be seen, a full page illustration of four Adam style chairs appears as No. 181 in section 52.

Nos. 72, 73 and 74 show different backs of Chippendale style chairs. Three backs are shown, instead of merely one as is usual, because it may be confusing to the amateur collector, as it was to the writer, to see three kinds of chair backs of such dissimilar appearance called by the one name of "Chippendale" without explanation.

No. 72 has a Chippendale style chair back with a solid splat. Here the line of the top rail follows the distinctively Chippendale "cupid's–bow" shape, with the two ends, or "ears," curved upwards; this is explained in notes 8 and 9 in this section.

No. 73 has the more familiar Chippendale style chair back with the "cupid's–bow" top rail, but with the splat pierced; this is the favorite kind of Chippendale style chair.

No. 74 has another form of Chippendale style chair back; here the top rail, instead of curving upwards at the ends, is rounded, and curves downward somewhat in the style of a Queen Anne chair; examples of this type are also in Nos. 91, 116 and many others. The legs here have been cut off slightly. This chair is also shown as No. 136.

No. 75 is in the style of Hepplewhite. The backs of chairs of this graceful style are almost always in the shape of a shield or a heart or an oval, with upright splats or banisters. Other shapes will be seen in section 53.

No. 76 illustrates the style of Sheraton. Here the back is not curved, but is rectangular. As in the banister–back chairs Nos. 44–49, and the transition chairs Nos. 41–43 and Nos. 82–84, the splat does not extend down to the seat rail, but rests upon a cross–piece. In the chairs of the Sheraton style the back was ornamented with designs of much charm, as will be seen in section 54.

The styles of three other chairs, Nos. 77–79, are derived mainly from French sources and are somewhat similar in certain features.

No. 77 is in the American Directory style, a style not yet fully appreciated for its influence upon our chairs; see sections 19 and 55. The curving lines of the entire framework, except the front of the seat, were copied in part in many American chairs. This chair appears also as No. 310.

No. 78 is a chair made by Duncan Phyfe. The French Directory style is seen in the curves of the framework as in the preceding piece. The lyre resting upon a cross–piece in the back is a feature taken from the Sheraton style. There is no "Duncan Phyfe style" for the reason explained in section 20.

No. 79 is one of the forms of the American Empire style chairs seen in section 57, in which various other forms are shown.

At the risk of going too much into details, certain matters may be mentioned here in regard to the American chairs in the Chippendale style. Some of these remarks may not be very interesting, but they will assist in knowing and appreciating the Chippendale style chairs.

Queen Anne   Chippendale   Chippendale

Chippendale   Hepplewhite   Sheraton

Directoire   Duncan Phyfe   American Empire

71 (UPPER) HAMMOND-HARWOOD
     HOUSE.
74 (CENTRE) MISS HARRIETT R. CHEW.
77 (LOWER) MRS. THOS. J. LINDSAY.

72 (UPPER) MR. J. F. H. MAGINN.
75 (CENTRE) HAMMOND-HARWOOD
     HOUSE.
78 (LOWER) ANONYMOUS.

73 (UPPER) MISS MARGARET C.
     PAINTER.
76 (CENTRE) DR. HENRY M. FITZ-
     HUGH.
79 (LOWER) MR. JOHN HINKLEY.

Wood. It is said that the fine American chairs in the Chippendale style were made almost exclusively of mahogany; but a few were made of walnut,[6] such as No. 123. Mahogany had two advantages; it is handsome and is well suited for carving.

Carving and inlay.[7] Chippendale was a master of carving and he used it as the only ornament for his designs of chairs and other articles; inlay was used only upon the request of a customer. In America as in England the presence of carving and the absence of inlay is characteristic of the Chippendale style chairs.

Top rail. As above mentioned, the form of the back determines whether or not a chair is in the Chippendale style, and the shape of the top rail is the distinctive feature of the back. An examination of the illustrations will make this matter much clearer than can be done by any printed description. It may be said, however, that two principal kinds of top rails are seen on Chippendale style chairs, as shown above in Nos. 72–74. In one kind, shown in No. 74, the top rail of the back is rounded, or almost rounded, at the ends where it joins the upright posts, or stiles; this kind is called a "rounded end" top rail. But the top rail which is particularly associated with the name of Chippendale is known as the "cupid's–bow,"[8] good examples of which are seen in Nos. 72 and 73. A feature of this top rail is the projection on each end beyond the stiles of the chair, forming what are called "ears."[9] It seems that a form of top rail somewhat similar to this one was used before the time of Chippendale; but it was he who perfected the design which is so much admired. A number of variations from the pure Chippendale style of backs and top rails will be noticed in the illustrations.[10]

Legs and feet. It is said that Chippendale used on his chairs either the cabriole leg[11] or the straight leg indiscriminately[12] at all times; and it is also said

6.   As to walnut see section 28; as to mahogany see section 29.

7.   As to carving see sections 36 and 37; as to inlay see section 33.

8.   The term "cupid's–bow" shape is given to top rails which, with or without carving or other ornament, have a convex, or upward, curve in the center, with a concave, or downward, curve on each side of the center, and also have at each end a little upward curve. Such a top rail has a close resemblance to the bow which was an attribute of Cupid in Roman art, differing from the Grecian form. There are many variations in form of these "cupid's–bow" top rails.

9.   The two "ears" on a Chippendale style chair are often interesting. They are the turned up extremities of the top rail. In some cases they extend out several inches beyond the stiles, as in No. 132; in other cases they are short. They are often carved, sometimes in a spiral form, with little projections upward and downward; when the top rail has this form it has the odd name of "swept whorl" top rail, a "whorl" being an unseen part of the ear in mankind; see Nos. 92 and 97.

      An obvious but seldom noticed point is that the top rail is a separate piece and is attached to the tops of the two upright posts, or stiles, and to the splat. Who notices that the front of a seat in almost all chairs is wider than the back?

      The words "stiles" and "uprights" are defined in note 3 in section 50.

10.   Occasionally we find chairs of the Chippendale style made with bowed, or flat, or almost flat, top rails, or with some other departure from the Chippendale style. Such variations are generally regarded as having been made in country districts where the influence of style was not so strong as in the cities.

11.   As to cabriole legs see section 24; as to ball and claw feet, see section 25.

12.   But certain special types of chairs, such as those in the Chinese manner, or in the French taste, always had certain kinds of legs which were suitable only for them, as will appear in the illustrations.

that in our country almost all of the chairs in the Chippendale style are found with either one or the other of these two kinds of legs. An extension of the rear ends of the side rails through the tops of the rear legs was often made, especially in Philadelphia, as in chairs in the Queen Anne style, mentioned in section 50, at note 7. Cabriole legs with Dutch, or club, feet were often used in the earlier part of the Chippendale period, as in Nos. 85–88, and sometimes later. Straight legs were first used about 1755, when the Chippendale Gothic designs came into vogue.

An interesting matter in connection with feet is that when Chippendale published his "Directory" in 1754, as mentioned in section 15, an advertisement of it stated that the designs were in "the newest and most fashionable taste"; but not a single ball and claw foot was shown in the volume. This indicates that these feet had passed out of style and were not in "the newest and most fashionable taste" at the time Chippendale's book was published. But nevertheless in England and in our country the ball and claw foot continued to be the favorite for the finer class of chairs. In many instances the ball is not much more than one–half of a sphere, being cut off at the bottom and thus making a flat surface. Ball and claw feet were used only on the front legs, where they could be seen to advantage; on the rear legs the feet were merely the lower parts of the back legs and were known as "stump feet"; these back legs were often in an oval form, especially in chairs made in Philadelphia.[13]

Seats. Curved seat frames were generally used on the chairs in the Queen Anne style, as appears in the illustrations in the previous section; but in the Chippendale period the frames were usually straight on all four sides, although occasionally the front seat rail was curved. This latter rail was sometimes ornamented with a carved shell, and in some chairs a carved ornament appears also on the top rail, or on the tops, or "knees," of the legs, as in Nos. 90 and 92. In some chairs the front seat is curved downward, as in Nos. 137 and 173, making a somewhat more comfortable resting place than the usual flat surface; this kind of seat is called "concave" or "dipped" and is seen also on later chairs, such as the Hepplewhite style chair No. 196. The seat itself was generally what we know as a "slip" seat, which could be lifted out of the frame. A slip seat was held in position by a molding. The molding was either cut in the solid wood of the seat frame, or was a separate piece which was attached to the frame. In many chairs the seat was

(NOTE 12, *continued*)

    Chairs of the same or very similar design, but with different kinds of legs or feet, are often illustrated together in this section for the purpose of showing that no one kind of legs or feet was exclusively used on such chairs.

    The cost of a chair with square straight legs was no doubt much less than the cost of one with cabriole legs and ball and claw feet; and this naturally influenced many customers in giving their orders.

    13. See section 25, note 2, D.

    Mr. Cescinsky, writing in "Antiques," November, 1925, pages 273–274, states that stump feet were abandoned in England in the Queen Anne period and more finished forms were used; and that the stump foot, called the "back leg crudity" was not intended as an economy, but was a deliberate style method which cost about as much as a more finished foot.

attached to the frame by carrying the upholstery down over the rails of the frame and attaching it with round–headed nails; this latter kind of seat is often called a "stitched up" seat. The seats were upholstered with various fabrics, such as silk or velvet or needle–point, and sometimes with horse hair; as to which see section 43, note 7, and also section 53, note 4, D.

Stretchers. These were often used with cabriole legs in the Queen Anne style as shown in the previous section, but only occasionally with those legs in the Chippendale style as in the chairs Nos. 120 and 155. In some cases there was only one stretcher, this connecting the back legs, as in No. 122. When straight legs were used, they were perhaps always joined by stretchers, the front stretcher, however, being "recessed," that is, set back a few inches from the front legs so as to connect the side stretchers instead of the front legs. See also section 26 and note 7 in section 50.

Curve of the back. Nos. 80–81. In the fine chairs in the Queen Anne and Chippendale styles the curves of the backs required the use of much wood. A chair back may appear from the front to be only an inch thick; but looking at the curve of the back from the side it will be seen that the back must have been carved from a piece of wood of much greater thickness. This is shown in the four illustrations Nos. 51, 64, 80 and 81.

In the note[14] are references to several well–illustrated magazine articles in which American chairs in the Chippendale style are considered.

We now begin to examine the illustrations[15] of chairs in the Chippendale style. In presenting these the aim has been to select as many different designs as possible within the limits of our space. Many of the pieces illustrated may be very similar in appearance, but on close inspection they will be found to differ in some respects, either in carving, or the top rail or the splat,[16] or the legs or feet or stretchers or

14. "Pre-Revolutionary Furniture Makers of New York City," by Rita Susswein; "Antiques," January, 1934, pages 6–10, 36.

"A Clue to New York Furniture," by Mr. Homer Eaton Keyes; "Antiques," March, 1932, pages 122–123. See also the issue of April, 1934, page 150.

"A Note on Philadelphia Chairs," by Mr. Homer Eaton Keyes; "Antiques," October, 1932, pages 146–147.

15. The illustrations are small, as the writer thinks the reader will prefer a large number of small illustrations to a small number of large ones. Unfortunately, the smaller the size, the less the clearness of details.

16. The splat is the feature in which the genius of Chippendale is most manifest. The graceful designs of the splats of his chairs constitute the principal charm of his work and are said to be his chief contribution to the art of the chair maker; quoted in part from Mr. Lockwood's "Colonial Furniture," volume 2, page 83.

Quoting further from the same page of Mr. Lockwood's book, it is said that "the chief fault in most of Chippendale's chairs is that the arms and seat rails are not sufficiently good for the back. . . In the Dutch period the seat rails were usually curved, so that the lack of ornamentation was not noticeable, beauty of line compensating for their plainness. On the Chippendale chairs, however, the seat rail was generally straight and, except in the finest specimens, did not sufficiently harmonize with the other portions of the chair, which were often carved."

seat rails or some other detail. These features are interesting and may indicate the place of origin of the chairs, whether New England or Pennsylvania or elsewhere; but the question of origin is not fully considered in this book for amateurs, as is mentioned in section 1 at note 5. In examining these illustrations it should be realized that the designs of the back and the splat are the principal features of a chair, although the legs and feet and other parts are not to be overlooked.

The illustrations are here arranged in seven groups; not, however, in the exact chronological order in which the various styles began to be in fashion in England. Nos. 80 and 81 are mentioned above.

1. The first group, Nos. 82–84, shows a transition from a popular American type of the Queen Anne style to the Chippendale style; this group has a splat, either solid or pierced, not extending down to the seat.

2. In the second group, Nos. 85–93, the splat is solid and extends to the seat.

3. The Chippendale Gothic style; Nos. 94–117.

4. The "Interlaced splat" style; Nos. 118–138.

5. Miscellaneous chairs; one with "ribband" designs; others in designs suggested by articles of Chinese origin; and others in designs which cannot well be classified. Nos. 139–162.

6. "Vertically–pierced splat" chairs; in these the splat is cut in vertical, not in curved, piercings. This type best shows the transition from the Chippendale style to the Hepplewhite style. Nos. 163–168.

7. The Chippendale–Hepplewhite transition chairs. Nos. 169–180.

1. Transition chairs; Queen Anne to Chippendale style. Nos. 82–84 show perhaps the earliest type of our chairs which may properly be called "Chippendale style" chairs.[17] They are in fact "transition" chairs, being mainly of the Queen Anne style, but with the Chippendale cupid's–bow top rail, which places them in the Chippendale style as mentioned above in this section under the heading "Top rail." In these three chairs the splat does not extend down to the seat, but is supported by a cross–rail, as in the chairs Nos. 41–43, which they resemble except as to the top rail. These three chairs are plain, but are interesting, as they show how the chairs changed from one style to another.

In No. 82 the stretchers and legs are "turned," and the feet are of the Dutch style called "Dutch," or "club," feet, as in the Queen Anne style chairs. The splat

17.   These chairs, which have a new style of top rail and are in the process of change from the Queen Anne style to the Chippendale style, are generally called "Chippendale style chairs"; they take the name of the style into which they were changing. But when the Chippendale style chairs began to take the Hepplewhite form, using the Hepplewhite style top rail, they did not take the name of "Hepplewhite style chairs," into which they were changing. They are known as "Chippendale–Hepplewhite transition chairs," as will appear in the text at the end of this section.

The transition from the cane chairs style to the Queen Anne style is shown in Nos. 41–43. For other "transitions" see the Index under that word.

See the comment on No. 168 in regard to the rule that the date of the latest style appearing in an article determines the earliest possible date of the article.

is not pierced, but is solid, as in most of those chairs. The cupid's–bow top rail is in a plain form. See also the corner chair No. 426. About 1740–1760.

In No. 83 the legs are square and straight. The splat is pierced in a design which seems to be an early form of that in No. 147. Here the curves of the top rail are more fully developed than in the preceding chair. About 1740–1760.

In No. 84 the top rail is fully developed in the cupid's–bow form; the splat is about the same as those in the later chairs Nos. 155–157. About 1740–1760.

2. Solid splat extending to the seat. This group consists of nine chairs, Nos. 85–93, in which the splat is solid, not pierced, and extends to the seat and does not rest upon a cross rail. The chairs with this type of splat are shown together merely for convenience, not as forming a separate class of chairs. Although the solid splat was a characteristic feature of the Queen Anne style, as shown in the previous section, it continued to be used in these Chippendale style chairs for years after the pierced splats became the fashion, even, it is said, until about 1760, perhaps because the solid splats were less expensive and less breakable than the pierced splats. The names "vase–back" and "fiddle–back" are applied to these splats as well as to the similar splats in the Queen Anne style chairs mentioned in section 50 at note 6.

In each of these nine chairs the top rail indicates the Chippendale style. All the front legs are cabriole in form except those in the arm chair No. 93 which are square and straight; and all have some form of Dutch feet except Nos. 91 and 92 which have ball and claw feet, and No. 93. The dates here given are merely approximate.

In No. 85 the top rail is a variation of the rounded end top rail, as is also the similar top rail in No. 91. The splat is in a form frequently seen in these chairs. The seat is straight and the bottom of the front rail is cut into for an inch or more, making what is sometimes called a "flat arch," often seen on highboys and lowboys. The feet are of the Dutch, or club, type. About 1750–1760.

In No. 86 the cupid's–bow top rail is seen in a variation of the usual form, the central portion being concave instead of convex. Here the seat is rounded at the front corners as in the Queen Anne style, and the three stretchers are flat and curved as in the Queen Anne style chairs Nos. 51 and 63. About 1750–1760.

In No. 87 the cupid's–bow top rail is seen in its more developed form, with a convex curve in the centre, here ornamented with a carved shell. The front seat rail is cut in curves somewhat similar to those on highboys and lowboys of the period, as in No. 645. About 1750–1760.

No. 88 is similar to the preceding chair in general appearance. The front seat rail is cut in cyma curves.[18] The width of the two stiles[19] decreases from the seat

18. As to cyma curves, see section 23.

19. The unfamiliar word "stile" was explained in note 3 in section 50 as follows: A stile and a back leg together form one upright piece of wood. The stile is the part above the leg. Stiles are also known as "uprights," meaning the rails which extend up from the back leg and are braced together at the top by the top rail. They almost disappeared in the chairs of Hepplewhite but are seen again in those of Sheraton and in later styles.

80 (UPPER) MR. JOHN C. TOLAND. 81 (UPPER) MISS HELEN H. CAREY. 82 (UPPER) HAMMOND-HARWOOD
83 (CENTRE) DR. JAMES BORDLEY, JR. 84 (CENTRE) MR. & MRS. H. L. DUER.   HOUSE.
86 (LOWER) DR. CLAPHAM PENNING- 87 (LOWER) MR. C. E. SNYDER.   85 (CENTRE) MR. J. F. H. MAGINN.
        TON.   88 (LOWER) MRS. JOHN S. GIBBS, JR.

to the top rail, as may also be noticed in other chairs. The "ears" at the ends of the top rail are well seen; see note 9 in this section. About 1750–1760.

No. 89 resembles the preceding chair in most of its features, but has a "flat arch" in the front rail of the seat as in No. 85. A carved design is on the top rail, and the splat is in a vase design. About 1750–1760.

No. 90 is finely carved with four shells, one on the top rail, one on the seat rail and two on the knees of the wide–spread legs. The feet are of the "three–toed" type shown in illustration No. 11, figure 11, in section 25. About 1760–1770.

In No. 91, a sturdy arm chair in the Chippendale style, the large plain splat is in the same form as that of No. 66 in the Queen Anne style. Other examples may be seen of splats which, like this one, were first used on chairs in the Queen Anne style, and were later used on chairs in the Chippendale style. About 1760–1780.

In No. 92, a side chair, and No. 93, an arm chair, the splats are about the same in design, indicating that a particular type of splat did not require a particular type of chair. In No. 92 the "ears" of the top rail are in a spiral form as described in note 9 in this section; carvings are on the top rail and the seat rail; and the front legs are wide apart, as in No. 90. About 1760–1780.

In No. 93 the top rail is in the plain form seen on Nos. 82 and 83; the legs are straight, but have not the stretchers which were generally used with straight legs. The arms are in the same shape as those on No. 154. About 1760–1780.

3. The Chippendale Gothic style; Nos. 94–117. About the year 1750 the Gothic architectural style was revived in England and was applied to architecture and furniture; and this revival led Chippendale and other cabinet makers to design and make chairs and other furniture "after the Gothic manner," as the expression is in his book, the "Director."[20]

In the illustrations of this type of chairs it is not easy to recognize the Gothic style as it appears in the great cathedrals of Europe.[21] The pointed Gothic arch in the splats is the principal feature showing any connection with the Gothic architectural style. Chairs with this arch were favorites in our country, and were made in considerable numbers throughout the Chippendale period, about 1755–1785. Good examples of this arch are in chairs such as No. 94, in which the top of the arch is attached to the centre of the top rail; here the arch is more easily seen than in many chairs in which the splat is crowded with other pieces used either for ornamental purposes or because they are needed to make the splat strong.

---

20.   As to this book see "The Chippendale style," section 15.

21.   The early Chippendale Gothic style chairs resembled the Gothic style much more clearly than the later ones which are shown in this section; but the early chairs were not popular in England and were apparently not made in our country and are not illustrated here.

Another revival of the Gothic style in furniture, including chairs, took place in England about the year 1825; and in our country a few years later a number of "Gothic" chairs were made, such as Nos. 355–357; see also the Gothic arches in the bureau No. 767. The Gothic style in other articles of furniture is referred to in the Index.

In his "English Furniture," volume 2, page 224, Mr. Cescinsky remarks that in the architectural work of the Gothic revival "the result can only be called Gothic by an excess of courtesy."

89 (Upper) Miss Mary D. Davis.   90 (Upper) Mrs. Miles White, Jr.   91 (Upper) Mrs. Miles White, Jr.
92 (Centre) Mrs. Miles White, Jr.   93 (Centre) Dr. M. A. Abrams.   94 (Centre) Mrs. Wm. M. Roberts.
95 (Lower) Hammond-Harwood   96 (Lower) Mr. John C. Toland.   97 (Lower) Mr. Albert G. Towers
          House.

147

Another feature of the Gothic style generally appearing in the splat is a "quatrefoil," which may be non–technically described as a four–part ornamental tracery used in Gothic architecture in windows. A "trefoil" is a three–part opening of a similar kind. The presence of a quatrefoil or a trefoil makes a chair a Gothic style chair even without a Gothic arch, as in No. 115. These graceful openings add much to the interest of a chair, although they are merely variations of the Gothic form and are seldom correct in an architectural sense. The lower openings in the splat of No. 114 is a good example of a quatrefoil.

Examining the twenty–four illustrations of these Gothic chairs, Nos. 94–117, we begin with Nos. 94–96, in each of which the Gothic arch is easily seen, being formed by curving the upper ends of the outer upright bars of the splat inward to a point in the centre of the bottom of the top rail, where they unite. The other parts are needed to strengthen the splat, and in doing so, they form smaller or subsidiary arches. Near the bottom of the splat is an opening supposed to represent a "quatrefoil."

Nos. 94 and 95 seem to be almost exactly the same in shape, but are different in appearance and quality[22] for the reason that No. 94 is not ornamented with carving, but No. 95 is carved on the top rail and legs, and its stiles are grooved. Both have cabriole legs with ball and claw feet. About 1760–1780.

No. 96, an arm chair, has straight legs with the straight stretchers which usually accompany such legs; and the arms are similar to those in No. 165 and others. About 1760–1780.

Nos. 97–99 are similar in having the sides of the splat cut in three concave curves, a feature which has no special significance. This kind of chair is said to have been very popular. No. 97 has cabriole legs and ball and claw feet. The "ears" at the ends of the top rail are of the same type as those in No. 92. The "quatrefoil" differs somewhat from that in the three preceding Gothic chairs, and is equally far from the correct architectural designs. About 1760–1780.

Nos. 98 and 99 have straight legs with the usual straight stretchers. Incidentally we notice that of the nine Gothic style chairs on the page containing the illustrations of these chairs all except No. 105 have straight legs and stretchers— an indication of the general usage. The Gothic arches are not as conspicuous as in the preceding chairs. About 1760–1780.

No. 100 has a graceful and too delicate splat. The carving on the top rail and the lines of beaded decoration on the outer edge of the front legs are not well seen in the engraving. This chair is probably of English make. About 1760–1780.

Nos. 101 and 102 have two concave curves on the sides of the splat. No. 101 has a historical interest which is mentioned in the note.[23] The Gothic arch is not

22.   In regard to "quality" see the comments on the chairs Nos. 116–117.

23.   This chair belongs to the Maryland Historical Society, Baltimore. On a plate on the top rail it is stated that the chair was the property of Charles Carroll of Carrollton, one of the Maryland Signers of the Declaration of Independence. See also the note to No. 173.

98 (UPPER) MR. J. G. D'A. PAUL.   99 (UPPER) DR. JAMES BORDLEY, JR.   100 (UPPER) MRS. T. J. LINDSAY.
101 (CENTRE) MD. HISTORICAL SOC.   102 (CENTRE) MR. ARTHUR E. COLE.   103 (CENTRE) MR. JOHN E. CAREY.
104 (LOWER) DR. JAMES BORDLEY, JR. 105 (LOWER) MR. ALBERT G. TOWERS.   106 (LOWER) MRS. PAUL H. MILLER.

as prominent in the splat as in some other chairs, but the "quatrefoil" is conspicuous at the base. About 1760–1780.

In No. 102 the carving and the beading on the top rail do not clearly appear in the illustration, but the Gothic arch and the two "quatrefoils" are conspicuous. Two fretwork brackets will be seen at the junctions of the front seat rail and the legs, a form of ornamentation frequently used in the Chippendale period, and seen on the chairs Nos. 106, 133 and others. About 1760–1780.

In Nos. 103–108 another form of Gothic arch splat is shown in which the upper curved part is much wider than the lower part. In No. 103 the base of the splat is pierced in an unusual curve and the top rail is of a plain character. No. 104 is daintily carved both on the top rail and the splat, and the latter is also decorated with beading at the edges; the "quatrefoil" in the base of the splat encloses a small pointed design. No. 105 is also a fine chair, with cabriole legs and ball and claw feet, a beaded and carved top rail and grooved stiles. About 1760–1780.

In Nos. 106–108 the arch is regarded as merely suggestive of the Gothic form. Perhaps these three chairs should appear in the next group, in which the "interlaced splat" chairs are shown; but the presence of the so-called "quatrefoil" seems to entitle them to a place with Gothic chairs. These three chairs have straight legs; Nos. 106 and 107 have "cupid's–bow" top rails, but No. 108 has an almost rounded one. About 1760–1780.

Nos. 106 and 107 have almost identical splats, top rails, stiles and ears, with well carved designs throughout. No. 106 has fretwork brackets with a straight front seat rail; No. 107 has a curved seat rail with a "stitched up" seat, and its front legs are ornamented with reeding and carved beads not visible in the engraving. The arm chair No. 108 has a splat of the same general design, and arms said to be characteristic of the finer chairs of the period of about 1755 in England.[24] About 1760–1780.

Still another form of Gothic chair is seen in Nos. 109 and 110. In these the splats are divided into upper and lower arches. In No. 109 there are three narrow arches above and two below, and the legs are square, with stretchers. In No. 110 there are three narrow arches in both the upper and lower portions; the legs are cabriole with ball and claw feet, and the seat is "stitched up"; this may be an English chair. In each the small Gothic arches are conspicuous, but the quatrefoils appear only in No. 110. About 1760–1780.

No. 111 has an elaborate splat with four long and narrow arched openings in the centre and numerous other arches above and below, forming an elegant and delicate piece of workmanship. The scrolled front seat rail and the small front stretcher may be modern. About 1760–1780.

Four other Gothic chairs, of different types, Nos. 112–115, compose another group. No. 112 is interesting in having in the upper part of the splat three curved

24. In Mr. Cescinsky's "English Furniture," volume 2, figure 246, a Gothic arch chair is shown with arms apparently the same as those in No. 108.

107 (Upper) Mr. Albert G. Towers. 108 (Upper) Dr. James Bordley, Jr. 109 (Upper) Coll. of Mrs. J.
110 (Centre) Mrs. T. J. Lindsay.   111 (Centre) Miss Agnes Walton.   Stabler.
113 (Lower) Mr. E. G. Miller, Jr. 114 (Lower) Dr. M. A. Abrams.   112 (Centre) Mr. Albert G. Towers.
                                                                         115 (Lower) Dr. H. M. Fitzhugh.

151

designs suggestive of a Gothic window; and if a fourth similar curved design were attached under these, there would be a fairly accurate "quatrefoil." The splat, the top rail and the outer edges of the stiles are all decorated with dainty carving.[25] No. 113 has an unusual type of splat, in the upper part of which an arch is seen; and two pointed designs, called "pinnacles" by Mr. Cescinsky, are in small arches in the base of the splat. In No. 114 there is one large arch within which there are three narrow ones. The small "quatrefoil" in this splat, showing the four sections, is perhaps nearer to the true Gothic design than any other seen in the illustrations.

No. 115 is the only one of the Gothic chairs here shown which does not have an arch, its character as Gothic resting chiefly upon two openings in the splat, the lower one, and perhaps the upper one also, being suggestive of a "quatrefoil." The knees are carved with a distinctive design seldom seen in our country, known as a "cabochon," which is an oval convex surface surrounded by ornamentation.[26] Two non–conclusive indications of Philadelphia origin are seen in the extension of the two ends of the seat rails through the rear legs, and the oval or rounded shape of these legs.[27]

The series of Chippendale style chairs "in the Gothic manner" closes with two chairs, Nos. 116 and 117, which were sold at auction[28] in New York in April, 1929. These are two of a group of six chairs believed to have been made about the year 1770, by Benjamin Randolph, of Philadelphia, whose label is shown as illustration No. 1 in this book. They are known as "Sample Chairs," and were probably made as advertisements of his skill and as models for other pieces of fine work. In each splat will be seen the familiar arch and quatrefoil. It will be noticed that the front feet of these two chairs are different from the feet on any of the chairs thus far illustrated. They are known as "French scrolled" feet, which were used by Chippendale and Hepplewhite on the chairs made by them in what they called the "French manner." In addition to the type of feet, these chairs differ from other fine Chippendale style Gothic chairs chiefly in the amount and character of carving which they display; in fact, the fine carving seems to furnish

25.   A chair similar to this appears in Mr. Lockwood's "Colonial Furniture," volume 2, figure 568, and a companion piece arm chair is on page 305 of the same volume.

26.   In Mr. Lockwood's "Colonial Furniture," volume 2, page 94, figure 558, is an illustration of a chair which is almost a duplicate of No. 115, and also of a label attached to the chair, bearing the name of James Gillingham, of Philadelphia. It is there said that the design of the chair is shown in Chippendale's "Director," third edition, plate 10, indicating that the book was used in Philadelphia.

In Mr. Cescinsky's "English Furniture," volume 2, pages 76–102, is a chapter entitled "The Cabochon–and–leaf Period, 1735–50." See section 14, note 5. The word "cabochon" is also applied, with a similar meaning, to a form of cutting precious stones.

27.   See these points mentioned in section 50, at note 7, and in this section at notes 12 and 13.

28.   At the auction sale of the Reifsnyder collection the chair No. 116 brought $15,000 and No. 117 brought $9,500. The chairs were illustrated in the newspapers on account of these prices. They have also been the subject of numerous articles in the magazines, as in "Antiques," November, 1925, page 273; May, 1927, page 366.

Another of the "sample" chairs was a "wing" chair which brought $33,000 at the auction sale; this is shown in this chapter as No. 406; see also note 2 in this section.

See section 175 for advice on buying.

their "quality,"[29] which is the main element of their great value. In form and in proportions these two chairs do not seem to be notably superior to certain other chairs of the Gothic type, such as No. 112 and perhaps others.

4. The "Interlaced splat" style; Nos. 118–138. A favorite form of splat of the Chippendale style is known as the "interlaced splat," of which there are many examples. Some of these are very pleasing, the parts twining in and around each other in graceful curves. In the comments on the illustrations we will not dwell particularly upon the details of the splat but will call attention to the more im-

116 (LEFT) ANONYMOUS.   117 (RIGHT) ANONYMOUS.

portant features of each chair as a whole. In these chairs the top rail is either in the "cupid's–bow" rail or the "rounded end" rail; and the legs and feet are either the cabriole leg with the Dutch, or club, foot, the cabriole leg with ball and claw foot or the straight square leg. As in other chairs in the Chippendale style, the kind of top rail and the kind of leg and foot seem to be whatever the cabinet maker or his customer preferred, the latter being influenced no doubt by the cost in many cases.

The form of the interlaced splat in Nos. 118 and 119 was used in England[30] as far back as 1730, and appears in the Queen Anne style chair No. 69. In the

29. "Quality" is defined by the Century Dictionary as "a distinguished and characteristic excellence or superiority."

30. Three illustrations are in Mr. Cescinsky's "English Furniture," volume 2.

(*Note 30 is continued on page 154.*)

hands of our cabinet makers working in the Chippendale style with the cupid's–bow top rail, these chairs take on a fine appearance, although some of the backs seem to be too high. We may assume that the large heart in the lower part of the splat of No. 118 indicates a full–brown romance; but the implication of the small one at the top is not obvious. It is said that the two carved shells on No. 118, one on the top rail and the other on the front seat rail, indicate a Philadelphia origin or influence as does also an unusually high back. About 1760–1780.

The designs of the interlaced splats of the nine chairs Nos. 120–128, although not all exactly the same, were evidently derived from the same source as those in the Queen Anne style chair No. 67. In these nine chairs we see three kinds of legs and feet, namely, cabriole legs with Dutch, or club, feet with and without stretchers; cabriole legs with ball and claw feet with and without a stretcher; and straight legs with stretchers; but it so happens that there is no variety in the form of the top rail, as each one is a "cupid's–bow" rail. Similar splats are in the corner chairs Nos. 431, 438, 439.

Nos. 120 and 121 have certain variations in the top rail, and the former has four stretchers of the type seen in No. 50. In these two chairs the cabriole legs terminate in Dutch, or club, feet. About 1760–1780.

No. 122 is an arm chair with ball and claw feet and a single stretcher between the rear legs, as in the Queen Anne style side chair No. 65 and others. The arms are of the same type as in Nos. 111 and 126. About 1760–1780.

No. 123 is notable for the reason that it is a walnut chair, not mahogany, a very unusual example of the employment of walnut in a fine chair in the period of Chippendale. The legs are carved on the knees. The top rail is ornamented with two horizontal cords and tassels, not well seen in the illustration, somewhat similar to those in the centre of the splat in No. 128. The chair descended to the present owner from ancestors in Philadelphia. See section 6, note 3. About 1760–1780.

In No. 124, in the centre of the interlaced splat, an additional ornament appears, said to resemble "a diamond caught among the scrolls" and also referred to as an "entwining design." The seat is "stitched up" and the four legs are unusually slender. About 1760–1780.

Nos. 125 and 126 are apparently companion pieces and are the property of one owner. The interlaced upper portions of the splats have lost some of their usual graceful forms by reason of the treatment of the outer curves. The relative

(NOTE 30, *continued from page 153.*)

An illustrated article on interlaced splat chairs is in "Antiques," March, 1929, pages 213–215, by Mr. Edward Warwick. In a note to this article reference is made to a difference between the designs of the English, the New England and the Philadelphia cabinet makers. In the English chairs the splat consists of two parts, one being the interlaced part above and the other the supporting part below, as in Nos. 120 and 124. The New England chairs are generally similar. In the Philadelphia chairs the interlaced portion seems to unite with the lower part as one piece, as in Nos. 121, 123 and others. See also Nos. 155–157 and 208–210.

Other illustrated articles on the subject in the same magazine are in March, 1932, pages 122–123, and October, 1932, pages 146–147.

118 (Upper) Mr. John C. Toland. 119 (Upper) Mr. John C. Toland. 120 (Upper) Dr. James Bordley, Jr.
121 (Centre) Mr. W. W. Lanahan. 122 (Centre) Mr. W. W. Lanahan. 123 (Centre) Mr. Wm. M. Ellicott
124 (Lower) Mr. Albert G. Towers. 125 (Lower) Mrs. Arthur Hale. 126 (Lower) Mrs. Arthur Hale.

sizes of an arm chair and a side chair are well seen here. The centres of the top rails and the knees of the legs are carved. About 1760–1780.

In No. 127 the interlaced splat is about the same in form as in several of the splats mentioned above, and the top rail is similar to that in No. 122; but it is the only chair of this type shown here in which the legs are straight, and in which there are four stretchers. We have now seen this form of interlaced splat with several styles of legs and feet. About 1760–1780.

No. 128 is a handsome chair very similar in form to No. 123. Here there is fine carving over the entire top rail and on the splat, on the legs and knees, on the front and side seat rails, and also above the knees, the latter an unusual feature. In the centre of the splat is a carved ribbon and tassel. The stiles, that is, the two upright posts of the back, are fluted. The bottom of the front seat rail has a molding. A very similar chair is No. 548 in Mr. Lockwood's "Colonial Furniture," in which he states that the chair "represents one of the best types found in this country." About 1760–1780.

In the next four chairs, Nos. 129–132, another pleasing type of interlaced splat is shown, having two concave curves on each side. This design appears, without a descriptive name, in Mr. Cescinsky's "English Furniture," figure 254, and in Mr. Lockwood's "Colonial Furniture," volume 2, page 306, dated about 1760. These may be compared with other splats having similar curves, as Nos. 101–102, and Nos. 161–162.

The two side chairs, Nos. 129 and 130, are almost the same in outline, and they are examples of what has been illustrated before, as in Nos. 94 and 95, namely, the same or a similar chair in a plain form and also in a more decorative form. No. 129 is not ornamented, but in No. 130 carving may be seen on the splat and the stiles are grooved. About 1760–1780.

In the two arm chairs Nos. 131 and 132 other differences of decorative treatment are noticed. No. 131 has carving and ball and claw feet; No. 132 is a plainer piece of more capacious size and with elongated "ears," as mentioned in note 9 in this section. This latter chair is an inherited piece belonging to a family which has owned and occupied the same large estate near Baltimore since about the year 1740. About 1760–1780.

In the next three chairs, Nos. 133–135, the interlaced splats are in elaborate and harmonious designs. No. 133, a side chair, and No. 134, an arm chair, are companion pieces, with finely carved top rails and with fretwork brackets at the junctions of the front legs and the front rail. No. 135, a side chair, is almost equally elaborate. On all three the legs are plain and straight and the four stretchers are necessarily of similar character. The cord and tassel in the innermost centre of the splat of Nos. 133 and 134 will be noticed, as in No. 128. These highly ornamental chairs may have been made in England or in the South from English designs.[31] About 1760–1770.

31.   Nos. 134 and 135 are illustrated by Mr. Lockwood in his "Colonial Furniture in America," volume 2, pages 305 and 306. On page 303 he remarks that it is "difficult to tell whether this chair (No. 134) was made in the South, or was imported when new from England."

(*Note 31 is continued on page 158.*)

127 (Upper) Dr. James Bordley, Jr.   128 (Upper) Miss H. H. Carey.   129 (Upper) Mr. Wm. M. Ellicott.
130 (Centre) Mrs. Miles White, Jr.   131 (Centre) Mr. John C. Toland.   132 (Centre) Family of Thos. C.
133 (Lower) Mrs. Miles White, Jr.   134 (Lower) Mrs. Miles White, Jr.   Cradock.
                                                                    135 (Lower) Mrs. Miles White, Jr.

Nos. 136–138 are the last of this group of Chippendale style chairs with inter-laced splats. The first two, Nos. 136–137, have very similar and graceful splats. No. 136 was also shown as No. 74, illustrating a top rail with rounded ends. Its legs were cut off a few inches in order to make it comfortable for a short member of the owner's family.[32] About 1760–1780.

In the design of its splat, No. 137 follows closely an English model which was popular in England, as shown in Mr. Cescinsky's "English Furniture," volume 2, figure 170. At the bottom of the oval opening under the centre of the top rail the small lines represent the Grecian honeysuckle called "anthemion," described in note 48, which was widely used on various articles of furniture, including chair No. 179 and others. The concave seat will be noticed. About 1760–1780.

In No. 138 the outline of the splat as a whole is in the vase form but the vase is not so well seen as in the solid splats in "vase–back" chairs, mentioned in section 50 at note 6. Two nearly oval forms, not purposely making the figure 8, are designs of two or three or four ovals, one above the other, which may be seen on fine English chairs, as in Mr. Cescinsky's "English Furniture," volume 2, No. 182. At the centre of the top rail is an opening "cut out." About 1760–1780.

In concluding these interlaced splat chairs it may be noted that several chairs made "after the Gothic manner" also have splats which might be regarded as interlaced, as mentioned in referring to the Gothic chairs Nos. 106–108.

5. Miscellaneous chairs; Nos. 139–162. Chippendale seems to have made his most elaborate chairs in the early part of his career, perhaps because he was then struggling to attract attention. An especially elegant kind of chair is that which he, in his book, the "Director," termed his "Ribband–Back" chairs. These are the rarest of his chairs, and are very elegant and expensive. Only a few genuine ones are now known, but numerous reproductions have been made. None of this type were made in our country so far as it is known.

No. 139 is a celebrated English ribband–back chair which is shown here because it is one of the most elaborate of the authenticated chairs of Chippendale. It is said that this chair was made by Chippendale himself, following his design in the "Director," and it has often been illustrated in the books. The "ribband" extends from the upper part of the splat to the seat rail, interlacing itself and giving the appearance of being tied with the cord from which the tassel is sus-pended. About 1755–1760.

(NOTE 31, *continued from page 156.*)

On page 304 Mr. Lockwood states that the chairs shown in this book as Nos. 130, 134 and 135 "illustrate the best of the Chippendale chairs found in the South from Colonial times, and should be compared with the Philadelphia chairs" shown in the chapter on chairs in his book.

Observing the very ornate and elaborate backs of these chairs and the plain legs and stretchers, we may refer to the remarks of Mr. Lockwood quoted in note 16 in this section and apply them to the legs and stretchers of these chairs—that is, the legs and stretchers "are not sufficiently good for the back."

32.   Chairs with short legs, purposely made short, are desirable; they are sometimes called "slipper chairs"; and chairs whose legs of normal length have been shortened sometimes are called, and pass as, "slipper chairs." If there are stretchers, as here, their distance from the floor may indicate the original length of the legs.

136 (Upper) Miss Harriett R. Chew.
139 (Lower) Anonymous.

137 (Upper) Mr. John C. Toland.
140 (Lower) Metropolitan Museum.

138 (Upper) Hammond-Harwood House.
141 (Lower) Victoria & Albert Museum.

The Chinese Chippendale style of chair is said to be one of the earliest developed by Chippendale, having been adopted by him a few years after the craze for Chinese designs began in England.[33] In the first edition of his volume, the "Director," published in 1754, he included designs for them and referred to them as being "after the Chinese manner"; by this he evidently did not mean that the chairs were copied from those made in China, but that the "Chinese manner" served as a suggestion for chairs which he could make for his patrons. Some chairs with Chinese features may have been made in our country,[34] but those found here were apparently made in England or were bamboo chairs of about 1800.

The illustrations Nos. 140 and 141 show the principal features of these chairs. Although cabriole legs and ball and claw feet are characteristics of Chinese furniture,[35] they here give place to straight legs, often pierced and fretted and with a bracket at the junctions of the legs and seat rails. In No. 140 the legs are formed of three columns in a cluster; in No. 141 the legs are straight and fretted. The splat, which in its many fine designs is the principal feature of the Chippendale style, was omitted, and its place is taken by fanciful forms of lattice work. About 1755–1760.

The so–called Chinese style of Chippendale was applied to other articles of furniture, several of which are illustrated in this book. The resemblance of these articles to the real Chinese forms is not supposed to be exact. Among the Chinese features in various articles are figures of Buddha, Chinese people in native costume and Chinese buildings.[36]

Chippendale chairs in the French style. These chairs are merely mentioned here, not illustrated, as they were very seldom made in America and only a very few have been found here. The designs of the backs were in many cases about the same as those used on other chairs in the Chippendale style, and the legs were generally cabriole; the principal French feature consisted of the scrolled French feet, examples of which are on the two American chairs Nos. 116 and 117. An

33.   The vogue of the Chinese style prevailed in England from about 1750 to 1765. In England a publication in 1757 by Sir William Chambers, who had travelled in China and had studied its arts and architecture, exercised a great influence upon English architecture and furniture.

34.   In volume 1 of "The Arts and Crafts in Philadelphia, Maryland and South Carolina," (as to which see section 45, note 5, A), page 169, is an advertisement of Peter Hall, "cabinet maker from London," in the South Carolina Gazette of December 19, 1761, stating that "gentlemen and ladies of taste may have made, and be supplied with, Chinese tables of all sorts, shelves, trays, chimney pieces, brackets, etc., being at present the most elegant and admired fashion in London." On page 187 is an advertisement of Thomas Woodin in the same newspaper of June 29, 1767, of "Chinese bamboo tea tables . . all London make."

As to bamboo furniture, see the Index, "Bamboo."

In Mr. Lockwood's "Colonial Furniture," volume 2, page 100, reference is made to John Briner, a cabinet maker at New York in 1762, who advertised that he made "Gothic and Chinese chairs." In the same volume are illustrations of four chairs in the Chinese manner, Nos. 571–574.

In the label of Benjamin Randolph, of Philadelphia, which is shown in illustration No. 1 and was made about 1770, Randolph states that he "makes all sorts of cabinet and chairwork . . performed in the Chinese and modern tastes."

35.   See sections 24 and 25 in which cabriole legs and ball and claw feet are considered.

36.   See the Index, "Chinese style."

142 (Upper) Mr. Lennox Birckhead.   143 (Upper) Mr. L. Birckhead.   144 (Upper) Mr. & Mrs. H. L. Duer.
145 (Centre) Mr. & Mrs. H. L. Duer.   146 (Centre) Mr. John C. Toland.   147 (Centre) Mrs. Miles White, Jr.
148 (Lower) Dr. M. A. Abrams.   149 (Lower) Hammond-Harwood   150 (Lower) Mrs. Thos. J. Packard.
House.

elaborately carved English chair in this style is illustrated in Mr. Lockwood's "Colonial Furniture," volume 2, No. 556, where it is said that this chair is "the best chair that has been found in this country and was probably made by Chippendale and imported."

The following "miscellaneous chairs" in this group are in the Chippendale style, as appears from the top rails, but the splats are so different from others that they seem to require a separate classification; but perhaps some of the illustrations should have been in the preceding groups. These chairs are arranged merely according to the general appearance of the splats.

In the side chair No. 142 and the arm chair No. 143 the splats are solid and are in the usual "vase–back" shape. The unusual features are that about one–half of each splat is covered with carvings, and that an oval opening is cut in the lower part of each splat. This method of decoration seems to be a survival of the designs in certain chairs in the Queen Anne style shown in Mr. Cescinsky's "English Furniture," volume 2, in figures 35–41. In the style of about 1750–1760.

In No. 144 the splat is of an unusual type and is almost entirely solid. On the upper portion a cord and tassel are carved on the surface, not pierced through it. The top rail and the arched cresting are fully carved as are also the knees of the legs and the seat rail. This chair, which is probably English, should be compared with No. 128, and also with figure 575 in volume 2 of Mr. Lockwood's "Colonial Furniture." About 1760–1780.

The design of the splats in the seven Chippendale style chairs, Nos. 145–151, is said to be somewhat unusual[37] in our country. The splats have a certain similarity, the upper portion generally being pierced vertically, the slender upright bars resting upon a base which in some cases is almost solid. The piercings of the bases are in several designs. In all of these chairs the top rails are in the usual forms. The legs are either in the cabriole or the straight form, the cabriole legs terminating in ball and claw feet.

In No. 145, a side chair, and No. 146, an arm chair, the upright bars rest upon almost solid bases which are rendered somewhat pleasing by pierced openings. In No. 145 the seat rail is curved, as in several other chairs, such as Nos. 65 and 148, and the top rail and other parts are carved. In No. 146 the upright bars are connected and strengthened by a horizontal "tie," as also in No. 165 and others. About 1760–1780.

The other five chairs of this type, Nos. 147–151, differ in the details of the splats, but need no special descriptions. In No. 147 the Chippendale style top rail is concave in the centre, as also seen on No. 86. In No. 148 the base is ornamented by a cut–out design and the front seat rail is curved. In Nos. 149 and 150 the bases are more fully pierced, and in No. 151, a fine arm chair, the bars in the splat are numerous and delicate. About 1760–1780.

---

37.   Little attention is given in the books to chairs of this type. In Cescinsky and Hunter's "English and American Furniture," page 123, an English example is shown in which the splat is in much the same form as in No. 145. In Mr. Wallace Nutting's "Furniture Treasury," volume 2, an example appears in No. 2200.

In illustration No. 83 an earlier splat of the same type is seen.

151 (Upper) Mr. Arthur E. Cole.
154 (Centre) Mr. Blanchard
    Randall.
157 (Lower) Dr. M. A. Abrams.

152 (Upper) Mr. & Mrs. E. H.
    McKeon.
155 (Centre) Judge F. N. Parke.
158 (Lower) Mr. John C. Toland.

153 (Upper) Mr. Wm. M. Ellicott.
156 (Centre) Mr. Albert G.
    Towers
159 (Lower) Mrs. Miles White, Jr.

In Nos. 152–154 a certain similarity in the outlines of the splats may be seen. In the upper part there is an unusual space which is not ornamented. In these chairs the different types of legs and feet are seen together. No. 152 has cabriole legs with Dutch, or club, feet and turned stretchers; No. 153 has cabriole legs with ball and claw feet with no stretchers; No. 154 has straight legs and feet with plain stretchers. In No. 153 two carved shells are seen, as in No. 118. No. 154 has a straight top piece, probably indicating the work of a country cabinet maker. Similar splats are in the corner chairs Nos. 427 and 433. About 1750–1780.

In Nos. 155–157 the splats are merely suggestive of those of the interlaced[38] Chippendale style chairs Nos. 118 and 119, but are of about the same design as that seen in the earlier transition style chair No. 84. These three chairs have certain differences, as Nos. 152–154 have; No. 155 has cabriole legs with ball and claw feet and turned stretchers; No. 156 has the same kind of legs and feet but no stretchers; No. 157 has straight legs and stretchers—all being in good styles of the period. In Mr. Lockwood's "Colonial Furniture," volume 2, figure 551, there is an illustration of a similar chair with cabriole legs and Dutch, or club, feet. Nos. 155–157 are often called "Salem" chairs; see "Antiques," December, 1934, page 241.

Five chairs of different designs, Nos. 158–162, are next illustrated. No. 158 is a handsome arm chair, with a finely carved top rail and with fretwork brackets under the seat rail which has a carved edge. The stiles, or uprights, are grooved, the splat is ornamented with a tassel, the vertical bars are connected by three small balls and the arms are similar to those in No. 131. About 1760–1780.

No. 159 has a pleasing splat, ornamented with three round openings with beaded edges, the upper one surrounded by a carved wreath; the top rail, however, is plain. About 1760–1780.

In No. 160 the splat is similar to that in No. 178, the rounded frame at the top of each splat containing a conventional design of the Grecian honeysuckle called "anthemion," a design which will be seen in connection with other articles, and which is regarded as typical of splats in the Hepplewhite style.[39] See note 48 in this section. In this chair and No. 178 the anthemion is in an "inverted" position, that is, it is upside down. Both of these chairs may be regarded as transitional, as are Nos. 169–180, being partly in the Chippendale style and partly in the Hepplewhite style. About 1785–1795.

In Nos. 161 and 162 the splats have two concave curves on each side. In No. 161 the upper curve is short and the lower one is long; in No. 162 the upper curve is long and the lower one is short. Resemblances to these forms may be seen in the Gothic style chairs Nos. 101 and 102, and in the interlaced splat chairs Nos. 129–132. The other features of No. 161 are the finely carved splat and top rail, a curved front seat rail, solid, not fretwork, brackets at the junctions of the seat rail and the legs, and the carved beaded edges of the legs. About 1760–1780.

38.   See the second paragraph in note 30.
39.   So stated by Mr. Cescinsky in his "English Furniture," volume 3, page 194, figure 218.

160 (Upper) Mrs. Miles White, Jr. 161 (Upper) Mr. Albert G. Towers. 162 (Upper) Mr. Albert G. Towers.
163 (Centre) Mrs. J. H. Whitely 164 (Centre) Dr. M. A. Abrams. 165 (Centre) Mr. Albert G. Towers.
    Est. 167 (Lower) Mrs. F. G. Boyce, Jr. 168 (Lower) Mrs. Bayard Turnbull.
166 (Lower) Family of Thos.
    Cradock.

6. "Vertically–pierced splat" chairs; Nos. 163–168. This somewhat awkward term is applied to chairs with splats of the type shown in the next six illustrations.[40] Although these splats are simple and plain, here is a certain attraction in them, particularly when the upright bars are very slender, as in No. 166. Moreover a special interest in them arises from the fact that in certain of these chairs the transition from the Chippendale style to the Hepplewhite style is most clearly shown, as will appear below. Similar splats are in the corner chairs Nos. 435 and 436.

Nos. 163 and 164 are very similar, each having in the splat five upright bars, called "uprights," which is also the word used to mean "stiles"[41] in chairs. In No. 164 the uprights are connected together by what has been termed a "tie." About 1760–1780.

The arm chair, No. 165, has an earlier form of top rail, slender cabriole legs and Dutch, or club, feet; and the front seat rail is cut in a curve. This chair may be compared with the Queen Anne style arm chair No. 68 and with the Chippendale style arm chair No. 151. About 1755–1780.

No. 166, with its fine beaded and carved top rail and stiles, and cabriole legs with ball and claw feet, and the carved "cabochon"[42] on the knees, is an attractive chair, probably English. There are seven uprights in the splat, connected at about the centre by a tie. About 1755–1770.

In No. 167 the five uprights in the lower part of the splat become six in the centre and enclose an oval opening. The chair has straight legs and a concave seat, "stitched up." About 1760–1780.

No. 168 is the last of the chairs illustrated in this section in which the two principal features of the Chippendale style appear, that is, a Chippendale style top rail and a splat resting upon the seat rail; and it is the first chair in which certain features of the Hepplewhite style appear, that is, the carved urn in the splat and the tapering front legs. No. 168 is in reality a transition chair mainly in the Chippendale style, and is purposely shown in this place in order to connect it with the next chair, No. 169. See also No. 187. About 1780–1790.

Here again we may mention that the date of the *latest* feature appearing in an article of antique furniture determines the date of the article, as stated in section 6 at note 4. Here, in No. 168, the Hepplewhite style urn and the Hepplewhite style tapering legs appear on an American chair whose other parts are in the previous Chippendale style, and as these Hepplewhite features were first used in our country about 1785 we must date the style of this chair at not earlier than that date. The chair itself, with Hepplewhite features, could not have been made before the Hepplewhite style began, but after that style began the chair might have been made at any time.

40. The "vertically–pierced splat" chair, shown as No. 68 in section 50, is copied by permission from Mr. Cescinsky's "English Furniture," volume 2, figure 31; it is dated 1725–1730.

41. This word means the two upright posts at the sides of the back; see section 50, note 3, also the present section, note 19.

42. See the text of this section at note 26.

7. Chippendale–Hepplewhite transition chairs;[43] Nos. 169–180. Many of these chairs are found in our country, probably copied from imported English chairs. They seem to have been very popular, especially the chair No. 171 which was a favorite in many homes.[44] The principal feature of the Chippendale style in these chairs is that the splat rests upon the seat rail; the principal features of the Hepplewhite style are the top rails shaped in a shield form, the design of the splat and the tapering of the front legs.

As mentioned in the comment, the preceding chair, No. 168, is a transition chair, mainly in the Chippendale style, having the characteristic top rail and a splat resting upon the seat rail. In No. 169 the Chippendale style splat continues to rest upon the seat rail, but the shield shape of the top rail, the carved urn in the splat and the tapering of the legs are in the Hepplewhite style; hence this chair also, having features of both styles, is regarded as being transitional, passing from the Chippendale style to the Hepplewhite style after the Revolutionary War was over, and therefore is termed a "Chippendale–Hepplewhite transition" chair.[45] See also No. 187, in which the complete change into a Hepplewhite style chair is made. About 1785–1795.

No. 170 has several points of similarity to No. 169. The splat rests upon the seat rail, as in the Chippendale style chairs; but the oval frame in the splat, the Adam urn and the festoons are features used by Hepplewhite. About 1785–1795.

In Nos. 171–174 the "vertically–pierced splats" resting upon the seat rails are in the Chippendale style, but the top rails and the tapered legs are in the Hepplewhite style and therefore these chairs are regarded as transition pieces.

In No. 171 the splat is less liable to breakage than those in the two preceding chairs and is more pleasing in appearance than those in the three following ones; and as mentioned above was a favorite type in our country. About 1785–1795.

In No. 172 the solid base of the splat is conspicuous, and different from others shown on the page. The design of the splat is somewhat more "vertically–pierced" than usual in chairs of this type. About 1785–1795.

No. 173, a side chair, and No. 174, an arm chair, were apparently made to match each other, as the splats are so similar and each chair has a concave seat. Here the splats are in the Chippendale style, but the other parts are in the style of Hepplewhite. The silver plate on No. 173 is mentioned in the note.[46] About 1785–1795.

43. Chairs in transition from the Queen Anne style to the Chippendale style are illustrated in the early part of this section, Nos. 82–84.

Other transitions, changing from one style to another, are referred to and illustrated in this book; see the Index under the word "Transition."

44. It is possible that many conservative purchasers, accustomed to the Chippendale style chair and not inclined to buy an entirely different kind, but also not inclined to be too old–fashioned, would prefer a chair of the transition type rather than one with the new–fangled shapes of Hepplewhite.

45. See note 17 for remarks upon this expression.

46. This chair is the property of the Maryland Historical Society, Baltimore. The silver plate states that at one time the chair was used in the Senate Chamber at Annapolis. In that room Washington resigned his commission as Commander–in–Chief of the American army in 1783. No. 101 is another historical chair belonging to the same owner. See also note 5 in section 1.

169 (Upper) Mrs. C. P. Rogow.   170 (Upper) Mr. D. R. Randall.   171 (Upper) Mr. C. W. L. Johnson.
172 (Centre) Dr. J. Hall Pleasants.   173 (Centre) Md. Historical Soc.   174 (Centre) Mrs. John Stokes.
175 (Lower) Mr. W. W. Lanahan.   176 (Lower) Mr. J. F. H. Maginn.   177 (Lower) Mr. Arthur E. Cole.

In No. 175, an arm chair, the oval frame which forms the upper part of the splat encloses a design of uncertain meaning but supposed to represent an anthemion, with eight vertical bars instead of four as in the supporting base below. Nos. 178–179 are interesting in connection with this chair. About 1785–1795.

The top rails in the above chairs, Nos. 169–175, are of the shape used on the Hepplewhite style "shield–back" chairs which are seen in section 53, No. 184 and others.

In the next five chairs, Nos. 176–180, sometimes called "camel–back" chairs, the top rails are in three convex curves, one in the centre and one at each end.[47] This form is seen on American transition chairs, chiefly in the Hepplewhite style, with the Chippendale style appearing in the splat which rests upon the seat rail and the straight legs which are not tapered.

178 (Left) Mrs. Alex. Armstrong.   179 (Centre) Mrs. E. N. Dunham.   180 (Right) Mr. & Mrs. H. L. Duer.

In No. 176, a side chair, and No. 177, an arm chair, the Chippendale style "vertically–pierced" splats resemble those in No. 171. The straight, not tapered, legs in the Chippendale style may be compared with the tapered ones on several preceding chairs. The top rails are in the Hepplewhite style which also appears in a small "anthemion" carved on the centre of the top rail of No. 176. About 1785–1795.

In No. 178 the Grecian honeysuckle, or anthemion,[48] in the splat, is in an inverted position, as in No. 160. In No. 230, in the section on Hepplewhite chairs, we see a similar splat in a chair which is more fully in the Hepplewhite style, having a hoop back and spade feet. About 1785–1795.

47.   Examples of these top rails are in "Furniture in the Olden Time," by Miss Frances Clary Morse, illustration 180; "Furniture Treasury," by Mr. Wallace Nutting, figures 2309, 2313, 2316A and 2317; "Antiques," March, 1928, page 223.

48.   The anthemion, or honeysuckle, was apparently first used in English furniture by Robert Adam who found it in his studies of ancient Greek and Roman architecture. (*Continued on next page.*)

In No. 179 the anthemion is in its upright position. The legs have been shortened a few inches, as is seen by comparing the height of the stretchers in this chair and the other two; but because of the thick upholstery on No. 179 the tops of the seats seem to be on the same level. About 1785–1795.

In No. 180 the splat contains an urn in the wider portion, as in Nos. 168 and 169, indicating the Hepplewhite style. Solid brackets connect the seat rail and the legs, and the outer corners of the legs are ornamented with carving, features which are in the Chippendale style. This chair is more elaborate than American chairs of this type, and was probably made in England.[49] About 1785–1795.

This section on chairs in the Chippendale style is now at an end. The next style in fashion in England was the Adam style. This style was never important in our country as a separate style, as mentioned in section 16, and few or no American chairs were made in that style, but because of its influence upon us through the Hepplewhite and Sheraton and later styles, it is desirable to examine briefly some of the Adam style features.

Section 52. Adam style chairs.—In section 16, entitled "The Adam style," a brief account of that style is presented, and it is said that in the chapter on chairs a full page illustration, No. 181, is given in order to show the Adam style in chairs and to enable the reader to see the source from which Hepplewhite and Sheraton derived some of their designs.[1]

In illustration No. 181 are four English chairs, marked A, B, C and D, which are examples of several types of the Adam style and school. In these chairs we

(NOTE 48, *continued from page 169.*)

    This Greek word means a flower, or a flower ornament. It is also known as the "honeysuckle" ornament from its supposed resemblance to that flower with unopened buds. It is an ornamental design, "varying in details, but constant in type, of very frequent occurrence in vase-painting, in jewelry and dress fabrics and in all other decorative work of Greek origin"; Century Dictionary.

    As mentioned in the comment on No. 160, the anthemion design is regarded in England as typical of the splats in the Hepplewhite style. It was also used in the Empire style.

    A good, although small, illustration of the usual form of anthemion is on the top of the Adam style oval mirror No. 1149; and another is on the oval mirror in the full–page illustration No. 4 which exhibits six articles of furniture in the Adam style.

    Among many examples are those in the chairs Nos. 160, 175, 178, 179, 230, 333, 336; the settee No. 523; on the bottom of the pedestal of the table No. 1554; on the sofa No. 566; and on the pieces of Adam furniture shown in Illustration No. 4.

    It is also an important architectural decoration of the cornice and other exterior parts of the handsome new "Enoch Pratt Free Library" of Baltimore, which was opened in January, 1933.

    See the Index, under the word "Anthemion," for other references.

    49. An English chair with a similar top rail and fretted legs, and with wheels instead of an urn in the splat, is shown in "Antiques," June, 1922, page 272, where it is said to be an example "combining elements of both Chippendale and Hepplewhite designs."

    1. It is hoped that the reader, before proceeding further, will read the remarks in section 16 and will observe illustration No. 4 which shows six articles in the Adam style.

    The Adam style is not well known in our country because no furniture in that style was apparently made here; but in England the style is one of the most important in furniture history. In England certain features which Americans regard as being in the styles of Hepplewhite or Sheraton are well known as the work of Adam.

ILLUSTRATION No. 181. CHAIRS IN THE ADAM STYLE.

see certain features which were not known in English or American furniture prior to their use by Robert Adam. Some of these features were copied by Hepplewhite and Sheraton in their books, mentioned in sections 17 and 18, and became well known to the English chair makers who followed the designs of those two masters.

The more important of the decorative features of the Adam style seen in these chairs[2] are the fluting, the patera,[3] the rosette,[4] the festoon, the lyre,[5] the square tapering legs with block feet and other ornamental features which were added to chairs made in the designs of the Chippendale and Hepplewhite schools. There are few chairs in a purely Adam style, distinct from the styles of Chippendale and Hepplewhite. The Adam types of ornamentation and designs seem to be less attractive in chairs than in certain other household articles such as tables, mirrors and chimney pieces. In these large illustrations the details are well seen.

The side chair A in No. 181 follows the style of Chippendale, with changes and additions in the Adam style such as the straight and fluted top rail, the rosettes, the paterae and the square tapering legs with enlarged square feet which have been called "Marlborough[6] legs." About 1770.

In the arm chair B in No. 181, the top rail is curved in the Chippendale style. The graceful lyre in the back, the numerous paterae on the flat surfaces and the four rounded legs and feet with much carving unite in making a handsome chair. About 1770.

The side chair C in No. 181 is a "wheel–back"[7] chair, a form which was very popular at the time and was a characteristic of the Adam school, but was seldom if ever made in our country. Here the fluting on the front rail and on the round front legs will be noticed. The back is connected with two supports in the same manner as in so many chairs in the Hepplewhite style. The legs are round and the seat is a "slip–in" one. About 1770.

2.   It is not meant that the designs of the four chairs here shown were drawn by Adam himself, but that they are in the general character of the designs of Adam as followed by the cabinet makers who worked in the Adam style and period. In other words, these designs are those of the "Adam school" of cabinet makers.

3.   The word "patera," plural "paterae," is an architectural term, meaning the representation of a flat round dish used as an ornament. Rosettes and other flat ornaments of various shapes, which bear no resemblance to dishes, are now often called by this name. From the Century Dictionary.

4.   A "rosette" is defined as any circular ornament having many small parts in concentric circles, or regularly arranged around the centre; or any object or arrangement resembling in form a full–blown rose. From the Century Dictionary.

5.   As to the lyre as an ornamental feature see section 44 and note 7 in section 171, and chair No. 183, which combines features of both the Adam and Hepplewhite styles; see also the Index under the word "Lyre."

6.   In "Philadelphia Furniture—1682–1807," by Mr. Wm. M. Hornor, Jr., chapter 6 is entitled "Marlborough, a refinement and rival of the cabriole" legs; pages 173–189. On page 174 reference is made to "Marlborough, with its straight legs—often ending in a square block, and decorated only with ancient or Gothic motifs." On page 179 it is said that the word is "loosely associated with all straight-legged furniture of the Chippendale period."

7.   The "wheel–back" chair obviously took its name from the back, which was in the shape of a wheel with ornamental spokes radiating from an oval hub.

The side chair D in No. 181, copied from figure 37 in volume 3 of Mr. Cescinsky's "English Furniture," is one of a set made in three sizes for the "Drapers' Company of London," the size of this chair being for the wardens, whose chairs were larger than those of less important members. The oval back[8] is attached to the rear seat rail by a board which, with the arms, makes the chair fairly secure. Here the legs are square and tapering and are connected by stretchers. In the oval in the back the emblem of the Company, a ram, is inlaid.[9] About 1770.

Section 53. Hepplewhite style chairs.—In the graceful chairs of the Hepplewhite style[1] we see articles of a very different appearance from those of the more stately Chippendale style. Instead of the almost rectangular backs of the Chippendale style, the cabriole legs with ball and claw feet, and the straight and plain legs and stretchers, we now see several forms of curved backs, straight legs tapering on the inside towards the bottom, spade feet[2] in many cases and occasional inlay. Some of the characteristic features of the Hepplewhite style chairs seem to have been entirely original with him and some other features were evidently taken from the designs of Robert Adam;[3] but whatever was the source of his inspiration, many of the chairs are very lovely, and in this respect are equalled only by some of the best designs of Sheraton.

The furniture designs of George Hepplewhite became popular in England about the year 1780; and, as mentioned in section 17, after his death in 1786, his widow, Alice, trading as "A. Hepplewhite & Co.," published in 1788 his book, or

8.   Another form of chair made in the style of Adam, but not necessarily from his design, had a padded oval back, and still another form had ovals in an open–work design in wood.

9.   One type of chair which we might expect to see in the classic Roman designs of Robert Adam is the chair with the "curule" form, but which seems to have been used later in the Empire style. The curule chair was used by the highest Roman magistrates in their official capacities. It was shaped like a folding camp–stool, with a flat seat without a back, and had crossed and curved legs. It was copied by Sheraton and was apparently a favorite of Duncan Phyfe.

Of the fourteen chairs made by Duncan Phyfe which are illustrated in the book of Mr. Cornelius, "Furniture Masterpieces of Duncan Phyfe," six have the curule form either in the back or the legs or in both, and each of the two window seats in the same book has the same form, derived from Sheraton. Four of the chairs are shown here in section 56, Nos. 320–323. The chairs with curule forms in the back are classified as being under the Sheraton influence; those with curule legs are regarded as "showing Empire influence."

The curule form is also seen in the Sheraton style chairs Nos. 490 and 491. It is seen with variations in some cases, in the bureau No. 756; in the two chairs Nos. 490–491; also in the bureau No. 756, and the tables Nos. 1590, 1591, 1592; and in various articles. It is mentioned also in section 24, note 2, I.

The "anthemion," or honeysuckle, ornamentation was apparently first used on English furniture by Robert Adam; see note 48 in the previous section, No. 51.

1.   It is suggested that section 17, entitled "The Hepplewhite style," be read in connection with this section.

In section 16 it is explained why in our country the furniture style passed from the Chippendale directly to the Hepplewhite, the Adam style not coming in between.

Wing chairs in the Hepplewhite style are shown in section 59.

2.   As to this kind of foot, see figure 17, in illustration No. 11. The spade foot tapers from its top to the ground, and is sometimes very short as in No. 212, and sometimes much longer as in No. 228.

3.   As in chairs Nos. 182 and 183.

trade catalogue, of his designs of various articles which had been, or could be, made in his shop. This publication, entitled "The Cabinet Maker's and Upholsterer's Guide," generally known as the "Guide," illustrated various designs of chairs which we now know as Hepplewhite style chairs. Even before the book was published, however, Hepplewhite style furniture had been imported into our country and had been advertised for sale in the newspapers, not under the name of "Hepplewhite style," but so described that no other kind could have been meant;[4] and later the book reached America. From these two sources our cabinet makers no doubt obtained their designs.

Chairs in the Hepplewhite style appear to have been first made in America about 1785, and they continued in vogue until about 1800 or later. During the latter part of this period the style of Sheraton was also in vogue, and it gradually superseded the style of Hepplewhite, which finally became old–fashioned and passed out. All the American chairs here illustrated may therefore be regarded as having probably been made between these dates, 1785 to 1800 or a few years later.

The backs of the chairs in the Hepplewhite style, as in other styles, are the distinctive features. Here the backs are in several shapes, each of which may be easily distinguished, and are known by names which explain themselves when the illustrations are seen, namely:

1. The "shield" back, Nos. 184–198, 200 and others; this is the shape most frequently found. It was made in two forms, one having a splat and known as a

---

4.   A.   In the "Arts and Crafts in Philadelphia, Maryland and South Carolina," volume 1, page 162, is an advertisement dated January 8, 1785, copied from the Pennsylvania Packet," by "Samuel Claphamson, cabinet and chair maker . . late from London," who "makes and sells . . oval and circular card tables"; at the date mentioned tables of this kind were not made in the Chippendale style, but were made in the Hepplewhite style. See also section 17, note 3.

      B.   The designs of Hepplewhite were copied by other cabinet makers in England, as were the designs of Chippendale and Sheraton. Hence, in the absence of documentary evidence, English chairs in the Hepplewhite style cannot be regarded as having been made by Hepplewhite himself or by the firm of "A. Hepplewhite & Co." In England the work of the "Hepplewhite School" was about 1780–1792; see Cescinsky, "English Furniture," volume 3, pages 138, 142, 174.

      C.   Although the backs of the Hepplewhite style chairs were often made somewhat stronger and heavier in our country than in England, as mentioned in note 4, B in section 45, it is justly said that the back is the weak feature and is a structural error. Owners who have allowed their more than a century and a quarter old Hepplewhite style chairs to be used by heavy or restless visitors who lean backwards will agree that the back is too liable to give way under pressure, generally at the points where the upright posts, or stiles, are attached to the back.

      D.   A remark in Hepplewhite's "Cabinet Maker's and Upholsterer's Guide" refers to horsehair coverings: "Mahogany chairs should have the seats of horsehair, plain, striped, chequered, etc., at pleasure." Mr. Cescinsky mentions that "horsehair appears to have been the fashionable material for coverings at this date"; that it was made in many patterns and colors; and that it has very great wearing qualities; "English Furniture," volume 3, pages 171–172. Nowadays some of us think of horsehair as an abomination of the Mid–Victorian period. See also section 43, note 7.

      E.   Mr. Cescinsky's opinion of Hepplewhite's designs of chairs is stated by him on page 200 of his "English Furniture," volume 3, as follows: "In spite of the claims which have been made for both Chippendale and Sheraton as designers of chairs—and there is no doubt that their schools produced many notable models—it is to that of Hepplewhite that the palm must be awarded for general high level of design, proportion and workmanship."

"splat back" and the other having "banisters" and known as a "banister back." In most of the shield back chairs the bottom of the back is rounded; in others it is pointed, the latter form being perhaps the more elegant.

2. The "interlaced heart" back, Nos. 226–228, which is a kind of shield back.

3. The "oval" back; Nos. 182, 183, 221, 231, 232.

4. The "hoop" back; No. 230.

The backs of the Hepplewhite style chairs, except the hoop back, do not connect with the rail of the seat, as do the chairs of the Chippendale style, but are merely attached to an upward extension of the rear legs. This method and the shape of the back are the outstanding features of the backs of the Hepplewhite style chairs. There are however some variations from the usual forms. These will be pointed out as they occur throughout the book.

Several other matters to be noticed in the illustrations are mentioned in the note[5] and are in some cases repeated in the text in referring to certain chairs.

The ornamental designs within the backs of the shield back chairs are of two principal types. One of these types, regarded as the earlier, is in the general form of a "splat,"[6] and some of these splats are very similar to the splats used in the Chippendale style chairs, and were no doubt copied from them and from the Chippendale–Hepplewhite transition style chairs; chairs with these splats are often called "splat back" chairs.[7] The other principal design consists of a series of three, four or five upright pieces, called "banisters,"[8] or "balusters," or "bars," which extend from the bottom of the back upwards; chairs with these may be called "banister back" chairs in the Hepplewhite style. There are also other ornamental designs used in the back, but the two above mentioned are the main ones.[9] It is

5. Almost all of the chairs have plain straight front legs which taper on the inside. Tapering of the legs was a feature of the Adam style, as mentioned in section 52, at figure 3. In some cases the front legs are ornamented with grooving or carving. The back legs are sometimes curved and placed close together, as in No. 188.

In almost all cases the chairs have plain straight stretchers; the front one connects the two side stretchers, not the front legs, and is called a "recessed" stretcher, as in many other chairs.

It has been said that any shield back chair with moldings on the front legs and *without* stretchers is of English make; but recently it has been definitely proved that chairs of this kind were also made in our country.

The seats are either slip seats or are upholstered over the front rail. The latter method is called "stitched up," and is sometimes finished with brass–headed nails, as in Nos. 215 and 232; and it may be concave as in No. 196, a method borrowed from Chippendale as in No. 137. The seat front rail may be either straight or convex.

A "half–rosette" is usually a half–circular piece of wood at the inside base of a shield chair back, to which the ornamental work inside the back is attached, as in No. 222 and others.

The form of the shield backs and oval backs of these chairs will also be seen on the mirrors of the dressing glasses in the Hepplewhite style in section 152, such as Nos. 1260 and 1262.

6. These splat back chairs are illustrated in Nos. 184 to 210.

7. These transition chairs are illustrated in Nos. 169 to 180 in the previous section.

8. The early banister back chairs are illustrated in Nos. 44 to 49 in section 49.

9. It should be understood that only a few of these designs appear in Hepplewhite's "Guide," which is referred to above in the text. The other cabinet makers of England and those of our country originated many designs of their own, following the general style of Hepplewhite.

sometimes uncertain whether a particular shield back chair should be termed a splat back or banister back chair.

With the two features in mind—the shape of the backs and the designs within the backs—the most convenient method of presenting the shield back chairs is to arrange them according to the character of the designs within the backs, beginning with the "splat back" chairs.

Before examining the illustrations of the purely Hepplewhite style of chairs we observe Nos. 182 and 183, two English chairs which are of much interest because of their elegant appearance and also because they combine features of both the Adam style and the Hepplewhite style. In No. 182 the Adam style is chiefly seen in the fluting on the seat rails and on the back in the Adam manner, as on the Adam style tables in the full–page illustration No. 4 in section 16; and the Adam style is also seen in the fluted legs and the rounded feet. The Hepplewhite style is seen in the design of the splat, which is somewhat similar to his "interlaced heart" pattern shown in Nos. 226 and 227; and the "sweep of the arms and the arm supports in unbroken curves" from the back to the square tops of the front legs is in the early Hepplewhite style.[10] Three "Prince of Wales" ostrich feathers,[11] or plumes, are at the top of the splat. This chair appears here through the courtesy of the Victoria and Albert Museum in London. About 1775.

No. 183, a painted chair, has a fine design with an oval back enclosing a lyre[12] splat and three plumes. Excepting the lyre, the form of the upper part of this chair is very similar to that of the preceding one. Two vertical flutings are seen at the bottom of the arms. About 1775.

Shield back chairs with splats, Nos. 184–210. As mentioned above, the shield back chairs with splats are probably the earliest of the Hepplewhite style. When they were first made, the Chippendale style chairs with splats were in vogue and it was natural that Hepplewhite should use splats, adapting them to the shape of the shield back and the other forms of his chairs; but the splat in the Hepplewhite style chairs does not rest upon the rear seat rail as the splat in the Chippendale style does.

10.   As also in the Chippendale style. In the later chairs in the Hepplewhite style the supports of the arms were generally not connected with the top of the legs, but were fastened to the outside of the side rails, a weaker method.

11.   This design was a favorite one "of which the firm of A. Hepplewhite & Co. appear to have been inordinately proud"; it is found on many chairs and on other articles in the Hepplewhite style, and was particularly mentioned in the "Guide." It was later used by Sheraton. The three feathers or plumes were an emblem of the Prince of Wales at the time and still continue to be. It has been said that this badge of three plumes was assumed by Edward, the Black Prince, of England, at the battle of Crécy in 1346. But it is now believed that this story is without foundation, and that "the origin of the badge must be sought elsewhere." See the Encyclopædia Britannica, under the headings "Crécy," and "John, King of Bohemia."

12.   It is said that Robert Adam was the first to use the lyre form in the splat, a style of ornament which was later used by Hepplewhite and Sheraton and still later by Duncan Phyfe. Notes on the lyre are referred to in the Index; especially see section 44 and note 7 in section 171.

A study of three lyres in the backs of chairs is in "Antiques," April, 1934, page 137.

182 (UPPER) VICTORIA & ALBERT MUSEUM.
185 (CENTRE) MR. & MRS. J. M. MATTHEWS.
188 (LOWER) MRS. G. FRANK BAILY.

183 (UPPER) ANONYMOUS.
186 (CENTRE) MR. JOHN C. TOLAND.
189 (LOWER) MR. J. F. H. MAGINN.

184 (UPPER) MR. & MRS. J. M. MATTHEWS.
187 (CENTRE) ANONYMOUS.
190 (LOWER) MRS. W. W. HUBBARD.

In the group of thirteen chairs, Nos. 184–196, we see several splats which will at once recall some of the "vertically–pierced splat" chairs of Chippendale, Nos. 163–168, and some of the "Chippendale–Hepplewhite" transition chairs Nos. 169–180.

Nos. 184 and 185, a side and an arm chair, companion pieces belonging to the same owners, have shield backs rounded at the bottom, with a straight and fluted cross–piece near the top of the splat. They have slightly tapering legs and the usual four stretchers, the front one being recessed, connecting the side stretchers and not the front legs. The splats may be compared with that of the transition chair No. 172. About 1785–1795.

In No. 186 the outline of the chair is similar to that of No. 184, but the splat is in a different design, with the cross–piece lowered. About 1785–1795.

No. 187 has the same kind of splat and shows the manner in which a complete change was made from the Chippendale style to the Hepplewhite style as mentioned in the note.[13] About 1780–1790.

No. 188, a side chair, and No. 189, an arm chair, have almost identical forms of splats, which closely resemble those in Nos. 192–193. In No. 188 the front legs are grooved and the back legs are curved and are very close together, a feature which will be noticed in many chairs in this section. In No. 189 the supports of the arms are attached to the side rails of the chair, as also in No. 185, not to the top of the front legs as in Nos. 182 and 183; see note 10. About 1780–1790.

In No. 190 the three arches in the splat are in the Gothic style, resembling to a certain extent the arches in some of the Chippendale style Gothic chairs. About 1785–1800.

In No. 191 the back is somewhat wider than in the preceding chairs. At the top of the central bar five ears of wheat, a distinctive ornamental feature of the Hepplewhite style, are carved, below which are carved flowers; but these small carvings are not visible in the engraving. The splat resembles the one in No. 171, except the base and the tie. About 1785–1800.

In the above chairs Nos. 184–191 in the Hepplewhite style with splats, the backs are in the shield shape, rounded at the bottom. In No. 192, a side chair, and No. 193, an arm chair, we see the same character of splats, resembling those in Nos. 188 and 189, but with a different type of shield back; the bottom of the back is not rounded, but has a central horizontal part supporting the splat, with a curved

13. In No. 168 the top rail and the splat resting upon the seat rail are in the Chippendale style, but the urn in the splat and the tapering front legs are in the Hepplewhite style. In No. 169 the Chippendale style top rail was superseded by the Hepplewhite style top rail, but the splat continued to rest upon the seat rail as in the Chippendale style. In No. 187 the Chippendale style back has changed to a Hepplewhite style shield back, and the splat does not rest upon the seat rail. The chair has thus wholly changed from the Chippendale style to the Hepplewhite style, except that the general design of the splat has not changed.

191 (Upper) Mr. C. E. Snyder.
194 (Centre) Mr. C. E. Snyder.
197 (Lower) Mrs. J. W. Williams.

192 (Upper) Mr. John Ridgely.
195 (Centre) Mrs. W. W. Hubbard.
198 (Lower) Anonymous.

193 (Upper) Mr. John Ridgely.
196 (Centre) Mr. Arthur E. Cole.
199 (Lower) Coll. of Mrs. J.
 Stabler.

part on each side.[14] This type of back is also seen on the banister back chairs Nos. 217–219. About 1790–1800.

In Nos. 194, 195 and 196 the splats are somewhat similar to the earlier ones of the Chippendale and transition styles, but they have certain Hepplewhite style features in addition to the shield back. No. 194 has the Prince of Wales plumes in the centre of the splat; No. 195 has a characteristic splat; and No. 196 has an oval medallion in the centre of the splat, carved wheat ears on the top rail, not visible in the engraving, and a concave seat which Hepplewhite "borrowed from Chippendale."

The next group of Hepplewhite style chairs with splats, Nos. 197–210, is interesting because of the elegance of many of the designs. Except Nos. 199, 203 and 204 the backs are all of the shield shape, with variations of form in some cases. It is possible that all of these chairs are of American make, although some of them may have been imported, especially those with the Prince of Wales plumes. In these chairs the principal characteristic designs and features of the Hepplewhite style appear, such as the shield back, the front legs tapering on the inside, the spade feet, the Prince of Wales plumes, the festoons of draperies, the urns and the inlaid medallions; unfortunately the small carvings on the back of the chairs or on the front legs are not well seen in the engravings. It must not be thought, however, that all of these features originated with Hepplewhite. Some of them, such as the draperies, the urns and the medallions, were used by Robert Adam, from whom Hepplewhite got them; and other designs were no doubt appropriated from the designs of Sheraton by the cabinet makers who worked in the Hepplewhite school. It is not always possible to determine whether certain chairs should be considered as being in the Hepplewhite or the Sheraton style, as, for example, No. 197; and in several other cases, the writer has hesitated to classify certain chairs as being in the one style or the other.[15]

In Nos. 197, 198 and 199 the draperies, favorite ornaments of Robert Adam, are a feature of the splats. In No. 197 the carved decoration on the back and on the front legs should be examined with a magnifying glass. On the central portion of the top rail are five feathers, not the three plumes of the Prince of Wales; this portion of the top rail is almost flat, as also in the similar designs of other fine shield back chairs in the Sheraton style.[16] About 1785–1800.

14.   A set of these chairs belonged to John Eager Howard, a Revolutionary War hero, afterward Governor of Maryland and United States Senator. These chairs have been in the possession of the Ridgely family for several generations. Other chairs similar to these are in Maryland and it is believed that they were made in Annapolis.

15.   See the remarks on this subject in section 17 entitled "The Hepplewhite style."

16.   This chair appears in this section of Hepplewhite chairs because it has a shield back, the familiar characteristic of the Hepplewhite style, and also because the design appears in the Hepplewhite "Guide" published in 1788; but almost exactly the same design appears in the "Drawing Book" of Sheraton, published some years after the "Guide," as is shown in the next section in illustration No. 233, figure 6; and figure 10 is somewhat similar. The chair may therefore be classified as being in either or both of the two styles. The five feathers were not a patriotic emblem, but merely a decorative feature; a three plume emblem of the Prince of Wales, being English, would not be desired by the owner, Charles Carroll of Carrollton, one of the Maryland Signers.

In No. 198 the splat is one of much delicacy and elegance of carving. The lower part of the back is not rounded but is pointed as in No. 202 and others. Excepting Nos. 182 and 183, which are of a transition type, this is the first chair in this section not having stretchers. As in No. 188, and other chairs, the rear legs are close together. About 1785–1800.

No. 199 is a plainer chair, having but little carving, but with a splat of the same kind as the preceding one. The back of this chair is in the oval shape, of which kind others will be seen in Nos. 221, 231 and 232. About 1785–1800.

Within the shield back of the chair No. 200 there is a separate narrow shield at the top of which is a carved oval medallion, over which the drapery hangs and forms a part of the interior shield. This much admired design does not appear to be in the books of Hepplewhite or Sheraton. A very similar chair is regarded as the work of Duncan Phyfe, and if the attribution is correct, the chair is especially interesting as being one of the very few surviving pieces of furniture made by Phyfe in the Hepplewhite style, his best work being almost altogether in the Sheraton, Directory and Empire styles.[17] About 1790–1810.

In No. 201 there is an even more distinct, although small, shield within the shield back and there is also the Prince of Wales emblem of three plumes. The legs have spade feet and there are no stretchers. About 1785–1800.

No. 202 is said to have been a popular form of chair in and around New York. The fleur-de-lis in the centre of the splat and the falling drapery contribute to the fine appearance of the back, which is pointed as in Nos. 198, 216 and others. The casters, as to which see section 27, seem to be a modern addition. About 1790–1800.

Nos. 203 and 204 should have appeared on a previous page with the Chippendale-Hepplewhite transition chairs Nos. 169–180, but by some mysterious accident they were misplaced. In No. 203, doubtless an English chair, the top rail and the Prince of Wales plumes are of the Hepplewhite style, but the splat rests upon the seat rail in the Chippendale style. The outline of the splat as a whole is in the form of a vase, and this and the drapery are both in the style of Adam. About 1785–1795.

In No. 204 the splat rests upon a curved cross rail instead of upon the straight seat rail, a form of support which may be a variation of the support in Nos. 192–193. The splat, by a coincidence, is very similar to that in the chair immediately above it, No. 201. About 1785–1795.

In No. 205 the arm chair has a shield back enclosing a splat in the form of a lyre which is "inverted," or "upside down," a position seen in the "anthemion," or honeysuckle, in No. 160. This lyre chair seems to be the same as that shown in figure 206 in volume 3 in Mr. Cescinsky's "English Furniture" where it is said to be

---

17. See section 20 entitled "The Duncan Phyfe Furniture." In "Antiques," April, 1934, pages 129–130, a very similar chair is examined; see also the issue of December, 1929, page 499. A similar splat is in the arm chair No. 591 in Mr. Lockwood's "Colonial Furniture," volume 2.

200 (Upper) Mrs. J. W. Wilson.   201 (Upper) Mr. W. W. Lanahan.   202 (Upper) Mr. H. O. Thompson.
203 (Centre) Mr. John C. Toland.   204 (Centre) Coll. of Mrs. J. Stabler.   205 (Centre) Mr. Geo. Shipley.
206 (Lower) Mr. John C. Toland.   207 (Lower) Mr. & Mrs. Wm. D. Poult-   208 (Lower) Mrs. F. G. Boyce, Jr.
                                      ney.

209 (Upper) Dr. Wm. P. E. Wyse. 210 (Upper) Mr. & Mrs. E. H. 211 (Upper) Mr. Arthur E. Cole.
212 (Centre) Miss E. H. Bartlett. McKeon. 214 (Centre) Mr. & Mrs. J. P. Reese.
215 (Lower) Hammond-Harwood 213 (Centre) Mr. & Mrs. J. Carey, Jr. 217 (Lower) Dr. James Bordley, Jr.
    House. 216 (Lower) Dr. James Bordley, Jr.

necessary, in order to adequately describe this type, to use the term . . "serpentine-top, shield–back lyre–splatted chairs."[18] About 1780.

In Nos. 206 and 207 there is a certain similarity in the shape of the splats, both of which are curved at or near the base. In No. 206 the back closely resembles that in figure 205 in Mr. Cescinsky's book, volume 3, and the splat has an outline somewhat resembling that in No. 197 in this book. These resemblances may not be of any real significance in the development of the chairs. A small urn in the centre of the upper part of the splat indicates the Adam–Hepplewhite style. The legs are round, as in Nos. 182 and 183, and there are no stretchers. About 1785–1800.

In No. 207 the top rail is ornamented with delicate carvings. The festoons of drapery are caught up in a small carved rosette. The two "U–shaped" uprights in the splat have the appearance of being much stronger than many of the other uprights in the splats of these shield back chairs. About 1785–1800.

In Nos. 208, 209 and 210 the designs of the interlaced splats have a certain resemblance to each other and to the splats in the Chippendale style interlaced chairs Nos. 120–128. In each of these three splats there is an upper part with one or more curves and also there are ovals which rest upon supports which are either merely supports or are essential parts of the designs, as mentioned in note 30 in section 51. Nos. 209 and 210 are inlaid at various points not well seen in the engraving, and each has a half–rosette at the bottom of the shield to hold the splat, that of No. 209 being inlaid and solid and that of No. 210 being pierced. It will be noticed that these two splats are very similar; that No. 209 has stretchers and plain square and slightly tapering legs, but No. 210, the arm chair, has no stretchers and has thin legs and spade feet.

At this point the group of Hepplewhite chairs with shield backs and with splats comes to a close and we proceed with other types.

Banister back chairs. Nos. 211–225. In this type of shield back chairs in the Hepplewhite style there is no splat in the proper sense of the word, and in place of a splat the back is occupied with three or four or five "banisters," also called "balusters" or "bars."[19] The central one of the three or five banisters rises vertically in the centre of the back and the side ones are generally curved in harmony with the sides of the back.

No. 211, unusual in having only three banisters, is a handsome arm chair. The banisters are straight, not curved, and are finely carved, the shield back is ornamented all around with carving, the arm supports and the front legs, to which the arm supports are attached as in Nos. 182 and 183, are fluted, and the back legs are curved as in No. 188. About 1785.

18.   Mr. Cescinsky also states, page 188, that "the use of the lyre for the decoration of the backs of chairs was one of the distinctly Hepplewhite motives which were borrowed by Thomas Sheraton." See references to other remarks on "lyres" in the Index.

19.   The "banisters" in chairs of this type may have been derived from the early "banister–back chairs" shown in section 49. Hepplewhite termed chair–back settees of this kind "bar–back." The present English term is "baluster," the correct word; Century Dictionary. See also note 1 in section 49.

No. 212 is a side chair and No. 213 an arm chair, each of which has four banisters, and is interesting in that the upper halves of the banisters are fluted and the lower halves are carved in another design. The feet are of the spade type. The arm supports of No. 213 are attached to the side rails of the seat, not to the tops of the legs, which are fluted. The rear legs of the arm chair are very close together. Both of these chairs may be dated about 1785–1795.

Nos. 214, 215 and 216 have five banisters, each set having a different form of carving. The backs in Nos. 214 and 215 are rounded at the bottom and that in No. 216 is pointed as in Nos. 198, 202 and others. These chairs differ as to stretchers. This type is perhaps the one most frequently seen. About 1785–1800.

In Nos. 217, 218 and 219 the backs are similar in shape to those of Nos. 192 and 193, and are of a Hepplewhite design.[20] In the first and second chairs, side and arm, the three banisters are pierced and carved; in the third there are no piercings; in each the banisters are ornamented with inlaid medallions. About 1785.

No. 220 is a shield back chair and No. 221 is an oval back chair, each with the same delicate and graceful form of pierced banisters, which resemble somewhat those in Nos. 217 and 218. They are included here among the banister back chairs with some uncertainty, as the central upright is not exactly a banister. Chairs with this type of back do not seem to be illustrated in the English or American books on antique furniture. About 1785–1800.

Shield back chairs of another type, here classified as banister back chairs but having features of both the splat back and the banister back, are illustrated in Nos. 222–225. The backs of the first two, Nos. 222 and 223, arm and side chairs, are close copies of a chair, shown in Hepplewhite's "Guide," which is termed by the leading English writer "baluster and central splatted."[21] The legs of the side chair are carved with flowers not easily seen in the illustration. The arm chair is not a companion piece, having round legs and turned arm supports which are attached to the top of the legs, as in Nos. 182, 183 and 211. Nos. 224 and 225, side and arm chairs, are of the same type, but with a somewhat plainer design, having only one simply carved ornament under the top rail, and no carved work on the banisters. The carved half–rosette on each of these chairs will be noticed. The supports of the arms in No. 225 are attached to the side rails, as to which see note 10 in this section. About 1790–1800.

20. In Mr. Wheeler's "Old English Furniture," page 498, is an illustration of similar English chairs, and illustration No. 247 in Mr. Cescinsky's "English Furniture," volume 3, shows a Hepplewhite chair in the French manner with the same form of banisters, dated about 1785.

21. Mr. Cescinsky, "English Furniture," volume 3, figure 208. On page 189 the author writes that the pattern was shown in the second and third editions of the "Guide," and that "they are useful as establishing Hepplewhite's right to be regarded as the originator of the shield–back chair in spite of the claims which have been made for Sheraton in this particular."

218 (UPPER) MR. JOHN RIDGELY.   219 (UPPER) MRS. WM. M. ROBERTS.   220 (UPPER) DR. CLAPHAM PENNING-
221 (CENTRE) MISS MARY K. HINKLEY. 222 (CENTRE) MD. HISTORICAL SOC.   TON.
224 (LOWER) EST. OF MRS. J. H.   225 (LOWER) EST. OF MRS. J. H.   223 (CENTRE) MRS. JOHN S. GIBBS, JR.
     WHITELY.   WHITELY.   226 (LOWER) MRS. THOS. J. LINDSAY.

227 (UPPER) MD. SOC. COL. DAMES. 228 (UPPER) MRS. JOHN S. GIBBS, JR. 229 (UPPER) MR. & MRS. W. A. DIXON.
230 (LOWER) MRS. ALEX. ARMSTRONG. 231 (LOWER) MRS. I. R. TRIMBLE. 232 (LOWER) DR. JAMES BORDLEY, JR.

Interlaced heart chairs. Nos. 226–228. This is one of the popular designs of Hepplewhite and also one of the most characteristic in the sense that it was not adopted by Sheraton or other cabinet makers in any of the design books or trade catalogues of the period. The first two of these chairs are good examples of the type, the design of the entire back making one heart in three interlaced divisions, each having a curving form of top. The back of each of the three chairs is pointed at the bottom. In the side chair No. 226 the central upright is inlaid with flowers and the other two uprights are carved and inlaid, all three meeting below in the inlaid half–rosette. The arm chair No. 227 is not a companion piece, having different legs and but little decoration. No. 228 is a variation of the interlaced heart design, having a shield shaped back and one of the interlaced divisions. About 1785–1800.

Other types of Hepplewhite style chairs. Four less known, but interesting, kinds of chairs, which cannot well be included in any of the groups already illustrated are shown as "other types." Some of these chairs bear little or no resemblance to what we thus far have seen of the Hepplewhite style.

No. 229, with a heart shaped back, is placed here in order to adjoin the interlaced heart chairs. This is a high back chair which it is believed was used by the President of the Senate of the Maryland Legislature at Annapolis at a date not definitely known; but the back with lines of inlay around the frame, the inlaid shell in an oval at the top, the arm supports attached to the side rails as in the next three chairs, the legs and the stretchers all indicate that the chair was made when the Hepplewhite style was the fashionable one in Maryland. A somewhat similar chair used in the old Hartford, Connecticut, State House is shown in "Antiques," July, 1928, page 31. About 1785–1800.

No. 230 is an arm chair with a so–called "hoop back," a type which is said to be a purely Hepplewhite conception. In the rounded upper part of the splat is a Grecian ornamental design called an "anthemion," or "honeysuckle," as to which see note 48 in section 51. In this chair the ornament is inverted, that is, the branches extend downward instead of upward. The legs are reeded and tapering, and end in short spade feet. The hoop back chair is said to be the only chair in a style of Hepplewhite in which the splat rests upon the back rail of the seat, as was the method in the Chippendale style chairs and in several in the Chippendale–Hepplewhite transition chairs[22] and No. 203. About 1785–1800.

No. 231 is an oval back arm chair of a kind seldom seen in our country. In the centre of the back is an oval carved rosette from which eight pierced banisters[23] radiate. Another fragile back is in the chair C in illustration No. 181. About 1780.

22.   These are in section 51, Nos. 169–180.

Almost a duplicate of this chair is illustrated in Mr. Cescinsky's "English Furniture," volume 3, figure 218.

This "hoop back" is not the same as the "hoop back" in the Windsor chair shown in figure 3 in illustration No. 440.

23.   A chair with eight pierced banisters of the same type as those in No. 231, but with a hoop back like that in No. 230, is shown in Mr. Cescinsky's "English Furniture," volume 3, figure 217.

No. 232 is also an arm chair with an oval back. The photograph of this chair was taken from the side in order that the shape and position of the arms might be well seen. The arms and supports are much like those in No. 182, but are attached to the sides of the seat rail. The front legs are grooved and the back legs are curved, as in several prior illustrations. About 1790.

The subject of chairs in the style made famous by George Hepplewhite is now concluded. The next style was that originated or developed by the genius of Thomas Sheraton.

Section 54. Sheraton style chairs.—We now approach a type of chairs very different from those seen in the previous sections. The chairs of the Chippendale style had passed out of fashion, having been superseded by the shield back chairs of the Hepplewhite school; and these latter in turn gave way to the square back chairs of the Sheraton style,[1] not suddenly, but gradually over a period of years. As mentioned in section 18, Sheraton published in sections a book of designs, the first part of which was issued in 1791, and was called "The Cabinet–maker and Upholsterer's Drawing Book,"[2] now generally referred to as his "Drawing Book." It is said in England that the test whether certain styles of chairs should be regarded as being in the Hepplewhite style or the Sheraton style is whether they appear in the books of the one or the other of these two men; but the principal visible difference is that almost all of the Hepplewhite style chairs have curved backs and almost all of the early type of the Sheraton style chairs have square, or at least rectangular, backs. In a general way, the back of the Hepplewhite style of chairs is one of curves and the back of the Sheraton style chair is one of straight lines;[3] but the designs of Sheraton include several curved backs, such as the shield backs marked 6 and 10 in illustration No. 233.

1.   It is requested that section 18 entitled "The Sheraton style" be read in connection with this section.

2.   This book, as mentioned in section 18, was a book of designs made by Sheraton chiefly for the use of cabinet makers in making furniture; it was not a trade catalogue of articles of furniture to be made by Sheraton for customers. Sheraton was a designer, not a cabinet maker except in a very small way; the furniture which we know as in the Sheraton style was made by cabinet makers from his designs. See also the comment on illustration 233.

A complete reprint of the third edition of Sheraton's "Drawing Book," published in 1802, with an "Appendix" and "Accompaniment," and all the engraved plates, "revised and prepared for Press by J. Monro Bell," was published by Gibbings & Co., London, in 1895. The furniture designs and the comments by Sheraton are interesting and well worth examination.

William Camp, a cabinet maker in Baltimore about 1800–1820, used a large label with illustrations copied from Sheraton's "Drawing Book." It is in the style of the label of Benjamin Randolph in illustration 1, but even larger and more pretentious, with a side board and a dressing table in the foreground so elaborate that all beauty of line vanishes.

3.   Chairs with straight line backs in the Adam style may be seen in illustration No. 181.

In Mr. Cescinsky's "English Furniture," volume 3, page 309, it is said that Sheraton borrowed freely from Adam, Hepplewhite and others in his designs of chairs "without the slightest acknowl-

(*Note 3 continued on page 190.*)

Another feature of the early Sheraton style chairs is that the vertical splats or the banisters, also called "bars," do not extend down to the seat rail, as in the chairs of the Chippendale style, but rest upon a cross–piece, as in some of the earlier chairs such as Nos. 41–43 and 82–84. Several other features are mentioned in the note.[4]

As mentioned in section 18, when we refer to a chair or other articles of furniture as being in the "Sheraton style" we generally mean the first and finest style of Sheraton such as is seen in the chairs in illustration No. 233 and also in a few chairs in illustration No. 234. In his last book, which was published in 1812 after his death, Sheraton followed the French Empire style, and his designs show such deterioration that they are now disregarded; but as a matter of interest twelve examples are presented in illustration No. 235.

In regard to the dates of American chairs and other articles in the Sheraton style it seems that the style became known from the designs in his first book, the "Drawing Book." This book was issued in sections at intervals from 1791 to 1793, as shown by the dates on the engravings. The furniture designs are not in the early sections; the first furniture designs are dated 1792 and 1793, a considerable time after the first section was issued in 1791 which year is generally stated to be the date of the book as though the entire book had been issued at one time.

The dates on the original engravings of the chairs and other articles seem to fix the dates at which similar articles could have been made. For example, the engravings of figures 3, 5 and 6 in illustration No. 233 are marked "Published by T. Sheraton, Aug. 1792," thus indicating the earliest date at which such chairs could have been made from these designs. It is apparent from the above dates that the Sheraton style of chairs began in England about 1792, and it is probable that in our country it became the fashion in the next two or three years.

(NOTE 3, *continued from page 189*)

edgment of his indebtedness." This borrowing sometimes makes it uncertain whether a particular English chair should be regarded as being in the style of Adam, or Hepplewhite, or Sheraton; but in our country, as mentioned in section 52, it seems that furniture in the pure Adam style was not made; any American chair showing the Adam style probably derived it from chairs made in the Hepplewhite or Sheraton style but with some feature copied from Adam.

4. The top rails of the chairs in the Sheraton style were occasionally curved, but were generally straight, and were very often raised in the centre, as in several backs in illustration No. 233, and in Nos. 249, 255 and others.

The legs were generally square, often tapering to the bottom or terminating in spade feet, as in Nos. 238, 245 and 256; but were often round and reeded as in Nos. 249, 253 and 270.

Inlay was sometimes used on the legs or back, generally in lines or flower designs, as in Nos. 236 and 255.

The seats were almost square, but were sometimes curved in front; in most cases they were entirely covered with upholstery, but slip seats were also used.

Stretchers were used or not, as preferred.

The shape and position of the arms in arm chairs is better understood from the illustrations than by printed description; see the comment on No. 237 and the other chairs there referred to.

Mahogany was used in making fine chairs in the Sheraton style, but minor woods are found in plain pieces. Beech was often used if the chairs were to be painted.

At the risk of taking too much space, almost three pages are here given of designs of chairs by Sheraton or by cabinet makers of the "Sheraton school" who worked in the "Sheraton style."

No. 233 is a group of twelve[5] designs made by Sheraton in his finest period. They are copied from his "Drawing Book" and are examples of the designs which were the inspiration of the large number of handsome chairs made in the early Sheraton style. It is interesting to compare these designs with the illustrations of our American chairs in this and other books. It should again be noted that these and all other designs were made chiefly for the use of cabinet makers, and do not represent chairs actually made by Sheraton, differing in this respect from modern catalogues showing articles of furniture on hand and for sale.

No. 234 contains thirty later designs said to be in the Sheraton style, some of which are called "late Sheraton." Several of these designs will be referred to as the models which were followed in some of our American chairs. Although most of these designs are of a plainer type of chair and have not the elegance of those of the earlier style, many of them have a very pleasing appearance. It will be noticed that none of the chairs have stretchers, except figure 30, and also that they are given the date "Early 19th Century" by Mr. Strange.[6]

In No. 235 are other drawings[7] made by Sheraton which were published in 1812, after his death. The chairs here shown are in his "decadent period" when he was compelled by the fashion of the day to follow some of the designs of the French Empire style, as mentioned above. Unfortunately a similar decadence is said to have occurred in the work of his follower, our Duncan Phyfe; but Phyfe's friends of today do not allow such work to be illustrated. It will be seen that there is almost nothing in these designs to remind us of the fine creations of the early style of Sheraton. The designs are shown here in order to complete the picture of the various styles of his chairs; but no chairs made in these latter designs are illustrated in this book and it is not likely that any were made in our country.

Not very many of our American chairs in the Sheraton style follow exactly the designs in his books. Our cabinet makers, as well as the English ones, developed many variations; but any chair which has the principal Sheraton features—the square back being the main one—is generally classed as a "Sheraton style" chair, although some other parts may have been appropriated by Sheraton from the work of Robert Adam or George Hepplewhite, or may have been designed by the cabinet maker who made the chair.

In the illustrations the chairs are presented in groups, according to the general designs of the backs; and the reader will at once observe the charm of many of

5. These designs are numbered here for convenience of reference in comparing them with others in this section.

As a general rule only the backs of the chairs are shown in Sheraton's book.

6. This page is a copy of page 345 in "English Furniture, Decoration," etc., by Mr. T. A. Strange.

7. These designs are on page 344 in the book of Mr. Strange and the design of figure 3, with its Directory style curves and its broad overhanging top rail, is seen in substance in the Directory style chairs Nos. 307–319.

233—Sheraton Chair Backs Copied from Sheraton's "Drawing Book," as arranged by J. M. Bell.

192

234—Copy of Page 345 in "English Furniture, Decoration, etc.," by T. A. Strange.

235—Copy of a portion of page 344 in "English Furniture, Decoration, etc.," by T. A. Strange.

these chairs. They have not the abundance of cyma curves of the style of Queen Anne, nor the stately dignity of the school of Chippendale, nor the fine curved lines of the style of Hepplewhite; but in the opinion of many persons, no other chairs are equal in elegance to those in the best style of Sheraton.

With the features of the Sheraton style chairs in mind, we now examine illustrations Nos. 236–304. Many of these chairs are very similar in appearance, but each one is different in one or more respects, showing a great variety of detail. The main features of each are briefly pointed out in the comments.

The chairs are arranged in four groups according to their principal characteristics, not in chronological order, as follows:

    1. Banister–back chairs; Nos. 236–253.
    2. Splat–back and banister–back chairs; Nos. 254–271.
    3. Late Sheraton style chairs; Nos. 272–289.
    4. Painted and stenciled chairs; Nos. 290–304.

1. Banister–back chairs. In this group, Nos. 236–253, we begin with ten chairs which have three banisters each; then follow the chairs having four or five banisters. This arrangement according to the number of banisters has no significance, but is a convenient method of observing close together the chairs of similar general appearance. All of these chairs may be dated at about the same years.

In No. 236 the top rail is straight. Lines of inlay are on the back, on the front rail of the seat, and on the front legs. The legs are gently tapered as in the Hepplewhite style of chairs. About 1800–1810.

No. 237, an arm chair, is not inlaid. The arm supports are concave and are attached to the side rails of the seat, as was usual in the period,[8] not to the front legs as in Nos. 249 and 265. The raised portion of the top rail, forming a panel, will be noticed, a feature which will be frequently seen in other illustrations. About 1800–1810.

In No. 238 the banisters are daintily carved and have a medallion in the centre. The tapering legs terminate in spade feet, as is often the case of Sheraton style chairs of this type, following the Hepplewhite style, as also in Nos. 241, 268 and others. About 1800–1810.

In No. 239 the top rail is curved in the manner of the shield back chairs of the Hepplewhite style; the central banister is carved with a string of flowers, and the other two banisters are reeded. About 1800–1810.

No. 240 has an arched top rail and carved banisters, each of which has a carved panel in the centre; the grooves in the legs are not well seen in the illustration. The large–headed nails on the front seat rail will be noticed. About 1800–1810.

No. 241, an arm chair, has a similar arched top rail with carved banisters having central panels. The supporting parts of the arms are concave as in No. 237. The legs end in spade feet. About 1800–1810.

8. See also note 10 in section 53.

236 (Upper) Mr. Wm. M. Ellicott.
239 (Centre) Mr. Blanchard
    Randall.
242 (Lower) Mrs. Wm. G. Weth-
    erall.

237 (Upper) Mr. James Dixon.
240 (Centre) Mrs. R. W. Petre.
243 (Lower) Mrs. John Stokes.

238 (Upper) Mr. & Mrs. E. H.
    McKeon.
241 (Centre) Mr. & Mrs. E. H.
    McKeon.
244 (Lower) Mrs. John S. Gibbs,
    Jr.

In the next four chairs, Nos. 242–245, the three banisters have one or more pierced openings which give to the chairs a slender and graceful appearance. In No. 242 the top rail is concave at the sides and flat in the centre. In No. 243 the centre also is concave, and the top rail and sides of the back are inlaid; this chair has no stretchers. In Nos. 244 and 245 the top rails are raised in the centre with a panel having vertical reeding. No. 244 has plain feet; No. 245 has spade feet and no stretchers. About 1800–1810.

In Nos. 246–251 the chairs have four banisters which in each case are carved or reeded to some extent, especially at the top. In No. 246 the two side banisters are continued a short distance above the top rail instead of terminating under the top rail, forming, with a connecting part, a slightly raised centre; a similar form of construction will be seen in Nos. 254, 256 and some others. No. 247 has a flat centre in the top rail, with concave sides, as in No. 242. About 1800–1810.

Nos. 248 and 249 are side and arm chairs and are companion pieces belonging to the same owner. These are the first chairs here shown in the Sheraton style having round, tapering and reeded front legs which are turned[9] and have rings near the feet. The arms in No. 249 are connected with the tops of the front legs, not attached to the side rails of the seat as in No. 237. The raised panel in each chair is decorated with carved drapery in the manner of Robert Adam. About 1800–1810.

Nos. 249, 250 and 251 illustrate three different types of construction of arms and their supports. In No. 249 the arms are horizontal and are connected by their supports with the tops of the front legs, as above mentioned. In No. 250 the arms slope down almost from the top rail; the arm supports are connected with the side rails of the seat and are vertical and vase–shaped, a favorite form in sofas in the Sheraton style, such as No. 564. In No. 251 the arms are horizontal and the supports are connected with the side rails. The top rails in these three chairs are in different forms which have been mentioned above. Such differences as these indicate that there was no inflexible requirement of detail in the American chairs in the Sheraton style. About 1800–1810.

Nos. 252 and 253 have five banisters. In No. 252 the top rail is similar to that in No. 251, having an arched top with horizontal ends. Slender banisters occupy the entire back, and the legs are grooved and slightly tapering. In No. 253 the banisters are connected at the top and form four arches, over which are carved festoons of drapery similar to those in No. 268. At the four corners of the back are small carved rectangular panels. The cresting on the top rail is a variation from the usual raised panel. The turned side posts of the back, called "stiles,"[10] are round, as are also the front legs. This is a handsome chair, but is perhaps somewhat overloaded at the top. It may be regarded as in the Hepplewhite style

9. As to "turnings" on chairs see section 46, notes 8 and 11, and section 35.

10. Repeating the definition in section 51, note 19, a "stile" and a back leg together form one upright piece of wood. The stile is the part above the leg. Stiles are also known as "uprights," meaning the rails which extend up from the back leg and are braced together at the top by the top rail. They almost disappeared in the chairs of Hepplewhite but are seen again in those of Sheraton and in later styles.

245 (Upper) Mrs. Miles White, Jr.
248 (Centre) Mr. H. O. Thompson.
251 (Lower) Mr. & Mrs. C. E. McLane.

246 (Upper) Md. Soc. Colonial Dames.
249 (Centre) Mr. H. O. Thompson.
252 (Lower) Mrs. Miles White, Jr.

247 (Upper) Mrs. F. T. Redwood.
250 (Centre) Mrs. John S. Gibbs, Jr.
253 (Lower) Hammond-Harwood House.

because it follows closely one of the designs in the third edition of Hepplewhite's "Guide," published in 1794; see also No. 271 and note 15 in this section. About 1795–1800.

2. Splat–back and banister–back chairs. We now examine the second main group of fine Sheraton style chairs, in which the back is ornamented with a splat and also with banisters. In these chairs, Nos. 254–271, the decorative skill of Sheraton and his followers is seen at its best, producing many pleasing designs The backs of several were obviously copied in whole or in part from Sheraton's designs shown in the full page illustration No. 233. The chairs are arranged here according to their similarity of design, in order that the variations may be easily seen.

In Nos. 254–257 the splats are in vase–shaped form, with banisters at the sides. The back of No. 254 is almost an exact copy of Sheraton's design in figure 5 in our illustration No. 233, above mentioned, the principal difference being that in No. 254 all of the festooned drapery is carved on the vase but in Sheraton's design[11] the ends of the drapery fall down on the sides. In Nos. 255 and 256 the design is almost the same as in No. 254, the main difference being that the vases are not solid, but are pierced, giving a lighter and more delicate appearance. In Nos. 254 and 256 the banisters are prolonged above the top rail, as was also noticed in No. 246. No. 255 has inlaid strings of flowers on the legs and lines of inlay on the top rail and sides of the back. The arms and supports in No. 256 are similar to those in No. 241, and the front legs are very much tapered and have long spade feet. In the first three chairs the plumes[12] above the vases will be noticed; these plumes, the vases and the strings of flowers were all taken by Sheraton from the designs of Adam or Hepplewhite or both. The dates of all three are about 1795–1810.

In No. 257 the pierced vase design is again seen and on its sides are curved pieces which suggest handles. The back is evidently copied from that shown as figure 2 in No. 233, which appears in Sheraton's plate No. 36, dated August, 1792, as mentioned in note 11. About 1795–1810.

In No. 258 we see a combination of features taken from Sheraton's designs, figures 3 and 4 in illustration No. 233. A small vase is in the centre of the splat, recalling the Adam style. The legs have lines of inlay. About 1795–1810.

In No. 259 the central banister supports a cross–piece, above which are two cornucopias tied with a cord. The banisters are delicately reeded, and the tapering legs are enlarged to a block suggestive of a spade foot. In this chair the corners of the top rail are "chamfered," that is, the corner angle is cut away as in No. 295 and as in bureaus and other articles. About 1795–1810.

11.   This design is in Sheraton's "Drawing Book" on plate 36 which bears the inscription "Published by T. Sheraton, Aug. 1792."

12.   These plumes seem to be "Prince of Wales plumes," mentioned in section 53, note 11; they were much used by Hepplewhite, as stated in the note referred to. A card table by Duncan Phyfe with carved plumes of the Prince of Wales is shown in Plate 19 of the book of Mr. Charles Over Cornelius entitled "Furniture Masterpieces of Duncan Phyfe"; see also section 56.

254 (UPPER) MRS. MILES WHITE, JR. 255 (UPPER) MRS. T. R. SLINGLUFF. 256 (UPPER) ANONYMOUS.
257 (CENTRE) MR. & MRS. JAMES 258 (CENTRE) MR. & MRS. JAMES 259 (CENTRE) MRS. I. R. TRIMBLE.
    CAREY, JR.   CAREY, JR. 262 (LOWER) MR. & MRS. CARROLL
260 (LOWER) MRS. M. S. HARTS- 261 (LOWER) MR. E. G. MILLER, JR.   VANNESS.
    HORNE.

In No. 260 a reeded column supports a small urn, and drapery hangs in festoons on the banisters. A curved design rises from the lower part of the reeded column. The legs are inlaid with lines. About 1795–1810.

No. 261 plainly resembles figure 8 in illustration No. 233. The column in the centre is carved with a string of flowers and the seven branches may represent the "anthemion," or honeysuckle.[13] About 1795–1810.

No. 262 is similar in plan to No. 260 except that it has not the curved design between the banisters as in the latter chair. The back of this and of several other chairs is not exactly rectangular as in many of the chairs of this type. About 1795–1810.

Nos. 263 and 264 are a side and an arm chair, companion pieces, in which drapery falls gracefully in festoons in the styles of Adam and Hepplewhite from the top rail across the five banisters. In each of the centre banisters is a small carved panel. The top rail is in a pleasing shape, as in No. 242 and others, with rosettes carved on the straight portion. In each chair a line of inlay is on the edge of the curved front seat rail, and a band of bright inlay is around the front legs near the bottom as in many chairs and tables in the Hepplewhite and Sheraton styles. The high arms in No. 264 and their grooved supports will be noticed. English chairs with the same design in the back are in Mr. Cescinsky's book, volume 3, figures 351 and 352. About 1795–1810.

No. 265 is an arm chair with a splat similar to the two preceding ones. The back is in the form of a shield[14] as in figures 6 and 10 in illustration No. 233 and as in the Hepplewhite style chair No. 197 in the previous section. It may be classified as being either in the Hepplewhite or Sheraton style, with a superior claim in favor of Hepplewhite because of the earlier date of his designs. The arm supports are attached to the front legs as in No. 249 above, and the legs are tapering and reeded and are enlarged near the bottom with a square block suggestive of a spade foot. About 1795–1810.

No. 266 is a finely made chair, with the stiles, or uprights, of the back reeded and the top rail delicately carved, with rosettes on the raised portion and on panels at the ends. The splat contains two arrows pointing downwards through Gothic arches. The seat is concave, the first one of this kind shown here in chairs in the Sheraton style. About 1795–1810.

No. 267 is somewhat similar to No. 266, the splat having arrows resting upon short cross–pieces above that which supports the banisters. The top rail is slightly raised in the centre, forming a panel which is ornamented with carving, as in the preceding chair. About 1795–1810.

13.   See section 51, note 48, as to this ornamental classic design.

14.   This shield shape appears in Sheraton's "Drawing Book" in plate 36 which is dated August, 1792, as mentioned in note 11 in this section. The Hepplewhite book of designs, the "Guide," was published at an earlier date, as stated in section 17. See also the comments on Nos. 253 and 271.

In his "English Furniture," volume 3, page 250, Mr. Cescinsky refers to the illustrations in our No. 233; stating that these are examples of Sheraton's chair backs, he remarks that they are "among his most happy creations. They serve to show that the shield back, in its various forms, which is so usually credited to Sheraton, belongs almost entirely to Hepplewhite."

263 (Upper) Mr. E. G. Miller, Jr.
266 (Centre) Mrs. R. W. Petre.
269 (Lower) Anonymous.

264 (Upper) Dr. J. H. Pleasants.
267 (Centre) Hammond-Harwood House.
270 (Lower) Anonymous.

265 (Upper) Mr. & Mrs. E. H. McKeon.
268 (Centre) Mr. E. G. Miller, Jr.
271 (Lower) Mrs. Francis P. Garvan.

No. 268 seems to be a variation of a design of Sheraton in his "Drawing Book" in which an arch appears, as in figure 11 in the full page illustration No. 233 and in No. 253. Under the raised portion of the top rail is a panel upon which festoons of drapery are carved. The square tapering legs terminate in spade feet. About 1795–1810.

Nos. 269 and 270 are English chairs shown in the third volume of Mr. Cescinsky's book on "English Furniture," Nos. 399 and 340. They exhibit two types of Sheraton style chair backs, the first having what is called a "diamond latticed" splat and the second having a splat which is a combination of the lattice and the banister. Chairs of these types do not seem to have been often found in our country. The arms and their supports show the same methods of construction as in Nos. 250 and 251, that is, the arm supports in No. 269 are attached to the front legs and in No. 270 the supports rest upon the side rails of the rounded seat. The arm supports are in the vase shape. About 1795.

No. 271, which may be regarded as in the Hepplewhite style,[15] has curved bars or banisters in the back, making a series of pointed arches. The top rail is in almost the same shape as in No. 251, and in its centre is a panel in which leaves and a basket of fruit are carved. About 1795.

The series of chairs in the early and fine style of Sheraton ends at this point and is followed by chairs in his "late" style.

3. Late Sheraton style chairs. Each of the thirty–six chairs thus far illustrated, Nos. 236–271, except No. 265, has a horizontal cross–piece in the lower part of the back, upon which a vertical splat rests, or several banisters, or both, not extending down to the seat rail. That characteristic feature of the early Sheraton style appears in ten of his designs in illustration No. 233, and is also seen in many of his later designs in illustration No. 234 in which the "Early 19th. Century" is given at the top of the page as the date for all of the chairs there shown.

The next group of illustrations, Nos. 272 to 289, is devoted to the "late Sheraton style" chairs, as modified and developed by our American cabinet makers during the years from about 1800 to 1820 or later.

As will be seen in the illustrations, the new features in the late Sheraton style chairs often make a complete change in the appearance of the chairs. The top rail is generally much broader, and often projects beyond the sides of the back, with a concave form as in No. 273; or the top rail may be a small round rail, generally reeded in the centre, as in Nos. 280, 284, 285. The backs are often lower than in the early style, as in Nos. 273–275. The front legs are generally round, are often reeded, and are sometimes spread outward or "splayed" as in No. 284 and Nos. 286–289; and other features will be mentioned in the comments.

15. The partly rectangular shape of the back, the carved panel and the curved banisters indicate the Sheraton style and is therefore shown in this section on that style; but almost this exact design of back appears in plate 9 in the third edition of Hepplewhite's book, "The Guide," published in 1794. In that book there are several other designs of chairs with square or rectangular backs, as in plates 3, 10, 13 and others. Possibly Hepplewhite and Sheraton both copied an earlier designer, perhaps Robert Adam. making a puzzle for posterity.

Nos. 272–276 are similar in certain respects to some of the chairs shown in illustration No. 234, especially in having broad top rails, all of which, except No. 276, extend beyond the side uprights, or stiles. They follow the structural plan of the earlier chairs in having a cross–piece upon which the banisters rest; but in other respects they are different. The upholstery on these chairs is modern. The backs are somewhat low, as is also the back in No. 277. The date of these chairs is regarded as about 1800–1820.

Nos. 272 and 273 have rounded seats and the front legs are reeded to a point within a few inches of the bottom, from which point the legs are bare, a peculiar and unattractive method which was followed in some of the chairs of Duncan Phyfe. In each chair the entire back is reeded, and in the arm chair the arms, beginning high on the sides, are grooved. The banisters form arches resembling those in Nos. 248–249. About 1800–1820.

Nos. 274 and 275, side and arm chairs, are companion pieces and belong to the same owner. The seats are rectangular and the tapering legs are round, without reeding. The backs are finely reeded, except the top rail. In No. 275 the supports of the high arms are attached to the side rails in the manner of those of No. 250. About 1800–1820.

In No. 276 the three banisters, forming two rounded arches and two half arches, rest upon a support which has cross–bars connected by a rosette. The legs are tapering, are reeded in part, and have a somewhat large ring near the feet which are almost pointed. About 1800–1820.

No. 277 is an arm chair with a cane seat, and also a cane back, the latter apparently being a simplified form of the oval cane back in the English chair, No. 289. This back has an unusually large amount of woodwork. The reeded legs are similar to those in the preceding chair, and the reeding also appears on the arms and their supports; these supports are somewhat in the form of a vase in an inverted position, and rest upon the front legs as in No. 265. About 1800–1820.

In No. 278 another arm chair is shown with a broad top rail, but with its other parts in slender and delicate lines. The splat has an interesting design of three diamonds, perhaps suggested by figure 16 in the illustration No. 234. In this chair the back legs are in the same form as the front ones, a very unusual treatment. About 1800–1810.

In No. 279 the back has a horizontal cross–bar, a form which will be seen in many chairs in the Sheraton and American Empire styles. The top rail and legs continue in about the same form as in the preceding chair. About 1800–1810.

In Nos. 280 and 281 are examples of top rails of a type seen in figure 15 in illustration No. 234. In this type of top rail the central portion is round and enlarged and is horizontally or spirally reeded and on each side is a horizontal turning resembling a vase. Somewhat similar top rails are on the Empire style chairs Nos. 343–345. About 1800–1810.

272 (Upper) Mr. John Ridgely.   273 (Upper) Miss Helen H. Carey.   274 (Upper) Miss L. C. Austen.
275 (Centre) Miss L. C. Austen. 276 (Centre) Mr. E. G. Miller, Jr.   277 (Centre) Mrs. C. H. Wyatt.
278 (Lower) Miss H. R. Chew.   279 (Lower) Mrs. I. R. Trimble.   280 (Lower) Mr. & Mrs. J. M.
                                                                               Matthews.

205

In No. 280 the diagonal cross–bars are of the type seen in figure 5 in illustration No. 234. They were also used by Duncan Phyfe, as in No. 325. About 1800–1810.

In No. 281 the design of the back partly follows that of the above mentioned figure 15 in illustration No. 234, having a rectangular panel for a painting under the top rail; and under the panel is a combination of arches. The legs are reeded and are connected by crossed stretchers, which are unusual. This chair may be an English one. About 1800–1810.

No. 282, although plain in design, is a finely reeded one, the top rail being particularly well done. The entire back is ornamented with reeding and also the front legs. About 1800–1810.

With the next five chairs, Nos. 283–287, the group of American chairs in the "late Sheraton" style comes to a close, except for the painted and stenciled chairs of this style, which follow. In these five chairs, most of which are of maple, the seats of rush or cane are rounded; the front legs are attached to the seat rails within the edge of the rails, and, except No. 283, the legs do not extend to the floor at a right angle, but are "raked," or "splayed," that is, they slant outwardly; and in Nos. 284, 286 and 287 they end in ball feet. In No. 285 only the lower portion of the legs are "splayed," as will also be noticed in Nos. 288 and 289.

No. 283 has a broad top rail with a fanciful horizontal design between it and the cross–bar; the legs are straight and reeded, and the front stretcher has a panel as an ornamental feature. About 1810–1815.

In Nos. 284 and 285 the top rails are similar to that described above in connection with Nos. 280 and 281. If these chairs were painted there might be a doubt whether they should be classified as in the late Sheraton style or in that known as the "Hitchcock style," referred to in section 57, which treats of chairs in the American Empire style; they may perhaps be regarded as transitional between the two styles, having some feature of both. About 1810–1820.

In Nos. 286 and 287, companion pieces belonging to the same owner, the large top rail is again seen, under which is an upper horizontal cross–piece connected by six balls, a frequent form of ornament in the chairs and settees of the period; and there is also a lower cross–bar. The front stretchers have three connecting balls. The fronts of the stiles, or side posts, are flattened as may perhaps be seen here, but examples will be more clearly seen below in some of the painted chairs. As in No. 284, the arms and their supports are attached to the sides of the seats, and the legs are too far within the seats to add to the appearance of the chairs. About 1810–1820.

Nos. 288 and 289, which are English painted chairs of the late Sheraton style, are copied by permission from Mr. Cescinsky's "English Furniture," volume 3, Nos. 360 and 356. These chairs appear here because they show clearly the models from which certain features of some of our American chairs were derived. In each of these chairs the lower parts of the legs are "splayed," that is, they curve outward, as in Nos. 285 and 297. In the upper parts of the front legs

281 (UPPER) MR. W. W. LANAHAN.   282 (UPPER) MR. WM. M. ELLICOTT.   283 (UPPER) MRS. J. S. GIBBS, JR.
284 (CENTRE) MR. WM. A. DIXON.   285 (CENTRE) MR. WM. A. DIXON.   286 (CENTRE) MR. A. MORRIS TYSON.
287 (LOWER) MR. A. MORRIS TYSON.   288 (LOWER) ANONYMOUS.   289 (LOWER) ANONYMOUS.

are three painted rings, called "collars," a form of decoration much favored in our chairs of the Empire style, as shown in section 57. In the arm chair the high arms begin almost at the top rail as in Nos. 250 and 273. The seat rail of No. 289 is painted with a design which Mr. Cescinsky terms a Grecian "Key pattern." About 1795–1800.

4. Painted and stenciled chairs. This group consists of chairs in the Sheraton style decorated with paintings or stenciled designs.[16] In England painted decorations were used long before the time of Sheraton; but in our country it seems that they began to be popular about the year 1800, when the Sheraton style was in vogue, and continued in favor for a number of years. A particular type was developed, known as "fancy chairs" which are illustrated below, Nos. 296–304. After about the year 1820, the use of a stencil[17] by factory employes, instead of a brush in the hand of an artist, enabled chairs to be decorated in quantity and at prices which brought them within the reach of the average householder.

The first six illustrations, Nos. 290–295, are of a fine type of chairs with painted designs.

No. 290, an arm chair, was made by a Baltimore chair maker whose name and history are at present not clearly established. This cane seat chair which is one of a set, and also No. 515, a settee of the same character, belong to members of a family for whose ancestor they were made. The Sheraton style is indicated by the design of the back, which resembles the back of figure 11 in illustration No. 233. The details of construction[18] are interesting, but the important feature is the elaborate decoration of each chair in the set. On the top rail in each chair is an oval in which is a painting showing a different residence in and near Baltimore. About 1800–1810.

No. 291 may be regarded as a "fancy chair" in the Sheraton style and it is shown here, instead of with the other fancy chairs in that style, Nos. 296–304, because of the resemblance of some of its painted decorations to those of No. 290, indicating perhaps the same artist and possibly the same chair maker. This chair is known to be the work of Robert Fisher, of Baltimore, whose name appears

16.   The chairs illustrated in this section are only those in the Sheraton style; other painted and stenciled chairs are shown in section 57, in which several American Empire style chairs are illustrated, such as the "Hitchcock" chairs.

17.   Three articles by Mrs. Esther S. Fraser entitled "Painted Furniture in America," in "Antiques," are mentioned in section 34, note 1, and for convenience are again mentioned here, as follows: "The Sheraton Fancy Chair, 1790–1817," June, 1924, page 302; "The Period of Stenciling, 1817–1835," September, 1924, page 141; "The Decadent Period, 1835–1845," January, 1925, page 15.

Section 34 is entitled "Painting; gilding; stencil work."

18.   The high and sloping arms resemble those in No. 250, but the supports of the arms are different. The rounded legs are similar to many others in this section, and all four legs are alike, as in No. 278. On either side of the residence are rectangular panels done in gilt. A panel in the central banister is decorated with bows and arrows, and the front seat rail is ornamented with an oval and foliage. Other painted decoration is on the arms and their supports, the banisters and the cross rail; and also at the top of the front legs and at the bottom of the stiles.

In an article by Dr. Henry J. Berkley in "Antiques," September, 1930, page 209, entitled 'Early Maryland Furniture," are illustrations of these chairs.

290 (Upper) Mrs. Wm. DeFord.
293 (Centre) Anonymous.
296 (Lower) Mrs. Thos. J. Lindsay.

291 (Upper) Mrs. Miles White, Jr.
294 (Centre) Mr. & Mrs. H. L. Duer.
297 (Lower) Mrs. Wm. G. Wetherall.

292 (Upper) Anonymous.
295 (Centre) Mr. & Mrs. E. L. R. Smith.
298 (Lower) Mr. Wm. M. Ellicott.

in the directories of that city from 1803 to 1812 as a "fancy chair maker."[19] On the top rail are two rectangular panels similar to those on No. 290, and between them is another panel ornamented with musical instruments; the central banister is suggestive of the vase splat in No. 254 and others; and the front stretchers and the front seat rail are decorated. About 1810.

No. 292 also may be considered as a fancy chair, resembling the next two in the form of the arms and their supports. On the top rail is an urn with festoons of drapery in the Adam style, details which Sheraton used almost as freely as did Hepplewhite. A somewhat unusual feature is the flat form of the front stretcher. About 1810.

Nos. 293 and 294 are finely decorated chairs, both perhaps being of English make. No. 293 is somewhat similar in design to chairs shown in the English books, in which the fluted legs and the feet are characteristic. The chair is painted black and the decorations are in gilt. The top rail is adorned with strings of leaves resembling a French style of decoration. About 1810.

No. 294 is a painted and gilded cane seat chair similar to figure 27 in illustration No. 234, and is of a type illustrated in several books.[20] The top rail is of the kind described in the comment on Nos. 280 and 281. The panels on the two horizontal cross–pieces are decorated, the lower one with musical instruments. About 1810.

No. 295 is an unfamiliar type of painted chair, one of a set of furniture which includes a table with a similar style of decoration, shown in section 166, No. 1432. It is painted white, with the Adam style festoons, the leaves and the rectangular panels in black, as are also the lines on the edges. In shape the chair is similar to other banister–back chairs of the early Sheraton style, with the rectangular back and the straight tapering legs; the ends of the top rail are "chamfered," that is, the corners are cut away, as in No. 259. The seat is cane. Perhaps about 1810.

Fancy chairs. Perhaps the most popular painted chairs in our country were those known as "fancy" chairs, the best of which were made in the Sheraton style; and after that style passed out of fashion, the "fancy" chairs were made in the American Empire style,[21] as will be seen in section 57.

19.   Three of these chairs are shown in Mr. Lockwood's "Colonial Furniture," volume 2, page 310; on page 311 are references to other pieces by the same maker, namely, a settee, a window seat and a card table, all of which are also shown in this book; the settee being our No. 516, the window seat No. 536 and the card table No. 1528.

20.   As in Mr. Cescinsky's "English Furniture," volume 3, No. 353; on page 326 it is said of this and another chair that these chairs are "typically English in character, and they are certainly the best of the creations of this period" of about 1795. A similar chair with slight variations is shown on the front cover of "Antiques," June, 1924.

21.   The term "fancy chair" apparently meant any type of painted chair and was not confined to those in the Sheraton style. In the Baltimore City Directory of 1842 is an advertisement of "Augustus P. Shutt, fancy and Windsor chair factory." At this date the Sheraton style was out of fashion and the Empire style was still in vogue. In the directory of 1849–1850, seven names appear under the heading "Chair manufacturers—Windsor and Fancy."

The term "Sheraton fancy chair," as generally used, means a brightly painted chair in the Sheraton style and of a particular type, with painted or stenciled decorations. The painting may have been in any one of a variety of colors, often black; the decorative designs were gilded, generally painted, but sometimes in gold leaf. The chair itself was not as heavy as the other chairs of the period, being made of light wood. The seats were either square or curved, rather wide in front, and were of cane or rush. The legs were round and turned. The top rail, the seat rail and the front stretcher were often shaped in such a way as to provide a panel for a painted design. These chairs were made from about 1800 to 1850.

It could not be expected that the original decorations of these chairs would survive the usage of more than a hundred years; and therefore much restoration and entirely new decorative work is often found; and as chairs of this type were made by a large number of "fancy chair makers"[22] in many widely separated cities and towns, it is natural that there should be a considerable variety of construction and decoration.

Nine of these "fancy chairs" are illustrated in Nos. 296–304 and Nos. 291 and 292 are of the same type. Their features exhibit the characteristics mentioned above and there is little more to be said by way of description.

Nos. 296–299 have rounded seats, which are esteemed more highly than the straight ones. The legs are placed within the edge of the seat rail, as in all the others except No. 304. The front surfaces of the upright sides of the backs, called stiles,[23] are flattened from the top to a point near the seat, perhaps to provide good surfaces for decoration. On each of the front legs are rings, or collars, generally painted.

In No. 296 the arms begin at the top rail and end in curves similar to those in the Directory style chair No. 309; and on the top rail is a painting of a landscape. About 1815.

In No. 297 the top rail and the seat rail are decorated with a stencil. The cross–pieces have ball ornaments, which are also in the front stretcher. The legs are partly reeded and are turned outward, or splayed, at the bottom, ending in rounded feet. This chair is more ornamental than many others. About 1815.

No. 298 is a simple form, but with the characteristic features of the style. It will be noticed that the same painted design appears more clearly on the flattened sides of the back than on the round legs. About 1810–1820.

In No. 299 we see a modified form of the top rail shown in Nos. 280, 284 and others; here a panel is provided for a painting. The cross–piece represents a bird, probably an American eagle,[24] resting upon the top of the northern hemisphere. This chair, which has a rounded seat, should be compared with No. 343 in section 57, which is classified as an American Empire style Hitchcock chair. About 1810–1820.

22.　The makers of these chairs called themselves "fancy–chair makers," not "fancy chairmakers." See on the subject of chair makers, note 5 in section 45.

23.　See note 10 in this section for the definition of this word "stile."

24.　As to the American eagle see section 33.

299 (Upper) Mrs. F. G. Boyce, Jr.
302 (Lower) Miss Harriett R.
    Chew.

300 (Upper) Miss Eleanor S.
    Cohen.
303 (Lower) Mrs. Alex. Arm-
    strong.

301 (Upper) Mrs. Wm. DeFord.
304 (Lower) Mr. John Ridgely.

In the next illustrations, Nos. 300 to 304, the Sheraton style is indicated by the banisters, which do not extend down to the seat rail, but rest upon a cross-piece, as mentioned in the second paragraph of this section.

In No. 300 the back seems to be copied from figure 17 in illustration No. 234. The painting on the top rail is a landscape. The cross–bars are brightly decorated, as is also the oval panel of the front stretcher. About 1800–1810.

The back of No. 301 is a simplified form of that of figure 8 in illustration No. 234. The decoration does not show clearly in our engraving. The design of the panel in the front stretcher seems to be in harmony with the design of the central banister in the back. About 1800–1810.

Nos. 302–304, arm chairs, are interesting pieces. In No. 302 the arms are bowed and have banisters, similar to those in the back, resting upon a cross–piece. Gilded lines will be noticed on the arm supports and on the front legs; but the other decorations are not well seen. About 1800–1810.

In No. 303 the top rail is broad and the banisters in the back are in about the same form as those in the next chair. The arms here are straight, with banisters. The decorations of gilded lines are similar to those in the previous chair. About 1800–1810.

No. 304 is a very fully decorated chair. The panels on the top rail, on the bottom of the stiles, on the front seat rail, at the top of the front legs and on the stretcher, are all daintily ornamented with flowers. The arms, sloping from near the top rail, and also their supports, resemble in shape those in the chair No. 275. A three–part settee belonging to the same set is shown as No. 518. About 1800–1820.

This concludes the section treating of the chairs in the Sheraton style, and we next consider the American Directory style, or as it is often called, using the French word, the "Directoire" style.

Section 55. American Directory style chairs.—In a previous section, No. 19, the American Directory style of furniture was considered and we are now to examine the American chairs in that style.[1] The Directory style came into vogue

---

1.   The reader is urged to read section 19 in connection with this section, because if it is not read, this section will not be fully appreciated.

The subject is considered in Mr. Holloway's "American Furniture and Decoration," published in 1928 by J. B. Lippincott Co., Philadelphia, in his chapter entitled "The American Directoire Style," pages 133–152. This chapter of Mr. Holloway, quoted in section 19, has suggested and made possible the separate treatment of the Directory chairs in this section; otherwise the chairs shown in this section would probably have been mingled with Empire style chairs with which they have little or no connection.

One effect of treating the Directory style chairs apart from the Empire style chairs is to reduce the number of chairs which might be regarded as being in the Empire style; see also section 57 at note 3.

See also note 7 in section 54 in regard to figure 3 in illustration No. 235; the design of this figure 3 is somewhat similar to that of the Directory style chairs in this section.

in England while the Sheraton style was the fashion, and Sheraton adopted some of its features in his books of drawings. Whether our cabinet makers derived their models from France directly or through English examples may be uncertain; but it is clear that the American chairs followed the general outlines of the French designs, and were made about the years 1805–1825. As will be seen in the next section certain chairs made by Duncan Phyfe in the Directory style, wholly or partly, have made the style prominent in our country.

Writers on American antique furniture have generally disregarded the Directory style and have included the chairs and other furniture of this style in either the late Sheraton style or the Early American Empire style. The result of this placement has been that many fine articles, especially chairs and sofas, which should be known as being in the American Directory style have been regarded as being in the American Empire style, and have not received the favorable attention to which they are entitled. Only recently has the Directory style become recognized as being worthy of separate treatment.

In order to see at once the important features which distinguish some of the chairs in the Empire and Directory styles we examine illustrations Nos. 305 and 306, which give a front and side view of a French Empire style chair, and compare that chair with No. 307 which is a good example of the American Directory style. Both of these chairs have been in the possession of a Baltimore family for several generations.

In the French Empire style chair, No. 306, the side view, the back is almost perpendicular; in the Directory style chair, No. 307, the back is curved from the top to the seat. In No. 306 the stiles, the upright parts of the back, are attached to the seat rails for a short distance but are not parts of the seat rails; in No. 307 the stiles continue as seat rails in curved lines to the front where they curve downward and form the front concave legs.[2]

In No. 307 there are thus two curves which are characteristic of the Directory style chairs. One is a series of curves from the two small ones at the ends of the top-rail down to the seat, then on to the front of the seat and then to the floor. The second characteristic curve is that formed by the line of the back and of the rear legs, which, like the front legs, are concave. The top rail and the cross-piece with balls[3] are also in curves both in the horizontal and upright directions. Every outline in this chair is curved except the front and back lines of the seat, and these are the only straight lines in the chair. The two rosettes at the top and the other two at the junctions of the side seat rails and the legs are of wood. About 1805–1820.

---

2. In other chairs, of course, the uprights of the back are generally continued downward below the seat and form the rear legs; here the uprights turn forward at the seat.

We also notice in Nos. 305–306 the brass "mounts" on the top rail and on the lyre and at the junction of the side seat rails and the front legs. These brass applied pieces were seldom used on American furniture. See section 38, entitled "Applied decorations; mounts."

One or more of the features of the American Directory style chairs continued to be used on our chairs for some years after the style itself passed out; examples are in Nos. 335, 347, 348 and others.

3. The cross-pieces connected by balls are seen in many chairs in the late Sheraton style; see No. 286.

305 (Upper) Mrs. C. H. Wyatt. 306 (Upper) Mrs. C. H. Wyatt. 307 (Upper) Mrs. C. H. Wyatt.
308 (Centre) Mrs. C. H. Wyatt. 309 (Centre) Mrs. Thos. J. Lind- 310 (Centre) Mrs. Thos. J. Lind-
311 (Lower) Mr. Wm. M. Ellicott.   say.   say.
                                 312 (Lower) Mrs. F. G. Boyce, Jr. 313 (Lower) Mrs. F. T. Redwood.

In each of the following American chairs illustrated in this section the two characteristic curves above mentioned, and also the concave front legs, are present although not clearly seen in the engravings, and need not be referred to again in these comments.

In No. 308, an arm chair, the features are the same as those in the companion piece No. 307; and it will be noticed that the arms and their supports are of about the same shape as those in the late Sheraton style chair No. 273. The Duncan Phyfe arm chair No. 327 is a more elegant chair of the same general character. About 1810–1825.

Nos. 309 and 310, arm and side chairs, are companion pieces. The reeding of the arms, legs and front seat rail may be faintly seen. The arms and their supports resemble in part those of the late Sheraton style chair No. 296. On each end of the top rails of these two chairs are wooden panels with carved designs resembling the "anthemion," or honeysuckle, which is mentioned in note 48 in section 51. About 1810–1825.

The next nine illustrations, Nos. 311 to 319, show the Directory style features in chairs which in other respects are in the late Sheraton style or the early American Empire style. In several of these chairs certain features were no doubt suggested by some of the Sheraton style chairs shown in illustration No. 234.

In No. 311 the cross–piece in the back is one of a favorite type in the Sheraton period, and its delicate design is more attractive than the somewhat coarse carving on many chairs. About 1810–1825.

In No. 312 the top rail is raised as in the Sheraton style chair No. 254 and others. Here the cross–piece is a solid one, with carved designs and a round panel carved with grooved circles. About 1810–1825.

No. 313 is another chair of similar character with a carved cross–piece in which there is an opening. As in other chairs of this type, the top rail is curved and paneled, giving an appearance more pleasing than that of a plain flat surface. About 1810–1825.

In Nos. 314 and 315 the front legs have a projecting knee which is well seen in the engravings; and this may also be seen in the late American Empire style chairs, Nos. 348, 353 and others. At the top of the front legs are carved wooden rosettes on both the inside and the outside of the legs. About 1815–1830.

In Nos. 316 and 317 are other examples of favorite kinds of cross–pieces in our American chairs. Many of these cross–pieces are well designed and have small panels with floral or leaf carvings. The slanting position of No. 316 gives a better view of the chair than the straight position of No. 317. About 1805–1825.

No. 318 has the Directory curves except in the front legs which are straight and are reeded in the late Sheraton style, as in Nos. 276–277. The seat rail also is reeded. The stiles, or uprights, of the back are in an unusual design and the cross–piece is in the form of two horizontal vases with a round piece between them. This chair may be considered as being in the late Sheraton style with features of the Directory style. About 1805–1825.

314 (UPPER) MRS. EDW. SHOEMAKER. 315 (UPPER) MRS. EDWIN B. NIVER. 316 (UPPER) MR. H. T. TIFFANY.
317 (LOWER) MISS M. S. SCHENCK. 318 (LOWER) ANONYMOUS. 319 (LOWER) MRS. JOSEPH WHYTE.

No. 319 is painted with classic designs and has the two principal Directory curves, but the large top rail is apparently not of the Directory type; a top rail with a similar design may be seen in the American Empire style chair No. 328. The top rail overhangs the sides and is larger than usual; and at each end it curves around, with small wooden knobs projecting from the top and bottom. About 1805–1825.

It may not be amiss to mention again that the Directory style chairs shown in this section have generally been called "late Sheraton" or "Empire" chairs and that in many publications the "Directory" style is not mentioned.

Section 56. Duncan Phyfe chairs.—It will be noticed that the title of this section is not "Duncan Phyfe *style* chairs." The reason for the omission of the word "style" is that it cannot properly be said that Duncan Phyfe originated or developed a new "style" of chairs or of other articles of furniture as Chippendale and Hepplewhite and Sheraton did.[1] The fine chairs which are known to have been made by Duncan Phyfe were not made in a new style; they all seem to be wholly or partly in one or more of the three styles which were in vogue during some portions of the period in which his best furniture was made, about 1800 to 1825, that is, the Sheraton style, the Directory style and the early American Empire style.[2] The most attractive chairs made by Duncan Phyfe are those in which the Directory style is closely followed, as in No. 326.

It is said that the chairs of Duncan Phyfe were of but few types and that the variations of these types were chiefly in the decorations, which consisted mainly of carving, veneering and reeding.[3]

1.   It is hoped that section 20, entitled "The Duncan Phyfe Furniture," will be read in connection with this section.

In the catalogue of the "Girl Scouts Loan Exhibition," held in New York in September, 1929, every chair made by Phyfe in the Sheraton style is called a "Sheraton style chair by Phyfe," not a "Phyfe style chair"; similarly a "Sheraton style card table by Phyfe"; and the same expression is used in regard to other articles made by him in the Sheraton style. Mr. Cornelius in his book, mentioned in the next note, uses the expression "chair showing Sheraton influence," an expression scarcely strong enough if Phyfe almost copied a Sheraton style chair and merely added some fine carving and reeding or acanthus leaves. Mr. Halsey, in his book entitled "Homes of our Ancestors," in a note to figures 115–118, remarks that the chairs there illustrated "show Phyfe's interpretation of Directoire designs."

2.   The fact that the Hepplewhite style was passing out in our country about the year 1800 may be the reason that few articles in that style were apparently made by Phyfe; or perhaps he did not admire the curves of Hepplewhite although he was very partial to those of the Directory style. One fine Hepplewhite style chair is regarded as having been made by Phyfe because certain details of workmanship were characteristic of his work; see "Antiques," April, 1934, pages 129–130.

3.   In the book entitled "Furniture Masterpieces of Duncan Phyfe," pages 62 and 52, by Charles Over Cornelius; published for the Metropolitan Museum of Art by Doubleday, Page & Company, 1922.

It is also said that the range of his designs is restricted to a "relatively small number of standardized and oft repeated motives, most of them equally applicable to any and all" the different articles which he made. This will be seen in the chairs in the book of Mr. Cornelius and in other publications.

It may be noticed that few reproductions of the best chairs of Phyfe seem to have been made; but his sofas and tables have been frequently copied.

It is difficult to arrange the chairs of Duncan Phyfe according to their probable dates of manufacture. Mr. Cornelius, in his book mentioned in note 2, estimates the dates of the chairs and of other furniture by Phyfe according to the date of the style, beginning with the style of Sheraton, and thus fixes the dates of all of Phyfe's fine pieces between 1800 and 1825, although pieces "with Empire features may be placed after 1813." Six of the chairs here shown are authenticated chairs from the workshop of Duncan Phyfe, but the makers of Nos. 322 and 325 are not surely known.

In the two chairs Nos. 320 and 321, side and arm, the Sheraton style is recognized by the rounded seats, such as are seen in the Sheraton style chair No. 270; also by the curule[4] type of cross-bars in the back, as in figures 1 and 30 in illustration No. 234; by the reeded back and seat rails; and by the general form of the supports of the arms as in No. 284. We notice, too, that the top rails are curved upwards and horizontally, and are carved with leaf designs, that the seat is cane, that the front legs are almost straight and are carved with Phyfe's characteristic flat acanthus leaves and that the feet are brass. About 1800–1820.

No. 322, also in the Sheraton style, is very similar to the side chair No. 320, the principal difference being that the front legs are round and reeded and have round feet somewhat similar to those in the Sheraton style chair No. 274. This chair is in the manner of Phyfe even if not made by him. About 1800–1820.

(NOTE 3, *continued*)

Many tables and sofas have been popularly and commercially attributed to Phyfe merely because they have the curved and reeded legs which Phyfe used when working in the Sheraton style.

In this connection it should be mentioned that the use of certain decorative designs does not indicate a particular designer or cabinet–maker. For example the classic "anthemion," or honeysuckle, (see note 48 in section 51), has been used for centuries in furniture designs and by many designers. It is said that it is not the use of certain designs "but the manner of their individual use and of their combination with other" features that "count in determining questions of period, nationality and personal authorship," as remarked in "Antiques," January, 1927, page 57. These details may be understood, even if not fully mastered, by the amateur collector if seen and examined on the articles rather than in an illustration.

Another example is the lyre on a chair or other article which is often thought to be proof in itself that the piece was made by Phyfe; but the lyre has been in use as a decorative feature from the classic age of Grecian art. See the references in the Index under the word "Lyre."

No chairs or other articles known to have been made by Phyfe after about 1825, except the desk No. 836, are shown in this volume. It is said that his admirers hope that his later furniture will not be brought to light. Let us especially hope that Sheraton's decadent style chairs shown in our illustration No. 235 were not demanded by Phyfe's customers.

Certain variations by Phyfe in the usual designs of chairs are not of a pleasing character and are merely mentioned here. One design is on plates V and VI in the book of Mr. Cornelius, in which the lower parts of the front legs are treated as animals' legs with growing hair and three toes, a kind of decoration used as far back as about 1725 in England. The growing hair design is also seen on the legs of certain sofas of the period. A very plentiful use of acanthus leaves on the legs of chairs is also noticeable.

4. In the book of Mr. Cornelius, plates 1–9, fourteen chairs are illustrated, six of which show the curule form either in the back or the legs.

As to the curule form see note 9 in section 52.

320 (Upper) Mr. Howard Mansfield.
322 (Lower) Mr. Edgar G. Miller, Jr.

321 (Upper) Mr. Howard Mansfield.
323 (Lower) Mrs. Francis P. Garvan.

324 (Upper) Mr. V. Everit Macy.   325 (Upper) Mr. W. W. Lanahan.
326 (Lower) Anonymous.   327 (Lower) Anonymous.

No. 323 is in the Directory style, except that the Sheraton style cross–bars in the back are of the curule type. Comparing this chair with the Directory style chairs Nos. 307–310, we notice the two characteristic curves[5] of the Directory style, although the curves of the rear legs are not well seen. The top rail is carved with flowers and leaves, but the curved front legs are plain. About 1800–1825.

No. 324 is in the Sheraton style, having the rounded and reeded seat rail and the round reeded and tapering legs. The top rail is carved with one of the favorite designs of Phyfe, known as the "thunderbolt," representing streaks of lightning. In the back are four reeded bars which are placed diagonally and make a double crossing. About 1800–1825.

In No. 325 also we see the Sheraton style in the same form as in the previous chair, the difference being in the two, instead of four, diagonally placed cross–bars in the back. The top rail is ornamented with vertical reeding. As with No. 322, this chair is in the manner of Phyfe, but is not authenticated by written evidence. About 1800–1825.

No. 326 is the most admired of the chairs of Phyfe. It is in the Directory style and has a lyre–shaped ornament in the back, two features which have made Phyfe's sofa No. 574 the most admired of his sofas. Here the top rail is plain, but the legs are ornamented with leaves of the acanthus plant as in Nos. 320 and 321. About 1800–1825.

No. 327, also in the Directory style, is a sturdy arm chair. The top rail, the panel in the back and the front of the arm supports are plain, but other parts of the front are fully reeded except the legs, which are grooved. The cross–piece in the back is plain, but in a graceful design. About 1800–1825.

In three chairs shown in plates 8 and 9 in the book of Mr. Cornelius the *legs* are in the curule form shown in the backs of Nos. 320–323 and are regarded as indicating the Empire style. Those chairs are interesting but are awkward and unlovely.

It is the opinion of the writer that although some of the chairs and sofas of Duncan Phyfe are among the finest American examples of those articles, the most pleasing of his creations are his tables; see the Duncan Phyfe tables in section 171, and those shown in the book of Mr. Cornelius.

Section 57. American Empire style chairs.—At first it is difficult to use the term "American Empire style[1] chairs," or, more briefly, "Empire style chairs," without thinking that in some way the chairs are in the style and period of the French Empire of Napoleon, 1804–1815, the only modern empire from which any of our American furniture styles were directly derived. But there is little resemblance between the chairs in the style of the French Empire of Napoleon

---

5.   These two curves are explained in the comments on No. 307.

1.   Section 21, entitled "The American Empire style," should be read in connection with this section.

and those in the style commonly called the American Empire,[2] as is shown by the illustrations in the books; in fact very few articles of furniture of any kind were made in our country in that French Empire style. In the case of American chairs, many of those called "Empire style" chairs are combinations of previous styles, with new features of doubtful merit. In this section the words "Empire style" in connection with American chairs should be understood to mean chairs made in the fashion of the period of about 1815 to 1840, the latter date being that of the beginning of the Victorian style. This dating may not be free from objection, but it at least has the advantage of excluding certain chairs of the earlier types, such as the late Sheraton and the Directory, which have sometimes been regarded as being in the "Empire" style.[3]

The mention of the American Empire style in connection with sofas, sideboards, tables and certain other articles, often suggests large size, heavy weight, and the legs and feet of some imaginary animal; but these unpleasant qualities do not appear in many of the American chairs of the period. On the contrary we find in that period many chairs which have features showing that the fine Directory style, although not exactly followed, was not forgotten; in fact, many of the chairs illustrated in this section show, more or less clearly, the influence of the Directory style, which is the subject of section 55. A large number of the chairs are painted or stencilled, including those known as "Hitchcock" chairs. Many others are made in the forms of earlier styles. The illustrations in this section, which are not arranged in exact chronological order, probably include examples of almost all of the important American Empire style chairs;[4] and although no one who is familiar with the previous styles will greatly admire all of our Empire style chairs, yet no one can fairly condemn them all as being "debased" or "clumsy"—words which are sometimes applied to almost all furniture made in the same period as the chairs.

No. 328 is a cane seat chair, painted in a light color with a style of decoration somewhat similar to that of No. 319 which is mainly in the Directory style. In this chair, as in No. 319, we see the curved and overhanging top rail, and also the characteristic lines of the stiles, or uprights, which curve forward and become part of the side seat rails as in the chair No. 307. The front legs, however, depart from the curved form of the Directory style, being straight, round, ringed near the foot, and decorated with flowers; these front legs, and certain less important details, prevent the chair from being regarded as in the Directory style. About 1825–1835.

2.   An even worse misapplication of words is to apply the word "Colonial" to the heavy sofas, bureaus, etc., of the period of about 1830–1840, as mentioned in section 1, note 1, A.

3.   The subject of American Empire chairs is not fully considered or illustrated in any of the books on antique furniture, doubtless because some of the chairs are not sufficiently old, and not sufficiently fine, to be worthy of much attention. The writer has found a woeful lack of information on the subject, which will account for his uncertainty and possible errors in several instances. See the Victorian parlor on page 65, also chairs Nos. 493 and 495.

4.   There may be other types of American chairs of the period which do not appear in our illustrations; but the writer has not found many such, either in books or in the numerous homes visited. There are, however, many variations in details. A few Victorian style chairs are also shown.

328 (UPPER) MR. ALEXANDER
    BROWN.
331 (CENTRE) MRS. M. S. HARTS-
    HORNE.
334 (LOWER) MRS. JOHN S. GIBBS,
    JR.

329 (UPPER) MR. & MRS. J. M.
    HARRIS.
332 (CENTRE) MRS. EDW. SHOE-
    MAKER.
335 (LOWER) MRS. JOHN S. GIBBS,
    JR.

330 (UPPER) MR. & MRS. J. M.
    HARRIS.
333 (CENTRE) MRS. RALPH ROBIN-
    SON.
336 (LOWER) MR. ALBERT G. TOW-
    ERS.

In the painted chairs Nos. 329, 330 and 331, the departure from the Directory style is more pronounced, all of the legs being straight and round, the front ones ending in ball feet as in the Sheraton style fancy chair No. 299 and in others of the late Sheraton style. In these three chairs the back legs make no curve with the sides of the back as in No. 328. In each of these three chairs the excellent painting or stenciling on the straight top rail gives a certain distinction to the plain design of the chair. About 1825–1835.

No. 332 is also a painted chair, but with a different form of top rail, of which two other examples immediately follow. In the back there is a solid splat in the form of an inverted vase such as is seen in the backs of the chairs No. 59 and others in the Queen Anne style, and upon the vase is a painting in the shape of a lyre— a revival of previous decorative designs. See also the splats in Nos. 348–349. About 1825–1835.

In the painted chairs Nos. 333, 334 and 335 the top rail is of the same form as that in the preceding chair. In these three illustrations we notice certain features already seen in some of the previous chairs; thus in No. 333 there is an upright carved design on the cross–piece in the back resembling the "anthemion," or honeysuckle, which is mentioned in note 48 in section 51. About 1825–1835.

Nos. 334 and 335 present two views of the same chair. The stiles, or uprights on the sides of the back, curve into the seat rail, as in the Directory style, but the front legs are straight and rounded as in some of the chairs in the Sheraton style; in this chair the front stretcher has a painted panel as in the Sheraton style chair No. 304 and others; and we also see on the upper part of the front legs a painted "palmette," a small palm leaf which will also be noticed in several of the chairs following. In these chairs the front rail of the seat is ornamented with vertical rings. The carved design on the cross–piece in the back of No. 334 consists of two cornucopias filled with fruits. This chair is here considered somewhat at length, not because it is of importance as a fine chair, but because it combines several interesting designs of previous years and illustrates the composite nature of many of the chairs of the period. About 1820–1835.

Nos. 336–338 are three painted chairs very similar in form to some of the preceding ones, having a rectangular and overhanging top rail. The cross–pieces in the back are interesting, each one having carved and gilded "anthemions," or honeysuckles, of somewhat different designs. Nos. 337 and 338 have "palmettes," which are mentioned in the preceding paragraph; the vertical rings on the front seat rails are conspicuous as are also the horizontal rings at the top of the legs; and the front stretchers have panels in the Sheraton style. About 1820–1835.

No. 339 is best described in the words of Mr. Lockwood in his "Colonial Furniture,"[5] in which he states that the similar chair illustrated by him is "a painted variety of the Empire chair such as is quite commonly found in the South. The back and rear legs are raked and are joined to resemble the folding bronze chairs found in Egypt. A brass rosette finishes the imitation hinge." The

5.   Volume 2, page 125, No. 615.

palmettes may be seen on the seat rail and on the front legs, which are often reeded. About 1820–1830.

No. 340 was originally a yellow chair, with a painting of leaves on the top rail. The stiles, or side uprights, extend upwards above the top rail. The five banisters and the solid and rounded seat will be noticed. About 1830–1840.

No. 341 is a fully decorated chair without any well defined style but of a popular type. The three banisters extend upwards only to the cross–piece, leaving a large open space in the back. About 1830–1840.

No. 342 shows a combination of styles; the top rail and the three banisters seem to be of about the same design as those of a "Boston rocker," as appears in No. 485; the stiles, or uprights of the back, and also the form of the side seat rails, resemble those in No. 331; the curved legs are like those of No. 333 and are decorated with "palmettes." About 1830–1840.

"Hitchcock" chairs. A group of American Empire style chairs of a certain type, painted in some parts and stenciled in other parts, are commonly known as "Hitchcock" chairs. These chairs were made from about 1826 to 1843, chiefly within the Empire period. They acquired the name of Hitchcock because they were first made in quantity by a chair maker of that name, who had a factory in Connecticut in a village bearing his name, as mentioned in the note.[6] The popularity of these chairs led to their imitation by other furniture makers in various parts of the country. It may be possible in many cases to distinguish chairs made by Hitchcock himself, or his firm, from similar chairs made by other makers. but it is enough to consider all chairs of this type under the name of "Hitchcock chairs," thus using the term to indicate the general type of chair rather than the chair of a particular maker. Three illustrations sufficiently show the character of this type of chair, but it is not meant that these three were the only kind made, as there were many variations in details.

6.   In an article in "Antiques," August, 1923, page 74, entitled "Hitchcock of Hitchcocks–ville," by Mrs. Guion Thompson, the story of Lambert Hitchcock and his chairs is given, with illustrations. It appears in this article that from about 1826 to 1829 he conducted the business of chair making by himself, and from 1829 to 1843 in a partnership called "Hitchcock, Alford and Company." Later "Alford and Company" continued the business. In the earlier years about one hundred persons were employed including women and children, the women doing the decoration. In 1866 the town of "Hitchcocks–ville" changed its name to "Riverton" in order to avoid confusion with a town called "Hotchkissville."

In the earlier period, 1826–1829, the chairs were stenciled on the back of the seat "L. Hitchcock, Hitchcocks–ville, Conn." In the second period, 1829–1843, the chairs were stamped "Hitchcock, Alford & Co. Hitchcocks–ville, Conn." In both of these periods the word "Warranted" is marked on the back. In the later period, after 1843, "Alford & Company" omitted the warranty. Chairs with the name and warranty have been made recently and have been sold as originals.

Very similar chairs were made during some of the years above mentioned, at a nearby town called Robertville, by a man named Camp. His chairs, and also many made by other makers, are said to be distinguishable from those of Hitchcock in several points, especially in having more horizontal reeding on the legs.

Other information on the subject in "Antiques" may be referred to; editorial in issue of December, 1923, pages 268–269; article in September, 1924, at page 144, by Mrs. Esther S. Fraser, in which some of the views expressed in the article above quoted are questioned; article by the same writer in issue of October, 1929, page 303, on Hotchkiss. Another well illustrated article by Mrs. Fraser is in the issue of August, 1936, pages 63–67.

337 (UPPER) MR. ALBERT G. TOW-
    ERS.
340 (CENTRE) ANONYMOUS.
343 (LOWER) MR. D. R. RANDALL.

338 (UPPER) MRS. RALPH ROBINSON.
341 (CENTRE) MRS. WM. G. WETH-
    ERALL.
344 (LOWER) MRS. M. S. HARTS-
    HORNE.

339 (UPPER) MR. & MRS. W. D.
    POULTNEY.
342 (CENTRE) MISS MARGARET
    STEELE.
345 (LOWER) REV. & MRS. A. C.
    POWELL.

The features of these Hitchcock chairs are better understood by observing the three illustrations Nos. 343–345, than by reading a description of them; but it may be said that they follow the style of some of the painted chairs in the late Sheraton style, especially in the top rails, as in Nos. 285 and 299. They were generally, but not always, painted black, but were brightened on the back, the seat, the front legs and on the front stretchers by brilliant stencil designs, mostly of fruits and flowers, in gold, color, or bronze. The chairs of this type first had rush seats but soon afterwards were made with cane and solid seats also. The legs were round, the front ones often bending outward at the bottom, with horizontal reeding on some parts, and frequently were tapered, in which latter case they often ended with a small ball foot. In these three chairs the seats are of rush and are square, not rounded. The stiles, or uprights in the back, are cut flat in front in order to have a good surface for the painted lines, as also in Nos. 298 and 299 which are classified as chairs in the late Sheraton style.

No. 343 is a pleasing example, having a cross–piece with two cornucopia designs painted in several colors, and a cross–bar below. The front legs are fully ornamented with horizontal reeding. No. 344 has a rectangular cross–piece with a classic design. No. 345 has a large cross–piece decorated with grapes and leaves. These three chairs may be dated at about 1826–1840.

On page 230 is a group of nine chairs, Nos. 346–354, all of a type of which a larger number are probably now in use than any other kind of semi–antique chairs. They were in fashion from about 1835 to about 1850 when they were superseded by the chairs of the Victorian period. These chairs do not receive the space here given to them because of any value as antiques, but because almost every one of them contains an interesting combination of features which we have seen in chairs of two former styles, the Queen Anne and the Directory. In point of style and elegance they are not desirable, but in durability and comfort they are generally satisfactory. These chairs are often regarded as being much earlier in date than they really are.

In many of these chairs the two curves which are characteristic of the Directory style of chairs are present, in part at least. As explained in the comment on the chair No. 307, one curve is the Directory curve which extends unbroken downward from the top rail to the seat, then to the front of the seat and then to the floor. In most of the chairs in this commonplace group the curve continues unbroken from the top rail to the floor, except at the knees of the front legs. The second Directory curve is that formed by the line of the back of the chair when seen from the side and by the line of the rear legs which, like the front legs, are concave. The similarity of these designs to those in the Directory style will be apparent by noticing the chairs in section 55.

Another feature of these chairs is the splat, many of which are similar to some which we have seen in the chairs in the Queen Anne style and the Chippendale style. Perhaps the resemblance of some of the splats to the earlier ones may have led the owners of chairs of this kind to think them of great age.

Other features taken from previous styles, generally combined with the Directory style features, will be noticed upon examining these chairs separately. All of the chairs Nos. 346–357 and 359 may be dated about 1830–1845.

In No. 346 the form of the splat and its position, resting upon the cross–piece and not extending down to the seat, remind us of some of the chairs in the Queen Anne and early Chippendale styles, such as Nos. 42, 43 and 82, and of course the chairs in the Sheraton style. The top rail is ornamented with a carved cresting which has an opening for the hand. About 1830–1845.

In No. 347 the top rail has a carved leaf design with a small heart–shaped opening. The splat is in a vase design and suggests the Queen Anne style. About 1830–1845.

In No. 348 the top rail is rounded and the splat is in another vase–shaped design. About 1830–1845.

No. 349 has the same rounded top, and the same shape of splat which has been cut into a lyre which roughly imitates the lyre in the Sheraton style chair in figure 13 of illustration No. 234. About 1830–1845.

In No. 350, a sturdy arm chair, the arms terminate in large curved supports which resemble those in the Directory style chair No. 309 and the Sheraton style painted chair No. 296. The vase–shaped splat here is solid. About 1830–1845.

No. 351 has a top rail with many curves and an opening for the hand. The cross–piece has piercings in the shape of hearts. About 1830–1845.

In No. 352 the top rail curves downward, and the scrolls cut in it and in the cross–piece produce openings which perhaps unintentionally resemble the figure 3 in a horizontal position. About 1830–1845.

In Nos. 353–356 the construction is different. The stiles, or upright sides, are not connected with the rear legs, but are attached to the front of the side rails of the seat. The rear legs are concave and are closer together than in the preceding chairs; and the backs are not very strong. In No. 353 the top rail is prolonged upward to a flat top and is concave.

In No. 354 the top rail is rounded and the splat is in a vase design. The curved rear legs are seen to be closer together than in the preceding chairs, being "raked," or "splayed," at the bottom. About 1830–1845.

Nos. 355 and 356 have splats which suggest the Chippendale style chairs "in the Gothic manner"[7] shown in illustrations No. 94–117; see note 21 in section 51. The central arch in these two chairs is in fact much more in the style of the arches seen in the Gothic cathedrals of Europe than are those in the Chippendale style chairs. The single arch in No. 355 is not pierced as are the three arches in the next chair. The two protuberances on the sides of the top rail in No. 356 may have been intended to represent the "ears" in many Chippendale style chairs, such as Nos. 107, 115 and in the ladder–back chairs Nos. 367 and 368. About 1830–1845.

---

7. In England about the year 1825, and afterwards in our country, an effort was made to revive the Gothic style, and the Gothic arch appears in a number of articles of furniture of the period. See also the Index under the word "Gothic."

346 (Upper) Mrs. I. R. Trimble.   347 (Upper) Miss Anna D. Ward.   348 (Upper) Mr. John Hinkley.
349 (Centre) Mr. John Hinkley.   350 (Centre) Mr. John Hinkley.   351 (Centre) Mrs. R. W. Baldwin.
352 (Lower) Mrs. Joseph Whyte.   353 (Lower) Mr. C. W. L. John-   354 (Lower) Miss M. S. Schenck.
son.

230

355 (Upper) Mrs. S. Johnson Poe. 356 (Upper) Mrs. Henry C. Miller. 357 (Upper) Mrs. Edwin B. Niver.
358 (Centre) Mrs. F. T. Redwood. 359 (Centre) Miss H. H. Carey. 360 (Centre) Mr. & Mrs. J. M.
361 (Lower) Miss Helen H. Carey. 362 (Lower) Mrs. John Stokes.   Matthews.
       363 (Lower) Mr. E. G. Miller, Jr.

In No. 357 the three arches are in a Gothic design. The French Empire style is suggested by the side rails which are treated in the manner mentioned in the comment on No. 306 in the Directory style. The front legs also seem to be of a French type, and have probably been shortened. About 1830–1845.

In No. 358 the ornamental treatment of the top rail faintly suggests the "inter-laced splat" designs in some of the chairs in the Chippendale style, such as Nos. 120–128. The round and tapering legs are similar to those in the Sheraton style chairs Nos. 278 and 279. About 1830–1845.

No. 359 is out of place here. The top rail and splat indicate a foreign design, probably French. The top rail is flat at the top and concave horizontally. The stiles, or upright sides, are attached to the front of the side rails of the seat as in No. 353. About 1810–1820.

No. 360 also is out of place at this point. It is a curly maple chair with a broad top rail, carved cross–rail and turned front legs which are raked, or slanting, at the bottom. The two piercings in the cross–rail are in the form of darts. Perhaps about 1820–1830.

Nos. 361 and 362 are arm chairs in which several familiar forms will be seen. In No. 361 the top rail is slightly curved in the manner of a shield back chair in the Hepplewhite style; the arms and their supports are somewhat in the shape of those in No. 327, which is a Directory style chair by Duncan Phyfe; the front legs are in an exaggerated form of those in the late Empire style chair No. 353 and are furnished with casters, as to which see section 27. Compare the arm chair No. 423. About 1830–1840.

In No. 362 we notice the presence of the Directory style in the curved back extending from the top rail to the front rail of the seat; we see arm supports similar to those in the Sheraton style chair No. 296 and terminating in a fantastic head; and the front legs which are square and tapered have spade feet in the style of Hepplewhite and Sheraton. About 1820–1830.

No. 363 is not well placed here. It seems to be a plainer and later American development of the French lyre–back Empire style chair shown as Nos. 305 and 306. The top rail is broad and overhanging, the lyre rests upon a cross–piece and all the legs are curved. See also No. 501. About 1810–1825.

Section 58. Ladder–back chairs.—Slat–back chairs such as those shown in section 47 probably suggested to Chippendale the type of chairs which are considered in this section; and under his master hand the plain slat–back became the graceful ladder–back.

These chairs are sometimes spoken of as though they were made only in the style of Chippendale; but the English books illustrate chairs of similar design made in the styles of Hepplewhite and Sheraton; and two examples in the latter style are illustrated later in this section, Nos. 389 and 390. Mr. Cescinsky states that in England the ladder–back pattern was "common to the trade from 1760 to

1790, and was embellished in a variety of ways in the hands of different makers."[1] In our country almost all of the chairs were in the Chippendale style, some of simple character and others of much elegance.

The dates of these chairs are probably from about 1760 to 1795 and these dates need not be repeated in the comments.

In chairs of the ladder–back type the important features are the designs of the top rail and of the other rails, or slats; these designs are usually about the same in form. The openings in the rails are called "piercings." Several of these chairs are very much alike, but it will be seen that they are different in details, some of which are not important. Mahogany is the wood in all cases; all of the chairs are in the Chippendale style with the exception of the two in the Sheraton style, above mentioned; and all have straight and square legs, sometimes grooved, in the Chippendale style, with four stretchers. The seats were either of the "slip on" kind or with the upholstery covering the seat rails.

Examining these chairs we see that in Nos. 364, 365 and 366 the top rail and each slat appear to have interlaced or entwined lines, recalling the manner of some of the interlaced splats in the Chippendale style chairs shown in Nos. 118–119. In No. 364, applied pierced brackets are seen at the junction of the legs with the front seat rail, as was also seen in several Chippendale style chairs, Nos. 106, 158 and others. In No. 365 the piercings are graduated in size, the largest being in the top rail; this graduation will also be noticed in several other chairs. In No. 366 there are but two slats in addition to the top rail; the front legs are grooved and the seat rails are covered with upholstery.

In Nos. 367, 368 and 369 the slats are slightly different from those in the preceding chairs, the inner ends of the lower branches of the piercings not being interlaced. In No. 367 the ends of the top rail are ornamented with "ears" as in the Chippendale style chairs Nos. 92 and 97; and there are also applied brackets as in No. 364 above. In No. 368, an arm chair, the top rail has "ears" and the sides of the back and the arms are grooved. No. 369 is also of a similar character, except that the top rail is rounded at the ends, as in many Chippendale style chairs such as No. 136 and in many of the ladder–back chairs here shown.

In the next six chairs, Nos. 370 to 375, the noticeable feature is that there are three piercings in the top rails and in each of the three slats, the central piercings being longer than those on the sides. In these chairs, except Nos. 374 and 375, the top rails are not in the bow shape, being rounded at the ends.

In Nos. 370 and 371 we see two forms of the piercings of the slats. The front seat rails and the front legs are plain, but the stiles, or uprights, of the backs are grooved.

---

1.   In his "English Furniture," volume 3, pages 197–198, where a ladder–back chair in the Hepple-white manner is shown. The Chippendale style chairs are illustrated in volume 2, figures 265–267, and are dated about 1760.

The name "ladder–back" seems to have been given to these chairs because of the similarity of the slats to the rungs of a ladder.

In England the words "rail" or "cross–rail" seem to be used instead of the word "slat."

364 (UPPER) MR. & MRS. H. L.
DUER.
367 (CENTRE) MR. JAMES DIXON.
370 (LOWER) MRS. JOHN S. GIBBS,
JR.

365 (UPPER) MR. & MRS. H. L.
DUER.
368 (CENTRE) MR. & MRS. M. P.
MORFIT.
371 (LOWER) MRS. J. H. WHITELY
EST.

366 (UPPER) MRS. MILES WHITE,
JR.
369 (CENTRE) MR. JOHN C. TOLAND.
372 (LOWER) MRS. THOS. J. LIND-
SAY.

373 (UPPER) MRS. JOHN S. GIBBS, JR.
374 (UPPER) MRS. MILES WHITE, JR.
375 (UPPER) MRS. E. N. DUNHAM.
376 (CENTRE) MR. JOHN C. TOLAND.
377 (CENTRE) MR. ALBERT G. TOWERS.
378 (CENTRE) MR. & MRS. H. L. DUER.
379 (LOWER) MRS. W. W. HUBBARD.
380 (LOWER) MR. JOHN C. TOLAND.
381 (LOWER) MR. & MRS. E. H. McKEON.

No. 372, an arm chair, is almost a companion piece to No. 371; the arm supports are grooved, but the back is not; the seat rails are covered with upholstery.

In No. 373, the bottom of the front seat rail is in a serpentine curve, and the seat rails are covered.

No. 374 and 375 have bow–shaped top rails in the Chippendale style, as mentioned a few lines above. The piercings on the slats of these two chairs seem to be almost the same; but the slats themselves are different, those in No. 374 being in an uninterrupted curve across the back, and those of No. 375 being broken into three separate divisions.

Nos. 376 and 377 are arm chairs, each having concave seats fully upholstered, with grooved arm supports and stiles, or uprights. The designs of the top rails and slats are somewhat similar, although the piercings of the top rails and the slats are not the same at the ends. Hence we notice the small Gothic "quatrefoil" pierc-ings which are seen in several of the Chippendale style chairs "in the Gothic manner," as in Nos. 110, 114 and others.

In No. 378 the top rail and slats are in four divisions, and in the centre of each is a small carved design resembling the "anthemion," or honeysuckle, which we have seen in several of the Chippendale style chairs, as in Nos. 178 and 179, and is described in note 48 in section 51.

Nos. 379–381 are three chairs with very similar top rails and slats. In No. 379 the piercings are long and are divided in the centre by a ball. In this chair the top of the rear seat rail is visible and is seen to be curved in the same serpentine line as the top rail and the slats; the front seat rail is in a single serpentine form.

Nos. 380 and 381 are much alike, but the former has a concave seat. On the top rail and slats of these two chairs, and also in Nos. 379 and 388, are tiny knobs, or points, which seem to divide the curves into separate portions. Similar knobs will be seen in the Chippendale style chairs Nos. 97, 112 and others.

No. 382 is interesting for the reason that each one of the piercings on the top rail and the slats is different in size and design; and the piercings are grad-uated, the smallest one being in the top rail.

Nos. 383 and 384, side and arm chairs, almost companion pieces, are of an-other type, the top rail being solid, not pierced. In these two chairs, as in No. 382, the piercings in the slats are each different in design. The shape of the arms in No. 384 is clearly seen. In these chairs the different curves of the three slats make an odd combination. In the arm chair the seat is concave and the outside edges of the front legs are grooved, as is faintly seen in the engraving.

In No. 385 the oval panels in the centre of the top rail and slats are sug-gestive of those in No. 378. The stiles, or uprights, projecting above the top rail, and the tapering of the front legs in the manner of Hepplewhite, seem to indi-cate a somewhat later date than the other chairs illustrated. This and No. 366 are the only chairs shown here which have but two slats in addition to the top rail.

No. 386, an arm chair, is the only chair shown here which has four slats, in addition to the top rail, all of which are pierced with one similar piercing.

382 (Upper) Mrs. Wm. M. Roberts.   383 (Upper) Mrs. Thos. J. Lindsay.   384 (Upper) Dr. James Bordley,
385 (Centre) Dr. H. J. Berkley.   386 (Centre) Dr. M. A. Abrams.   Jr.
388 (Lower) Mrs. W. D. Steuart.   389 (Lower) Mr. John C. Toland.   387 (Centre) Mr. John C. Toland.
                                                                          390 (Lower) Mr. J. C. D'Arcy
                                                                               Paul.

Nos. 387 and 388 are of still another type, having both the top rail and the three slats entirely solid and unpierced. In No. 387 the back is finely ornamented with eight carved rosettes and the top rail is carved with a string of leaves. No. 388 is a plainer chair with somewhat wider top rail and slats. Here will be seen the same kind of small projecting knobs or points as in Nos. 379–381.

Nos. 389 and 390, arm and side chairs, are regarded by scholars as being in the Sheraton style. They are obviously not in the Chippendale style nor in that of Hepplewhite; and the graceful design of the back and the carved oval panel with the five plumes indicate the school of Sheraton. A three–chair back settee of the same design appears as No. 512.

Section 59. Wing chairs.–-These chairs,[1] generally known as "easy"[2] chairs in the period in which they were made, were popular in our country for more than one hundred years, about 1700 to 1810. The distinctive features in all types of wing chairs are the high backs, the arms and the "wings." The wings were meant not only to make the chair comfortable, but also to protect the occupant from the strong drafts which must have resulted from the open fires in the homes of our ancestors. The upholstery of the chair was as important as the cabinet work, and in the homes of well–to–do families the best needlework was often used, covering the entire visible surface of the chair except the legs and feet; and even these were sometimes hidden by a valance, which protected the feet of the occupant, as in No. 403.

The American wing chairs may generally be classified in three types, which differ chiefly in the arms and legs. In the first style, the Queen Anne, shown in Nos. 391–395; the arms terminate in an almost vertical rounded form; the wooden framework of the arms, which is covered by upholstery, is attached to the wings, not to the back of the chair; the legs are cabriole, generally with club feet, which are also called "Dutch" feet; and stretchers are often used. The wood was walnut.

In the second style, the Chippendale, shown in Nos. 396–398, the arms are similarly attached to the wings, but the upper part of the arm makes an outward turn or scroll;[3] the legs are cabriole, generally with ball and claw feet in the

1. A wing chair is defined as an upholstered easy chair with side wings or ear–pieces to support the head.

2. This name was no doubt very suitable in the early part of the eighteenth century, as perhaps no other chair was then made which could be called an "easy" chair; but now the word "easy" is equally appropriate to other styles of chairs. The word "wing" chair is more descriptive; and even more so is the term "winged arm chair," which is sometimes used in England. Another term is "fireside." The names "grandfather" or "grandmother" were also given to these chairs, doubtless indicating the principal occupants.

These chairs were somewhat expensive, requiring much material for the coverings. They were chiefly used in the bedroom, and were listed in the court inventories with the other furniture of that room, as far back as 1710. Now, however, these chairs, covered with elegant fabrics, are worthy of a place in the drawing room.

3. A similar shape of arm was used in English chairs before the time of Chippendale and again became prominent after being adopted by him. Examples of these earlier chairs are in Mr. Cescinsky's

earlier chairs, and with straight legs in the later ones, as in other Chippendale style chairs. Mahogany was the usual wood in this type of chairs.

In the third style, the Hepplewhite and Sheraton, shown in Nos. 399–402, the arms extend all the way to the back of the chair, not only to the wings. The wings are generally larger than in the two previous types and rest upon the arms. The legs on these chairs are square and straight as in other chairs of the Hepplewhite style, but sometimes they are round in the Sheraton style; and occasionally a wing chair in the American Empire style is seen.[4] Mahogany was used in these chairs.

These differences, which will be seen in the illustrations, are sufficient to identify the style of chair in most cases; but in some instances a chair may have features of more than one style, making it uncertain whether it should be regarded as being in one style or the other, as is mentioned in the comments. Moreover, as there was no inflexible rule requiring chair makers to make a wing chair in exactly one manner and no other, the chairs may be found with variations from the standard designs.

Nos. 391 and 392 are in the Queen Anne style, their distinctive features being the almost vertical arms ending in a rounded form, or "roll," and without any indication of the arms extending further back than the front line of the wings; and also the four cabriole legs, each terminating in a club foot. Each of the front legs is ornamented, No. 391 with carving and No. 392 with beading. The stretchers which are often seen in the Queen Anne style wing chairs are not present here. In No. 391 the seat is rounded in front and was made to hold a cushion; the seat of No. 392 is also rounded, but is higher and a cushion is not used. About 1740–1760.

Nos. 393 and 394 have the arms of the Queen Anne style, and also stretchers in the shape which is characteristic of the style, as may be seen on other chairs of the period, as in Nos. 50 and 52. Each chair has a straight seat front and a cushion. No. 393 has club feet in front and straight feet in the rear; in No. 394 we see ball and claw feet on the front legs. In England the ball and claw foot was used in the later chairs in the Queen Anne style; but in our country they were apparently first used on chairs in the Chippendale style. In No. 394 the arms are in the Queen Anne style and the legs and feet are in the Chippendale style; these details of the two styles are combined and seem to show a transition from the Queen Anne to the Chippendale style. These two chairs, and the next one, No. 395, with their fine upholstery, are very handsome pieces. About 1745–1760.

(NOTE 3, continued)

"English Furniture," volume 1, No. 96, etc.; and in Mr. Lockwood's "Colonial Furniture," volume 2, figure 507. On page 75 Mr. Cescinsky states that it is most unusual to find these chairs with the original upholstery; that loose cushions were generally used on the seats; and that spring seats were not known in England until about 1750.

4. An example is in Mr. Lockwood's "Colonial Furniture," figure 515, with animal's claw feet.

391 (UPPER) MRS. JOHN S. GIBBS, JR.   392 (UPPER) MRS. BAYARD TURNBULL.
393 (CENTRE) MRS. MILES WHITE, JR.   394 (CENTRE) MRS. JOHN S. GIBBS, JR.
395 (LOWER) MRS. JOHN S. GIBBS, JR.   396 (LOWER) MR. A. MORRIS TYSON.

In No. 395 the arms are almost vertical, in the Queen Anne style; the front legs with ball and claw feet indicate the Chippendale style, and the rear legs with club feet suggest the Queen Anne style; this chair, also, may thus be considered a transition piece. Here there are no stretchers; the seat is rounded and the knees are carved with a shell. About 1745–1760.

We next examine three chairs in the full Chippendale style. In these chairs, Nos. 396–398, as in the Queen Anne ones, the framework of the arms does not extend further back than the front lines of the wings; but the arms are not vertical, and the upper part of the arms turns outward in a scroll form. This form of arm will also be seen in the sofas Nos. 540–543 in the Chippendale style shown in section 70.

In No. 396 we see the kinds of legs and feet used in so many other chairs in the Chippendale style, the front legs being cabriole in form, ending in ball and claw feet, and the rear legs being plain. In Nos. 397 and 398 the cabriole legs terminate in types of the club foot, such as the foot shown in illustration No. 11, figure 11, in section 25. In each of these three chairs the seat is rounded in front, and the first two have cushions. The stretchers seen in some of the Queen Anne style chairs are not used. The Chippendale style chairs are perhaps the most elegant in appearance of any of the wing type. Their dates are about 1755–1785.

In the next group are five wing chairs in the Hepplewhite and Sheraton styles, Nos. 399–403. These chairs exhibit the characteristics mentioned above, namely, that the wings are generally larger than those in the chairs in the Queen Anne and Chippendale styles; and that the arms extend to the back of the chair and support the wings which appear to be separate from the arms, as though they had been added after the arms were put in place. In the Hepplewhite wing chairs the legs are square and straight and are strengthened by stretchers; but in the Sheraton type there are no stretchers and the legs are rounded as in some of the late Sheraton style chairs. These chairs are all very similar in form, except as to the legs and some minor details; but the pleasing variety in the upholstery designs seems to justify the number of examples here shown, although the chairs are not as handsome as those in the previous styles. About 1785–1810.

Nos. 399 and 400 are in the full Hepplewhite style, with straight legs. In the first chair the upholstery on the sloping front of the arms and on the seat rail is ornamented with large-headed nails. About 1785–1800.

In Nos. 401 and 402 the construction of the arms and wings is about the same as in the two preceding chairs; but here we see the round legs of the Sheraton style instead of the straight ones of the Hepplewhite style. In No. 401 the legs are in the usual round form; in No. 402 they have a spiral carving. About 1795–1810.

In No. 403 the construction of the arms is not as well seen as in the four preceding chairs; and the feet are not seen at all, being hidden by the valance. It is said that this style of covering was used in the period of about 1790 to 1800.

Nos. 404 and 405 are not strictly wing chairs, but they are sufficiently like them to be shown here rather than elsewhere.

397 (Upper) Mr. & Mrs. H. L. Duer.
399 (Centre) Hammond-Harwood House.
401 (Lower) Mr. & Mrs. J. M. Berry.

398 (Upper) Mrs. Miles White, Jr.
400 (Centre) Mr. F. Highlands Burns.
402 (Lower) Mrs. I. R. Trimble.

403 (Upper) Mr. & Mrs. Lennox Birckhead.   404 (Upper) Mr. & Mrs. H. L. Duer.
405 (Lower) Mrs. Miles White, Jr.   406 (Lower) Anonymous.

In No. 404 the wings and the back are made in a semi-circle, with nine vertical divisions, thus resembling somewhat the inner side of the half of a barrel, and for that reason the chair has been called a "barrel–back" chair.[5] The round and reeded front legs are in the Sheraton style and the rear legs are curved. This may be an English chair. About 1795–1810.

No. 405 also has a rounded back with extensions at the sides which are not visibly separated from the curved portion of the back or from the arms. The front legs are of the straight type and the rear legs curve outwardly. About 1785–1800.

The next chair, No. 406, is a handsome wing chair said to be in the French style of Chippendale, with fine carving on the arm supports, the seat rails and the legs and feet.[6] It appears here instead of with the other Chippendale style wing chairs because it is of a very different type. It is one of the six celebrated "Sample" chairs which are attributed to a noted Philadelphia cabinet maker, and it came into wide public notice because it brought at an auction sale the highest price ever paid for an American chair.[7] About 1770.

Section 60. Other upholstered chairs.—Having examined one type of fully upholstered chairs in the preceding section on "wing" chairs, we now see other types of such chairs. At the time when the fine chairs shown in this section were made, the fabrics used in their covering were generally of an elegant character, and as the frames were of fine proportions, the chairs present a handsome and dignified appearance.[1] Most of the chairs here illustrated are in the Chippendale style, and their dates are from about 1755 to 1780.

5.   A similar chair with square and plain legs is shown in Mr. Percy Macquoid's "English Furniture," volume 4, figure 177; probably on account of the kind of legs the chair is referred to as in the style of Hepplewhite; our chair No. 404 is regarded as in the style of Sheraton because of its reeded legs. In Mr. Macquoid's book the chair is called a "tub" chair.

6.   In this chair we notice the serpentine form of the top rail. The uncovered arms have supports which are curved inwards and are carved with leaves. The front seat rail is finely carved with scrolls and leaves, and with a man's head which may have been intended to represent Benjamin Franklin. The front legs are in the cabriole form and have paw feet, and the rear legs flare outward.

7.   At the Reifsnyder auction sale in New York in April, 1929, this chair was sold for $33,000. It is said that it was made about 1770 by Benjamin Randolph, of Philadelphia, whose label is shown in illustration No. 1 in this book.

Illustrated articles in which this and the other five sample chairs are discussed are in the magazine "Antiques," November, 1925, pages 273–275, by Mr. Cescinsky, and in May, 1927, page 366, by Mr. S. W. Woodhouse, Jr.

See also section 51 in this volume, in which two of the "Sample" side chairs are illustrated, Nos. 116 and 117.

1.   It has been said that many arm chairs appear to be side chairs with arms added; but this does not apply to the arm chairs here shown, as in size and design they seem to have been constructed purely as arm chairs. A similar remark, made in regard to rocking chairs, is that a rocking chair often appears to be a side chair with rockers added; as to rocking chairs, see section 63.

In several of these illustrations casters will be seen on the feet of the chairs; these additions should be disregarded in examining the illustrations. As to casters, see section 27.

Chairs of this type with very wide seats recall the type known as "drunkards'" or "lovers'" chairs, two of which are illustrated as Nos. 61–62 in section 50 and are referred to in note 8 in that section.

No. 407 has legs in cabriole form terminating in club, or Dutch, feet in the Queen Anne style, but the general design, the arms and the arm supports are in the Chippendale style.[2] As in perhaps all others of these arm chairs, the back slants slightly backward from an upright position, the technical term for which is "canted."[3] The top of the back is in a serpentine curve. The large-headed tacks will be seen on the seat rail. About 1760.

Nos. 408 and 409 are handsome arm chairs in the Chippendale style, and are probably of English origin, like No. 407.

No. 408 is elaborately ornamented with carving on the seat rail and on the legs which are in an early form, the feet having an inward scroll.[4] This chair was inherited from an ancestor of the present owner. About 1745–1760.

No. 409 has ball and claw feet and is regarded as being pre–Chippendale in style, as to which see section 15, note 6. It has much carving on the arm supports and on the legs which are somewhat shorter[5] than in some other chairs shown here. The curve of the arm supports in this and the two preceding chairs are of a similar character and are well seen in the engravings. About 1740–1750.

In Nos. 410 and 411, the former an arm chair, we see the straight and plain legs and stretchers which were introduced by Chippendale about the year 1755 and which are seen on so many of the chairs of that style in section 51; and in No. 411 the legs are in the same shape but are grooved. Each of these two chairs has solid corner brackets which are parts of the legs and connect the legs with the seat rails. These solid brackets were used to strengthen the legs and also were often ornamental; but the fragile pierced brackets shown on the next two chairs and on several others shown in section 51, were entirely ornamental. About 1755–1770.

The next three chairs in the Chippendale style, Nos. 412–414, have ornamental fretwork in one or more parts. This fretwork may be solid or pierced; the solid may be carved on the solid wood of the arms or legs or may be cut from

2. A chair of the same design, with club feet on the front legs, is shown in Mr. Cescinsky's "English Furniture," volume 2, figure 191, page 191, and is regarded as a Chippendale style chair. It is dated about 1760.

3. "Canted" means tilted or slanted, or inclined to one side; Century Dictionary.

4. In Cescinsky and Hunter's "English and American Furniture," page 126, is shown an English chair with the same kind of scroll feet, but without the pad underneath; the date is given as about 1745.

5. A chair almost exactly the same as this in design and carving is illustrated in Mr. Symonds' "Old English Walnut and Lacquer Furniture," plate 20, opposite page 108, and is dated 1735.

On page 127, in a note, Mr. Symonds remarks that the reason that these chairs "have short legs is owing to their seats being fitted with squabs, (a loose cushion seat for a chair or couch), and this increased height in the upholstery necessitated a reduction in the height of the leg." And on the same page it is said that "a number of single chairs will be found converted into arm chairs by the addition of spurious arms, as the arm chair is not only more valuable than the single but far more salable. To detect such a chair will not, however, require much circumspection, as owing to its narrow seat and back it will lack the proportions of the genuine arm chair."

407 (Upper) Dr. James Bordley, Jr.
409 (Centre) Dr. James Bordley, Jr.
411 (Lower) Mrs. Miles White, Jr.

408 (Upper) Mr. & Mrs. E. H. McKeon.
410 (Centre) Mr. & Mrs. H. L. Duer.
412 (Lower) Dr. James Bordley, Jr.

wood and applied[6] on the arms or legs; the pierced fretwork was cut out of several thin sheets which were glued together to prevent warping or breakage, as in the furniture of John Belter, of New York, who is mentioned in section 22, note 3.

In No. 412, a side chair, handsomely upholstered, are three examples of this work; the pierced fret brackets at the junction of the legs with the seat; the applied fret designs on the legs; and the pierced fret stretchers.[7] About 1760–1770.

No. 413, an arm chair, also has pierced fret brackets, resembling those in No. 367, connecting the legs and the seat rail; the stretchers are of the kind used on the Chippendale style chairs having straight and plain legs. About 1760–1775.

In No. 414 the arm supports and the legs are ornamented with carved and applied fretwork not well seen in the engraving. The form of the block feet will be noticed. In this chair the top of the back is straight; in the others here illustrated the form is serpentine. About 1760–1775.

Nos. 415, 416 and 417 are representative and very similar arm chairs in the Chippendale style, without special features except that in No. 415 the arm supports are ornamented with carving. In Nos. 416 and 417 will be seen a decorative method of placing the large–headed tacks on the seat rail, in about the same manner as in No. 407. In No. 416 the concave shape of the arm supports is well shown. The legs of No. 417 are grooved. About 1770–1780.

In No. 418 the seat is concave, as in some of the Chippendale style chairs shown in section 51, as, for example, No. 137. The legs are grooved, as also are the arm supports which are in the same shape as those in Nos. 407 and 408. About 1770–1780.

"Martha Washington" arm chairs. A chair at Mt. Vernon, supposed to have been used there by Martha Washington, has received her name, and this name has for many years been given to chairs of a similar character.[8] In their general style these chairs seem to have been based upon the Chippendale style chairs above illustrated; but their slightly tapering square or round legs, and the shape of their arms and arm supports, indicate the Hepplewhite style. A noted writer refers to

6.   In many cases the fretwork on the legs and other parts of chairs and tables is not carved, but is "applied," as are the streamers on the fine Philadelphia style highboys shown in section 87, where the subject is mentioned. Mr. Cescinsky devotes chapters 12 and 13 in his "English Furniture," volume 2, to "Chippendale's Gothic and Fretted Furniture," pages 224–311.

7.   An arm chair of very similar design is shown as figure 295 in volume 2 of Mr. Cescinsky's "English Furniture." In his comment on that chair Mr. Cescinsky writes that the chair "is the decorative limit reached in these square–leg fretted arm chairs, where the under framing and the brackets are pierced and the fronts of the arms and the legs are all decorated with applied frets." Fretwork was much used during the prevalence of the Chinese taste in England, as in the Chippendale style chair No. 141.

8.   In the absence of written evidence, some doubt may prevail as to the connection of these chairs with Martha Washington; but the "Mother of her Country" seems to be entitled to have at least one pleasing object of domestic life named in her honor in addition to sewing tables, such as Nos. 1557–1565.

413 (Upper) Dr. M. A. Abrams.
415 (Centre) Mr. Arthur E. Cole.
417 (Lower) Mrs. Howard Sill.

414 (Upper) Mr. Albert G. Towers.
416 (Centre) Mrs. Miles White, Jr.
418 (Lower) Mr. Arthur E. Cole.

248

419 (UPPER) MR. C. EDWARD SNYDER.
421 (CENTRE) ANONYMOUS.
423 (LOWER) MRS. EDWIN B. NIVER.

420 (UPPER) MR. DANIEL R. RANDALL.
422 (CENTRE) MRS. BAYARD TURNBULL.
424 (LOWER) ANONYMOUS.

them as "the Hepplewhite overlapping with the Sheraton."[9] These chairs are all very similar in appearance; the high back tilts slightly to the rear; there is no upholstery on the arms, differing in this respect from the Chippendale style upholstered arm chairs; the top of the back is generally in a serpentine curve; the arms and their supports are curved; and stretchers are generally used.

No. 419 is a good example of this type, with the characteristic features above mentioned. Here the arm supports and the legs are grooved and the legs are slightly tapered in the Hepplewhite style. No. 420 has a high back, with other features as in No. 419, including the tapered legs. In the engraving the rear stretcher is hidden by the front seat rail. In No. 421 the curve of the arm supports is more clearly seen than in the previous two examples. Here also the legs are tapered. The dates of chairs of this type are thought to be about 1790–1800.

Later chairs. In these illustrations, Nos. 422–424, are three upholstered arm chairs which have certain designs similar to those in chairs shown in other sections of this volume, as mentioned below.

No. 422 is a tall chair in the Sheraton style, having the characteristic shape and reeding of the legs and the reeded ends and supports of the arms. The high back suggests that the chair was perhaps made for the use of a chairman of a legislative or other assembly;[10] and it may be compared with the Hepplewhite style chair No. 229, which was probably used for that purpose. The brass feet are appropriate here. A somewhat similar chair with rockers is shown as No. 482; see also No. 499. About 1800–1820.

In No. 423 the influence of the Directory style appears in the curve of the back, which continues unbroken from the top rail to the end of the seat, as in No. 362 in the section on the Empire style chairs. The arm supports are in the shape of a swan's neck, an Empire design which appears also in sofas of the period, as in No. 588. The legs may have been shortened. About 1830–1840.

In No. 424 the sloping sides of the back are similar to those in the Empire style chair No. 353, to which are added the arms and their supports and the upholstery. About 1830–1840.

Section 61. Corner chairs.—These chairs were intended to stand in corners[1] of a room and their special features are two; first, the seat comes to a point, or a

9. Mr. Cescinsky in "English and American Furniture," page 274. A few chairs of this type were made definitely in the Sheraton style, with reeded arm supports and legs; one is in the Metropolitan Museum of Art and is shown in "The Homes of Our Ancestors," figure 164.

10. A chair almost the same is shown in an article entitled "Jefferson's Furniture at Monticello," in "The Antiquarian," July, 1930, on page 40, where it is said that the chair was used by Jefferson when vice–president, which was from 1797 to 1801. The same chair appeared in "Antiques" in the issue of December, 1927, page 485.

1. This gave the name "corner" chair. They are also called "roundabout" chairs, a name which indicates the shape of their backs. Mr. Lockwood mentions, in his "Colonial Furniture," volume 2, pages 69–70, that the corner chair may be derived from a round chair known as a "wheel" chair, which had stretchers radiating like the spokes of a wheel, and also a semi–circular back, illustrated in his book as the frontispiece and as figure 516.

small curve, in the centre of the front, where it is supported by the front leg; and, second, the back consists of a horizontal, semi–circular and heavy rail[2] which is generally supported by extensions upwards of the rear leg and the two side ones.

In the hands of Chippendale and the cabinet makers of his school these chairs reached their highest standard of design. They are not shown in his "Director," perhaps for the reason that the corner chair was not in the latest style in the year 1754 when his book was published.[3]

In addition to their interest as a fine type of chair, these corner chairs are important to us because from them the "Windsor" chair was perhaps developed, which was one of the most popular chairs made in our country, as will appear in the next section. The dates of the corner chairs here illustrated are from about 1725 to 1775 or later.

The American corner chairs were made in three successive styles,[4] with several features which we have seen in certain chairs previously illustrated; first, in a transitional style with Spanish feet and "turned" legs and stretchers such as those illustrated in chair No. 41; second, in the Queen Anne style with the solid splat and the club, or Dutch, feet similar to those shown in the chair No. 42; and, third, in the Chippendale style with the ball and claw feet and pierced splat such as those shown in the chair No. 153. Many variations in details were made by the American chair makers.

The semi–circular top rail in these corner chairs is generally made of three curved pieces of wood; the lower two of these pieces are connected at the centre of the back and form the lower and flat portion of the top rail; the third, the upper piece, is put on the lower ones; this method of construction was also followed in the early types of Windsor chairs, such as Nos. 442 and 443.

No. 425, in the first style, is in a transitional design, having front stretchers and three Spanish feet of the period of about 1725, as shown in the chairs Nos. 39–41. There are no splats between the arm supports as there are in all of the other chairs here shown. This chair is of maple, with a rush seat, and is dated at about 1725. It is of very plain character but shows well the period features. This illustration appears here through the courtesy of the Essex Institute, at Salem, Massachusetts.[5] About 1725–1750.

2. This kind of rail was also used in the early type of Windsor chairs; see the next section, Nos. 442 and 443.

3. As to this book see "The Chippendale style," section 15.

4. A corner chair in the Sheraton style is shown in Mr. Cescinsky's "English Furniture," figure 365, and it is said that a corner chair was an unusual form at the period of the chair, about 1795–1800. The two splats were lyres. It is possible that corner chairs were made in the Sheraton style in our country, but the writer has never seen one.

5. The Essex Institute publishes catalogues of its large collections of photographic negatives of New England buildings, exterior and interior, furniture, glass, metal work and other antiquities; from these negatives photographic prints are made on order at small cost. The Institute is in a town which is perhaps the most interesting in New England. In architecture of the eighteenth century Salem is almost in the class of Annapolis but has no houses of equal elegance.

No. 426 is another transitional chair of about the same date, showing the Queen Anne style in several respects, such as the Dutch front foot and the solid splats which do not rest upon the seat rails as in the next chair, but are supported by a cross–rail as in the Queen Anne style chairs Nos. 82–84. The rush seat, the turnings of the legs and of the double stretchers are similar to those in the preceding chair. This chair is illustrated here through the courtesy of Mr. Luke Vincent Lockwood, in whose "Colonial Furniture," volume 2, it appears as figure 518. About 1725–1750 or later.

The second style of corner chairs is the Queen Anne style, of which four examples are shown, Nos. 427–430.

In No. 427 the front leg is in the cabriole form, with a foot of the club, or Dutch, type; the other three legs have the same foot, but are straight and rounded as in the table No. 1308. The two splats in this chair are not solid, being pierced in a design which is very similar to that in the Chippendale style chairs Nos. 153 and 154. The seat rail comes to a point in the centre of the front of the square seat. The skirts under the seat rails are very large, indicating that the chair was intended for a bedroom. The seat itself is of the "slip in" type as in perhaps all corner chairs, the seat rail and the skirt not being well suited for a covering of upholstery. About 1740–1750.

In No. 428 the front of the seat is not pointed, but is shaped in a rounded form, making a more graceful appearance than the pointed seat. The vase–shaped splats are solid, as in many of the Queen Anne, and in some of the Chippendale, style chairs. The front leg is in the cabriole form with a club foot, but the other three legs are straight. The smooth rounded knee may also be noticed. A particular feature is the use of crossed stretchers, often called X stretchers. The arms of the top rail are flat and terminate in an extended and rounded form, as in most of the other corner chairs. About 1740–1750.

No. 429 has a solid splat and a deep skirt with an extension, as in No. 427. The front leg is cabriole in form and has a Dutch, or club, foot; the other three legs are turned in a form which resembles that of a vase, and which is also seen in No. 435. About 1740–1750.

In No. 430 the front leg is cabriole in form, ending in a grooved Dutch, or club, foot; the three other legs are turned and have small ball feet similar to the rear feet in No. 426. The skirt of the chair is deep but has no extension such as that in Nos. 427 and 429; and the splats are solid. About 1740–1750.

In the remaining chairs, Nos. 431–439, various features of the Chippendale style are seen. The splats are generally similar to those of the usual type of Chippendale chairs of the same period. As mentioned in section 51, at note 12, the Chippendale style chairs with cabriole legs and ball and claw feet were in style for some years before those with straight legs which were used after about 1755; but it does not follow that all chairs with ball and claw feet were earlier in manufacture, as for some years both kinds of legs and feet were made simultaneously. Beginning with the earlier style, we see the cabriole legs, ending in ball and claw feet. About 1755–1785.

425 (UPPER) ESSEX INSTITUTE, SALEM.
428 (CENTRE) MRS. MILES WHITE, JR.
431 (LOWER) HAMMOND-HARWOOD HOUSE.

426 (UPPER) ANONYMOUS.
429 (CENTRE) MR. & MRS. H. L. DUER.
432 (LOWER) MR. E. G. MILLER, JR.

427 (UPPER) MR. JOHN C. TOLAND.
430 (CENTRE) MRS. BAYARD TURN-BULL.
433 (LOWER) MR. ALBERT G. TOW-ERS.

In Nos. 431 and 432 there are four cabriole legs with ball and claw feet. The design of the splat in No. 431 is similar to that in the Chippendale style chair No. 120 and certain others; see the comments on No. 120; the splat is also similar to that in No. 439. In No. 432 the splat is very simply pierced. The knees in both chairs are carved. The arm supports in No. 431 are turned and upright as in the previous chairs; in No. 432 they are in the form of cyma curves[6] and resemble cabriole legs "inverted" meaning "upside down"; and here also we see a deep skirt under the rails of the seat. About 1755–1785.

In Nos. 433 and 434, the former maple and the latter mahogany, each has a cabriole leg in front with ball and claw feet, but the other legs are plain and straight. In No. 433 the splats are similar to those in No. 427, and those in No. 434 are also in the Chippendale style. In No. 434 the front seat rails are ornamented with a carved shell of the type sometimes seen on chairs of the Chippendale style, as, for example, in Nos. 90 and 118; and the ends of the arms are carved with "knuckles." About 1755–1785.

In Nos. 435, 436 and 437 different details are seen. In No. 435 the front leg is straight and square, but the other three are turned in the vase form noticed in No. 429. The splats resemble those in the Chippendale style chair No. 167. The skirt has semi–circular extensions as in No. 427. About 1755–1785.

In No. 436 all the legs are straight and square in the Chippendale style. The splats are similar to those in the chair No. 165. About 1755–1785.

No. 437 has four straight and square legs and the vase–shaped splats are solid, resembling the vase portion of the splats in Nos. 56 and 59 in section 50. The seat rail extensions are large, are shaped in curves, and are ornamental as well as useful. About 1755–1785.

No. 438 is a plain corner chair with a rush seat and large and heavy square legs and arm supports and stretchers. The splats are similar in design to those in the chairs Nos. 155–157, but are different from those shown in Nos. 120–123 and Nos. 431 and 439. About 1755–1785.

This series of corner chairs ends with No. 439, a fine Chippendale style chair with an extension above the top rail.[7] This extension has the appearance of being the back of a small Chippendale style chair placed on top of the back of the corner chair. The splat in the extension and those in the two splats below are of the same design, which resemble those in No. 431 and also those in No. 120 and others in section 51 on the Chippendale style chairs. The crossed stretchers will also be noticed. About 1755–1785.

6.   As to cyma curves see section 23.
7.   In the English book entitled "A Glossary of English Furniture," by Messrs. Penderel–Brodhurst and Layton, in the definition of corner chairs is the cross reference "See Barber's chair." In this latter definition it is said that a barber's chair is "a corner chair . . with a rest for the head rising from the back portion of the semi–circular arm–rail. . . These so–called barber's chairs, often elaborately carved and upholstered, were very popular in the eighteenth century."
       See also the "combs" on Windsor chairs, mentioned in note 8 in section 62, and an illustration in "Antiques," February, 1935, page 74.

434 (UPPER) MRS. WM. DEFORD.
437 (LOWER) MD. SOC. COLONIAL
    DAMES.

435 (UPPER) MRS. MILES WHITE, JR.
438 (LOWER) MR. JOHN S. McDAN-
    IEL.

436 (UPPER) MRS. BAYARD TURN-
    BULL.
439 (LOWER) DR. JAMES BORDLEY, JR.

Section 62. Windsor chairs.—Whether the designs of the early American Windsor chairs were derived from the English form of Windsor chair, or whether they came to us directly from the "corner chair" is a matter upon which opinions may differ, and which need not be discussed here; but the illustrations of an English chair, No. 441, and of the early corner chairs Nos. 425 and 426, may suggest the probability that our earliest Windsor chairs were indebted in part to both sources for their designs. Their American place of origin, however, is not uncertain, for it seems clear that American Windsor chairs were first made in Philadelphia, and that the date of their appearance was about the year 1725. Strange to say, little attention has generally been given to them in the books; recently, however, the researches[1] of students have produced much information, and have apparently raised the Windsor chair from a lowly position to one of some importance.

The plainer types of Windsor chairs were low-priced articles, suitable for farm houses and other modest dwellings. Only the finer Windsor chairs were

1. A. In an article by the late Mr. J. B. Kerfoot, entitled "American Windsor chairs," published in the magazine "Country Life in America," October, 1917, pages 65–70, with sixty–one illustrations, a clear analysis of the chairs is made, dividing them into six classes; and the chairs are sufficiently described. The classification of Mr. Kerfoot is followed in this section.

B. In the book entitled "Knowing, collecting and restoring early American furniture," by Mr. H. H. Taylor, published by J. B. Lippincott Co., 1930, pages 73–82 are devoted to the restoration of Windsor chairs, with incidental information of a practical kind.

C. In "The story of American furniture," by Mr. T. H. Ormsbee, published by The Macmillan Company, 1934, pages 193–220, more pages with illustrations and drawings are given to Windsor chairs than to any other kind of chairs.

D. Mr. Walter A. Dyer contributed to the magazine "The Antiquarian," October, 1929, page 29, an article with twenty–five illustrations, entitled "A short history of the Windsor chair," which contains a discussion of the subject.

E. In "The Pennsylvania Museum Bulletin," December, 1925, pages 46–58, is an article by Mr. J. Stogdell Stokes, with illustrations of twenty–six chairs. In the same issue, on pages 58–60, is an article by Mr. Fiske Kimball entitled "Thomas Jefferson's Windsor Chairs." Both of these articles are valuable and interesting. The article of Mr. Stokes appears also in "Antiques," April, 1926, page 222. It is referred to again in note 11 in this section.

F. Mr. Wallace Nutting's book entitled "American Windsors," published in 1917, contains one hundred and ninety–two pages and about one hundred illustrations of chairs, with comments. In his "Furniture Treasury," almost two hundred, Nos. 2514–2705, are shown—the largest collection published, but not all arranged in groups.

G. Advertisements of makers of Windsor chairs are in the two volumes of the books entitled "Arts and Crafts in Philadelphia, Maryland and South Carolina," published by the Walpole Society, and mentioned in section 45, notes 5, A and 5, C.

H. In some cities Windsor chairs were advertised "as good as those made in Philadelphia" or as "Philadelphia made Windsor chairs." On page 179 of volume 1 of "Arts and Crafts" is an advertisement in 1784 in a South Carolina newspaper of "Philadelphia Windsor chairs, either armed or unarmed, as neat as any imported, and much better stuff." On page 189 is an advertisement in 1766, from the same newspaper, in which it is said: "Imported from Philadelphia. . . A large and neat assortment of Windsor chairs . . well painted, high back'd low back'd, sack back'd, and settees or double seated, fit for piazzas or gardens, children's dining and low chairs. Also walnut of the same construction."

I. In the Baltimore City directories many cabinet makers are classified as makers of Windsor chairs, and in the directory of the late date of 1849–1850 seven names are listed as "Chair manufacturers—Windsor and Fancy." This is also stated in section 54, note 21.

received in the houses of people of means, and then not often in the drawing room, but in the less important rooms or on the porch.[2] But at the present time, being antiques, they are more highly esteemed, and are sometimes given a rank to which they may not be entitled; for example, in any room where there is other furniture in the style of Chippendale or Hepplewhite or Sheraton, or even in the early Empire style, a Windsor chair, no matter how fine, seems to be out of place.[3]

A number of matters of interest in connection with Windsor chairs are mentioned in the note,[4] perhaps in more detail than is desirable; but so many Windsor chairs are seen that it is well to understand them somewhat fully.

2.   It appears that General Washington had thirty Windsor chairs for his guests on the east portico at Mt. Vernon; and that Thomas Jefferson in 1801, while President, bought for $192.00 four dozen Windsor arm chairs, which he called by the English name "stick" chairs, a more descriptive but less elegant term than "Windsor" chairs; and previously, in 1800, in a letter written by him, he drew a sketch of the style of chair he desired. These items are in the article on "Thomas Jefferson's Windsor chairs," by Mr. Fiske Kimball, in the "Pennsylvania Museum Bulletin," mentioned above in note 1, E. On page 60 Mr. Kimball writes: "Jefferson's large use of Windsor chairs at a period when he was in the full tide of prosperity tends to confirm the views that they were by no means poorly regarded, but occupied an honorable place in the finest houses of the day." Two illustrated articles entitled "The furnishing of Monticello," by Mrs. Marie Kimball, are in "Antiques," November, 1927, page 380, and December, 1927, page 482; these are mentioned also in note 1, H, in section 11.

3.   The use of a Windsor chair "in connection with the better grade of furniture is a decorative error" in the opinion of Mr. Holloway, as stated in his "American furniture and decoration," page 57.

4.   A.   A Windsor chair has been said to be only a "wooden chair with a common wooden seat." Formerly a cushion was often used to make the seat more comfortable. The chair is light in weight and very durable. According to a tradition which is not taken too seriously, it derived its name from the town of Windsor, England, where King George the First, 1714–1727, saw one and took it to his castle and made it famous.

B.   It does not seem possible to fix exact dates for the various types of these chairs, because of the similarity of designs for a great number of years, with no change in the distinctive features. Mr. Lockwood, "Colonial Furniture," volume 2, pages 73–80, places all of his illustrated chairs in the last half of the eighteenth century, about 1750 to 1800, except two showing the Sheraton influence, such as our No. 469, which is assigned to the first quarter of the nineteenth century. These approximate dates are sufficient for our purpose. In the foreword of the catalogue of the sale of the celebrated Reifsnyder collection in 1929 it was stated that no attempt was made to fix the dates other than "eighteenth century."

C.   In the fine chairs in the Queen Anne, Chippendale and other important styles the wood used on all visible parts of the chair was of one kind, such as walnut or mahogany; but for the various parts of the Windsor chair such woods were selected as were best suited for the purpose. The parts which were bent in various shapes, such as the bow and the arms, were usually of hickory or oak; the spindles, which should yield to the pressure of the back of the occupant were of the same wood. The seat was generally made of a single piece of pine, a wood which was not so liable to shrink or warp as other woods. For the legs and stretchers either maple or birch was generally used.

D.   In very many Windsor chairs the seat is in a shape which is called a "saddle" seat. From the centre of the front of the seat the wood is cut away slightly in a downward slope to the sides. Examples will be seen in No. 447 and others.

E.   The spindles are the round sticks which extend from the seat to the rim of the back of the chair; the term "stick chairs" was used by Thomas Jefferson, as referred to in note 2. In arm chairs the spindles under the arms, not including the "arm support" under the end of the arm, are known as "short spindles." As many as eleven spindles may be in one back; and a noted collector lived in hopes of finding one with thirteen, but never found it. The spindles were sunk into holes made in the rim and the seat in such manner as to make the backs slant backward. In some cases the spindles were gracefully curved; and in the later chairs they were often ornamented with rings in the style of a bamboo stalk.

(Note 4 continued on page 258)

Windsor chairs are best classified by arranging them in groups according to the designs of the backs, as has been attempted in this book in considering other styles of chairs. The shape of the seats is also to be noticed, as certain early types

(NOTE 4, *continued from page 257*)

F. Windsor chairs were generally painted dark green, but other colors were also used. Only occasionally were they finished in the natural colors of the woods. In refinishing an old Windsor chair, black may be added to the list of suitable colors, although it was not often used; but white paint was apparently never used.

G. Rockers now found on Windsor chairs are almost always additions of a later date than the chair itself; see section 63 on "Rocking chairs." The rockers and the lower stretchers in the "converted" chairs are generally too close together.

H. The "turnings" of the legs and stretchers are important features. There are many varieties. Those which cut deeply into the wood are preferred; and chairs without good turnings are not highly esteemed. In New England the favorite types were those in the "vase" design or in the later "bamboo" style; the latter was used in Philadelphia from about 1763. The Pennsylvania turnings will be noticed on the chairs made in that State, such as the comb back chairs Nos. 444–446. See section 35 on turnings.

I. The legs are always connected with the seat at a point about two or three inches in from the edges of the seat, and almost always extend entirely through the seat to the top; and they are "raked," that is, they slant outward.

J. Chairs of several kinds made with short legs are often called "slipper chairs"; and Windsor chairs whose legs have been shortened by accident or otherwise may be represented as being original slipper chairs.

K. The "braced back" type of chair is highly regarded. The "braces" are spindles which rest on a rear extension of the seat and support the back, making the chair stronger than otherwise. Braces were used on several of the six types of chairs; their presence does not constitute a separate type of chair.

L. In purchasing a painted Windsor chair there is always the danger that the chair has been too abundantly "restored." A leg, a stretcher, or a spindle or two, may have been substituted; a broken seat may have been succeeded by a perfect one; parts from several damaged chairs may have been combined to make a new one; or other defects may be present; and yet under the protection of a coat or two of paint none of these "restorations" may be visible. See section 10 as to restorations.

M. Children's chairs and babies' chairs generally followed the designs of full sized chairs; but in babies' chairs the legs were longer so as to give the seat for the baby the proper height for the dining table. These chairs are not illustrated here; many are shown in Mr. Nutting's books mentioned in note 1, F. The legs are very "raked," or slanting, reducing the likelihood of upsetting the chair.

N. Almost all the outlines of good Windsor chairs are curved or slanting, not rectangular. The top rail, the spindles, the legs and the stretchers depart from the right angle; and the holes in which the slanting spindles and legs are placed are necessarily slanting.

O. Fresh green wood was much used in making certain parts of Windsor chairs instead of seasoned wood, especially in the seat. The upper ends of the legs were inserted in holes bored in the seat to receive them. Frequently the tops of the legs are seen in the seat. The same method was used in placing the stretchers. If well seasoned wood was used, the legs were fastened in the hole in the seat by wooden pins and wedges, as may be noticed in some cases.

P. Several minor differences may be seen between the Windsor chairs made in Philadelphia and those made in New England, the principal one being in the form of the leg turnings.

Q. It is said that in side chairs the grain of the wood of the seat was always at right angles to the front of the seat, but that in arm chairs the grain was generally parallel with the front, except in the New England arm chairs such as Nos. 451 and 452.

of Windsor chairs generally have certain kinds of seats.[5] It will be found that the backs of these chairs may be satisfactorily divided into at least six groups, although this arrangement does not include the variations of style in certain chairs which are here collected together in a seventh group under the vague and comprehensive term "miscellaneous." The names here used to designate these six types of backs are sufficiently descriptive to make the names appropriate; but at present there seems to be no standardized names for the six types, and writers on the subject in certain cases use different names for the same type of chair, and this may cause some confusion to those not familiar with the subject.

In order to present these six types of Windsor chairs clearly to the eye in groups, one example of each group appears in illustration No. 440, as follows:[6]

1. Low back chair	4. New England arm chair
2. Comb back chair	5. Fan back chair
3. Hoop back chair	6. Loop back chair

"Miscellaneous Windsor chairs," which are variations of the above six types, are in a seventh group.

In the first three of these groups it will be noticed that there is a semi-circular horizontal rail in the back; in the other groups the horizontal rail is not used. This difference in construction of the back, when once noticed, becomes very apparent to the eye, and tends to simplify the subject. The number of spindles, or the presence of a comb, or braces, or other special features, do not determine the type of a Windsor chair.

(NOTE 4, *continued*)

R. It may be added that Windsor chairs are even now made in great numbers by the furniture manufacturers, which shows that these chairs are still in demand and that they have had a more extended period of popularity than any other type of chair; perhaps its only rival is the slat–back chair, side or rocking, which may be seen in so many country homes. The Windsor has been termed a "universal" chair.

S. Names are occasionally found burnt on the bottom of the seats of Windsor chairs and on other types having wooden seats. A name may be that of the maker of the chair or of a dealer or even of the owner. On some chairs the bottom of the seat has two names. Labels were sometimes used on chairs of this type.

T. In Windsor chairs the spindles are generally odd in number and an even number is said to be unusual. Twelve spindles are seldom found, being an even number and a high one; and a chair with thirteen spindles is a rarity.

5. In the later chairs the particular kinds of seats were not always used with particular kinds of backs, and therefore too much importance should not be given to their seats as indications of dates or place of origin. The seats are not often mentioned in the comments in this section, as the subject is somewhat confusing; but of course a well–shaped seat is a desirable feature.

6. The classification and names here adopted are those of the late Mr. J. B. Kerfoot in his magazine article referred to in note 1, A. The division into these six classes is also used by Mr. J. Stogdell Stokes in his article in "Antiques," April, 1926, page 222, where it is said, page 223, that they are "the six fundamental types of Windsor backs. All others are variants of these." The article by Mr. Walter A. Dyer, also referred to in the same note, 1, D, arranges the chairs in nine groups.

1. Low back   2. Comb back   3. Hoop back

4. New England arm   5. Fan back   6. Loop back

440 The Six Kinds of Windsor Chairs.

For purposes of comparison, the main features of the English type of Windsor chairs are illustrated in the English chair[7] No. 441. The most noticeable difference between the English chairs and the American ones is that the English back generally has a pierced upright splat extending from the centre of the rear of the seat to the centre of the top rail, in addition to the spindles; in the American chairs the space within the frame of the back is occupied only by spindles. The front legs of the English chair are placed at the very corners of the seat, whereas the legs of the American are always two or three inches within the edge of the seat; and the legs of the American chairs are much more raked, or slanting, than the English ones. Other differences of a less conspicuous character might also be mentioned. This English chair has cabriole legs, but the later ones have straight and rounded legs. About 1750–1775.

We now proceed to the types of American Windsor chairs in the order above mentioned.

1. Low back Windsor chairs. Nos. 442 and 443. These chairs are examples of the earliest type of American Windsor chairs. The back is so similar to that of the earlier corner chair No. 425 in section 61, and to others in that section, that the design of the Windsor low back chair was apparently based upon the design of the corner chair. This low back Windsor type of chair was apparently not made in England. It was not very popular in America and not many examples of it are found; but the later forms of American Windsor chairs were developed from it and it is therefore important to us.

The two illustrations, Nos. 442 and 443, show the character of these low back chairs, a special feature being the horizontal, semi–circular and heavy top rail of the back, resembling that of the corner chairs. In No. 442 the supports at the ends of the arms are vertical, as was often the case in the corner chairs and in some of the comb back Windsor chairs; but in No. 443 and in other types they are slanting. No. 442 has seventeen spindles and No. 443 has nine. The seat of the latter chair is somewhat higher than in the former. As in the corner chairs, the top rails are made in three pieces, a central raised portion and two arms, the joints being barely visible in the illustrations. About 1750–1800.

2. Comb back Windsor chairs. Nos. 444–449. In this type of chair the "comb" is the particular feature.[8] A comb back chair is in reality a low back chair with the addition of extensions upwards of the spindles supporting a comb. In the comb back chairs, except the earliest, such as No. 444, the horizontal top rail of the back is made of one piece of bent wood of moderate thickness, differing from the thick and heavy rail used in the corner chairs and in the low back Windsor chairs Nos. 442–443.

7. This chair is No. 526 in Mr. Lockwood's "Colonial Furniture," volume 2, page 74, and appears here through his courtesy.

8. These combs were sometimes added to other types of Windsor chairs for ornamentation, as perhaps in No. 460, and also for "glorification," as to which see section 7.

See also note 7 in section 61, in regard to "barber's chair."

441 (Upper) Anonymous.
444 (Centre) Mr. A. Morris
    Tyson.
447 (Lower) Dr. James Bordley,
    Jr.

442 (Upper) Mr. Albert G. Tow-
    ers.
445 (Centre) Mrs. Wm. M. Rob-
    erts.
448 (Lower) Mrs. F. T. Redwood.

443 (Upper) Dr. James Bordley,
    Jr.
446 (Centre) Mr. E. G. Miller, Jr.
449 (Lower) Sheppard, etc. Hos-
    pital.

In No. 444 we notice the same kind of thick horizontal and semi–circular top rail as is seen on the two preceding low back chairs, through which rail the spindles extend upward and support a comb. This chair is in the nature of a transitional[9] one, and shows the new features of longer spindles and a comb; in the next chair the thick top rail disappears and the new thin and flat rail begins. This chair is provided with rockers, which may or may not be original.[10] The arm supports are in an English form as in the chair No. 108 and others. Chairs of this character are highly esteemed.[11] About 1740–1780.

Nos. 445 and 446, almost identical except for the rockers and stretchers, are examples of the best Philadelphia comb back chairs, which are said to be "probably the noblest and most dignified of the Windsor family."[12] This praise is no doubt based upon the symmetrical design with nine spindles, the ample seat, the graceful comb with carved "ears"[13] at its two ends, and the fine workmanship; moreover, the comfortable seating qualities should not be overlooked. About 1750–1780.

No. 447 is of the same general type, but with six spindles, instead of the nine in the previous chairs; the comb seems almost too large; the arm supports are more slanting and the turnings of the legs and stretchers are different from the previous ones. About 1750–1800.

In No. 448 the comb is in a plainer shape and is without ears. Under each arm there are four short spindles and in the back are nine. The comb, the arm supports and the legs are now decorated with gilt painting over the dark background. The chair is somewhat low, the legs having apparently been cut down. About 1750–1800.

In No. 449 the upper edge of the comb is cut in the form of two cyma curves.[14] The two braces, attached to an extension in the rear of the seat and to the comb, add strength to the back. Chairs having these braces are sometimes called "braced back Windsor chairs," as though the braces constituted a type of Windsor chair; but as braces are used on several types of Windsor chairs their presence does not create a separate type. This chair is properly called a "braced back comb Windsor." About 1750–1800.

9. The nature of "transitional" chairs is stated in section 48, at illustration No. 41, in connection with the change from the English style chairs to the Dutch style; and in other places noted in the Index under the word "Transitional."

10. As to original and converted rocking chairs, see the next section, No. 63.

11. A full page illustration of a chair apparently a duplicate of No. 444, except that it has no rockers, is shown in the "Pennsylvania Museum Bulletin," of December, 1925, page 50, mentioned in note 1, E in this section. On page 49 Mr. J. Stogdell Stokes, the author of the article, writes that the chair is usually regarded as the most graceful of the Windsor family; and that "we may call attention to the well carved oak knuckles, the outward flare in the lower plain portion of the legs, and the graceful oak ram's–horn arm supports. This type of support is derivative of English construction, but has taken on a form still more gracious." This article, as stated in note 1, E, appears also in "Antiques," April, 1926, page 222.

12. Quoted from the article mentioned in the preceding note.

13. "Ears" are also seen on the ends of the top rails of chairs in the Chippendale style, as in Nos. 118–126; see also section 51, note 9.

14. As to the cyma curve, see section 23.

3. Hoop back Windsor chairs. No. 450. These chairs, also called "bow back" Windsor chairs, and the loop back chairs shown as Nos. 457–461 in this section, are among the favorites of the Windsor type. The hoop back[15] chair resembles the low back and the comb back in having a horizontal semi–circular rail; upon this rail rests an upright semi–circular top rail which is also supported by spindles projecting upwards through the horizontal rail. Although chairs of this type are numerous, and were made in various sections of the country, they all seem to be of about the same form, but occasionally have a small comb at the top, and sometimes a high back. These chairs are sufficiently represented by No. 450, in which the ends of the arms are carved in the shape of knuckles, or fingers, and the legs are very raked. Chairs of this type are reproduced in great numbers. About 1750–1800.

We now leave the three groups of chairs having a horizontal semi–circular rail in the back and take up the other types of Windsor chairs.

4. New England Windsor arm chairs. Nos. 451–452. This type of chair, originated and chiefly made in New England, is a simpler, and more graceful, form of the preceding type, the hoop back. Comparing the hoop back chair No. 450 with these arm chairs Nos. 451 and 452, we see that in the latter two chairs the semi–circular horizontal rail is omitted and that the top rail and the arms are combined in one piece of bent wood. These chairs were sometimes ornamented with a small comb or were strengthened by braces, but their distinctive feature is that the top rail and the arms are in one piece. Chairs somewhat similar to these, but easily distinguishable, will be seen in the group of loop back chairs below, some of which were furnished with arms of a different kind. About 1750–1800.

No. 451 has seven spindles in the back and No. 452 has nine, all in addition to the supports under the arms. In No. 452 the legs and stretchers are finely turned, and the back is braced. The construction of these New England arm chairs is such that the arms frequently break at the bend where they turn upward to form the back. About 1750–1800.

5. Fan back Windsor chairs. Nos. 453–456. This type of chair, like the comb back, is said to be of Philadelphia origin; but it was also made in New England and elsewhere. It is thought that these chairs were made as side chairs to the comb back chairs, for the reason that the top rails of the fan back chairs follow so closely the designs of the combs of the comb back chairs. Some of the later chairs of this fan back type have arms or combs or rockers, none of which additions improve their appearance. The four illustrations present a pleasing group of which the seats are all cut in on the sides and the legs are all widely raked.

15. The term "hoop back," as used in connection with this Windsor chair, does not indicate the same form of back as it does in the Hepplewhite style "hoop back" chair No. 230 in which the top rail and the stiles, or uprights, make a continuous curve from one back leg to the other. Nos. 457 and 458 are hoop back Windsor chairs in the English sense, but are called "loop back" by Mr. Kerfoot, whose classification is followed in this book as mentioned in note 6.

450 (UPPER) MD. SOC. COLONIAL DAMES.

451 (UPPER) MR. EDGAR G. MILLER, JR.

452 (UPPER) MR. & MRS. JOHN S. GIBBS, JR.

453 (CENTRE) MRS. J. S. GIBBS, JR.

454 (CENTRE) MR. JAS. DIXON.

455 (CENTRE) MR. JAMES DIXON.

456 (LOWER) MRS. FRANCIS P. GARVAN.

457 (LOWER) DR. JAS. BORDLEY, JR.

458 (LOWER) DR. JAMES BORDLEY, JR.

No. 453 is interesting because of the small seat which is cut in on both sides, the high spindles, the high turned stiles, or uprights, at the sides and the raked legs which extend much beyond the sides of the seat. About 1750–1800.

In No. 454 the special feature is the comb which has scrolled "ears" at the ends as in No. 445, a design much used in Philadelphia. About 1750–1800.

No. 455 has eleven spindles, the two end ones serving as stiles, or uprights, without ornamentation by turnings. About 1750–1800.

No. 456 is a New England chair with a braced back, a type of back which was very popular in that section; the top rail is cut in cyma curves and has up-turned ears, and the stiles and legs are finely turned.[16] Said to be about 1790–1800.

6. Loop back Windsor chairs. Nos. 457–461. It is said that this type of chair was first made by New England makers as side chairs to go with their arm chairs which are illustrated above, Nos. 451 and 452. A comparison of the two chairs, Nos. 451 and 457, will show that the supposition is natural, because if the bent rail of the back of the New England arm chair No. 451 were continued down to the seat instead of extending forward to make the arms, a loop back chair such as No. 457 would be produced. It is said that although at first these chairs were made without arms as companion, or side, pieces to arm chairs, they themselves were later made with arms, as will be seen in Nos. 460 and 461. Moreover these loop back chairs were not only made with arms, but occasionally with a comb and also with braces. All the legs in this group are well "raked." These chairs are sometimes called "bow" or "balloon back" Windsor chairs; they were very popular, as mentioned in connection with hoop back chairs.

Nos. 457 and 458 are much alike in the lower parts with their bamboo turn-ings, but differ somewhat in the backs. No. 457 has the more usual form of back and has nine spindles. In No. 458 the curve of the back is somewhat more pro-nounced and graceful and there are seven spindles. The types of spindles will be noticed, being very daintily turned and tapering to small ends at the top. The bamboo turnings seem to mark the beginning of decadence in these chairs. About 1770–1800.

In No. 459 the back is wider than in the previous chairs, making a more fully rounded appearance. About 1750–1800.

Nos. 460 and 461 are loop back chairs with arms, mentioned a few lines above. Comparing these with the "New England arm chairs" Nos. 451 and 452, it will be seen that in these loop back arm chairs the arms are attached to the sides of the back, and if the arms and their supports were removed there would still be a loop back chair; but in the New England arm chairs the arms are a continuation of the sides of the back, all being made of the same piece of bent wood. Perhaps the loop back chairs made with arms attached were less expensive or more durable

---

16.   This chair is a small one, but is of a character to cause a learned and impartial critic to refer to it enthusiastically, in part as follows: "This is the kind of thing that gives the collector a thrill, whether the medium be pine or oak, walnut or mahogany, pewter or silver. Of diminutive size (but at the same time intended for grown–ups) these delightful chairs have all the frills of their larger brethren and yet retain perfect proportion. Well raked legs always make for character and these have otherwise plenty of it in the seat, turnings and cresting rail."

459 (Upper) Mr. Albert G. Tow-
    ers.
462 (Centre) Mrs. Wm. G. Weth-
    erall.
465 (Lower) Mr. James Dixon.

460 (Upper) Mr. E. G. Miller, Jr.
463 (Centre) Mr. John S. McDan-
    iel.
466 (Lower) Mrs. John S. Gibbs,
    Jr.

461 (Upper) Mr. Wm. M. Ellicott.
464 (Centre) Mrs. Howard Sill.
467 (Lower) Mrs. John S. Gibbs,
    Jr.

than those made in the New England arm chair style. In No. 460 there is a small comb in simple form. The seat of No. 461 is almost rectangular and the sides are grooved. About 1780–1800.

At this point the six definite types of Windsor chairs come to an end and we proceed with several variations.

7. Miscellaneous Windsor chairs. Nos. 462–473. In this group the first eight are Windsor chairs made in the period when chairs in the late Sheraton style were in vogue, in which the straight line type of back was the conspicuous feature. These Windsor chairs are not in the true Windsor style, having certain features of the Sheraton style; but they are more in the nature of Windsor chairs than in the nature of Sheraton chairs, having spindles and seat and legs and stretchers in the Windsor style, and hence they are commonly called Windsor chairs. The bamboo turnings are not well seen in the engravings. It will be noticed that the legs of all these chairs are raked. They were all probably made between 1800 and 1825.

In Nos. 462 and 463 the Sheraton style appears both in the straight line backs and in the panels which were no doubt decorated with stencil designs or paintings. The top rails in the first chair are straight and in the second are curved. The spindles and legs of these two chairs, and also of others, are turned in the bamboo style. No. 463 is a small chair intended for a child; it may be compared with No. 301 in the Sheraton style. About 1800–1825.

In the arm chair No. 464 the spaces between the top rails are divided into four parts by an extension of three spindles. In No. 465 the spindles are shortened and over them are three upright panels. About 1800–1825.

Nos. 466, 467 and 468 are arm rocking chairs having a certain similarity. The rockers in the first two chairs are perhaps later additions; those in No. 467 are in about the shape of rockers used on cradles, as on the cradle No. 1085. No. 466 is a plain form. No. 467 has a plain top rail and a high and plain comb. No. 468 has a painted comb in a shape and design which follow that of the top rail. In these arm chairs and others it will be noticed that there is but one spindle between the back and the arm support at the end of the arm. Other rocking chairs are seen in Nos. 478–486 in section 63. About 1800–1825.

No. 469 departs still further from the Windsor designs, but perhaps for lack of a better name it has been called a "Sheraton Windsor." It combines features of the Windsor chair and of the American "fancy" chairs. About 1800–1825.

Nos. 470 and 471, side and arm chairs, are unusual,[17] having a loop back similar in shape to that in Nos. 457 and 458; but the back is supported by two curved spindles connected by three pierced slats which remotely resemble those in the ladder–back chair No. 385 and others; and there is a pierced opening at the

17. Chairs of this type are illustrated in Mr. Kerfoot's article mentioned in note 1; and are also shown in "Antiques," November, 1930, page 432. The fact that they are unusual and rare may indicate that only a few were made because they were not popular; see the remarks on "rarity" in section 175, paragraph 13.

468 (Upper) Dr. James Bordley, Jr.
471 (Lower) Mr. J. S. McDaniel.

469 (Upper) Dr. H. M. Fitzhugh.
472 (Lower) Dr. James Bordley, Jr.

470 (Upper) Mr. J. S. McDaniel.
473 (Lower) Mr. J. S. McDaniel.

top. The arms in No. 471 are attached to the back as in the loop back arm chairs Nos. 460 and 461. About 1800–1825.

Nos. 472 and 473 are revolving, or swivel, chairs with features of Windsor chairs. No. 472 is a small chair suitable for a child; its back indicates a Windsor chair with turned legs. No. 473 is plain and later in design. About 1800–1825.

Windsor writing chairs. Nos. 474–477. The earliest chairs of this type seem to be the comb back ones, which in the course of years were followed by chairs in which the comb back was superseded by a straight back with a rectangular panel top rail. A comb, upon which the occupant might rest his head, may have been pleasant for meditation, but was certainly not very useful while he was writing. From the standpoint of the collector these writing chairs with comb backs are desirable; they are not often seen, and are not illustrated here. The later and more usual kinds of chairs are shown in the four illustrations Nos. 474–477. These chairs are similar in their general construction, the most noticeable difference being that in Nos. 474 and 475 the front leg under the writing arm is placed under the seat,[18] but in Nos. 476 and 477 the front leg is placed under the extension which projects from the seat; this latter arrangement causes the front legs to be far apart, making an awkward appearance. None of these four chairs were made for left-handed writers. All of these chairs have bamboo turnings on some parts.

No. 474 is of simple design, without a drawer under the writing arm and without painted decorations. In No. 475 we see a panel on the front stretcher and also the round and tapering front legs, both suggestive of the later type of Sheraton and Empire style chairs. This chair also is painted, and the drawer, the panel on the stretcher and the top rail are all decorated with painted lines. Each of these chairs has five spindles. About 1800–1825.

No. 476 is also of simple design, and has no drawer, but is painted and in several parts is decorated. In No. 477 the original paint has been removed and the wood is in the natural light color; and there are two drawers, one under the writing arm and the other under the seat. The width of this chair at the widest part across the front is thirty-two inches. About 1800–1825.

Section 63. Rocking chairs.—The origin and history of rocking chairs seems at present to be somewhat uncertain.[1] It is believed that they are of American invention, mainly because such a chair was not known in Europe until long after

18. A chair with this construction is illustrated and pleasantly described in "Antiques," December, 1928, page 514.

1. A book entitled "The Rocking chair: an American Institution," by Mr. Walter A. Dyer and Mrs. Esther Stevens Fraser, 127 pages published by the Century Co., 1928, contains much information on the subject, with many illustrations. The second part of the book, by Mr. Dyer, is devoted to the "Boston Rocker." The book includes material from articles by the authors in the magazine "Antiques."

In the magazine "House and Garden," September, 1929, page 96, is an article entitled "The Rocking Chair—a history" by Mr. Dyer, with a number of illustrations.

The writer is much indebted to the above mentioned book and article for assistance in the preparation of this section. See also "Antiques," February, 1935, page 49.

474 (UPPER) DR. H. M. FITZHUGH. 475 (UPPER) MD. SOC. COLONIAL DAMES.
476 (LOWER) JUDGE F. N. PARKE. 477 (LOWER) MR. EDGAR G. MILLER, JR.

it was a common article of furniture in our country. This seems strange in view of the fact that cradles with rockers were used in Europe for many years before rocking chairs were made in America. Mr. Lockwood, in his "Colonial Furniture," volume 2, figure 422, shows an American rocking chair, reproduced here through his courtesy as illustration No. 478, which he believes was made from about 1650 to 1700 because of the similarity of its turnings and slats to those of certain slat-back chairs of that period.

The earliest type of which any considerable number have been found are those having slat backs[2] of the period of about 1725 to 1750, one of which, through the courtesy of Mr. Lockwood, appears here as No. 479. It has been shown by written evidence that as far back as 1762 rocking chairs were in common use in our country and that rockers were being added to rockerless chairs in order to convert them into rocking chairs.[3]

In many instances it is difficult to decide whether a particular chair which is now a rocking chair was made originally as a rocking chair, or whether the rockers were added later, making it a "converted" chair. There are certain features of original rocking chairs which are not found in the converted ones; one such feature is an enlargement of the bottom part of the rear legs as in No. 478, through which the rockers pass, indicating that the legs were intended to hold rockers;[4] but genuine rocking chairs with this or other convincing features are seldom found. Another aid is a comparison of the wood of the rocker, and the paint if any, with that of the other parts of the chair in order to determine whether there is a difference between them. Moreover, as the conversion requires the cutting off of a few inches of the legs in order not to raise the height of the seat, the lower side stretchers may be brought too near the rockers. These matters should be examined by a cabinet maker experienced in antique chairs, and even such a person may not be able to reach a correct conclusion.

A point of difference between the early and later styles is in the shape and length of the rockers. In the early chairs the rockers generally extend about the

2.   Slat-back chairs are illustrated in section 47.

3.   See article in "Antiques," May, 1928, page 409, by Mr. C. F. Luther. In the notes to this article reference is made to previous articles in the magazine on the same subject.

The idea that the rocking chair was invented by Benjamin Franklin is regarded as unfounded.

Rocking chairs, like Windsor chairs, seem to have always been of a homelike character, not for the best rooms of the houses of the well-to-do. None were shown in the books of designs of the great cabinet makers, from Chippendale to Sheraton. They are essentially for ease and comfort, not for elegance or display.

It seems strange that there are so few rocking chairs old enough to be considered antique. With the exception of the converted Windsor chairs, rocking chairs are seldom mentioned or illustrated in the books on antique furniture. Even in the great collection of illustrations in Mr. Nutting's "Furniture Treasury," there are very few rocking chairs other than Windsors.

4.   This chair appears here through the courtesy of Mr. L. V. Lockwood in whose "Colonial Furniture," volume 2, figure 422, it is shown.

An original slat-back rocking chair with this construction is shown in Mr. Nutting's "Furniture Treasury," volume 2, No. 1866, and in the same author's "Furniture of the Pilgrim Century," Revised Edition, No. 396, where it is said that wooden pins were used in these rockers instead of nails.

same short length beyond the front and the back and also have the same shape; but in the later types of rockers the rear ones project much further than the front ones, making the chairs safer to rock in.[5]

Examining the illustrations, we see in No. 478, the rocking chair mentioned above, in which the rear legs are enlarged at the bottom in order to hold the rockers. It is difficult to imagine any other purpose for which this enlargement could have been intended, and it was in fact availed of for this purpose. The shape of the slats and the turnings of the stiles, or uprights, and of the finials at their tops are of the period mentioned above, about 1650 to 1700; and it is therefore reasonable to believe that this chair was made at about that time.

In No. 479 there are three slats; and chairs with somewhat similar slats, but without rockers, are shown in Nos. 27 and 28. Here the rockers are in grooves cut in the bottom of the legs, through which the rockers pass, which is the method perhaps most frequently found in old rocking chairs, both original and converted.[6] The arms are short and the arm supports pass down through the side rails of the seat and into the upper stretchers in the same manner as is seen in the early chair No. 29. About 1725–1750.

5. A. Of course a rocker with a longer projection at the rear may be shortened, either because the owner liked it better that way, or because some one wanted to make the chair appear to be more ancient and therefore more valuable.

B. In certain chairs there is only a very light projection of the front of the rocker beyond the leg. A long projection is often unpleasant for the ankles of visitors.

C. Most of the old rocking chairs are apparently converted. The date when the conversion was made is of course impossible to determine, unless there is some clear indication of a particular period. The practice of converting rockerless chairs into rocking chairs has been common for many years and will no doubt continue for years to come. The manufacture in large numbers of chairs made with rockers seems to have begun about the year 1800. From that date, rocking chairs have been made in the late Sheraton style, in the Empire style and in the later styles; a few of such chairs are illustrated here, although not yet quite old enough to be antique.

D. A number of rocking chairs of the Windsor chair style are found, some made originally with rockers and others converted later into rocking chairs; see Nos. 466–468 which are illustrated in the section on "Windsor chairs," rather than in this section on "Rocking chairs," because their Windsor features, not their rockers, are their distinctive characteristics. Windsor style rocking chairs made in the period in which painted furniture of the Sheraton and Empire styles was popular were often painted and decorated.

6. The two chairs above described, Nos. 478 and 479, are the only very old ones here shown in which the rockers may with certainty be regarded as original. If the rockers in any particular chair were evidently made with the chair, the value is of course greater than if they were made and attached later; yet as probably a majority of the rocking chairs made before about the year 1800 are "converted," but are nevertheless regarded as "rocking chairs," they are not always looked upon as having much of a blemish on their character.

In his article entitled "The Rocking Chair—a history," referred to in note 1, Mr. Dyer writes that the practice of applying rockers "appears to have started at some time subsequent to the year 1750 and to have continued for half a century"; but that not until after 1800 were true rocking chairs, meaning chairs made with rockers, at all common.

A large proportion of the rocking chairs made before 1800 illustrated in the book entitled "The Rocking Chair; an American Institution," mentioned in note 1, are converted chairs.

478 (Upper) Lockwood, Col. Furn. 422.

481 (Centre) Mrs. F. T. Redwood.

484 (Lower) Mr. E. G. Miller, Jr.

479 (Upper) Mr. L. V. Lockwood.

482 (Centre) Mr. & Mrs. Wm. D. Poultney.

485 (Lower) Mr. & Mrs. J. M. Berry.

480 (Upper) Mrs. Paul H. Miller.

483 (Centre) Mrs. Edwin B. Niver.

486 (Lower) Jones Library, Amherst.

The next four rocking chairs, Nos. 480–483, have features similar to those of certain chairs without rockers, illustrated in previous sections.

No. 480 is a slat–back chair of the Pennsylvania type seen in Nos. 31–33. Here there are five slats, graduated in size, and the front stretcher is ornamented with large ball turnings. The turnings of the arm supports are unusual. The seat is of rush. The date of this chair is said to be about 1760.

The painted chair No. 481 bears a resemblance in some respects to the Shera-ton style painted chair No. 287. In each chair the rounded seat, the cross–pieces in the back with balls between them, and the round, ringed and tapering front legs and arm supports, indicate its connection with the late Sheraton period. The sides of the legs have been cut into in order to hold the rockers. About 1810–1820.

No. 482 resembles in many respects the arm chair No. 422 which is in the Sheraton style. In addition to the upholstery and the high back, each of these two chairs has similar curved arms, vase–shaped arm supports and round legs, all of which are features of the late Sheraton style. In No. 482 the exposed parts are decorated with stenciling. As in the Boston rockers Nos. 484 and 485, the legs are made to fit into holes cut in the rockers. About 1820–1830.

No. 483 has several features of the chairs Nos. 347–354 in the American Empire style, with the addition of the rockers which here were made as a part of the chair. The top rail and the vase–shaped splat are familiar objects in chairs of this type. About 1830–1840.

The "Boston rocker"[7] type of rocking chair is shown in Nos. 484 and 485. It seems to have been developed from the Windsor rockers such as Nos. 444 and 446 shown in the preceding section. No. 484 is in the usual late form, and has six spindles in the back and one under each arm. Both the Windsor rocker and the Boston rocker have the solid wooden seat, the thin spindles in the back and the large top rail; but the Boston rocker is more decorative than the Windsor rocker, as the former has designs of fruits and flowers and landscapes done in stencil or painting or both. A special feature of the Boston rocker is the form of the seat, which curves up at the back and down in the front, the curved portions being separate pieces attached to the flat portion of the seat. This kind of seat is called a "rolling" seat. A chair of this type without arms is known as a "Little Boston rocker." About 1840–1850.

---

7. The most popular of all the rocking chairs—among the public, not among connoisseurs—is the "Boston rocker," the word "rocker" as here used meaning the chair, not the rocker on which the chair rocks. The term "Boston" doubtless indicated that most of this type of chairs originated, or were most largely made, in that city, just as the term "Philadelphia highboy" is given to the type of elaborate high-boys made in that city; but these chairs were made in other places also. At the present time the chair cannot properly be called an "antique," nor can it be regarded as an object of much elegance or beauty. But it possesses one important feature not often found in the older chairs—that is, it is comfortable; and, furthermore, it is homelike. These chairs were apparently first made in their standardized form about 1840 and continued to be made until a very recent date. It is said that in certain localities they were made as late as 1890.

An illustrated article entitled "The Boston Rocker," by Mr. Walter A. Dyer, is in "An-tiques," May, 1928, pages 389–392; see also note 1 in this section, and "Antiques," January, 1925, page 15.

In No. 485 instead of the usual spindles there are four somewhat wide up-right slats which are shaped to fit the back of the occupant and are no doubt more agreeable to lean upon than are the spindles. A side chair in the Empire style with similar slats is No. 342. About 1850.

No. 486 is a rocking chair made by the Shakers[8] and now owned by the Jones Library at Amherst, Massachusetts, through whose courtesy the engraving appears here. This plain chair resembles in form other slat–back chairs such as Nos. 26–28. The backs of Shaker chairs of this type were often fitted, over the top slat, with a cushion rail from which a cushion or shawl could be suspended. Chairs of this type were made and sold for a great many years, especially after about 1852.

Section 64. Miscellaneous chairs.

—Under this indefinite title are fifteen illustrations, some of which might properly appear in other sections as variants of certain styles of chairs; others perhaps ought not to appear anywhere in a book on "American Antique Furniture." With this confession and apology the chairs are presented with but little comment and with no attempt to fix doubtful dates.

No. 487 is entitled to lead the group. It is an Egyptian chair more than three thousand years old, found in the tomb of Iuia and Tuiu, a king and queen of the eighteenth dynasty, about 1600 to 1300 B. C., and now in the great museum at

---

8. An interesting illustrated book by Dr. Edward D. Andrews, entitled "The Community indus-tries of the Shakers," was published in 1933 by The University of the State of New York, in Albany, New York. The price in paper covers is forty cents.

In the book of Dr. Andrews it is said, page 233, that "The Shakers were among the first in this country to equip chairs with rockers. They were designed principally for the comfort of invalids and the aged. The rockers were short and gracefully cut in profile. . . Heavier rockers of the 'sled' type were sometimes used for the brethren's chairs." The subject of chairs is considered on pages 229–248 of the book. On page 239 it is said that "the business of making chairs on a large, almost wholesale, scale goes back to about 1852."

The Shakers also made other chairs. They were not influenced by changes in style and they continued to make the same kind of chairs for many years without material change, so that it is almost impossible to give their dates.

An illustrated article entitled "An interpretation of Shaker furniture" by Edward D. and Faith Andrews is in "Antiques," January, 1933, pages 6–9.

See also section 47, note 2, for other remarks on slat–back chairs and for references to maga-zine articles.

The Shakers are the members of an American religious sect which was an offshoot of the English Quakers. The real founder of the sect was Ann Lee who called herself "Ann, the Word." With her husband and others she came to America in 1774. In 1787 the first American Shaker Society was organized at Mt. Lebanon, near Albany, New York. The early members in England "when wrestling in soul to be freed from the power of sin and a worldly life, writhed and trembled so much that they won the name 'Shaker'; their trances and visions, their jumping and dancing, were like those of many other sects" in Europe. Communities were formed in several other places in America. The society was celibate and communistic, and their communism "was an economic success, and their cleanliness, honesty and frugality received the highest praise." They wear a plain uniform and are often seen at northern resort hotels in the summer offering their articles for sale. The historical statements made here are taken from the "Encyclopædia Britannica," title "Shakers," eleventh edition, volume 24, page 771, where the literature on the subject is given.

It is said that now there are only seventeen members of the Shaker sect.

Cairo. After the conquest of Egypt by Napoleon[1] in 1798, objects such as this inspired the French artists and cabinet makers in producing their Empire style of furniture, referred to in section 21. Observing the high "pads" or "shoes" under the animals' claw feet of the chair, we see that the device was not a new invention when it appeared on the Queen Anne style table shown as No. 1288.

We next see two Baltimore chairs of about 1850, Nos. 488 and 489, known as "spool chairs" or "beaded chairs," in which the entire back, the arms, arm supports and legs are "turned" in a form somewhat resembling spools. The back is not vertical, but slopes backward slightly. According to a local tradition, chairs of this type were brought from Norway by a Baltimorean who was in the diplomatic service of our country. These chairs were found so comfortable, strong and light in weight, that they were often copied in Baltimore and are now seen in many homes, generally painted black. In each illustration the rear cushion, covering the back, is removed in order that the construction may be seen. In No. 488 the arms extend about two-thirds of the distance from the back to the front; in No. 489 they extend all the way to the front. The turnings on these two chairs are different in form and size. Chairs of this type do not seem to be known in other cities.

No. 490 is in the manner of the Roman curule chair which was a chair of State and was used only by high officials. The type of chair here shown seems to approach the arched form of the Roman chair more closely than any other chair found in our country. The form is seen in the collection of drawings of Sheraton style chairs in illustration No. 234, figure 30; and the style of Sheraton was copied by Duncan Phyfe and others who made many chairs and other articles with curule legs. See note 9 in section 52 in reference to the curule form and also the comment on the chairs Nos. 320 and 321. See also the Index under the word "Curule." The date of this chair is probably about 1820–1830.

The arm chair No. 491 shows the curule design in the legs. The very sloping back seems to indicate that that chair was made mainly for peaceful repose—a back very different from the stiff vertical backs which were used in the various furniture periods considered in this book. It is said that the chairs of this type generally have rockers. This is commonly called a "Sleepy Hollow" chair. See "Antiques," September, 1935, pages 126–127. The date may be about 1820–1830.

No. 492 has been regarded as a ladder-back chair with variations from the usual style, or as a Sheraton style chair because of the rounded seat, the reeded seat rail and the concave form of the legs; but it was found to be a piano stool upon

1. An interesting feature of Napoleon's expedition was that with his army were several French savants who were engaged to study the antiquities of Egypt. It is said that in the battles the orders to the soldiers were: "Form a square; savants and asses in the centre." In this way the learned men and the donkeys were protected. This is also mentioned in note 2, D in section 21, which is on the subject of the American Empire style.

487 (Upper) Anonymous.
490 (Centre) Mrs. Edw. Shoe-
    maker.
493 (Lower) Mr. John Hinkley.

488 (Upper) Dr. J. Hall Pleas-
    ants.
491 (Centre) Mr. & Mrs. E. H.
    McKeon.
494 (Lower) Mr. Blanchard Ran-
    dall.

489 (Upper) Mr. & Mrs. Carroll
    Van Ness.
492 (Centre) Sheppard, etc., Hos-
    pital.
495 (Lower) Anonymous.

the discovery of a chair precisely the same, and still having the original stretchers and a long metal screw by which the height of the seat could easily be changed. About 1800–1820.

No. 493 is a Victorian style chair, with the upper part of the back enclosing a painting on papier maché, not well seen in the engraving. This material, composed of paper pulp compressed into a form, was much used from about 1830 to 1860. See the fifth paragraph of section 44 in regard to the use of the material. About 1840–1860.

In No. 494 the back is not cut down, but is complete in itself, with a scroll at the top and the bottom of the back. The four concave legs are similar to those on the chairs of the Directory style chairs Nos. 307–310 and others. It has been suggested that perhaps a chair without a back was agreeable to ladies in arranging their long hair. Another theory is that it is a piano stool. About 1810–1830.

No. 495 is a highly carved Victorian chair with a number of curves in the form of a "C," a favorite design of the Chippendale period; other examples are referred to in the Index under the letter "C." The legs and feet resemble some of those in the French models in the Hepplewhite style. Perhaps about 1850–1870.

Nos. 496 and 497 are two French chairs which have probably been in our country for more than a century. They are very similar in form and the difference in appearance is chiefly caused by the abundance of brass mounts in Napoleonic designs in the first chair and the absence of mounts in the second. The mounts in No. 496 consist mainly of two sphinxes and the "anthemion," or honeysuckle, designs on the front seat rail and on the tops of the legs; these latter designs are considered in note 48 in section 51. In No. 497 the frame of the chair recalls that of No. 353. About 1810–1820.

No. 498 is a French arm chair, semi–circular in form, with a low back and finely decorated with brass mounts, some of which are similar in design to those on No. 496. The raised portion of the back recalls those on the much earlier corner chairs Nos. 425–439 and the Windsor chairs Nos. 442–443. The mounts on the front ends of the top rail represent animals' heads and the feet are of the animals' claw type. About 1810–1820.

No. 499, with its high back, may have been intended for the chairman of an assembly, as was apparently No. 422. The reeded front legs, continuing upwards as arm supports, present the longest straight reeded part seen on any chair in this chapter. The reeding and the slanting rear legs indicate the Sheraton style. The legs terminate in brass feet and casters, as in No. 422. About 1800.

No. 500, an arm chair, should have appeared with the upholstered chairs in section 60. It is said to be regarded as in the Hepplewhite style, or as a transitional Chippendale–Hepplewhite chair such as Nos. 176–177 which it resembles in shape. The legs are square and straight as in the Chippendale style. About 1785–1800.

No. 501 is very similar in form to No. 363, with the exceptions that the former has no lyre in the back and has the Sheraton style round front legs seen in Nos. 274–280 and the broad and concave top rail of those chairs. About 1820–1830.

496 (Upper) Mrs. Wm. DeFord.   497 (Upper) Mrs. F. T. Redwood. 498 (Upper) Mr. H. T. Tiffany.
499 (Lower) Mrs. F. T. Redwood. 500 (Lower) Mrs. J. H. Whitely 501 (Lower) Mrs. Bayard Turn-
                                         Est.   bull.

The chapter on chairs has now reached its end. It is the longest chapter in this book and has the greatest number of illustrations and pages of text and notes. For the writer it has been a difficult chapter, because the subject required the proper classification and description of so many chairs in the various styles and transitional styles from the time of William and Mary to that of Queen Victoria. Here may be repeated a statement made at the beginning of this chapter: "the amateur collector who knows the styles of chairs knows the styles of almost all other articles" of household furniture.

Chapter VI

DAY–BEDS; SETTEES; WINDOW SEATS

Section 65. Day–beds
Section 66. Settees with backs
Section 67. Settees without backs
Section 68. Window seats

Section 65. Day–beds.—The word "day–bed" is defined as "a bed used for rest during the day." A similar article is known in France as a "chaise longue," meaning a "long chair." In our country they were known as "couches" in the period in which they were made, which was from about 1640 to 1780; and that name is preferred by the leading writer[1] on American antique furniture. The term "day–bed" is used in England[2] and seems to be more descriptive of the use to which the piece was put than any other word; but the term "chaise longue" more fully describes its appearance, as it is in fact a "long chair."

A day–bed may be described as a long chair without a back lengthwise, but having at one end a head–piece or a back "similar to a chair back of the period to which it belongs, with three pairs of front legs, making an elongated chair"; thus in the period of Chippendale the head–piece resembled the back of a Chippendale style chair. It was often so constructed that the head–piece was adjustable and could swing backwards or forwards, supported by chains or straps, giving a reclining position for the head of the occupant. The seat and head–piece were of cane or rush in the early pieces, and were furnished with cushions; but the later ones were often upholstered. The wood was that used in the period, generally walnut in the earlier and mahogany in the later; but other woods were sometimes used.

No. 502 is the earliest of the day–beds illustrated here. The carved cresting on the back at the end, and the carved stretchers between the legs, are in the style seen in the cane chairs Nos. 36–38, which were of about the same period. The cane in the back and the seat will be noticed. The length of the three divisions made by

---

1. Mr. L. V. Lockwood, "Colonial Furniture," volume 2, page 141. It is said here that these pieces were more common in the South at an early date than "among the more sturdy New Englanders." But it would seem that later they were more frequently made in New England.

2. Cescinsky, "English Furniture," volume 3, pages 323–324. It is here said that "the day–bed as an article of furniture had lost its vogue by the close of the seventeenth century, when the use of the bed–chamber as a reception room had also gone out of fashion." As to this use see "Bedsteads," section 133, note 3.

In Shakespeare's "Twelfth Night," (1601), act 2, scene 5, line 45, Malvolio says: "having come from a day–bed where I left Olivia sleeping."

In Mr. Wallace Nutting's "Furniture Treasury," volume 1, are numerous illustrations of day–beds, Nos. 1586–1620.

282

502 (Upper) Metropolitan Museum of Art.   503 (Centre) Mr. Wm. M. Ellicott.   504 (Lower) Mr. L. V. Lockwood.

283

the legs and stretchers about equal the width of the seats of three chairs. Some of the day–beds of this type have scrolled feet in the Flemish style, such as are seen in the cane chairs mentioned. These early day–beds are seldom seen outside of museums. About 1670–1680.

No. 503 is in a later style which was favored in Pennsylvania. The back at the end somewhat resembles the banister–backs which are shown in the chairs of that type, such as No. 49. Ten stretchers may be counted, seven of which are well turned. The seat is furnished with a cushion. About 1700.

No. 504 is also a Pennsylvania day–bed, showing how the back swings and is held in position by chains. The two upright posts at the back, known as "stiles," are plain, and the three vase–shaped splats resemble the splats in the Queen Anne style chair No. 50. About 1700.

In No. 505 the Chippendale style is seen in the back, although the cabriole legs and the club feet are in the Queen Anne style which is also represented in the "cyma"[3] curves which are cut on the bottom (the skirt) of the seat rail. About 1750.

No. 506 will be recognized at once as being entirely in the Chippendale style. The back resembles the backs of the Chippendale Gothic style chairs Nos. 94–96, and the legs are of the square and plain type seen in so many of the Chippendale style chairs. The "godroon" molding on the skirt of the seat is similar to that on the Chippendale style chairs Nos. 117, 144 and others. Stretchers crossing each other in the form of an "X" are seldom seen in articles in the Chippendale style; see section 51, page 142. About 1775.

Day–beds of the kind above illustrated, having a chair back at the end, were apparently not made in the lighter and more delicate styles of Hepplewhite or Sheraton; they were, however, made in the late Empire style, much changed in appearance, as shown in No. 507. Here we see the chair back in a form somewhat resembling in outline the chair backs in Nos. 307 and 308, and the "roll–over" sofa arms in Nos. 566 and 576. The legs are in the late American Empire style, such as are seen in the sofas Nos. 593 and 594, in section 76, also in the miniature Empire bureau, No. 774, shown in section 100, page 423. This illustrates the principle that the date of the latest feature shows the earliest possible date of its manufacture; the article could not have been made before that latest feature began to be used.[4] This day–bed may be dated about 1830–1840.

But although the day–bed with a chair back end was apparently not made in the periods and styles of Hepplewhite or Sheraton, the need for a comfortable lounging piece of furniture was in part at least supplied by the article which is sometimes known as a "Grecian sofa" and which is the subject of section 75.

---

3. As to the "cyma curve" see section 23.

4. See text of section 6, at note 4.

505 (UPPER) MR. L. V. LOCKWOOD. 506 (CENTRE) METROPOLITAN MU- 507 (LOWER) MRS. PAUL H. MILLER.
SEUM OF ART.

285

Section 66. Settees with backs.—In the early years of our country the word "settee" had a wider meaning than it now has, as it then included the pieces of furniture which we now call sofas. In fact, the two words seem to have had the same meaning; and even now the English books appear to use the words as synonymous terms.[1] But the leading American author[2] uses the word "settees" to mean the pieces which do not have upholstered backs, and he applies the word "sofa" only to those which do have them; and these definitions are followed in this book.

Settees may be conveniently classified in two divisions. In one group they have backs, and in the other they do not have backs. In the early settees of the first group the backs resemble those of two or more chairs placed together, but with a single seat.[3] A settee having two chair backs may be called a two–back settee; if three, a three–back settee. Pieces of this kind were made from about 1700 to 1800, with chair back designs in the successive styles of that long period. Settees without backs are considered in the next section.

Beginning with settees having chair backs in the Chippendale style,[4] No. 508 is a settee with three backs having the familiar type of top rail, splat, square legs and other features seen in chairs of that style. The three backs are separated by two inside stiles, and there are four front legs. The splats are in a pleasing design; and there are ten stretchers. About 1760–1780.

No. 509 is a three–back settee in the Chinese manner of Chippendale; two chairs in this manner may be seen in section 51, Nos. 140 and 141. Here the three backs are not separated by a single stile, as is No. 508, but each back is complete and has its own stiles, leaving two open spaces between. The middle back is some-

---

1. Thus in Mr. Cescinsky's "English Furniture," volume 2, figures 33, 60, 354 and others are termed "settees," but would now be known as sofas in our country.

2. Mr. Lockwood, in his "Colonial Furniture," volume 2, page 127.

3. These settees do not appear to the writer to be very interesting pieces. It seems unnatural to join together in one article two or more chair backs; and each chair back seems to lose something of its individual attraction.

Settles. These pieces of furniture may be mentioned in connection with settees, but are not illustrated here. Two are illustrated in Mr. Lockwood's "Colonial Furniture," volume 2, figures 618 and 619, the first a very rare one finely carved in a manner similar to that of the early chests shown in section 77, and the other of a very plain character. Settles appear to be chests with a high back and with arms at the sides. The top of the chest portion lifts up, but when not up it serves as a seat or may be used as a bedstead. It was placed in front of the open fire place, generally in the kitchen. The high back and the chest portion protected the occupant from drafts. They were used until about 1760. Those now seen at country auctions are generally very plainly made. Several are shown in Mr. Nutting's "Furniture Treasury," volume 1, Nos. 1621–1631.

A certain kind of settee with a back, called a "wagon seat" or "rumble seat," was made and used in country districts. The backs were either in the usual form of a settee or with two–chair backs in the manner of the settees Nos. 508–510. These seats were strongly built, without ornamental features. An illustrated article entitled "Ancestral Rumble Seats" is in "Antiques," June, 1931, pages 464–465, by Ada Hemstreet. Examples are shown in Mr. Wallace Nutting's "Furniture Treasury," No. 1735 and others.

4. Settees with chair backs in the Queen Anne style, and even earlier, some dating from about 1675, are seen in several museums, but are seldom found elsewhere. They show the Queen Anne style chair, with legs of the same style.

what wider than those at the ends. In this piece and in the one above, the under-bracing is strongly made, with many stretchers. Here there are only three front legs. About 1760–1780.

No. 510 is a graceful settee in the Hepplewhite style, the characteristic features being the shield back and square tapering legs. Here the two backs are tied together without touching each other. The front rail of the seat is in a serpentine curve. The splats are in the same graceful design as in the Hepplewhite style chair No. 198. A fine eight-back curved settee in the Hepplewhite style is shown on the front cover page of "Antiques," January, 1922, and in Mr. Nutting's "Furniture Treasury," No. 1672. About 1785–1800.

No. 511 is in the Sheraton style, with four chair backs which have splats in the same design as in the Sheraton chair No. 262. The backs are separated by single stiles as in No. 508. Having only three legs in front, this settee does not appear to resemble a group of chairs so closely as does the next example. A carved rosette is at the top of the outer legs, and there are no stretchers. About 1795–1810.

No. 512 is a ladder-back settee in the Sheraton style. The three chair backs are the same in design as those of the Sheraton style side and arm ladder-back chairs Nos. 389 and 390 in section 58. These three pieces—the two chairs and one settee—if together, would make a very pleasing group. Here the stiles are separated, leaving an open space between the backs as in No. 509. The eight legs and seven stretchers seem more than sufficient for three persons. About 1795–1810.

No. 513 is a cane settee in the Sheraton style from the workshop of Duncan Phyfe. The sofa No. 573, illustrated in section 74, has the same characteristic Phyfe features as appear in this settee; that is, the top rail in three panels carved with the "thunderbolt" design and with drapery festoons, the fine reeding at almost every available point, and the general shape of the arms and the legs. If the back were upholstered, the piece would be called a sofa.[5] The cane seems to give a lighter and more dainty appearance than is seen in a sofa. About 1800–1825.

No. 514 is a Windsor settee in the Sheraton style,[6] with a back having four divisions which, as also in the preceding settee, are not chair backs. There are twenty-six spindles in the back, in addition to the five heavier upright posts, all of which slope backward in a graceful curve. Ten short spindles support the arms. All the spindles and posts, and also the legs and stretchers, are turned in the bamboo style.[7] The under surface of the seat is stamped[8] "Warranted J. Cole, 1827."

5.   This is in accordance with the definitions mentioned at the beginning of this section.

6.   Arm chairs of the Windsor type are occasionally found with a square back in the Sheraton style, having a plain straight top rail, one of which is illustrated in Mr. Nutting's book entitled "American Windsors," pages 76–77; a small settee, or "love seat" is shown on page 186. Other Windsor settees are in the same author's "Furniture Treasury," Nos. 1635–1655. It is not thought advisable to exhibit other Windsor settees here, as the main features are similar in all.

7.   As to the bamboo style of turning see the word "Bamboo" in the Index.

8.   A similar stamp is found on many Windsor chairs, as mentioned in section 62, note 4, S.

508 (Upper) Dr. James Bordley, 509 (Centre) Mrs. E. N. Dunham. 510 (Lower) Mrs. Edw. Shoemaker.
Jr.

511 (UPPER) MRS. TOWNSEND SCOTT. 512 (CENTRE) MR. W. W. LANA- 513 (LOWER) MRS. FRANCIS P. GAR-
HAN. VAN.

The next five settees with backs, Nos. 515–519, are decorated with paintings or stencils. Several of these settees have features which resemble those of the "fancy chairs" shown in section 54 and 57.

The first painted settee, No. 515, is a very handsome one in the Sheraton style.[9] It is fully decorated with various designs. The top rail has four rectangular panels, between which are three paintings of mansions in the neighborhood of Baltimore. The three upright splats and the cross–pieces supporting them are daintily decorated with flowering vines; four oval rosettes are at the base of the upright posts of the back and four others are at the tops of the legs. The curved seat rail is ornamented with three paintings of a bow and arrows and a quiver. This settee is a companion piece to the painted Sheraton style arm chair No. 290, and both are inheritances in the same family. The painted designs on the next settee are similar, suggesting that they were both made by the same Baltimore cabinet maker and painter. About 1820–1825.

No. 516 is another fine settee in the Sheraton style. It is notable for the paintings in ovals on the top rail, all being similar to those on the companion "fancy chair" No. 291 in section 54. Another feature is that many of the parts are in pleasing curves, especially the ends of the seat, the arms and the end stretchers. The top rail has six rectangular panels and three oval ones, which are not clearly seen in the small engraving. The form and decoration of this settee, and of the preceding one and of the chair above referred to, indicate that they were probably made by the same cabinet maker, Robert Fisher, of Baltimore.[10] This settee may be compared with No. 518 and No. 536. About 1810–1820.

The next three settees with backs, Nos. 517, 518 and 519, are good examples of painted settees of a more familiar type than the previous ones.

No. 517 has four chair backs, and five front legs with the same number in the rear. The top rail is decorated with paintings of classical designs; the two–bar cross–pieces enclose other designs, including a laurel wreath, and the seat rail is decorated with leaves. The two–bar front stretchers enclose gilded balls. The background of this settee is painted black. A Sheraton style chair with a back in a somewhat similar design is shown as No. 286 in section 54. About 1815–1830.

No. 518 is a fully decorated settee with three chair backs which are of the same general design as that of the arm chair belonging to the same owner, No. 304 in section 54. A settee without a back, but of the same general character, also belonging to the same owner, is No. 526 in the next section. The urn shaped banisters, the three painted panels on the top rail, and the six others on the seat rail and front stretchers will be noticed; also the four panels at the top of the legs,

---

9.   This settee and its companion chairs are illustrated in "Antiques," September, 1930, page 210, in an article by Dr. Henry J. Berkley.

10.   This settee, and also the companion chair and the window seat above referred to, are illustrated in Mr. Lockwood's "Colonial Furniture," volume 2, pages 310, 313, 315. As to Robert Fisher, see section 68, note 4.

514 (Upper) Dr. Henry M. Fitz- 515 (Centre) Mrs. Wm. DeFord. 516 (Lower) Mrs. Miles White,
  HUGH.   Jr.

291

four at the bases of the back posts and three in the central splats; twenty panels in all. About 1800–1820.

No. 519 is a plainer settee than the preceding ones. The top rail has stenciled designs in the three sections, under which are the three–bar cross–pieces enclosing balls; under these are cross–bars and twenty–four spindles. On the legs are "palmette" designs, that is, small designs of palm leaves which were seen on many chairs in the Empire style, as in Nos. 337 and 338. The spindles and stretchers are turned in the bamboo style. About 1810–1820.

Section 67. Settees without backs.—Some of these settees in the French style, inherited by families in Baltimore, may have been made in France; but the painted settees with backs, Nos. 515 and 516, shown in the previous section, indicate that there were in that city cabinet makers, or their foreign employees, who were entirely capable of producing them.

The first four settees, Nos. 520–523, and also No. 525, are those referred to above. They are apparently in the style of the French Empire, but in certain features we may see suggestions of the style of the Directory.[1]

Nos. 520 and 521 belong to a set of furniture, comprising also chairs and tables, which has similar painted decorations.[2] On the seat rails are classic designs of swords, and on the panels over the legs are winged objects with darts or arrows The feet of each are in the same shape. In No. 520, fully upholstered, the arms, with the "roll over" tops, are decorated with painted leaves. No. 521 has a cane seat. It has no arms, as also No. 523, with only a ledge at the ends. Probably about 1810–1820.

Nos. 522 and 523 are fully decorated and upholstered settees without backs, belonging to the same owner. Their painted designs are almost the same as those on the Directory style sofa No. 566, in section 73; the Greek "anthemion," or honeysuckle, referred to in section 51, note 48, will be noticed in these pieces on which it is in both vertical and horizontal positions. In No. 522 the arms curve inward as in No. 524. The legs are in a form commonly known as the "cornucopia" leg, which is often seen on the sofas in the Directory and later styles in this chapter and is referred to in note 7 in section 73, and in note 5 in section 74. About 1810–1820.

No. 524 is a simplified American settee of the same type as No. 522, with both arms curving inward, but having rounded legs. The painted lines on the arms and the seat rail take the place of the highly decorative designs on the preceding pieces. About 1810–1820.

1. The writer cannot speak with certainty in regard to the origin of some of these settees, for the reason that he has been unable to find, in any available book on French or English furniture, either illustrations or descriptions of similar settees.
2. All of these belong to the same owner. A chair of the set is shown as No. 328 in section 57.

517 (Upper) Mrs. A. N. Turnbull. 518 (Centre) Mr. John Ridgely. 519 (Lower) Mr. Edgar G. Miller, Jr.

293

520 (Upper) Mr. Alexander Brown.   522 (Next to Lower) Mrs. P. L. C. Fischer.
521 (Next to Upper) Mr. Alex. Brown. 523 (Lower) Mrs. P. L. C. Fischer.

524 (UPPER) MR. WM. M. ELLICOTT.   525 (CENTRE) MR. & MRS. JAMES P.   526 (LOWER) MR. JOHN RIDGELY.
REESE.

No. 525 is a settee in which the round upholstered ends resemble the "squabs," or cushions, seen on the sofas Nos. 568, 591 and others in section 76. The front seat rail is decorated with painted designs. The front legs are reeded and gilded, but the back legs are plain, indicating probably that the piece was intended to be placed against a wall, where the legs would not be conspicuous. The legs seem to have been cut off a few inches.[3] About 1815–1825.

No. 526 is in the late Sheraton style and is a part of the same set of painted furniture as the chair No. 304 in section 54, and the settee with a back, No. 518, in the previous section. The panels on the seat rail of this settee, on the stretchers and at the top of the legs, are all of the same type as those in the articles cited. The arms here are small and vertical. About 1800–1820.

Nos. 527 and 528 are later and plainer designs of a type somewhat similar to that of the preceding settee. The arms have developed into more substantial supports. In some respects No. 527 resembles a small bedstead such as No. 1077 in section 137. No. 528 is more distinctly a settee, being too narrow for a bedstead. About 1820–1830.

The last settee without a back, No. 529, is an unusual and somewhat fragile looking piece, with arms which suggest the "roll over" arms of the Directory style, shown in section 73. Brass rosettes are on the seat rail and on the ends of the arms. The curule[4] type of chair, such as is seen in No. 490 in section 64, may have suggested the form of this settee. About 1800–1825.

Section 68. Window seats.—These dainty little seats are in reality small settees, without backs, generally made of a size suitable to be placed in the deep window recesses in the thick walls of the fine houses of the eighteenth century. It is said that although they were common in England they were not often made in our country. They were probably first used in the style of Chippendale, and became even more the fashion by the designs of Robert Adam which were followed by Hepplewhite who illustrated, in his volume known as the "Guide,"[1] several examples showing the Adam influence. Apparently all the window seats found in America are without backs, although in England the name is also given to very small seats having upholstered backs.[2] Several small settees without backs,

---

3. A similar settee but with a back, shown in Mr. C. R. Clifford's book entitled "Period Furnishings," page 197, is regarded as being in the Adam style "in which the classic spirit is emphasized."

A handsome settee of this type appears also in Mr. Nutting's "Furniture Treasury," volume 1, No. 1731; it is clearly in the Adam style.

4. As to "curule" chairs, see note 9 in section 52, and also the Index.

1. As to Hepplewhite's "Guide," see section 17; in that book they are called "Window stools."

2. As in Mr. Cescinsky's "English Furniture," volume 3, figures 193 and 194, which are only about three feet in length across the front of the seat.

known to have been made by Duncan Phyfe[3] and regarded as window seats, have arms made in the style of the backs of chairs, as in No. 537. There may be at present a tendency to give the name of "window seat" to antique settees not small enough to be placed in the recesses of American windows; but whatever their name many of these pieces are attractive and look well in any part of a room.

Nos. 530 and 531 are window seats in the Chippendale style. In each piece the roll of the arms resembles that in the sofas in the Chippendale style in section 70 and in the wing chairs in section 59. The legs are square and plain as in the later style of his chairs and sofas. No. 530 is somewhat larger than No. 531 and the slope of the arms is different. No. 531 is very graceful and pleasing, although the legs seem somewhat heavy. About 1760–1780.

Nos. 532–535 are in the Hepplewhite style, as shown particularly by their tapering legs. In No. 532 the front of the seat is in a serpentine form; the arms are straight, with a slight roll at the top which is ornamented with a rosette. An extra leg under the seat rail provides for unusual weight above. About 1785–1800.

No. 533 is in a similar design, but smaller in size and with a straight front. Here also a rosette is seen on the roll of the arms. About 1785–1800.

In No. 534, as in the two preceding pieces, the upholstery covers the front seat rail. The legs are tapering and are grooved. The arms are more sloping than in the two preceding pieces and are grooved above the seat rail. About 1785–1800.

In No. 535 the arms form graceful curves and are ornamented with lines of inlay, as are also the seat rail and the legs. Four rosettes are seen, two of which are at the top of the arms and the other two at the points where the legs connect with the rail. The curves of the arms, flowing into the seat rail, suggest the Directory style chairs seen in section 55, but the straight legs are not in that style. About 1785–1800.

No. 536 is in the Sheraton style, as particularly shown by the round and tapering legs. That it was intended to be used as a window seat appears from its construction, the arms turning outward and extending beyond the seat which goes into the recess of the window. The painted designs on the seat rail and arms are in somewhat the same style[4] as those on the chairs Nos. 290 and 291, shown in section 54, and those on the settees Nos. 515 and 516 in section 66. About 1800–1820.

No. 537 is an example of the type of window seats which have arms in the form of chair backs, giving the appearance of two chairs facing each other. The broad top rails of these arms and the splats resting on a cross–piece, not on the

3.   Three of the six now known are illustrated in the catalogue of the "Girl Scouts Loan Exhibition," held in New York in September, 1929, Nos. 758, 769 and 791. Two are shown in "Furniture Masterpieces of Duncan Phyfe," by Mr. Charles O. Cornelius, plates 10 and 11, opposite page 22; on page 65 it is said that these "little window benches are more closely related to chairs than they are to sofas. The arms are simply reduced replicas, in line and detail, of the chair backs."

4.   Most of these fine articles are known to have been made by Robert Fisher, of Baltimore, who was a chair maker from about 1800 to 1814, and for some years appeared in the directories as a "fancy chair maker."

527 (Upper) Mrs. Edwin B. Niver.   528 (Centre) Mr. F. H. Burns.   529 (Lower) Mrs. Alexander Arm-
STRONG.

530 (UPPER) DR. M. A. ABRAMS.   531 (CENTRE) MRS. MILES WHITE, 532 (LOWER) MRS. MILES WHITE,
JR.   JR.

533 (Upper) Miss Evelyn P. Bon- 534 (Centre) Mr. J. S. McDaniel.   535 (Lower) Mr. John E. Carey.
SAL.

300

536 (Upper) Mrs. Miles White, 537 (Centre) Col. of Mrs. Jordan 538 (Lower) Mrs. E. N. Dunham.
Jr. Stabler.

seat, indicate the Sheraton style, as shown in section 54. This type of window seat was made by Duncan Phyfe, as mentioned above at note 3. The white lines in the illustration are photographic reflections. About 1800–1820.

No. 538 is in the late American Empire style, about 1830–1840, and shows the heavy construction which was characteristic of the period and is seen in the sofas Nos. 593 and 594 in section 76. The legs are suggestive of the "sabre" legs of the sofas of the Directory style shown in section 73, as is also the roll of the arms, which, at the top, are ornamented with a rosette. This window seat may be compared with the American Empire style day–bed No. 507.

The sections on day–beds, settees and window seats are now at an end and we next take up the subject of sofas of the various styles, from the Queen Anne to the Victorian.

539 (Upper) Mrs. John S. Gibbs, Jr.   540 (Centre) Mrs. Miles White, Jr.   541 (Lower) Mr. John Ridgely Jr.

arms resemble those of the wing chairs in the Chippendale style illustrated in section 59. About 1760–1780.

No. 541 is a large sofa of handsome proportions. Here there are eight square, not tapering, legs, in the later Chippendale style, with stretchers; the front legs are grooved. At the junction of the legs with the seat rail are carved brackets such as have been seen in chairs of the period.[4] The back is in a series of graceful curves and there is more of a "roll" in the arms than in the previous example. About 1760–1780.

No. 542 is also a large sofa, with eight plain legs, connected by stretchers. The back is arched in the curve characteristic of these pieces. The seat is movable, as in No. 539. About 1760–1780.

No. 543 is a smaller sofa of the same type, with six legs. The back and arms are in much the same graceful designs as in No. 542. About 1760–1780.

No. 544 is a small sofa of a different type, the back and the arms being in an unbroken curve. The fronts of the arms are not upholstered and they connect with the legs. The carving on the arms and the paneling of the legs, which terminate in a form of block feet, will be noticed. The precise period and style of this sofa is not very clear.[5] It appears to be of English origin and was inherited by the present owner from Philadelphia ancestors. About 1780.

Section 71. Hepplewhite style sofas.—In these sofas, dating from about 1785 to 1800, two principal types will be seen. In the earlier type the "roll over" arms and the serpentine curve of the back follow closely the sofas of the Chippendale style illustrated in the previous section; but the Hepplewhite style is indicated by the legs, which are slightly tapered. Two sofas of this kind are illustrated here, Nos. 545 and 546. In some sofas of this type it may be difficult to determine at first sight whether a particular piece is in the one style or the other.

In the second type Nos. 547–549, the designs are very different from those of the Chippendale style sofa. Here the designs follow closely those in the Hepplewhite volume, published in 1788, commonly called the "Guide," which is referred to in section 17. The back is in different curves and the "roll over" arms are superseded by arms, without upholstery on their fronts, which connect with the front legs; and the legs are more tapered and in some cases are inlaid.[1]

4.   See the chairs in section 60, Nos. 411 and 412.

5.   It may be in a design transitional from the Chippendale style to the Hepplewhite. The square legs, not tapered, are in the Chippendale style; but the back and arms are in the Hepplewhite style, as appears in the next section. As to transitional styles, see the Index "Transitional styles." A very similar sofa, but with tapered legs, appears in Mr. Cescinsky's "English Furniture," volume 3, figure 185, in the chapter on Hepplewhite's sofas and is dated "about 1780."

1.   Some of the English sofas in the Hepplewhite style have round legs, either fluted or turned; examples are in Mr. Cescinsky's "English Furniture," volume 3, figures 184 and 188.

A group of fine sofas in the Hepplewhite style is shown in an article entitled "Furniture Carvings by Samuel McIntire," by Mr. Fiske Kimball, in "Antiques," December, 1930, page 498, figures 6–9. These sofas have carvings made by Samuel McIntire whose work is mentioned in connection with No. 564 in the next section.

542 (Upper) Miss Margaret C. Painter.   543 (Centre) Mr. J. F. H. Maginn.   544 (Lower) Mr. & Mrs. E. H. McKeon.

307

In Nos. 545 and 546, the sofas of the first type, the resemblance to the Chippendale style sofas Nos. 542 and 543 is obvious, but it will be noticed that the legs of the Hepplewhite type are tapered. These two Hepplewhite style sofas are almost the same in general design, each having the serpentine back, the roll over arms, the movable seat and the tapering legs with stretchers; the principal differences are in the height of the back of No. 546, a slight variation in the arms and perhaps in the character of the upholstery. The front legs of each are grooved, although this is not easily seen in the engravings. About 1785.

Nos. 547, 548 and 549 are of the second type. In No. 547 the back rail has a series of graceful curves which continue over the arms, and is not covered with upholstery; nor are the arms, which are in a characteristic Hepplewhite design. There are eight legs, without stretchers, the front ones being grooved and tapering. The "flaring," or "splayed," outside rear legs will be noticed in each of these sofas. About 1785–1800.

No. 548 is of the same general character; but the back is somewhat differently shaped and is entirely covered with upholstery,[2] as is also a portion of the arms. A dainty oval of satinwood inlay ornaments the top of each end leg; and the edge of the seat rail is lined with a row of nails with large heads very close together The legs are decidedly tapering and were fitted with brass cups and casters. About 1785–1800.

In No. 549 the back is in a single curve of pleasing design. The rail, as in No. 547, is not upholstered, and the concave lines of the arms continue downward to the tapered legs which are ornamented with a string of carved flowers. The feet have brass cups and casters. About 1785–1800.

No. 550 is in another form and is said to be a later example of the Hepplewhite style, approaching the designs of the Sheraton style shown in the next section.[3] Here the line of the back does not continue in a curve with the arms, which go forward at right angles; and the entire frame of the sofa, excepting the eight legs, is covered with upholstery. The legs are tapered and are decorated with lines of inlay in a form similar to that seen on various articles in the Hepplewhite style, such as the sideboard No. 964. About 1785–1800.

Section 72. Sheraton style sofas.—From the large number which have been found, it seems that sofas in the Sheraton style were the favorites in the period of about 1795 to 1825; and the elegance of many of these pieces is the obvious reason for their popularity. The details of the sofas will be seen in the illustrations, but certain characteristics may be mentioned here. In general, it may be said that the rectangular form appears in almost all of the Sheraton style sofas; the rail of the

2.   Horsehair was the proper material for upholstery on sofas in the Hepplewhite, Sheraton and Empire styles. This material is referred to in section 43, note 7, and in section 53, note 4, D. Horsehair is now made in good quality and designs and is very different from the horsehair used on the sofas and chairs of the Victorian period.

3.   A similar sofa is shown in "Antiques," December, 1929, page 506, with a note by the editor.

545 (Upper) Mr. & Mrs. H. L. Duer.   546 (Centre) Mr. F. H. Burns.   547 (Lower) Mr. Albert G. Towers.

548 (UPPER) MR. BLANCHARD RAN-
DALL.
549 (CENTRE) DR. J. HALL PLEAS-
ANTS.
550 (LOWER) MRS. MILES WHITE,
JR.

310

back, frequently reeded, is generally straight, often with a raised and carved portion in the centre; the legs are sometimes square and tapered, as in the Hepplewhite style, but generally are round and tapered, and if so are usually reeded; stretchers were apparently not used; and the arms were most frequently supported by a vase-shaped column,[1] often reeded, a design which appears in Sheraton's "Drawing Book" and seems to have been previously published in Hepplewhite's "Guide."[2] The features which most frequently identify the Sheraton style are the straight back, the arm supports and the round and reeded legs; these features were used by Duncan Phyfe from about 1800 to 1825 and formed the basis of his finer sofas.

Observing the illustrations, we see two sofas, Nos. 551 and 552, which have square and tapered legs, such as were previously used on the sofas and chairs in the Hepplewhite style. It is sometimes thought that square and tapered legs of this type belonged only to the Hepplewhite style and were not used on Sheraton style furniture; but this view is incorrect, as shown by these two sofas and by many chairs.

In No. 551 the top rails of the back and arms are exposed, not upholstered. The raised portion of the top rail, here fluted vertically, recalls the similar feature in many chairs in the Sheraton style, such as Nos. 254–258; the arms are in concave curves; the lower edge of the seat is ornamented with a row of nails with large heads; and there are eight legs, the front ones ending in brass cups with casters. About 1795–1815.

In No. 552 the back and almost all of the arms are covered with upholstery, and the raised portion in the centre of the back is also covered. The vase-shaped arm supports are turned, but not reeded. There are seven legs, four in front and three in the rear, as also on some other sofas in this section; in No. 555 there are six legs; and in Nos. 559 and 560 there are only four, although these are long sofas. About 1795–1815.

With No. 553 we begin a group of sofas in the Sheraton style having the round, and generally reeded and tapering, front legs which are seen in almost all of the sofas and in many of the chairs of that style such as Nos. 249, 269 and 280. Here, as in No. 551, the top rail of the back is not upholstered; and this top rail has a raised portion in the centre which is ornamented with three delicately carved festoons of draperies. The arms come down to the front seat rail in curves; and the four round front feet, not reeded, terminate in brass cups with casters. About 1795–1815.

No. 554 is a small sofa, with vase–shaped and reeded arm supports and front legs, and over the latter are carved panels. The back rail is raised in the centre and the arms flow forward in a graceful curve. About 1795–1820.

---

1. This design appears also in arm chairs in the Sheraton style; as in No. 250 in section 54.
2. These two books are referred to in sections 17 and 18 which treat of the styles of Hepplewhite and Sheraton.

551 (UPPER) MR. & MRS. H. L. DUER.   552 (NEXT TO UPPER) MRS. ARTHUR HALE.
553 (NEXT TO LOWER) MR. A. E. COLE.   554 (LOWER) MR. A. E. COLE.

312

555 (UPPER) MRS. W. W. HUBBARD.   557 (NEXT TO LOWER) MR. ALBERT G. TOWERS.
556 (NEXT TO UPPER) MRS. BAYARD TURNBULL.   558 (LOWER) BISHOP E. T. HELFENSTEIN.

No. 555 is interesting, the surfaces of the seat rail, the panels over the legs, and the exposed portions of the arms being in a light wood, giving a pleasing touch of color with which the upholstery harmonizes. The reeded legs of this sofa have turnings of a type which is seen also on certain chairs of the Sheraton style, such as No. 275 and 279. It will be noticed that there are only two rear legs, as also in No. 557 and in later ones. About 1800–1810.

In No. 556 and several following sofas the top rail becomes a straight un-broken piece, often reeded in whole or in part; and the seat rail is similarly orna-mented. The small knobs at the ends of the top rail will be noticed, as also in the next sofa and No. 579; this ornamentation was adapted by Sheraton from French models of the time of Louis the Sixteenth. The reeding is not only on the top rail and seat rail but also on the arms, the arm supports and the tapering legs. The fine sofas made by Duncan Phyfe in the Sheraton style are not more fully reeded than this one and some others of the Sheraton type; and the common idea that Duncan Phyfe originated this abundance of reeding in American sofas or that it is in a Phyfe style, rather than the style of Sheraton, is manifestly erroneous. The best sofas made by Phyfe in this style show, however, more delicate workman-ship. See the comment on No. 573. About 1800–1820.

No. 557 is a small sofa, about fifty–four inches long. The top rail is in three divisions or panels, a favorite form with Duncan Phyfe; the central panel is reeded and the two others are plain. Small knobs are at the ends of the top rail, as in No. 556. The arms, arm supports and legs are reeded in whole or in part, but not very delicately. The seat rail is plain. About 1810–1820.

Nos. 558–561 are sofas in the later Sheraton style, and are not as fine as the previous ones. The changes are easily seen and indicate the growth of less attrac-tive types of designs.

In No. 558 the top rail and arms are about the same as in the previous examples but the legs are thicker and heavier and their reeding is not so delicate; the round rear legs are seen to be of about the same diameter as the front ones, but not being reeded or tapered they appear to be somewhat large and heavy. About 1815–1825.

In No. 559 the seat rail is nicely reeded, as are also the arms and a portion of the supporting columns, which are in an unusual form; but the top rail is not reeded. The most prominent indication of a change of style, however, is seen in the legs and feet, which extend forward and terminate in animals' paw feet which were afterwards used so frequently in the Empire style furniture. About 1815–1825.

In No. 560 the top rail appears to be divided into four panels, which, how-ever, are not ornamented. The curved arms follow the design of certain chairs in the Sheraton style, such as No. 296 in section 54. The arms, the seat rail and the legs are reeded, but not delicately. The two front legs project forward beyond the line of the seat and are furnished with brass feet and casters. About 1815–1825.

No. 561 is in a form which is said by a noted writer[3] to be "transitional from English Empire to Early Victorian"; and the sofa is referred to as "American, early nineteenth century." It may be somewhat difficult to realize the approach of the Victorian period in this sofa; but we notice the top rail of the back is not straight, having a long and gentle curve, and that the legs are without any fineness of design. In some other respects, however, this sofa closely resembles several good examples of the Sheraton style. About 1815–1825.

In Nos. 562 and 563 the designs of their arms and arm supports are in a form[4] which has been used on arm chairs in the Sheraton style, such as No. 273. These arms extend in a curve from the top rail over the arm supports which connect in a concave curve with the tops of the legs in the usual manner. In No. 562 the top rail is fully carved with large festoons of leaves; the arm supports and the legs are also decorated with carved leaves, below which the legs are reeded in the central parts. No. 563 has a plain top rail and seat rail, and only the panels over the end legs are carved. The legs are reeded. About 1800–1825.

No. 564 is a fine sofa in the Sheraton style, with carvings by Samuel McIntire, the celebrated architect and builder, of Salem, Massachusetts, who died in 1811. In the note, reference is made to a lengthy discussion[5] as to whether McIntire was also a cabinet maker and a carver who was employed to make carvings on articles of furniture made by various cabinet makers. The opinion at present is that he made many skillful carvings and also that a few articles of furniture were probably made by him.[6]

3. Mr. Herbert Cescinsky in "English and American Furniture," page 277, where the frame of a sofa, apparently the same in form as this, is illustrated without upholstery; only the feet are different, those shown by Mr. Cescinsky being in the round Sheraton reeded form.

4. A sofa in the same form, but more elegant in detail, is figure 661 in Mr. Lockwood's "Colonial Furniture," volume 2.

5. The discussion was in the magazine "Antiques," between Mr. Fiske Kimball and Mrs. Mabel M. Swan. Many illustrations, and extracts from original receipted bills in the Essex Institute, add to the interest of the articles.

Mr. Kimball's articles were in the following issues: November, 1930, page 388; December, 1930, page 498; January, 1931, page 30; March, 1931, page 207; January, 1932, page 23.

Mrs. Swan's articles were in the issues of November, 1931, page 280; December, 1931, page 338; February, 1932, page 86; October, 1934, page 130.

Other articles on the subject were by Mr. Charles Messer Stow, in "The Antiquarian," February, 1929, page 36; and by Dr. A. M. Frankfurter, in the same magazine, November, 1930, page 41. More recent articles are in "Antiques," December, 1933, page 218, and October, 1934, page 130.

6. As usual when several fine articles of furniture are identified as the work of a certain cabinet maker, many other similar articles are attributed to him without any proof except a resemblance to the identified pieces; on this subject see section 6, note 13. Many carved objects have been attributed to McIntire merely because of the resemblance of the carvings to those known to be the product of McIntire, as though his carvings could not have been copied by others.

In the absence of documentary evidence, no sofa or other article should be attributed to Samuel McIntire as its maker; the best that can be said with certainty is that the carving on the article is in the manner of McIntire.

A book of forty–four pages has been written by Mrs. Swan, entitled "Samuel McIntire, Carver, and the Sandersons, Early Salem Cabinet Makers." This book was published in 1934 by the

(*Note continued on page 318.*)

559 (Upper) Mr. & Mrs. H. L. Duer.
560 (Next to Upper) Mr. G. B. Simmons.
561 (Next to Lower) Mrs. Howard Sill.
562 (Lower) Mr. John C. Toland.

563 (UPPER) MR. WM. M. ELLICOTT.   564 (CENTRE) MRS. FRANCIS P.   565 (LOWER) MR. JOHN C. TOLAND.
GARVAN.

In Nos. 564 and 565 the ornamentation of the back is the most distinctive feature.[7] Above the upholstery in each is a line of rosettes and flutings, and above the centre of this line is a carved rectangular panel, on each side of which is another carved panel in a curved form; each of these panels has a "stippled," or "punched," background, a treatment which was used many years previously in chairs in the Chippendale style[8] in order to make the carving appear more distinctly by preventing reflections. The central panel in No. 564 is ornamented with a carved basket of fruit, and in No. 565 with a rosette. The side panels have carved designs of fruits and drapery; and the arms terminate in a scroll. In No. 564 the legs are round and in No. 565 are square and tapered. In No. 565 the back is divided into three rectangular sections with projecting cushions, following a Sheraton design.[9] About 1800–1810.

We now close the section devoted to sofas in the Sheraton style; but in section 74 are illustrations of sofas made by Duncan Phyfe in the Sheraton style; and in section 66, No. 513, appears a settee of like character by him.

Section 73. Directory style sofas.—In many sofas, as well as in chairs,[1] the French "Directory," or "Directoire," style, is very evident; but it has generally

(NOTE 6, *continued from page 315.*)

Essex Institute, Salem, Massachusetts. It appears that much of the furniture made by the Sandersons was carved by Samuel McIntire. In an "Introductory note," not by Mrs. Swan, it is said that the book "establishes quite conclusively the fact that while the Salem carver was not a cabinet maker, he did carving for various Salem furniture makers. . . The contention has been that because designs known to be McIntire's have appeared on furniture, the piece must have been made by him. Now, we have the proof." A similar remark is applicable to many other pieces of furniture—those resembling Duncan Phyfe's for example.

Samuel Field McIntire, a son of Samuel McIntire, continued the carving business in Salem after his father's death in 1811. It is said that his carvings and those of his more distinguished father have often been confused, those of the son being taken for the work of his father. An article on the son's carvings, written by Mr. Fiske Kimball, is in "Antiques," February, 1933, page 56.

7.   Five sofas with a similar ornamentation are illustrated in an article on "Furniture carvings by Samuel McIntire," written by Mr. Fiske Kimball, in "Antiques," December, 1930, page 498, mentioned in note 5, paragraph 2.

8.   Examples are in Mr. Cescinsky's "English Furniture," volume 2, figures 74 and 75, dated about 1745.

Some persons have thought that stippling or punch marks of a certain form were indications or proofs that the article was made by McIntire; but many articles made by various cabinet makers were stippled or punched. Views on this subject are expressed in "Antiques," December, 1930, page 514.

9.   In Sheraton's "Drawing Book," plate 35, a sofa of this kind is shown, with three cushions. In the description of this piece Sheraton wrote, page 318: "The loose cushions at the back are generally made to fill the whole length (of the sofa) which would have taken four; but I could not make the design so striking with four, because they would not have been distinguished from the back of the sofa by a common observer. These cushions serve at times for bolsters, being placed against the arms to loll against."

1.   See section 55 in which the subject of chairs in the Directory style is considered; and also section 19 in which the style itself is explained. In the present section there is a certain duplication of what has been said in those sections.

been treated as a part of the Empire style, not as a distinct style in itself. Recently, however, the style has been more generally recognized, both in England and in our country.[2] For example, some of the chairs made by Duncan Phyfe are described in the leading book[3] on his furniture as being "of the Directoire type," or as "showing Directoire influence"; and some of his sofas are described as being made under the "Directoire influence," as mentioned in section 74. It is therefore impossible to ignore the Directory style; and the subject will be more appreciated, and much more clearly understood, by the amateur collector, if sofas in the Directory style are treated as being in that style and not as being merely in the Empire style. Such at least is the experience of the writer.

As in chairs, the main feature of the Directory style in sofas is a fine continuous curve. In chairs the curve extends from the top rail to the front of the seat,[4] and in the sofas it extends from the tops of the arms to the seat rail. This curve[5] will be seen in all of the sofas illustrated in this section; and so much favored was the design that it continued to be used on sofas, with variations, throughout the Empire period and until the Victorian style became the fashion. Moreover the same feature is seen in the graceful type of sofas shown in section 75, known as "Grecian" sofas. In our American sofas illustrated in this section some of the features, such as the back and the legs and feet, are in the Sheraton style or the Empire style, but the most interesting features are the curved lines of the "roll over" arms in the Directory style.

Examining the illustrations,[6] we see in No. 566 a painted French sofa in which the Directory style curve is seen in the "roll over" arms, the same curve which is

2.   Especially in "American Furniture and Decoration" by Mr. Edward Stratton Holloway, in his chapter entitled "The American Directoire style," quoted in the sections mentioned in the previous note. In France the style is definitely treated as a separate style; and in England also, to a certain extent.

See note 2 in section 75, in which the "Regency" furniture is referred to.

3.   In "Furniture Masterpieces of Duncan Phyfe," by Mr. Charles Over Cornelius, mentioned in the sections referred to in note 1.

4.   See the chairs in section 55 and the group of late American Empire style chairs of about 1830–1840, illustrations Nos. 347–352, in some of which the curve is seen.

5.   It is said that the design of the Directory style sofa appeared in the work of Robert Adam some years before the Directory style was developed in France; and that both Adam and the French cabinet makers derived the design from Greek and Roman sources. The style was adopted by Sheraton, and appears in his "Cabinet Dictionary," which was published in 1803. Duncan Phyfe followed the Adam or French or Sheraton models, with embellishments of his own; and other American cabinet makers apparently used the same designs, with variations. See note on "Regency" furniture in section 75, note 2.

In "English Furniture," etc., by Mr. T. A. Strange, page 239, is a drawing of an Adam sofa of the same type as the Directory sofas here shown; the date given is "about 1780."

6.   A type of handsome sofas, said to be another type of the Directory sofas, not illustrated here, is shown in Mr. Nutting's "Furniture Treasury," volume 1, No. 1709, and in Mr. Holloway's "American Furniture," plate 104. In this sofa the upholstered arms are high and straight, not in the usual "roll over" form; they extend forward to the seat rail, flaring slightly outward. This type, which is not often seen, was made by a Philadelphia cabinet maker named Henry Connelly, as appears in an article in "Country Life in America," September, 1929, page 47, by Mr. W. M. Hornor, Jr.

seen in the Directory style chairs Nos. 307, 308 and others. These "roll over" arms, with a rosette at the ends of the rolls, appear in the sofas shown in this section. The legs, terminating in brass casters, are in a form resembling cornucopias.[7] In this sofa the back is not as pleasing as the other parts, being high at each end with a deep concave curve in the centre. The painted designs on the arms, and on the seat rail and the legs, are based upon those used in classic times; and the design at the top of each leg will be recognized as the Greek "anthemion," or honeysuckle,[8] which was seen on some of the chairs in the style of Chippendale, as Nos. 178 and 179, and on the two settees without backs, Nos. 522 and 523 in section 67. About 1800–1820.

No. 567, the back not being upholstered, is a "settee" according to the strict definition given in section 66, even though the arms are upholstered on the inside; but its back, covered with cane, may entitle it to be called a "sofa," which it more closely resembles. The arms are of the "roll over" type, the curves flowing into the seat. The legs are similar to those in the fine sofa No. 574. The arms, the seat rail and the legs are cut in a manner to resemble the wood of the bamboo, but the reflections have made the grooves in the wood appear to be inlay. The seat, which is hidden by the movable cushion, is caned. About 1800–1820.

In No. 568, the reeding on the arms and seat rail is characteristic of sofas and other articles in the Sheraton style; but the main outlines of the sofa are in the Directory style, and therefore this sofa may be conveniently called a "Directory style sofa," meaning a sofa in which the Directory style predominates. Because of the abundant reeding, sofas of this type are sometimes erroneously thought to be the work of Duncan Phyfe, which is considered in the next section. Two "squabs" are seen on this sofa.[9] About 1800–1820.

In No. 569 the Sheraton style is seen in the raised portion of the rail of the back, which resembles one of his published designs; the two long and graceful cyma curves, (as to which see section 23), of this rail will also be noticed. Other parts are in the Directory style, with carving on the arms, the seat rail and the legs; above the latter are two rectangular carved panels. About 1810–1825.

7. The "cornucopia," meaning "horn of plenty," was a classic Roman ornamental design in the shape of a horn. It was generally filled with fruits and flowers and was an emblem of prosperity and abundance.

     As to the other names for this type of legs, see note 5 in section 74.

8. The "anthemion," or honeysuckle, design is more fully mentioned in section 51, note 48.

9. A squab of this kind is a thickly stuffed cylindrical cushion made for use in connection with a sofa, to which it may or may not be attached, especially the sofas having "cornucopia" shaped arms such as in No. 589. As an adjective the word "squab" means "fat, short and stout, or plump," features which to some extent are seen in the squabs of this type.

     In older furniture, a squab was merely a loose cushion used on chairs and settees before the upholstered seats were made about 1700.

566 (UPPER) MRS. JAMES W. WILSON.   568 (NEXT TO LOWER) MR. & MRS. CARROLL VAN NESS.
567 (NEXT TO UPPER) MRS. JAMES W. WILSON.   569 (LOWER) DR. M. A. ABRAMS.

No. 570 is a curly maple sofa of pleasing Directory design unaided by any ornamentation except the panels over the legs[10] and the lines of molding around the edges of all the exposed parts. The top rail here is a plain panel extending the entire length of the sofa. About 1810–1825.

In No. 571, also of curly maple, the top rail, the arms and legs and the seat rail are deeply reeded. The legs appear to be shorter and less graceful than similar ones on the previous sofas; they are ornamented with rosettes of the same design as those on the "roll over" arms. The top rail is cut in a curve at each end where it joins the arm, as also in the next example. About 1810–1825.

In No. 572 the Directory features begin to disappear. The arms and seat rail are not in a continuous curve; the seat rail is broken in the centre by a panel; and the molded and reeded legs are in a late Sheraton or Empire design. About 1810–1825.

In section 76 we examine the American Empire style sofas, in almost all of which are reminders of the curved Directory arms, although in heavy and sometimes coarse designs, and with feet of wholly different types.

Section 74. Duncan Phyfe sofas.—In section 20, entitled "The Duncan Phyfe furniture," it is said that at the time when Phyfe began his career in the city of New York, about 1795, the Sheraton style was the new and fashionable one in furniture; a few years later the designs of the French Directory style appeared; and in the early part of the next century some of the prominent characteristics of the French Empire style were seen.[1]

With these three styles at hand, Duncan Phyfe, carrying on his business for the purpose of making his living, not for the purpose of creating a new furniture style, naturally made his furniture in either the Sheraton or Directory or Empire style,

10.   The name "sabre" is sometimes given to similar legs. See note 5 in section 74 on pages 324 and 326.

1.   These remarks, in substance, were also made in section 20 above referred to, but their repetition here is perhaps allowable for convenience and in view of the somewhat erroneous popular ideas on the subject. See also section 56 in regard to chairs made by Phyfe.

In the book "Furniture Masterpieces of Duncan Phyfe," by Mr. Charles Over Cornelius, more fully referred to in section 20, a chapter on sofas is on pages 67–71. There is no index to the book, but the pages containing illustrations of the sofas are sited in the list following the table of contents.

It is said in the book of Mr. Cornelius, pages 67–70, that the sofas made by Phyfe are in three types. The first and most usual is the type in the Sheraton style, as seen in Nos. 573 and 575. In these the rail on the back is straight and generally in three panels and is ornamented with carving; and there are six or eight round reeded legs.

The second type is in the Directory style, or under the influence of the Directory style, as in No. 574; chairs in that style are shown in Nos. 307–317, 323, 326.

The third type has features of the Empire style. A sofa in this style is not shown here, but in one of those shown in the book of Mr. Cornelius the principal Empire features are the legs in curule form, as in the Sheraton style chair marked 30 in illustration No. 234. The curule form is also seen in the backs of the chairs Nos. 320–323; see also the Index under the word "curule."

570 (Upper) Mrs. John S. Gibbs, 571 (Centre) Mr. John S. McDan- 572 (Lower) Mr. Edgar G. Miller,
Jr.   iel.   Jr.

323

as desired by his customers; and thus we may see in his work the designs of one or another of these styles, in some cases two of the styles being combined in one sofa. A sofa made by Phyfe in the Sheraton style may thus be called a "Duncan Phyfe sofa showing Sheraton influence"; but perhaps a better expression is a "Sheraton style sofa made by Duncan Phyfe";[2] or, if not made by Phyfe, such a sofa may be called a "Sheraton style sofa made in the manner of Duncan Phyfe."

Two sofas, Nos. 573 and 574, known to have been made[3] by Duncan Phyfe, are illustrated here, and also a third sofa, No. 575, whose maker is not known.

No. 573 is in the Sheraton style, having the characteristic features which are seen in that type. We observe the straight top rail, the reeded tops of the arms and their supports, the reeded seat rail and the reeded legs, all of which appear also in some other Sheraton style sofas, such as No. 556. Certain other details, however, give to the sofa a most elegant appearance and indicate the work of Phyfe. The top rail of the back, ornamented in three panels, is particularly fine; the central panel is carved with festoons of drapery, a feature of many designs by Robert Adam, and the two side panels with designs of arrows or darts, also known as "thunderbolts," a conventional term for strokes of lightning.[4] The ends of the arms in this particular sofa turn slightly inward, a detail which Phyfe sometimes used, instead of continuing them forward in a straight line. The reeding is especially to be noticed. It is not merely *reeding;* it is *fine reeding,* very delicately done. Moreover, the handsome upholstery covering adds not a little to the elegance of this piece. About 1800–1825.

No. 574 may be called a "Directory style sofa made by Duncan Phyfe." Here we see the characteristics of that style, as shown in the previous section. The "roll over" arms, the graceful curve of the arms flowing into the seat rail, and the legs in the "cornucopia"[5] form, are in the Directory style, as mentioned in the comment

2.   This is the method used in the catalogue of the "Girl Scouts Loan Exhibition," held in New York in September, 1929, which is generally regarded as the finest exhibition of American antique furniture ever held.

3.   Of course it is not meant that Phyfe made these two sofas with his own hands. He employed a large number of skilled cabinet makers in his shop to carry out his designs. Chippendale's work was done in the same manner; see section 15, note 1.

A cane settee made by Phyfe is shown as No. 513 in section 66.

4.   Different carved designs on the three panels are the main variations in sofas of this type; examples are carvings of cornucopias, ears of wheat and festoons of drapery.

5.   There seems to be a difference of opinion as to the proper name for a certain type of legs on sofas in the Directory style and on the "Grecian sofas" shown in the next section.

The curved legs on the Duncan Phyfe Directory style sofa No. 574 are said to be "made up of scrolls in cornucopia form" in the book of Mr. Cornelius entitled "Furniture Masterpieces of Duncan Phyfe," page 69. The same legs on the same sofa are shown in plate 107 in the book entitled "American Furniture and Decoration," by Mr. E. S. Holloway, and on page 147 it is said that "all the American sofas illustrated here have the graceful 'sabre' legs." In Mr. Lockwood's "Colonial Furniture," volume 2, figure 663, the same legs and sofa are illustrated and it is said that "the legs are scroll–shaped and reeded." The term "cornucopia" legs, meaning legs in the shape of a horn of plenty, seems to be the most descriptive of these particular legs and similar ones such as those on Nos. 576 and 577.

(*This note is continued on page 326.*)

573 (UPPER) ANONYMOUS.   574 (CENTRE) ANONYMOUS.   575 (LOWER) MR. C. EDW. SNYDER.

on No. 566. The fine reeding is conspicuous, but is not used on the top rail. The graceful arms, enclosing lyres, are perhaps the most important feature of this sofa. The use of the lyre as an ornamental feature has been seen in other articles, especially in chairs of the Sheraton type, as in figure 3 in No. 233; see also section 44, paragraph 3, and also other chairs made by Phyfe, such as No. 326. Whether seen from the front or the sides, this sofa is a handsome object; and it has been more widely illustrated than any other American sofa. About 1800–1825.

No. 575 has not been proved to be a product of the shop of Duncan Phyfe, but it is so similar to one made by him and shown in the leading book on the subject, that it may be used here to illustrate the general character of his work. It is in the Sheraton style, and has many of the features of No. 573. The three panels of the top rail, however, are ornamented in a different manner; the central panel has the same festoons of drapery, but the side panels are fluted vertically.[6] The reeding on the seat rail is very delicate. About 1800–1825.

Sofas made by Duncan Phyfe in the latter part of his career followed the unattractive fashions of the Empire style. His best work was apparently done between 1800 and 1825. Examples of his furniture made after about 1825 are not admired. He died in 1854.

Section 75. Grecian sofas.

—The "Grecian" style sofas seem to have originated in England with Sheraton,[1] or perhaps with Robert Adam, whose classic designs were often copied by Sheraton; and Robert Adam may have secured the designs from Greek examples; or the designs of Sheraton may have come from the French

(NOTE 5, *continued from page 324.*)

The term "sabre legs" has been given to certain legs because of a resemblance of the shape of the legs to that of the curved sword known as a "sabre" or "saber," both spellings being approved in English; the first spelling is also French. This word is used by Mr. Holloway, as mentioned in the preceding paragraph, and seems to be appropriate to several of the legs which have somewhat the form of a curved sword, such as the legs on the Directory style sofas Nos. 569 and 570.

Variations in the form of a horn of plenty will be noticed, but all may be recognized by the gradual widening from the bottom to the top, as in the horns in the Grecian sofas Nos. 580–583.

6. This top rail is similar to that in the sofa shown in plate 13, opposite page 26, in the book of Mr. Cornelius above referred to, entitled "Furniture Masterpieces of Duncan Phyfe." The vertical flutings and the festoons are in each sofa; but the feet and certain other details are different.

1. On pages 137 and 139 of the book entitled "Chippendale, Sheraton and Hepplewhite furniture designs," arranged by Mr. J. Munro Bell and published in London, designs by Sheraton in his "Cabinet Dictionary" are given of these sofas, called "Grecian beds," and the designs are referred to on page XI as illustrations "of the classic revival which followed the advent of Napoleon the First."

A sketch of a sofa of this kind is also in the book of Mr. Strange, entitled "English Furniture," etc., page 346.

The only sofa in Mr. Lockwood's "Colonial Furniture" of the type here shown is in volume 2, page 321. This sofa resembles No. 583 in form and is called a "Couch, Sheraton style, about 1810."

Sofas of the type shown in this section have been called "Madame Recamier" sofas. Illustration No. 586, at the end of this section, may correct this error.

who got the inspiration from classic sources. In England the Grecian sofas are regarded as being in the period and style of the "Regency."[2]

In applying the word "sofa" to some of these "Grecian" pieces, we are departing from the definition of "sofa" given in section 69, as some of these "sofas" have no upholstery on the back and others have only one arm.

The principal feature in the Grecian sofas is that the back does not extend over the entire rear of the sofa, but leaves a portion of the seat without a back, indicating that the sofa was intended to be used for reclining, not as a sitting place. Another feature is that the two arms are of different sizes, the arm at the foot being

2. In this section on Grecian sofas reference should be made to the so–called "Regency" style of furniture which is an English development of several styles in the period of about 1795–1820. Historically the word "Regency" refers to the period of 1811–1820 when the Prince of Wales was Regent, becoming King in 1820 on the death of his insane father George the Third. This style is sometimes included in the English Empire style, and our late Sheraton style and American Empire style are partially within the period, as appears in section 21. An English book entitled "Regency Furniture, 1795–1820," by Miss M. Jourdain has recently been published by "Country Life, Limited," of London.

Mr. Charles Messer Stow, in commenting on this book "Regency Furniture," in the New York Sun of March 2, 1935, remarks that "it is strange that so little attention has been paid to Regency (styles) in this country. Generally speaking, in making attributions, students skip from late Sheraton to Victorian, not remembering that a period of great importance came in between." Mr. Stow also remarks that "one of the best workers in the Regency style was our own Duncan Phyfe, who may be credited with developing in this country the equivalent of the current mode in England."

In some of our Grecian sofas illustrated in this section certain features of the French Directory style are noticed, and in the English book referred to are illustrations of several Grecian sofas with the same distinctive features; these sofas, plates Nos. 60, 61c, 62, 63, are apparently regarded in England as being in the English Regency style. It thus appears that the American cabinet makers who made furniture with these features must have invented the features or followed either the French Directory designs or the English Regency designs. The similarity could not have been accidental.

An obv'ous adoption of the English Regency designs is shown by the fact that one of the Phyfe side chairs with curule legs shown in plate 8 in the book of Mr. Cornelius entitled "Furniture Masterpieces of Duncan Phyfe" is almost the same in design as one of the chairs in plate 37 of "Regency Furniture."

In the preface of the English book it is said that the most important factor in the early years of the Regency style was Henry Holland, an architect, who borrowed elements from the French Directory style; and that after the death of Holland in 1806, designs were borrowed from the excavations at Pompeii, among which were couches. The Regency designers utilized these forms of Roman bronze and marble for wooden furniture. Moreover the Regency was the last consistent and recognizable style that designers employed before the Victorian.

After the death of Holland the classical revival was given a Grecian direction by the book of Thomas Hope, entitled "Household Furniture," and the word "Grecian" became part of the furniture maker's vocabulary.

In addition to the Greek revival of furniture designs in this period there was an Egyptian revival and also a Chinese revival, in which certain ornamental features of the furniture of Egypt and China were used. Later, about 1825, a Gothic revival was attempted in England and in our country, but was not successful, as mentioned in section 21, note 3, C.

The book "Regency Furniture" has 173 excellent illustrations, but without much descriptive information in regard to them. Many are shown sideways, requiring the book to be turned around if the illustrations are to be examined.

smaller than the one at the head; this difference increases in later pieces and in No. 585 the arm at the foot has entirely disappeared.

Nos. 576 and 577 are in the Directory style, the outlines of which are seen in section 73. Here the curves of the "roll over" arms continue into the seat rail, and the legs, which are supposed to resemble cornucopias, are curved; see note 5 in section 74. There is no upholstery in these two pieces, even the back having merely an uncovered bar. In No. 576 the entire front portion is decorated with painted designs.[3] No. 577 is painted white, requiring a dark background for photographing, and is ornamented with lines of gilt. In each piece the seat is of rush and was apparently meant to be furnished with a cushion. The cross–pieces of both arms are in designs which we have seen in the chairs in the Sheraton style, such as Nos. 286 and 312, and the curve of the bar in the back is similar to that in the arm chair No. 296. About 1810–1825.

No. 578 is a sofa from South Carolina, made chiefly of fine curly maple. The Directory style is less definitely followed than in the two previous examples, the legs with gilded wings and the black paw feet being in the Empire style, as appears in the following section. The seat, the arms and the back are caned and the seat was perhaps covered with a movable cushion, as in No. 567. The back extends further towards the other end than in Nos. 576 and 577. About 1810–1825.

In No. 579 the Directory style almost disappears, the curve of the arms not continuing into the seat rail, resembling somewhat in this respect the sofa No. 593 in the Empire style shown in section 76. The ornament at the junction of the back with the arm will be noticed, resembling those in the sofas Nos. 556 and 557. About 1820–1830.

In Nos. 580 and 581 another type is seen. At the foot of each sofa is a decided "roll," not an arm, turning inward, perhaps merely an ornament. The Directory style is seen in the curve of the arm and in the design of the legs. In each of these sofas continuous lines of reeding extend from the rosette at the end of the arm to the end of the seat rail, and onward to the rosette at the end of the small "roll." The legs are of the cornucopia type; those of No. 580 are fluted and those of No. 581 are carved. It will be noticed that in No. 580 the head of the sofa is at the right and in No. 581 the head is at the left, as though they were made in a pair, perhaps for opposite sides of a large room. About 1810–1825.

Nos. 582 and 583 are of still another type, differing from the two preceding sofas mainly in having a solid "roll" with a "built in" squab at the foot of the sofa. Here the Directory style is closely followed in the curve of the arm and the character of the legs. In No. 582 there is a variation in the top rail, which has a rectangular panel in three parts, upon which designs of ears of wheat and festoons of drapery are carved, resembling the style of the decorative treatment by Duncan Phyfe in No. 573. The roll at the foot of the seat is ornamented with a large rosette. In No. 583 the back is larger than in any of the previous sofas. In each of these two

3. In Mr. Holloway's "American Furniture," plate 105, a similar sofa, but not decorated, is shown, entitled "American Directoire Grecian Sofa, made in the South."

576 (Upper) Anonymous.
577 (Next to Upper) Mrs. W. G. Wetherall.

578 (Next to Lower) Mrs. Benj. H. Read.
579 (Lower) Miss Helen H. Carey.

329

580 (UPPER) MISS B. COHEN ESTATE.　　　　582 (NEXT TO LOWER) ANONYMOUS.
581 (NEXT TO UPPER) MD. SOC. COLONIAL DAMES.　　583 (LOWER) MR. MORRIS WHITRIDGE.

584 (Upper) Mrs. S. S. Buzby.   585 (Centre) Rev. & Mrs. A. C.   586 (Lower) Mme. Recamier Sofa.
Powell.

331

sofas the slope or slant of the arm is greater than in any of the others shown in this section. About 1810–1825.

The next three sofas, Nos. 584, 585 and 586, are not quite like those above. No. 584 is not strictly a Grecian sofa, but resembles one in some respects. It is different in that the back extends solidly all the way from the head to the foot. This is doubtless merely a variation of the Grecian sofa designs, giving a longer back to lean against. The front surfaces of the wood are all reeded and carved; and the legs and feet are in the Empire style, as shown in the next section. The arm at the foot is much smaller than that at the head, where a "squab" is placed. A debased form of this type became a prime favorite with the furniture makers and buyers of the early Victorian era. About 1810–1825.

In No. 585 there is no "roll" or arm at the foot of the sofa, which at this point is entirely open. The curve of the back is somewhat similar to that of the upper curve in the preceding sofa. The curved arm is carved in the figure of a dolphin[4] and does not continue into the seat rail, resembling No. 579 in this respect. A fine example of a dolphin sofa is in figure 667 in volume 2 of Mr. Lockwood's "Colonial Furniture." The winged legs are ornamented with carving. About 1810–1825.

No. 586 is an illustration of the celebrated portrait of Madame Recamier seated upon a sofa, painted by Jacques Louis David, (1748–1825), court painter to Louis the Sixteenth and Napoleon. We are more interested in the sofa than in the lady, for this is the "Recamier" sofa designed by David himself in the style of the Directory.[5] It will be noticed that the sofa is not a long one and that it has no back. The two arms are somewhat high and are of equal height. In several magazine articles and catalogues the term "Recamier" sofa has been applied to the general type of the sofas shown in this section; but the illustration of the painting by David shows that the "Recamier" sofa is a very different one, resembling a settee without a back.

Section 76. American Empire style sofas.—In considering the American Empire style chairs in section 57 it is said that few articles of American furniture are clearly in the style of the French Empire; and it is also to be said that the type of sofas known as the American Empire style type has but little to suggest the French Empire type except, in some cases, size and weight, especially in the later sofas of the period.

4. Dolphins as ornamental features are seen in the table No. 1556 and the girandole mirror No. 1242.

5. "Could anything be more simple in arrangement or graceful in pose than the furnishings and figure in this picture? The plain white gown without ruffle or lace, against the pale yellow of the cushions, and the outline of the whole figure intensified by the empty background, make a picture so vivid in its severe simplicity and transparent color that even the memory of it gives a thrill of pleasure"; from "Pictures and their Painters," pages 331–332, by Lorinda Munson Bryant, published by John Lane Co., New York, 1907. On page 333 is an illustration of Gerard's painting of Madame Recamier sitting upon a chair whose back resembles the arms of the sofa in the painting by David.

Almost all the sofas of the American Empire type, however, suggest the curve of the "roll over" arms of the Directory style, showing that our cabinet makers continued for some years to use that style in connection with features of the Empire style. But the fine curve soon lost its character and the arms of the later sofas assumed a variety of heavy and unlovely shapes; and the curved feet shown in the previous section were superseded, first by heavy animal paws and large wings and later by even heavier plain scrolls. Some of these later sofas are not deemed worthy of illustration in the books on antique furniture, both on account of their poor design and their insufficient age; but in this book for amateur collectors a number of illustrations of such sofas are given in this section in order that the reader may see what are *not* regarded as fine antiques. Moreover they form a part of the history of American furniture, and on that account should not be entirely disregarded.[1]

All the Empire style sofas here illustrated are believed to have been made between the years 1810 and 1830, except the last two.

In No. 587, the first example of the American Empire style, we observe the continuance of the Directory style in the curve of the arms and in the shape of the legs.[2] All of the other features are in the Empire style, and they remove the sofa from the earlier Directory style. The seat rail is a plain panel between the lower ends of the arms. At the top of the back is a rounded rail with a carved scroll at each end turning downward, sometimes called a "bracket"; a similar feature will be seen on the tops of the head–boards on certain bedsteads of the period, as in No. 1067 and others in section 137. In this sofa there is a large panel, not upholstered, under the rounded rail. The variety of carved designs will also be noted. About 1810–1830.

In No. 588, as in the preceding sofa, the Directory style is suggested by the shape of the arms. The sofa is known as a "swan's neck" sofa, from the design of the arms, a design which was also used in some of the arm chairs of the Empire style, as in No. 423 in section 60, in which there is an opening in the upper part, showing the neck and head more clearly. As in the previous sofa, there is a rounded rail on the back with a scroll at each end. Connected with the inner side of each leg with its animal foot, is a bird's wing, said to be in imitation of an Egyptian style or of a winged griffin,[3] a popular form of ornamentation in the Empire period. About 1810–1830.

1. As mentioned in sections 5 and 21 the books on antique furniture generally close the subject of American Empire furniture at or about the year 1825; but there is an increasing tendency in the magazines to publish articles on sofas and other furniture of a later date.

In "Antiques," January, 1927, pages 41–44, is an illustrated article by Mr. Homer Eaton Keyes, the editor, entitled "Concerning some Empire sofas." The Directory style is not considered as a distinct style. On page 43 it is said that "the quality of an American Empire sofa is determined very largely by the skill with which its variously curving lines are harmonized in flow, the character of the wood used and the relative excellence of the carving."

The mahogany used in sofas during the Empire period was of a fine character, whether solid or veneer. Sometimes the wood was finished in a reddish color, as mentioned in note 1, E in section 29.

2. As to this type, see the comment on No. 566 and note 7.

3. As to a "griffin" as used in antique furniture, see note 12 in section 193.

587 (Upper) Bishop E. T. Helfenstein.   589 (Next to Lower) Mr. Daniel R. Randall.
588 (Next to Upper) Mrs. Edwin B. Niver.   590 (Lower) Mrs. E. N. Dunham.

591 (UPPER) DR. HENRY J. BERKLEY.
592 (NEXT TO UPPER) MRS. THOS. J. LINDSAY EST.

593 (NEXT TO LOWER) MRS. JOHN D. C. DUNCAN.
594 (LOWER) MR. JOHN HINKLEY.

No. 589 is known as a "cornucopia"[4] sofa having arms in the shape of that symbol of prosperity and abundance, a design which was in favor from about 1810 to 1830. The top parts of the cornucopia arms are ornamented with fruits and flowers. The curve of these arms is no doubt a debased form of the Directory style arm curve shown in section 73. Each arm curves outward and then inward and has an upholstered top surface, forming a space below in which a "squab" may be placed. In this sofa the legs and feet resemble those in the previous piece. The central part of the seat rail and the same part of the top rail is finely reeded in the Sheraton style. About 1810–1830.

No. 590 is a fanciful sofa at all points, with much carving. The upholstered seat is too high to allow a "squab" to be used in the place provided for it. The curious feet apparently with hair growing on them will also be noticed. About half way up on each arm is a V–shaped carving which in the next illustration is much enlarged; or perhaps the design here is a small survival of the next one. About 1810–1830.

In No. 591 the arms divide into two curved ends, making the V–shaped forms referred to in the previous paragraph, and thus providing two suitable spaces for the squabs. The usefulness of the V–shaped design is not clear. The panel in the back rail is within reeded lines; and the arms and legs and feet are carved, the latter very elaborately. About 1810–1830.

No. 592 has a back rail in two panels and on each side is a rounded and curved rail with a rosette at the inner end. Here the curved and upholstered tops of the arms are very large, and of no apparent utility and leave no space for a squab. About 1820–1830.

No. 593, having no carving, is a plain sofa, less expensive than those with carving. The curves of the arms suggest those of the Directory style, but they do not connect with the seat rail in a continuous curve, and are separate from it as in No. 579 in the previous section. The tops of the arms are not enlarged as in No. 589 and in other sofas in this section, but "roll over" in a graceful curve. The heavy scroll legs are in the late Empire style; and on the principle that the latest feature in an article of furniture determines its date,[5] this sofa should be regarded as of the date of the legs. About 1830–1840.

No. 594 has features similar to those in the preceding sofa, but the "roll over" arms of that sofa are superseded by those with large upholstered tops as in No. 592. The small squabs find no resting place under these arms. As in the preceding sofa, there is here no carving on any part. About 1830–1840.

4.   In No. 587 the term is applied to the legs; in No. 589 it is applied to the whole sofa.

5.   See the subject of "Dating Furniture," which is considered in paragraph 5 in section 6. This principle has not been strictly observed in connection with the sofas shown in this chapter.

Following the style of No. 594, many other late Empire style sofas were made. These are not illustrated here, as the words "American Antique Furniture" cannot be stretched further. They were in turn superseded by sofas in the early Victorian style which began about 1840. An example of the latter sofas, made by John H. Belter, of New York, may be seen in illustration No. 7, which is one of the views of alcoves furnished in the style of the early Victorian era, in the Metropolitan Museum of Art. See also note 3 in section 22 in regard to Belter.

Chapter VIII

CHESTS AND CHESTS OF DRAWERS
(NOT INCLUDING HIGHBOYS, LOWBOYS OR BUREAUS)

Section 77. New England chests; and two others
Section 78. Pennsylvania Dutch chests
Section 79. Early chests of drawers
Section 80. Tall chests of drawers on frames; and others
Section 81. Chests–on–chests

Section 77. New England Chests; and two others.—The early chests mentioned in this section are full of interest to the connoisseur, and many pages and illustrations are given to them in the books. But as this book has been prepared mainly for the pleasure of amateurs, and as the chests are seldom seen outside of museums, the subject is only briefly referred to. It is said that no museum, exhibition or book dealing with American antique furniture is complete without "chests."[1]

1. A. The subject of chests is treated at length, with many illustrations, in Mr. Lockwood's "Colonial Furniture," 3rd. edition, 1926, volume 1, pages 22–51, and 335–344. Also in Mr. Nutting's "Furniture Treasury," Nos. 1–120, and "Furniture of the Pilgrim Century, 1620–1720," Revised edition, Nos. 1–85.

B. A chest is defined as a large box of wood or metal with a hinged lid. Next to the chair and the bed, chests are said to be the earliest articles of domestic furniture. They were the receptacles for clothes and valuables, and were also used as a seating place, a chair being somewhat of a luxury in days when the chest was an almost universal possession. Chests were frequently made to contain the store of linen which a bride took to her husband upon her marriage. Perhaps no other articles of furniture were brought from England by the early settlers in such numbers as the "ship chests," being the indispensable pieces in which to transport clothing and valuables; containing these articles the chests took but little more of the limited space of the small ships of the period than did the articles themselves.

C. Boxes. As boxes were generally small chests, they are often mentioned in connection with chests. They were made to hold papers and books, especially Bibles. Like chests they had a hinged top. In America they were generally made of oak and pine. They were ornamented with carving and painting in much the same way as chests. Many illustrations of these boxes are in Mr. Nutting's "Furniture Treasury," Nos. 121–173.

Desk writing boxes may be regarded as a form of desk. They are referred to in the chapter on "Desks," section 101, note 2, B.

See the early box type of desk No. 775, shown in section 102.

D. Certain chests on frames. These are small pieces, often about three feet high and two feet wide, consisting of a flat–top box with one drawer underneath, built on a frame–work somewhat like that of a table. The top lifts up, as in chests. They are sometimes called "pilgrim chests." Just what they were used for is not altogether clear, but their decorative character indicates that they were

338

The earliest type of chests made in our country seems to have been copied from pieces brought over from England; and the similarity in design and appearance between them is so great that in some cases it may be difficult to determine whether a piece is of English or American make, even by an examination of the kind of wood used. The principal feature of chests is the decoration of the panels on the fronts, and also on the "stiles," which are the four vertical posts at the corners of the chest and which, when prolonged several inches below the body of the chest, form the feet.

The dates of the making of these chests are rather indefinite, ranging from about 1650 to about 1750; the style of the decoration is said to be the least uncertain test. The English pieces were generally made of English oak throughout; some of the American pieces were also made altogether of oak, but the bottom, the back and the top were often made of pine. The height of the chests without drawers was usually about thirty inches, and the length about four or five feet. The addition of drawers, of course, increased the height, but in order to keep down the bulk the length was reduced somewhat.

Whether or not the earliest chests were all made without drawers may be uncertain, but more of the chests with drawers have been found than those without drawers; and chests with one drawer seem to be earlier than those with two or more; but no exact periods of making chests with one or two or more drawers can be given.[2] Much carving was used in the decoration of chests; in some cases the entire front was covered. The carving is generally flat and curious rather than artistic; in fact it may be termed crude, but was perhaps creditable to the colonial carpenters or cabinet makers of the time and place.

The four chests here shown are representative of the principal kinds. All of these chests seem to have been made in New England.

No. 595, a chest without drawers, is more ornamental than some others, being carved "all over" the front. The central one of the three panels has leaves and scrolls, and the two outer panels have a decoration known as the "tulip decoration." The cyma curves[3] will be noticed in the top of the central panel and on the carved

(NOTE 1, *continued*)

of some importance. It is believed that they were made about 1670–1700. Only a few of these pieces have survived and they have all been found in New England. They are illustrated in Mr. Nutting's "Furniture Treasury," Nos. 207–217.

E. A "settle" is said to be a form of chest with a high back and with arms at the sides, as mentioned in section 66, note 3; see Mr. Lockwood's "Colonial Furniture," volume 2, pages 127–128, and Mr. Nutting's "Furniture Treasury," volume 1, Nos. 1621–1634.

2. Of the four chests, Nos. 595–598, the first has no drawer and the other three have drawers.

As appears in section 79, a chest having drawers which do not occupy the entire space within is a "chest *with* drawers"; and when it developed into a chest consisting entirely of drawers, with a fixed top instead of a lid, it became a "chest *of* drawers" which we call "bureaus."

Two illustrated articles, entitled "The American Chest," by Mr. Walter A. Dyer, are in "The Antiquarian" in the issues of October, 1931, page 36, and November, 1931, page 45.

3. As to the cyma curve, see section 23. See also the carving on the wainscot chair No. 22 and note 7 in section 46.

brackets at the junctions of the feet with the bottom of the chest. As in other chests, the top lifts up. The very sturdy appearance of this chest will be noticed. This piece and the next two are in the Bolles Collection in the Metropolitan Museum of Art. About 1650–1675.

No. 596 has one wide drawer, which has the appearance of being two separate drawers. The carving on the three panels is in a rectangular design with four circular designs on the sides, and other carvings will be noticed above and below the panels. Bands of dark wood are on the uncarved upright and horizontal portions of the front. The probable date of this chest is believed to be the same as that of the preceding chest, about 1650–1675.

No. 597 is a chest of the Hadley[4] type, so called because many pieces of this character have come from the neighborhood of the town of that name in Massachusetts. The feature of this type is that the entire front of the chest is covered with rather crude and shallow carving of simple designs, usually of tulips, vines and leaves, and that they almost always bear the initial letters of a name, as the letters "E C" in this piece. It is said that these chests were generally wedding gifts. Some of them have no drawer, but most of them have one, two or three drawers, and are usually made of oak with some parts of pine. Three rectangular, carved and sunken panels are generally on the upper part of the front. About 1700–1720.

No. 598 is a chest of the type commonly called the "Connecticut sunflower chest" for the reason that it has been found chiefly in that State and because the central one of the three panels on the front is often carved with three circular designs supposed to represent sunflowers or asters. The two side panels are usually carved with designs of tulips. Perhaps the most conspicuous feature is the other ornamentation on the front, consisting of, in this chest, six half–spindles which are called "half" or "split" spindles[5] because each one is one–half of a round spindle as are the banisters in banister–back chairs,[6] and also eight separate oval ornaments

---

4. An article, with ten illustrations, entitled "The Secret of the Hadley Chest," by Mr. Walter A. Dyer, is in "The Antiquarian" of February, 1930, page 27. See also "The Hadley Chest" by Rev. C. F. Luther, published in 1935.

Hadley chests have aroused much interest in recent years and their values have greatly increased. Their origin is still somewhat obscure, but most of them have been found in Massachusetts and Connecticut. Very extensive searches and much publicity have increased the known number at the present time to an even one hundred examples, which are now in various parts of the country. They are referred to by the initials on the front, the one shown in No. 597 being known as "E C." Most of the study and investigation has been done by Mr. Luke Vincent Lockwood and the Reverend C. F. Luther; the latter contributed articles on the subject to "Antiques," October, 1928, page 338, and September, 1929, page 202.

An illustrated article entitled "Chests of our New England Grandmothers," by Mr. Malcolm A. Norton, is in "Antiques," August, 1922, page 76.

5. The spindles are the vertical columns or pillars, one at each end and four between. They are sometimes called balusters or banisters.

6. See the chairs Nos. 44–45 and others.

595 (Upper) Metropolitan Museum of Art.
597 (Centre) Metropolitan Museum of Art.
599 (Lower) Dr. James Bordley, Jr.

596 (Upper) Metropolitan Museum of Art.
598 (Centre) Mrs. Francis P. Garvan.
600 (Lower) Mr. J. G. D'Arcy Paul.

called "bosses"[7] on the two drawers; all of these spindles and bosses were applied[8] with glue. These spindles and bosses were originally painted black. There are two wide drawers with small wooden knobs, one of which is missing on the lower drawer on the right. About 1675–1700.

Nos. 599 and 600 are not closely connected with the four preceding chests and are of a more recent and familiar form, such as the form of the Pennsylvania Dutch chest No. 603. There is no ornamentation of any kind on either of the two chests now being examined. In the American chests of this type, at the front upper left corner of the interior, there was often a "till" or "treasure box" in which money or small articles of value might be placed. On these two chests the brass handles will be noticed.

In No. 599 the feet seem to be a variation of an early type of foot known as a "ball" foot, which may be seen in figure 3 in illustration No. 11. The date may be about 1725–1750. The miniature chest or box has bracket feet of a later date and may be dated at about 1750–1780.

No. 600 is in the Queen Anne style, having cabriole legs and club feet. By reason of the legs, the two drawers and the upper part of the chest were raised and made more accessible without bending over. The skirt of the under–frame is cut in cyma curves, as to which see section 23, similar in part to some of those seen in the illustrations of the lowboys of the Queen Anne period, such as No. 684. This chest is of cedar wood and has certain features which indicate that it is one of a type made in the island of Bermuda.[9] About 1740–1760.

7.   Also called "turtle backs," or "eggs." A "boss" is defined as an oval or circular protuberance applied on a surface as an ornament. A round brass one, called a "boss," was often used on the brass dials of English grandfather clocks on which boss the maker's name and location was given. For discussion of brass mounts, ormolu, "Boulle work," handles and their attachments, see section 38.

8.   As to "applied" decorations, see (as above) section 38.

   Several illustrated articles on the subject of the "Sunflower" chests may be cited. In "The Antiquarian," July, 1930, page 52, is an article entitled "Sunflowers," by Mr. Walter A. Dyer and Reverend C. F. Luther; in the same magazine, October, 1931, page 36, is an article entitled "The American Chest—seventeenth century" by Mr. Dyer. In "Antiques," January, 1931, page 20, is an article entitled "A newly discovered Connecticut Chest," by Mr. Luther; and in the issue of April, 1935, page 140, is an article by Mr. Dyer entitled "The Tulip–and–Sunflower Press Cupboard," in which the sunflower chest is precisely described.

   In Connecticut, about 1700, it seems that certain chests were painted with various designs and in different colors; these are not connected in origin with the painted chests known as the Pennsylvania Dutch chests referred to in section 78.

9.   The engraving is not large enough to show clearly the two front corners of this chest where there is a peculiar form of dovetailing by which the front and side boards are held together. The ends of the side boards project through the front board and are cut in such a way as to show, from the front, a series of toothed or saw–like ends. Illustrated articles on this type of chest are in "Antiques" of February, 1925, page 80, and December, 1929, page 487; see also a somewhat similar chest in walnut by William Savery, of Philadelphia, in the issue of February, 1929, page 137, dated about 1760.

   Many old chests of a plain character, very often made of pine, are found in the country shops and auction sales. They are even now useful for the storage of almost anything, including firewood. Many are country–made pieces of no particular style, except sometimes in the feet or handles, if original; and it is difficult to determine their date. These pieces are not interesting as antiques and are not illustrated in this book.

Section 78. Pennsylvania Dutch chests.—To the southeastern section of Pennsylvania there came, during a number of years after 1683, many immigrants from Germany, who, and also their present descendants, are commonly known as "Pennsylvania Dutch."[1] Bringing with them the customs and ideas of their homes in the old country, they also brought their German chests, decorated with painted designs, which they followed in making other chests in later years. Most of these later chests were made from about 1770 to 1810. They are usually ornamented on the front in two or three panel designs, with painted flowers, especially tulips,[2] and with various fruits and birds; and many bear initial letters, supposed to be those of the brides for whom they were made, or the names of the men owners.[3] These chests are not elegant in character and are regarded as "peasant furniture."

1. These people were not "Dutch" in the sense of coming from Holland, but in the colloquial sense, meaning "German." Many of their conversational expressions are very queer. A number of the towns have German names, as Mannheim, the home of Baron Stiegel, whose glass is so much in demand. At Ephrata, near Lancaster, is an interesting "cloister" built in 1740, where printing, book–binding and other work was carried on. The religious sects, such as the Amish, Dunkards and Mennonites still survive, and their members may be known on the streets by their style of dress, all odd to our eyes, and some very odd, such as clothing without buttons. A visit to Lancaster is well worth while, especially to the market on market days when the country people come to town with their produce. The style of the beards of the older men has apparently continued without change since the early settlers arrived. They are thrifty and prosperous people and good citizens. The present younger generation is not quite so strict as their parents in clinging to old customs. These remarks are a digression from "American Antique Furniture"; but after seeing these "Pennsylvania Dutch" people one becomes more interested in their painted boxes and chests.

Interesting illustrated articles by Mrs. Esther Stevens Fraser entitled "Pennsylvania Bride Boxes and Dower Chests" are in "Antiques," July, 1925, page 20, and August, 1925, page 79. In the latter article the various decorative designs on chests made in five countries are discussed; see also the issue of September, 1926, page 203. Three other illustrated articles by the same writer, entitled "Pennsylvania Dower Chests," are in the same magazine, February, 1927, page 119, April, 1927, page 280, and June, 1927, page 474. An illustrated article entitled "Antiques of the Pennsylvania Germans," by Mr. W. L. Stephen, is in the same magazine, "Antiques," June, 1926, page 407. In the same magazine of July, 1927, page 36, is an illustrated article by Mr. Adolphe Riff on "Old Alsatian Marriage Chests," showing the resemblance of the Pennsylvania pieces to the Alsatian. In "The Antiquarian," May, 1930, page 35, is an illustrated article by Mr. H. D. Eberlein entitled "Bridal Furniture of the Pennsylvania Germans."

The word "polychrome" is often used in connection with these and other painted articles. The word means "having several colors"; the first four letters "poly" mean "many," as in the word "polygamy," and the other letters, "chrome," refer to colors, as in the word "chromo."

Interesting tales of the Pennsylvania Dutch have been written by Mrs. Helen Reimensnyder Martin. A popular one is "Tillie: A Mennonite Maid."

Considerable faking has been done in these chests, such as repainting the designs on old chests, and even the manufacture of both chests and painting; and many chests and other kinds of peasant furniture made in Sweden and Germany have been imported and sold as American. See the remarks in section 8, note 2.

2. Mr. Nutting, in volume 1 of his "Furniture Treasury," at figure 55, has a note on the "tulip motive" in furniture decoration in which it is said that in addition to being painted on wood, it is found on iron utensils, on fabrics, and in carvings on wood. From some points of view it appears to have three leaves and to have a religious motive.

3. A. In a note at figure 119 in the same book, Mr. Nutting writes in regard to calling these chests "Dower chests," that "There is no significance in the common term 'dower chest' unless the initials of a lady appear. More chests were acquired after marriage than before." (*Continued on next page.*)

These chests have no connection with the New England chests mentioned in the previous section, and have no period styles except that the earlier and the later chests show certain differences. Whatever decorative style they had was that of their own Pennsylvania county, although the form of the chest itself may follow the style of other large boxes with lids. These chests, especially if fully decorated with the original decorations, are much in demand in Pennsylvania. They were generally made of poplar (tulip) wood, with or without one or more drawers, and often the dates of their making were painted on the front.

The four chests Nos. 601–604 are of a more elaborate character than many others; some chests are of the same shape, without any decoration. In size they range from about 22 to 25 inches high and from 40 to 50 inches long.

No. 601 is the earliest chest. It is dated 1774 and bears the name "Johann Esleman." On the three panels with arched tops, like the arched dials of many clocks, are painted tulips in vases. Originally there were probably four feet. There were no drawers. 1774.

No. 602 has three sunken panels on the front and two on the ends, making five arches. In the central panel a gorgeously arrayed man with very thin legs is walking with a staff; in the other front panels are tulips and birds. The lock is dated 1785. This piece has no drawers. 1785.

No. 603 has two drawers and is dated 1795. The two side panels contain vases of tulips and the central one is a heart with (no doubt the appropriate) birds, and the name of Benjamin Hammer, the man for whom probably it was made. Stars and scrolls add to the decoration. This chest, No. 492 in the Reifsnyder collection, was sold at auction in the boom year 1929 for $2,000. 1795.

No. 604 is probably a foreign chest. It bears some initials and the date 1832. There are no feet and no panels, but the front is divided into two equal parts, each decorated with vases containing fanciful figures supposed to represent flowers. The lid is curved, not flat as in the other chests. 1832.

Section 79. Early chests of drawers.—As mentioned in the text and note 2 in section 77, some of the early chests were made without drawers and others were

(NOTE 3, *continued*)

B. Here, as on several other pages in this book, the writer indulges in some elementary legal remarks in regard to the use of words. The words "dower chest," in connection with furniture, are erroneously used, unless we think that by continued misuse the word "dower" has changed its meaning. The word "dower," as applied to a chest, is wrong because throughout English and American legal history the word "dower" applies only to real estate, that is, land, and means a widow's legal interest in the real estate of her deceased husband. A "dower chest" is as meaningless as a "dower dinner" or a "dower excursion."

The word "dowry" is sometimes used to mean "dower," but legally it means property of any kind which a woman owns and brings to her husband at the time of her marriage, whether the property is real estate or other property, and whether owned by her prior to her marriage or given to her upon her marriage. It corresponds with the French "dot." Any reader who cares to pursue the subject of wrong words in matters of antique furniture may find several references in the Index under "Words."

601 (UPPER) ANONYMOUS. 602 (UPPER) ANONYMOUS.
603 (LOWER) ANONYMOUS. 604 (LOWER) ANONYMOUS.

made with one or two drawers, all being under the box part of the chests. In the course of time it was found desirable to fill the entire chest with additional drawers, and to make the lid a stationary top. In this way a chest *with* drawers developed into a chest consisting entirely *of* drawers, that is, a "chest of drawers," or, as we now term it, a bureau.

These changes would perhaps be better seen in the simpler forms of early chests than in the finer ones whose elaborate decorations may absorb our attention; but the simpler and less valuable ones have apparently not survived the years, so that it is necessary to use some of the finer ones as illustrations.

Nos. 605–607 are examples of the highly ornamented chests of drawers of the period of about 1675–1700. These three pieces appear here through the courtesy of the Metropolitan Museum of Art. It will be seen that No. 605 has two drawers with floral carvings, with the tulip designs in evidence. The box part of the chest has disappeared and the piece consists only of drawers; the lifting lid is gone and a stationary top has taken its place. The decorations and the feet, however, continue about the same as in the chests. About 1675–1700.

No. 606 has three drawers. The front is covered with carved scroll designs and the feet are of the same kind as in the preceding chest. Two plain wooden knobs are on each of the drawers. About 1675–1700.

In No. 607 the elaborate front is different from that of the two pieces above mentioned, having no similar carving, and having much panelling. Each one of the four drawers is ornamented with different designs. The feet are not simply prolongations of the upright supports at the corners, called "stiles," but are of the ball type. About 1675–1700.

No. 608 is so different in appearance from No. 607 that it seems at the first glance to have but little connection with it; but the difference consists largely in the absence of the ornamentation seen on the front of No. 607 and the division of the upper drawer into two smaller drawers. The feet of each are of the ball type, which are seen in figure 3 in illustration No. 11. Except for the feet and the brasses on the drawers, this piece might almost be taken for a modern bureau; but it was made in the style of over two hundred years ago, that is, about 1700. A revival of the style may be seen in No. 752 in the chapter on bureaus.[1]

---

1. An article on a chest of drawers similar to No. 608 is in "Antiques," November, 1925, page 270, entitled "Pedigreed Antiques—Desire Cushman's Chest." The story is that Desire Cushman was born in 1673, and when she was a little girl of about eight or nine years of age this small chest of drawers, about twenty–seven inches high, was presented to her, and after her death it "passed on to a young girl in each succeeding generation, never to a boy." It is said in the article that Desire married a man named Kent and that she was "a woman from whom hundreds trace descent and whose ancestry has been one of the greatest of the New England genealogical puzzles." Strange to say, the chest was not brought over on the "Mayflower"; see the "Mayflower joke" in note 1, G, in section 11.

A chest of drawers decorated with paintings and with the larger drawers at the top and the smaller ones below is shown in the frontispiece in "Antiques," September, 1926. It is thought to be a Connecticut piece of the seventeenth century.

605 (Upper) Metropolitan Museum of Art.
607 (Lower) Metropolitan Museum of Art.

606 (Upper) Metropolitan Museum of Art.
608 (Lower) Anonymous.

No. 608 is the last of four illustrations of early chests of drawers, sufficient in number, however, to show how the modern bureau[2] developed from the chests. It is said that these early chests of drawers passed out of style about 1725 and that their place was taken by highboys and lowboys, which in turn went out of style and were superseded by a revival of the chest of drawers of the type of No. 608, as mentioned in section 96 in the comment on No. 752.

Section 80. Tall chests of drawers on frames; and others.—The height of the chests of drawers mentioned in the previous section was generally not more than about forty inches; but influenced perhaps by the popularity of the tall high-boys,[1] taller types of chests of drawers were developed, which are the subjects of this section.

In one type of these chests there was a tall chest of drawers which was placed upon a low "frame," also called a "stand" or "table." If this frame contains one or more drawers, the article may be called a "highboy"; but if there are no drawers in the frame it is called a "tall chest of drawers on a frame," or "highdaddy," and in the words of Mr. Lockwood, it is "literally a chest of drawers on a frame, for the table part has no drawers."[2]

In another type of tall chests of drawers, there is no frame below. This type is of a later date than those on frames; and their style has a relation to the style of bureaus, as will be seen in illustrations Nos. 615 and 616.

In Nos. 609 and 610 the upper parts containing the drawers are similar to those of some of the highboys in the Queen Anne style, such as No. 641 and others, having flat tops, cabriole legs and club feet. The legs of No. 609 are very short, making it possible to have six drawers within a convenient height. The drawers are graduated in size, the smallest being at the top. The skirts, or aprons, of the front rails of the frame, are of the same general character as those of the high-boys. About 1740–1750.

No. 611 is of a somewhat later style, having ball and claw feet. The almost straight skirt, or apron, is in the manner of those on some of the lowboys illustrated in the chapter on that subject, such as No. 673. At the front corners are rounded columns. About 1750–1770.

The remaining chests in this section, Nos. 612–616, are not strictly "tall chests of drawers on frames," because they do not rest upon frames in the usual manner, but rest directly upon their feet.

Nos. 612–614 have bracket feet only, instead of legs and feet, and the drawers are thus nearer to the floor. The feet on No. 612 are known as "ogee" bracket feet, as

2. The subject of bureaus might properly be included in this chapter on chests of drawers, as a matter of historical development, as is often done in the books on antique furniture; but the subject of bureaus, with its numerous illustrations in sections 93–100, seems to be more interesting when treated by itself than when connected with the subject of ancient chests.
1. See "Highboys," section 82 and note 4.
2. In "Colonial Furniture," volume 1, page 87, figure 81.

609 (UPPER) MRS. MILES WHITE, JR. 610 (UPPER) MRS. JOHN S. GIBBS, JR.
611 (LOWER) MRS. MILES WHITE, JR. 612 (LOWER) MRS. HOWARD SILL.

shown in figure 9 in illustration No. 11. It has a row of three drawers at the top, then a row of two drawers and below are four drawers which, as usual, are graduated in size. At the front corners are fluted columns. About 1750–1770.

No. 613 is unusual in having the large number of thirteen drawers, four of which at the top are under arches and are themselves gracefully arched. The feet here are of the plain "straight bracket" type, the front corners being straight, not curved; this kind of foot is shown in figure 6 in illustration No. 11, cited in the preceding paragraph. The wood is walnut. About 1750–1770.

No. 614, which is inlaid at the top with the figures "1793," is said[3] to be "the latest–made piece of Chippendale furniture yet discovered." The letters "D H" will be noticed in the central top drawer, and it is said that these probably indicate that the piece was a "marriage chest." It may also be surmised that it was made to please a customer who was fond of old–fashioned furniture and that it does not indicate a continuance of the Chippendale style as the fashionable style of the period. In the front corners are fluted columns. 1793.

Nos. 615 and 616, the last two illustrations in this section, are of a different kind of tall chests of drawers. As remarked above, these do not rest upon separate frames, but directly upon their feet. In design, but not in size, they seem to be related to the bureaus of the Hepplewhite and Sheraton periods.[4] About 1790–1810.

In No. 615 the French bracket feet[5] and the cyma curved skirt, or apron, are similar to those seen in bureaus of the period above mentioned. It it also interesting in having inlaid decorations on the front corners and on the top and bottom rails, and also inlaid ovals on each of the nine drawers. The same form of oval inlay may be seen on the bureau No. 742 and others. About 1790–1810.

No. 616 is a very tall piece, about eight feet, rivalling the highest of the highboys. Here also we notice the French bracket feet and the cyma curves of the apron, or skirt, and especially the twelve inlaid ovals within which are the brass handles. The inlaid squares and half–squares are of finely figured wood. The lower portion has a large compartment within the two doors, in this respect differing from a bureau. This is a very handsome piece, to which a small engraving cannot do justice.[6] About 1790–1810.

Section 81. Chests–on–chests.—These articles of furniture are exactly what their name indicates, that is, one chest on another chest; and they may also be recognized by the name of "double chest of drawers." The illustrations show that a chest–on–chest differs from a highboy in that the lower part consists of a chest of

3. By Mr. E. S. Holloway in his "American Furniture," published in 1928, page 93, and plate 41.
4. See the illustrations in the chapter on "Bureaus," sections 95 and 96.
5. As to French bracket feet see figure 8 in illustration No. 11.
6. This piece is of English make, and was imported into South Carolina by the ancestor of a well known family now living in Baltimore, to one member of which it now belongs.

613 (UPPER) MR. J. G. D'ARCY PAUL.
615 (LOWER) MISS ELISABETH H. BARTLETT.

614 (UPPER) ANONYMOUS.
616 (LOWER) MISS ELEANOR S. COHEN.

three or four large drawers, somewhat wider than the upper ones, and extending close to the floor, thus being a more massive and capacious article of furniture than the highboy, but much less graceful, although stately and dignified. It may also be regarded as the upper portion of a highboy upon a chest of drawers.

Chests–on–chests were made in England[1] many years before they were apparently made in our country. They were popular in America[2] from about 1750 to almost 1800, which years included the final period of the highboy. It was therefore natural that chests–on–chests should show a similarity to the highboy in some respects, and this similarity may be seen, for example, in their respective styles of flat top, scroll top, finials, carving and various details. In order to see these similarities it is suggested that the next chapter, on highboys, be examined in connection with this section.[3]

In one respect, however, the chests–on–chests surpassed the highboys and developed a feature which is regarded as one of the finest products of American cabinet work, that is, the "block–front"; and it is said that in chests–on–chests the block–front reached its most impressive form. In the books on American antique furniture the block–front chests–on–chests are generally considered in connection with the other chests–on–chests; but in this volume it seems best to consider all of the articles of block–front furniture in a separate chapter,[4] in order that the subject may be presented as a whole, making the block–front the principal feature. But in order that block–front chests–on–chests may not be entirely omitted from this section, one example is shown in illustration No. 624.

Examining the illustrations, we see first the four "flat top" chests–on–chests Nos. 617–620; these are plain in design and were probably much less in price than

1. In Mr. Cescinsky's "English Furniture of the Eighteenth Century," volume 1, pages 152–154, are three illustrations, figures 167–169, of these chests, called "double chests" on page 162, and the dates given are from 1700 to 1715. These have flat tops and are about 5 feet 9 inches high. On page 161 it is said that these pieces, also called "tall–boys," were made in England during the whole of the eighteenth century.

    Numerous illustrations of American chests–on–chests are in Mr. Lockwood's "Colonial Furniture," page 115 and others, and in the "Supplementary Chapter," page 352 and others. In Mr. Wallace Nutting's "Furniture Treasury" the illustrations are Nos. 297–324.

    It has been said that the chests–on–chests became fashionable after the highboys went out of style; but this statement seems to be erroneous.

2. It is said that almost all of the American chests–on–chests are in the style of Chippendale, but that some have been found with certain details of the Queen Anne style. It is also said that some chests–on–chests were made later in our country in the Hepplewhite style, perhaps following designs in Hepplewhite's "Guide," which is mentioned in section 17.

    An illustrated article entitled "The American Chest–on–chest," by Mr. Walter A. Dyer is in "The Fine Arts," March, 1932, page 36.

    The wood used in the Chippendale period was mainly mahogany, as in other furniture made in that period; but maple, walnut and cherry were also used.

3. Especially the sections treating of highboys with flat tops, with scroll tops and those in the Philadelphia style, sections 84–87.

4. See "Block–front furniture," sections 114–119; section 115 is entitled "Block–front chests–on–chests."

Nos. 621–624 which have decorative features of several kinds. These first four pieces are similar in general appearance but they differ in some details, such as the number and arrangement of the drawers in the upper and lower portions, the feet and the shape and moldings of the cornices.

In No. 617 the upright columns on the corners of the upper chest are fluted. Around the edges of each of the nine drawers a band of veneered wood may be faintly seen. The feet are of the "straight bracket" type which is mentioned in the comment on No. 613. About 1760–1780.

In No. 618 the corners of the four upright fluted columns are cut off, or "chamfered," as in the preceding piece, an ornamental feature on various articles, for example, on the handsome bureau No. 713 which belongs to the same owner. The elaborate brass handles and the short ogee feet will be noticed. About 1760–1780.

In No. 619 the columns at the four corners are rounded and fluted. The moldings on the top, the bottom and at the central part where the upper chest rests upon the lower chest are in an unusual number of forms. About 1760–1780.

In No. 620 the top is ornamented with a band of light colored wood veneer, below which is a line of flutings, which with the French bracket feet indicate the Hepplewhite style. The corners of the upper chest are chamfered. About 1785–1800.

No. 621 has a "scroll"[5] top, without a "hood"[6] behind the scrolls. The cornice is not a part of the front, but is separated from it by a molding, making a "pedi-

5. The word "scroll" is applied to such dissimilar curves that its meaning is not easily understood. The definitions in the books often use technical words which are equally, or even more, unfamiliar than the word "scroll" itself. In the "Century Dictionary," for example, it is said that a scroll is "in furniture and woodwork, a carved volute or spiral," and in "The Furniture Collectors' Glossary," page 44, the definition is "a convolved or spiral ornament." However, the forms of scrolls may be seen in illustrations. On each of the chests-on-chests Nos. 621–624 is a "scroll" top, consisting of two curved pieces which extend towards each other from the sides of the top but do not meet. The curves of these two pieces are "scrolls" and the pieces themselves are "scrolls."

In Webster's International Dictionary it is said that the word means "any of various spiral or convoluted forms," and "any ornament of such a form." Also that "spiral" means "winding or circling round a centre or pole, and more or less gradually receding from it; as, the spiral curve of a watch spring."

Familiar "scroll" tops will be seen on the highboys in sections 86 and 87, on the secretary-bookcases in section 109, on the highboys from No. 649 through No. 668; also on the secretary desks Nos. 842 and 843, through No. 851. The scroll tops vary widely in elaboration, but they are all scrolls. Other forms of scrolls include the "C" scroll which was much favored in the Chippendale period and may be seen on mirrors, such as Nos. 1103–1106; and there is also a "S" scroll. Another form is known as the "Flemish" scroll which is seen on the feet of certain chairs; see figure 16 in illustration No. 11 and the comment. See also the Index, under the word "Scrolls."

These scroll forms may be cut out of solid wood or may be painted or inlaid. The fanciful applied designs on the highboys and lowboys in the Philadelphia style seen in sections 87 and 92 are largely composed of scrolls.

6. The word "hooded" is applied to scroll top pieces of furniture, such as the chest-on-chest No. 622, in which the top is partly covered by an extension backwards of the scroll, covering most of

(*Note 6 is continued on page 356.*)

617 (UPPER) MR. F. HIGHLANDS BURNS.
619 (LOWER) MR. ARTHUR E. COLE.

618 (UPPER) MRS. MAURICE F. RODGERS.
620 (LOWER) MR. & MRS. E. H. MCKEON.

621 (UPPER) HAMMOND–HARWOOD HOUSE. 622 (UPPER) MR. & MRS. BAYARD TURNBULL.
623 (LOWER) MR. ALBERT G. TOWERS. 624 (LOWER) METROPOLITAN MUSEUM OF ART.

355

ment" similar to those seen on certain highboys, such as No. 666 and others. Two of the three finials are at the extreme ends of the top. About 1760–1780.

In the next two pieces, Nos. 622 and 623, the tops are "scrolled" and "hooded," and the central top drawers are ornamented with carving in the "rising sun" or "sunrise" pattern.[7] In No. 622 the upper lines of the two outer top drawers are cut in a curve which follows the lines of the scrolls above. There are no streamers on the cornice of these chests–on–chests such as are seen in the contemporaneous highboys in the Philadelphia style shown in section 87; nor are any of the corners of either the upper or lower portions fluted as in Nos. 617–619. About 1760–1780.

No. 624 is an early style of block–front chest–on–chest, shown here merely to avoid the appearance of having overlooked the most important class of chest–on–chests, as mentioned above in the third paragraph of this section. Other chests–on–chests appear in section 115 in the chapter on "Block–front furniture." Here the good "blocking" is on the three drawers in the lower section; the blocking in the upper section is not approved. At the top a "sunrise" is carved. The two flat corner columns, called "pilasters," on the upper part, are fluted. About 1750–1770.

(NOTE 6, *continued*)

the top from the front to the back. Tops of this kind are also known as "bonnet tops." Examples of this type of top will be seen in several illustrations of block–front chests–on–chests in section 115, and secretary–bookcases in section 118.

7. The words "sunrise" and "sunburst" are applied to carvings on these and other articles of furniture. It is said that the word "sunrise" is applied to carvings of less than a circle, with rays issuing from the centre of the bottom of the carving, and that a "sunburst" is round, with rays issuing from the centre of the circle. It is also said that the conventional "shells" were more or less circular in the Pennsylvania pieces and half–round in the New England pieces.

As to the "rising sun," see a remark of Benjamin Franklin in note 12 in section 85.

CHAPTER IX

HIGHBOYS

Section 82. In general.—The word "highboy" is said to be purely an American term, used in contradistinction to "lowboy." In England the word "tall–boy" is used. An American term more descriptive of the character of the piece is "high chest of drawers"; and the English expression "chest of drawers on stand" is even more explanatory. These terms have about the same meaning and are used by scholars as they prefer;[1] but in our country the word "highboy" is generally used, and is less formal than the other terms.

It seems that the highboy was developed from a chest of drawers[2] which was placed upon a stand[3] so that a person could open the lower drawers of the chest without stooping over. When the upper part of the stand was fitted with one or more drawers, a new article of furniture, the chest of drawers on stand, or highboy,[4] was created.

1. In Mr. Lockwood's "Colonial Furniture in America," volume 1, the subjects of "high chests of drawers," (highboys), "dressing tables," (lowboys), "chests–on–chests," and "chests of drawers," (bureaus), are all treated in one chapter entitled "Chests of Drawers," pages 52–148. Mr. Lockwood generally uses the expression "high chest of drawers," avoiding the word "highboy," and mentions, page 60, that the word "highboy" was "never used in the (probate court) records and probably was given in derision after their appearance had become grotesque to eyes trained to other fashions." The word "highdaddy" is not in the dictionaries, but is understood to mean a chest of drawers on a frame without drawers, such as No. 609 in section 80. The word "tall–boy" was sometimes used in our country, as in the "Maryland Gazette" of February 24, 1774.

   There is no reference to an article of furniture under the word "highboy" in the great Murray's English Dictionary. The word is marked "obsolete." Its meaning was "one who lives high"; also "a partisan making high claims for his party."

2. See section 79 for the early type of chests of drawers.

3. In connection with this chapter on highboys, the next chapter, on lowboys, should be examined, where it will appear that the lowboy and the stand, or frame, of the highboy developed in about the same manner, changing from one style to another at about the same time.

4. If the stand, or frame, has drawers *above* it but no drawers *within* it, the piece is not regarded as a highboy, but as a chest of drawers on a stand, or frame; as in section 80. If the stand has no drawers *above* it, but has drawers *within* it, the piece may be regarded as a lowboy.

In the three small illustrations on one line, we see a chest of drawers No. 625; a highboy No. 626; and a writing desk[5] No. 627; all are of the period of about 1700–1710, and we notice that the design of the upper part of the highboy, the design of the lower part of the writing desk and the design of the chest of drawers are all about the same. It is interesting to note from these illustrations[6] that if a stand with drawers is placed *under* a chest of drawers, we have a highboy; if a writing compartment is placed *over* a chest of drawers, we have a desk. The points of resemblance between these articles gradually disappeared as the articles developed in later years.

It is believed that English highboys were first imported into our country during the latter part of the seventeenth century, about 1690–1700, and were

625   626   627

copied by our cabinet makers. Later, the American pieces, especially certain highboys made in Philadelphia, developed into a style quite different from that of the English models. For about one hundred years highboys were popular in our country, finally going out of fashion about 1780–1790, when the purposes for which they were used were served by the chests of drawers which we now call bureaus.[7]

5. See the writing desks Nos. 777–778.
6. The chest of drawers No. 625 is similar to No. 608, and the highboy No. 626 is illustrated in this chapter as No. 632.
7. See section 93 in the chapter on bureaus.

       A fine highboy, like a fine grandfather clock, has a certain dignity which makes it attractive in the home. In order to present the best appearance, a highboy should be placed in a large room; in a small room the highboy will dominate the room and detract from the other furniture. A question often arises whether the highboy should be placed in a hall or bedroom on the second floor, or in a hall or living room on the first floor. For at least two reasons the latter position may now be preferred; first,

Section 83. The four kinds of highboys.—A convenient classification of the four kinds of highboys is attempted here, the dates overlapping and being merely approximate, the making of highboys probably continuing until about 1790.

First: section 84; flat top highboys with stretchers and six legs about 1690–1720; Nos. 632–634.

Second: section 85; flat top highboys with four cabriole legs without stretchers; about 1720–1760; Nos. 635–650.

Third: section 86; scroll top highboys; about 1730–1775; Nos. 651–659.

Fourth: section 87; "Philadelphia style" highboys, which are more highly ornamented highboys of the third kind; about 1750–1775; Nos. 660–668.

The small illustrations,[1] Nos. 628–631, show the four kinds in their order and the principal points of each style, all of which will appear more in detail as we proceed.

This classification of the kinds of highboy is not altogether satisfactory as to styles and dates. It is possible to consider them according to their styles, as the William and Mary Style, the Queen Anne style, and the Chippendale style,[2] but this is somewhat confusing, because some of the styles of our highboys overlap

(NOTE 7, *continued*)

because the highboy, being now a fine and valuable ornament, and not merely a receptacle for the storage of clothing, deserves a conspicuous position in the household, where it may be enjoyed by visitors; and second, in case of fire it may be possible to remove the highboy from the first floor, but it is probably too heavy to be removed quickly from an upper floor.

In the recent book by Mr. Wm. M. Hornor, Jr., entitled "Philadelphia Furniture, 1682–1807," it is said on page 110 that none of the pretentious old city residences or country mansions in or near Philadelphia had the highboy on the first floor, except in rare cases.

In about the second quarter of the eighteenth century there was a custom of placing on the top of flat top highboys a series of three or four wooden steps on which china, glass and other ornamental objects were exhibited. These steps were graduated in size, the largest one being at the bottom. This display suggests that the highboy was not in a bedroom where its exhibits would not be generally seen.

The amateur collector should be very careful in buying a highboy; indeed the advice of a cabinet maker experienced in working on antique furniture should be obtained. In some cases the original legs may have been broken accidentally, or removed purposely in order to reduce a too lofty height, and shorter legs made of old wood may have been substituted. Sometimes the tops have been partly removed because of the insufficient height of the ceiling, as in No. 665. Shells or sunbursts or other ornaments may have been recently carved on a plain highboy for the purpose of "glorifying" it. See also sections 7 and 10 in this book.

1. The first highboy, No. 628, appears in section 84 as No. 632; the next, No. 629, is No. 639 in section 85; No. 630 is No. 656 in section 86; No. 631 is No. 662 in section 87. Comments on these highboys are made in connection with the illustrations.

2. Classification by styles is used in the next chapter, on lowboys, sections 88–92, and may be found more satisfactory; see note 1 in section 89.

Some writers refer to the late Queen Anne style and the early Chippendale style as "Early Georgian," a term which is somewhat vague and is not familiar to all American readers. See section 14.

Designs of highboys were not shown by Hepplewhite or Sheraton in their books which are referred to in sections 17 and 18.

considerably, an earlier style continuing for many years after a later one became the fashion. It was not possible for all the cabinet makers, and all their customers, to change from one style to another at the same time. Therefore only an approximate date of the making of certain kinds of highboys can be given.[3]

It should be remembered also that the cabinet makers in small towns, as well as their customers, were almost always some years behind the fashions of the large cities. This is true of many articles of furniture, including the cases of grandfather clocks; and the fact is referred to in several chapters of this book. For example, in the case of highboys of an early date, much importance may be attached to the styles of moldings[4] as indications of date; but it is said that sometimes a certain type of molding was used upon a highboy made long after the molding passed out of general fashion in the larger cities.

628   629   630   631

Section 84. Flat top highboys with stretchers and six legs.—These high-boys, Nos. 632–634, in the style of William and Mary,[1] were the earliest made and were in vogue from about 1690 to about 1720. At about 1710–1720 the Queen Anne style furniture, as to which see section 14, became the fashion and there was a

3.   In regard to the dates at which the various highboys were actually made (not the dates when the *styles* began and ended) it is likely that many highboys of the second and third kinds were simultaneously made during the period of about 1740–1770. It must not be thought that, at a given date, only the kind of highboy was made which was then the latest fashion. The cost, as well as the style, would influence the customer's choice. The second kind was no doubt the least expensive, and the fourth kind was certainly the most expensive. See "Dating antique furniture," section 6. Rules are given here for determining the approximate dates of antique furniture.

4.   The subject of moldings is briefly considered in section 41 of this book; see also the Index. It may be mentioned here that the early pieces, including both highboys and lowboys, generally have what is known as a single–arch molding attached to the framework around the drawers; this molding is a strip of wood rounded in front in the shape of an arch. The next early kind, called a double–arch molding, is in the form of two smaller arches around the drawers. See also section 93, note 3.

1.   This style is stated in section 13.

632 (Upper) Mr. & Mrs. C. E. McLane.   633 (Upper) Hammond–Harwood House, Annapolis,
634 (Lower) Mrs. Elizabeth N. Dunham.   635 (Lower) Mr. & Mrs. George Shipley,

change in the number and style of legs as well as in some less important features, as will be seen in the next section.

Examining the six–legged highboys, Nos. 632–634, we observe that the stands upon which the chests of drawers are placed are of the same general character as the lowboys of the same period,[2] that is, the period of William and Mary. The turned legs, known as "inverted cup," or "cup," legs because of the resemblance of the larger turnings[3] to cups turned downward, are connected by flat curved stretchers[4] in front and on the sides, and by one straight stretcher in the rear.

The front part of the stand, below the top of the stand and between the end legs, through which part the drawers extend, is commonly called the "apron" or "skirt." The bottom of this apron is cut in various designs, almost always having cyma curves.[5]

In No. 632 the front and side stretchers are cut in the same curves as the apron, as was a frequent method.

These three highboys are not exactly of the same period, No. 632 being the older in style, having one wide drawer in the stand; Nos. 633 and 634 have three smaller drawers. The brass handles of Nos. 632 and 633 are of the "drop" type; No. 634 has "bail" handles.[6] Each has ball feet, not of quite the same design.[7] The moldings cannot be well seen in photographs of this small size. The wood is generally walnut; and in some cases a fine walnut veneer was used on the drawer fronts, as in No. 634. As above mentioned, the dates are about 1690–1720.

2. See the lowboy No. 669.

3. As to "turnings," see section 35.

   Another style of turning, less frequently found, is known as "trumpet" turning on account of a resemblance of the larger turnings to a trumpet. The trumpet turning is illustrated in the lowboy No. 672. Illustrations are in Mr. Lockwood's "Colonial Furniture," volume 1, figures 65 and 69.

4. Some highboys of this type have stretchers in the form of a capital X, instead of running at right angles to each other. These are not illustrated here, but may be seen in lowboys Nos. 670–672.

5. As to cyma curves, see section 23.

6. See "Brass handles," section 39.

   After two hundred years or more of usage it cannot be expected that all the handles, stretchers, and other parts should be the original ones. As the highboys were repaired or refinished from time to time, there would naturally be restorations or replacements of lost or injured parts. In the case of substituted handles, sometimes the proper period ones would be put on and sometimes wrong ones would be used. See the remarks on "Restorations," in section 10.

   In Mr. Nutting's "Furniture Treasury," a highboy, figure 342, bears this note: "The only example known to be original throughout."

   Highboys of the type of Nos. 632, 633 and 634 are illustrated in Mr. Lockwood's "Colonial Furniture," volume 1, figures 57–71, and on pages 344–345; and in Mr. Nutting's "Furniture Treasury," figures 329–339.

   A rare form of scroll legs in the shape of the letter "S" is illustrated in Mr. Lockwood's "Colonial Furniture," page 345, and in Mr. Nutting's "Furniture Treasury," No. 327. As to "scrolls" see note 5 in section 81.

7. As to "Ball" feet, see figure 3 in illustration No. 11.

Section 85. Flat top highboys with four cabriole legs without stretchers.— The new feature in this group of highboys, Nos. 635–650, is the change from the six straight legs with stretchers to four cabriole[1] legs without stretchers.

These cabriole legs and their feet were of two kinds. The first cabriole legs were of the Queen Anne type, often somewhat long, but almost always graceful, sometimes apparently too slender for the weight of the frame and drawers above, as mentioned in note 5, and generally terminating with "club," also called "Dutch,"[2] feet; these legs and feet were first used on highboys about 1710–1720, and they continued in favor until about 1750–1760. The second kind of cabriole legs were in the style of Chippendale and were generally shorter and stronger and had ball and claw feet; they were first used on highboys in our country about the year 1750, and continued to be made until highboys passed out of style, which was about the year 1790 or later.[3]

The wood used was generally walnut in the earlier years and mahogany in the later ones; but other woods were also used, especially cherry, and the customer's choice no doubt prevailed. Nos. 641–642, 644 and 647 are of curly maple.

Several of these flat top highboys with four cabriole legs are very similar in appearance, but each one has certain points of difference which make it interesting. Most of these differences may easily be noticed and it therefore seems unnecessary to describe all of them, or to point out what is obvious to the reader. Unfortunately the small size of the illustrations makes it difficult, without a magnifying glass, to clearly see the details of the moldings, one of which, under the cornice, is known as a "torus"[4] molding, which is generally the front of a concealed drawer.

The illustrations Nos. 635–647 are of highboys having a flat top and four cabriole legs[5] terminating in club, or Dutch, feet, commonly called Queen Anne style highboys; Nos. 648–650 are of a similar form except that the legs are generally shorter and stronger and terminate in ball and claw feet.

On Nos. 635 and 636 will be noticed the borders of lighter wood around the drawers, the fronts of which are finely veneered. About 1725–1750.

    1.   As to cabriole legs see section 24.

    2.   As to the kinds of feet, see section 25.

    3.   In Mr. Lockwood's "Colonial Furniture," volume 1, page 351, there is an illustration of a scroll top highboy, as to which see the next section, to which the dates "1750–1775" are given. This latter year is the last date given by Mr. Lockwood for any highboy illustrated in his book.

    4.   This concealed drawer extends across the entire width of the highboy, and is shallow. The word "torus" is an architectural one, meaning a large convex molding; Century Dictionary. See the Index under "Torus."

    5.   It will be noticed that in many of these highboys the cabriole legs seem to be too long and slender; and indeed many of them have been broken. Examples of slender legs are shown here and in Mr. Nutting's "Furniture Treasury," Nos. 347, 350, 351.

        A learned commentator has remarked that in these highboys in the later style of Queen Anne the form of the piece is not satisfactory, which may be due to the inharmonious combination of the slender curved legs and the considerable size and weight of the upper portion; and that in the New England highboys a heavy cornice often destroyed the symmetry of the piece, and in Pennsylvania the larger upper portion is out of proportion to the lower portion.

636 (UPPER) MRS. MILES WHITE, JR.   637 (UPPER) MRS. ELIZABETH N. DUNHAM.
638 (LOWER) MRS. JOHN S. GIBBS, JR.   639 (LOWER) MR. J. F. H. MAGINN.

640 (Upper) Mr. & Mrs. Henry Lay Duer.
642 (Lower) Mr. John S. McDaniel.

641 (Upper) Mrs. John S. Gibbs, Jr.
643 (Lower) Mr. J. G. D'Arcy Paul.

Nos. 637–640 are very similar to each other. No. 637 has one drawer at the top; Nos. 638 and 639 have two, and No. 640 has three. No. 638 is maple, which appears too dark in the engraving. On each highboy the "apron," or "skirt," is cut in different curves, but the cyma curve, mentioned in section 23, is always present. About 1735–1760.

On the "aprons," or "skirts," of Nos. 635–637 and No. 639 we see two pendant[6] drops or acorns or other ornaments, some of which may or may not be the original ones, at about the points where the two inner front legs of the six–legged highboys Nos. 632–634 are placed; on Nos. 638 and 640 the ornaments are missing, but the projections to which they were attached when the highboys were made are still in position. In other pieces, such as Nos. 641–647, pendants were not to be used, and the aprons were cut in designs without places for them; and thus the last reminder of the two inner front legs of the earlier type disappeared. About 1725–1760.

In Nos. 641 and 642 the aprons are cut in cyma curves and, as above stated, there are no places suitable for pendants. No. 641 has one large lower drawer in the stand instead of the usual three small ones. In No. 642 there is a carved rising sun design, and the legs are very slender, as mentioned in note 5, and may be compared with those on the lowboy No. 680. About 1730–1750.

Feet of the kind on No. 643, not well seen in the engraving, have been given the name of "three–toed," or "drake," or are simply called "three–pointed";[7] a better example may be seen on the lowboy No. 692. They are said to be found chiefly in Pennsylvania, New Jersey, Delaware and Maryland. A somewhat similar foot is in the curly maple highboy No. 644. A curly maple lowboy, companion piece to No. 644, is shown as No. 694 in the next chapter. About 1740–1760.

The feet of No. 645, somewhat resembling a form of Spanish feet,[8] are of an unusual type; and above each foot is a molding which is sometimes called a "bracelet,"[9] although it does not surround the leg, being on the two outer sides only. The legs are not round, but almost rectangular. About 1720–1730.

On several highboys here shown the club feet are "cushioned," that is, there is a wooden "cushion," or "shoe," under, and a part of, each foot as a protection against breakage.[10] Examples are in Nos. 638–642.

Nos. 646 and 647 are very tall, about eight feet high,[11] without an unusual width. No doubt a step–ladder was kept near at hand. The legs of each are very

6.   In note 2 in section 86 "pendants" and "finials" are more fully mentioned. Pendants were used on flat top highboys, but finials were not used.

7.   In regard to these "three–toed" feet, see section 25, figure 11, in illustration No. 11.

8.   Spanish feet may also be seen on lowboys Nos. 673–674.

9.   Similar feet with "bracelets" are shown in Mr. Lockwood's "Colonial Furniture," volume 1, figures 84–85, and in Mr. Nutting's "Furniture Treasury," figures 358, 383, 421–422, etc.

10.   A still larger cushion is occasionally found under the feet of tables of this period, as in No. 1400.

        A "cushion" or "shoe" is a piece of wood on the bottom of a foot, and is mainly used on a club foot, as in the Queen Anne style chairs Nos. 68, 69.

11.   The height of the very tall Sheraton style chest of drawers, No. 616, is about the same.

644 (Upper) Mrs. Daniel Miller.   645 (Upper) Mr. Edgar G. Miller, Jr.
646 (Lower) Mr. C. Edward Snyder.   647 (Lower) Mr. Albert G. Towers.

short, perhaps to make the upper drawers more accessible. The stands of each are very similar, but the upper portions are different. Their ornamentation consists of carvings supposed to represent a "rising sun,"[12] one on No. 646 and two on No. 647. The drawers on which the "rising suns" are carved are sometimes called "sunrise drawers." There are apparently fourteen drawers in No. 647, but in reality only twelve, the lower "sunrise" and the two sides being one drawer,[13] as also in No. 646. About 1730–1750.

Nos. 648–650 are examples of the second kind of highboys having flat tops and four cabriole legs, but with ball and claw feet instead of club feet or other kinds.[14] As mentioned in the second paragraph of this section, the ball and claw foot first appeared about the year 1750, and continued as long as highboys were made, that is, until about 1790.

In No. 648 a well carved shell appears under the central drawer of the stand, somewhat similar to the shell in No. 662. The knees of the legs are carved and the corners of the stand are fluted. No. 649 has only one drawer, but a large one, in the stand, and the skirt is ornamented with a line of beading. No. 650 has an unusual arrangement of drawers in the stand, the long one being below, instead of above, the small ones; and the legs are fully carved. It will be seen that the legs of these pieces are somewhat short compared with many of the Queen Anne type with club feet, as shown above. In No. 648 the ball of the foot approaches a perfect sphere, but in the other two only about two–thirds of a sphere is used. About 1750–1775.

Section 86. Scroll top highboys.—The next important change in the style of highboys took place when the scroll top[1] became the fashion about the year 1730; but flat top highboys, such as those in the previous section, continued to be made for many years after that date.

12. The "rising sun" recalls a remark of Benjamin Franklin at the Convention in Philadelphia in 1788 when the Constitution of the United States was adopted after many difficulties, as told by James Madison. "Whilst the last members of the convention were signing, Dr. Franklin, looking towards the president's chair, at the back of which a rising sun happened to be painted, observed that painters had found it difficult to distinguish in their art a rising from a setting sun. 'I have often in the course of the session looked at that behind the president, without being able to tell whether it was rising or setting, but now at length I have the happiness to know that it is a rising and not a setting sun.' "

It is said that the carved "sunburst" or "rising sun" is almost the only decorative feature of New England highboys in the Queen Anne style; and that the presence of these carvings indicates that a highboy is a New England product, or a copy of one.

As to "rising sun" see also section 81, note 7. The highboys Nos. 622 and 624 are good examples of the popular "rising sun" design for carving.

13. This maple highboy, No. 647, is shown as No. 355 in Mr. Nutting's "Furniture Treasury," where it is concisely described as "Very high, maple, three tier lower section, 1730–1750."

14. Only one highboy with flat top and ball and claw feet appears in Mr. Lockwood's "Colonial Furniture," volume 1, figure 100, a block–front piece. In Mr. Wenham's "Collector's Guide" four examples are shown, Nos. 198, 201, 206, 209.

1. As to scrolls, see the long note 5 in section 81. Compare the scroll tops on mirrors, secretary–bookcases, corner cupboards and other articles; study the Index for further information about various types of "Scroll tops" for furniture.

648 (Upper) Mr. John C. Toland.   649 (Upper) Mr. James Dixon.
650 (Lower) Mr. Albert G. Towers.   651 (Lower) Mr. & Mrs. E. H. McKeon.

As shown in the illustrations, this scroll top consists of an arch extending over the top of the highboy, except in the centre where it is broken into two parts in a graceful design, leaving an open space between them. In this space was a carved ornament such as a flame or urn, and a similar ornament was generally placed on the two outer ends of the arch. These three ornaments are "finials," a word which is applied to any decorative device at the top of any kind of upright part.[2]

In many of these scroll top pieces the top is partly covered over by an extension of the scroll running from the front of the highboy to the back, as is well seen in the illustrations Nos. 652 and 653. These highboys are said to be "hooded"; and the word "bonnet–top" is also used to describe them.

Certain differences have been observed between highboys of this type made in New England and those made in other sections of the country. The earlier New England pieces are said to have less carving than those made about the same period in Pennsylvania, and few of them have ball and claw feet; but these New England pieces were often ornamented with one or two "rising suns," which are referred to in the previous section at note 12 as almost the only decorative feature of New England highboys. Other differences are that the "shells" made in Pennsylvania were generally round, but those made in New England were generally half–round; and in New England the fluted corners were seldom made, but were often used in Philadelphia.

The earlier highboys of this scroll top type were supported by cabriole legs in the Queen Anne style, generally with club, or "Dutch," feet, as was the rule with those of the flat top kind; but, as also with the flat top kind, those legs and feet were in time superseded in the better class of highboys by cabriole legs with ball and claw feet, and this latter kind was in fashion from about 1750 until highboys were no longer made.

Examining the illustrations, we observe that No. 651 is an early type with slender cabriole legs and club feet in the Queen Anne style and with the drawers of walnut veneer with light borders. The central drawer of the stand is partly concave, and two projections on the apron are seen to which the missing pendants were attached. About 1725–1750.

No. 652 is another fine New England example of the same period. The hooded top, the three long spiral finials at the top, and the two "sunrise drawers" of the same size, are prominent features. The pendants are missing here also. See the lowboy No. 679, a companion piece. About 1735–1750.

2. A "finial" is an ornament on the top, pointing upward. A similar ornament on the bottom of the "skirt," or "apron," pointing downward, is known as a "pendant," that is, a hanging ornament. Both finials and pendants were generally used on the fine scroll top highboys. The "finials," being at the top and out of the way of children and domestics, were often undisturbed, but the "pendants" were seldom saved from destruction. Compare No. 653 with its finials and pendants with Nos. 652 and 654 with finials but without pendants, although we notice the projections to which pendants were attached; see also the comment on Nos. 635–637 and others. Of course, excellent finials and pendants and other wooden ornaments may now be made to order in old mahogany. See also section 37 on carving and finials.

652 (Upper) Mr. Morris Whitridge.   653 (Upper) Mr. & Mrs. George Shipley.
654 (Lower) Mr. Paul R. Powell.   655 (Lower) Coll. of Mrs. Jordan Stabler.

No. 653 has a similar design in curly maple, which gives the appearance of inlay along the top of the stand. The hood is enclosed at the back. The apron, or skirt, of this highboy and of Nos. 652 and 654 are cut in three straight lines under the drawers, a design also seen on the lowboy No. 679. This highboy is the last one in the Queen Anne style shown in this book. About 1735–1750.

The next six scroll top highboys, Nos. 654–659, are of a somewhat later style, having ball and claw feet instead of the club feet of the previous pieces. The legs are generally shorter than those in the Queen Anne style, and in this and the next section some of the legs may be thought to be out of proportion to the massive structures of which they are parts. On this matter see also the comment on lowboy No. 708. Ball and claw feet are regarded as indicating the influence of the Chippendale style, and are seen on the legs of all the other highboys in this and the next section.

No. 654 is in about the same form as No. 653 with the exception of the ball and claw feet. The "rising sun" carvings on the upper and lower rows of drawers indicate the New England origin. The handles on the drawers shown in this and the next section include examples of fine hardware, such as is seen in illustration No. 13. About 1750–1770.

No. 655 has architectural "pilasters" at the sides of both the upper and the lower portions of the highboy, in the style of flat fluted columns. Other examples of pilasters are seen on the scroll top chest–on–chest No. 624 and on the block–front pieces Nos. 900 and 901. The treatment of the central part of the apron, or skirt, is unusual. The knees of the cabriole legs are fully carved with leaves. About 1750–1770.

No. 656 has ball and claw feet in front, with club, or Dutch, feet in the rear, a combination which is occasionally found.[3] In these ball and claw feet the balls are almost round. The apron is cut in concave and convex curves, is ornamented with a carved shell and has no projections for pendants. About 1750–1775.

No. 657 is plain in design, with spreading legs and with large drawers in the stand. The apron is cut in a variety of concave and convex curves and small scrolls. The usual two handles appear on the large drawers, but there are no escutcheons of the same type. About 1750–1775.

No. 658 has a very high top and large and high scrolls at the inner ends of which are carved rosettes, a decorative form which will also be seen in the next section. The finials at the sides are placed at the extreme outside ends, as was sometimes done. There are thirteen drawers in this highboy. About 1750–1775.

No. 659 has come down to the present owner from a Philadelphia family. The scrolls at the top are large and heavy as in the preceding piece. There are twelve drawers with handsome brasses. A carved ornament is under the apron, as also in Nos. 648 and 662, and the knees of the legs are carved. About 1750–1775.

3. A highboy which is almost a duplicate is illustrated in Mr. Lockwood's "Colonial Furniture," volume 1, page 351, and it is said that the cornice and the finials are the typical Goddard ones. As to Goddard and Townsend, Rhode Island makers of block–front articles, see section 114.

656 (Upper) Hammond–Harwood House.
657 (Upper) Mr. Henry Scott Baker.
658 (Lower) Mr. & Mrs. Lennox Birckhead.
659 (Lower) Mrs. Wm. M. Roberts.

373

Section 87. "Philadelphia style" highboys.—Certain cabinet makers[1] of Philadelphia in the eighteenth century, about 1760–1775, who made furniture of mahogany in the Chippendale style are justly celebrated as among the most skill-ful and artistic of our country, equalled only by cabinet makers of about the same period in Newport, Rhode Island.[2] Indeed it may be said that their furniture rivalled the best products of the English shops. Their highboys and lowboys, especially, are regarded as among our finest examples of workmanship and design. These articles were not copies of the works of English cabinet makers, but were originated and developed in Philadelphia.[3] In this section the highboys are treated,

1. A few years ago the outstanding cabinet makers of Philadelphia then known, or believed, to have been the makers of the finest furniture in the Chippendale style were William Savery and Benjamin Randolph.

The discovery of the label of Savery upon a fine lowboy and upon four chairs of superior workmanship established his reputation for a time as the leading cabinet maker of Philadelphia. The result was the "Savery vogue," and a large number of articles in the Chippendale style and resembling in some details the labeled Savery pieces were attributed to him. Further research, however, and the finding of labels of other Philadelphia cabinet makers on other articles of high character, changed the views previously held, and his importance has suffered a decline, although the few known products of his shop have not lost their high position. An article by Mr. W. M. Hornor, Jr., in the Pennsylvania Museum Bulletin of February, 1928, discusses the chairs of Savery; another article by the same author is in "The Antiquarian," July, 1930, page 29; and in Mr. Hornor's book entitled "Philadelphia Furniture, 1682–1807," the subject is further considered.

Later the name of Benjamin Randolph held for a while the commanding position in the list of the master cabinet makers of Philadelphia. He was believed to have been the maker of six fine "sample" chairs in the Chippendale style, three of which were in the Reifsnyder auction sale in April, 1929, but now there seems to be some uncertainty as to their maker. Two of these side chairs are illustrated as Nos. 116 and 117 in section 51. Another, a wing chair, brought the sum of $33,000, the highest price ever paid for an American chair; it is shown as No. 406 and is referred to in various sections of this book, as one of his 6 famous "Sample" chairs. His fine label is shown with comments in illustration No. 1 in section 6 of this book. Articles on the subject by Mr. S. W. Woodhouse, Jr., are in "Antiques," May, 1927, and January, 1930.

At the present writing Thomas Affleck seems to be the most important of the Philadelphia cabinet makers. This man was a Scotchman, as Duncan Phyfe was, and came to Philadelphia in 1763 and died there in 1795. In Mr. Hornor's book above mentioned, it is said on page 73 that Affleck was "the paramount figure in the cabinet– and chair–making craft and was by far the leader of the Philadelphia–Chippendale school." In the exhibition at the Pennsylvania Museum of Art in May, 1935, a fine highboy by Affleck was shown, and also several other labeled pieces by him. Mr. Fiske Kimball, the Director of the Museum, remarked that the authentication of various articles by particular cabinet makers "will make and unmake values and reputations" and that "we may expect a new crop of assertion and conjecture, with faking of pieces and labels, so that henceforth buyers should be doubly on their guard."

Other Philadelphia makers of high class furniture in the Chippendale style were James Gillingham, Thomas Tufft, Jonathan Gostelowe and Edward James. Perhaps further discoveries may elevate one or more of these men, or others not now known, to the present rank of Thomas Affleck. Mr. Hornor suggests as possibilities the names of John Folwell, David Evans, Daniel Trotter, Samuel Walton and William Wayne.

2. John Townsend and John Goddard, of Newport, are the principal makers. See the reference to them in connection with block–front furniture, section 114. Job Townsend was also important.

3. Mr. Herbert Cescinsky, in "English and American Furniture," writes, page 175, that "there is little or no kinship between a Philadelphia highboy and anything ever made in England."

for convenience, as a separate class, although in reality they are chiefly a more highly decorative type of the scroll top highboys shown in the previous section. The fine character of the pieces and the widespread interest they have aroused have caused a demand which has raised the monetary value of the best examples to a point not reached by any other kind of American furniture, culminating in the price paid at an auction sale of the last highboy illustrated, No. 668.

The principal features of the best type of these "Philadelphia style" highboys will be seen by examining the full page illustration No. 660. Every part of this handsome piece is finely made. The central drawer of the lower portion, the stand, is carved with a shell design, from which streamers extend in graceful curves. The apron, or skirt, is cut in cyma and other curves, with a carved design in the centre. The legs are somewhat short and the knees of the legs are finely carved. The balls in the claw feet are almost round. The front corners of both the stand and the upper section have fluted columns. The handles are large, as they should be on a large article of furniture. The inner ends of the scrolls terminate in carved rosettes. Under and between the scrolls is an elaborate design of finely carved flowers and leaves, not carved out of the wood, but separately made and then "applied."[4] The two finials at the sides are urns. In the centre is an original Chippendale style carved form, of graceful design, often called a "cartouche,"[5] enclosing a bird. The entire top above the three small drawers may be removed by sliding it forward, as also in Nos. 666 and 667. The hood, or bonnet, of this highboy is missing, but grooves in the backs of the scrolls show that the piece was made with a hood. About 1760–1775.

Other highboys in the "Philadelphia style" are next illustrated. They differ in the extent and fineness of decoration as well as in exact design, and they are all interesting pieces.

Almost equal in importance to No. 660, the highboy above described, is another, No. 661, which is the property of the same owner. The principal differ-

(NOTE 3, continued)

    The making of all the highboys and lowboys of the "Philadelphia style" seems to be attributed to cabinet makers of that city; but it seems reasonable to suppose that the cabinet makers of other cities, such as Baltimore, may have copied the Philadelphia style. Several cabinet makers in Baltimore came from Philadelphia, as appears from their advertisements. For example, Gerrard Hopkins, "cabinet and chair maker from Philadelphia," advertised in the "Maryland Gazette" on April 9, 1767, that he made "chests of drawers of various sorts . . with or without carved work." See also note 3 in section 29.

    4. The word "applied" means laid on or put on, as mentioned in section 38. The French word "applique" is used in the same sense in connection with dress and upholstery. In furniture a wooden part may be applied to another part by tacks or by gluing; a metal ornament may be applied by a tack, as on French Empire pieces of various kinds. The steamers and rosettes on these highboys are generally applied.

    5. As here used, the word "cartouche" means a carved ornament of fanciful form. It has no similarity in meaning to a cartouche of the Egyptian kings. Ornaments of this kind were used in England, one on a tall secretary–bookcase dated about 1740 being shown in Mr. Cescinsky's "English Furniture," volume 2, figure 118.

660 MR. JOHN C. TOLAND.

661 (Upper) Mr. John C. Toland.
663 (Lower) Episcopal Diocese of Md.

662 (Upper) Baltimore Museum of Art.
664 (Lower) Miss Mary S. Schenck.

ence is in the treatment of the top, this having a drawer, carved with a shell, similar to the drawer in the stand. The top has no applied streamers; in fact the size of the shell drawer prevents much decoration at that point. The design between the scrolls is a cupid upon an urn. About 1760–1775.

Another fine highboy is No. 662. Here the scroll top is made higher and permits a decorative design of streamers on the two spaces which were left plain in the preceding piece; and a shell in the apron, or skirt, matches in style the shell in the large top drawer above. A similarly placed shell is in No. 659 and also in No. 648. This highboy was acquired from the estate of the late Howard Sill by a group of his friends, and presented to the Baltimore Museum of Art in his memory. Mr. Sill was the leading authority in Maryland on antique furniture. About 1760–1775.

In No. 663 the ornamentation of the top is by two sets of graceful streamers applied over the entire available space; and by two shell drawers, under the lower of which, in the stand portion, is a third shell. This highboy was presented to the Episcopal Diocese of Maryland by Mrs. Francis T. Redwood, of Baltimore. About 1760–1775.

Other highboys illustrated as Nos. 664–667 are less elaborate in decoration than those above mentioned, but may all be regarded as in the "Philadelphia style" or at least influenced by it. In these highboys the legs seem to be too short, giving an inharmonious appearance.

No. 664, lacking finials, has two well designed shells with applied streamers; and the heart–shaped opening below the shell drawer in the stand is a pleasing variation in adornment. About 1760–1775.

No. 665 is an unusually tall piece, so tall in fact that the upper portion of the scroll top had been cut off when found by the present owner, who restored it to its former appearance. About 1760–1775.

Nos. 666 and 667 are in a somewhat different style, the top in each being separated from the front of the upper section by a molding, giving the appearance of an addition to a flat top highboy. This method may also be seen in the chest–on–chest No. 621. These two pieces were made without a hood. The edges of the skirts are ornamented with beading. No. 666 has bail handles and is of walnut.

In No. 667 some of the streamers are carved into the wood, a method not used in fine highboys. It is shown here as a "warning."

The last highboy illustrated, No. 668, appears here as a matter of general interest, being the highboy which brought the highest price at auction of any American piece of furniture. It is the celebrated Reifsnyder highboy, which was sold on April 27, 1929, for the sum of $44,000. In point of elegance,[6] workmanship

6.   See note 2 in section 92 in which the "rococo" ornamentation is mentioned.

As remarked by Mr. Wm. M. Hornor, Jr., in his "Philadelphia Furniture, 1682–1807," pages 102–103, "a paucity of decoration does not indicate a lack of skill, nor does the liberality of flourishes, shells, torches, flowers and leaves on certain highboys prove to be an asset," referring to a highboy on which was "an abundance of carving on every conceivable space."

(*Note 6 continued on page 380.*)

665 (Upper) Mrs. Alexander Armstrong.
667 (Lower) Anonymous.

666 (Upper) Mr. John S. McDaniel.
668 (Lower) Reifsnyder Collection.

and rarity, it surpasses certain other highboys to a limited extent only, if at all
About 1770.

At this point there is a temptation to indulge in a few remarks about auction sales and values and prices; but another section[7] will be a more appropriate place for these comments.

The chapter on highboys is now closed.[8] Lowboys, the subject of the next chapter, will be found to be very similar to highboys in the development of style, and it is suggested that the two chapters be considered together.

(Note 6, *continued*)

The description of this highboy in the sale catalogue includes the following features: scrolled pediment with rosettes on the inner ends of the scrolls; two flaming vase finials; a scrolled cartouche; the frieze above the drawers with applied rococo scrolls; festoons of flowers; drooping stalactites; five small drawers above three large ones; fluted pilasters at the corners; on the stand are four drawers, a long one above three small ones, the centre small one with a shell carving with scrolls; leaf carvings on the skirt, or apron; cabriole legs with carved acanthus leaf, terminating in ball and claw feet. Original brasses with bail handles. In the description it was also said that this highboy was in original condition, and "is one of the outstanding pieces of Chippendale furniture in the rococo taste in America. The elegance of the proportions and the delicate restraint and originality of the applied carving indicate the work of the first among the master craftsmen of Philadelphia." The height is almost 8 feet and the width is 45 inches. A large illustration, showing the details, is in "Antiques," April, 1930, page 328.

7.   See sections 1 through 10, also 175.

8.   The story of highboys ends at the time when the highboy had reached the summit of its long career. How fortunate that it did not survive to the period of the late American Empire style and became debased in the style of 1840.

Other remarks upon the "Philadelphia style" are in the next chapter, on lowboys, section 92.

Chapter X

LOWBOYS

Section 88. In general.—The word "lowboy," like the word "highboy" mentioned in the previous chapter, is purely an American[1] term. It means a low chest of drawers on legs, as distinguished from a high chest of drawers on legs; and, like the word "highboy," it is said to be of somewhat recent origin, apparently not having been used during the long period in which it was made in America.[2] This period, like that of highboys, was from about 1690 to 1790 or later.

As will appear in the illustrations, the designs of lowboys at different periods were about the same as the designs of the stand or frame of a highboy of the same periods; the styles changed together. The lowboy was a very useful piece of furniture, as it combined the advantages of a small chest of drawers and of a table, having a flat top upon which various articles could be placed.

With these features, it was natural that ladies sitting at, and partly under, these dainty pieces of furniture, should find them useful as dressing tables, with a dressing glass[3] on the table and a looking glass on the wall in front; and the words "dressing table"[4] for many years were very appropriate. In their later design,

---

1. In Murray's English Dictionary, the word "lowboy" is first defined as "one who supports the low party, in opposition to the 'high–fliers' or 'high boys.'" The second definition is: "U. S., a low chest of drawers."

   In Mr. Lockwood's "Colonial Furniture," volume 1, pages 67–113, the term "dressing table" is generally used, although the word "lowboy" appears in the supplementary chapter of the third edition, page 350.

   As was suggested in the previous chapter, on highboys, section 82, note 3, that chapter and this may well be read together, as the subjects are closely related.

   Lowboys, or small tables, with slate tops, are mentioned in section 154, note 2.

2. As with highboys, lowboys were much more popular in America than in England. In our country large numbers of lowboys have survived to the present time, many more than the number of highboys.

3. Dressing glasses are illustrated in section 152.

4. The term "dressing table" is sometimes applied also to a table with a top which lifts up, disclosing a mirror and places for various accessories of the toilet; also sometimes called a "Beau Brummel" dressing table. This, of course, is not a lowboy. See the illustrations in section 168, Nos. 1473–1476.

   Another kind of dressing table is of the "knee–hole" type, sometimes made in the block–front form; see sections 168 and 119.

however, the fronts of these dressing tables, especially those in the "Philadelphia style" illustrated in section 92, were made so low that one could not conveniently sit at them. Hence, it is said, they were then much used as side tables, and were apparently placed in any part of the house where such a table was desired.

Occasionally a lowboy and a highboy were made as companion pieces,[5] the lowboy following the design of the stand of the highboy, but of somewhat smaller size.[6] In some cases when the upper part of a highboy has been destroyed or injured, the stand of the highboy has been fitted with a top like that of a lowboy, and offered for sale as a lowboy and it may be difficult to determine the real character of the piece.

In every lowboy we see the cyma curve, the curve which Hogarth called the "Line of beauty."[7] It appears in the William and Mary style in the aprons, or skirts, and in the stretchers; in the Queen Anne and later styles in the aprons and legs. In some pieces two cyma curves are united in the lines of the apron. To every lowboy it gives grace and elegance, but seeing it so often we may not notice or appreciate it.

Section 89. Style of William and Mary.—We begin the illustrations of lowboys with the style called the William and Mary[1] from the names of the king and queen in whose reign, (1689–1702), the style was in vogue in England.[2] These lowboys are almost the same in design as the stands of the six–legged highboys of the same period, illustrated in section 84 except that these lowboys have a top which could be used as a table.

The lowboys of this period are among the most interesting and desirable pieces of American furniture, although not so valuable as those in the "Philadelphia style," which are illustrated in section 92.

It could not be expected that many of these lowboys should survive to our day in their original condition. Their stretchers furnished a convenient resting place

5.   As the maple highboy No. 644 and the maple lowboy No. 694, both belonging to the same owner. Companion pieces may have been frequently made, but they are very seldom found together.

6.   In Miss Morse's "Furniture of the Olden Time," page 31, the measurements of a certain lowboy and the stand of its companion highboy, both owned by the authoress, and dated about 1740, are given as follows: the height of the lowboy is 28 inches, of the stand 36 inches; length, 30 inches, 37 inches; depth 18 inches, 21 inches. These differences are easily seen when the two pieces are together. The height of lowboys ranges from about 28 to 30 inches. These comparative measurements may be important when a lowboy is offered for sale.

7.   See section 23.

1.   As to this style see section 13.

      The corresponding highboys in section 84 are not classified as being in the William and Mary style, but as "flat top highboys with stretchers and six legs." See note 2 in section 83.

2.   It does not follow that all the American lowboys of this type were made in these years. The styles in our country were of course somewhat later than in England; and moreover a lowboy of any style may have been made on the order of a customer some years after the style itself passed out. See the remarks in the chapter on "Highboys," section 83, note 3.

for several generations of feet; the somewhat insecure wire fastenings of the brass handles no doubt often gave way; and any veneering was liable to fall off in the course of time. Hence almost all of these pieces have required restorations[3] to a greater or less extent.

The wood in these pieces is generally walnut.

The first illustration, No. 669, is of the six–legged[4] type, similar to the stands of the highboys in Nos. 632–634. Very few lowboys of this kind have apparently survived. There are three drawers, which is the number in almost all of the lowboys of this period; the drawers at the sides are narrower and deeper than that in the centre. These drawers have borders of light wood and around them are double arch moldings.[5] The six legs have turnings in the form of inverted cups, and the feet are of the ball type.[6] It will also be noticed that the curves of the stretchers in front and at the sides follow the general design of the curves of the apron, or skirt, at the front and sides. This lowboy is of walnut, having been made in the "Age of Walnut,"[7] but in this period other woods were also used. About 1700.

The next three lowboys, Nos. 670–672, may be a few years later in style. It will be seen that instead of having six legs, as No. 669, these lowboys have four legs, and that the places occupied by the two inner front legs in No. 669 are ornamented with two pendants. This change also took place in the highboys of the period, as was mentioned in section 85 in the comment on Nos. 635–637; and this ornamentation by pendants continued in vogue for many years after the William and Mary style passed out and the style of Queen Anne came in, as will be seen in the next section. About 1700–1710.

These four lowboys are in the same general style, differing in some details. In No. 670 the moldings around the drawer are known as "single arch" moldings; in the other three pieces the moldings are of the "double arch" type.[8] Nos. 669 and 670 have drop handles; Nos. 671 and 672 have bail handles; all these were originally held in place by wires.[9] No. 672 has trumpet[10] turned legs instead of the inverted cup turnings of the other three pieces. The stretchers should also be noticed.[11] The dates are about 1700–1720.

3.   The danger in much restoration is referred to in section 10.

4.   This illustration is given here not only because of the high character of the lowboy, but also because there are two inside legs attached to the bottom of the apron, or skirt, at places which were later utilized for the two "pendants" as shown in Nos. 670–672.

5.   These moldings are mentioned in section 83 note 5.

6.   See figure 3 in illustration No. 11 and the feet in the highboys Nos. 632–634.

7.   See this referred to in section 28.

8.   These moldings are mentioned in note 5 in section 83.

9.   As to these handles, see illustration No. 12 in section 39.

10.   See section 84, note 3, in the chapter on highboys.

11.   In three of these lowboys the stretchers are in a form suggestive of the letter "X," and are therefore commonly called "X" stretchers. Each stretcher has the appearance of being made from one piece of wood but each is really made from a number of pieces glued together in such a manner as to

(Continued on page 386.)

669 (Upper) Anonymous.
671 (Centre) Anonymous.
673 (Lower) Dr. James Bordley, Jr.

670 (Upper) Mr. J. S. McDaniel.
672 (Centre) Anonymous.
674 (Lower) Mr. Wm. M. Ellicott.

675 (Upper) Dr. James Bordley, Jr.
677 (Centre) Mrs. John S. Gibbs, Jr.
679 (Lower) Mr. Morris Whitridge.

676 (Upper) Mrs. Elizabeth N. Dunham.
678 (Centre) Mrs. John S. Gibbs, Jr.
680 (Lower) Hammond-Harwood House.

Lowboys of this type are not often seen outside of museums. Great care should be exercised in purchasing any lowboy, or indeed any article of furniture, appearing to be of this period, and the advice of some one experienced in antique furniture should be secured in regard to the extent of the restorations.

Section 90. Style of Queen Anne.—Soon after Queen Anne came to the throne in 1702 the Dutch style of furniture became the fashion in England, superseding the style of William and Mary. This Dutch style, known to us as the Queen Anne style,[1] continued in vogue in England for about forty years, when it in turn yielded to the style which we know as the style of Chippendale.[2] About 1715–1720, the Queen Anne style became the fashion in our American colonies and made a great change in the designs of various articles of furniture, as in chairs,[3] highboys[4] and lowboys. The period of the Queen Anne style, lasting with us until about 1755–1760, is a portion of the "period of the cabriole[5] leg," and the presence of cabriole legs and club, or Dutch, feet identify the highboy and the lowboy as being in the style of Queen Anne.

In a general way the date of a Queen Anne style lowboy may in some cases be indicated by the presence or absence of the two projections for holding pendants on the apron, or skirt, at the points where the two inside front legs of a six–legged lowboy were placed, as referred to in the comments on Nos. 670–672. A lowboy with pendants would seem to be of an earlier date than a lowboy made without pendants; but it must not be thought that lowboys having pendants, or places for them, are in all cases earlier in date to other lowboys not having pendants or places for them; some lowboys with pendants are dated[6] in the books as late as 1750–1760.

(NOTE 11, *continued*)

make the stretcher as strong as possible. The joints are concealed by a veneer. The shape of the stretchers gives room in the front for a person to sit down at the lowboy comfortably, which could not well be done when there was a front stretcher as in No. 669.

1. For convenience, there is here and elsewhere a certain repetition of what is said in previous sections. The Queen Anne style, for example, has been considered in section 14.

2. See section 15 as to this style.

3. See the chairs illustrated in section 50.

4. See the highboys in section 85.

5. See sections 23–24. The cabriole legs include not only those in the Queen Anne period but also those with ball and claw feet which were in fashion from about 1750 to the end of the Chippendale period, about 1785.

The cabriole legs of the lowboys made in the Queen Anne style were very similar to those of many of the highboys of the same period; for example, they were often long and slender; and they were well suited to the moderate weight of the lowboys.

Walnut was the favorite wood in the Queen Anne period, but other woods were much used, especially maple and cherry in New England. A recital of the names of the other woods used for various parts of articles of furniture is almost equivalent to a list of all of the usable trees then grown on the Atlantic seaboard. See also section 30 entitled "Pine, maple and other woods."

6. As in Mr. Lockwood's "Colonial Furniture," volume 1, figures 101, lowboy, and 96, 99, highboys; also in Mr. Nutting's "Furniture Treasury," Nos. 398–400. In several of these the pendants are missing.

Before examining the illustrations of lowboys with pendants, we should notice Nos. 673–674, made in the early Queen Anne period, and in a somewhat uncommon form without pendants and having a type of foot known as "Spanish."[7] The legs are in the cabriole[8] form, but are almost rectangular, not rounded, and are ornamented on the front and outer sides with a "bracelet" or "collar" above the Spanish feet, as was also noticed in the highboy No. 645. The aprons, or skirts, are cut straight except for the curved projections which were obviously not made for pendants. These two pieces are said to be of the period of about 1710–1730.

The next six lowboys, Nos. 675–680, have, or had, pendants hanging from projections in the bottom of the apron, or skirt; on the last two lowboys of this group the pendants were doubtless on the projections but are now missing.

In Nos. 675 and 676 the middle drawer is partly concave. On No. 676 the top may not be the original one, the overhang being very small and the edge not being cut in a molding such as, for example, a thumb–nail molding seen on the table No. 1289 and on other lowboys, and mentioned in section 41, note 3, A. The very small round pendants probably are substitutes. On the drawers are bands of light wood. There are two drawers in the upper row.[9] The difference in the thickness of the legs in these two pieces is considerable. About 1740–1760.

In Nos. 677 and 678 the three small drawer fronts will be noticed, with a "rising sun," or perhaps a "fan" design. In each the wood is maple. Except for the projections for holding the pendants, the bottoms of the aprons of Nos. 675–677 are cut in straight lines, as in many highboys and lowboys. In No. 678, as in No. 682, all the feet point to the front. About 1740–1760.

Nos. 679 seems to be a companion piece to the highboy No. 652, and both have been in the possession of the same family for many years. The cushions, or shoes, under the club, or Dutch, feet are thicker than usual, as also in the highboy referred to. About 1735–1750.

No. 680 has very slender legs, rivalling those on the highboy No. 642, and the top seems to be a substitute, having an unusually large overhang. About 1730–1750.

In the succeeding illustrations in this chapter the pendants and the projections to which the pendants were attached, which perhaps have received too much attention, have disappeared, because the aprons, or skirts, were cut in such designs that pendants were unsuitable.[10]

In Nos. 681–690 another group of lowboys in the style of Queen Anne is presented. These pieces are all of the same general appearance; the legs are all in the cabriole form; the feet are of the club, or Dutch, type, or variations of them;

7.   For illustrations of other articles with Spanish feet see the Index under "Feet, Spanish"; see also figure 18 in illustration No. 11 in section 25.

8.   See also Mr. Lockwood's "Colonial Furniture," volume 1, figures 84–85; and Mr. Nutting's "Furniture Treasury," Nos. 358, 419, 421, 422.

9.   Compare the lowboy referred to as "Veneered, inlaid Queen Anne, 1740–1760," in Mr. Nutting's "Furniture Treasury," No. 400.

10.   This matter is also mentioned in connection with highboys Nos. 635–637.

681 (Upper) Dr. James Bordley, Jr.
683 (Centre) Mr. Albert G. Towers.
685 (Lower) Mrs. R. W. Petre.

682 (Upper) Mr. Albert G. Towers.
684 (Centre) Hammond–Harwood House.
686 (Lower) Family of Thos. Cradock.

388

687 (Upper) Mr. E. G. Miller, Jr.
689 (Centre) Mr. & Mrs. J. P. Reese.
691 (Lower) Mrs. Miles White, Jr.

688 (Upper) Dr. James Bordley, Jr.
690 (Centre) Mr. & Mrs. C. E. McLane.
692 (Lower) Mrs. Miles White, Jr.

the size and shapes are about the same. In spite of these points of similarity, however, each one of these lowboys is different in some respects and presents to the eye a graceful and pleasing object. The aprons, or skirts, are cut in a great variety of designs, almost every one of which has a form of the cyma curve; and the number and shape of the drawers are varied.[11]

In examining Nos. 681–690, it will be seen that they are arranged to some extent according to the style of the arches and curves in the apron; this method merely presents together the lowboys which have points in common, and is not intended to indicate the dates of the pieces.

In Nos. 681–683 the centre of the apron is cut somewhat in the shape of an arch of the period of about 1720–1750.

No. 681 has three small drawers but not the usual large one above, in this respect resembling the early lowboys Nos. 669–672. The wide and high arch in the apron will be noticed. About 1720–1750.

In No. 682, as in No. 678, all the feet point to the front, although this is not very clearly seen in the illustration. Here there are five drawers. About 1730–1750.

In No. 683 the apron is cut in cyma curves and half–circles, as also in No. 686. The feet here are of the three–toed type, which is referred to in note 12 in this section. About 1740–1760.

In Nos. 684–689 the central arch gradually becomes smaller and in No. 690 it almost disappears.

In No. 684 the apron, or skirt, is cut in two flat spaces somewhat resembling those in Nos. 673 and 674; the rounded projections are not intended for pendants, as referred to in the comments on the highboys Nos. 635–637. About 1740–1760.

In No. 685 the drawers are inlaid, as also in No. 690 and in the dressing table No. 1475. The oval handles now on this lowboy are in the later styles of Hepplewhite and Sheraton, as shown in illustration No. 15 in section 39. About 1740–1760.

No. 686 has a delicate beading upon the edge of the apron, which is cut in two series of cyma curves, with a semi–circular arch in the centre. About 1740–1760.

In Nos. 687 and 688 the central arch and the two somewhat similar ones on the sides make harmonious groupings. In No. 688 the large and finely pierced brass handles add to the appearance. About 1740–1760.

On No. 689 also are fine brass handles. Here we see the three–toed feet, which are variations of the usual form of club, or Dutch, feet of the Queen Anne style, and are well seen in No. 692 and in figure 11 in illustration No. 11, in section 25; and see note 12 below. About 1740–1760.

11.   It does not seem necessary to give full descriptions of all of the lowboys in this or the following groups, nor to mention the various features which distinguish one from another; these are obvious to the eye of the reader. In some few cases there have been restorations or replacements which are apparent, such as a rectangular edged top without a molding; or the handles may not be of the exact period.

In No. 690 as in Nos. 681 and 692, there are only three small drawers, which were used also on the early lowboys Nos. 669-672. Inlay is on the drawers, as in No. 685. About 1740-1760.

The last series of lowboys in the Queen Anne style is Nos. 691-698. These are apparently of the period from about 1750-1790, and about the latter date the lowboy and the highboy went out of style and ceased to be made, the modern bureau taking their places.

In No. 691 the apron, or skirt, is cut in a series of curves, without the cyma curve; the edges of the drawers are beaded and the central drawer and the two knees are decorated with carved shells. About 1740-1775.

In No. 692, a small and dainty lowboy with three drawers, there is a delicate bit of carving, called a half-rosette, on the central drawer, under which is a carved ornament known as a "fish tail," from a fancied resemblance to one, as also in the next illustration.[12] About 1750-1775.

Nos. 693 and 694 are of curly maple. The legs of the first are much too thick, and a fish tail is faintly seen in the centre of the apron; the second is a companion piece of the maple highboy No. 644 and belongs to the same owner. About 1740-1760.

In No. 695 the apron, or skirt, has so many curves and arches with edges that it seems dangerous to the body and raiment of one sitting at or partly under it; and in No. 696 the apron, or skirt, is well supplied with cyma curves. About 1750-1775.

In No. 697 the apron, or skirt, is cut in a design somewhat like that in No. 673. A very unusual type is seen in No. 698 which has a deep central drawer and a large and bare apron which is cut in four "C" curves. Here we may compare examples of legs, those of No. 697 being thick and strong and those of No. 698 being slender and probably weak. About 1740-1760.

Section 91. Lowboys with ball and claw feet.—In this and the next section the lowboys illustrated are those with ball and claw feet. This type of feet[1] came

12. Nos. 691 and 692 are illustrated in Mr. Lockwood's "Colonial Furniture," volume 1, pages 348 and 349, the dates of each being given as 1750-1775.

In regard to No. 692 it is said, in Mr. Lockwood's book, page 350, that "the legs terminate in the thin pointed feet so often found in Pennsylvania and New Jersey."

No. 695 is the same as No. 416 in Mr. Nutting's "Furniture Treasury," where the foot is termed a "drake foot," which in his No. 415 is said to be "regarded as coming from the Delaware Valley."

See also the comment on No. 689 and the reference to section 25.

1. See section 25, entitled "The kinds of feet."

Pendants and projections for pendants having passed out of style were not used on these lowboys.

It is said that aprons, or skirts, cut in arched forms were out of style in the Chippendale period; an example to the contrary, however, is in No. 699 in which the arched apron and the Chippendale style ball and claw feet are both present.

693 (Upper) Mr. J. S. McDaniel.
695 (Centre) Hammond-Harwood House.
697 (Lower) Mr. John C. Toland.

694 (Upper) Mrs. Daniel Miller.
696 (Centre) Dr. James Bordley, Jr.
698 (Lower) Mr. Albert G. Towers.

699 (Upper) Mr. & Mrs. E. H. McKeon.   700 (Upper) Mr. J. S. McDaniel.
701 (Centre) Mr. J. F. H. Maginn.   702 (Centre) Mrs. I. R. Trimble.
703 (Lower) Mr. & Mrs. R. L. Cary.   704 (Lower) Mrs. Miles White, Jr.

into general use in our country about the year 1750 and continued in vogue until about the year 1785 when the Hepplewhite style of feet came into fashion. In this period the lowboys and highboys with ball and claw feet reached their highest development. The use of ball and claw feet in our country indicates the style of Chippendale, although in England these feet were in use for a few years prior to the time of Chippendale.[2]

In this section the twelve pieces shown as Nos. 699–710 are examples of fine lowboys without reference to their place of origin, and in the next section are illustrations of two representative lowboys of the type known as the "Philadelphia style" which is referred to in section 87 in connection with highboys.

Some of the lowboys shown in this section may have been made at the same time, and by the same cabinet makers, as the more elaborate pieces in the "Philadelphia style." The chief difference between the lowboys shown in this section and those in the "Philadelphia style" is that the latter are more highly decorated with carvings and applied "streamers" and scrolls.

No. 699 has unusual brass handles, an arch in the centre of the apron with graceful cyma curves on each side and much carving on the legs. Around each of the finely veneered drawers are bands of lighter wood. See the remarks in note 1. This lowboy, inherited from Philadelphia ancestors of the present owner, may be of English origin. About 1740–1750.

In No. 700 the apron is cut in a design resembling that in No. 684. The knees are carved with acanthus leaves. About 1750–1770.

No. 701 resembles No. 691 to some extent in the form of the apron and also has a similarity to the form of the apron in No. 712, excepting the shell in the apron of the latter. The brass handles are in an elaborate design and the central drawer is of a greater size than usual. The fluted columns on the two front corners of this and other lowboys are referred to in note 1, D, in section 92. About 1750–1770.

In No. 702 the design of the apron is very unusual having two long projections which prevent any possible usage of the space under the frame by one sitting upon a chair in front. About 1750–1770.

No. 703 and the next three lowboys, Nos. 704–706, are distinguished by the somewhat similar carvings at the bottom of the aprons, representing shells of different kinds. We may also notice that on each of these lowboys the fine brass handles are of a different type, that the knees of the legs of the latter three are carved and that fluted columns are on the corners of the fronts of all except No. 704. About 1750–1770.

In Nos. 707–710 we approach nearer to the "Philadelphia style," which is in the Chippendale style with the addition of decorative features of certain kinds. In these four lowboys the size, the shape and the various details of the drawers, handles, aprons, legs and feet are about the same as those in the more elaborate

2.   See section 15, entitled "The Chippendale style."

705 (Upper) Mr. Arthur E. Cole.
707 (Centre) Mr. & Mrs. H. L. Duer.
709 (Lower) Mrs. James W. Wilson.

706 (Upper) Mr. John C. Toland.
708 (Centre) Md. Soc. Colonial Dames.
710 (Lower) Mr. W. W. Lanahan.

"Philadelphia style" lowboys, but are without the "fine feathers" which are referred to in note 6 in section 87.

In No. 707 the edge of the front of the apron, or skirt, is beaded and is carved in "C" scrolls, in the centre of which is a shell which is more elaborately carved than any other one previously shown here. The knees of the legs are fully carved with leaves. At the corners are fluted columns which are referred to in note 1 in the next section. About 1750–1775.

In No. 708 the apron is cut in a series of curves with points which, as in No. 695, might endanger the comfort of one sitting in front of the lowboy. The legs of many lowboys in the Chippendale style are shorter than those of the lowboys in the Queen Anne style seen in the previous section. In lowboys in the Queen Anne style, the effort was apparently to give as much "knee–room" as possible, but in the lowboys in the "Philadelphia style" the "knee–room" was reduced. A concave shell is carved on the central drawer. About 1750–1775.

In No. 709 there is a carved concave shell in the central drawer and another shell is at the lower end of the apron, extending nearer to the floor than any other apron here shown; similar shells are seen on the highboys Nos. 648 and 662. The handles are in an unusual design. About 1750–1775.

Lastly, in No. 710, the central drawer is carved with a fine design around which are a few streamers which are the most distinctive feature of the highboys and lowboys in the "Philadelphia style." About 1750–1775.

Section 92. "Philadelphia style" lowboys.—In section 87 mention is made of the "Philadelphia style" highboys and of several of the cabinet makers who have made Philadelphia and themselves famous in the annals of American furniture in the Chippendale style. Much of what is there said about highboys applies equally well to lowboys.[1] Without meaning to depreciate in any way these masterpieces of American furniture, it may be said that the importance of these lowboys does not seem to be based upon their superiority in form or workmanship as much as upon

1. A. In these lowboys the legs seem to be even shorter than in the previous ones, apparently indicating that they were not made primarily as dressing tables; see the third paragraph in section 88 and the comment on No. 708.

B. Only two lowboys of this type are shown here for the reason that the "stands," or lower sections, of the "Philadelphia style" highboys Nos. 660–668 are substantially the same as lowboys and are sufficiently representative of them.

C. The fine brass handles contribute to the elegant appearance of these lowboys.

D. The front corners are in some cases ornamented with carved designs and in other cases they have fluted columns. These fluted columns are similar to those seen on the sides of grandfather clocks of the period, except that the columns on the clocks often have brass mounts at the top and bottoms. Brass mounts were not used on the lowboys or highboys.

E. A fluted column of this type is called a "quarter–round" column, being a quarter of a round column, in the shape of a round lead pencil, cut lengthwise in four equal parts. It is said that in England in the Chippendale period this form of ornamentation was used chiefly on grandfather clocks, but that in our country it was also used on many other articles. See mirror, No. 1115; chair, No. 182; and table, No. 1429.

F. The wood in all of these lowboys is mahogany.

711 (Upper) Miss Margaret L. Myers.
712 (Lower) Mr. John C. Toland.

the fanciful carving and applied designs that have been lavished upon them; in other words, upon their "rococo"[2] ornamentation. Passing from this somewhat unorthodox remark, we turn to two examples of the "Philadelphia style." These lowboys, although not so elaborate as some others in the books,[3] illustrate the fine features of the style and are representative of the type. They are regarded as having been made in the period of about 1760–1775.

The distinctive features of these lowboys will be noticed in Nos. 711 and 712, resembling the "stands," or lower portions, of the "Philadelphia style" highboys in general appearance. There is a carved design on the central drawer, generally a shell or something similar to a shell. Around the shell are applied streamers in graceful curves. The apron, or skirt, is carved more or less elaborately in pleasing lines, generally, in fact almost always, with a shell. The cabriole legs are finely carved and terminate in ball and claw feet, the ball being generally about two-thirds of a sphere, or less, and therefore somewhat flat. The size[4] of these lowboys is about the same as that of others less elaborately ornamented.

No. 711 is the more ornate of the two here shown. It has the usual features above mentioned; the apron, or skirt, is of superior design, consisting of a series of "C" scrolls which were so popular in the Chippendale period, as shown especially in the mirrors such as Nos. 1103–1106; and in the centre are two "C" curves with an open space between. About 1760–1775.

In No. 712 the central drawer is somewhat more fully decorated with carving, having several "C" scroll streamers. The apron, or skirt, is cut in a number of cyma curves, as to which see section 23, resembling in form Nos. 691 and 701 with the addition of a carved shell in the centre. In this and the preceding lowboy the large and finely designed handles are to be noticed. About 1760–1775.

This closes the chapter on lowboys which, like highboys, passed out at the summit of their career.

2.   In the Century Dictionary, the "rococo" ornamentation is rather severely described as "generally a meaningless, though often a very rich, assemblage of fantastic scrolls and crimped conventional shell work, wrought into irregular and indescribable forms, without individuality and without expression apart from its usually costly material and surroundings. The style has a certain interest from its use in a great number of sumptuous European residences and from its intimate association with a social life of great outward refinement and splendor. Much of the painting, engraving, porcelain work, etc., of the time has, too, a real decorative charm, though not of a very high order in art." The words "baroque" and "rocaille" have a somewhat similar meaning. These styles prevailed in Europe, especially in the time of Louis the Fifteenth, 1715–1774. The word "rococo" is said to be derived from the French words "roc," a rock, and "coquille," a shell, as the work is characterized by shells and often by a rocky background. See also section 87, note 6.

Whether we like or dislike the rococo style of ornamentation we should remember that it was adopted by Chippendale in some of his elaborately carved work and by the cabinet makers of his period, and that the Philadelphia cabinet makers followed Chippendale.

3.   A collection of illustrations of fine lowboys in the "Philadelphia style" is shown in Mr. Nutting's "Furniture Treasury," Nos. 423, 424, 426, 427, 429–442.

4.   As to the size, see section 88, note 6.

Chapter XI

BUREAUS

Section 93. General remarks.—The word "bureau" in our country now means a chest of drawers for holding clothing or other articles, whether or not a mirror is attached to the top. If there is no mirror, the bureau is in reality only a chest of drawers; if a mirror is attached, instead of being separate as it formerly was, there is a combination of a chest of drawers and a mirror; but in both cases the article is now commonly known as a bureau. It is said that in the early part of the eighteenth century, both in England and America, the word "bureau" was used in its original sense, meaning a desk,[1] which is a chest of drawers with a writing compartment on the top, or a flat table for writing with drawers at the sides. In England at the present time the word "bureau" still retains its original meaning of "desk."[2] The reason for the American change in the meaning is not clear.

1. See the next chapter, on "Desks," section 101; also the chapter on "Highboys," section 82, at note 5.

In the "Maryland Gazette" of April 9, 1767, and June 1, 1769, both "bureaus" and "desks" are offered for sale in the same advertisements, from which it seems that "bureaus" and "desks" were not then exactly the same.

In Mr. Lockwood's "Colonial Furniture," volume 1, pages 231–233, the early meaning of these words is discussed.

2. In Mr. Cescinsky's "English and American Furniture," pages 163–172, American desks with slanting lids are illustrated, and are called by the English name, "bureaux," and the American bureaus without a mirror attached are called "chests of drawers."

Commode. This word in England at one time meant a chest of drawers, designed chiefly in the French style. The French commodes were very ornamental, often with ormolu mounts, and finely inlaid; and the English commodes were generally very decorative. In the books of designs of Chippendale and other contemporary English cabinet makers a number of drawings of commodes are illustrated, showing serpentine fronts and elaborate carvings, and larger than the chests of drawers of the period; but the commodes themselves are not readily distinguishable from the finer chests of drawers, except by their more ornamental character. They were also made in the later styles of Adam, Hepplewhite and Sheraton; a favorite form, and the one most frequently seen in English books, was in a half–circular shape with doors opening like those of sideboards, or with drawers, and handsomely decorated with

 (*Note 2 continued on page 400*)

Bureaus may be considered in four types, according to the shape of their fronts, namely, the serpentine front, the reversed serpentine front, the swell, or bow, front and the straight front.

These four types of bureau fronts are best understood from the illustrations, but may be briefly described here. The word "serpentine" is used to indicate a waving curve. This curve appears in two forms, one of which is simply called "serpentine" and the other "reversed serpentine." The "serpentine" curve is convex in the centre and concave at the two sides, as is well seen in illustrations Nos. 714 and 726. The "reversed serpentine" curve is the opposite of the "serpentine" curve, being concave in the centre and convex at the two sides,[3] as is well shown in Nos. 717–720. In each of these curves a form of the cyma curve, shown in section 23, may be seen. These two kinds of serpentine curved fronts show the play of light and shade, and the grain of the wood, to better advantage than either of the other two kinds of front. The reversed serpentine form is the most highly esteemed.

The bureaus known as block–front bureaus should perhaps appear in this chapter; but, as mentioned in section 81 in connection with chests–on–chests, the writer thinks that all the block–front pieces, such as chests–on–chests, bureaus, desks, secretary–bookcases and dressing tables, should be presented in one chapter where they may be conveniently examined together, rather than in separate chapters. In such pieces the "block–front" is the real feature of interest; apart from the "block–front," their style is not very different from that of other bureaus and desks in the Chippendale period. The "block–front" bureaus are illustrated and considered in section 116.

(NOTE 2, *continued from page 399*.)

paintings or inlay and often veneered with satinwood. Sheraton wrote in a book published in 1803 that the word "commode" applies to pieces of ornamental furniture to stand under a glass mirror in a drawing room; and that it also applies to articles "used by ladies to dress at, in which there is a drawer fitted up with suitable conveniences for the purpose." Commodes were not popular in our country and very few have been found. They are said by Mr. Cescinsky to be "merely glorified chests of drawers"; "English and American Furniture," page 145. See "Antiques," February, 1936, page 51.

3. A. Because of its shape this front is sometimes called "ox–bow" or "yoke"; these words refer to the yoke of a pair of oxen and are well understood in farming communities but are not known to many dwellers in cities. The expensive reversed serpentine bureaus were probably not made by country cabinet makers.

B. In perhaps a large majority of cases the drawers of bureaus and desks were "graduated" in size, the deepest one being at the bottom and the others "gradually" diminishing in depth.

C. Mention may be made here of the moldings on the drawers of bureaus, highboys and other articles. The early moldings were strips of wood with an arched front and were "applied." In section 83, which treats of the early highboys, it is said in note 5 that the first kind of molding used on highboys was a single–arch one and that at a later date two strips were sometimes used making a double–arch molding, as in the miniature bureau No. 769. These moldings were applied upon the framework surrounding the drawers, not upon the drawers. Later, in the Hepplewhite and Sheraton periods, the moldings, consisting chiefly of narrow semi–circular strips called "beading," or "cock–beading," were applied upon the drawers, not upon the framework surrounding the drawers; but in many cases moldings were not used exactly as here stated. See the comments on Nos. 713, 714 and 752; also section 41, in which various moldings are described; also section 83, note 5.

D. The lower portion of the desks and of certain other articles shown in the next chapter closely resemble the corresponding portions of the bureaus shown in this chapter.

The "swell," or "bow," front is one with a single sweep of a convex curve from one side of the bureau to the other, such as is well seen in Nos. 733–736. Both the terms "swell front" and "bow front" are used by careful writers and in this book. Modified forms are in Nos. 746–749.

The two kinds of serpentine fronts and the bow fronts were more expensive to make than the straight front, because they were necessarily made out of thick blocks of wood, much of which was cut away and lost in making the curves; and the time required was of course greater. These fronts were often veneered.

The term "straight" front explains itself, being a front without curves, as in Nos. 722 and 723.

The wood used in the better class of bureaus was almost always mahogany from about 1750, the beginning of the Chippendale period, until rosewood became popular in the Victorian style about 1845; but cherry was also used at various times in sections where the wood was plentiful.

In section 79 a chest of drawers, or bureau, No. 608, of the style of about 1710 is illustrated, and it is said that this type passed out of fashion a few years later and was apparently not in style again until about 1750. The present chapter begins at about this latter date; but the reader is invited to examine the chest of drawers above mentioned in order that he may get a view of the early bureau.[4] The change from the simple article No. 608 to the handsome bureaus Nos. 713 and 714 is one which could hardly occur without having passed through a transitional period; but no transitional pieces are illustrated or referred to in the books. Perhaps the design of the fine later American bureaus was not developed from the style of 1710, mentioned above, but was taken by our cabinet makers from the designs of Chippendale. A revival of the simpler form is seen in No. 752, which is in the Sheraton style.

Section 94. Chippendale style bureaus.—The two handsome bureaus, Nos. 713 and 714, are worthy of particular attention. We notice that the fronts are in the serpentine form, which consists of two concave curves at the sides, meeting

(NOTE 3, *continued*)

        E.   Overlapping. If the front edges of a drawer are cut to extend a short distance over the edges of the opening in which the drawer slides, the drawer is said to "overlap" the opening. This overlapping is said to be of use in keeping dust from the interior of the drawer. It was apparently popular in the Queen Anne and Chippendale periods. The overlapping part was generally cut in a "thumb–nail" molding, which is referred to in the comment on the lowboy No. 676 and is mentioned in section 41, note 3, A. Drawers of this kind are sometimes called "lipped" drawers.

        4.   It is said that after these early chests of drawers passed out of fashion, as above mentioned, their place was taken by the highboy and the lowboy, until the Chippendale period, which began in America about 1750. This may have been the case in well–to–do families who could afford the more expensive articles; but it is probable that the useful and inexpensive chests of drawers, or bureaus, continued to be made throughout those years.

        The lower portions of many desks, secretaries and secretary–bookcases are of the same type as those of bureaus of the period. The principal kind of desk is in fact a chest of drawers, or bureau, with a compartment above for writing, as is illustrated in section 82, No. 627, in the chapter on highboys. In the chapter on desks and secretary–bookcases this is mentioned in section 101.

as a convex curve in the centre; and that the tops are in the same shape, following the curve of the fronts. The corners are cut off, so as to form a flat surface and thus avoid sharp edges which would otherwise be made by the junctions of the curved front and the straight sides; in other words, to use the technical term, the corners are "chamfered." These chamfered corners are ornamented with fretwork, as are the pieces just referred to. In some cases the fretwork may be cut out separately and "applied" with nails and glue; but these are carved on the solid wood. The feet are in the bracket form and are known as "ogee" bracket feet, which are similar to figure 9 in illustration No. 11; and although they are the best of their kind, they are somewhat large and awkward.[1] The brasses on No. 713 are in the "willow" pattern and those on No. 714 are of the bail type, as shown in figures 27–29 in illustration No. 14 in section 39. The fine moldings at the top and bottom of No. 714 will be noticed. In these bureaus, and in the desks of the same period, there is often a small rounded molding on the frame work surrounding the drawers, not on the drawer itself, as mentioned in note 3, C, in the previous section. The top drawers of bureaus of this type were often fitted with small drawers and compartments. The wood used is generally mahogany. About 1765–1785.

In the next two bureaus, Nos. 715 and 716, the fronts are also in the serpentine form. The tops follow the curves of the drawers, and the handles are of the bail type. In No. 715 the chamfered corners may be seen, but are narrower than in the two previous pieces, and are not decorated with fretwork. The feet are in a different bracket form and their corners are chamfered. In No. 716 the corners are not chamfered and the piece is supported by very short cabriole legs with ball and claw feet, which may be compared with those on No. 721. These two pieces may also be dated about 1765–1785.

In the next four bureaus, Nos. 717–720, the fronts are in the "reversed serpentine" form, in which, as mentioned in the previous section, the curves on the sides of the front of the drawers are convex and the curve in the centre is concave; see also the reversed serpentine fronts on the desks Nos. 787–789. In each of these four pieces, as in the previous ones, the curve of the top follows the curve of the drawers.

In Nos. 717 and 718 the fronts of the drawers are flush with the sides of the bureau for an inch or two and the curve of the drawer then begins. The feet are in the ogee bracket form, referred to in the first paragraph above, but are not chamfered, as the corners above them are not treated in that manner. The handles

1. It is said that bracket feet, instead of ball and claw feet, were generally used on bureaus and desks made in the southern part of our country. See also section 25, entitled "The kinds of feet."

Feet of this kind are the subject of editorial comment in "Antiques," September, 1927, pages 201–202, with a humorous account of the career of William King, a cabinet maker of Salem, Massachusetts, about 1790, who devised a more graceful type, which, however, would probably not have pleased Chippendale.

Two somewhat similar fine walnut bureaus in the Chippendale style made by Jonathan Gostelowe, a leading cabinet maker of Philadelphia, are illustrated in "Antiques," June, 1926, pages 387 and 388, in an article by Mr. Clarence W. Brazer.

713 (UPPER) MRS. MAURICE F. RODGERS.　714 (UPPER) MR. JOHN C. TOLAND.
715 (CENTRE) MR. ALBERT G. TOWERS.　716 (CENTRE) MR. C. E. SNYDER.
717 (LOWER) MR. ALBERT G. TOWERS.　718 (LOWER) DR. M. A. ABRAMS.

on No. 717 are in the willow pattern, with brass plates and escutcheons; on No. 718 the handles are of the bail type, as on No. 714. About 1765-1785.

Nos. 719 and 720 are in the usual form of the reversed serpentine pieces without special features in the upper part. Both have bail handles. In No. 719, however, a small carved fan or shell is seen in the centre of the base; and the feet are in the ogee bracket form. In No. 720 the feet are of the straight bracket type; and the bead moldings on the frames surrounding the drawers are clearly seen, as mentioned in section 93, note 3, C. About 1765-1785.

In Nos. 721-723 the bureaus have straight fronts and are thus of a simpler form than those with serpentine or reversed serpentine forms. In No. 721 are two drawers at the top instead of the usual one drawer. The supports, too short to be called legs, terminate in a very flat type of ball and claw feet. Under the base, as in No. 719, there is a carved fan or shell ornament. In No. 722 the corners are cut off and fluted columns are attached. Here the feet are in the ogee bracket form. The handles have solid plates which are probably of an earlier style than the bureau itself; compare figures 9-11 in illustration No. 13 in section 39. The elaborate moldings at the top and bottom will be noticed. No. 723 is somewhat similar, having the same type of feet and corners with columns. A feature not seen in previous bureaus is a shelf which pulls out, intended no doubt for holding articles, being too high for use as a writing shelf. These three may be dated about 1765-1785.

No. 724 is a bureau in what is called a "bombé," or "kettle," shape. This form will also be seen on Nos. 898 and 899 and on the two secretaries Nos. 896 and 897. It was much used in English, French, Dutch and German furniture. The lower part swells out in front and on the sides, and the entire front from side to side is serpentine—interesting but not handsome. It is said that some of the best English pieces in the Chippendale style were made in this form; but only a few bureaus of the type have been found in this country. See the Index under the word "Bombé." About 1760-1780.

Section 95. Hepplewhite style bureaus.—As is also mentioned in section 104 in connection with desks and secretary-bookcases in the Hepplewhite and Sheraton styles, and in section 127 on sideboards, the features of the Hepplewhite and Sheraton schools are often so similar that it is difficult to decide whether certain pieces are in the one style or the other. The same difficulty applies to some extent to bureaus. Some writers therefore refer to certain pieces as being "of the Hepplewhite-Sheraton period," which is sufficient for those who are not particularly interested in the precise classification of every piece. In the present section on bureaus in the Hepplewhite style some of the bureaus may possibly be regarded as being in the Sheraton style; but it is certain that all of the bureaus in the next section are in the Sheraton style and not in the Hepplewhite style.

At the beginning of the vogue of the Hepplewhite style, which in our country was about the year 1785, some of the bureaus seem to have been made with certain features of the previous style of Chippendale. Thus in Nos. 725 and 726 we see

719 (Upper) Mr. Albert G. Towers.
721 (Centre) Hammond-Harwood House.
723 (Lower) Dr. James Bordley, Jr.

720 (Upper) Mrs. Miles White, Jr.
722 (Centre) Miss Helen H. Carey.
724 (Lower) Rhode Island School of Design.

feet resembling the bracket feet of the Chippendale period.[1] The bail handles on No. 726 are generally seen on somewhat earlier pieces. In both bureaus the corners and feet are "chamfered," as in the Chippendale style bureaus Nos. 713 and 714; and the front surfaces are ornamented with inlay, which also decorates the bracket feet of No. 726 and the small projection below the base. In both of these pieces, and in the next six, the fronts are in serpentine form in which, as mentioned in the previous section, the central portion is convex. About 1785–1800.

In bureaus in the Hepplewhite style the usual wood was mahogany, but walnut, cherry and maple and other woods were also used.

In the handsome bureau No. 727 the feathered satinwood veneer covers the fronts of the drawers. This decorative wood needs no assistance in making the piece a most ornamental one; but the fine grain of the framework surrounding the drawers adds to the elegant appearance. The French bracket feet, a prominent characteristic of the Hepplewhite style, also often used on pieces in the Sheraton style, are somewhat higher than in some other examples. This bureau is believed to be a New England product. As in almost all of the Hepplewhite style bureaus a line of inlay appears on the base. About 1785–1800.

No. 728 is ornamented with finely grained satinwood veneer on each of the twelve large panels. These panels are bordered with dark wood in such manner that the dark wood is always between light wood. This bureau is similar in design to No. 736 in certain respects. About 1785–1800.

No. 729 is a graceful bureau. The long horizontal lines of inlay with rounded ends[2] on the drawers, the bright color of the top, the round ring handles, the line of inlay on the apron, or skirt, and the flowing curves of the French bracket feet and the skirt, all combine to give a pleasing effect. About 1785–1800.

No. 730 has a finely figured veneer on the drawers, and lines of inlay decorate the sides and the skirt, on which there is also an inlaid fan in a reversed position. A few inches of the French bracket feet seem to have been cut off. About 1785–1800.

Nos. 731 and 732 are also Hepplewhite style bureaus with serpentine fronts. No. 731 resembles No. 729 somewhat in form, but has light rectangular inlay on the edges of the drawers. The grain of the mahogany veneer of the drawers gives an interesting appearance. No. 732 is a plain piece without inlay. Around the

---

1. On almost all of the bureaus and desks in the Hepplewhite style and on many in the Sheraton style, the curved French bracket foot will be seen, as in the bureau No. 727 and others. When this foot is used there is almost always a curved or scroll apron, or skirt, the feet and the skirt making a series of graceful curves, as will be seen in the illustrations referred to. But where a straight bracket foot was used, as in the bureaus Nos. 725 and 726 and others, only a base was generally used, without an apron, or skirt. Designs showing these two different methods are in the "Guide" of Hepplewhite, as to which see section 17, and are also shown on pages 240–245 of the book "Chippendale, Sheraton and Hepplewhite furniture designs," by Mr. J. M. Bell.

Small dressing glasses in the Hepplewhite style, made to stand upon bureaus, are illustrated in section 152.

2. As to this form of inlay, see section 96, note 1.

725 (Upper) Mrs. Edwin B. Niver.   726 (Upper) Mr. John C. Toland.
727 (Centre) Mrs. Francis P. Garvan. 728 (Centre) Anonymous.
729 (Lower) Mrs. Miles White, Jr.   730 (Lower) Mr. Daniel R. Randall.

edges of the drawers are bead moldings, and the skirt is cut somewhat in the form of double cyma curves. The feet on both pieces are in the French bracket form. About 1785–1800.

Six examples of swell front, or bow front, Hepplewhite bureaus are shown in illustrations Nos. 733–738.

The first two, Nos. 733 and 734, are very similar in design. The principal difference is in the fine veneer in light woods, covering almost the entire fronts of the drawers and surrounded by bands of wood of darker color. These two similar bureaus illustrate what is mentioned in other places in this book, that is, that two articles may be shown which are so similar that one may represent the type as well as two; but if both are attractive in appearance, as these are, it is difficult for the writer to decide which one should be omitted—and perhaps the reader may be pleased to see both. In No. 733 the line of inlay in the base matches the edge of the top and the drawers have brass knobs such as those shown in illustration No. 17 in section 40. About 1785–1800. In No. 734 the skirt is decorated with inlaid flowers and the brass handles are of the familiar oval type shown in illustration No. 15 in section 39. About 1785–1800.

No. 735 is highly decorated with inlay. Each of the drawers is veneered and inlaid in three sections, two large ones being on the sides and a smaller one in the centre. The four inner corners of each of the large sections are ornamented with fan designs; and an oval inlay, apparently a shell, is in the skirt which shows a form of the cyma curve. About 1785–1800.

No. 736 resembles No. 728 in having the front divided into twelve panels, each of which is covered by a satinwood veneer. On the skirt there is a small panel which interrupts the graceful curves between the French bracket feet. The beading on the edges of the drawers will be noticed. About 1785–1800.

Nos. 737 and 738 are very similar, having swell fronts, inlaid designs with rounded ends, mentioned in note 1 in section 96, oval brass handles and French bracket feet; the principal difference is that in No. 737 there is a curved skirt, but in No. 738 the base is plain. The remark in the comment on Nos. 733 and 734 in regard to illustrations of similar objects is applicable to these two bureaus. About 1785–1800.

The straight front bureaus in the Hepplewhite style are shown in Nos. 739–744. These are more frequently found than those with curved fronts, doubtless because they were less expensive, as mentioned in section 93, and more of them were made.

Nos. 739 and 740 are ornamented with rectangular lines of inlay on the drawers. No. 739 has straight bracket feet, similar to those in No. 725, probably indicating a transitional form; the handles are of the bail type. In No. 740 there are two drawers at the top and the skirt is cut in the favorite curves. Again we see the characteristic line of inlay on the base. About 1785–1800.

731 (Upper) Mr. W. W. Lanahan.   732 (Upper) Mr. Edgar G. Miller, Jr.
733 (Centre) Mr. & Mrs. Henry L. Duer.   734 (Centre) Mr. & Mrs. Richard L. Cary.
735 (Lower) Mr. John C. Toland.   736 (Lower) Metropolitan Museum of Art.

No. 741 is in a different form, having two shallow drawers at the top, under which is a large drawer resembling those in the "bureau desks" Nos. 827 and 828, and also those in the secretary–bookcases Nos. 857–859. The base is ornamented with a straight line of inlay and the skirt is cut in cyma curves. About 1785–1800.

In No. 742 each of the four drawers has inlaid horizontal lines with rounded ends which are mentioned in note 1, C, in section 96. The top, the skirt and the feet are also ornamented with lines of inlay, those on the feet being unusual, as in No. 726. Here, too, the cyma curves appear on the beaded skirt, and may also be seen on the left side. About 1785–1800.

No. 743 is not provided with inlay, but has interesting original handles which are octagonal in shape, a type which is referred to and illustrated in section 39. On each of these handles a beehive appears and the words "Nothing without labor," which reminds us of the maxims of Benjamin Franklin. The beading on the edges of the drawers is well seen. The usual curved skirt is not seen here. About 1785–1800.

Perhaps No. 744 should have been placed next to No. 735, both being plentifully supplied with inlaid fans in the corners. At the centre of each drawer is a small square of inlay within which is an inlaid six pointed design, not a keyhole, in different colored woods; and the same design on a larger scale is at the centre of the skirt. The skirt itself is cut in double cyma curves, as to which see section 23. The handles are of an earlier period, as appears in illustration No. 13 in section 39. About 1785–1800.

Section 96. Sheraton style bureaus.—In these eight bureaus, Nos. 745–752, two distinctive features of the Sheraton style appear, one being the round corner columns projecting beyond the body of the bureau, as in Nos. 745–748, and the other being the round and tapering feet, which are seen in perhaps all cases.[1] In this connection the remarks at the beginning of the previous section in regard to the "Hepplewhite–Sheraton period" should be read.

1. A. Two drawings by Sheraton of bureaus are on plate 15 of the "Appendix" to his "Drawing Book," opposite page 382 in the edition by Mr. J. M. Bell.

B. In one of these drawings the round front columns are placed forward beyond the line of the body of the bureau, are reeded, and continue down to form the feet. This is the design which is copied in Nos. 745–748. The same design appears on the Sheraton style tables Nos. 1521, 1585 and 1610, on the sideboards Nos. 991–993 and on other articles.

C. In the other drawing is the form of parallel lines of inlay which are rounded at each end. These are seen in the bureaus Nos. 741–742 and others, and in the desk No. 827 and others and in many sideboards. This form of inlay seems to have been copied by Sheraton from a design of Shearer; see section 127, note 6. The form was also used by our cabinet makers in combination with Hepplewhite designs, as in the bureaus above cited.

D. The veneer on the drawers was generally of mahogany, but other kinds of wood were used, such as the expensive satinwood and the inexpensive cherry and maple.

E. Small dressing glasses in the Sheraton style, used on bureaus, are shown in section 152.

737 (UPPER) MRS. F. G. BOYCE, JR.   738 (UPPER) MR. J. F. H. MAGINN.
739 (CENTRE) MR. BLANCHARD RANDALL.   740 (CENTRE) MR. EDGAR G. MILLER, JR.
741 (LOWER) DR. JAMES BORDLEY, JR.   742 (LOWER) SHEPPARD & ENOCH PRATT HOSPITAL.

411

No. 745 is a handsome bureau with a straight front. The particular features are the drawers, each veneered with two pieces of crotch satinwood and surrounded by bands of mahogany with small pieces of satinwood at intervals; the columns are outside the body of the bureau, are "ringed" at the top and are then reeded, and continue down to form the feet—a method much used in New England. The top of the bureau is so shaped at the corners as to cover the tops of the columns. On the edge of the top and on the skirt are lines of inlay and the skirt is cut in cyma curves. Casters are properly found on the feet, but are not essential. The handles are of an earlier period. About 1795–1810.

In No. 746 the drawers, finely veneered with curly maple, are in a "swell," or "bow," shape, the curves of which are most clearly seen at the ends. The columns are "ringed" at intervals, and continue down to form the feet as in No. 745. The drawers have bead moldings on all edges, and brass knobs. About 1795–1810.

No. 747 is in the same general form, but with a straight front and skirt. The reeded projecting columns terminate in round feet, as in the two previous pieces. Each of the drawers is veneered with two pieces of fine matched[2] mahogany. The brass handles are of the "ring" type, and are suspended from the top as shown in section 39, figure 46. About 1795–1810.

No. 748 also has a swell front with reeded projecting columns, and the legs are also partly reeded. The drawers have wide lines of light inlay, around which are thin inlaid lines. The handles are of the oval type, and the base is plain. About 1800–1815.

It may be repeated here that the designs in the books of Chippendale, Hepplewhite and Sheraton were seldom copied exactly in our American pieces, and that the cabinet makers who made furniture in the periods in which the styles were in vogue adopted the general characteristics of the styles, but often with modifications. Their collective work is known as furniture in the "school" of Chippendale, or Hepplewhite or Sheraton.

In Nos. 749 and 750 the fronts are in the swell, or bow, shape; the front of the former is similar to that of No. 746. In No. 749 there are no projecting columns, but the upright parts at the sides, called "stiles,"[3] are reeded down to the legs. On the left side of this bureau a sunken panel will be noticed and others will be seen in Nos. 751 and 757. No. 750 is a plainer bureau, of the same general design, frequently seen in our homes. About 1800–1815.

No. 751 is taller than other bureaus shown in this chapter, having five rows of graduated drawers instead of the usual four. The wood is curly maple; over the reeded "stiles" are small rectangular panels; and the sides are paneled as in No. 749. The bails of the handles are attached at the top, not at the sides, as also in figure 45 in illustration No. 16. About 1800–1815.

2.   As to "matched" pieces of wood, see section 32, note 2.

3.   In section 51, note 19, a "stile" in a chair is described as follows: "A stile and a back leg together form one upright piece of wood. The stile is the part above the leg." The word is also applied to other upright parts, as in this bureau.

It is said that sunken side panels in late eighteenth century bureaus and other pieces imply cheaper construction and relatively late date.

743 (Upper) Mr. & Mrs. Mason P. Morfit.
744 (Upper) Dr. James Bordley, Jr.
745 (Centre) Miss Mary K. Hinkley.
746 (Centre) Mr. & Mrs. William A. Dixon.
747 (Lower) Mrs. Edwin B. Niver.
748 (Lower) Mr. Charles Morris Howard.

749 (Upper) Miss Dora L. Murdoch.
751 (Lower) Mrs. John S. Gibbs, Jr.

750 (Upper) Mr. Edgar G. Miller, Jr.
752 (Lower) Miss Mary S. Kimmel.

In No. 752 we see a simple type of bureau which is interesting because of its resemblance, exclusive of feet, legs and handles, to the bureau, or chest of drawers, No. 608 which was made in the style of about 1700–1710, and is referred to in sections 79 and 93. After the passing of about one hundred years, the form and general appearance of the early bureau returns, with different kinds of moldings, legs and feet and with glass knobs instead of drop handles. The moldings are attached to the frame of the drawer, not to the framework enclosing the drawers which was the earlier style as mentioned in section 93, note 3, C. About 1800–1820.

Section 97. Sheraton style bureaus with mirrors attached.—The four interesting pieces, Nos. 753–756, shown in this section, are called "dressing tables" by some writers and merely "bureaus" by others; but a more descriptive term is adopted as the title of this section. For a long period it was the custom to hang a mirror on the wall over a lowboy or bureau, to assist in the arts of the toilet, and later it was the fashion to place on a bureau a tier of two or three small drawers, with a swinging mirror attached, as mentioned in section 152; but in the early part of the nineteenth century the mirror itself was made a part of the bureau, and was supported by upright posts, as in the illustrations here shown. In our modern usage the term "dressing table" seems to apply to a piece of furniture which resembles a table to some extent at least; and therefore "dressing tables" are not discussed in this chapter on bureaus, but in the chapter on tables, section 168, and the four pieces here illustrated are termed "Sheraton style bureaus with mirrors attached."

In Nos. 753–755 the prominent features of the bureaus are in the style of Sheraton; but in No. 756 there are indications of the Empire style, as is mentioned in the comment. The dates of these pieces are regarded as being from about 1800 to 1820.

The description in section 96 of the bureau No. 745 in the Sheraton style is partly applicable to No. 753, namely: "the columns are outside the body of the bureau, are 'ringed' at the top and are then reeded, and continue down to form the feet—a method much used in New England. The top of the bureau is so shaped at the corners as to cover the columns." The body of this early Sheraton style piece has two long and two short drawers instead of the four long ones generally found in bureaus; and the drawers begin more than the usual distance above the floor. On the top is a tier of three small drawers, made as a part of the bureau, upon which a mirror is supported by two upright reeded posts to which are attached scroll brackets and a form of the letter "C" which is mentioned in the next paragraph. This piece is delicate and handsome throughout, except that the wooden knobs seem to be somewhat plain for their surroundings.[1] About 1800–1820.

1. This bureau appears as No. 545 in the catalogue of the noted auction sale of the antiques of the late Howard Reifsnyder, of Philadelphia, in April, 1929. Another handsome example, said to be of about 1800–1810, appears as No. 713 in the catalogue of the "Girl Scouts Loan Exhibition" in New York, in September, 1929, where it is termed a "Sheraton style bureau." Another bureau almost identical with No. 754 was found by the writer in a private house in Baltimore, making the fourth bureau of this type in Maryland.

No. 754 is of the same general character, but is probably of a somewhat later date than the preceding piece for the reason that the spiral legs are heavier and less delicate. There are four small drawers in the body, and under the mirror are two drawers instead of the three in the previous piece. A panel of light wood extends across the front underneath the top. The mirror and the posts and brackets supporting it are similar to those in No. 753. The letter "C," a popular design[2] of an earlier period, appears on the side of each of the two posts supporting the mirror. Here also the knobs are of wood. About 1810–1820.

In the next bureau, No. 755, the early Sheraton style is again seen, especially in the finely reeded and projecting columns ending in brass feet, and in the outlines of the piece as a whole. In some respects the body bears close resemblances to two serving tables made in the Sheraton style by Duncan Phyfe and illustrated in the chapter on tables, Nos. 1444 and 1445. Here the shape and fine reeding of the legs and the posts supporting the mirror, and the elegance of the piece, suggest the skill of the New York maker. The brass handles are of the lion's head and ring type. Instead of the usual tier of two or three small connected drawers under the mirror, the two drawers are separated; and a shelf is under the lower drawer. About 1810–1825.

No. 756 is of a different type, in which we see both the early and the later Sheraton styles and the Early American Empire style. In this piece, as in the previous one, the early Sheraton style is shown in the shape and the delicate reeding of the legs. The later Sheraton style is indicated by the somewhat heavy spiral carvings of the thick posts supporting the mirror and of the stretcher connecting the legs. The legs are of the "curule" type, derived from the ancient Roman "curule" chair, which is seen in the style of Sheraton in figure 30 in illustration No. 234, and in designs of Duncan Phyfe in the backs of the chairs Nos. 320–323. This "curule" design is regarded as an Empire style feature,[3] as are also the feet of the paw type. About 1810–1820.

Section 98. Empire style bureaus.—The early type of the bureaus which are commonly said to be in the "Empire" style had the benefit of several desirable features of the previous Sheraton styles; but in a few years these desirable features gave way to the forms of the style which we call the "Early American Empire." A few years later, about 1830–1840, the American cabinet makers degenerated into the "Late American Empire style" which was followed by the Victorian and later styles. These styles were all briefly discussed in sections 18–22, and are now again mentioned because the gradual changes in styles are perhaps more

2.   See for example, the letter "C" in the frame of mirrors in the Chippendale style, such as No. 1103; also see the Index, under "Scrolls."

3.   The Empire influence is seen in the curule legs on other chairs made by Duncan Phyfe; see plate 8 and page 64 in the book of Mr. Cornelius entitled "Furniture Masterpieces of Duncan Phyfe." See also note on curule chairs in section 52, note 9.

   Similar curule legs supporting a table appear in a design by Sheraton which is shown in the English book entitled "Chippendale, Sheraton and Hepplewhite furniture designs," arranged by Mr. J. M. Bell, page 160.

753 (UPPER) ANONYMOUS.   754 (UPPER) MRS. E. P. BRUNDIGE.
755 (LOWER) MRS. PAUL H. MILLER.   756 (LOWER) MRS. E. P. BRUNDIGE.

clearly seen in bureaus than in some other articles. The classification of the bureaus illustrated in this section may not be precisely correct in all respects; most of them are not discussed in the books on antique furniture, not being of sufficient age; but in this book for amateur collectors they are entitled to be exhibited. For the purpose of this section, eight bureaus, Nos. 757–764, may be regarded as being in the Early American Empire style, which lasted from about 1815 until about 1825–1830. The Late American Empire style is represented by the two pieces Nos. 765–766, and also by the miniature bureau No. 774. Nos. 767 and 768 are in the Victorian style. A great many bureaus in these different styles, with numerous variations, are seen in our homes and it has been difficult to make a selection.

In Nos. 757 and 758 the two small drawers at the top extend forward beyond the three larger ones below, that is, they "overhang" the lower drawers. These overhanging parts are supported by columns, parts of which are finely carved and reeded and are beyond the line of the body, or frame, of the bureaus. In No. 757 the lower part of the columns is reeded, above which are "rings" and carved designs; and above the columns are small carved panels. The feet are ringed, and a large sunken panel will be noticed on the side as also in Nos. 749 and 751. Some of these features, but not the overhang, appear in somewhat similar forms on the bureaus in the Sheraton style shown in section 96. In No. 758, also, the columns are reeded and are carved at the top and bottom, with small panels above; and the feet are reeded. The drawers of each of these bureaus are veneered with fine mahogany, especially noticeable on No. 757, in which the mahogany is "matched";[1] and each has round wooden knobs. The large drawers are in the swell, or bow, form in No. 757, and are straight in No. 758. The base of each of these pieces is straight and plain, as in almost all bureaus in the Empire style,[2] and in No. 757 is thick and heavy. About 1810–1820.

No. 759 shows a more decided change from the Sheraton style to the Empire style. The top has become prominent, with its tier of three small drawers for toilet articles and with a plain upright back above. The overhang continues in the manner seen in the two preceding pieces, supported by two columns which are less delicately ornamented than in the preceding ones, having rings instead of reeding. Brass knobs are on the drawers and the feet are ringed. As usual in this period, the mahogany veneer is very good. About 1820–1830.

Nos. 760 and 761 are shown here through the courtesy of Mr. L. V. Lockwood, in whose book entitled "Colonial Furniture in America," volume 1, they appear as Nos. 146 and 144. In No. 760 the columns are beyond the frame of the bureau and extend down, forming the feet, as in the Sheraton style bureaus Nos. 745 and 746. The columns are ornamented at the top and bottom with a cylindrical and carved design known as "pineapple" and supposed to represent that fruit. This design is similar to that seen on the bedstead No. 1070 in section

1.   As to "matched" wood, see note 2 in section 32.

2.   The base and the overhang give to these two bureaus a date in the Empire style on the principle that the date of the latest part of a piece of furniture determines the date of the whole, as mentioned in section 6.

757 (UPPER) MRS. MURRAY STEUART HARTSHORNE.   758 (UPPER) MRS. MAURICE F. RODGERS.
759 (CENTRE) MR. & MRS. C. E. MCLANE.   760 (CENTRE) LOCKWOOD, COL. FURN., FIG. 146.
761 (LOWER) LOCKWOOD, COL. FURN., FIG. 144.   762 (LOWER) MR. EDGAR G. MILLER, JR.

137. The central parts of the columns, which appear too light in the illustration, are carved in a twisted or spiral form. Above the top are two small drawers and a curved back. The drawers are ornamented with lines of inlay, and oval brass handles are in the Hepplewhite and Sheraton styles. The skirt is cut in cyma curves. About 1810–1820.

No. 761 is a bureau of a popular type of the period. In front of the upright sides are half–round columns which are heavily decorated with carved designs of leaves, and near the top with pineapples and of a more familiar kind than that in the preceding bureau. The three small drawers at the top slightly overhang the four large drawers below. Here we see the first example on a bureau of the animals' claw, or paw, foot, which was a favorite in the Empire style and in other chapters is seen on tables, wardrobes and other articles. The handles are of the ring type. About 1810–1820.

In Nos. 762, 763 and 764 the same general form of bureau continues. There is a slight overhang of the upper drawers in these pieces. No. 763 has a tier of two small drawers with a mirror above; the columns are without carving. In the next bureau the columns are ornamented with brass pieces at the top and bottom. In Nos. 762 and 764 the feet are of the animals' claw, or paw, type, but in No. 763 they are in a ball form, such as those on the lowboy No. 672, a type of feet which was revived after about one hundred years. Nos. 762 and 763 have glass knobs on the drawers and No. 764 has brass ring handles. The fine veneer of the drawers in each piece will be noticed. No. 764 has a high mirror attached, which requires the illustration to be on a smaller scale than the previous ones. The carved pieces attached to the feet in Nos. 764 and 766 are suggestive of the wings on the feet of some of the sofas of the period, as in Nos. 591–592 and others. About 1820–1830.

In Nos. 765 and 766, and the miniature bureau No. 774, we see examples of the Late Empire style which are not now admired and are regarded as "coarse and massive."[3] They well illustrate the changes for the worse in the style of the furniture of the Late Empire period, a style which has been ignorantly called by the patriotic name "Colonial," as mentioned in section 1, note 1 in this book.

In No. 765 the body of the bureau has a rounded overhanging top drawer, the front being in a form of the "torus" molding mentioned in note 4 in section 85 in connection with highboys. The round and short columns are thick and heavy. The mirror is supported by upright posts with brackets in cyma curves resembling somewhat those in No. 754. About 1820–1840.

No. 766 is not so heavily built. The upper drawer overhangs the two large lower ones. Carved wings are attached to the paw feet, as mentioned in the comment on No. 764. The curved brackets supporting the mirror are assisted in maintaining their position by two marine animals, probably dolphins, such as are seen on the card table No. 1556. The knobs on this and the preceding bureau are of

3. The "coarse and massive" character of these bureaus was not adopted for any purpose for which a bureau was used; but we may at least admire the fine mahogany veneer with which the furn'ture was ornamented and also the good workmanship which is seen in the cabinet work.

763 (Upper) Mrs. Rignal W. Baldwin.   764 (Upper) Miss Mary S. Schenck.
765 (Centre) Miss Eleanor S. Cohen.   766 (Centre) Coll. of Mrs. Jordan Stabler.
767 (Lower) Maryland Society Colonial Dames.   768 (Lower) Mrs. C. E. Henderson.

glass.[4] Two separate drawers are under the mirror, as in No. 755, instead of a tier of drawers as in No. 753. About 1830–1840.

The miniature bureau No. 774, mentioned in section 100, is of a type frequently seen in the Late Empire period. Instead of heavy round columns in front it has still heavier (in proportion) supports in the form of scrolls, and also heavy scroll feet. The sides are paneled, as in No. 757 and others.[5] About 1840.

Section 99. Victorian style bureaus.—These two bureaus, Nos. 767 and 768, are too modern to call for our attention as antiques; but they are interesting because each one combines in one piece several designs which were suggested by, or copied from, earlier styles, and which were apparently mingled together according to the fancy of the cabinet maker. This method of design has been noticed in a group of chairs, Nos. 346–358, which are classified in this book as "American Empire style" chairs but are of about the same date as these Victorian bureaus, that is, about the year 1840, or later. Without spending too much time and space on this subject it is worth while to point out in the notes certain features of these two bureaus, beginning with No. 767, in which several different styles are apparent.[1]

No. 768 shows other points of similarity to earlier styles.[2] These two bureaus and some other pieces made in the Victorian period are interesting puzzles if we try to discover the "why and wherefore" of their designs. Their makers may have had at hand some "old-fashioned" articles of furniture made in the styles of Chippendale and Sheraton; but the furniture in the Hepplewhite style was apparently not appreciated.

4.   See section 40, entitled "Knobs of brass, glass and wood."

5.   A discussion of a similar miniature piece is in "Antiques," May, 1926, page 299.

1.   In No. 767 the large mirror and the long and narrow mirrors in the upright posts have arches which were doubtless suggested by arches in certain Chippendale Gothic style chairs, such as Nos. 94–105, and in the Late American Empire style chairs Nos. 355–357. At the top of the mirror is a small carved design of an "anthemion," or honeysuckle, which is seen on the chairs Nos. 178–179, and on the settees Nos. 522–523; see also note 48 in section 51. On the front corners of the bureau we notice projecting columns suggesting those seen on the corners of the bureaus in the Sheraton style, Nos. 745–748; and also that the marble top is cut in a form covering the tops of these columns, as was the wooden top in the bureaus referred to. The reeded feet resemble those on the Sheraton style bureau No. 758 and others. The panel on the side is like that of No. 757. Other features of previous styles may be seen or imagined on this bureau; those mentioned seem to indicate that the maker of this Victorian piece was familiar with the work of some of his predecessors and saw no reason why he should not combine any and all the features which he liked best. About 1840–1850.

2.   The elaborate uprights supporting the mirror consist of several small "C" curves and two large "S" curves; the "C" curves are seen on many articles in the Chippendale period, such as the mirrors Nos. 1103–1106, and on the label of Benjamin Randolph which is illustration No. 1. The "S" curves are an earlier type of decoration. On the body of the bureau we see that the corners are cut in a rounded form, as are also the corners of the small outside drawers under the mirror; similar corners are seen on the bookcase No. 875 and the desk No. 836. The curved fronts of the three small drawers combine to make a serpentine curve. Finally the cyma curve, seen in section 23, is not overlooked, as the outline of the frame of the mirror consists of several curves of that kind; and the apron, or skirt, of the bureau is in the form of two cyma curves, with two "C" curves in the centre. Moreover, the shape of the glass is about the same as that in the mirror No. 1118. About 1840–1860.

For other Victorian matters, see section 22 and the Index under the word "Victorian."

Section 100. Miniature bureaus.—Articles of antique furniture made in small sizes may have been intended for children as toys[1] or for grown people as curiosities or for the safe–keeping of small possessions. They were made in about the same designs as those of the larger pieces; and the six bureaus here illustrated in Nos. 769–774 will be seen to resemble some of the full sized pieces shown in previous sections of this chapter. Without mentioning in detail the particular features of these miniature or small bureaus, we will briefly notice their styles. For the purpose of this section the illustrations are of about the same size, although the bureaus are of different sizes.

769 (Upper) Mrs. Miles White, Jr. 770 (Upper) Dr. Henry M. Fitz- 771 (Upper) Mrs. John S. Gibbs, Jr.
772 (Lower) Mr. Blanchard Ran-   hugh.   774 (Lower) Mrs. Edward Shoe-
       dall.   773 (Lower) Mr. Arthur E. Cole.   maker.

No. 769 is about ten inches high. The drop handles, the ball feet and the moldings on the frames surrounding the drawers are all of the period of about 1700–1720.

1. In Mr. Lockwood's "Colonial Furniture," volume 1, figure 1, is an illustration of an English "doll house," made about 1700 to 1725, furnished in the Queen Anne style of the period. The front walls of the house are removed and the three floors are seen with the furniture in position. There are three bedrooms, each having a bedstead heavily draped. In some of the rooms are small figures of the family (and the cook) dressed in the styles of the period. An American "doll house" of the period of Hepplewhite or Sheraton would be very interesting.

Several dolls' houses in the Victoria and Albert Museum in London are illustrated in "Antiques," December, 1930, pages 494–497.

No. 770 is a small bureau, but not exactly a miniature. The style of Chippendale is seen in the straight bracket feet, the moldings at the top and bottom and the large willow style handles. About 1760–1780.

No. 771 is a miniature piece, also in the Chippendale style, made of a light wood. The straight bracket feet and the moldings will be noticed. The wooden knobs have no doubt been substituted for the original brass handles. About 1760–1780.

In Nos. 772 and 773 we reach the style of Hepplewhite. On these pieces may be seen the French bracket feet, the curved aprons, or skirts, the mahogany veneer on the drawers, and the line of inlay on No. 773, all of which features may be seen in one or another of the bureaus in section 95. The original oval brass handles on these two pieces seem to have been replaced with others of a later type. About 1785–1800.

No. 774 has been referred to in the last paragraph of section 98, which treats of the bureaus of the American Empire style. This piece is the latest in point of date of these miniatures, being in the style of about 1840. See also the desk portion of the secretary–bookcase. No. 867.

CHAPTER XII

DESKS; SECRETARIES; SECRETARY–BOOKCASES; BOOKCASES CHINA CABINETS

Section 101. Definitions and general remarks.—In the previous chapter, entitled "Bureaus," section 93, it is said that the word "bureau" in its original sense meant a desk, in which sense the word is now used in England; and that the most usual type of desk is in reality a chest of drawers with a writing portion above.[1] Various words have been used in our country and England for pieces of furniture made for writing purposes, as mentioned in the note.[2]

1. See the chapter on "Highboys," section 82, illustrations Nos. 625–627, in which a chest of drawers, a highboy and a slant top desk all of about the year 1710, appear together in order to show their similarities and differences.

2. A. Without stating the various meanings given to the word "desk" in the books of Chippendale and Sheraton and in the modern English books and dictionaries, we may refer to Mr. Lockwood's "Colonial Furniture in America," volume 1, page 233, where it is said that in our country in the first part of the eighteenth century "there were four words used interchangeably to denote a piece of furniture for writing purposes, viz., desk, scrutoire, escritoire and bureau." In the Century Dictionary the word "scrutoire" is defined as an "obsolete erroneous form of 'scritoire' for 'escritoire.'"

B. In Mr. Lockwood's book it is also said on pages 210 and 217 that prior to about the year 1700 the word "desk" meant a box for holding writing materials and also for holding the family Bible. Some years before that date a new piece of furniture for writing purposes, called a "scrutoire" or "scriptoire," began to appear in the inventories of the estates of deceased persons. This word "scrutoire" is the equivalent of "desk." Mr. Lockwood's chapter is entitled "Desks and scrutoires," and includes the pieces which in this chapter are called "secretaries" and also "bookcases." See also section 77, note 1, C, in regard to the early boxes, and note 1 in the next section.

C. Mr. Cescinsky in his "English and American Furniture," page 146, remarks: "I object to the name 'desk,' as used in America, to indicate pieces as varied as a writing table, a bureau, a secretary or a slope fronted chest with an upper part in cabinet or bookcase form."

The terms used in this chapter, "Desks; secretaries; secretary–bookcases," seem to be more appropriate than certain others of indefinite meaning which are frequently employed. The reader of English or American books and magazine articles on antique desks, whether illustrated or not, is liable to be confused by the different terms employed. Every writer, including the present one, uses the words which he thinks most appropriate.

In its largest sense the word "desk" may apply to any article of furniture which is intended for writing purposes, but it is most frequently applied to a chest of drawers with a writing portion, as mentioned above.

A slanting lid desk furnished with a cabinet above, containing pigeonholes and drawers for papers, but not long shelves for books, is here called a "secretary";[3] and a piece having a similar outside appearance but having mainly shelves in the upper portion, and for books only, or chiefly, is here called a "secretary–bookcase."

A "secretary–bookcase" becomes a "bookcase" if, instead of a desk below, it has a cabinet with doors and drawers. These pieces are now sometimes used for china instead of books.

A "china cabinet" often resembles a bookcase; it is intended for china but is often used for books.

Several pieces with variations in form from the usual type of desks have names descriptive of some special feature, such as "cylinder" desks, "tambour" desks, "bureau" desks and "fire screen" desks; all of which, and others, appear in this chapter.[4]

The most familiar type of desk consists, as mentioned above, of a chest of drawers with a writing compartment above. In most of these desks the lower portion, under the writing compartment, will be seen to resemble the bureaus made in the same period. For example, the lower portion of the desks in the Chippendale style resemble closely the bureaus in the Chippendale style; and so also the desks and bureaus in the Hepplewhite style. In each style the fronts of the desks, like those of the bureaus, may be straight or serpentine in form; the kind of

---

3.   A fine example is shown in Nos. 839–840, open and closed.

In the Century Dictionary a "secretary" is defined as "usually a high cabinet–shaped piece (of furniture) as distinguished from a writing table or desk."

Instead of the word "secretary" Mr. Lockwood uses the expression "slant–top scrutoire with bookcase top," or "slant–top scrutoire with cabinet top"; and Miss Morse in her "Furniture of the Olden Time," pages 128–137, uses for the same piece the words "desk" and "desk with cabinet top" as well as "secretary." It is said that there is no etymological connection between the words "secretary" and "escritoire" or "scrutoire."

In "Antiques," October, 1926, pages 272–273, this matter of names is discussed in an editorial entitled "Concerning desks."

See note 5 to the tambour piece No. 825, in section 106, in which a quotation is made from the will of George Washington, referring to "my bureau, or as cabinet makers call it, tambour secretary."

4.   In "The Furniture Collectors' Glossary," by Mr. Lockwood, seventeen types of desks are mentioned. In the English book entitled "A glossary of English Furniture" the words "Secretary, Bureau, Escritoire, Scritoire, or Secretaire" are placed together and are defined as "A desk with writing appliances."

feet and handles will be seen to be the same, or similar; and inlay was used as a decorative feature in both articles when inlay was in style. These similarities will be pointed out in the comments on some of the desks and other pieces.

A peculiarity of many antique desks with slanting lids is that the lid when opened for writing is too high for the convenience of one sitting on a modern or antique chair of the average height. It will also be noticed that in some desks the lid is more upright than in others; and that the drawers are generally "graduated," as mentioned in connection with bureaus in section 93, note 3, B.

Desks with slanting lids passed out of style in our country about 1800–1810, but slanting lids were used later in secretary–bookcases, as in the Victorian style piece No. 868.

Section 102. Early types of desks.—As mentioned in note 2, B, in the previous section, the word "desk," prior to about the year 1700, meant a box for holding books and writing materials. These boxes, however, are seldom found outside of museums, and although important from a historical standpoint are not generally interesting to the amateur collector, and are therefore merely mentioned here.[1] We therefore begin the subject of desks with articles which may be easily recognized as intended for writing purposes.

In our country three types of early desks have been found, which may be described as follows: those with a vertical, or straight, front, the upper part of which falls forward and down; those on a frame and with a slanting lid, or top, and turned legs; and those with a slanting lid, or top, and round ball feet. These three types are illustrated in this section.

No. 775 is an example of the first type,[2] having a straight front, the upper part of which falls forward and down. This desk, dated about 1700, is made in two parts. The lower part has three large drawers, drop handles and ball feet and resembles the chest of drawers of the same period, No. 608, which is mentioned also in the second paragraph below. In the upper part, the front when open, as here, discloses pigeonholes and small drawers, and provides a writing surface which is supported by metal rods which fold up when the front is closed. This form of desk was copied from English pieces of the period.[3] A century or more later a similar form was used in desks Nos. 835 and 836, shown in section 108. About 1700.

1. Boxes of this kind are mentioned in the chapter on "Chests," section 77, note 1, C. Knife boxes are illustrated in connection with sideboards, section 131. See also the Index and note 2, B, in the preceding section.
2. This is copied by permission from Mr. Lockwood's "Colonial Furniture," volume 1, figure 238.
3. In Mr. Cescinsky's "English Furniture," volume 1, figures 130, 153, 154, English desks of this type are shown, handsomely ornamented with marquetry and veneer, dated about 1700. The American desk is a very plain copy.

   The rounded "torus" molding below the cornice is the front of a drawer, supposedly concealed, of which other examples are seen on highboys of about the same period, as on No. 636 and in the Empire style bureau No. 765.

The second type of early desks, shown in No. 776, has a slanting lid and "turned"[4] legs, with stretchers. In some cases the desk and the frame below are in two parts; but in this one they are both made as one piece. The slanting lid, being closed, conceals the pigeonholes and drawers. The date is about 1700–1725.

The third type, which is the most usual one, having a slanting lid, ball feet and drop handles, is illustrated in Nos. 777 and 778, a desk which is shown closed and open. This type is also seen in No. 627 in the chapter on highboys. The lower part of this desk has much the same features as in No. 775 and as in the chest of drawers No. 608. The slanting lid falls forward and down and when opened is supported by "pulls" which in early pieces are small and square. The pigeonholes with ornamental "curtains" at the top are pleasing in design. Two special features will be seen; in the writing compartment the pigeonholes and drawers at each end extend forward beyond the line of the others, being, as it is said, "advanced" or "stepped"; and in the lower portion, above the two smaller drawers, there is an enclosed space, not a drawer, called a "well," which may be opened by pushing back a "slide" as is shown in No. 778. In some of the later pieces both of these features may be seen; and bracket feet may be used instead of the ball feet, as appears in the next section. It will be noticed that in this there is no central compartment with a door, separating the pigeonholes, as is generally seen in later desks; nor are there any "secret" drawers, unless the "well" be regarded as one. Finely veneered desks of this type are occasionally found. A molding *around* the drawers, not *on* the drawers, will be noticed; and also the heavy molding on the base in front, and on the sides. About 1700–1710.

Section 103. Desks; later and Chippendale styles.—After about the year 1725 the types of desks shown in Nos. 775 and 776 in the previous section passed out of fashion; but slanting lid desks of the type shown in Nos. 777 and 778 continued in style with various changes in form until they finally ceased to be made in the early part of the nineteenth century. In this section we continue the subject of slanting lid desks from about the year 1725, above mentioned, to the end of the Chippendale period which in our country was about the year 1785.

In order to explain in advance the three groups in this section we first examine the two desks Nos. 779 and 780 which show the later development of the desk No. 778, and which have the "advanced" or "stepped" drawers in the writing portions; secondly, we see four slanting lid desks of various sizes, Nos. 781–784, which have one or more drawers which do not extend near to the floor, and are supported by separate frames on long or short legs as may be required for a convenient height; and, thirdly, there is a group of eighteen desks, Nos. 785–802, which are commonly said to be in the Chippendale style, a term which serves as a name for perhaps all American desks of this same general character until those designed in the style of Hepplewhite came into vogue and displaced those of the Chippendale style after their long period of fashion.

4. As to "turnings" and turned legs, see section 35.

775 (Upper) Met. Museum of Art.
777 (Lower) Mr. Edgar G. Miller, Jr.

776 (Upper) Mr. L. V. Lockwood.
778 (Lower) Mr. Edgar G. Miller, Jr.

No. 779 resembles the preceding desk in having a "well," not clearly seen, and also in having "advanced," or "stepped," small drawers in the writing portion; but other features show a change from the style of the earlier type. In the centre between the small drawers is a compartment with a lock; straight bracket feet take the place of the ball feet; and the handles on the large drawers are of a type which succeeded the "drop" style, as shown in the illustrations in section 39. About 1730–1750.

No. 780 also has the "advanced," or "stepped," small drawers in the writing portion, but the "well" has disappeared and there is thus room for another large drawer. The design of the interior is interesting; all of the small drawers are concave in form; the central compartment has no door; and the two architectural "pilasters" on the sides of the compartment are the fronts of vertical drawers. It is said that one of the vertical drawers was for paid bills and that the other was for those which had not received attention. In some desks these drawers appear to be books, as in No. 808 and others. The legs are of the short cabriole style, with club, or Dutch, feet; and the frames surrounding the large drawers have a small beaded molding. About 1730–1750.

In Nos. 781–783 we see three desks of a type which was made from about 1740–1750 and perhaps later. The frame is made separately and the writing portion is set in a molding around the top of the frame. In each of these desks the frame portion resembles in some respects a lowboy or the lower part of a highboy, and the "skirt" is cut in designs which resemble some seen in the illustrations of those pieces.

No. 781 is a pleasing desk which may be regarded as in the Queen Anne style, because of the character of the legs which, however, are not exactly in the cabriole form, being almost straight,[1] terminating in club, or Dutch, feet, which in this case all face to the front, as in the lowboys Nos. 678 and 682; and also because of the "skirt" of the frame which is cut in cyma curves and furnished with pendants, as in the highboys and lowboys of the period. There is only one drawer, which is in the writing portion. The small "pulls" which support the slanting top when opened are of the same type as those in No. 777. About 1740–1750.

In No. 782 there are two drawers in the writing portion which rests upon a frame, the skirt of which is cut in a flat design. The legs are in the cabriole form and terminate in club, or Dutch, grooved feet. In this desk the "pulls" which support the lid are larger than in the previous pieces, being about the same in height as the drawer between them; this form of pulls continues in almost all of the later desks. About 1740–1750.

No. 783 differs from the two preceding desks in having one drawer in the writing portion and another in the frame; and also in having cabriole legs and ball and claw feet in the Chippendale style; all the legs terminate in ball and claw feet. On the slanting lid are three inlaid but almost invisible six–pointed stars, an early form seldom seen in the books. The skirt of the frame is cut in cyma curves and resembles that of the highboy No. 642. About 1760–1770.

1.   Legs of this type may also be seen in certain tables of the period, as in Nos. 1289 and 1308.

In No. 784 we see another form of desk, in which the framework is lowered because of the increased number of drawers, in this case three. The frame rests on short cabriole legs having club, or Dutch, feet. The skirt, as in other pieces, is cut in a scrolled form, somewhat similar to that used on some of the highboys and lowboys of the period. This desk is of curly maple. About 1740–1750.

The next eighteen illustrations, Nos. 785–802, are of slanting lid desks in the Chippendale style. Many of these pieces are handsome and all of them are interesting, although they are in the same general form, differing mainly in the kinds of feet and handles, and in the design and arrangement of the interior of the writing portion. The cabinet makers seem to have been very ingenious in designing these interiors in such a variety of ornamental forms, and also in devising and locating the secret drawers.[2]

In the desks here shown the lower portions follow the general form of the bureaus of the period, such as Nos. 717–720. Almost all the desks have straight fronts, although several reversed serpentine fronts appear, such as Nos. 787–789. The feet are of either (1) the ball and claw type or (2) the bracket type, the latter being either straight or in the "ogee" form, as seen also on the bureaus of the period in the previous chapter. The expensive ball and claw feet were not always used on the more elaborate pieces; for example, only one of the three fine reversed serpentine front desks mentioned above has ball and claw feet; the other two have ogee bracket feet.[3] The wood in the finer Chippendale style desks is almost always either mahogany or walnut.[4]

In many of the desks in the Chippendale style there is a small rounded, or "bead," molding on the frame surrounding the drawer; but when there is a molding upon a desk made in the later style of Hepplewhite the molding is upon the drawer itself, not upon the frame. This matter is also mentioned in connection with bureaus and other articles in section 93, note 3, C.

"Block–front" desks in the Chippendale style are regarded as the most important and valuable of our American desks. These are not shown in this section, but in section 117 in the next chapter, entitled "Block–front furniture," for the reason that the "block–front" is the main subject of interest.

Examining the illustrations Nos. 785 and 786 we see two fine desks with straight fronts and ball and claw feet. In the former the "knees" above the feet are carved, which is an unusual treatment; in the latter the handles are of the bail type. The fine grain of the mahogany will be noticed. About 1755–1785.

2.   Most of the secret drawers or boxes are placed behind the central compartment which is almost always found in desks in the Chippendale style. In one of the desks, No. 792, there are thirty–seven drawers and boxes. The vertical drawers on the sides of the central compartment are not regarded as secret. Naturally these hiding places could be discovered without much difficulty.

3.   See section 23, entitled "The cyma curve," in which the "ogee" form is explained.

4.   No particular method of arrangement of these desks has been followed, except that those with ball and claw feet and those with reversed serpentine fronts are first shown. The others are particularly interesting because of the interiors of the writing portions; but no special importance can be attached to these interiors as indicating exact style or date.

779 (Upper) Mrs. John S. Gibbs, Jr.
781 (Centre) Mrs. John S. Gibbs, Jr.
783 (Lower) Metropolitan Museum.

780 (Upper) Dr. M. A. Abrams.
782 (Centre) Mrs. Miles White, Jr.
784 (Lower) Dr. James Bordley, Jr.

785 (Upper) Dr. M. A. Abrams.
787 (Centre) Mr. John S. McDaniel.
789 (Lower) Dr. M. A. Abrams.

786 (Upper) Mrs. G. Frank Baily.
788 (Centre) Mr. Arthur E. Cole.
790 (Lower) Collection of Mrs. Jordan Stabler.

In Nos. 787–789 the curve of the fronts of the lower portion is in the reversed serpentine form, that is, the curve is concave in the centre and convex at the sides; in this respect they are very similar to the bureaus Nos. 717–720 in the previous chapter.

In No. 787 even the bottom line of the slanting lid is in the reversed serpentine form, following the lines of the drawers; but the curve may not be visible in the illustration. In this piece the moldings on the framework surrounding the drawers are clearly seen; as also in the next three desks. The feet are of the ogee bracket type; and the "graduated" scrolls next to the feet are of an unusual form, somewhat similar to those seen in several lowboys, such as No. 708. As in the previous desk, the handles are of the bail type. The wood is cherry. About 1755–1785.

In No. 788 the reversed serpentine curve begins a short distance from the ends of the drawers, as in the bureaus Nos. 717 and 718 in the previous chapter; and an ornamental projection, or pendant, is at the centre of the base as on the bureau No. 719. The convex portions of the top drawer are shaped at the top in a manner to avoid ending in unsightly flat surfaces, as also in Nos. 789 and 790. The feet are in the ogee bracket form. About 1755–1785.

In Nos. 789 and 790 the feet are of the ball and claw type. No. 789 is furnished with large brass handles on the sides as aids in moving the desk. The convex portions of the reversed serpentine drawers are shaped at the top as in the previous piece.[5] About 1755–1785.

In No. 790 the front is in an unusual form, having three convex curves with two concave curves between them; the central convex portion is wider than those on the sides; and the shaping of the tops of the three convex curves is in a different form from that in the two preceding desks. Apparently this desk was not finished, as there are no handles. About 1755–1785.

In the next twelve illustrations, Nos. 791–802, the desks are very similar in the construction of the lower portions. They have four drawers, and even five in cases where there are two small drawers at the top instead of one. The feet are in the bracket form, either plain or of the ogee type. In some desks the front corners

---

5. A curious historical error is made by attaching the name "Governor Winthrop" to certain antique reversed serpentine front desks with a slanting lid and with drawers underneath and ball and claw feet, such as No. 789, in the style of Chippendale. There were three governors named Winthrop; John Winthrop, 1588–1649, governor of Massachusetts Bay Colony; his son John Winthrop, 1606–1676, governor of Connecticut; and the latter's son Fitz–John Winthrop, 1639–1707, governor of Connecticut. All of these governors died long before this type of desk was made. To scholars and other well informed persons this error is almost as objectionable as the error in the use of the word "Colonial" in connection with furniture of the Empire style made about 1830–1840. See a note on certain words in section 1, note 1, A.

The term "Governor Winthrop desk" when applied to reproductions is merely a trade name used by manufacturers in their advertisements of desks similar to No. 789. The words "Miles Standish desk" or "John Alden desk" would be equally appropriate.

The desire to use names of celebrities is also seen in "Martha Washington chairs," as in No. 419, and "Martha Washington sewing tables," as in No. 1557.

are cut into and "quarter-round" fluted columns are "applied" in the cuts made in the corners, which are said to be "recessed." In all of these desks, and in others having slanting lids, it is apparent that a desk of this type consists of a chest of drawers below, with a writing portion above, as mentioned in section 101. Because of the similarity of the lower portions, the comments on these desks will generally refer particularly to the writing portion, in which the small drawers and pigeonholes are in a great variety of designs and constitute the particular features of the pieces. The curved forms at the tops of the pigeonholes are called "curtains." Between the pigeonholes there is generally a compartment with a door, behind which are small drawers, and often secret drawers, or boxes; and on each side of the compartment there is generally a vertical drawer, as was seen in No. 780. The partitions between the pigeonholes are not well seen in the engravings, but should be noticed when examining a desk; in the fine pieces they are thin and dainty, and the front edges are cut in curved designs.

In No. 791 are two groups of four small drawers each, with concave fronts which begin about an inch from the sides. At the tops of the eight pigeonholes are "curtains" cut in an arched form seen on the skirts of many highboys and lowboys. The central compartment is enclosed by a concave door with shell carving at the top, and is flanked by "pilasters" which are in reality the fronts of the two vertical drawers. Fluted columns are applied on the "recessed" corners. About 1755–1785.

No. 792 is the desk referred to in note 2 of this section in which there are thirty-seven drawers and boxes, of which twelve are not visible, and seven although visible may not be thought to be drawers. The dark open door of the central compartment, which pulls out, shows four small drawers, behind which are twelve secret drawers, or boxes, cleverly arranged in places in the back which would otherwise be empty, in a manner which cannot be fully understood without seeing them. Each of the six "curtains" over the pigeonholes is the front of a drawer, two on the left being partly open; and the arched top of the compartment also pulls out as a drawer. The two pilasters flanking the compartment are, as usual, the fronts of vertical drawers. Eight small drawers are under the pigeonholes; and there are four large drawers in the lower portion of the desk. An eight-pointed inlaid star on the front of the lid, and one on and two over the door of the compartment, are not visible in the engraving. In some desks of this type secret drawers may be found in almost every hollow place in the back, and the drawers in front which conceal them may be removed only when released by pressing a hidden spring, or by some other contrivance. About 1755–1785.

In No. 793 three small drawers are grouped at each end with a round arched door effect. In the centre are two half-round columns, which are the fronts of vertical drawers, between which is a large pigeonhole, not a closed compartment. Three wide drawers rest on the floor of the writing surface, and above them are other drawers and pigeonholes. The curtains are cut in cyma curves. About 1755–1785.

791 (Upper) Mrs. Howard Sill.
792 (Upper) Mr. Edgar G. Miller, Jr.
793 (Centre) Mr. Albert G. Towers.
794 (Centre) Mr. Albert G. Towers.
795 (Lower) Mr. Edgar G. Miller, Jr.
796 (Lower) Mr. Edgar G. Miller, Jr.

797 (UPPER) MR. J. GILMAN D'ARCY PAUL.
799 (CENTRE) ANONYMOUS.
801 (LOWER) ANONYMOUS.

798 (UPPER) MR. EDGAR G. MILLER, JR.
800 (CENTRE) MR. EDGAR G. MILLER, JR.
802 (LOWER) ESTATE OF MRS. THOS. J. LINDSAY.

No. 794 also has two columns in the centre, enclosing a group of small drawers above which is a carved shell design, and still above is a fluted surface. The four pigeonholes are wide and the curtains over them are in scroll designs and are pierced with ornamental openings. This desk is of curly maple. About 1755–1785.

No. 795 is a plainer desk, having in the upper portion five drawers with straight fronts and two drawers with curved ones on the sides of the central compartment. The curtains over the eight pigeonholes are curved in a simple design. The skirt is shaped in large cyma curves and the too large feet are of the straight bracket kind. About 1755–1785.

In No. 796 four drawers on each side of the central compartment are in curves sloping inward. The partitions between the pigeonholes are in graceful curves. In the lower portion of this desk there is a deep drawer at the bottom, then two smaller drawers, above which is a larger one. Here the "pulls" supporting the lid are not of the usual kind, but are boxes or drawers which may be pulled out and in which pens and other writing accessories may be kept. The corners are "recessed" and fluted quarter–round columns are "applied" as in No. 791 and others. About 1755–1785.

In the central compartment of No. 797 there is an arched door between the usual two vertical drawers, and above the compartment is a wide and shallow drawer somewhat in the manner of the drawer in No. 798. On each side of the vertical drawers are two drawers resting on the writing floor, and beyond are two other drawers. All of these drawers, except the wide one, have curved fronts. The curtains over the pigeonholes are cut in designs not seen in other desks. This desk is made of curly maple. About 1755–1785.

No. 798, also, has an unusual form of interior, there being under the top a row of four small drawers and a large one. Perhaps the cabinet maker thought that the space occupied in other desks by the "curtains" could be used to better advantage by inserting drawers. On each side of the centre compartment is a vertical drawer with small brass knobs; and next are two quarter–round columns which are the fronts of two other adjoining vertical drawers without knobs, which can only be opened by—but that is a secret! The walnut wood here is of a light color. About 1755–1785.

No. 799 is an attractive curly maple desk of moderate size. At the two sides of the interior are small square drawers with fronts carved in round designs, over which are pigeonholes. Four other pigeonholes are above two drawers which make a graceful concave curve; and in the centre are two columns, the fronts of vertical drawers, between which are three drawers, the upper one of which is carved in a shell design, as in No. 794. The skirt is of the same type as that of No. 793. About 1755–1785.

In No. 800 there are two curved drawers at each end, one above the other; the compartment and one drawer on each side are placed above the level of the writing floor, leaving a wide space in which a ledger or other long book may be kept. About 1755–1785.

No. 801, also, has a wide space suitable for a large book, on either side of which is a plain drawer. Above are eight other drawers, three of which are ornamented with shell carving. The central portion is flanked by columns, which are the fronts of vertical drawers. It will be noticed that the shell carving appears more frequently than any other decorative treatment in these interiors, and that many drawers are curved and arranged in curved lines; these features disappear in the desks in the Hepplewhite style which are shown in the next section. About 1755–1785.

No. 802 is apparently an English desk, in which the interior, now altered somewhat, has a curved compartment elevated from the floor of the writing surface, making a space below for a large book as in the previous two desks. This compartment has three divisions enclosed within curved doors. The handles are very elaborate. About 1755–1785.

Section 104. Desks; Hepplewhite style.—As will be seen in the illustrations Nos. 803–808, the slanting lid desks in the Hepplewhite style are different in appearance from those in the Chippendale style, although in each style the general form is about the same. In the lower portion containing the large drawers, these desks in the Hepplewhite style are often in the same designs as those of the chests of drawers, or bureaus, of the Hepplewhite style described in section 95. We see French bracket feet with curved skirts and a long line of inlay above, as on the bureaus, and the same kind of inlaid decoration on the drawers.

Whether certain of the desks shown in later sections should be regarded as strictly in the Hepplewhite style, and others as in the Sheraton style, may not be entirely clear, because several features were used in each of the two styles in this class of furniture, such as the French bracket feet, the curved skirt, the kind of inlay and the handles. By some writers such desks are merely said to be "of the Hepplewhite–Sheraton period," which is perhaps sufficiently definite. In some cases the cabinet makers seem to have combined in one piece such features of the two styles as they desired; and we thus see desks which in some parts appear to be in the Hepplewhite style and in other parts seem to be in the Sheraton style.

Desks with slanting lids and with drawers in the lower portion were apparently not in fashion in styles later than the Hepplewhite style; but in the style of Sheraton other types with drawers below were made.[1]

1.   Desks with slanting lids are not shown in Sheraton's "Drawing Book," published in 1792, (as to which see section 18), in which he wrote that desks with drawers under them "are nearly obsolete in London." This quotation appears in "Furniture of the Olden Time," page 146, by Miss Frances Clary Morse; and in the English book of Mr. Burgess, entitled "Antique Furniture," pages 242–243, it is said that when Sheraton's book was published the desks which had been so popular in earlier times were not much in demand.

Desks clearly in the Sheraton style, with tambour slides which were previously used by Hepplewhite, are shown in this book in section 106; and secretary–bookcases in the Sheraton style, with desks in the lower portion, are seen in section 110.

In the writing portion of the desks in the Hepplewhite style the drawers, the pigeonholes and the other details are very plain in comparison with the handsome interiors shown in the preceding section. Inlay takes the place of carving and the fronts are straight, not serpentine or curved.

In Nos. 803 and 804 we see a desk with a slanting lid in the Hepplewhite style. On the lower portion are the French bracket feet, with a skirt in the form of two cyma curves and a long line of inlay over it. On the four drawers the long parallel lines of inlay with rounded ends are said to be in the style of the English cabinet maker Shearer whose design was copied by Hepplewhite and Sheraton, as mentioned in section 96, note 1, C. This inlaid design is better seen on the bureau desk No. 827. The oval line of inlay on the lid encloses a design of the American eagle with a striped shield, outspread wings and legs, and claws holding two arrows and a branch of a tree, probably a branch of an olive tree, the emblem of peace and plenty. On the streamer held in the eagle's mouth are sixteen cross-marks, or stars, supposed to indicate the number of States in the Union at the time, just as the forty-eight stars on our flag now indicate the number of our States.[2] The sixteenth State, Tennessee, was admitted in 1796, and the seventeenth State, Ohio was admitted in 1803. If the cabinet maker was correct in his political history, and intended the stars to represent the number of States at the time, this desk was made between 1796 and 1803; but stars may not be a reliable index. Reasons for this have already been pointed out elsewhere.

In Nos. 805 and 806 the feet are of a bracket type[3] and as usual in such cases there is no skirt on the base. A small sliding brass cover for the keyhole in the lid is not well seen. The inlaid eagle is not in such detail as in the previous design and holds only one arrow in one claw, with a branch of a tree in the other, probably an olive tree as in the preceding desk. There are seventeen marks, or stars, on the streamer, which may indicate that the desk was made during the period between the admission of the seventeenth State, Ohio, in 1803, and the admission of the eighteenth, Louisiana, in 1812. The latter date would be late for the Hepplewhite style. About 1803–1810.

No. 807 is a somewhat plainer desk, having little decorative inlay. The French bracket feet and the long line of inlay between them are seen here as on the other desks, and also on bureaus, of the Hepplewhite style. The skirt is in a curve. The interior differs from that in desks in the Chippendale style, the pigeon-holes and small drawers being in a straight line, not curved; and in this piece there are no vertical drawers on the sides of the central compartment, on the door of which is a five-pointed star. About 1790–1800.

In No. 808 the characteristic features are the same as in the previous desks, with the addition of rectangular forms of inlay on the somewhat heavily-built sides. In the upper portion, on each side under the three pigeonholes, are two small drawers under which is a large drawer; and in the centre is the usual compartment with a vertical drawer on each side. The fronts of these vertical

2. See section 6, entitled "Dating antique furniture," at note 12.
    Due to the strong symbolic appeal of stars and eagles to early Americans, they became the most popular of all decorative designs. Other examples of the use of stars to indicate the number of States are referred to in the Index under the words "Stars" and "Eagles."

3. In the Hepplewhite style bureau No. 725 and others the feet are of the same bracket type as in this desk.

803 (Upper) Miss Ethel M. Miller.
805 (Centre) Mr. Edgar G. Miller, Jr.
807 (Lower) Dr. James Bordley, Jr.

804 (Upper) Miss Ethel M. Miller.
806 (Centre) Mr. Edgar G. Miller, Jr.
808 (Lower) Mr. George H. Powell.

drawers resemble books,[4] and on close inspection it is seen that they are labeled "Life of Washington," "Volume 1" and "Volume 2." The words "John Dereks—cabinet maker" appear on this desk. The skirt is cut in cyma curves and others. About 1790–1800.

Section 105. Cylinder desks.

—These desks are not now often seen in our country in the first form in which they were made, that is, with a solid "cylinder," so called, which is a lid in a curved form,[1] as shown in illustrations Nos. 809 and 810, which are of one desk, shown open and closed. An objection to this form was that the solid cylinder required as much space in the back of the desk as it did in the front; but it is said that in the hands of the cabinet makers of the Hepplewhite and Sheraton schools the loss of space was avoided by the use of the "tambour" lid which is the type now known to us as the "roll–top," and in England is called a "reed–top." The subject of "tambour" desks is treated in the next section.

In the handsome desk above referred to, shown closed and open, we see an abundance of inlay. The large inlaid oval on the lid, the rectangular forms on the drawers and the ends, the line of inlay on the base, the French bracket feet, and the oval handles are all characteristic of the style of Hepplewhite. In the interior some of the same forms of inlay are repeated, together with the small crossed lines which in the illustration are reflected below. The raising of the cylinder enables a slide to be drawn out for writing purposes, in the same manner as in Nos. 811, 825 and others. In some desks the raising of the cylinder moves the slide outward. The similarity in some respects between this desk and No. 808 will be noticed, especially in the graceful form of the skirt with its cyma curves. The finely "matched"[2] mahogany on the front of the drawers is well shown in the engraving. About 1790–1800.

Section 106. Tambour desks and secretary–bookcases.

—The word "tambour" when used in connection with antique furniture refers to a series of small strips of wood glued on a piece of canvas or strong cloth in such a manner as to make a flexible sheet. The familiar "roll–top" in modern desks is constructed

4. In several other pieces shown in this chapter will be seen similar vertical drawer fronts, as in No. 828, in which the supposed books are labeled "History of America"; other examples are in Nos. 835 and 867.

This pleasantry on the vertical drawers recalls the markings on the backs of certain liquor bottles made in the form of books in the so–called Bennington ware. One of them is marked "The book of departed spirits."

1. This type of desk was invented in France about 1750. It reached its highest development in design, workmanship and elegance in the celebrated desk, the "Bureau du Roi," made for Louis the Fifteenth, which is one of the treasures of the Louvre in Paris. This desk is "a large cylinder desk elaborately inlaid in marquetry of woods, and decorated with a wonderful and ornate series of mounts consisting of moldings, plaques, vases and statuettes of gilt bronze. . . It is as remarkable for the boldness of its conception as for the magnificent finish of its details." "Encyclopædia Britannica," eleventh edition, volume 8, page 96, "Desks."

2. As to "matching," see section 32 on "Veneer," note 2.

809 (Upper) Mr. & Mrs. J. Morrison Harris.   810 (Upper) Mr. & Mrs. J. Morrison Harris.
811 (Centre) Mrs. Isaac Ridgeway Trimble.   812 (Centre) Miss Helen H. Carey.
813 (Lower) Mr. Wm. Wallace Lanahan.   814 (Lower) Mr. Edgar G. Miller, Jr.

on somewhat the same principle. In the previous section it is mentioned that the cabinet makers of the Hepplewhite and Sheraton schools generally used this tambour lid in preference to the solid "cylinder" lid because the tambour lid, being flexible, falls down perpendicularly when it is pushed back, and thus takes much less space. Several desks of this tambour type are shown in the illustrations Nos. 811–814.

A second form of tambour desk is shown in illustrations Nos. 815–824 and No. 826, in which the tambour work is in the form of "slides" which move horizontally along the front of the small drawers and pigeonholes and disappear into the sides of the desk. These desks are regarded as among the most attractive of the smaller pieces of furniture made for writing purposes; and from the financial standpoint they seem to be decidedly the most desirable, as mentioned in the comment on No. 824.

The first four illustrations, Nos. 811–814, are of tambour desks in the Sheraton style. In No. 811 the characteristic forms of the desks of this type are seen. The tambour lid, partly open, covers the writing surface which may be pulled out, for which two small knobs are provided. The two drawers have oval handles which are suspended from the top. The desk is plain in appearance, having little inlay. On desks of this kind a plain cabinet top containing shelves, not in keeping with the daintiness of the desk, was sometimes placed; such desks are not illustrated here; similar cabinets are referred to in note 1, B, in this section. About 1795–1810.

No. 812 is a more elegant piece, ornamented with brilliant veneer on the fronts of the small drawers in the interior. The light–colored band is the front of a shallow drawer. The curved sides of the writing portion are finely reeded, as are also the legs, a prominent feature of the Sheraton style; and over the legs are vertical forms of inlay. The front of the desk has an arched kneehole in the centre as in No. 825. A white sheet is on the writing surface. About 1795–1810.

No. 813 is a table desk, the desk being built upon a table. The tambour lid, enclosing three small drawers, is at the back; and a large drawer with bands of inlay is in the front. The legs are rectangular, tapering gracefully. This may be an English piece. About 1795–1810.

No. 814 is a small portable desk, intended to be placed upon a table or stand. The tambour top is connected with the slightly open drawer in such a manner that when the drawer is opened the tambour also opens. The sloping lid of the desk is on hinges and may be opened, providing a writing surface, beneath which is a compartment for papers; and there are also spaces for pens and ink. The tambour lid in desks of this kind is at times difficult to open or close on account of expansion or contraction caused by atmospheric changes. About 1795–1810.

We now come to the second type of tambour desks, Nos. 815–824, in which, as mentioned above, the tambour work is in the form of two slides which may be moved horizontally, also known as "shutters." Whether each one may be definitely stated to be in the Hepplewhite or the Sheraton style is perhaps uncertain because the same conspicuous features often appear in both styles. In some of these desks the door of a small compartment in the centre separates the slides; in others, the slides touch each other in the centre. There seems to be no significance in this difference of construction; but for convenience of comparison the two kinds are presented in separate groups. In all of these pieces a writing surface is made by opening the hinged lid which, when open, is supported by two "pulls" as in the slanting top desks shown in previous sections. A considerable sameness will be noticed in this group of desks, but, as mentioned in connection with bureaus and other articles, the reader will probably be interested in all of them.[1]

In the upper portion of No. 815, under the cornice, is an ornamental line of light-colored wood. The two tambour slides, opened to show a part of the interior, enclose pigeonholes on each side and also drawers above. In the centre is a compartment with a door ornamented with lines of inlay, within which is an oval in which the American eagle appears. At the ends of the upper section are two upright inlaid columns, resembling or imitating "pilasters," a feature which is repeated next to the pulls which support the lid when it is opened. The three large drawers are ornamented with a bead molding in light wood, and have rectangular inlay with fan-shaped designs at each inside corner, as in the bureaus Nos. 735 and 744. The legs, sharply tapering, are decorated with inlaid designs and terminate in spade feet. The lower one of the three large drawers extends so near to the floor that it is not suitable for one to sit at and write. This desk is regarded as being in the Hepplewhite style. About 1790–1810.

No. 816 is decorated with lines of inlay around the door of the compartment, on the sides of the cabinet and on the two drawers in the lower portion; and inlaid bell–flowers are on the legs and on the uprights above them. The handles are oval and are stamped with festoons. A desk of this character may be said to be in the Sheraton style.[2] About 1790–1810.

In No. 817, as in the previous desk, there are only two large drawers, presenting a more dainty and light appearance than a larger number does, as in No. 820. The open tambour slides disclose two large pigeonholes, with small drawers above, on each side of the central compartment. Inlay is on the door of the compartment, and on the legs and on the large drawers. This desk may be regarded as in the Sheraton style. About 1790–1810.

1. A.   Other desks were made in much the same form but with solid doors instead of tambour slides; these are generally plain and are not so interesting and are not illustrated here. A desk of the same general character, but without tambour slides or doors, is shown in No. 833.

B.   Upon the upper portion of some desks made with horizontal tambour slides, a bookcase cabinet was built, the entire piece thus resembling, but in shape only, the secretary–bookcase No. 826. Some pieces of this type, if finely designed and ornamented, may be handsome and attractive, the design and ornamentation overcoming the somewhat top–heavy and ungainly appearance. Some of these desks have plain solid doors instead of tambour slides. Examples of these pieces are not shown in this book, but may be seen in Mr. Wallace Nutting's "Furniture Treasury," volume 1, Nos. 729–731.

2.   In "American Furniture and Decoration," by Mr. E. S. Holloway, a desk almost identical with the above is illustrated in plate 79 and is described as a Sheraton style desk of New England origin, of about 1800. At the auction sale of the Reifsnyder collection in April, 1929, the desk was sold for $3,900. Compare the sale price of No. 824 mentioned in note 3.

815 (UPPER) MR. & MRS. GEORGE SHIPLEY.　　816 (UPPER) MRS. CHARLES WOOLLEN.
817 (CENTRE) MRS. ALEXANDER ARMSTRONG.　818 (CENTRE) MISS MARY K. HINKLEY.
819 (LOWER) MRS. FRANCIS T. REDWOOD.　　820 (LOWER) MR. EDGAR G. MILLER, JR.

In No. 818 one of the tambour slides is entirely open, showing three pigeon-holes and two small drawers. The door of the central compartment is ornamented with an inlaid oval, and inlay is also seen on the two large drawers. On the brass oval handles are cornucopias, a favorite design of the period. A band of inlay is under the large drawers and around each of the four legs near the bottom. The light color of the slide on the right is due to the position of the photographer's high-powered electric lamps. About 1790-1810.

No. 819 is also a graceful piece between whose closed slides is a compartment door with an oval inlaid panel of finely grained mahogany. Here also are lines of inlay around the two large drawers, and bell-flowers on the legs, above which are three vertical lines of inlay, not well seen. The two ends of the tambour section are reeded, in keeping with the reeded appearance of the slides. About 1790-1810.

No. 820 is a less desirable type, having four large drawers extending almost to the floor as in a bureau, which the lower part resembles. The feet are of a French bracket type, with a curved skirt between them. Two large pigeonholes, with small drawers above, are on each side of the compartment door, which has an oval inlay. The lid is opened, supported by the pulls. The mahogany tambour slides and the reeded pilasters appear almost white in color, owing to the position of the strong electric lights used in taking the photograph. The brass handles on the large drawers are ornamented with cornucopias. About 1795-1810.

In the next four tambour desks, Nos. 821-824, there is no compartment in the centre separating the slides, so that the slides meet each other when closed, as shown in No. 824. Whether this type or the previous one is the more attractive depends of course upon the taste of the individual.

In No. 821 there are three large drawers, the front of each of which is veneered with a finely grained light wood which is also seen on other parts. The open slides disclose a different arrangement of pigeonholes and drawers from those in the previous desks, made possible by the larger space available on account of the absence of a central compartment. About 1795-1810.

No. 822 is somewhat similar to No. 817 in the inlaid ornamentation of the lower part, and has a band of inlay on the lower part of the legs. The principal differences are that in No. 822 there is no compartment between the tambour slides and that in No. 817 the inlay is less conspicuous in the engraving. About 1795-1810.

No. 823 is an English piece, the feature of which is the convex form of the tambour portion, making it necessary for the lid to have the concave form in order to fold over. This type of desk does not seem to have been made in our country, but is illustrated in English publications. About 1800.

No. 824 is a fine tambour desk which has attracted wide attention because of its elegance, but mainly because of the price which it brought at an auction sale of fine antiques.[3] The important features observed in the preceding pieces in this

3.   The sum of thirty thousand dollars ($30,000.) was paid for this desk No. 824 at the auction sale of the collection of the late Philip Flayderman, of Boston, held in January, 1930, at the American

(Note 3 is continued on page 448.)

section are seen here in their finest development. As in No. 815 we see the inlay imitating pilasters; as in No. 821, the fine fronts of the large drawers; as in No. 822, the decorative inlays on the drawers and legs. The particular features of distinction in No. 824 are the graceful inlaid festoons in light wood on the tambour slides, the ring handles with plates of decorated Battersea enamel, the brackets at the inner corners of the legs, and the label of "John Seymour & Son." This desk is regarded as being in the Hepplewhite style, and is dated about 1790–1800.

The next two pieces, Nos. 825 and 826, are called secretary–bookcases because each is furnished with a bookcase; but as the desk portion in each has a tambour lid, or slides, they are included in this section on tambour desks instead of being placed in section 110 which treats of the usual types of secretary–bookcases in the Hepplewhite and Sheraton styles.

In each of these two fine examples of the Sheraton style the "pediment," which is the decorative feature above the cornice, has two concave curves. In No. 825 the pediment is rounded in the centre and in No. 826 the centrepiece is rectangular. Remarks upon this type of pediment are in the note.[4]

In No. 825 the desk portion is similar to that in No. 812, having an arched kneehole in the centre as in dressing tables of the period in section 168 in the chapter on tables. The open tambour lid discloses the drawers, pigeonholes and writing board. The glass front of the bookcase portion is divided into graceful forms of a Gothic type.[5] The handles are of the ring form. About 1795.

In No. 826 the fine design is accompanied by a liberal inlay of curly maple which adorns the pediment, the cornice, the door and drawers of the desk portion, the three large drawers and the upright parts. The tapering of the legs

(NOTE 3, *continued from page 447.*)

Art Association—Anderson Galleries, Inc., in New York. In the foreword of the catalogue it is said that this "Hepplewhite secretary by John Seymour (and Son) of Boston, is unquestionably as fine as anything existing of its type, and is one of the two known labeled pieces by this maker." Compared with the price of $3,900. brought by the tambour desk No. 816, mentioned in note 2, this Seymour desk, with its label, was, financially speaking, more than seven times as fine as No. 816. See also the comment on the celebrated "Reifsnyder highboy," No. 668, shown in section 87; also the remarks on buying antiques found in opening sections and in section 175.

4. This type of pediment is shown in Mr. Cescinsky's "English Furniture" on a "bureau-bookcase," No. 293 in volume 3; it is also twice illustrated in "English and American Furniture" by Cescinsky and Hunter, pages 240–241. In Mr. Holloway's "American Furniture and Decoration" the pediment is shown on plates 85, 86, 87, the latter illustration being about the same as our No. 825.

It is said that in our country this form of pediment has been much used. It is shown in this book on the desks Nos. 825, 826 and 864, and variations from these forms are seen in No. 858. Figure 298 in Mr. Lockwood's "Colonial Furniture" is about the same as our No. 826, with its graceful lines and interesting finish. The apparent absence of information in the books concerning the origin of this interesting design is the reason for this note.

5. A sketch of a tambour secretary–bookcase, belonging to George Washington, with a pediment and other features somewhat similar to No. 825, appears in the book "The Home of Washington," by Mr. Benson J. Lossing, published in 1870. On page 228 of that book the following extract from the will of Washington is quoted: "To my companion in arms and old and intimate friend, Dr. Craik, I give my bureau (or as cabinet makers call it, tambour secretary)." For this reference the writer is indebted to Mr. James Gustavus Whiteley, of Baltimore, the owner of No. 825.

821 (Upper) Mr. George Bradford Simmons.
823 (Lower) Mr. & Mrs. Edward H. McKeon.

822 (Upper) Mr. John C. Toland.
824 (Lower) Anonymous.

on the inside is well seen. The writing table when open is supported by pulls in the usual manner. The arched forms in the bookcase doors will also be noticed. About 1800.

Section 107. Bureau desks.—This type of desks consists of a chest of drawers, generally containing three drawers of the usual size, over which is a larger drawer the front of which opens forward and downward and is held in position by metal supports in the shape of a quarter of a circle, called "quadrants," such as are seen and described in connection with Nos. 856–860. This large drawer is fitted out as a desk, the inner surface of the front when opened serving as a writing surface. These pieces are not very important in themselves, but were often made with a bookcase cabinet above, thus forming a "secretary–bookcase," as will be seen in illustrations Nos. 856–859 and others in section 110.

The two pieces here shown, Nos. 827 and 828, indicate the character of these bureau desks. No. 827 is a handsome piece and, except the top drawer, resembles the bureau No. 737 shown in the preceding chapter. The two large horizontal ovals on the top drawer resemble those on the secretary–bookcase No. 856 in this chapter. The parallel lines of inlay with rounded ends, on the lower drawers, are of the type referred to in section 96, note 1, C. The entire front is veneered with finely grained mahogany. The wooden knobs on the drawers are probably of a later period. About 1790–1810.

In No. 828 the front of the top drawer is open and pigeonholes and small drawers are seen, as in other desks. The "quadrants" which supported the front of the top drawer are missing. The door of the central compartment is ornamented with an inlaid shell. The fronts of the two vertical drawers on the sides of the door are made to resemble the backs of books and are marked "History of America," and are numbered "volume 1" and "volume 2." Similar book drawers are referred to in the comment and note on No. 808. About 1790–1810.

Section 108. Other kinds of desks.—In this section are shown several desks of special character which may be conveniently considered together.

In Nos. 829 and 830 we see the same desk, closed and open. It is a "fire screen" desk, intended to serve both as a fire screen[1] and a desk. When closed, the front is upright and is seen to be ornamented with lines of inlay and a diamond–shaped design in the centre. When open, the front is horizontal, disclosing a writing surface and places for paper and pens. This dainty piece may be an English one in the style of Sheraton. About 1795–1810.

No. 831 is of the same general design, but is later in date and plainer in appearance; moreover the illustration does not show the grain of the mahogany. On the sides, at the top, are reeded rosettes which give a touch of decoration.

---

1. These should not be confused with the tiny "pole screens," which were equally deficient as protectors from the heat of the fireplace.

825 (Upper) Mr. James Gustavus Whitely.
826 (Upper) Mr. & Mrs. George Shipley.
827 (Lower) Mr. & Mrs. W. Hall Harris.
828 (Lower) Mrs. John Stokes.

Real protection from the heat of a fire is furnished by the board at the back, reaching nearly to the floor. We see here the heaviness of the late Empire style in comparison with the delicacy of the early type of Sheraton, as shown in the charming little pieces Nos. 829, 830, and 834. About 1830–1840.

No. 832 is a knee–hole desk or writing table. It closely resembles in form the knee–hole dressing tables Nos. 1463–1466, but that it is a desk is shown by the lid on the top and the two pulls below. The knee–hole portion is wide enough to enable a person to sit in front and write, and in the rear of this space is a cupboard with shelves. This illustration appears through the courtesy of the owner, Mr. L. V. Lockwood, who regards it, partly on account of the original brass handles, as having been made in the Sheraton period. Similar desks were made as far back as about 1725, as shown by comparing figures 253 and 295 in volume 1 of Mr. Lockwood's "Colonial Furniture." About 1795–1810.

No. 833 is similar in certain respects to some of the tambour desks, such as No. 818, shown in section 106, but it is made without tambour slides and therefore is not shown in that section. The lower portion has the usual lid which, when opened, provides a writing surface. The lid is supported by two wide pulls which are placed horizontally instead of vertically. The pigeonholes are separated only by round columns; and above them are four drawers. The piece is well decorated with inlay. About 1785–1810.

No. 834 is a pleasing writing desk in the style of Sheraton. As in the previous piece the hinged lid opens and is supported by the pulls. In the upper portion are three compartments faced with light wood and decorated with dark ovals in which are painted female figures; above these is a shelf with a back which is also decorated with a figure in an oval inlay. This is doubtless an English piece, but it has been in the family of the present owner for several generations. About 1795–1810.

In Nos. 835 and 836 we see two desks with a "fall front" or "straight front" of the same type as in No. 775, which is the first desk shown in this chapter and which was made about the year 1700. In No. 835 the Sheraton style particularly appears in the reeding on the top and other places and in the rounded and tapering feet. On each side of the central section are two vertical drawers with fronts in the form of books, as in Nos. 808 and 828, but without names. The lid is not supported by "quadrants" as in No. 858, or by pulls, but by an interior arrangement which is not visible, as in the next piece and in the secretary–bookcase No. 868. About 1810–1820.

No. 836 is believed to have been made in the workshop of Duncan Phyfe in his last period; it was purchased by the present owner from one of his descendants. In this finely made desk of the Victorian period the interior has eight drawers, two closed compartments and a large open one in the centre, all veneered with maple. The front opens and is held in position in the same manner as No. 835. The rounded corners are of the same type as is seen in the bookcase No. 875 and in the bureau No. 768. This piece is regarded as having been made about 1840–1850.

829 (Upper) Mr. Herbert T. Tif-   830 (Upper) Mr. Herbert T. Tif-   831 (Upper) Collection of Mrs.
    Fany.   Fany.   Jordan Stabler.
    832 (Centre) Mr. L. V. Lockwood.   833 (Centre) Mr. Edgar G. Miller, Jr.
    834 (Lower) Miss Ethel Knight.   835 (Lower) Dr. Henry M. Fitzhugh.

No. 837 is a very elaborately carved English flat top desk, called a "pedestal writing table" in Mr. Cescinsky's "English Furniture," volume 2, figure 300, from which, through his courtesy, the engraving is taken. This type of desk no doubt suggested the form of the Washington desk next mentioned, and is probably also a model from which so many of our modern desks are made. On each side is a "pedestal" with three drawers, between which is a central drawer. This desk, having pedestals with drawers, and a space between, seems to be a development of the kneehole type of desk shown in No. 832, omitting the cupboard. There seems to be some doubt as to the date of this desk.

No. 838 is a flat top mahogany desk which was used by George Washington after he became President[2] of the United States in 1789. It is in charge of the Art Commission of the City of New York, which has furnished the photograph for this book. The desk may be seen in the Old City Hall in New York. That it is in the Sheraton style is shown by the round, fluted and tapering legs and the rosettes, twelve of which are faintly seen on the side which is toward the reader. The other side is similar and either side may be used as the front. There are seven drawers on each side. On each end there are six handles which, with the moldings, not plainly seen in the engraving, give the appearance of drawers; but these are "sham" drawers and are examples of a device of the period. The two shelves at each end are no doubt intended for papers, but are not very satisfactory for that purpose. About 1795.

Section 109. Secretaries and secretary–bookcases; Queen Anne and Chippendale styles.—As mentioned in paragraph 4 of section 101, a slanting lid desk furnished with a cabinet above, containing pigeonholes and drawers for papers, but not long shelves for books, is called a "secretary" in this book; and an article having a similar outside appearance but with only shelves in the upper portion, and for books only or chiefly, is here called a "secretary–bookcase." Both of these types are considered in this section.

It is said that in most of the secretaries and secretary–bookcases made in our country during the Chippendale period, about 1755–1785, the doors of the upper portion were made of solid wood, although in England the use of glazed doors was common in that period. The solid wooden doors were generally paneled in various forms, or in some cases, as in No. 839, mirrors were placed in them. The top in almost all cases, as in No. 842, was curved in two "scrolls" in which the cyma curve is seen, as to which curve see section 23; and there was a space in the centre in which a carved urn or "flame" was placed; in these respects there is a resemblance to the scroll top highboys shown in section 86. The design and orna-

---

2. Washington was President from 1789 to 1797. The Sheraton style became popular in our country about 1795; see section 18, entitled "The Sheraton style."

    In his office the writer uses an exact reproduction of the desk. It is a very satisfactory piece; but one regrets that there are no slides on each side above the top drawers, as in the modern American desks. Slides appear in a reproduction which was widely advertised as an exact copy of the original.

836 (Upper) Mrs. Reginald Perry Rose.
837 (Centre) Anonymous.
838 (Lower) Art Commission of City of New York.

mentation of the top contributed a large part of the handsome and dignified character of these pieces. The desk portion follows the form of the desks Nos. 785–802 in the Chippendale style shown in section 103, and we see the same exterior and interior designs as in those pieces. This similarity is of course because the desks and the secretaries were made at about the same time and in the same Chippendale style.[1]

The wood used in these secretaries and secretary–bookcases was generally mahogany or walnut, but sometimes other woods. On some pieces, such as No. 844, there is a "hood" or "bonnet" at the top, similar to that seen on the highboy No. 652 and others. The feet are generally of the bracket type, either "straight" or "ogee," but occasionally cabriole legs with club feet, or ball and claw feet, are found. A noticeable feature in the upper portion of many of the pieces is the very inconvenient height of the pigeonholes and shelves, doubtless requiring the use of a ladder.

"Block–front" secretaries and secretary–bookcases. These are more esteemed than any other type. They are considered and illustrated in the next chapter, entitled "Block–front furniture."

In Nos. 839 and 840, shown open and closed, we see a fine secretary–bookcase which has features of the Queen Anne style, the principal one being the shape of the door panels and of the mirrors and their frames, such as are seen in the mirrors Nos. 1091–1096. The top is arched, and in the centre it is "broken" and holds a gilded figure; and at the two ends are gilded flames on urns[2] which rest upon small pedestals.[3] Between the upper portion and the desk portion are two candlestick slides which pull out. The desk portion is similar in outline to those in the Chippendale style shown in section 103. The feet are of the straight bracket type. Observing the interior of the desk portion we see the "advanced," or "stepped," drawers, as in the earlier pieces Nos. 778–780, and also the "well," as in No. 778, and the nine drawers and eight pigeonholes. The upper portion is fitted with vertical divisions, perhaps for account books, and has many pigeonholes and vertical drawers. The upper portion of this piece was evidently intended for writing and bookkeeping purposes rather than for a bookcase, and is therefore called a "secretary."[4] About 1730–1750.

1. A few secretaries and secretary–bookcases of the "bombé" type have been found, but are not illustrated here. The lower part of these pieces consists of a bombé chest of drawers, or bureau, such as is seen in No. 724 in the chapter on bureaus, with a slanting lid and a writing compartment above, thus making a desk, and above this is a cabinet enclosing pigeonholes and drawers, or shelves for books. Three examples are shown in Mr. Lockwood's "Colonial Furniture," volume 1, figures 279–281.

2. These ornaments on the top are called "finials," which mean "end pieces pointing upward." They are mentioned in the chapter on highboys, section 86, note 2.

3. The rule against using technical words in this book, unless necessary, should not be broken in favor of a certain word which means a pedestal and an urn or other ornament placed thereon. That word is "acroterium"—which will not be mentioned again! These pedestals are also seen in the illustrations of highboys, as in No. 652 and on various other pieces.

4. An English Queen Anne style secretary–bookcase with a curved "broken arch," and very similar to No. 839 in other respects, is illustrated in Mr. Edward Wenham's "Collector's Guide to Furniture Designs," No. 347; see also No. 368.   (*Note 4 is continued on page 458.*)

839 (UPPER) MR. & MRS. BAYARD TURNBULL.   840 (UPPER) MR. & MRS. BAYARD TURNBULL.
841 (LOWER) DR. JAMES BORDLEY, JR.   842 (LOWER) DR. RANDOLPH WINSLOW.

No. 841, also, has "advanced," or "stepped," drawers in the lower portion, curved in graceful lines, and the usual fittings, except that there are no "curtains" over the pigeonholes. Under the compartment in the centre there is a small drawer, and at the sides are the usual vertical drawers. On the upper portion we notice the flat top, the two lines of molding under the cornice and around the side, and the fluted columns at the corners, next to which are fluted pilasters, a third pilaster being in the centre. On each of the doors there are two panels, a feature seldom found in these pieces. The handles and hinges should be noticed. About 1730–1750.

In No. 842 the top is "scrolled" and in the centre is a pedestal upon which there is an urn. The doors have long panels which have arched tops resembling those in No. 845. In the lower portion of the two small drawers at each end are "advanced" and the pigeonholes above are wide, with arched curtains. About 1730–1750.

Nos. 843 and 844 are unusual in having glazed doors, with panes rectangular in form and plain in design. Their plainness in comparison with the ornamental character of the other parts might suggest that they are not the original doors and have been substituted; but doors of the same type appear in a fine English secretary–bookcase illustrated in the leading American book;[5] and an examination of these two American pieces gives no indication that the doors have been changed.

In No. 843, which is regarded as a Pennsylvania piece, and is of cherry, the top has two scrolls whose inner ends are ornamented with large carved rosettes; and three urns and flames on their pedestals are the finials. An unusual carved design is in the centre over the doors. In the lower portion, on each side of the central compartment, is a pedestal with a flame which is the front of a vertical drawer; and on the door of the compartment is a carved design representing shells. The "curtains" over the eight pigeonholes are the fronts of drawers which pull out; and below are eight small drawers with serpentine fronts. Fluted columns are on the corners of both the upper and lower portions. About 1760–1780.

No. 844 is also an interesting piece. The top is scrolled and is continued to the back of the piece, forming a "hood," or "bonnet," such as is seen in the highboys Nos. 652, 653 and others. Through the glass in the arched top of each of the doors may be seen a row of lofty pigeonholes. In the lower portion there are eight pigeonholes in groups of two each, over which are small drawers which

(NOTE 4, *continued from page 456.*)

In the definitions in this section and in section 101 the difference between a "secretary" and a "secretary–bookcase" is this: if the upper portion is furnished with pigeonholes and drawers, as in No. 840, the article is a secretary; but if the upper portion is furnished with long shelves for books, as in No. 852, it is a secretary–bookcase. In the illustrations in this section the doors of the upper portion are generally of solid wood and are closed, so that the contents of the upper portion are not seen; but, as a matter of fact, most of the upper portions are furnished with pigeonholes and drawers, not with shelves for books. Moreover, the illustrations were purposely taken with the doors shut because the fine designs of the doors are more important to us than groups of pigeonholes and drawers.

Several of the upper portions have a few pigeonholes or drawers and also long shelves for books; examples are in Nos. 851, 857 and 864.

5. See Mr. Lockwood's "Colonial Furniture," volume 1, figure 285.

843 (Upper) Mr. John C. Toland.
845 (Lower) Mr. Albert G. Towers.

844 (Upper) Mr. C. Edward Snyder.
846 (Lower) Mrs. Murray Steuart Hartshorne.

pull out and are carved with four concave shells. In the central compartment the door is concave with a shell in the same pattern as the others; and the fronts of the two vertical drawers are fluted. In the second row of drawers there are two smaller drawers as also in No. 850 and others. About 1760–1780.

No. 845 is made of maple. The desk front is in a reversed serpentine form and has bail handles and ball and claw feet, in these respects resembling the desk No. 789. In the centre is a compartment containing three concave drawers, without a door in front; the upper drawer is carved with a shell. As in the preceding piece the top is scrolled and the finials are missing. The panels in the doors are arched in a manner similar to those in No. 842. On the left side of the upper portion is a handle for use in moving. About 1760–1780.

In No. 846 the desk portion has a straight front. The straight bracket feet and the entire base seem to be substitutes. Two candlestick slides support the candlesticks. The tops of the doors in the upper portion are cut in cyma curves, not well seen in the illustration, the forms resembling cabriole legs in a horizontal position. The finials on the top are missing. About 1760–1780.

In No. 847 the front of the desk portion is in the reversed serpentine form and there are short ball and claw feet as in No. 845. The tall upper portion has a scrolled top on which are three urns and flames, and carved rosettes are applied on the inner ends of the scrolls; somewhat smaller rosettes are almost always used on similar scrolls of fine articles of furniture. A round carved shell is under the central flame. The tops of the doors are arched and there is a candlestick slide. About 1760–1780.

In No. 848, also, the inner ends of the scrolls at the top are ornamented with rosettes. The usual three finials are missing. The doors and their panels are arched at the top. The handles on the desk portion and the escutcheons on the doors of this and other secretaries of this kind are worthy of the aid of a magnifying glass. Two candlestick slides are seen at the extreme ends of the desk portion; in almost every piece their positions are different. The feet here are of the ogee bracket kind, which are better seen on the next piece. The upper portion is unusually high, rivalling the height of No. 853. About 1760–1780.

No. 849 has several distinctive features. In addition to the scroll top with the rosettes and the large flames, we see the latice work, instead of the usual solid wood, between the scrolls and the tops of the doors. The sunken panels in the doors are cut in a series of cyma curves and other curves, somewhat similar to those seen on mirrors, such as Nos. 1139–1141. In the lower portion, at the front corners, are fluted columns as in No. 791 and others. About 1760–1780.

In No. 850 the tops of the two doors form an arch under which are panels cut in the same arch design. Two escutcheons are on the doors and two candlestick slides are below. The desk portion has a pleasing interior with eight small serpentine front drawers and eight pigeonholes and also a compartment with small drawers. The arrangement of the large drawers is similar to that in No. 844 and others, there being two small drawers, instead of one large one, under the upper drawer. About 1760–1780.

847 (Upper) Hammond–Harwood House.
849 (Lower) Mr. C. Edward Snyder.

848 (Upper) Mr. & Mrs. Charles E. McLane.
850 (Lower) Mrs. James V. Wagner.

No. 850 is the last "secretary" in the Chippendale style shown in this chapter, as the word is defined in section 101 and at the beginning of this chapter, namely, "a desk furnished with a cabinet above, containing pigeonholes and drawers for papers, but not long shelves for books." See also note 4 in this section.

The next two illustrations of pieces in the Chippendale style are of a similar form, but the upper portion contains only or mainly shelves for books and are therefore called "secretary–bookcases."

In No. 851, a secretary–bookcase, the upper portion contains mainly long shelves for books, but through the lower part of the glass doors several small drawers and pigeonholes may be seen. In each of the doors the four large panes of glass enclose a small diamond–shaped glass panel somewhat resembling the small panel in No. 865. On the top is a "broken pediment" with an urn in the centre. The feet are of the ogee bracket type. About 1760–1785.

In No. 852 the upper portion has a flat top and the doors have diamond–shaped panes, through which china articles are seen on the full length shelves. This piece was no doubt intended to be used as a desk and a bookcase, in other words, a secretary–bookcase; it does not seem likely that a china cabinet and a desk would be made as one piece; but shelves intended for books were often used for china. On one of the two candle slides is a candlestick and candle. On the front corners of the desk portion are fluted columns. The handles are of the bail pattern, and the feet are of an animal type. About 1770–1785.

Section 110. Secretary–bookcases; Hepplewhite and Sheraton styles.—In this section it is evident that the upper portion of each article here shown has long shelves for books, and that the lower portion, whatever its form and contents, was intended for writing purposes. Under the definitions given in sections 101 and 109, the articles should therefore be called "secretary–bookcases"; but too much importance should not be given to the names of the articles, or to their styles,[1] whether Hepplewhite or Sheraton, as the reader has no doubt already discovered.

For convenience, the sixteen articles illustrated in this section may be examined in three groups. In the first group of three pieces, Nos. 853–855, the desk portion has the type of slanting lid seen in previous sections. In the second group, Nos. 856–860, the desk portion is a "bureau" desk in which, as shown in section 107, there is a large upper drawer, the front of which opens forward and downward and is held in position by curved metal supports called "quadrants" which are described in connection with Nos. 857 and 858. The third group consists of

1. In this section we meet with the same difficulty as in section 104, namely, the uncertainty in determining whether certain pieces should be regarded as in the Hepplewhite style or in the Sheraton style, on account of the similarity between them. Some of these secretary–bookcases are easily recognizable as being in one or the other of the two styles, but with others it is safer to regard them as examples of the influences of both styles; and therefore they may be referred to as being merely in the "Hepplewhite–Sheraton period," which is perhaps sufficiently definite, as mentioned in the section above cited.

851 (LEFT) HAMMOND–HARWOOD HOUSE.   852 (RIGHT) COLLECTION OF MRS. JORDAN STABLER.

smaller and more delicate pieces, Nos. 861–864, which have one or more drawers which do not extend as near to the floor as desks do, and have a writing lid which opens and folds back and is supported by pulls. The upper portion of almost all of the second and third groups contains only movable shelves for books, without pigeonholes or small drawers; and hence the articles should not be regarded as "secretaries" but as "secretary–bookcases," as above mentioned, although they are now frequently used for holding china.

The ornamental designs of the glass doors[2] contribute to the interest of many of the pieces shown in this and later sections of this chapter. The designs most frequently found on our American pieces are those having thirteen or fifteen panes of glass, as in Nos. 857 and 858 and others.

The interior of the desk portion in the pieces shown in this section has not the finely curved small drawers seen in the pieces of the previous style. The interior is generally built with straight lines, with the exception of the "curtains."

Two handsome secretary–bookcases, fitted with a tambour cylinder or slide, are shown in Nos. 825 and 826 in section 106, entitled "Tambour desks." They should perhaps appear in this section, but the tambour feature distinguishes them from other pieces.

No. 853 is tall and with a scroll top, in the centre of which is an urn; under the curved open portion are inlaid designs of vines with flowers at the ends, barely visible in the engraving. The high solid wooden doors and the slanting lid are ornamented with rectangular lines of inlay, with fan designs at the inner corners, as in the desk No. 815 and others. The four large drawers are inlaid in the same design as in the desk No. 808, and the feet are of the same French bracket type. The line of inlay at the base and the curve of the skirt are in the usual form of the Hepplewhite style. The handles are in the Chippendale style. About 1785–1800.

No. 854 also has a slanting lid on the desk portion. The four drawers and the lid are bordered with lines of light wood and the handles are in the proper oval form. The feet are short ones of the French bracket type and between them the skirt is cut in a series of cyma curves, as to which see section 23. On the upper portion we see under the top a molding of dainty Gothic arches,[3] the partitions between which end in designs which apparently represent acorns. Some of the

2. In "English Furniture," by Mr. T. A. Strange, pages 152–155, one hundred and sixty–one designs of glazed doors are shown, mainly from the designs of Chippendale, Hepplewhite and Sheraton; and others may be found under the words "Bookcases" and "China showcases" in the index to that book.

Mr. Wallace Nutting, in his "Furniture Treasury," volume 1, in a note to No. 736, a secretary–bookcase of about 1800, remarks that "there is positively no limit to the variety of the designs of this period. Whatever the experience of others, the author has never seen two pieces precisely alike."

3. In Mr. Cescinsky's "English Furniture," volume 3, figure 170, it is said that a cornice of this kind "originated as a usual detail about 1775–1780, and became a favorite one with the Sheraton school." In the American pieces the divisions between the arches often terminate in what are supposed to be "acorns." Other illustrations of this molding are in Nos. 855 and 872.

See note 2 in section 41 for a confession of the writer on discovering that these arches and acorns were not carved on the wood but were merely glued on; see also note 3, G, in the same section.

panes of glass are in the diamond shape. The shelves are adjustable, sliding in grooves in the sides, as usual in modern bookcases. About 1785-1800.

No. 855, also with a slanting lid, has at the top an arched "pediment"[4] carved in the design of a fan. Here also, as in the preceding piece, is a line of Gothic arches, with the partitions terminating in acorns. The graceful arrangement of the interlacing[5] ovals in the two doors closely follows Sheraton's design No. 6 in plate 27, page 302, in his book referred to in note 4. The two small oval panels in the centres add to the elegance of these doors. Other designs will be seen in Nos. 860, 870, 875 and 879. A similar design used by Hepplewhite, but without the small oval panels, is shown in Mr. Cescinsky's "English Furniture," volume 3, figure 164, and is dated "about 1790." In the corners of the desk portion are fluted columns. About 1795-1810.

In the secretary-bookcases Nos. 856-860 the desk portions are not of the slanting lid type, but are "bureau" desks such as Nos. 827 and 828. In these secretary-bookcases the upper drawer is a deep one which may be pulled forward and the front may then be opened downward, disclosing the usual writing equipment, and is held in position by curved metal supports called "quadrants." It is said that these secretary-bookcases gradually became more popular than those with the slanting lids, perhaps because in the slanting lid type a person may neglect to pull out the "pulls" upon which the lid rests, in which event the hinges on the lid may be broken.

In No. 856, closed, and No. 857, open, we see the operation of the bureau desk. But we first notice that the cornice of No. 856 is ornamented with two straight lines of inlay, beneath which are two rows of inlaid designs consisting of interlacing half-circles, those in the upper row having their convex sides downward and those on the lower row having their convex sides upward, forming the diamond-shaped spaces which may seem more conspicuous than the half-circles. The desk portion is ornamented with four large ovals, the two on the upper drawer

4. A "pediment" is a decorative form above the cornice, as mentioned in connection with Nos. 825 and 826.

This pediment is shown in the "Drawing Book" of Sheraton, (as to which see section 18), third edition, revised, 1802, plate No. 28, page 305. Sheraton calls his piece a "secretary and bookcase," and says that "the use of this piece is to hold books in the upper part, and in the lower it contains a writing-drawer and clothes-press shelves." The design is dated 1791.

5. In Mr. Cescinsky's "English Furniture," volume 3, page 153, it is said that the design of "intersecting ovals" was "a favorite one with the cabinet makers of both the Hepplewhite and Sheraton periods."

It may be noted here that in all well made pieces each of the glass panes is cut out separately and is separately placed in position in the space made for it. In some modern reproduction and fakes there may be one single pane of glass placed behind the whole rectangular space within the door frame; and some English pieces were made in this manner, one of which is illustrated in Mr. Cescinsky's "English Furniture," volume 3, figure 297.

It may also be mentioned here that the writer has several times seen a desk which was made simply as a desk, upon which has been placed a bookcase top taken from another piece; or, if the desk was originally made with a bookcase top, a different type of top has been substituted; these defects may generally be discovered by close inspection.

853 (Upper) Mr. Austin McLanahan.
855 (Lower) Mrs. Alexander Armstrong.

854 (Upper) Mr. John C. Toland.
856 (Lower) Mrs. Wilbur W. Hubbard.

857 (Upper) Mr. & Mrs. Richard L. Cary.
859 (Lower) Mrs. Paul H. Miller.

858 (Upper) Estate of Mrs. Thomas J. Lindsay.
860 (Lower) Mr. & Mrs. J. Marsh Matthews.

resembling those in the bureau desk No. 827. The label of "Stitcher and Clemmens, cabinet and chair makers, Baltimore" was found on the bottom of one of the drawers. A larger illustration of this piece is in an article by Dr. Henry J. Berkley in "Antiques," September, 1930, page 211. About 1795–1810.

Thirteen panes of glass are seen in each of the doors of No. 856 and other pieces. These thirteen panes are sometimes thought to represent the thirteen original States of the Union. This, however, is a fallacy which becomes apparent when we see in the English books illustrations of glass doors with thirteen panes on pieces made years before there were any American States.[6] But American cabinet makers no doubt found the number "thirteen" a popular one in the early days of the young Republic and used it as a patriotic feature. These thirteen panes are generally arranged in such a manner that an eight–sided figure is formed in the central portion of the two doors, with a four–sided figure within.

In No. 857, in which the writing portion is open, the top is flat and there are thirteen panes of glass in each door, as in the previous piece. Inside, at the bottom of the upper portion, the six indistinct light–colored rectangular surfaces, separated by dark framework, are six drawers in two tiers. In some pieces similar drawers are not concealed, as in No. 851; in others they are hidden by pieces of silk; and in others by wooden panels, as in No. 864. The same light–colored wood appears on the fronts of the smaller drawers in the writing portion. About 1795–1810.

No. 858 is another secretary–bookcase with an open desk of the bureau type. The design of the "pediment," at the top, is a variation of a characteristic Sheraton feature which will be seen in Nos. 825, 826 and 864. Fifteen panes of glass are in each door, requiring a more intricate design than in the doors having thirteen panes. The feet and the skirt are of the familiar type which seems to have been the common property of the cabinet makers of the period. About 1795–1810.

No. 859 has a flat top and fifteen panes in each glass door, very similar in design to those in the preceding pieces; and the large upper drawer opens as in the previous piece, disclosing the writing portion. All the drawers have lines of inlay and on the ends of the framework are long vertical inlaid rectangular forms. The brass handles are of the oval type generally seen on the furniture of the period. The skirt is cut in several cyma curves. About 1795–1810.

In No. 860 the doors with interlaced ovals are very similar to those in No. 855, but the small oval panels are of clear glass. Apparently there are five drawers, but in reality there are only four, as those seeming to be two upper ones with four handles are the front of the writing portion. The borders in light wood around the drawers add to the interest of the piece. The handles are of a type occasionally seen in the period. On the cornice and on the skirt are lines of inlay. Between the French bracket feet there is, as usual, a skirt cut in cyma curves. About 1795–1810.

6. In Mr. Cescinsky's "English Furniture," there are several examples; in volume 2, a bookcase, figure 124, dated about 1755; another dated about 1765–1770, figure 342. In volume 3, figure 122, there is a bookcase dated about 1770–1780 with panes in the same design as in our Nos. 856 and 857.

Nos. 861–864 are secretary–bookcases according to our definitions in sections 101 and 109, but are of a different type from those previously seen. In each of these four pieces the upper portion has shelves intended for books and the lower portion is meant for writing purposes, as appears from the folding lid which may be opened, forming a writing surface supported by two pulls. The first three are in the Hepplewhite style and the fourth is in the Sheraton style.

No. 861 is an elegant and dainty piece in the Hepplewhite style.[7] At the top are scrolls resembling those in No. 853, between which is an urn on a pedestal. In the glazed doors the upper panes are in Gothic forms. There is one drawer with a finely figured mahogany veneer on the front. On each side is a brass handle to be used in moving the piece. The appearance of height in the tapered legs is caused by there being but one drawer instead of several. All of the front is decorated with lines of inlay. About 1790–1800.

No. 862 is a handsome secretary–bookcase with two drawers in the lower portion and a lid and pulls. In the upper portion there are thirteen panes of glass; the shadows of some of the partitions between the panes are more easily seen in the illustration than the partitions themselves. Under the doors are three drawers. Delicate inlay is seen over the entire front. A shell is in the centre of the top, four groups of four leaves each are on the ends, four strings of bell–flowers are on the upper and lower ends, rectangular forms are on the large drawers and bands are on the legs near the floor. About 1790–1800.

No. 863 is in the same general form as the preceding piece, but is smaller and not so fully decorated. In each of the doors are eight panes of glass, the arrangement of which is similar to that in the preceding piece, but with fewer panes; here also the shadows of the partitions are conspicuous in the illustration. The lower portion is finely decorated with inlay on the drawers and legs. The narrow lines of inlay on the drawers are within wider ones on the edges. About 1790–1800.

In No. 864 are seen two features plainly characteristic of the Sheraton style. One is the pediment,[8] consisting of a high central portion from which concave curves extend to the ends where there are two small pedestals with urns. The other feature is seen in the reeded columns projecting beyond the line of the drawers and terminating in rounded and tapering legs and feet, much the same as in the bureaus Nos. 745–748. The arched panes of glass in the bookcase portion extend downwards almost to the finely grained panels of light wood which conceal the drawers or pigeonholes within. About 1795–1810.

7. A piece of similar design but more elaborately inlaid and with the usual thirteen panes, is shown as No. 707 in the catalogue of the "Girl Scouts Loan Exhibition" held in New York in September, 1929. The piece has no lid or pulls and thus has no writing facilities, and is therefore called a "china cabinet." Its date is given as 1790–1800, and its place of origin is said to be "probably Baltimore."

8. See Nos. 825–826 and notes 4 and 5 in section 106.

861 (Upper) Mrs. S. S. Buzby.   862 (Upper) Mrs. A. Morris Carey.
863 (Lower) Mr. C. W. L. Johnson.   864 (Lower) Mr. & Mrs. Bayard Turnbull.

865 (UPPER) MR. JAMES E. STEUART.
867 (LOWER) MISS DORA L. MURDOCH.

866 (UPPER) MISS HELEN H. CAREY.
868 (LOWER) MR. EDGAR G. MILLER, JR.

Section 111. Secretary–bookcases; later styles.—In this section are shown four secretary–bookcases of a later type which are not generally admitted to the books on antique furniture because they are not of sufficient age or elegance, but which appear here in order to present examples of the Empire and Victorian styles. In these pieces several features taken from previous styles will be seen.

In No. 865, a mixture of styles, the upper portion is from a small bookcase with two scrolls between which there is an urn. These scrolls resemble somewhat in form those seen on No. 858 in the previous section. In each door there are four rectangular panes of glass and at the intersection of the frames there is an ornamental panel as in No. 851. The design of the upper portion is copied from plate 47, dated August 6, 1792, in Sheraton's "Drawing Book,"[1] the piece being called a "cylinder desk and bookcase," in describing which Sheraton wrote that "the square figure of the door is much in fashion now." Below the doors are two small drawers. The desk portion has a solid cylinder top of the type shown in No. 809, but with glass knobs. The round legs and the ball feet are of the same type as those on the Empire style bureau No. 763. About 1825–1830.

In No. 866 the lower portion resembles somewhat the Empire style bureau No. 766, having a large overhanging top drawer, short round columns and animals' claw feet. The front of the top drawer pulls out and down, disclosing pigeonholes and drawers as in the next piece and in the "bureau desk" No. 827. The wooden knobs will also be noticed. The doors of the bookcase portion above have many panes of glass, mostly in the diamond shape. The date of this Empire style piece is probably about 1830.

In No. 867 the bookcase portion has a high cornice, as in the previous piece, here supported by long round columns. The lower portion is in the form of a "bureau desk" in which the open front is supported by "quadrants," as explained in connection with Nos. 856–860. The interior drawers and pigeonholes have curly maple fronts. Two "books" in the centre serve as vertical drawers, as in No. 808 and others. The lower portion resembles the miniature bureau which is shown in No. 774, with massive scrolled sides and feet. The date of this piece in the late Empire style is about 1830–1840.

No. 868 is a later piece, being in the Victorian style of about 1860. We may imagine the cabinet maker using various designs which he had seen in earlier pieces, some of which were then old fashioned, as is also mentioned in connection with the two bureaus Nos. 767 and 768. Other comments are in the note.[2] The

1. As to this book, see section 18.

2. The desk portion has a slanting lid, which had apparently passed out of style many years before, and which in 1792 was "nearly obsolete in London," as mentioned in section 104, note 1. The pediment is not very different in general shape from that in No. 865, although solid and much more ornamented. The lid when open is not supported by pulls or quadrants, as in No. 858, but is firmly held by an interior arrangement as in Nos. 835 and 836. The two large round panels on the square lower doors are no doubt copied from inlaid oval panels in pieces like No. 856, or on the doors of the Hepplewhite and Sheraton style sideboards such as Nos. 971 and 975; and indeed on a square door a round inlay is more harmonious than an oval one. This will be easily demonstrated by a glance at Nos. 856 and 868, in comparison with some of the other pieces.

fanciful forms of carved decorations placed on so much of the available surface on the front were made separately and were "applied" with glue. We may admire the "rococo," and even the "baroque,"[3] designs in their proper places, but not on Victorian furniture. Much of this ornamentation seems meaningless and coarse, but nevertheless this secretary-bookcase has a certain dignity. About 1850-1860.

Section 112. Bookcases.—The shelves in the upper portion of the secretary-bookcases shown in sections 109-111 provided such a convenient place for the few books which were sufficient for the ordinary house of the eighteenth century that it is not strange that there was but little demand for separate bookcases. For many of the more pretentious homes, however, in our country, as in England, large bookcases were made. They were often in three sections, the central one being wider than the other two, called "wings," and projecting forward beyond them. In many cases the bookcases were made without feet.

Nos. 869, 870 and 871 are examples of these large bookcases, each of which has a capacity for several times the number of books which could be placed in a secretary-bookcase of the size shown in the three sections above cited; and some bookcases were much larger.[1] The bookcase No. 869 originally had two additional "wings" which were recently removed and put together as another bookcase which is now in the home of a descendant of the original owner, Colonel John Eager Howard, of Baltimore, 1752-1827, of Revolutionary War fame and Governor of Maryland. About 1780-1800.

In No. 870 we see glass doors which are familiar to us, being similar to those in the secretary-bookcases Nos. 855 and 860, having interlaced ovals with small panels in the centre. On both ends of the projecting central section and at the outer ends of the wings are reeded flat columns called "pilasters." At the top of the lower portion is a light-colored band, in the central part of which is a shallow drawer with a keyhole. The four cupboards below have sunken panels with an arch and "pilasters" at four points. The feet are of the ball type. About 1800-1820.

In No. 871, also, the doors in the central section are in a familiar pattern, having thirteen panes of glass in each, as in the secretary-bookcases Nos. 856 and 857; and each of the doors in the wings has eighteen panes. In the lower portion there are two small drawers in each wing; in the centre is a large drawer containing a writing compartment as in the bureau desk No. 828; and there is a vertical drawer on each side. Under the drawers are four cupboards. All of the drawers have wooden knobs. As in the previous piece, the feet are of the ball type. About 1800-1820.

3. As to the meaning of these words, see section 92, note 2.

1. In No. 869 the panes of glass in the four doors are in fanciful forms which are difficult to describe. The doors in the central section have at the top and bottom a row of interlaced circles between which are three small circles on the sides, with large and somewhat intricate figures occupying the other spaces. The doors in the wings are cut in other forms, the largest of which is in a diamond shape, and there are other small circles on the sides. Thirty "quatrefoils," which are described in the chapter on chairs, page 148, are on the front of this bookcase and are similar to those on the Gothic chairs in the Chippendale style, such as No. 114 and others. There are four cupboards in the lower portion, with paneled doors.

869 (UPPER) MR. BENJAMIN CHEW HOWARD.
870 (LOWER) MR. & MRS. LENNOX BIRCKHEAD.

The smaller type of bookcases, such as Nos. 872-875, became popular about the year 1800. The favorite type had a cabinet top with movable shelves, under which there is generally a wide drawer, and under the drawer is a cupboard with two doors within which are shelves or partitions.

No. 872 is a pleasing bookcase now used as a china cabinet. Under the cornice is an applied molding with Gothic arches and acorns as in Nos. 854 and 855. This molding continues around the sides of the bookcase. There are eight rectangular panes of glass in each door. There is no drawer between the upper and the lower

871—Mr. John Ridgely.

portion as there is in the next three pieces here shown. Two cupboard doors, showing a fine grain of mahogany, are in the lower portion, within which are shelves. The feet are of the straight bracket type, which continued to be used in many pieces in the Hepplewhite and Sheraton styles. About 1790–1810.

No. 873 is recognized at once as being in the Sheraton style because of the kind of pediment, which we have seen in the secretary–bookcases Nos. 826 and 864. The three brass urns which were on the top are missing. Nine panes of glass are in each door, the upper ones having Gothic arches. In the lower portion are two small drawers with glass knobs. Below the drawers are the doors of two cupboards which enclose shelves. On each end is an inlaid string of flowers. The feet are of the round and tapering type which are characteristic of pieces in the Sheraton style. About 1795–1810.

In No. 874 the top is flat, with a line of inlay which continues around the sides. In each door are nine rectangular panes of glass, above which are interlacing designs of Gothic arches. In the lower portion are two drawers with inlaid lines, below which are two cupboard doors as in the previous piece. The feet are of the ogee bracket type and their curves are also seen on the left side. About 1790–1800.

No. 875 is a later type of bookcase, as shown by the rounded corners of both the upper and lower portions, resembling in this respect the desk No. 836 and the Victorian bureau No. 768. Features of several previous styles will be seen, as in No. 868. The glazed doors have interlaced ovals as in two previous pieces, Nos. 855 and 860. In the lower portion there is one long drawer under which are two cupboard doors in the usual form. The upper portion is not as deep as the lower one, and thus leaves a flat surface above the drawer, as in the china cabinets in the next section. The "matched" mahogany veneer on the cupboard doors of this and the preceding bookcase will be noticed; see note 2 in section 32. About 1840–1850.

Section 113. China cabinets.—Very little information is found in the books on American antique furniture in regard to china[1] cabinets; and the few which are illustrated are not easily distinguishable from certain secretary–bookcases and bookcases whose shelves and glazed doors were as well adapted to the display of china as of books. China was also kept in corner cupboards, as will appear in the illustrations in sections 122–123.

The principal features which distinguish the four china cabinets Nos. 876–879 from the bookcases Nos. 872–874 in the previous section are that the cupboards of the china cabinets do not extend to the floor or near to it, and that in each of the china cabinets the top of the lower portion provides a flat surface on which articles may be placed temporarily, as in the bookcase No. 875. Whether or not these pieces were originally made for china cabinets, they are elegant and pleasing and have been used for china for very many years by the families of the present owners.

1. In Mr. Cescinsky's "English Furniture," volume 2, page 309, it is said that the word "china" has, through custom, lost its original significance, which was porcelain imported from China or Japan, and that Chippendale seems to have regarded furniture made in the "Chinese manner" as the only suitable style for cabinets to hold china. The "Chinese manner" is referred to in section 51 at chairs Nos. 140 and 141.

On page 310 in Mr. Cescinsky's book are illustrations of "china shelves" made to hang on the wall.

Cabinets, or closets, for china were occasionally placed on the tops of sideboards; fine examples are in volume 1 of Mr. Lockwood's "Colonial Furniture," pages 201 and 202; on his page 376 is a handsome example. One is shown in this book as No. 1007 in the chapter on sideboards.

A large central drawer in sideboards, as in the bookcase No. 871, was occasionally fitted out with writing materials. Other large pieces resembling sideboards, but known as "Salem secretaries," were furnished with similar writing drawers; examples are illustrated in an article in "Antiques," May, 1933, by Mr. Fiske Kimball.

872 (Upper) Mr. John C. Toland.
874 (Lower) Est. of Mrs. Thos. J. Lindsay.

873 (Upper) Mr. & Mrs. W. Hall Harris.
875 (Lower) Mr. & Mrs. W. Hall Harris.

876 (Upper) Mrs. Townsend Scott.   877 (Upper) Mrs. G. Frank Baily.
878 (Lower) Mrs. Isaac Ridgeway Trimble.   879 (Lower) Miss Eleanor S. Cohen.

No. 876 has the popular doors with thirteen panes of glass which we have seen in the secretary–bookcase No. 856 and others. The pediment has scrolls with an urn upon a pedestal in the centre. The front of the lower portion is in the serpentine form, such as is seen on the bureaus Nos. 725–730 and others. The two drawers are furnished with glass knobs. Lines of inlay are on the doors and drawers; inlaid shells are on the pediment and on the ends of the lower portion. The tapering on the inside of the legs will also be noticed. About 1790–1800.

No. 877 is a similar piece with a straight front in the lower portion. The scrolls on the pediment, with an urn in the centre, below which is an inlaid American eagle, the thirteen panes of glass, the two drawers and the two cupboards below, are in the same style as in the previous piece. There is also a line of inlay under the cupboards, and on the tapering legs are strings of flowers and bands near the bottom. About 1790–1800.

No. 878 is somewhat smaller than the two preceding pieces; the top is straight; the doors have the familiar thirteen panes of glass, and we see the usual style of inlay, the tapering legs with inlaid bands near the bottom, and the oval brass handles. About 1790–1800.

In No. 879 we recognize some of the features of the late Sheraton style and of the later American Empire style. The pediment is in a form which appeared in Sheraton's last book,[2] published in 1812, and is not provided with pedestals to receive urns. The ends of the upper portion are ornamented with long lines of reeding as in the bookcase No. 870. The lower portion, however, with its heavy spiral legs, ball feet and square blocks above the feet, is of a later date than that of the upper portion, as in Nos. 763 and 865. The glass doors are in the design seen in the secretary–bookcases Nos. 855 and 860, and in the bookcase No. 870, with carving[3] in addition. This piece is regarded as a china cabinet, but is now used as a bookcase, reversing the more frequent usage of a bookcase as a china cabinet. Probably about 1810–1830.

2. This type of pediment appears in the book "Chippendale, Sheraton and Hepplewhite Furniture Designs," arranged by Mr. J. M. Bell, page 168; the design was in the book of Sheraton published in 1812, after his death; see section 18 regarding the books of Sheraton.

3. The carved design on the partitions around the six–sided central panel is copied almost exactly from design No. 6 in plate 27, page 302 of Sheraton's "Drawing Book," which is referred to in connection with No. 855.

A piece very similar in certain respects appears in "The Antiquarian," October, 1930, page 66. The editor states that he believes the date of the piece to be about 1825 to 1835.

Chapter XIII

BLOCK–FRONT FURNITURE

Section 114. Preliminary remarks.—As mentioned several times in this volume, the subject of block–front furniture is not considered in the chapters treating of the various articles on which the block–fronts appear, but is considered in this one chapter where all the articles may be conveniently examined together. The reason for this method is that in such articles the block–front is the principal subject of interest; and except for the block–fronts the articles having them are not very different from those of the same period without them. At present, in the opinion of connoisseurs, the fine block–front pieces are among the best products of American cabinet makers.[1]

One block–front design has been found in England, as appears from the illustration of the desk in the note;[2] but it is now regarded as an American product and the date is thought to be about 1760–1775.

1. Mr. Herbert Cescinsky, the author of "English Furniture," writes in "English and American Furniture," pages 146–147: "Although these Philadelphia highboys and lowboys bring enormous prices at public auctions, if I were asked to select the finest examples of American furniture, my choice would fall on the block–fronted bureaux from Newport and Rhode Island." In English usage the word "bureau" means a "desk," as is mentioned in section 101.

In "Antiques," October, 1923, page 176, in an article entitled "The Block–Front in England," Mr. Cescinsky suggests that the origin may be traced to Holland.

The writer has seen in the ancient cathedral at Havana, Cuba, a number of large chests of drawers which at least suggest the block–front. An illustration of a group of these chests of drawers, connected as one very long chest, is in the "Furniture Treasury" of Mr. Wallace Nutting, volume 1, No. 260; see also No. 712 in the same volume.

2. This illustration is copied from "English Furniture," by Mr. Percy Macquoid, London, 1906, volume 3, No. 39. The date is given as "about 1720." The comment states that "the front is divided into four drawers, the tubbed and recessed surfaces entailing a sacrifice of three and a half inches of the

Almost all block–front pieces of furniture were made in New England and the finest have been traced to Newport, Rhode Island. In that city, a rich one in the latter part of the eighteenth century, two cabinet makers, John Townsend and John Goddard produced the pieces which have made their names famous, and have given to Newport a position almost equal to that of Philadelphia in the history of American furniture. Certain facts regarding these men are mentioned in the note.[3] In the neighboring State of Connecticut, also, many fine pieces were made by various cabinet makers of that State who were competent to follow, in part at least, the designs of the Townsend and Goddard shops. A number of minor differences in style and workmanship have been observed in the various pieces made by Townsend and Goddard respectively; but it is said that unless the pieces are labeled or otherwise identified it may not be possible to determine whether a particular piece was made by Townsend or Goddard or copied from their designs by other cabinet makers. For this reason certain pieces are attributed merely to "Townsend or Goddard," or are said to be "Rhode Island pieces" or pieces of the "Newport school" or "Connecticut pieces." Many block–front pieces were made by other cabinet makers in various parts of New England and although these pieces did not have the distinctive features of the work of Townsend and Goddard, they are often fine in design and workmanship and are much desired by collectors.[4]

(NOTE 2, *continued*)

wood." The height is about three feet and six inches. The lower portion of the desk may be compared with the bureau No. 887.

3. John Goddard was born at Newport in 1724 and died there in 1785, insolvent. Besides his importance as a cabinet maker he is noted as the father of fifteen children. John Townsend, born in 1733, worked in Newport. The theory that he moved to Middletown, Connecticut, at some date after 1769, is not now favored. The exact date of his death is not known. These two men were cousins–in–law.

Further information on the subject of Townsend and Goddard will be found in Mr. Lockwood's "Colonial Furniture," third edition, 1926, pages 117, 354–358; in the magazine "Antiques," April, 1929, pages 275–277, December, 1930, page 513, and June, 1931, pages 435–436; and in the "Metropolitan Museum Studies," 1928, part 1, page 72.

For several years it was commonly thought that John Goddard was the sole originator and developer of the block–front style, and it became the custom in catalogues and magazine articles to attribute to Goddard almost every fine piece of block–front furniture, just as William Savery in Philadelphia was at one time popularly regarded as the maker of almost every fine highboy and lowboy of the Philadelphia style. But it now appears that credit for these fine pieces should be divided between John Townsend and John Goddard, and that the latter was perhaps not the master maker. See also the remarks in notes 1 and 2 in section 87.

Advertisements offering block–front furniture for sale have helped to make the name of John Goddard almost as famous as the names of William Savery and Duncan Phyfe. A great number of pieces have been fearlessly attributed, without documentary proof, to Goddard as the actual maker. Gradually the advertisements became less positive, as is shown in the following quotations. A certain bureau "was made by Goddard, the famous Newport cabinet maker." A desk was "undoubtedly by Goddard, of Newport." Another piece "bears many characteristics of the work of Goddard." One was merely "attributed to John Goddard," and another was "attributed to the master cabinet maker without the slightest doubt." A kneehole desk was "undoubtedly a production of the Goddard school." In a desk "Goddard's handiwork is particularly to be noticed."

4. In Mr. Nutting's "Furniture Treasury," volume 3, pages 431–447, is an illustrated discussion of John Goddard and his work. On page 438 Mr. Nutting remarks that "No other specimens of furni-

(*Note 4 continued on page 482.*)

A block–front on a drawer was cut in such a way as to make a "raised" surface at each end of the drawer and a "depressed" surface in the centre, somewhat similar in this respect to the reversed serpentine fronts of the drawers of bureaus and desks shown in the two preceding chapters. A block–front was frequently cut from a single thick piece of wood. It is said, however, that on certain pieces the raised shells were "applied" with glue, and that in some cases the raised flat surfaces were similarly attached;[5] but shells which were depressed below the line of the front of the drawer were cut out from the solid wood.

The articles of furniture made with block–fronts were mainly chests–on–chests, bureaus, desks, secretaries and dressing tables, all of which are illustrated in this chapter in the order named.[6] The blocked articles follow the general style of the same unblocked articles of the period. Thus the feet of the block–front bureaus and desks are of the same type as those on the bureaus and desks of the same period, shown in the two preceding sections. The wood used was generally mahogany, sometimes maple or cherry, the latter being used in many pieces made in Connecticut. Neither inlay nor veneer were used.

The dates of perhaps all of the block–front pieces range from about 1750 to 1780, in the Chippendale period. After the Chippendale style passed out of fashion and the Hepplewhite style came in, the block–front pieces were no longer made.

Block–front pieces of the finest type, that is, with the carved block shells and other features made only in the Rhode Island style of Townsend and Goddard,[7] are more often seen in museums than in private houses; but pieces not made in that style are frequently seen in private collections and at auction sales.

(NOTE 4, *continued from page 481*)

ture are so impressive as a block–and–shell high secretary or a chest–on–chest. These are the aristocrats of furniture"; and page 439, that "where the blocks lack the shells the blocks appear incomplete, and that their attractiveness may fairly be questioned."

Certain differences have been noticed in block–front articles of furniture between the pieces made in Rhode Island and those made in Connecticut, the former being more favorably regarded. These differences are stated in detail in Mr. Nutting's book mentioned above, pages 443–445.

5. In "Antiques," March, 1925, pages 127–128, instances are mentioned in an article by Mr. Malcolm A. Norton. Other illustrated articles, by the same writer, on the subject of block–front furniture are in the issues of February, 1923, page 63, and March, 1927, page 192.

6. In addition to the block–fronts on the five kinds of furniture considered in this chapter, the cases of grandfather clocks were ornamented with block–fronts. See also "Antiques," July, 1933, frontispiece and pages 3 and 4.

Block–fronts on other kinds of furniture have occasionally been used, but were not favored. A lowboy in the Queen Anne style with a block–front is illustrated in "Antiques," September, 1929, page 182, and a highboy and a lowboy are shown in Mr. Lockwood's "Colonial Furniture," volume 1, figures 100 and 101.

7. A. The carved shells are the most noticeable feature of the Townsend and Goddard pieces, which are often referred to as "Rhode Island pieces" or as pieces of the "Newport school," as above stated. Certain other features are also mentioned here and will be referred to in the comments.

B. It is said that the most specific characteristic in the chests of drawers, (the bureaus), is a molding beneath the top, as in Nos. 884 and 885; and in the high "hooded" pieces, a molding on

After these preliminary remarks we proceed with the illustrations, for many of which the writer is indebted to the Metropolitan Museum of Art and to Mr. Luke Vincent Lockwood who has kindly given his permission to copy from his "Colonial Furniture" in which many examples are shown.

Section 115. Block–front chests–on–chests.—In section 81, in which the usual types of chests–on–chests are considered, a block–front piece, No. 624, is shown as a reminder that the block–front type of chests–on–chests should not be overlooked; and in this section the subject is continued. It is suggested that the section above cited be read in connection with the present one.

No. 880 is a handsome block–front chest–on–chest[1] and has the most elaborate blocking of any of the pieces shown in this chapter. On this large piece, regarded as having been made by Townsend or Goddard, there are the unusual number of nine shells, the three inverted ones on the lower drawer of the upper portion not being found on other pieces. At the top are two large box-like supports[2] for the pedestals, urns and flames, a treatment which is also seen on the next piece; these finials are said to be substitutes, not being in the Townsend–Goddard style. On the top drawer of the upper portion are three shells, the outer ones "raised" and the inner one "depressed," which is the usual method in all block–front objects. On the upper drawer of the lower portion there is the same arrangement of the three similar shells. On each of the front bracket feet is a small circular scroll, mentioned in note 7, C in the preceding section, and not well seen in the engraving; examples of such a foot are shown in the small engraving in the note.[3] The

(NOTE 7, *continued*)

the curved openings under the scrolls in the top, as in the chest–on–chest No. 881 and the secretary, No. 896. See "Antiques," April, 1931, page 324.

C.   Another characteristic is that the front feet are in the bracket form with a scroll addition on the inside, ending in a small circular scroll at the bottom, as is shown in the small engraving on this page.

D.   The urns and flames at the top of the chests–on–chests and secretaries are different from those on other pieces, as in Nos. 881 and 896.

E.   When a shell is used on a bureau, as No. 884, or desk, as No. 890, the front of the top is made in a straight line; but the base of the piece is always shaped in a manner to conform to the vertical lines of the blocking above.

1.   This is shown on page 353 of volume 1 of Mr. Lockwood's "Colonial Furniture." In an article in "Antiques," January, 1922, page 17, it is No. 1 in a series of "Little–known Masterpieces," with comments on page 18.

2.   A box of this kind was also used on the top of some of the grandfather clocks of the period. where it was often most effective.

3.   In the article mentioned in note 1 the circular scroll is referred to as being a part of an extra foot ending in a small volute, or spiral scroll; and Mr. Lockwood refers to "the bracket feet with the extra feet carved on the inside." The small illustration is an enlargement of feet on No. 905.

large and elaborate brass handles were doubtless imported from England. Two other large handles for moving purposes will be seen on the side. The surfaces of the blocked parts of the drawers are flat, not curved. The date of this piece is regarded as about 1760–1780.

No. 881 is also of the Townsend–Goddard type. It has four carved shells, one at the top and three below, the latter being arranged as usual with two "raised" shells on the ends and a "depressed" one in the centre; the single shell at the top is also depressed. On each end of the upper portion is a fluted column. The box–like supports of the end finials are similar to those in the previous piece, and the finials are in a form peculiar to the Rhode Island pieces. The top is "scrolled" and "hooded" as also in Nos. 882, 883, 896 and 897. The molding around the curved openings at the top is a characteristic feature as mentioned in note 7, B in the previous section. About 1750–1775.

No. 882 has no raised block shells nor any molding around the curved openings at the top, and is therefore not regarded as being in the Townsend and Goddard style; but it is a stately and handsome piece. The inner ends of the scrolls in the top are furnished with carved rosettes with leaf sprays. At the ends of the upper portion are fluted pilasters. The shell at the top is not in the same design as those in the previous two pieces. In the lower portion the four drawers are blocked and arranged in the usual manner. About 1770–1780.

No. 883 is somewhat plain in comparison with the previous pieces. The central drawer at the top has no ornamentation. On each side of this central drawer is a smaller drawer whose top is in a curved line, similar to those in the chest–on–chest No. 622. The pilasters on the ends are fluted on the upper part and reeded on the lower part, a design which is sometimes seen in other pieces, as in No. 896, and is seen in the corner columns of many grandfather clocks. The handles and escutcheons are in an open–work form. The feet are in a plain straight bracket form. This also is not in the Townsend and Goddard style. About 1760–1775.

Section 116. Block–front bureaus.—In the six bureaus, Nos. 884–889, shown in this section, the first two were presumably made by Townsend or Goddard, judging from the appearance of the blocks and the carved shells, the separate line of molding under the top of each bureau, and the scrolls carved on the front feet as shown on the small illustration in note 3 in the previous section, but not well seen here. The other four bureaus have not these distinctive features, but seem to be excellent examples and are apparently the work of skillful cabinet makers. Many more bureaus of this latter type are found than those of the expensive Townsend–Goddard type. In each of the bureaus there is a resemblance to those in the Chippendale style shown in section 94, excepting, of course, the blocking.

Nos. 884 and 885 are similar in general appearance, except that the former has four drawers and the latter has three. Small lines of molding will be seen on the framework *around* the drawers, not *on* the drawers, a feature of the Chip-

880 (Upper) Lockwood Col. Furn., Page 353.
882 (Lower) Lockwood, Col. Furn., Page 360.
881 (Upper) Lockwood, Col. Furn., Page 121.
883 (Lower) Metropolitan Museum of Art.

884 (Upper) Metropolitan Museum of Art.
886 (Centre) Hammond-Harwood House.
888 (Lower) Mr. Albert G. Towers.

885 (Upper) Metropolitan Museum of Art.
887 (Centre) Mrs. Francis P. Garvan.
889 (Lower) Mr. John C. Toland.

pendale and earlier styles.[1] The number of the "radiates," or rays, in the shells is not the same in each piece. The shells on the ends of the top drawer of each piece are "raised," as usual, and the central shell is "depressed." In each case the blocked portions and the shells above them give the appearance of a continuous vertical panel from the top to the bottom. Under the top is the separate line of molding referred to in note 7, B, in section 114. The fronts of the tops are straight, not conforming to the blocking below; but the base conforms. In block–front pieces the blocking of the drawers begins about one or two inches from the ends of the drawers, as in the drawers of certain bureaus having reversed serpentine fronts.[2] On each bureau there are two escutcheons with bail handles on the top drawer between the shells. About 1750–1775.

Nos. 886 and 887 are very similar block–front bureaus. In these and the two following pieces there are no carved shells nor any other of the special features of the style of Townsend and Goddard as mentioned in note 7 in section 114. In each of these two bureaus the top and the base are shaped in a manner to conform to the blocking of the drawers, in this respect differing from the two preceding pieces. The plain feet are in different forms of the straight bracket type. The blocked surfaces are arranged in the usual manner, the depressed block being in the centre. In No. 886 the brass handles seem to be very large for the drawers, as in No. 893, but this will also be noticed on several other pieces in this chapter. About 1760–1775.

In Nos. 888 and 889 we see a different type of block–front bureaus. Here the three blocked surfaces are not flat, but curved, the two at the ends curving forward in a convex form and the central one curving slightly inward in a concave form. The top and the base conform to the drawers in shape, as in the two previous bureaus. No. 888 has plain bracket feet with modern casters and No. 889 has ball and claw feet. About 1760–1775.

Some of the forms of bureaus shown in this section are seen again in the block–front desks and secretaries shown in the next two sections. It will be recalled that the lower portion of the desks and secretaries in sections 101 and 109 are generally in about the same form as a bureau.

Section 117. Block–front desks.—Of the six desks, Nos. 890–895, shown in this section, only Nos. 890 and 891 have indications of having been made by the master makers of block–front furniture, John Townsend and John Goddard. We especially notice the bracket feet mentioned in note 7, C in section 114. On the slanting lid of No. 890 there are three carved shells, below which are large flat blocked surfaces. This type of blocking on the lid will also be seen in Nos. 896 and 897 in the next section. The shells and the flat blocked surfaces in some pieces of this kind not made by Townsend or Goddard seem to have been

1. See this mentioned in the chapter on bureaus, section 93, note 3, C. These moldings on the framework around the drawers are on most of the block–front pieces shown in this chapter, but may not always be well seen on account of the small size of the engravings.

2. Examples are in the bureaus Nos. 717 and 718.

890 (Upper) Metropolitan Museum of Art.   891 (Upper) Anonymous.
892 (Centre) Metropolitan Museum of Art.   893 (Centre) Metropolitan Museum of Art.
894 (Lower) Mrs. Alexander Armstrong.   895 (Lower) Mrs. Maurice F. Rodgers.

"applied," as mentioned in the text, section 114 at note 5. The two keyholes have small sliding brass covers, as there is no space available for large escutcheons. About 1760–1775.

In No. 891, shown open, an indication of the Townsend and Goddard style is given by the three shells at the top of the lower portion and by the bracket feet with carved scrolls ending with small circular scrolls as illustrated in section 115, note 3. There are no blocked shells on the lid. The arrangement of the raised and the depressed blockings is as usual. The handsome interior is not well seen in the engraving, but we notice the two rows of drawers, and the arched "curtains" of the pigeonholes. A vertical drawer is on each side of the central compartment which, as usual, contains several drawers, the upper one having a shell design. These features of the interior are all familiar, as numerous illustrations of them were seen in the previous chapter, sections 103 and 109. About 1760–1775.

On No. 892, regarded as a typical piece, there is no blocking on the slanting lid, but the four graduated drawers are blocked in the usual manner, with the depressed form in the centre; the blocking extends down through the molding into the brackets of the legs, as in several other pieces. Here the four feet are of the ball and claw type and at the centre of the base is a scrolled ornament; these features were apparently not used by the Newport cabinet makers. Three large handles are on each of the drawers, so large in fact that they are bent over on the top drawer; and a handle for moving is on the side. About 1760–1775.

Nos. 893 and 894 are interior views of similar desks. At the ends of each interior are concave drawers with shells and in the centre is a concave compartment, with a shell on the door. These shells, the columns, (which are the fronts of vertical drawers), and the fronts of the small drawers, are all in much the same form as in the desk No. 801 in the previous chapter. The feet are of the ball and claw type and on the base of No. 893 is a carved shell.[1] About 1760–1775.

No. 895 appears to be somewhat plain in comparison with the other desks, mainly because the lid is closed and because there are no handles on the central part of the front and the oval handles are of a later period than the desk. Here the feet are of the ball and claw type, much flattened as in numerous instances. The central blocking is wider than that on the ends, and the blocking is continued down through the moldings to the base, as in other pieces. About 1770–1780.

Section 118. Block–front secretaries.—In this section we see several fine examples of the block–front "secretary," which word, as mentioned in section 101, means a desk with a cabinet above containing pigeonholes and drawers for papers, but not long shelves for books. As the features of these block–front secretaries are about the same as those shown in section 109 in the chapter on desks, with the addition of the block–front feature, they need not be repeated here.

1. In "Antiques," April, 1929, page 276, are shown two interiors which somewhat resemble that in No. 893, with remarks by the editor.

In No. 896 the top is "scrolled" and is also "hooded," that is, it has a hood or covering made in the same curve as that of the scrolls, as in the highboy No. 653 and the chests–on–chests Nos. 881–883; this form is often called a "bonnet" top. The finials, that is, the pedestals, urns and flames, are in a style peculiar to the Townsend and Goddard pieces as mentioned in note 7, D in section 114, and in the comment on the chest–on–chest No. 881. Around the edge of the curved openings under the inner ends of the scrolls are moldings which are characteristic of the same makers, as mentioned in section 114, note 7, B. Under the scrolls are two raised panels. There are three doors, two of which are hinged together, the purpose of having three being to provide spaces for three shells which would harmonize with the three shells on the lid of the desk and with the three blocked drawers. On the top of each of the two outer doors there is a carved "raised" shell and on the central door there is a carved "depressed" shell. On the corners are columns which on the upper part are fluted and on the lower part are reeded, as in the chest–on–chest No. 883. The lid is ornamented with three carved shells, the outer ones being raised and the central one depressed; and under the shells are large blocked surfaces, as in No. 890. There are also two escutcheons on the doors and two others on the lid. The lower portion has three drawers with blockings which extend down through the molding to the feet. On the ends of the feet are the characteristic scrolls of Townsend and Goddard, mentioned in section 114, note 7, C and illustrated in note 3 in section 115. About 1760–1775.

No. 897 is a similar secretary which is regarded as having been made by Townsend or Goddard. It differs from the previous example in certain details. The scrolls at the top have rosettes on the inside ends; the columns at the corners are fluted throughout; under the lid is a slide which pulls out; the pulls which support the lid are very small, as in No. 896 and in the early desk No. 777 which is shown in the previous chapter on desks; and the molded partitions around the drawers and on the base are of a darker color than the fronts of the drawers. The finials are in the same style as in the previous piece. The upper portion of this secretary seems to be of great height, but it is said to exhibit a happy medium between some which are too high and others which are too low. About 1760–1775.

In Nos. 898 and 899, closed and open, we see a block–front secretary in the "bombé" type, which type is also seen in the bureau No. 724. The blocking is only on the lower portion where the four drawers curve outward.[1] About 1750–1775.

1. The "pediment," at the top, is a "broken pediment" such as is also seen in the secretary-bookcase No. 851 in the chapter on desks. The architectural molding in the form of small rectangular blocks is called a "dentil" molding, from its supposed resemblance to a row of teeth. The "pilasters" at the outer sides of the doors are fluted. The beveled panels in the doors are cut in the form of cyma curves, as to which see section 23, and as in Nos. 849 and 900. The interior of the upper portion has twenty–five pigeonholes, three large open sections and four drawers; this arrangement may be compared with that in the fine secretary No. 840 in the chapter on desks. The characteristic features of the secretaries made by Townsend or Goddard are not seen in this piece.

896 (UPPER) METROPOLITAN MUSEUM OF ART.   897 (UPPER) MRS. FRANCIS P. GARVAN.
898 (LOWER) METROPOLITAN MUSEUM OF ART.   899 (LOWER) METROPOLITAN MUSEUM OF ART.

491

900 (Upper) Mr. George Bradford Simmons.
901 (Upper) Mr. John S. McDaniel.
902 (Lower) Mr. John C. Toland.
903 (Lower) Metropolitan Museum of Art.

492

Nos. 900 and 901 are also fine examples of block–front secretaries, differing from each other chiefly in the design of the upper portions; the Townsend and Goddard features are not found in these pieces. In No. 900 the inner ends of the scrolls terminate in carved and applied rosettes. The panels in the doors are cut in cyma curves in a manner similar to those in Nos. 849 and 898, and in the mirrors Nos. 1139–1141; and the two pilasters are fluted. Two candlestands are under the doors. The blocked drawers are in the usual form. About 1760–1780.

In No. 901 the space in the centre under the scrolls is ornamented with a carved shell. The doors are paneled and arched as in the secretary No. 845 and others in the previous chapter; and each door has two fluted pilasters which give an appearance of height. The blocking of the drawers is in the usual form. It will be noticed that the finials—the urns and the flames at the top—are in a different design from those on the Rhode Island pieces such as Nos. 896 and 897 and others. About 1760–1780.

No. 902 differs only in detail from the preceding secretary. There is a circular carved ornament in the centre of the top and the doors are arched and paneled. The two escutcheons on the doors, and the two candlestands, will be noticed. The tall finials assist in giving an appearance of height which in the two previous pieces was secured by the fluted pilasters. About 1760–1775.

No. 903 is an unusual piece and is made of cherry instead of the usual mahogany. The very short legs and the feet are in the Queen Anne style and are similar to those on the desk No. 780. This style of feet and legs was out of date in the cities in the block–front period. The brass balls on the top are doubtless substitutes for the original wooden ones. The handles are larger than many others. The most conspicuous peculiarity is the insufficient height of the upper portion, which is too short for "complete harmony with the lower portion." About 1760–1775.

Section 119.   Block–front kneehole dressing tables.—Kneehole dressing tables of the usual type are considered in section 168 in the chapter on tables; in the present section only those with block–fronts are shown. In these examples the main features of the block–front are of the same general character as in the articles shown in the preceding four sections, except, of course, as modified by the knee-hole portion which occupies the place taken by the central recessed blocking in other block–front pieces.[1]

Whether an article of furniture of this type should be termed a "kneehole dressing table" or a "kneehole desk" is not always clear. If there is any indication that the piece was intended for writing purposes, such as a lid supported by pulls when open, as in No. 832 in the chapter on desks, it is of course a desk, wholly or

1.   In Mr. Lockwood's "Colonial Furniture," volume 1, page 123, it is said that "when the block–front type of chests of drawers came into use, the popularity of the highboy and lowboy was on the decline, and consequently a different form of dressing table had to be adopted, which brought about a revival of the earlier kneehole type" shown in illustration No. 113 in his book, which is similar to No. 1463 in this book.

partially; but if there is no such indication, as in the great majority of cases, the piece may safely be called a dressing table. Perhaps in some cases they were found suitable for both writing and dressing; but in either case it is difficult to see how the knees of any person of an average size could be comfortably placed within the narrow kneehole space; certainly some of us could not possibly adjust ourselves to that position. At the rear of the kneehole space, there is a small cupboard, with a door which is generally ornamented in keeping with the design of the other parts. There are usually six feet, four in front and two in the rear, a wide drawer under the whole width of the top and a section of three small and narrow drawers on each side of the kneehole.

The first illustration, No. 904, is of a block–front kneehole dressing table which has been appropriately termed a "masterpiece." [2] That it was made by Townsend or Goddard, or in their style, appears from the presence of special features which we have seen in other block–front pieces of those cabinet makers, that is, the molding under the top, the carved shells on the wide top drawer and the bracket feet with a scroll carved on the inside, not well seen in the illustration, ending in a small circular scroll, as shown in this chapter in section 115, note 3. Examining other features, we see the carved lattice–work on the top drawer with the three shells; the depressed shell at the top of the cupboard door; the four columns at the corners of the two sections on the sides of the kneehole, each column being fluted on the upper portion and reeded below, as in Nos. 883 and 896; the six blocked drawers with the blocked surfaces; and the molding of the kind known as "godroon," [3] across the bases. The door in the kneehole portion is depressed and within the door is a small cupboard. There are two keyholes and escutcheons in the top drawer, so placed as to be in proper balance, as in No. 884 and others. About 1760–1775.

No. 905 is similar in form to the preceding piece and contains the principal features which indicate the handiwork of Townsend or Goddard, that is, the molding under the top, the carved shells and the bracket feet with scrolls, all of which are mentioned in note 7 in section 114. This piece, however, is not ornamented with some of the features seen in No. 904, such as the lattice work, the godroon moldings and the corner columns. The moldings on the framework are around the drawers, not on the drawers, as is also seen in Nos. 884 and 885 and others. About 1760–1775.

No. 906 presents no indications of the style of Townsend or Goddard, but it is an attractive piece without features of special elegance. The door of the cupboard is arched and paneled as are the doors in Nos. 901–903, and is supported by large H hinges. Above the kneehole opening is a shallow drawer, under the

2. This kneehole dressing table is illustrated and discussed in a series of "Little Known Masterpieces," in "Antiques," September, 1922, pages 111–112. Another example is shown in the same magazine, January, 1932, page 28. It is also seen in part in the magazine for October, 1923, page 180.

3. The word "godroon" comes from a similar French word meaning a plait or ruffle. As used in connection with a furniture molding it means a molding in a ruffled or fluted form. It is sometimes erroneously spelled "gadroon"; Century Dictionary.

904 (Upper) Mr. John C. Toland.
906 (Lower) Metropolitan Museum of Art.

905 (Upper) Metropolitan Museum of Art.
907 (Lower) Anonymous.

wide top drawer. The feet are of the straight bracket type, and are very plain in comparison with those in the two preceding pieces. The top of this dressing table is shaped to conform to the blocking below. We notice that there is a somewhat wider opening for the knees than in the previous pieces. About 1760–1775.

No. 907 resembles the previous piece in several respects, the principal difference being in the convex blocking on the side drawers, as in the block–front bureaus Nos. 888 and 889. Here also the opening for the knees appears to be almost comfortable and over it is a small shallow drawer. The beading on the framework around the drawers is clearly seen. Several of the large brass handles are without keyholes, as may be noticed also on No. 905. About 1760–1775.

CHAPTER XIV

CUPBOARDS

Section 120. General remarks.—In England and our country cupboards of various kinds have been in use for several hundred years. The original cupboards seem to have been a series of horizontal boards or shelves upon which cups and other eating and drinking utensils were kept.[1] In this chapter the more important forms of cupboards found in our country are presented, with special attention to "corner" cupboards which for the past one hundred years have been the favorite kind and the most numerous, exclusive of cupboards of the kitchen type. Corner cupboards of fine character are often seen in private homes and are more interesting to us than the earlier and rarer cupboards which are seldom seen outside of a museum.

---

1. A. The word "cupboard" is defined in the Century Dictionary, in substance as follows: originally, a table on which cups and other vessels for household use or ornament were kept or displayed; later, a table with shelves, open and closed, used for such purpose; in modern usage, generally a series of shelves, enclosed or placed in a closet, for keeping cups, dishes and other table–ware.

B. The word "cupboard" not only means a familiar piece of furniture but also means an enclosed compartment in another piece of furniture. There may thus be a cupboard in a cupboard. In each of the block–front dressing tables Nos. 904–907 there is a cupboard; the enclosed lower portions of a sideboard are called cupboards; so also cupboards are seen in the bookcases Nos. 870 and 871; and other similar "cupboards" may be mentioned.

C. Mr. Lockwood in his "Colonial Furniture," volume 1, page 149, remarks that in the old records "the spelling of the word (cupboard) is various enough to suit all tastes: cubboard, cubberd, cubbord, cubbert, cupbard and cubart are some of the spellings employed."

D. The exact meaning of the old word "beaufet," with its various spellings, seems to be uncertain, but may be about the same as "corner cupboard," or perhaps may indicate a more elegant piece. The values given to "beaufets" in the inventories of the estates of deceased persons were higher than those of corner cupboards. They were generally placed in a corner, but were also "built in" a side wall, as stated by Mr. Lockwood on pages 179, 180 and 184 of his book.

E. A "livery" cupboard is mentioned occasionally in the books. One meaning of the word "livery" is "an allowance of food or other provisions stately given out, as to a family or horses"; Century Dictionary. A livery cupboard was often a small stand with an open front with shelves upon which a supply of food and drink was placed; Encyclopædia Britannica, eleventh edition, page 634. See also Mr. Lockwood's "Colonial Furniture," volume 1, pages 149–150.

F. It is said that the names "court cupboard," "press cupboard," "wardrobe cupboard," "livery cupboard" and other names, have often been used without exactness, which is not surprising.

Section 121. Certain early cupboards.—In this section are illustrations of four early cupboards. The first and second, Nos. 908 and 909, present an example of a "court" cupboard and a "press" cupboard; these pieces bear little or no resemblance to a "cupboard" as we now understand the word. No. 910, a New York Dutch "kas," and No. 911, are mainly for clothing; the latter has been called a "clothes" cupboard. It is customary in the books on antique furniture to consider all of these four articles as early forms of cupboards.

"Court" cupboards and "press" cupboards [1] were made from about 1650 to 1700 and are the earliest examples of fine cupboards found in our country. They were generally of oak, with pine in some parts. Cloths upon which glass and silverware were placed are frequently mentioned in the inventories of the estates of deceased persons in connection with the cupboards, but none of these cloths have been found.

No. 908 is a "court"[2] cupboard. The distinctive feature of this type of cupboard is that the upper portion is enclosed and the lower portion is open. The ends of both portions are supported by large and heavy columns. In the upper portion are two compartments[3] with paneled doors, between which is a panel with two applied ornamental columns. In the central portion are two drawers. The skirt, or apron, of the lower shelf is cut in cyma curves. These cupboards are seldom found and are quite valuable. About 1650–1675.

No. 909 is a "press"[4] cupboard. In this type of early cupboard there are compartments or drawers in the lower portion as well as in the upper. Here the

1. Several illustrated articles discussing these cupboards in detail are in the magazines as follow: "The tulip-and-sunflower Press Cupboard," by Mr. Walter A. Dyer, in "Antiques," April, 1935, page 140, in connection with which the Connecticut sunflower chest No. 598 and note 8 in section 77 should be examined; "The American Press and Court Cupboard," by Mr. Dyer, in "The Fine Arts," December, 1932, page 18; "The individuality of Connecticut furniture," by Mr. Homer Eaton Keyes, in "Antiques," September, 1935, page 110.

Ten press cupboards are illustrated and described by Mr. Lockwood in his "Colonial Furniture," figures 162–171, and one on page 370.

2. The word "court" as used in this connection has no reference to royalty or the judiciary. It is the same as the French word "court" which means "short." It is said that in England what we call a "court" cupboard is known as a "standing buffet"; and what we call a "press" cupboard is known as a "court" cupboard.

In Mr. H. H. Taylor's "Knowing, Collecting and Restoring Early American Furniture," page 24, a court cupboard is mentioned in connection with his statement that "the greater the rarity, the greater the permissible restorations"; and he mentions that "a court cupboard, might—to exaggerate— lack dozens and dozens of parts and yet be most acceptable."

3. In some "court" cupboards there is a central compartment which projects forward with sloping sides as in the "press" cupboard No. 909.

4. The name "press" is said to be given to these pieces because of their drawers which may serve as a "press" in the sense of a clothes press.

An illustrated article entitled "The Anatomy of a Cupboard," by Mr. Homer Eaton Keyes, is in "Antiques," March, 1931, pages 200–203. This article is a skillful analysis of a pedigreed "press" cupboard, which the author proves to have been begun as a court cupboard and before completion, or soon after, was changed into a press cupboard.

In the same magazine, April, 1930, pages 312–316, is an article by Mrs. Esther Stevens Fraser in which are illustrations of press cupboards of a plain type made in Hampton, New Hampshire.

908 (Upper) Metropolitan Museum of Art.
910 (Lower) Wadsworth Athenaeum, Hartford.

909 (Upper) Metropolitan Museum of Art.
911 (Lower) Mr. L. V. Lockwood.

compartment in the upper portion is made with sloping sides. Two arches are on each of the sides. As in the preceding cupboard the top is supported by heavy columns. In this piece the lower portion is occupied by three drawers, forming a chest of drawers which resembles somewhat in form, but not in decoration, the chest of drawers No. 606, which is of about the same period. The paneling of the three drawers and the nine pairs of blackened vertical columns upon them will be noticed. More of these pieces have been found than the court cupboards, but they are seldom offered for sale. At the centre of the base are the figures "1699," doubtless indicating the year when the piece was made.

No. 910 is a "kas"[5] which was a Dutch form of clothes cupboard; the name often appears in the inventories of the estates of the early Dutch owners in New York and New Jersey. The kas was a large piece of furniture and was made in several forms often painted in gay designs and bright colors. The noticeable features in this kas are the large overhanging cornice, the paneled front, the two doors in the upper portion, the two drawers in the lower portion and the ball feet. The wood is walnut. About 1700–1750.

No. 911 is a clothes cupboard of a type made from about 1725 to 1750. The cornice has an elaborate series of moldings, and another molding is on the top of the lower portion. On the four doors are four large arched panels and on each side of the doors are narrow arched panels, not well seen in the illustration; these eight panels are all "applied" on the frame. The feet are of the same type as those seen on many of the desks, bureaus and secretaries shown in previous chapters, known as "ogee" bracket feet, as to which see sections 23–25. The keyhole escutcheons and the H hinges are original and are in the style of those seen on other articles of the period.

Section 122. Corner cupboards.—These cupboards are among the few articles of furniture which have remained in fashion in the same general form for the long period of about one hundred years. From about 1725 they were made continuously until the Empire period, about 1820, with little change in shape although with various changes in ornamental treatment. They are among the most abundant of the larger pieces of furniture and in many cases have survived with little damage except in their doors, probably because the cupboards were seldom moved from place to place and were only exposed to careless treatment in the front.

In this section are twenty–four illustrations of corner cupboards;[1] these cannot be arranged exactly in chronological order, as it is not possible to give all

5. Other examples are in Mr. Wallace Nutting's "Furniture Treasury," Nos. 480–482. Mr. Nutting remarks in connection with No. 481 that "the kas has never been popular as an article to collect. This might not be the case if collectors had great rooms and much bare space. As it is, collectors are jealous of their rooms, which are usually overcrowded anyway." And also it is said that the kas is usually held together with large wooden pins or wedges which may be knocked out and the kas may thus be taken apart and moved easily.

1. The name "corner" cupboard was given to these pieces because the cupboard was intended to stand in a rectangular corner. It was built in a triangular form and the shelves were in the same form.

dates with certainty.[2] Many of the pieces shown are very similar and some may not be important, but the writer thinks that the reader will be pleased to see them all.

The various furniture styles from the Chippendale to the Empire style are not so distinctly recognized in corner cupboards as in many other articles; but it is possible to see the influence of the Chippendale style in some examples and to see the later styles in others.

Corner cupboards were generally movable so that they could be placed in one corner or another as desired, but were also built in a corner, forming a part of the house and not movable, as shown in section 123.

The interesting features of these corner cupboards are not only the exterior, but also the interior with curved and scalloped shelves and sometimes with the ceiling, or top, in the form of a half of a dome and carved in the design of a shell as in Nos. 936–938. Occasionally a domed ceiling without a shell was painted a light blue color. In a few cases the door of the upper portion is of solid wood, as in No. 912, and only the exterior can be seen; but the doors are almost always glazed, and through the panes we see the china and glass of the household. The design of the panes often contributes to the elegance of the cupboard; but the arched top of the doors prevents as great a variety of graceful forms as are seen in the rectangular doors of the secretary–bookcases in section 110 in the chapter on desks. The lower portion of the corner cupboard always had one or two paneled or ornamental doors enclosing a cabinet with shelves. A plain corner cupboard, made of a common wood such as pine, and not painted or ornamented, was generally intended for the kitchen. In many cases, however, a corner cupboard made of pine was built in the dining room, but a handsome cupboard made of mahogany would naturally not be used in a kitchen but only in a dining or other suitable room. This distinction should of course be observed at the present time.

No. 912 is a narrow corner cupboard with several features not often seen in other pieces. At the top is a "broken pediment" formed by a heavy molding, similar in shape to those in No. 917 and in the secretary–bookcase No. 851 and in other pieces. The upper door is solid and is arched at the top in the Queen Anne style, as is also the arched molding above, which rests upon the "capitals" above the fluted "pilasters" at the sides.[3] The lower door has four panels, as also in the next piece. We notice that the capitals at the top of the pilasters are not fluted, nor are the lower portions under the pilasters. In the centre of the arched molding is the "keystone." The date of this piece may be about 1750.

2. The dates cannot be definitely stated because the cupboards were made in a similar style, although with different details, during such a long period of time. Mr. Wallace Nutting in his "Furniture Treasury," volume 1, gives merely the "eighteenth century" as the date of some of the pieces illustrated by him. The examples showing the style of Hepplewhite and Sheraton may be more closely dated, as appears later in this section.

3. This and other features may be compared with those of the "corner cupboard" which is No. 5 of the "Little–known Masterpieces" in "Antiques," May, 1922, pages 209–210.

912 (UPPER) MRS. JOHN S. GIBBS, JR.   913 (UPPER) MRS. JOHN S. GIBBS, JR.
914 (LOWER) DR. JAMES BORDLEY, JR.   915 (LOWER) MRS. JOHN S. GIBBS, JR.

916 (Upper) Judge F. N. Parke.
918 (Lower) Mrs. Alexander Armstrong.

917 (Upper) Dr. James Bordley, Jr.
919 (Lower) Mrs. Edwin B. Niver.

503

No. 913 is a handsome piece without an upper door, and is carved or ornamented at almost every visible point of the woodwork, except on each side of the
arch in the upper portion, in which is the usual keystone. On each side is an
upper and a lower fluted pilaster. The width of the door with four panels is
less than that of the open part above. A small heart applied above the door is a
pleasant ornamentation. The edges of the curved shelves are carved, which is an
unusual feature. About 1730–1750.

No. 914 is a narrow corner cupboard with one large solid door having three
panels, extending from the cornice almost to the shallow drawer below. The rat
tail hinges are not often seen on cupboards. The corners are much cut off, or
"chamfered," a treatment which appears on many bureaus such as Nos. 713 and
714. Below the door a molding divides the upper portion from the lower one
in which there is a single drawer with a brass handle. About 1740–1760.

No. 915 is unusual in having the front in an angular[4] form, giving somewhat
more depth than if the front were straight. The corners are not cut off, or "chamfered," owing to the shape of the front. Two doors, each with four panes of
glass, are above, and two solid paneled doors are below. The hinges are of the
H type which are shown in section 42, and which it is said were used on certain
articles of furniture until about 1800. About 1740–1760.

No. 916 is regarded as being "architectural" because it has several features
which are architectural[5] in design, the principal one here being the four fluted
"pilasters," two in the upper portion supporting the arched moldings, and two in
the lower portion, the latter not being continuations of the former. Here there
are two glazed doors which unite in forming an arch resembling a Gothic type
in part and in a design which is often used in these pieces; and the glass panes
are in shapes which are often seen, with modifications in many cases. Over the
glazed doors are semi-circular moldings, with a keystone in the centre. The
corners of both the upper and the lower portions are cut off, or "chamfered." The
top is flat, with moldings below. In the lower section are two drawers with bail
handles, under which are two paneled doors enclosing shelves. The feet are of the
scrolled bracket type. About 1730–1750.

In No. 917 the top is in the form of a "broken pediment," which was seen
also in No. 912. In the centre of the pediment are two rounded openings which
are ornamented with moldings suggestive of those on the block–front chests–on–
chests and secretaries made by Townsend and Goddard many years afterwards, as
shown in the chapter on block–fronts, Nos. 881 and 897. The two wide fluted
pilasters have at the top a "capital" in the forms seen in Ionic columns; the lower
portion is not ornamented with pilasters. There is only one door in the upper
portion. The H hinges and the two escutcheons on the lower doors will be
noticed. The feet are in the ogee bracket type. About 1730–1750.

4.   A somewhat similar corner cupboard is in Mr. Nutting's "Furniture Treasury," No. 489.

5.   In Mr. Cescinsky's "English Furniture," volume 2, pages 103–129, is a chapter entitled
"Architects' Furniture from 1720 to 1750." It is said that in much of the English furniture of the
period "the hand of the architect is apparent in numberless small details. . . The result is necessarily
incongruous, furniture and buildings having obviously totally different functions to fulfill."

In No. 918 the architectural pilasters are reduced in importance, although still seen on the upper portion; under them on the lower portion are panels instead of pilasters. On the cornice and also above the single door are moldings in the "dentil" form. There is one glazed door with Gothic arches at the top. One large door with two panels is in the lower portion instead of the two doors in the preceding pieces. Here also are H hinges. About 1740–1760.

In No. 919 the pilasters are omitted and the arched molding over the two glazed doors is supported by small brackets. This molding, and the molding and keystone in the cornice, are the only ornamental features. Here, as also in No 917, the panes of glass at the top of the two doors are separated by straight partitions instead of the curved Gothic arch partitions seen in Nos. 918 and 920. The corners are chamfered, as usual. In the lower portion there is one wide drawer, with two doors below, enclosing a cupboard with shelves. The feet are in the ogee bracket style. About 1740–1760.

In No. 920 are two scrolls at the top, the inner ends terminating in rosettes between which is a pedestal supporting an urn with flames; and the two openings are faintly seen to be ornamented at the bottom, in this respect resembling No. 917. The molded arch over the door rests upon fluted pilasters of very small size in comparison with those previously seen. The wood is light-colored. About 1740–1760.

No. 921 has a scroll top, with an inlaid ornament on and under the pedestal supporting the urn. Here the place of pilasters in other corner cupboards is taken by a long panel on the side of each of the two doors; and at the edge of each of the chamfered corners is a very small spiral column which extends down to the feet. The horizontal space between the upper and lower portions is ornamented with vertical fluting. The glass doors unite in forming arched designs, the one at the top being in a reversed position. In the lower portion a large drawer is above two finely paneled doors which enclose shelves. About 1740–1760.

No. 922 seems to have been made in England judging from its elaborate design, but it has acquired American citizenship from long residence in Maryland. Under the scroll top having rosettes and a carved pineapple is a horizontal fretwork in the Chippendale style. On the chamfered corners of the upper portion are fluted pilasters with carved Corinthian style capitals, and the same carving and flutings are on the lower portion. The glazed door is in a difficult and handsome form. A drawer fluted vertically, and with small round carvings, is over the lower door which has a panel in the shape of a Gothic arch with carvings at the upper corners. Much carving is seen on the skirt and the bracket feet. This piece is somewhat similar to figure 190 in Mr. Lockwood's "Colonial Furniture," volume 1. About 1750–1775.

In No. 923 are two scrolls on the top, leaving in the centre scarcely sufficient space for the pedestal or urns and the flaming finials. The corners are chamfered and on the front we notice on each end, instead of a wide pilaster, a slender molding in a rope form extending from the scrolls to the top of the lower portion. On

920 (Upper) Mr. C. Edward Snyder.
922 (Lower) Mr. H. Oliver Thompson.

921 (Upper) Mr. Albert G. Towers.
923 (Lower) Reifsnyder Collection.

924 (Upper) Mrs. John S. Gibbs, Jr.
926 (Lower) Rt. Rev. Edw. T. Helfenstein.

925 (Upper) Mrs. F. G. Boyce, Jr.
927 (Lower) Anonymous.

the large single door in the lower portion may be seen the knotty wood, said to be cherry or poplar. The height of this corner cupboard is seven feet and the width of the lower portion is almost four feet. About 1750.

No. 924, perhaps a country–made cupboard, is interesting because of its peculiar decoration. The line of molding over the door is of an unusual type. On each side of the single door a vine is cut into the wood and blossoms into a flower above, as in No. 934; it is probably a tulip such as is seen on the "Pennsylvania Dutch" chests Nos. 601–603, shown in section 78; and other similar vines are cut into the lower portion on each end. The small spots over almost the entire surface are painted. The crude panel in the centre of the lower door is in the form of cyma curves. About 1750–1775.

No. 925, in the Hepplewhite style, has one of the principal architectural features of the earlier pieces, that is, the four fluted pilasters, which are here on the "chamfered," or "cut off," corners instead of on the front, and extend down to the base. The piece is brightened by the lines of inlay on the scroll top and other parts. Above the doors of the upper portion are two inlaid parallel lines rounded at the outer ends, a style of inlay mentioned in section 96, note 1, C, of the chapter on bureaus; and below the doors are other inlaid lines. The two glazed doors have diamond–shaped panes as in the secretary–bookcase No. 852. The feet are of the straight bracket type which continued to be used in the Hepplewhite period, as in Nos. 928 and 929. The date of this piece may be about 1780–1800.

No. 926 is a later piece, showing no prominent features of the architectural style. The corners are chamfered in the usual manner. Each of the glazed doors has one large pane. The brass rectangular pieces at the corners of the doors will be noticed; these are said to be a decorative feature of the Empire period or a later one.

No. 927. This corner cupboard is out of place at this point, as it is earlier in style than Nos. 925 and 926. It is said to be a good example of a corner cupboard of the Queen Anne period, with solid doors instead of glazed ones. The cornice has a "dentil" molding, as in No. 918 and others, and the usual keystone of the period. The two upper doors are arched and have six panels; in the lower portion also the two doors are paneled. The date of this piece is said to be about 1750.

The seven corner cupboards Nos. 928–934 are ornamented with inlay, indicating, with other features, that they are in the style of Hepplewhite and Sheraton; and on account of their similarity in some respects it may be doubtful whether certain of the pieces should be classified as being in the one style or the other, as mentioned in section 110, note 1, and section 127 in connection with desks and sideboards. These seven pieces may be dated within the period of about 1785 to 1815, which approximately covers the Hepplewhite, Sheraton and part of the American Empire styles, as stated in sections 17, 18 and 21.

Except for the tops and the number and arrangement of the panes of glass in the upper doors, Nos. 928 and 929 are very similar. In No. 928 the top is scrolled, with a central panel on which an American eagle is in a small oval inlay; and other inlays are around the doors and on the chamfered, or cut off, corners and elsewhere. Each of the doors has thirteen panes of glass, as in many secretary–bookcases of the type shown in No. 856 and others. The fallacy that this number of panes necessarily referred to the thirteen American colonies or the thirteen original States of the Union is mentioned in section 110, at note 6. Three shelves may be seen within the glass. About 1785–1800.

In No. 929 the top is flat and there are eighteen panes in each of the upper doors. The same design of inlay is on the doors of the lower portion as on No. 928. The feet of this and the preceding piece and No. 925 are of the straight bracket type which were used for some years after the Hepplewhite style began. About 1785–1800.

No. 930 is a pleasing corner cupboard, especially because of the abundance of inlay. The top is scrolled and inlaid as in No. 925, and underneath is a "dentil" molding. Thirteen panes are in each of the two upper doors, and the shadows of some of the partitions appear in the engraving. A large number of glasses are on the shelves. The doors below are decorated with inlaid ovals. On the base is the inlaid line which is generally seen on the bureaus and desks of the Hepplewhite style, as appears in sections 95 and 104. The skirt has a series of cyma curves, as to which see section 23, and in the centre is a half–circle with inlaid leaves. The feet are in a form of the French bracket foot which is seen on so many pieces in the Hepplewhite and Sheraton styles. About 1785–1800.

No. 931 has a flat top. Each of the two upper doors has twelve panes of glass wholly or partially in the diamond shape; and a thirteenth may be seen if the large diamond beginning at the top and extending to the bottom of the door is counted, which may not be proper as it contains partitions which make four of the twelve panes. The skirt is in the form of cyma curves and the feet are similar to those in the previous cupboard. The inlaid designs on the "chamfered," or cut off, corner on the right will be noticed. About 1785–1800.

Nos. 932 and 933 are narrow corner cupboards which were doubtless suitable either for corners in the walls or at the sides of a chimney projecting a short distance.

In No. 932 are twenty–one panes of glass in the single glazed door. The top is flat and under it are inlaid lines forming four diamond–shaped designs and five sections of circles which are repeated in wood under the door, but are not seen clearly in the engraving; these resemble somewhat the inlay in No. 856. In the lower portion the door is inlaid in a rectangular form enclosing a design which contains eight sections of small circles. The skirt is curved and the feet are of the bracket type. About 1785–1800.

No. 933 is even narrower than the previous corner cupboard. The glazed door contains twenty rectangular panes of varying sizes, giving a better view of the contents within than the more elaborate doors seen in other pieces. The lower

928 (Upper) Hammond–Harwood House.
930 (Lower) Mr. & Mrs. Ralph Robinson.

929 (Upper) Mr. John S. McDaniel.
931 (Lower) Mr. C. Edward Snyder.

932 (Upper) Anonymous.
934 (Lower) Mr. & Mrs. Edward H. McKeon.

933 (Upper) Mrs. Elizabeth N. Dunham.
935 (Lower) Mr. & Mrs. Wm. A. Dixon.

door is finely inlaid with an urn in which woods of three colors are used. The inlay on the chamfered corners is faintly seen. The feet here are of the straight bracket type. About 1785–1800.

In No. 934 the top has scrolls with inlaid rosettes at the inner ends, and under the pedestal, which doubtless supported an urn, is an oval inlay. As in the preceding piece the panes of glass are rectangular. Under the single upper door and at the base are lines of inlay as in No. 930. The lower door has rectangular inlaid forms enclosing oval inlays. On each side of the upper door is an inlaid vine with a flower at the top, probably a tulip, in this respect resembling No. 924 and indicating a Virginia or Pennsylvania origin. About 1785–1800.

No. 935, the last of the corner cupboards illustrated here, is partly in the American Empire style as shown in the lower portion by the animals' claw feet, the spiral columns and the rounded front of the wide drawer. The upper portion, however, is in the usual form of the cupboards of the Hepplewhite and Sheraton styles.[6] About 1800–1830.

Section 123. "Built–in" cupboards.—Cupboards of this type were built in the walls of rooms as in our modern houses. The "architectural" character, mentioned at note 5 in the previous section, is more apparent in some of these "built–in" cupboards than in the usual movable corner cupboards because the "built–in" cupboards were generally made to match the paneling or other architectural features of the walls of the rooms. These "built–in" cupboards were sometimes placed at a corner of a room, but more frequently in a side wall; they were of course not movable and were in fact a part of the house and not an article of furniture. The dates of these pieces are said to be from about 1725 to 1760, judging from the probable dates of the houses in which they were built. During this period and later the corner cupboards of the usual type were also made and they continued in vogue until about 1820. The wood of the built–in cupboard was generally pine, painted in the color of the other woodwork.

For two illustrations of New England "built–in" cupboards, Nos. 936 and 937, the writer is indebted to Mr. L. V. Lockwood, in whose "Colonial Furniture" they appear in volume 1 as figures 185 and 186, and are called "side" cupboards, being built in the side walls of the houses.

In No. 936 we see the surroundings of the cupboard. The woodwork of the walls of the room is painted white, as usual in New England, and so also is the cupboard. The panels in the lower portion follow the design of those on the wall. The open door discloses a dome–like shell which has a large carved rosette in the centre. The blue color of the interior, the gilded edges of the shell and the two gilded cupids, too small to be well seen in the engraving, indicate that the owner

6. The reader will notice that in this book are several illustrations in which a mixture of styles is seen, not as a transitional style, but a combination of two or more different styles in one article. Such a combination is not acceptable to collectors. Another example is in the secretary–bookcase No. 865, in which the upper portion is copied from a design of Sheraton and the lower portion has features of the Empire style. These and other illustrations are shown in this book as warnings to the amateur. Uninjured parts of two or more damaged pieces in different styles have often been combined to make one piece. See the Index under the word "Warning."

936 (Upper) Anonymous.
938 (Lower) Connecticut Soc. Colonial Dames.

937 (Upper) Anonymous.
939 (Lower) Md. Soc. Colonial Dames.

was not fond of the "somber simplicity" of the style of Queen Anne. This house was built at Saunderstown, Rhode Island, in the period from about 1725 to 1750.

No. 937 is a built–in cupboard in a Connecticut house which was probably erected about 1750. Here also there is paneled woodwork surrounding the cupboard. The outline of the shell at the top of the interior is clearly seen, and the carving is in the pattern known as "scalloped." The wood above the shell seems to be in one large solid piece; but when viewed from the rear it is apparent that several boards were glued together to the necessary size and thickness and the shell was then carved in the curves desired. The back of the cupboard is in the shape of a semi–circle in the fine pieces. The upper three shelves are seen to be scalloped. On the kettle we see the form of the "bail," or handle, which is referred to in connection with brass handles on furniture in section 39, note 2, A; see also illustration No. 14.

No. 938 is a fine built–in cupboard in which the interior is well seen. The domelike top, with the lines radiating from a central half–circle, seems to resemble a rising or setting[1] sun rather than a shell. The three curved and scalloped shelves, the paneled woodwork on the door on the left side and on the cornice, and the large cross on the door are noticeable features. This cupboard is in the Webb House at Wethersfield, Connecticut, which is owned and occupied by the Connecticut Society of Colonial Dames to which the writer is indebted for a photograph. About 1750.

No. 939 is in "Mount Clare," at Baltimore, built in 1754 and now in charge of the Maryland Society of Colonial Dames. The open doors, extending to the floor, disclose a plain interior with two inside glazed doors. On the door to the right, at the top, is a bolt which may be raised or lowered by means of the attached iron bar below. Five concave shelves provide space for china and glass. This cupboard is on the side of a fireplace and on the other side is a similar one. Over the cupboard is a cornice reaching to the ceiling, the lower line of the panels being in curves to match the curved top of the cupboard. About 1754.

Section 124. Hanging cupboards.—In this section the term "hanging cupboard" is applied to small cupboards which were made to hang on a wall, in a corner or otherwise. As in other cupboards, the doors of the early hanging ones were made of solid wood and the later ones were glazed; but no doubt many of the later ones had solid doors because they were less expensive than the glazed ones. In the six examples here illustrated, the first four have wooden doors. All except Nos. 944 and 945 were made in a shape to hang in a corner. Some of the cupboards had open shelves at the top and others had them at the bottom; but most of them had no shelves except in the interior.

Nos. 940 and 941 are plain hanging cupboards made of pine; a somewhat ornamental appearance is however given by the panels on the front and sides and

1. See the remark of Benjamin Franklin quoted in section 85, note 12, in connection with the "rising sun" designs on highboys.

940 (Upper) Mrs. John S. Gibbs, Jr. 941 (Upper) Mr. Edgar G. Miller, Jr.
942 (Centre) Mrs. John S. Gibbs, Jr. 943 (Centre) Mr. C. Edward Snyder.
944 (Lower) Mrs. John S. Gibbs, Jr. 945 (Lower) Miss Eleanor S. Cohen.

by the moldings at the top and bottom. In No. 940 the large diamond–shaped panels are interesting. In No. 941 the hinges are secured by iron bolts with large heads, a method which is said to have been common in Pennsylvania pieces. Over the door are two carved flowers, probably tulips, with an oval between them. The dates of these two pieces and the next one are difficult to estimate, but were probably about 1750 if they are not modern Swedish pieces made for American collectors of antiques.

No. 942 is of somewhat the same plain character as are the two previous cupboards. The two outside shelves are supported by a back which is cut in a series of curves. The panel in the door is rectangular and the door is attached by H hinges. About 1750.

The next three pieces, Nos. 943, 944 and 945, are of a different character. In No. 943 the top has scrolls with the inside ends terminating in simple rosettes, between which is a brass urn. The narrow columns at the corners are cut in a spiral design, above and below which they are fluted. The moldings in the scrolls at the top are continued around the entire front and sides. The portion of the front under the scrolls is too dark in the illustration. Here also the hinges are of the H type. The date may be about 1760.

No. 944 was made to hang on a wall, but not in a corner. The eight panes of glass on the front and sides, the arched design in the front, the drawers with the three brass handles and the curved shelves within are all interesting. This piece is probably an English one and the date may perhaps be about 1750–1775.

No. 945 is also not a corner cupboard, but a rectangular cabinet made with feet so that it might be used either on a table or hung on a wall, as was not unusual. The glass on the sides is cut in a pattern similar to that of the front. The lines of inlay on the top and around the door, the strings of inlaid bell flowers on the front ends, and the thirteen panes of glass in the front door recall the glass doors in the secretary–bookcases in the Hepplewhite and Sheraton styles in section 110. This piece and the previous one are of mahogany. The date is uncertain.

Section 125. Open cupboards.—Only two open cupboards are shown here. These were doubtless made for the kitchen, having few, if any, ornamental features except curves and panels. Such pieces were probably made throughout the eighteenth century and perhaps later.

No. 946 is a pine corner cupboard of Pennsylvania origin. In the upper portion there is no top and no front and the shelves are without any protection from dust. The sides are cut in half–round arches of the type which are seen on the skirts of highboys and lowboys of about the period. The lower portion has a small paneled door with H L hinges such as are illustrated in section 42, and the corners are cut off, or "chamfered," as in many fine cupboards such as No. 916. Said to be about 1725.

No. 947 is not a corner cupboard, the back having been made to stand against a side wall. The front is open in the upper portion where the frame is cut in curves in which the cyma curve predominates; here also, as in the preceding piece, the designs of the curves resemble those on the skirts of highboys and lowboys of the period and constitute the most interesting features of cupboards of this type. The door is paneled and the base is cut in a manner to serve as feet. The wood is pine. The date is said to be about 1720–1750.

946 (Left) Pennsylvania Museum of Art.   947 (Right) Anonymous.

The subject of these open cupboards might be continued at length with illustrations and descriptions of details, but they are not important in the study of American antique furniture and are neither fine nor interesting. The same remark applies to the subject of "dressers" which are generally large pieces with no elegance of design. Readers desiring to see illustrations of open cupboards and dressers are referred to Mr. Wallace Nutting's "Furniture Treasury," volume 1, figures 498, 572 and others.

Chapter XV

SIDEBOARDS; KNIFE URNS AND KNIFE BOXES; CELLARETS

Section 126. Introductory remarks.—The word "sideboard" as we now use it needs no definition; but in order to understand what it really means we should know that in its literal and original sense a "sideboard" was a "side borde," which meant a "side table," and that a "side table" was a table placed on the side of a dining room and used as a serving table. These serving tables were called "sideboard tables" and illustrations of them are in the books[1] of Chippendale, Hepplewhite and Sheraton. These "sideboard tables" were often very handsome pieces, frequently with marble tops which would not be injured by hot dishes. They are seldom seen in our country,[2] and, if seen, are not readily distinguishable by an amateur from other large and heavy tables, as there is little in their appearance to associate them with "sideboards" as we understand that word; these tables are therefore not considered here.

In order to present a clear view of the development of the sideboard, three pieces are shown in illustration No. 948, marked A, B and C. It is not certain, however, that the sideboard was developed exactly in the manner indicated by these illustrations, because there may be evidence to the contrary. The subject is somewhat complicated and uncertain.

In No. 948, A, we see the first step in the direction of a modern sideboard.[3] It is said that this step was taken by Robert Adam when he placed at each end of a "sideboard table" a pedestal, or cupboard, upon which an urn[4] was mounted.

---

1. These books are mentioned in sections 15, 17 and 18.

2. It is suggested that section 166 in the chapter on tables be consulted in reference to certain tables which may bear a resemblance to sideboard tables. Several forms are known as "hunting tables," "hunters' tables" and "serving tables."

3. This is copied from Mr. Cescinsky's "English Furniture," volume 3, figure 178, where it is referred to as a "five piece pedestal sideboard" of the Hepplewhite–Adam period. It is placed here in order to show the development of the sideboard, but not all of the features are in the style of Robert Adam, especially the large ovals on the pedestal cupboards. The date is given by Mr. Cescinsky as about 1790.

4. Urns and boxes used for keeping knives and other articles are shown in section 131.

948. A, Adam Sideboard Table and Pedestals; B, Adam Sideboard; C, Shearer Sideboard.

The pedestals were not connected with the table, nor were they connected with the urns, so that there were five separate pieces—the sideboard table, the two pedestals and the two urns.

The next step, shown in No. 948, B, was the connecting of the pedestals with the sideboard table, thus making three pieces instead of five;[5] this also, it is said, was the work of Robert Adam.

The next form of the sideboard, shown in No. 948, C, was the work of Thomas Shearer, who was a contemporary of Hepplewhite. This piece appears in a book containing several of Shearer's designs of sideboards, as mentioned in the next section. In this example the front of the table part of the sideboard is in a "swell," or "bow," shape and the pedestals are raised somewhat from the floor, and are plainly cupboards, and a back–board is added.

Two other designs by Shearer are A and B in illustration No. 949, in which the pedestals, the back–board and the urns disappear and in their stead are the ends with drawers and small cupboards, making the sideboard as we now know it. These designs were issued in 1788, as mentioned in the next section at note 6.

The name and designs of Shearer have unfortunately been so overshadowed by the greater names and more numerous designs of Hepplewhite and Sheraton that they are not generally known or appreciated. The two masters copied, and have generally received the credit for, the designs of Shearer.[6] They made little improvement over his designs, except in the decorative features.

The period in which sideboards were developed and made was a part of the "age of mahogany" and this wood was almost always used in the better class of pieces. The outside visible parts, such as the front, sides, legs and top were sometimes veneered with mahogany on a less expensive wood, although in some cases they were solid mahogany. In New England maple and cherry were also used, and in Pennsylvania and the South walnut pieces are found. The inlay was mainly of satinwood or maple, with other less familiar woods in many cases.

Section 127. Uncertainty as to styles.—The uncertainty whether certain bureaus, desks and secretary–bookcases should be regarded as in the style of Hepplewhite or of Sheraton has been mentioned in previous sections.[1] In the case of many fine sideboards of the period of about 1790 to 1800 this uncertainty

5.   This illustration is copied from the book of Mr. T. A. Strange, entitled "English furniture, woodwork, decoration, etc., during the eighteenth century," page 241.

6.   In his book entitled "English Furniture," from which this illustration is copied, Mr. R. S. Clouston states, page 226, in reference to the Shearer design that "it may or may not have been the first attempt to combine a sideboard and the pedestal and vases which went with it, into one article, but it is certainly first as regards date of publication."

It should be mentioned that it was the custom to affix a date to each of the designs, which were generally issued in a series and later were published in book form. Sometimes a design was issued and dated a year or more prior to the date of publication of the whole book, so that the design was probably in use before the book was published.

1.   See "Bureaus," section 95; "Secretary–bookcases," section 110; "Knife Urns and Boxes," section 131.

is still greater; and as more than sixty[2] sideboards in these two styles are illustrated in this chapter and are classified as in the one style or the other, often doubtfully and in some cases perhaps erroneously, it seems proper to consider the matter somewhat fully.[3]

It would seem that the question whether a sideboard or any other article of furniture should be considered to be in the Hepplewhite or the Sheraton style ought to be easily answered by the drawings in the books of those great designers; but a comparison of these designs with either the English or American pieces[4] shows that it is not always possible to distinguish the styles with certainty. As those books or their reprints are not easily accessible, we present here six designs[5] of sideboards in illustration No. 949; two, marked A and B, are by Thomas Shearer[6] in the book entitled "The Cabinet Makers' London Book of Prices," published in 1788; two, marked C and D, are from the "Guide" of Hepplewhite,[7]

2. The writer ought not to say so, but he thinks that in no other book are so many fine sideboards illustrated.

     Possibly too much attention is given here to the question whether a sideboard is in the Hepplewhite or the Sheraton style; but the question is a matter which so frequently arises, and about which there is such a difference of opinion, that it should be presented as clearly as possible.

3. This subject is considered with skill and learning by Mr. Edward Stratton Holloway in his "American Furniture," pages 116–123, with drawings and illustrations. Several statements made in this section are derived from Mr. Holloway's book.

4. The English and American cabinet makers did not follow these drawings closely. They often combined one or more designs of each style and also made variations of their own invention.

5. The designs in the books of the cabinet makers often show on one article two or more different kinds of legs, feet, handles or other parts, or two or more styles of inlay or other decoration, as in No. 949, A. This was done in order to present a variety of treatments which would be suitable on the article. A similar method of showing different plates for brass handles appears in the illustrations 27–29 in section 39, No. 14.

     The perspective in some of these designs is not good, owing, it is said, to the incompetence of the draftsman or engraver.

6. This design by Shearer of a semi–circular sideboard marked "A," with four legs, is especially interesting because of the different types of inlay shown, almost all of which will be seen in the illustrations of the sideboards made in the styles of Hepplewhite and Sheraton. On the upper drawer on the right is an inlaid form of parallel lines rounded at the ends, a favorite design on the sideboards and other pieces in the Sheraton style, and which is frequently referred to in the comments in this chapter. Under this is an oval form which was very popular in both the Hepplewhite and Sheraton styles. To the left of these two drawers are two vertical forms of inlay which were frequently used on the upright parts over the legs. On the central drawer over the arch the *corners* of the parallel lines are cut out in concave form; this also was popular in both styles. Adjoining this central drawer on the left are three vertical bars, as in Nos. 955 and 968. On the upper drawer to the left the *ends* of the form are cut in a concave shape; this design was seldom seen on our sideboards. On the lower drawer on the left the *corners* are cut in a concave form. With this design before him a customer could make his selection of the kinds of inlay.

     The design marked "B," also by Shearer, is the only one in the books of the three designers in which the top is serpentine in form and "unbroken," that is, with no "break" in the serpentine line and with concave ends; and the serpentine form of the top is followed in the arch in the centre.

7. The designs marked "C" and "D," by Hepplewhite, illustrate the *concave* ends which are the distinctive feature of the Hepplewhite style as mentioned in the text.

published in 1789; and two, marked E and F, are from the "Drawing Book" of Sheraton,[8] published partly in 1791. As to the time of publication of these books see note 6, paragraph 2 in the previous section.

An examination of almost any American sideboard of the period will show points of resemblance to some one of these six designs; and may show that an American sideboard which has been regarded as in the Hepplewhite style has features which are only seen in the designs of Sheraton, and hence should be classified as in the Sheraton style; and, vice versa, a piece supposed to be in the Sheraton style may be found to be in the style of Hepplewhite. This analytical method may cast doubt upon the correctness of a family tradition or a personal opinion as to dates, but is likely to furnish a proper view of the subject.

Because of the difficulties in determining whether certain pieces should be classified in the one style or the other some writers prefer to consider many sideboards as being in the "Hepplewhite–Sheraton style," or in the "Hepplewhite–Sheraton period." In this chapter, however, an effort is made to present the illustrations of the two styles separately; and even if some of the illustrations are misplaced we can nevertheless admire the sideboards.

Two features are often regarded as determining whether a sideboard is in the one style or the other, namely, the inlay and the kind of legs; but these do not definitely indicate the style.

As to the inlay, it has sometimes been said that the Sheraton style sideboards do not have inlay. But Sheraton's books show much inlay on sideboards as well as on other pieces; and Hepplewhite's designs also are fully inlaid. So far as the books indicate, therefore, the style cannot be determined by the presence or absence of inlay. Many of the Sheraton style sideboards have no inlay; but this does not mean that all those *with* inlay are in the Hepplewhite style. Moreover it has been said that in pieces made in the style of Hepplewhite the design of the inlay was not generally the same as in those in the style of Sheraton; for example in the use of certain oval, circular, rectangular or other inlaid forms. This is no doubt true in many cases; but any cabinet maker working in either style could suit his own taste in the use of any type of inlay and any combination of types.

The kind of legs is also not a positive test of the style. It is often thought that square and tapering legs, frequently with spade feet, always indicate the Hepplewhite style, and that sideboards in the Sheraton style always had round legs. This was, indeed, the usual treatment, especially in the American pieces, although some pieces clearly in the Sheraton style have square and tapering legs and spade feet as in illustration No. 949, E; but apparently the sideboards in the Hepplewhite style did not have round legs. The fact is that both of these types of legs were the common property of all cabinet makers to use as they preferred. In this connection Nos. 972 and 973 should be examined, with the comments on them, in the next section.

8.   In the designs marked "E" and "F," by Sheraton, the ends are *convex,* which is the distinctive feature of the Sheraton style of sideboards, as stated in the text. On one side of F is an open cupboard for holding dishes. The design E is on a plate marked October, 1792, and the design F is dated December, 1791. See note 6, paragraph 2, in section 126.

949. A AND B, SHEARER SIDEBOARDS; C AND D, HEPPLEWHITE SIDEBOARDS; E AND F, SHERATON SIDEBOARDS.

523

In seeking to distinguish the sideboards made in the styles of Hepplewhite and Sheraton we may therefore generally disregard as immaterial the presence and character of inlay and also the presence of square or tapering legs, because many sideboards of both styles were made with these features.

In the designs in the books of Hepplewhite and Sheraton, however, we find one clear indication of what is the Hepplewhite style and what is the Sheraton style, namely, in the designs of Hepplewhite the ends of the sideboards are *concave,* as shown in C and D in illustration No. 949, but in the designs of Sheraton the ends are *convex,* as shown in E and F. It is said that in England this distinctive feature between the two styles is recognized by scholars, although not always by others.[9] In the American books and essays, however, the distinction is not always regarded as the decisive feature; but the distinction may well be applied to the American pieces. In this chapter, therefore, the sideboards with *concave* ends are placed in the style of Hepplewhite and those with *convex* ends are placed in that of Sheraton. In cases where the ends are neither concave nor convex, but straight, as in Nos. 968–971, certain other features must be considered.

A favorite form of sideboard is one with a top in an unbroken serpentine curve, which is a curve with concave ends and a convex centre, without any break or projection in the curve from one end to the other. This form of top was apparently first designed by Shearer and appeared in the "Book of Prices" above mentioned, and is shown as B in illustration No. 949. The tops of sideboards Nos. 950

9.   The following quotations from two English writers are of interest.

In his book "The present state of old English furniture," page 112, Mr. R. W. Symonds writes: "The sideboards that the collector is most likely to meet with are usually called 'Sheraton' without any justification whatever, as these sideboards were made by all the principal cabinet makers for about ten years before Thomas Sheraton became known. The difference in the design of these sideboards is mainly in the shape of the front."

In Mr. Wheeler's "Old English Furniture," third edition, pages 505–506, it is said that "Hepplewhite and Shearer evolved the regulation sideboards which are generically known today as 'Sheraton.' . . It is quite evident that the vast majority of so–called Sheraton sideboards of finest quality and most pleasing outline were produced between 1775 and 1790; (which was before the time of Sheraton); in other words Sheraton had nothing whatever to do with their design and execution."

Many English dealers are said to regard certain sideboards as being in the Sheraton style which in our country are considered as being in the Hepplewhite style.

In "Antiques," December, 1928, page 516, is an article entitled "Ten important American sideboards," by Mr. William Stuart Walcott, Jr., with illustrations, descriptions and biographical and historical notes. The pieces are in the Hepplewhite and Sheraton styles and a book by an English writer, Mr. R. Davis Benn, is referred to as making a statement that "the Hepplewhite sideboard always employs the concave corner. The Sheraton sideboard, on the contrary, always has the convex corner." This statement is too broad for American sideboards, as it disregards the straight–front type such as Nos. 968–971. The words "always" and "never" are dangerous if it is stated that a particular article of furniture has "always" been made or has "never" been made in a specified place or manner or period.

Whether a concave or a convex end should determine whether a sideboard is in the style of Hepplewhite or that of Sheraton has of course no application to sideboards of the type known as "deep–end sideboards," which are illustrated here as Nos. 1000–1005, nor to other sideboards which have neither a concave nor a convex end.

to 961 are in this form, and having concave ends are regarded as in the Hepple-white style, although the design was doubtless originated by Shearer and should probably be called by his name.

Section 128. Hepplewhite style sideboards.—In this section no attempt is made to arrange the sideboards according to their exact dates, as such an arrangement would be merely imaginative; but it is safe to say that they were in style in our country from about 1785 to 1805, the approximate period of the Hepplewhite style.

In all of these sideboards the ends are *concave,* or at least *not convex.* This feature is regarded as the one which distinguishes the Hepplewhite style of sideboards, as actually made,[1] from those made in the Sheraton style, as mentioned in the previous section. The legs are square[2] and tapered, some terminating in spade feet, as in the chairs and tables of the Hepplewhite style; but, as mentioned in the previous section, this type of legs and feet is not a distinctive feature, as it was also used in many pieces in the Sheraton style. All the sideboards are inlaid, as were very many in the Sheraton style. The handles shown are all of brass and mainly in the oval or round form, as also in the pieces in the Sheraton style, although, as seen in illustration No. 949, C and D, the drawings in the book of Hepplewhite show other forms; but our cabinet makers generally used the ovals.

The front line of the tops of these sideboards may for convenience be considered in three groups: the "unbroken serpentine" line which is in a serpentine[3] curve without a "break" in the line; the "broken serpentine" line which is broken by two projections near the centre; and the "straight" line which is without a curve. In these three groups the twenty–two illustrations of sideboards in the Hepplewhite style will now be examined.

In the first group, Nos. 950–961, are twelve sideboards with "unbroken" serpentine front lines, that is, lines in a serpentine curve without a "break" in the curve.

The first four sideboards, Nos. 950–953, have an arch in the central portion, a form of construction which is also seen in several sideboards in the Sheraton style in the next section. The arch was apparently made in order to allow a cellaret,

---

1. Mr. Cescinsky, in his "English Furniture," volume 3, page 102, writes that "we are compelled to refer to furniture as being in the style of Hepplewhite rather than from his hand. . . Of his actual work absolutely nothing can be stated with certainty"; and "there is no single example of absolutely accredited Hepplewhite workmanship."

2. In some cases the front legs do not present their flat sides to the front, but are so placed that their corners are to the front; in this manner the legs conform to the line of the framework above. In a few cases these legs are triangular. See design D in illustration No. 949, and the tables Nos. 1431, 1432 and 1437.

3. The serpentine curve, concave at the ends and convex in the centre, the favorite curve in the Hepplewhite style sideboards, is much the same as the curve of the top of some of the Hepplewhite style chairs. This similarity may be easily seen by holding a chair in such a manner that the curve of the top is parallel with the curve of the top of the sideboard.

950 (UPPER) MRS. MILES WHITE, JR.   951 (CENTRE) MR. ARTHUR E. COLE.   952 (LOWER) MR. BLANCHARD RAN-
DALL.

526

953 (Upper) Mr. S. Johnson Poe.   954 (Centre) Dr. Edw. B. Fenby.   955 (Lower) Mr. & Mrs. Geo. Shipley.

527

also called a "wine–cooler," to be placed under the sideboard.[4] By reference to illustration No. 949, A, it will be noticed that this arch appears in one of the designs of Shearer, and the inference is that it was copied by the cabinet makers who were working in the styles of Hepplewhite and Sheraton. In each of these four pieces the strings of inlaid flowers on the square and tapered legs will be noticed; this was the most popular design for long and narrow vertical surfaces, as also on the legs of tables and other articles in the Hepplewhite style. In each piece there is one drawer over the arch. The front corners of the top are often cut off in order to avoid a pointed corner, as also in the serpentine front bureaus shown in No. 713 and others.

In No. 950 the inlay has a very pleasing appearance, especially the four large ovals enclosing panels of a darker wood; and there are also four smaller ovals under the top. A narrow band of light wood is near the bottom of each of the legs. The drop handles are in an oval form with plates adorned with urns. There are two deep drawers, one on each side of the central drawer. About 1790–1805.

No. 951 is of the same general type but has less decorative inlay. The slender legs, however, instead of having a narrow inlaid band near the bottom, are ornamented with a band of light wood extending several inches above the floor. At each end is a cupboard with a door supported by hinges. One cupboard was doubtless for bottles and the other for dining room requisites. About 1790–1805.

In No. 952 the fronts of the drawers are brilliantly veneered with light wood. Around the edge of each of these drawers there is a small "bead" molding, a type which is referred to in connection with bureaus in note 3, C, in section 93. The handles are in ring form without a plate behind them. About 1790–1805.

In No. 953 there appear to be four drawers on the ends, but in reality they are two cupboards with doors supported by hinges.[5] Here the arched portion is decorated with bands of inlay. The eight inlaid ovals will also be noticed. About 1790–1805.

The next eight sideboards, Nos. 954–961, also have "unbroken" serpentine fronts, but without an arch in the centre. Here the space between the end portions, occupied by an arch in the previous pieces, is taken in some cases by drawers but generally by cupboards.

In No. 954 the drawers are ornamented with bands of light wood around the edges; these bands, with eight inlaid ovals, and the usual strings of flowers and

---

4. See section 132, the last in this chapter, for cellarets.

5. In many sideboards the fronts of two drawers are apparently at one or both ends, but often these form the front of a single cupboard or of a single deep drawer. If hinges are on the side they indicate that the front is that of a cupboard, but if there are no hinges the front is that of a deep drawer. Many owners would be pleased to have these deep drawers, often with heavy contents, run on rollers or otherwise made easier to open and close. The same methods of construction are seen in sideboards in the Sheraton style. In some cases these cupboards or drawers are referred to in the comments. In regard to "shamming," see Pembroke table No. 1409 and note 5 in section 163, and the Washington desk No. 838.

other inlaid work on the legs, furnish abundant decoration. On the right end we apparently see the fronts of two drawers, but they in fact form the front of a cupboard as is shown by the two almost invisible hinges. On each side of the lower central drawer is a rectangular inlaid form resembling the vertical "bottle drawers" seen in the same position in later illustrations. About 1790–1805.

No. 955 is a handsome sideboard which is ornamented in a different manner from the previous pieces. Inlay in light wood is on the legs, the base and the four uprights, near the top of which are four American eagles in green. Over the eagles are inlays of six vertical bars, as in the Shearer design No. 949, A; and see No. 968. Seven ovals are on the drawers and two on the doors of the cupboard, all in finely grained mahogany veneer. About 1790–1810.

In No. 956 three forms of rectangular inlay are above and four are below, the latter enclosing two large ovals on the ends and two almost circular forms in the centre. On the uprights above the legs are inlaid panels and on the legs are flowers of a delicate design. At the ends are two cupboards, each having the appearance of two drawers. The only drawer is in the centre above the central cupboard. About 1790–1805.

In No. 957 all the inlay on the upper portion is rectangular. On the legs are inlaid forms, not seen on other sideboards, resembling the designs on No. 976 in the Sheraton style and on certain tables in the Hepplewhite style, such as No. 1490. There is a central drawer above, under which is a wide cupboard with two drawers; two other cupboards are on the ends. On the edges of the doors and drawers the bright lines of bead moldings are well seen, as in No. 952. The handles are round instead of oval. About 1790–1805.

No. 958 is of the same character as in the previous piece in some respects, all the line inlay in the upper portion being rectangular, but of a different design. The handle–plates on the drawers are eight–sided, a type which is shown in section 39. Strings of flowers are on the legs which terminate in spade feet. About 1790–1805.

In No. 959 the central portion is somewhat more curved than in many other pieces. As in the two previous sideboards, the inlay is rectangular in form. Between the two small drawers at the ends is a wide one, and below are two deep drawers at the ends and a cupboard in the centre. Oval designs are inlaid at the top of the four uprights, and flowers are inlaid on the legs. The handles are of glass, perhaps renewals. About 1790–1805.

No. 960 is of a similar appearance, with rectangular inlaid forms. On each side of the cupboard in the central portion is a small decorated space which in some other sideboards was enlarged and used as a bottle drawer as in No. 963. The legs are unusually slender and are ornamented with inlaid designs of a vine. The handles are of an earlier period. On the right is a cupboard, as shown by the two hinges, and on the left is a deep drawer. About 1790–1805.

No. 961 is the last illustration of the group of Hepplewhite sideboards with "unbroken" serpentine fronts. The two cupboards at the ends and the small one

956 (Upper) Mrs. Isaac R. Trimble. 957 (Centre) Dr. M. A. Abrams. 958 (Lower) Mr. C. Edw. Snyder.

959 (UPPER) MRS. TOWNSEND SCOTT.   960 (CENTRE) MR. MORRIS WHIT-   961 (LOWER) MR. DANIEL R. RAN
RIDGE.   DALL.

in the centre are decorated with inlays in ovals. On each side of the smaller cupboard is a drawer which is ornamented with inlaid rectangular lines with fans at each of the inside corners. The "brackets" at the junction of the inside legs with the base of the central portion also have fans; similar brackets are in the original designs in illustration No. 949. The legs terminate in spade feet. The handles and escutcheons are of an earlier period. This sideboard and No. 971 should be examined together, both being from Annapolis. About 1790–1810.

In the next six sideboards in the Hepplewhite style, Nos. 962–967, we see the "broken" serpentine tops, that is, those in which the serpentine curve is interrupted, or broken, by projections which will be noticed in the outlines of the tops. The original Hepplewhite design is shown in C and D in illustration No. 949.

No. 962 is a handsome sideboard in which the "broken" serpentine front feature is seen in the top at two points, above the inside legs. These two breaks in the line divide the serpentine front top into three curves, two concave ones on the ends and a serpentine one between them. In the centre is a large drawer under which is a "skirt," or "apron," in a curved form, resembling two cyma curves, which are shown in section 23. On the central drawer are two inlaid designs in the form of parallel lines which are rounded at the ends, a form which apparently first appeared in the design A in illustration No. 949, by Shearer, and was very often used on furniture in the Sheraton style, as referred to in the comment on No. 972, and will be seen in several sideboards in the next section. At the left end is a deep drawer and at the right end there is a cupboard with hinges. About 1790–1810.

No. 963 is an elaborate sideboard in which the serpentine curve is "broken" into five sections. There are two concave cupboards at the outer ends, next to which are two small straight sections in which are vertical drawers, with handles, known as "bottle drawers," and between these is a "recessed" cupboard. Above are five shallow drawers, the wide one in the centre overhanging the "recessed" cupboard below and having the appearance of three drawers. The fine inlay is abundantly supplied at all points. A very similar sideboard but without inlay and in the Sheraton style, No. 987 in the next section, may be compared with this one. About 1790–1810.

No. 964 has one wide drawer in the centre, under which is a cupboard of the same width and at the ends are cupboards. The handles are of the same round type as in No. 957. The edges of the drawer and cupboards have bead moldings of a bright color. The inlaid forms on the drawers and cupboards, with the corners cut in curves, are all of the same type and are similar to those in Nos. 958 and 967. This design is most frequently found on various pieces in the Hepplewhite style, but is also seen on those in the style of Sheraton, as in the sideboard No. 976 in the next section. Above the legs are vertical bars of light wood as also in No. 974 and others. About 1790–1810.

962 (UPPER) MR. ALBERT G. TOW-
ERS.   963 (CENTRE) ANONYMOUS.   964 (LOWER) HAMMOND-HARWOOD
HOUSE.

In No. 965 the central portion is reduced almost to the same width as the end portions, not making a pleasing contrast to the usual form. At each end is a cupboard and in the centre is a third, each ornamented with a familiar form of line inlay. About 1790–1810.

No. 966 is another example of a central drawer overhanging a "recessed" portion, as in No. 963. There are two small drawers at the ends, under which are deep drawers. The legs terminate in sharply tapered feet. Although not highly ornamented with inlay, this is a pleasing piece, with finely grained mahogany. About 1790–1810.

No. 967 also has a front of brilliantly grained mahogany. The same type of design in inlay as in No. 964 is seen on the drawer and on the four doors of the three cupboards. The "break" in the serpentine top is not clearly seen in the engraving. The central portion is straight, not curved, and may be regarded as introductory to the next group of pieces. About 1790–1810.

The next four sideboards, Nos. 968–971, have straight fronts. It may be uncertain whether these pieces should be classified as in the Hepplewhite style or in that of Sheraton. It is said that as a general rule Hepplewhite used the curve and Sheraton used the straight line, as in their respective styles of chairs; but neither of these masters, nor Shearer, show in their books any sideboards with straight fronts. The sideboards with straight fronts in the Sheraton style, illustrated in the next section, are identified by the characteristic round legs of that style or by other tests; but in the four pieces here shown the legs are in the square and tapering form which was used by both Hepplewhite and Sheraton. In the absence of any contrary indication of style, we may assume because of the form of the legs, the type of the inlay and the opinion of some collectors, that these four pieces are in the style of Hepplewhite.

No. 968 has three shallow drawers above with a deep drawer at each end and a slightly recessed cupboard below. The type of inlay is somewhat similar to that in No. 981 in the Sheraton style; and as in No. 955 in this section, there is an inlay of vertical bars, here five, under the top, as in the Shearer design No. 949, A. About 1790–1810.

In No. 969 there is a small arch in the centre, similar to that in No. 953, but with a different kind of inlay. In the centre of the arch is an inlay which suggests the "keystone" seen in many cupboards, as in Nos. 918 and 919. The other inlay is similar to that in the following sideboard and in No. 967. At the right end there is a deep drawer and at the left is a cupboard. The tapering legs have spade feet. This piece may be compared with No. 994 in the Sheraton style. About 1790–1810.

No. 970 is highly decorated with inlay and well supplied with drawers. Three long drawers are in the centre, on each side of which are two vertical drawers of unequal height, presumably for contents of different sizes. At each end there is a narrow drawer under which is a cupboard. The central portion, between the two inside legs, is of unusual length. About 1790–1810.

965 (UPPER) MR. & MRS. A. ADGATE
DUER.   966 (CENTRE) MRS. WADE HAMPTON
FROST.   967 (LOWER) SHEPPARD & ENOCH
PRATT HOSPITAL.

968 (Upper) Col. Washington Bowie, Jr.

969 (Centre) Dr. Wm. P. E. Wyse.

970 (Lower) Mr. & Mrs. C. E. McLane.

In No. 971 the central portion of the front is advanced somewhat beyond the line of the ends. In this portion there is a small cupboard with an oval inlay, on each side of which is a drawer; and at each end there is a cupboard. Inlaid brackets are at the junctions of the inside legs with the base of this portion. The three large inlaid ovals are the main decorative feature. The square tapering legs terminate in spade feet. The glass knobs are sunk in a metal cup as explained in section 40. This sideboard resembles No. 961 in several respects, the chief differences being that in this one the inlay is more restrained, and that the front is in straight lines, whereas in No. 961 the front is an unbroken serpentine curve. Pasted within No. 971 is the label of John Shaw.[6] Both of these pieces are from Annapolis. About 1790–1800.

971. Mr. Blanchard Randall.

Section 129. Sheraton style sideboards.—The presence of any one of four main distinctive features will enable us to identify sideboards as being in the Sheraton style with certainty.[1] These features are as follows: first, *convex* ends,

6.   An article by Mr. W. M. Hornor, Jr., entitled "John Shaw, of the great days of Annapolis," in the "International Studio," March, 1931, page 44, discusses the work of John Shaw, and illustrates this sideboard and other pieces. This sideboard is now at the Baltimore Museum of Art.

The label of John Shaw is ornamental, in marked contrast to many of the labels of the New England and Philadelphia cabinet makers. In the centre of the upper border thirteen stars are in an oval panel. In the lower border are the letters "F. C.," under which is "T. Sparrow." In handwriting are the figures "1797." The most interesting label thus far discovered is that of Benjamin Randolph, of Philadelphia, which is illustrated as No. 1 in section 6. Other labels are referred to in the Index under the word "Labels." They are often extremely interesting and provide a fascinating glimpse into the life of those days.

1.   A.   Some of the sideboards here shown have more than one of these four features, and others may not have any of them, in which latter case some other feature is present from which an inference may be drawn, although uncertainly. In studies of this kind it must be remembered that the cabinet

(Note 1 continued on page 538)

or at least *not concave* ends, shown here in Nos. 972–990, which are in contrast with the concave ends in the Hepplewhite style, as shown in the previous section; second, columns and legs projecting beyond the body of the sideboard, as shown in Nos. 991–993, a type which we have also seen in the bureaus Nos. 745–748; third, round and tapering legs, often reeded or fluted, as shown here in Nos. 994–999; and, fourth, "deep ends," which are seen on many sideboards of the late Sheraton style and are shown here as Nos. 1000–1006.

The dates of these Sheraton style sideboards range from about 1795–1815; in some cases more definite dates are given.

In the first group, Nos. 972–990, are nineteen sideboards which are regarded as being in the Sheraton style because of their convex ends, or at least not concave ends, as mentioned a few lines above. This convex feature in the "Drawing Book" of Sheraton, is copied in our illustration No. 949, E and F. In almost all the sideboards in this group the legs are square and tapering.

Nos. 972 and 973 are particularly interesting when seen together. Here are two Sheraton style sideboards, each having the convex ends which place them in the Sheraton style as shown by the drawings in his book, but each having a different kind of leg. The legs of the first are in the round and tapering form which is only seen on pieces in the Sheraton style, and the legs of the second are in the square and tapering form which is found in both the Sheraton and Hepplewhite styles. The inlaid designs on the convex ends are of two kinds, the first consisting of circles, the second being rectangular with their corners concave. These two pieces show that it is not possible to classify a sideboard as being in the Hepplewhite style because of its having square and tapering legs or because it has a rectangular form of inlay, as referred to in section 127 on page 522.

In No. 972 the central portion is serpentine, with a drawer above a wide cupboard with two doors. On each side is another cupboard, in a long convex curve which extends to the back without a break, as also in the next two pieces. The four legs, instead of the usual six in the Hepplewhite style pieces, are in the Sheraton style, being round and reeded, with rounded feet. The inlay on the cupboards consists of two ovals and four circles two of which are not fully seen. On the drawer the inlay is in the form of parallel lines rounded at the ends, a

(NOTE 1, *continued from page 537.*)

makers were in business to make a livelihood, not to exhibit a particular style, and they would naturally make a sideboard, or any other article, with any features which the customer desired. They were not interested in leaving a style record for posterity.

B. The sideboards in the Sheraton style cannot be satisfactorily arranged in the same groups as those in the Hepplewhite style in the previous section. Those in the Sheraton style differ from each other much more than those in the Hepplewhite style do.

C. One feature of sideboards in the Sheraton style which was not generally adopted in our country was the ornamental and useful brass rail at the back, and sometimes also at the sides. China plates and silverware were leaned against this rail and candles were attached to it. Our cabinet makers often used a back–board which served a similar purpose, but was not attractive; and in some cases the back–board was continued around the sides. See the rail in the Adam sideboard in illustration No. 948, B.

D. A seeming distortion of inlaid ovals, due to the curved surfaces, may be noticed on No. 972 and others.

972 (Upper) Mr. J. Ramsay Speer. 973 (Centre) Mrs. Wilbur W. 974 (Lower) Sheppard & E. P.
Hubbard. Hospital.

design referred to in the comment on No. 962 in the Hepplewhite style. The curved line of the top is "broken," as in several of the sideboards shown in the previous section. On the uprights over the front legs are designs in a form similar to those in No. 975 and others. This sideboard is seventy–four inches long. About 1800–1815.

No. 973 also is a handsome sideboard, with about the same structural lines as in the previous example. The same lines of inlay are in the central portion, but on the doors of the side cupboards the form is different. Broad bands of light–colored veneer are along the base of the body and under the top and on the uprights and the horizontal partitions. The four square and tapered legs are decorated with inlaid flowers, and the grain of fine mahogany is clearly seen. This sideboard is seventy–eight inches long. About 1800–1815.

No. 974 is a small and elegant sideboard. Between the convex ends is a concave central portion in which there is a long drawer, the front of which is of a lighter color than the other surfaces. Under the drawer is a cupboard and at each end is another cupboard in a convex curve. The uprights above the four legs are of a light wood. The drawer and the doors of the cupboards have bands on the edges; and on the edge of the base is a line of delicate inlay. The legs are square and tapered and are inlaid with a long string of flowers. It is said that similar sideboards with four legs were chiefly made in and around Philadelphia. About 1800–1815.

In the next seven sideboards, Nos. 975–981, the curves of the ends do not extend all the way to the back as in the previous three pieces, but are "broken" at two points over the two additional front legs, six or eight legs being used instead of four as in the previous three pieces. The outlines of the tops of these seven pieces are about the same as some of the Hepplewhite style "broken front" sideboards shown in the previous section, such as No. 962, except, of course, those in the Hepplewhite style have concave ends and those in the Sheraton style have convex ends.

No. 975 is unusual, having two very large inlaid circles on the cupboards at the ends; and also in having three separate cupboards in the centre, instead of the usual two, each of which has an inlaid circle. The central portion is in a serpentine curve. Over the central cupboards is a long drawer having an inlaid form of parallel lines rounded at the ends, which has been referred to in connection with No. 972 and others. The straight sides and six legs are seen here for the first time in the pieces in the Sheraton style. About 1800–1815.

No. 976 is a pleasing piece, with inlay on the wide drawer, on the two vertical "bottle" drawers and on the three cupboards in rectangular forms with concave corners. On the legs is the same form of inlay as on No. 957 in the Hepplewhite style; the uprights over the legs are also inlaid and there is the usual line along the base. The central portion is "recessed" and is in a serpentine curve as in the previous piece. About 1800–1815.

No. 977 is an elaborate sideboard with the unusual number of eight legs, not all necessary to sustain the weight of the upper portion, the additional two per-

975 (Upper) Hammond-Harwood House.   976 (Centre) Dr. James Bordley, Jr.   977 (Lower) Metropolitan Museum of Art.

541

haps being to avoid too large an open space in the front. Seven drawers are seen, one a long one in the centre, one small and one large vertical drawer on each side and one on each of the convex ends. There are also the usual cupboards. The front of the central portion is straight, instead of being in a serpentine form as in the two previous pieces. The decorative inlay is in at least ten different designs. An excessive amount and variety of inlay is sometimes noticed in sideboards made by some of our cabinet makers, especially those working in the Sheraton style. Another eight–legged piece is shown in No. 983. It has been said that "most collectors dream of owning an eight–legged sideboard."[2] About 1800–1810.

In Nos. 978–980 the central portion of the fronts is in a straight line, as in the previous piece, instead of in a serpentine one, as in No. 976 and others. In No. 978 the long drawer at the top has a straight front with a form of inlay which has been referred to in the comment on No. 962 and others. This drawer over-hangs the cupboard below, which is "recessed" somewhat and is ornamented with inlaid circles. At each convex end is a cupboard, not a deep drawer, as may be known by the hinges. About 1800–1810.

In No. 979 instead of only the central cupboard being "recessed" as in the previous piece, the top and the long drawer and the cupboard are all recessed in a straight line, not curved or overhanging as in No. 966. A cupboard is in the left end and a deep drawer is in the right one. Banding is used on the edges of the drawer and other places in the central section; an inlaid design on the legs is in a form similar to that in No. 976; and large ovals are on the convex doors at the ends. About 1800–1810.

No. 980 is a small sideboard which may be regarded as in the Sheraton style. As in the previous two pieces the central portion is straight, or nearly so; and the curve of the ends is somewhat less convex than in some of the previous pieces. The arch in the central portion is similar to several in the Hepplewhite style, such as Nos. 951 and 969, and to others in the present section, such as Nos. 986 and 994. The feet are in the spade form. About 1800–1810.

In No. 981 the curve of the top is "broken" at two points and then continues to the sides; the curve of the ends is less convex than in previous pieces. The eight inlaid ovals, in two different forms, are arranged in parallel lines, and the oval brass handles are stamped with cornucopias. About 1800–1810.

In Nos. 982 and 983 the central portion is convex but each of the ends is straight. Sideboards of this design are not shown in the books of the cabinet makers nor are they commonly seen in the books on antique furniture. It may be proper not to classify them in either the style of Hepplewhite or of Sheraton, but to consider them as variations made on the established styles, but they have been given a place in this section on the Sheraton style because they seem to approach nearer to that style than to the style of Hepplewhite.

2. Illustrations of other eight–legged sideboards, in Hepplewhite or Sheraton styles, may be seen in Mr. Nutting's "Furniture Treasury," volume 1, figure 750; in Mr. Lockwood's "Colonial Furniture," figure 207; in the catalogue of the "Girl Scouts," No. 716; and in "Antiques," September, 1935, page 113.

978 (Upper) Mrs. Wm. G. Wether-   979 (Centre) Mrs. Alexander   980 (Lower) Mr. & Mrs. Edward
ALL.   Armstrong.   H. McKeon.

No. 982 is a small sideboard in which there is a central convex portion containing a cupboard; and on each side of the cupboard is a straight section with a drawer above and a cupboard below. Rectangular inlays enclosing oval ones are on each of the doors and drawers; and a line of inlay is under the top and another one is at the base. The uprights above the legs are of the same type as those in Nos. 973 and 976. The handles and escutcheons are of an unusual design and are said to be modern. About 1800–1810.

No. 983 is a large sideboard having straight ends in which are cupboards. The central portion is convex and contains a wide drawer and also a cupboard which extends lower than the cupboards on the ends. The unusual number of eight legs support this sideboard, differently arranged from those in No. 977. The inlay consists of four large ovals containing brilliant oval designs, sixteen corner fans or shells, four fans on brackets at the junctions below the side cupboards, and also lines on the drawer and other parts. On the top there is a low back–board with sides, and spade feet are on the square and tapering legs. About 1800–1810.

The next four sideboards, Nos. 984–987, have "swell" or "bow" tops and fronts such as are seen on some of the bureaus of the period, as in Nos. 733–738. These four pieces have not the concave ends of the Hepplewhite style, nor the convex ends of the Sheraton style; but the whole design seems to approach nearer to the Sheraton style than to that of Hepplewhite. Perhaps these pieces are not "in" the style of either of the masters, but only "after" their styles.

No. 984 is a handsome sideboard of the type mentioned, that is, the top and front is in a "swell" or "bow" shape. On the drawer in the centre is an inlaid design of two parallel lines with rounded ends, referred to in No. 962. Under the drawer is an arch in a serpentine curve, under which a cellaret may be placed. On each end is a deep drawer inlaid with a square enclosing an oval. Above each of the four front legs is an inlaid bar of light wood as in Nos. 974, 976 and others. The brass handles are of the ring type. A sideboard of this design seems to have no distinctive features belonging only to the Hepplewhite style or to the Sheraton style; perhaps it should be classified merely as being in the "Hepplewhite–Sheraton" style, or period. About 1800-1815.

No. 985 resembles the previous sideboard in general appearance, except that it has no inlay at any point and has oval instead of round handles. Minor differences consist of a cupboard on the right end instead of a deep drawer, and two drawers on the left. The absence of inlay is characteristic of many Sheraton style sideboards of a somewhat later date. Here we may admire the fine design and proportions of the piece without the distraction of brilliant decoration. About 1800–1810.

No. 986 also has a bow front. An arch is in the centre, over which is a drawer, and on each end is a deep drawer resembling two smaller drawers. On the edges of the drawers are bands of mahogany, (not well seen), surrounded by lines of light wood. The legs have lines of inlay and on the uprights above are inlaid oval fan designs. The legs terminate in spade feet. The form of the escutcheons will be noticed. About 1800–1810.

981 (UPPER) MR. JOHN C. TOLAND.   982 (CENTRE) MISS MARGARET   983 (LOWER) MR. & MRS. BAYARD
                                              STEELE.   TURNBULL.

984 (UPPER) MR. WM. M. ELLICOTT.   985 (CENTRE) MRS. MILES WHITE, JR.   986 (LOWER) MISS HARRIETT R. CHEW.

987 (Upper) Mr. Wm. Wallace Lanahan.   988 (Centre) Mr. & Mrs. J. M. Matthews.   989 (Lower) Mrs. John S. Gibbs, Jr.

No. 987 also is a bow front piece without decoration by inlay. In form it is similar in some respects to the Hepplewhite style sideboard No. 963. There are five drawers of various sizes in the upper row, the central one overhanging a recessed cupboard below, two cupboards at the ends and two bottle drawers. About 1800–1810.

No. 988 is a very different form of sideboard, almost in the shape of a half–circle,[3] but flattened in the central portion of the front. The drawers at the top

990. Miss Eleanor S. Cohen.

are inlaid with the design mentioned in the comments on No. 962 and others; and on the cupboards below are six very large ovals which are also seen on some other pieces in the Sheraton style. Look at its other features and you see the front feet are curved on both sides and seem to be in a modified form of French bracket feet; the skirt is cut in a series of scrolls formed of cyma curves, as to which see section 23. The mahogany veneer is of a fine color and grain. This piece may be an English one. About 1800–1810.

3.   A somewhat similar sideboard, semi–circular in form, is shown as No. 767 in Mr. Nutting's "Furniture Treasury."

An interesting sideboard, somewhat similar in design, is in "Antiques," January, 1931, page 39. See also the issue of February, 1936, frontispiece.

No. 989 is also nearly semi–circular,[4] as is the previous piece. The compartments at the rear on each side are small cupboards which are supported by hinges. In this piece, as in some others, there is no inlay of any kind. The handles are of a somewhat earlier period. About 1800–1810.

No. 990 is probably a combined sideboard and cabinet[5] of the Sheraton style of about 1800, made in England, which has been in our country in the family of the present owner for several generations. In this highly decorated piece the unusual features are the mirror and the small satinwood drawers below between the handsome rectangular boxes,[6] probably for knives and silverware, which are almost as high as those in No. 1008 in this section. The sideboard portion is very similar to No. 975 in its characteristic inlay decorations and convex ends. A pull–out shelf is seen over the large drawer. The brass handles are eight–sided. About 1800–1810.

This concludes the illustrations of sideboards which are identified as being in the Sheraton style because they have convex ends, or, at least, ends which are not in the concave style of Hepplewhite.

In the next three illustrations, Nos. 991–993, are sideboards with a feature which is regarded as of Sheraton origin and usage, that is, reeded or fluted columns which project beyond the body of the sideboard and extend down from the top as tapering legs, the top being shaped to cover the upper ends of the columns. This feature is mentioned and illustrated in connection with Nos. 745 and 753 in the chapter on bureaus and may be seen in the Sheraton design in illustration No. 949, F.

No. 991 shows these mahogany columns projecting from the body of the sideboard and extending downward as reeded and tapered legs. Fine "crotch" and "feathered" mahogany veneer ornaments the fronts of the three upper drawers, the two vertical bottle drawers and the three cupboards. About 1795–1810.

In No. 922 the four projecting columns are reeded and their tops are carved with leaf and flower designs; these carved tops are repeated at the ends of the two upper drawers which are set back a short distance from the front edge. We again see an arch in the centre with a carved scroll in cyma curves in the keystone position. The cupboards approach nearer to the floor than in preceding side-

---

4.   This piece resembles in some points, especially in showing the framework under the centre drawer, a Sheraton style semi–circular sideboard in Mr. Cescinsky's "English Furniture," volume 3, figure 277, the date of which is given as about 1795–1800; but in the English piece there are only four legs.

     Semi–circular sideboards of this general type are also seen in a Shearer drawing in illustration No. 949, A; in "Antiques," March, 1931, page 210, in an article by Mr. Fiske Kimball on "Furniture Carvings by Samuel McIntire"; and in "English Furniture, Woodwork, Decoration, etc., during the eighteenth century," pages 298–299, by Mr. T. A. Strange.

5.   The decorative features in the upper portion of this piece are too numerous to be described here. The paintings, the various colored woods, the eagle and the urn finials, the diamond–shaped designs and other decorations, are of fine workmanship. The piece seems to have been based upon a design in Sheraton's "Drawing Book," plate 49, dated May, 1792, opposite page 332.

6.   Knife urns and knife boxes are considered and illustrated in section 131.

991 (UPPER) ANONYMOUS.   992 (CENTRE) MISS MARGARET C.   993 (LOWER) MRS. JOHN S. GIBBS,
PAINTER.   JR.

994 (Upper Left) Anonymous.
996 (Centre) Mr. John S. McDaniel.

995 (Upper Right) Mr. John S. McDaniel.
997 (Lower) Mr. & Mrs. Carroll Van Ness.

boards. A back–board, or "gallery," shaped at the ends, protects china or silver-ware which may be leaned against it. The handles on the drawers are numerous and modern. The legs are tapered and reeded. The carvings on the upper parts of the columns seem to be in the style of Samuel McIntire, of Salem.[7] The date may be about 1800–1810.

In No. 993, a combination of a sideboard and a bureau, the projecting columns are seen to be finely reeded. The sideboard portion is below and consists of two vertical bottle drawers between which is a cupboard with two doors. This cupboard and the inner portions of the two drawers above the cupboard project forward and the top and the base are similarly advanced, somewhat in the manner of a plain block–front. Oval handles and round brass knobs are noticed. This piece is of maple. About 1800–1810.

In the next group, Nos. 994–999, the principal feature which places the sideboards in the style of Sheraton is the round, tapering and often reeded type of leg, terminating generally in a small "turned" foot; and the absence of much inlay is also an indication of the style. This kind of leg for sideboards was first designed by Sheraton, and is shown in his books; in this connection see illustration No. 949, E and F. It appears on the Sheraton style sideboard No. 972 and on the three pieces Nos. 991–993; but on those pieces there are other features distinctive of the style. As indicated above, there is no inlay on these pieces, except on the edges of No. 999.

No. 994 is an attractive small sideboard of finely grained mahogany with a straight front and an arch under the drawer. At each end is a cupboard. Above the reeding the legs are "ringed" horizontally, and above the rings the uprights are fluted. This piece may be compared with No. 969 in the Hepplewhite style. About 1800–1810.

No. 995 is also a small straight front sideboard with fluting and reeding, as on the previous piece, and also on the edge of the top. A back–board, or "gallery," is at the back and extends forward on the sides; the rear portion may be a variation of the general form of the "pediment" at the top of the Sheraton style secretaries seen in No. 825 and others. There are five drawers, two of which are vertical bottle drawers, and a cupboard is in the centre. The brass handle plates are eight–sided, as in No. 958 in the Hepplewhite style. About 1800–1810.

No. 996 has convex ends and on that account might have been shown in the group having that distinctive form of the Sheraton style; but as it has round and tapering legs it may equally well appear with others having the same feature. The front is in the form which is called "reversed serpentine," and may be seen on the bureau No. 717, having a curve which is convex at the ends and concave

7. As to Samuel McIntire, (1757–1811), and his carvings see section 72, note 6.

A similar sideboard, but without an arch, is twice illustrated in "Antiques," August, 1932, page 49, and September, 1933, page 91, in connection with the Salem furniture makers and carvers, especially Samuel McIntire.

The carvings on the sewing table No. 1587 may be compared with those on this sideboard; see also the last mentioned article in "Antiques."

in the centre. There are four drawers and three cupboards. The legs are reeded and the uprights above are fluted; the edge of the top is also reeded and the brass handle plates are eight–sided, as in the previous piece. About 1800–1820.

In No. 997 the front is convex in the centre and straight at each end, in this respect resembling Nos. 982 and 983. The legs are in the usual rounded and tapering form but have no reeding, as is also the case with the next several sideboards. There are brass knobs on the drawer and brass handles on two of the three cupboards; either of these two types are suitable. About 1800–1820.

No. 998 is somewhat similar, having a convex centre and straight ends, and also round and tapering legs without reeding; but the uprights above the legs are fluted. There are three drawers with glass knobs, and three cupboards. A backboard and sides are on the top. About 1800–1820.

In No. 999 the round legs become shorter because the cupboards at the ends are made somewhat deeper than in previous pieces. The top is straight, except the central portion which projects forward. There are five shallow drawers of three sizes and also two deep vertical bottle drawers, between which is a curved and recessed cupboard. The fine crotch mahogany veneer is noticeable. Here there is inlay on the edges of the top and the base. About 1800–1820.

In the next six sideboards, Nos. 1000–1005, the cupboards on the ends are deeper than those on the previous pieces and for this reason the pieces bear the descriptive name of "deep end" sideboards. This feature was probably derived by our cabinet makers from some of the designs in the books of Sheraton.[8] Although the change in appearance is considerable, the only real change is the addition of a few inches to the depth of the end cupboards. The dates of these pieces are about 1800–1820.

In No. 1000 the ends are straight and the central portion is convex. The three drawers above and the three cupboards below are ornamented with inlay. The legs are tapered on the inside, a method seen in many of tne sideboards and other articles in the Hepplewhite style. Brackets are under the ends of the central cabinet as in later pieces of this type. The two small drawers are perhaps over–supplied with handles as in No. 992. About 1800–1820.

In No. 1001 two shallow drawers are placed on the top; these drawers were doubtless intended to support knife boxes as well as to contain silverware, and are inlaid with oval panels of satinwood with small shell ovals on the sides. The central drawer is curved and overhangs a recessed cupboard on each side of which is a wide vertical drawer capable of holding more bottles than the other bottle drawers seen in these illustrations. The six doors have dark inlaid oval panels. The short legs are square and tapered, with inlaid bands. About 1800–1820.

8. This type of "deep–end" sideboard seems to have been first designed by Thomas Shearer. It appears in the book entitled "Cabinet Maker's London Book of Prices," which was published in 1788, before the books of Hepplewhite and Sheraton were issued. Shearer's design in illustration No. 948, C, was appropriated by Sheraton in his book and was doubtless used by the cabinet makers who used the book of Sheraton.

998 (Upper) Mrs. Murray Steuart   999 (Centre) Mr. & Mrs. Wm. A.   1000 (Lower) Mr. Benjamin Chew
  Hartshorne.   Dixon.   Howard.

1001 (UPPER) MR. & MRS. HENRY 1002 (CENTRE) DR. GEO. E. HARDY. 1003 (LOWER) MR. & MRS. JAMES
LAY DUER. CAREY, JR.

No. 1002 has two shallow drawers on the top and two others under the top. A small slide for candle stands is seen on the left, as also in Nos. 1004 and 1012. Round brass knobs are used instead of oval handles. On each side of the end cupboards are "applied" reeded columns, giving the appearance of projecting columns such as those seen on Nos. 991–993; and the top is shaped so as to cover the upper ends of the columns. About 1800–1820.

No. 1003 is similar in general form to No. 1000, excepting the back–board and also the round legs, which are "ringed" and reeded. The doors of the deep end cupboards contain panels somewhat in the form of a Gothic arch, a method of ornamentation which will be seen in other pieces of the period having large surfaces, as in the bookcase No. 870. The brass handles consist of a brass oval plate from which is suspended an oval brass "pull" in a form not appearing elsewhere in this book. About 1800–1820.

In No. 1004 the cupboards at the ends are in a different form from those seen on other sideboards, the fronts being almost semi–circular. The design was doubtless taken from one of Sheraton's later illustrations[9] in which a "deep end" cupboard appears. The central portion has a convex drawer overhanging a recessed cupboard. Two shallow drawers, also with rounded fronts, are on the top, and the back–board has two scrolls with an urn between them. On the left, one of the two slides is seen, as in No. 1002. The feet are of the brass claw type which were popular about 1820. There is no inlay on this piece. About 1810–1820.

No. 1005 is a small sideboard, rectangular in outline except for the curved space under the central cupboard, and is without inlay. As in the next sideboard its plain appearance is relieved only by the four applied reeded columns on the deep end cupboards. The handles are of an earlier period. About 1810–1820.

No. 1006 has four reeded and applied Sheraton style flat columns which extend from the top down to the base as in No. 1005, and also has short round "ringed" legs. The central portion is built down to the base, there being no arched space under the central cupboard. The doors of the cupboards are paneled as in several other sideboards of the period, such as Nos. 1009–1010 and others. The three brass handles on the drawers are of the "lion and ring" pattern. The fine mahogany veneer is not well seen in the engraving. About 1810–1830.

Nos. 1007 and 1008 may not be recognized at first glance as sideboards although each consists of a sideboard of a certain type with a large china cabinet above.[10] This type of sideboard with a china cabinet is very similar in design to a "Salem secretary."[11]

9. The illustration is in Mr. J. M. Bell's "Chippendale, Sheraton and Hepplewhite furniture designs," page 147.

10. Three similar fine sideboards with china cabinets are illustrated and explained in Mr. Lockwood's "Colonial Furniture," volume 1, figures 214, 215 and on page 376.

11. A finely illustrated article in "Antiques," May, 1933, pages 168–170, by Mr. Fiske Kimball, is entitled "Salem Secretaries and their makers." One of the objects illustrated, No. 6, is very alike in design to our No. 1007 and is called, page 169, a "Salem secretary." In the other objects the lower portion is not in the form of a sideboard. The term "Salem secretary" is not used by Mr. Lockwood.

A "butler's" sideboard is one having a deep drawer in the centre which was furnished as a desk in which the butler kept the papers and accounts of his department in the household.

1004 (Upper) Mr. & Mrs. James 1005 (Centre) Miss Dora L. Mur- 1006 (Lower) Dr. Henry M. Fitz-
Carey, Jr. DOCH. HUGH.

No. 1007 is seen to be in the Sheraton style because of its deep ends and by a certain similarity of the design of the wide "pediment" at the top to the pediments on the Sheraton style secretary–bookcases Nos. 825–826, and others. Four brass urns and another ornament are missing from the pediment. The three white panels under the cornice are of painted glass and are decorated with flowers and a country scene, and under these are the doors with diamond–shaped panes of glass. In the centre of the sideboard portion is a desk drawer whose front pulls out and down as in the open and closed bureau desk Nos. 827–828, and within the drawer are the usual desk arrangements. A shallow drawer and a cupboard are at each end. The entire front is ornamented with finely grained inlaid forms in mahogany. About 1810–1820.

No. 1008 is a well–made sideboard of mahogany, with a china cabinet resting on two shallow drawers. On each side is a tall box for dining room articles, supported by a shallow drawer. The glazed doors of the cabinet are cut in diamond–shaped panes as in the preceding piece. The central part of the sideboard portion contains a deep drawer under which is a recessed cupboard. On the ends are two cupboards, each with a shallow drawer above and below, the latter being an unusual feature. Four finely fluted corner columns are supported by rounded legs and feet in the familiar style of Sheraton. The edges of the drawer fronts and of the various doors are banded with a light–colored wood. About 1810–1820.

Section 130. Empire style sideboards.—In these sideboards, as in several other articles, we see changes which were made under the influence of the French Empire style, by which the Sheraton style was superseded, as appears in section 21. The sideboards gradually became larger and heavier and the fine decorative inlays in oval and other forms were no longer used. The principal features of the new style were the heavy columns, either plain or carved in spiral form or with leaves or other decorations, and the feet which changed from the round and tapering type to animals' claw feet or to some fanciful design. On the other hand, the sideboards were generally well made of fine mahogany, and the flat surfaces, usually veneered, were brilliant with color, sometimes too highly stained red. In the French Empire style pieces fine brass ornaments were used, but these were seldom adopted by American cabinet makers, only the handles and sometimes the feet being made of brass.

In this section the first three sideboards, Nos. 1009–1011, may be regarded as in the Early American Empire style in which certain features of the Sheraton style will be noticed, and Nos. 1012–1016 will be seen to be in the Late American Empire style; some of the former, although burdened with the name "Empire," may be called handsome in design and fine in wood and workmanship. In considering furniture in the Empire style it is customary to condemn it all; but this condemnation is too broad.[1] Some of the admired pieces of Duncan Phyfe show

1. The "American Empire style" is the subject of section 21 in chapter 3 entitled "Styles of American Antique Furniture." Comments upon the style are made in connection with various articles of furniture; see also the Index, "Empire Style."

1007 (Upper) Anonymous.   1008 (Lower) Mr. Wm. M. Ellicott.

prominent features of the Empire style.[2] We should try to see the best features in the Empire style pieces and not concentrate our attention on the worst.

In No. 1009 we see two reeded corner columns at the top of which are carved vase–like designs; these columns resemble those seen in bureaus of the Empire period, such as Nos. 757 and 758. The feet remind us of several in the Sheraton style seen on the sideboards in the previous section, such as No. 1006. On the top is a back–board with railings at the sides. Three drawers of equal size, with banded edges and with glass knobs, slightly overhang the lower portion as in the bureau No. 757 and later bureaus. Under these drawers are four small and one large cupboard. The fronts of these drawers and cupboards are paneled, as in almost all of the pieces shown in this section, and are veneered with fine crotch mahogany. The straight and heavy base is a feature of the Empire style which will also be seen on other sideboards and bureaus of the period. About 1810–1820.

Nos. 1010 and 1011 are handsome sideboards with fine crotch mahogany veneer on the flat surfaces. No. 1010 has a back–board with side railings as in the previous piece. The larger one of the usual three drawers, here with glass knobs, is in the centre; and there are three cupboards. Four reeded columns, supporting the overhanging drawers, are carved at the top. The carved legs are in an unusual form adapted from the French, and have brass claw feet. A panel may be seen on the right side; similar panels are on many other Empire style sideboards but are not all seen in the engravings. About 1810–1820.

In No. 1011 the smaller one of the three overhanging drawers is in the centre. Under these three drawers are two large cupboards and two drawers. The two columns are carved with leaf designs. The round and carved feet are supplied with casters. On the doors of the two cupboards are large oval panels of fine crotch mahogany veneer, but these ovals are not easily seen in the engraving. Glass knobs are on two of the drawers. About 1810–1830.

The next five sideboards, Nos. 1012–1016, may be regarded as in the Late American Empire style. The first three have plain and heavy columns and either animals' feet or ball feet. These pieces have the same fine veneer work as the previous three sideboards, but having no carving on the columns they appear to be more massive and heavy.

No. 1012 has a shallow drawer over each end of the top, resembling in this respect No. 1008 and others; these drawers were intended to hold table–ware and to support a pair of knife boxes. Five other drawers are under the top, the three in the centre being recessed, and underneath the drawers are three cupboards. The four columns rest upon a heavy base under which are animals' claw feet. On the doors of the cupboards are arched panels in almost the same form as in the next illustration in which the panels are better seen. A small pull–out shelf is on the right side, as in No. 1004. About 1820–1830.

2. See the chairs Nos. 320–323, in which Phyfe combined Sheraton and Empire designs, adding his own elegant carving and other features, including brass feet.

1009 (UPPER) MRS. C. E. HENDER-   1010 (CENTRE) MR. & MRS. CARROLL   1011 (LOWER) MISS E. H. BARTLETT.
SON.   VAN NESS.

1012 (Upper) Miss Helen H. 1013 (Centre) Mrs. F. G. Boyce, 1014 (Lower) Judge F. N. Parke.
Carey.   Jr.

1015 (UPPER) ANONYMOUS.   1016 (CENTRE) ANONYMOUS.   1017 (LOWER) MRS. S. S. BUZBY.

563

No. 1013 has a back–board with side railings as in No. 1010, three drawers under the top and four plain round columns under which are animals' claw feet. Three arches are seen in the panels on the cupboard doors, four others over the columns and two others on the ends of the back–board. The row of three drawers is ornamented in an unusual design, having panels which were perhaps suggested by the inlaid parallel lines with rounded ends seen in many pieces in section 128, such as No. 962 and others. About 1820–1830.

In No. 1014 there is no carving and no curved line except on the two plain and round columns and the two ball feet. On the three drawers are glass knobs. The three cupboards are in a straight line. Each of the doors of the cupboards is paneled in a rectangular form. About 1820–1830.

In No. 1015 the back–board is in the form of a broken arch, somewhat resembling that in No. 1004. Between the inner ends of the scrolls is a panel of the same type as those in the row of three drawers. These drawers are finished with "lion's head and ring" handles. Each of the four columns is carved in a spiral or "rope" form, and below the small platform the carving continues to the floor. The cupboards are recessed under the overhanging drawers and on each one there is a panel with an arched top.[3] About 1820–1830.

No. 1016 is a small sideboard of a type which was popular in New England. As in the previous piece the columns are in a spiral or "rope" form, below which are "ringed" feet. Over the columns are panels cut in lattice–work design. Between two small vertical drawers is a large and deep one, which was sometimes a desk within, as in the bureau desks Nos. 827–828. About 1820–1830.

Other types of sideboards in the Late American Empire style may be seen in private houses and in antique shops; but those here shown illustrate the more important kinds. Some have mirrors on the back; others are in fantastic forms; few are desirable for the amateur collector.

No. 1017 is a small Victorian sideboard of about the year 1850, which, like some other Victorian pieces,[4] is interesting because of the attempts to combine various earlier good features with some later ones which we do not admire. In this sideboard the Hepplewhite and Sheraton styles of inlaid ovals, such as those in Nos. 955, 968, 981 and 988, are imitated by the six oval and recessed panels in this piece. The four round and projecting columns on the lower portion and the similar but smaller columns above, and the space between, seem to have been suggested by those in No. 992 and others. The heavy base follows the form of the Empire pieces, and the brass feet resemble those in No. 1010. The moldings around the ovals and elsewhere seem to be of the type which were easily made by a machine invented about 1840. The fine grain of the veneer will be noticed. About 1850–1860.

3. This and the next sideboard are copied, by permission, from Mr. Lockwood's "Colonial Furniture," volume 1, figures 218 and 223.
4. The use of earlier designs on articles made in the Victorian period is also seen in bureaus Nos. 767 and 768; in secretary–bookcase No. 868 and in others. See also the Index, under the word "Victorian."

Section 131. Knife urns and knife boxes.—Illustration No. 948, A, shows a sideboard table with separate pedestals and urns,[1] the first step in the direction of a modern sideboard, as mentioned in the comment on that piece; later the table, pedestal and urns were combined in one piece as in No. 948, B, making an early form of sideboard as we know it. The early urns were generally made as parts of the sideboard; but in the designs of Hepplewhite and Sheraton the urns became separate and movable pieces. Urns with various decorative features are shown in Hepplewhite's "Guide,"[2] and in Sheraton's "Drawing Book." The difference in shape between the two styles is not great; but the urns of Hepplewhite were

1. The urn was either fitted with a faucet and lined with lead or other material for holding water, or made with a top which could be raised on a shaft, with "terraces" which were cut out to hold knives, forks and spoons. The latter type was the usual one with Hepplewhite and Sheraton, and is shown in Nos. 1018 to 1023. Adam generally designed his sideboards, which were often large, with two or three slope–top knife boxes in addition to the pair of urns, an imposing picture with the silverware, glass, candles and an ornamental rail in the rear.

Urns are also seen in illustration No. 948.

2. A. Hepplewhite also made sideboards with pedestals and urns, or, as the latter were called, vases, with faucets. In describing them in his "Guide" he states that "the vases may be used to hold water for the use of the butler or iced water for drinking; . . or may be used as knife cases; . . the height of the vases is about 2 feet 3 inches." It seems that the ice–water habit of the American people was inherited from our eighteenth century English ancestors!

B. The urns were apparently not made to any great extent after the modern sideboard was developed, although they are shown in the books of Hepplewhite and Sheraton, as appears in the text; and the urns were gradually superseded by the boxes. Being intended for the two pedestals at the ends of the side–tables, the urns were of course made in pairs; and when knife boxes came into use they also were made in pairs.

C. These urns and boxes were generally made of mahogany, although sometimes of the more expensive satinwood. Their construction was difficult and that of the urns required such a high degree of technical skill that in London they were made only by cabinet makers who were specialists in such work.

D. The finest urns and boxes were made in England. While it is probable that some excellent ones were made in our country, the number does not seem to be large. In some cases they are adorned with handsome silver fittings, as in No. 1029 and others. Most of the urns and boxes shown here are apparently English.

E. No uniformity as regards feet on the boxes appears in the designs in the books or in the pieces as made. In No. 1027 there are five feet, in No. 1028 there are four, in No. 1029 there are three and in others there are none; and the kind of feet differs in many cases, the brass ones being most usual.

F. Two finely illustrated articles entitled "Knife cases," by Mr. Gregor Norman–Wilcox are in "Antiques," October, 1934, pages 133–136, and December, 1934, pages 222–225.

G. In Mr. Nutting's "Furniture Treasury," volume 1, Nos. 202–206, are illustrations of knife boxes. Two are stated to be "solid mahogany, top and front veneered in crotch grain." One is referred to as "American, from Alexandria, Virginia."

H. A few years ago the town of Snow Hill in Maryland came into prominence in the field of antique furniture, but not because of its snow or its hill—as it has little snow and no hill. Its importance was on account of an elaborate sideboard which was to be sold at auction in New York—a sideboard which the sale catalogue stated was a product of the eighteenth century and was made in Snow Hill, Maryland. Alas, some doubting antiquer discovered and proved that the sideboard was not from Snow Hill or any other place on a map of the United States, but that it was a product of the

(*Note 2 continued on page 566.*)

often more elaborate than those of the Sheraton type. In Nos. 1018–1023 closed and open urns in both styles are shown.

Knife boxes are for the same purposes as knife urns, but are of a different type; most of them have a top, or lid, the front of which slopes down, and they are therefore often called "slope top" knife boxes. Designs of these in the books of Hepplewhite and Sheraton are shown in Nos. 1024–1028; but the boxes as made did not often exactly follow the designs, and, as in the case of the urns, the styles are not always easily distinguishable. In this section the examples of these knife boxes are shown without attempting to classify all of them.

The dates of the urns and knife boxes in the style of Hepplewhite are from about 1785 to 1800, and of those in the Sheraton style from about 1795 to 1810.

The urns Nos. 1018–1020 are English and are in the style of Hepplewhite. It is said that the urns in this style are not as graceful as the typical ones in the Sheraton style, but that they are generally more fully decorated. In No. 1018 the ornamentation of the upper portion is very attractive, but the form of the lower portion is almost in the shape of a part of an egg.[3] About 1785–1795.

Illustration No. 1019 is a design in Hepplewhite's book of an open urn, in which the construction may be seen.[4] The top rises on a central shaft, and is held in position by a spring. At the top of the lower portion are two round raised blocks and these, with the surface of the lower portion, form three "terraces" in which are numerous openings for knives, forks and spoons. About 1785–1795.

No. 1020 is a design, also from Hepplewhite's book,[5] of an urn which was made to stand upon a pedestal of the early type of sideboard. The urn is ornamented with festoons, leaves and other designs. It was not made for knives, but for water for the use of the butler, or for "iced water for drinking" as mentioned in the quotation from Hepplewhite's "Guide" in note 2, A, in this section. At the bottom is a faucet for drawing out the water. About 1785–1795.

(NOTE 2, *continued from page 565.*)

far off Philippine Islands. As some amateur readers may not recognize the furniture of the Philippines it would be well to consult the magazine "Antiques," July, 1930, at page 31.

 I. Although called knife urns and knife boxes, these boxes were used for the keeping of forks and spoons as well as knives. They were generally purchased in pairs and one urn or box was placed on each end of the sideboard, and the lids were sometimes kept up in order that their contents might be seen. They were a very popular article of furniture in the latter part of the eighteenth century, so much so that Hepplewhite wrote in his book that their "universality" rendered a particular description unnecessary. Urns and boxes were often used on the same sideboard at the same time.

 J. A material called "shagreen," made of the untanned skin of sharks or horses or certain animals, was much used as a cover for knife boxes and other small articles. It was made and used in Philadelphia from about 1700 to 1760 according to the investigation by Mr. Wm. M. Hornor, Jr., as mentioned in his book "Philadelphia Furniture," page 62. The skin was finished with a granular surface and was generally colored black or green. Shagreen covers were imitated and leather was much used in its place.

 3. This is copied from Mr. Cescinsky's "English Furniture," volume 3, figure 287, page 262.

 4. This is from a drawing in Hepplewhite's "Guide," plate 39.

 5. This is from a drawing in Hepplewhite's "Guide," plate 36.

1018 (Upper) Anonymous.
1021 (Lower) Mr. Albert G.
     Towers.

1019 (Upper) Anonymous.
1022 (Lower) Mr. Albert G.
     Towers.

1020 (Upper) Anonymous.
1023 (Lower) Miss Helen H.
     Carey.

Nos. 1021 and 1022 are a pair of knife urns, or vases, in the Sheraton style. These urns are made of satinwood, with rectangular inlays of a darker wood on the upper portion. There are five "terraces" in which are openings for knives, forks and spoons. The fine wood, workmanship and design of these urns unite in making them very pleasing. About 1795–1810.

No. 1023 is an urn in what is said to be the later Sheraton style.[6] The upper portion resembles somewhat that of the previous piece, with the "finial" and the round dome. The lower portion suggests a modification of form of some of the knife "boxes" seen in the next group. About 1800–1810.

The next twelve illustrations show knife "boxes," three of which, Nos. 1024–1026, are copies of the drawings of Hepplewhite in his "Guide"; two others, Nos. 1027 and 1028, are copies of the drawings of Sheraton in his "Drawing Book"; and seven, Nos. 1029–1035, are engravings of existing pieces. The drawings establish the respective styles of Hepplewhite and Sheraton, and with their aid the reader may perhaps satisfy himself whether a particular box in which he may be interested is in the one style or the other; but it may be easier to avoid uncertainty and error by taking refuge in the classification of "Hepplewhite–Sheraton period."[7]

Examining Nos. 1024–1026, which are copies of drawings and outlines in Hepplewhite's book,[8] we see the highly decorative treatment of the front portions of knife boxes, or cases. These decorations are of course not essential parts of the boxes, and in fact were seldom made. Under the boxes are the outlines, or "plans," of the three fronts. Two of these "plans" follow the distinctive outlines of the Hepplewhite style sideboards having concave ends,[9] and the outline in the centre has no concave curves. It may be that the boxes were purposely made in harmony with the lines of the sideboards on which they were to be placed. About 1785–1795.

Nos. 1027 and 1028 are Sheraton's drawings.[10] In No. 1027 there is a resemblance to two of the drawings of Hepplewhite in having concave ends;[11] in No. 1028 there is the familiar Sheraton feature of two fluted column–like projections, such as are seen on several of the bureaus and other pieces[12] in the

---

6.   An urn apparently about the same as this, except having feet instead of a pedestal, is shown on plate 139 of Mr. F. S. Robinson's "English Furniture."

7.   See the remarks on this subject in "Bureaus," section 95; "Secretary–bookcases," section 104; and section 127 in this chapter.

8.   In his "Guide," plate 38; the printing under the "plans" reads as follows: "London. Published September 1st., 1787, by I. and J. Taylor, No. 56, High Holborn."

9.   The outline on the left is an "unbroken serpentine" curve; the outline in the centre has straight ends with a convex curve in the centre; the outline on the right is a "broken serpentine" curve. These outlines are also seen in the illustrations of the Hepplewhite style sideboards in section 128.

10.   These are in his "Drawing Book," plate 39.

11.   In this chapter the view has been presented in section 127 that sideboards with concave ends should be regarded as being in the style of Hepplewhite and that those with convex ends are in the style of Sheraton, as shown by the drawings in the books of those two masters; but this distinction does not seem to apply to knife boxes, as the designs of Sheraton show knife boxes with concave forms as well as convex forms.

12.   See "Bureaus," Nos. 745 and 753, and "Sideboards," Nos. 991–993.

London. Published Sep.r 1.st 1785. by I.k. J.Taylor, N.o 56. High Holborn.

Plans.

1024 (Upper) Anonymous.
1027 (Lower) Anonymous.

1025 (Upper) Anonymous.
1028 (Lower) Anonymous.

1026 (Upper) Anonymous.
1029 (Lower) Mrs. Miles White, Jr.

Sheraton style. The front outlines of these boxes do not appear to resemble closely those of any of the sideboards in Sheraton's style. Each box is supported by brass feet. About 1791–1810.

Examining the slope front and partly flat top knife boxes, Nos. 1029–1035, we see in No. 1029 a fine example of a plain design with handsome fittings. The handle on the lid, the two handles on the sides, the escutcheon in two parts on the front and the three feet are all of silver and are pierced in delicate designs. The tiny ball and claw feet and the C curves over the front foot seem to indicate that this knife box was made before the influence of the Chippendale style had entirely passed away. This is probably an English piece and is regarded as having been made about 1770–1780.

Nos. 1030 and 1031 give an open and closed view of an elegant pair of knife boxes, finely inlaid on all edges and with a shell on the lid. The centre of the front is concave and on each side of this portion is an inlaid column; and beyond the columns the form becomes serpentine. The silver escutcheons are in a graceful design, resembling in part those of No. 1028. In the open box we see the numerous openings for knives and forks and spoons, each opening being edged with lines of inlay. The inner side of the lid in the better class of boxes was often inlaid, sometimes with a star, thus avoiding a plain appearance when the lid was raised. About 1795–1805.

No. 1032 is in an unusual form, the corners being curved in an unbroken line. On the lid there is an oval shell inlay, under which is a silver handle; and an ornamental silver lock in two parts will be noticed. About 1790–1800.

No. 1033 shows a familiar form of knife box which was apparently very popular. The front is in the form of an unbroken serpentine curve and on each side of this there is a concave curve. A silver handle is on the lid and a silver escutcheon is below. About 1795–1805.

No. 1034 is a plainer kind of knife box, having a flat top instead of a sloping top. Here the book designs of Hepplewhite and Sheraton do not definitely appear. The central portion, with a silver escutcheon as in No. 1030, is concave, and on its sides are flat panels, beyond which are convex portions. The four upright panels are inlaid with lines. The feet are small ones of the ball type. About 1795–1805.

No. 1035 resembles the previous knife box, having a flat top. It is open here in order to show clearly the curves of the front, which are three concave ones, with a convex curve on each side. The form of escutcheon and the ball feet are the same as that seen on the previous piece. About 1795–1805.

Section 132. Cellarets.—In addition to the knife urns and knife boxes, the sideboards of the eighteenth century and the early part of the nineteenth were often accompanied by cellarets,[1] or "wine–coolers," as they were also called. In

---

1. In the English books the word "cellaret" has two meanings. The one with which we are familiar is a box, lined with lead or other metal, for bottles; this is a "wine–cooler" and is also called a "sarcophagus." The other meaning of "cellaret" is a deep side drawer of a sideboard, such as those seen in this chapter, fitted with divisions for bottles; this latter meaning is not in use in our country.

(*Note 1 continued on page 572.*)

1030 (Upper) Anonymous.
1033 (Lower) Miss Elisabeth H. Bartlett.

1031 (Upper) Anonymous.
1034 (Lower) Mrs. F. T. Redwood.

1032 (Upper) Mr. & Mrs. Chas. E. McLane.
1035 (Lower) Mr. Blanchard Randall.

the days when a "side table" was used, either alone or later with pedestals and vases, as mentioned in section 126, the wine–coolers were generally box–like pieces, sometimes with brass bands around them, and with a lid, often with the sides slanting inward. These were of a height which permitted them to be placed under the side–table.

1036 (UPPER) DR. JAMES BORDLEY, 1037 (UPPER) MRS. MILES WHITE, 1038 (UPPER) MRS. JOSEPH WHYTE.
        JR.   JR.   1041 (LOWER) MR. JAMES E. STEU-
1039 (LOWER) MRS. J. H. WHITELY 1040 (LOWER) SHEPPARD & E. P.   ART.
        EST.   HOSPITAL.

A later form was that made by Hepplewhite and others of his time, having an eight–sided or oval or round form, often bound with brass, as in Nos. 1038–1040. If these were too high to be put under a sideboard having a drawer in the central portion, they were placed at the side. The interiors of these cellarets were partitioned into several divisions in which the bottles were placed, with also a

(NOTE 1, *continued from page 570.*)

In "Southern Antiques," by Mr. Paul H. Burroughs, pages 68–75, seven cellarets are shown, all of which are rectangular boxes on stands, some having a drawer and a mixing slide.

Other cellarets resemble a small rectangular table with drawers; but these drawers and their handles are "sham," as the piece within is fitted for bottles and the top lifts up as a lid. No. 1041 is a somewhat similar piece.

division for the ice, and a faucet or other appliance by which the water from the ice could be removed.

No. 1036 is a "cellaret on frame" in the Chippendale style, as shown by the square and straight legs with block feet, the "C" brackets connecting the legs and the base, and the "cut–off," or "chamfered," corners of the legs and box portion. These characteristic features may also be seen in other pieces in the Chippendale style, such as tables and bureaus.[2] About 1770–1785.

No. 1037 is said to be apparently in the late Sheraton style, having reeded corners. The feet are in a form of animals' claws, and above them are carved moldings. The designs are seen in English books.[3] The date seems to be somewhat uncertain.

No. 1038 is in almost the same shape, with sloping sides. It is furnished with brass claw feet and with brass bands at the corners. The very short legs are tapering. Here also the date seems to be doubtful.

No. 1039 may be in the "Sheraton" style. It is the same as one in Hepplewhite's "Guide," except that this piece has round legs in the Sheraton style instead of the square and tapering ones shown by Hepplewhite. It is eight–sided and is securely held together by brass bands which entirely surround it, not merely holding the corners as in the previous piece. The inner lining of metal appears in the engraving. About 1795–1810.

No. 1040 is an oval cellaret, with tapering and inlaid legs. On the front is an oval inlay of light wood enclosing a panel of darker wood; and the fine veneer of mahogany rivals that in the next piece. On the ends are brass handles as in most of the previous cellarets. About 1785–1800.

No. 1041 is of a different type and is somewhat larger than the previous pieces. The box portion is rectangular, with figured mahogany veneer, and with rectangular lines of inlay and also an oval. In the centre of the front is an oval brass handle which is for ornament only, as the front is fixed and the top opens. The legs are square and straight, with a barely visible tapering on the inside. About 1785–1800.

2. See for example the bureaus Nos. 713–714.
    This cellaret No. 1036 resembles in several respects the piece described on plate 3 which is on page 69 of the book of Mr. Burroughs.
3. On pages 148 and 149 of "English Furniture," by Mr. T. A. Strange, are drawings of cellarets in which each of the features above mentioned appears. The pages are titled "Side tables and wine coolers. T. Chippendale, Ince and Mayhew, Manwaring and others." Some of the wine–coolers shown are round, some are oval and others are six–sided. Cabriole legs and ball and claw feet are also seen and in some pieces there are feet without legs.

Chapter XVI

BEDSTEADS; CRADLES; BED STEPS

Section 133. In general.—Although a few high–post bedsteads[1] in the Queen Anne style, about 1710 to 1735, with cabriole legs and club feet have been found in our country, the story of fine American bedsteads really begins at about 1735 to 1750 with those having square block feet, or ball and claw feet, in the Chippendale style. Before the Queen Anne period the bedsteads made in America were generally of a very plain character,[2] often merely a frame to hold the mattress and other furnishings; but with the increase in wealth and the building of fine houses the high–post bedstead became an article of elegance in our country as it was in England, where the bed room was for a long time one of much importance.[3]

1.   The word "bedstead" means the wooden frame; the word "bed" means the mattress. In the early inventories of the estates of deceased persons, the valuations of the "feather beds" were generally much higher than those of the "bedsteads."

2.   In Mr. Lockwood's "Colonial Furniture," volume 2, pages 243–252, an account is given of the English and American bedsteads of the seventeenth century; see also pages 333–334 of the same volume.

Examples of the huge oak bedsteads of the time of Queen Elizabeth, 1558–1603, and until that of William and Mary, 1688–1702, may be seen in some of the books. In several early pieces the posts in front rested upon large pedestals and were elaborately carved with "bulbous" forms. In the time of William and Mary the style changed and high slender posts, elaborate cornices and much drapery became the fashion. Some of the bedsteads of this period were from sixteen to twenty feet high. Very few such bedsteads have survived and apparently none of the type were made in America.

3.   In "English and American Furniture," by Cescinsky and Hunter, page 144, Mr. Cescinsky writes that in England after the Restoration of the Monarchy by Charles the Second in 1660 the bed room was "one of the important rooms in the house, in which the lady held formal morning receptions, perhaps because it was the only room in which one person, at least, (the occupant of the bed), could be assured of keeping warm. It was anything but a private chamber, as the huge elaborate bedsteads of the period indicate. It maintained this importance and publicity until almost the close of the eighteenth century, after which the four–poster went out of fashion (in England). These draped bedsteads were devised for semi-privacy rather than as a defense against draughts, and they must have been horribly stuffy in summer weather. At the same time they are decorative pieces of furniture . . in their glory of velvet, silk, fringe, braid and tassel." Mention of several fabrics is made in section 43, note 3.

In the time of Sheraton there was a fad for combining two or more purposes in one piece of furniture. For example, a table might have a folding step ladder concealed under the top. In the bedrooms there were washstands which could serve as bookcases, tables which opened out to form a

The wood used in the finer bedsteads in America was generally mahogany, but maple has often been regarded as particularly suitable for a bed room and hence many excellent pieces were made of that wood. Besides these two woods, other woods which were plentiful in particular localities were used both on account of convenience and expense; for example, it is said that maple and birch were generally used in northern New England.

The English bedsteads were often furnished with a cornice above the tester,[4] and many of these cornices were elaborate and handsome examples of skillful carving; but in our country only a few bedsteads seem to have received this kind of ornamentation.

(NOTE 3, *continued*)

writing desk, bureaus which held card tables and articles of folding furniture which contained much in small space. The designs of these may be seen in Sheraton's books of drawings. An example is in the bed steps, No. 1084. "Shamming" is described in section 163, note 5.

4. A. The word "tester" is defined as "the frame which connects the tops of the posts in a four–post bedstead." The word is the English form of the old French word "testiere" meaning a head–piece or helmet; Century Dictionary. One spelling of the word was "teester," which perhaps explains the usual pronunciation.

B. The word "valance" means "a short curtain used upon a bedstead, or in some similar way, either around the frame upon which the mattress rests, (a base valance), or around the head of the canopy, (a tester valance)"; Century Dictionary. The word "valanced" was used by Shakespeare figuratively in Hamlet, act 2, scene 2, line 411; "thy face is valanced since I saw thee last," meaning "fringed with a beard."

C. Almost all of the designs of bedsteads by Chippendale, Hepplewhite and Sheraton show a curtain at the back of the bedstead. Curtains of this kind are seen here in Nos. 1045–1047 and others. The long curtains on the sides could be moved as desired, sliding on rods.

D. It is sometimes said that what we know as "twin beds" were not made until recently; but the idea was developed by Sheraton in his "summer bed" shown below in illustration No. 1066.

E. An unfamiliar type of bedstead is that known as a "wall" bedstead, one side of which, not the head end, was placed against a wall. The posts of this side were almost of the height of a high–post bedstead, but the posts towards the room were low. Drapery suspended from a nail in the wall fell in graceful curves over the high–posts. An illustration of a bedstead of this type, adapted from a design of Sheraton by Duncan Phyfe, is No. 770 in the catalogue of the "Girl Scouts Exhibition," held in New York in September, 1929.

F. Bedsteads made by Duncan Phyfe in his best period followed the styles of Hepple–white and Sheraton, with no original features of design, but with distinctive forms of his favorite carved decorations, especially reeding, leaves and drapery. Very few of his bedsteads have been identified.

G. A type of folding bedstead sometimes found in our country was known as a "press bedstead" or a "cupboard bedstead." This was similar in principle to some now used in small apart–ments. When not in use it was kept fastened upright in an alcove or cupboard in the wall, and when needed it was tilted forward and lowered into the room. One is in a house in Shrewsbury, Massachu–setts, built as late as 1797. It was also known as a "slaw–bank," a Dutch word. A full description is in Mr. Lockwood's "Colonial Furniture," volume 2, page 248.

H. The amateur collector should be on his guard in purchasing bedsteads. The clever faker has little difficulty in converting plain and heavy posts of the Empire period into handsome posts, with carving and reeding of the Hepplewhite or Sheraton styles. This is the "glorifying" process mentioned in section 7. Moreover, high posts have been cut down and the bedsteads passed off as original low–post bedsteads; and other changes and additions have been made which are not easily discovered by the amateur.

I. The number of fine antique high–post bedsteads now seen in museums and private houses is small in comparison with some other large objects of household furniture. Very many must

In each style of high–post bedsteads the posts, legs and feet are the distinguishing features; and it will be noticed that in each style, except the Empire, most of the foot–posts, meaning the posts at the foot of the bed, are fluted or reeded. In the Chippendale and Adam styles, fluting was the favorite ornamental feature of the foot–posts, but in the later styles of Hepplewhite and Sheraton fluting was not so much used on bedsteads and its place was taken by reeding. In some of the illustrations it may be difficult to determine whether the work on the posts is fluting or reeding. In this connection it may be useful to examine section 41, in which the subjects of fluting and reeding are considered.

Another feature is that although the foot–posts may be ornamented with carving, the head–posts, meaning the posts at the head of the bedstead, are often entirely unadorned. This was because the head–posts were generally so concealed by the drapery that a decorative treatment would not be seen; but foot–posts were made to be seen.

The presence of elegant drapery adds greatly to the appearance of a bedstead, no matter how fine the woodwork may be; and it must be confessed that several illustrations are given here more on account of the fine drapery than on account of the style, wood and workmanship of the bedsteads themselves; moreover, the other furnishings seen in the bed rooms often make a pleasing picture. But much of the drapery is not quite worthy of the bedsteads, nor of the period.

The subject of drapery is not included in this book.

Section 134. Chippendale style bedsteads.—In the text of the previous section it is said that the fluting of the foot–posts was a feature of the bedsteads in the Chippendale style, but that reeding is seen on bedsteads in the Hepplewhite and Sheraton styles.

Another feature of the Chippendale style is that the bedstead has either the cabriole leg with ball and claw feet, or the straight square leg, not tapering, with a square block foot, as will be seen in the illustrations. A square leg, often with a spade foot, appears also in the Hepplewhite style, as shown in the next section. In regard to the tapering of the four posts, few of the designs shown in Chippendale's book, the "Director," have any tapering, and if they have, it is very slight;[1] but the posts in the American bedsteads in the Chippendale style are generally tapered, although not as much so as those in the Hepplewhite style.

(NOTE 4, *continued*)

have been destroyed after they passed out of style about 1820. It was no doubt difficult to dispose of them, as they were too large to be used in small houses and were somewhat expensive to equip with fine drapery. It is said that in the South they and other pieces of antiquated furniture were often given to the slaves, who found them excellent for firewood. Other pieces of furniture may be used in various rooms, but a bedstead can generally only be used in a bed room; and if not wanted there its chance of preservation is very slight.

J. "Day–beds" are more closely related to chairs than to bedsteads. They are considered and illustrated in section 65.

1. In the ten designs of bedstead posts in the Chippendale style in the book of Mr. T. A. Strange entitled "English Furniture," etc., page 198, none of the posts taper noticeably; nor in the designs of bedsteads on pages 199–201. Compare the eight posts of Hepplewhite in illustration No. 1048 in the next section.

1042 (UPPER) MR. A. MORRIS TYSON.   1043 (LOWER) MR. ALBERT G. TOWERS.

1044 (Upper) Mrs. Maurice F. Rodgers.   1045 (Lower) Mrs. John S. Gibbs, Jr.

1046 (UPPER) MR. & MRS. HENRY LAY DUER.   1047 (LOWER) ANONYMOUS.

579

Nos. 1042–1044 have cabriole legs with the ball and claw feet which indicate the Chippendale style, although these legs and feet do not appear in Chippendale's book, as mentioned in section 15.

In No. 1042 the "knees" at the tops of the front cabriole legs are carved with a shell design. The foot–posts are fluted and the head–posts are round and without ornamentation. The head–board is cut in scrolls in which the cyma curve is prominent. At the junctions of the front and back with the sides, over the legs, are round brass pieces which slide over and conceal the bolts which hold the frame together. Casters have been put on the feet. This bedstead is an inheritance by the owner from Philadelphia ancestors. About 1760–1780.

No. 1043 is very similar, the chief difference being that the foot–posts are fluted from the top down about two–thirds of their length to a point at which they are reeded; but the reeding is not well seen in the engraving. Other differences are that the plain head–posts are rectangular, not following the round form of the foot–posts, that the head–board is in a simpler form, and that the "knees" are not carved. About 1760–1780.

In No. 1044 the upper parts of the foot–posts are fluted as in the preceding pieces, and each of the head–posts is ornamented in the same manner, as though they were not to be covered with drapery. Under the fluting is a vase–shaped portion carved with leaves. This vase–shaped portion is not generally seen on bedsteads in the Chippendale style and does not appear in the designs[2] of Chippendale, but does appear in those of Hepplewhite, as shown in the next section. The head–board is also unusual in having a pierced fretwork at the top. About 1775–1790.

No. 1045 has square legs, terminating in square block feet, not tapering, which at first sight may appear to be tapering spade feet such as were used by Hepplewhite and Sheraton on sideboards and other pieces. The foot–posts are fluted, but the head–posts are plain columns. All of the posts taper slightly. The curtain at the back will be noticed, and also the covering of the top. About 1770–1785.

No. 1046 has the usual fluted foot–posts which become reeded below, as in No. 1043. Below the reeding is a carved vase–shaped portion as in No. 1044. The legs are straight and square and terminate in block feet. The head–posts are covered by the curtain. Above the tester is a cornice, and the top is covered. This bedstead is an English piece. About 1770.

No. 1047 also is a fine English[3] bedstead in the Chippendale style. The fretwork of the cornice is pierced in designs in the manner of Chippendale. The drapery covers almost all of the wood work, except the cornice and one fluted foot–post, and also covers the entire back. This foot–post is fluted from the top down to a carved vase–shaped part, as in No. 1044, below which is a square leg, not tapering, terminating in a large square block foot. About 1760–1770.

2.   Nor in any of the ten designs mentioned in note 1 in this section.
3.   This is copied from Mr. F. S. Robinson's "English Furniture," plate 114.

Section 135. Hepplewhite style bedsteads.—In illustration No. 1048 are eight designs of high posts which appear in Hepplewhite's "Guide."[1] The four designs on the right are the more familiar ones. The tapering of all the posts is clearly seen, the upper ends being very small. The five designs on the left have square legs and square block feet, following the Chippendale style, and only on the three designs on the right is there a tapering leg and a more or less developed spade foot. None of the designs show a cover for the bolts which hold the lower part of the frame together and which were generally used in our American pieces. The distinctive features in each of the posts are the tapering, the type of legs and feet and, except in the first one on the left, a vase form on the lower part of the post; and in three of the posts there is a carved form under the vase.

With the aid of these designs in No. 1048 we may recognize the bedsteads in the Hepplewhite style. But the American cabinet makers did not follow these designs in all details; and hence we see in this section several posts which do not resemble precisely any of these eight designs but which do resemble them sufficiently to show that the main idea came from Hepplewhite.

The designs in the book of Sheraton are different from those of Hepplewhite, but in many cases the pieces, as made, are difficult to classify in the one style or the other.[2]

In this section the bedsteads which are similar to the designs in the book of Hepplewhite are regarded as in the Hepplewhite style, although some of them may be thought to be in that of Sheraton. In one matter, however, the bedsteads in the Sheraton style are distinctive, namely, the round and tapering legs, which were apparently not used by Hepplewhite; Sheraton used other kinds of legs and feet also, but whenever these round and tapering legs appear the bedstead is classified as in the Sheraton style. Matters of ornament, head–boards, inlay, carving and other details are not convincing in making these classifications, as the same designs were used by the cabinet makers of both schools.

No. 1049 is very similar to some of those in the Chippendale style and perhaps should be regarded as in that style. For example, the foot–posts are fluted above, and below the fluting they are reeded, as in the Chippendale pieces Nos. 1043 and 1046; under the reeding is a carved vase, as in No. 1046; the legs are square with block feet as in several of the Chippendale style; and the head–board is almost the same as that in No. 1045. But all these features, except the head–board, are seen in Hepplewhite's designs in illustration No. 1048. In this bedstead, however, there is a detail not seen on the pieces in the Chippendale style, which becomes more conspicuous in the next piece, namely, the corners of the

1.   This illustration is copied from the book "Chippendale, Sheraton and Hepplewhite furniture designs reproduced and arranged by J. Munro Bell," page 256.

2.   This Hepplewhite–Sheraton difficulty in classification appears also in connection with bureaus, section 95; secretary–bookcases, section 110, note 1; sideboards, section 127; and other pieces. Perhaps some of these bedsteads may be wrongly classified here.

1048 (UPPER) EIGHT DESIGNS BY HEPPLEWHITE.   1049 (LOWER) MR. ARTHUR E. COLE.

582

1050 (UPPER) DR. M. A. ABRAMS.   1051 (LOWER) MRS. MILES WHITE, JR.

lower parts of the foot–posts are cut off, or "chamfered."[3] The applied panels on the legs cover the holes for the bolts which hold the frame together. About 1785–1795.

In No. 1050 the foot–posts are ornamented with reeding on the upper portion, and below is a carved vase design, under which is another form carved with festoons and leaves. The corners of the lower part of the posts are cut off, or chamfered, as in the preceding bedstead, and the legs are square, with block feet. The head–posts are the same as the foot–posts, except that the vase–shaped portions are not fully carved. The head–board is in the familiar "scroll" form with a broken arch and a pedestal supporting an urn, in this respect resembling several other pieces in this chapter and very many elsewhere, as in the highboys in section 86, and in the secretary–bookcases Nos. 849–850; see also note 5 in section 81. An old French damask spread is on the bed. About 1785–1795.

In No. 1051 the foot–posts are reeded, with a leaf carving at the lower end of the reeding, below which is a vase form with festoons of drapery. The legs are sharply tapered without spade feet. The head–posts are of the same shape as the foot–posts, but are without ornament, and on the back is a curved head–board. The drapery and spread are pleasingly decorated with trees and flowers. About 1785–1790.

In No. 1052 both the foot–posts and the head–posts are reeded and the upper parts swell out more than usual. The vase part is delicately carved with festoons of drapery. The legs are tapered and have spade feet. The head–board is scrolled in cyma curves and is carved as in No. 1062. About 1785–1795.

In No. 1053 the foot–posts are reeded and swell out as in the preceding bedstead, and below is a reeded portion; the head–posts are rectangular and plain. A bedstead with similar features but with round legs in the Sheraton style is shown in No. 1061 which belongs to the same owner. About 1785–1795.

In No. 1054 the four posts are the same in shape. The foot–posts are reeded and have a vase portion carved with leaves, but the head–posts are plain. The corners of the lower parts of the foot–posts are cut off, or "chamfered," making an eight–sided form, the beginnings of which were seen in Nos. 1049 and 1050, and which will also be seen in later pieces. The hangings are believed to be original pieces of "toile de Jouy," a fabric which is mentioned in section 43. About 1785–1795.

In No. 1055 the foot–posts are reeded in a spiral form which is to be distinguished from the spiral twist on some of the Empire style bedsteads, such as Nos. 1069 and 1070. Under this spiral reeding is a plain vase part; and, below, the corners are cut off. The legs are tapered and end in spade feet. The head–posts are rectangular and plain. About 1785–1795.

---

3.   This treatment is seen more fully developed in Nos. 1054 and 1063 in this chapter. Other examples are seen in the bureaus Nos. 713–714, and in the cupboards Nos. 914 and 916.

No. 1056 is a handsome inlaid bedstead which was probably made in the South.[4] The foot–posts are eight–sided, with a vertical line of inlay at each corner; the lower portion is in the form of a vase, with a ring above; and the head–posts are also eight–sided and inlaid. The design of this bedstead with square legs decorated with panels of light inlay, and terminating in a form of tapering feet, may have been inspired by the three posts at the right in the Hepplewhite designs in illustration No. 1048. The head–posts are similarly inlaid with panels on each side of the head–board. This head–board is inlaid with designs resembling those on various articles in the style of Hepplewhite and Sheraton, such as bureaus, desks and tables. A carved ornament is on the top of the head–board. About 1785–1800.

No. 1057 is also inlaid, but less abundantly, the inlay being only on the tapering legs and feet. Near the bottom of each foot–post there is a band of maple, such as is often seen on the chairs and sideboards and tables in the Hepplewhite style. The plain head–posts and foot–posts are round slender columns of similar design. An inlaid bedstead in the Sheraton style, with similar round posts, but with round legs, will be seen below in No. 1064. About 1785–1800.

In No. 1058 are two maple "field" bedsteads of plain design and without carving, but of graceful and pleasing appearance. This type[5] of bedstead differs from the usual "four–poster" merely in omitting the rectangular tester and in its stead placing on the tops of the four posts a framework having an arched form which was supposed to resemble a field tent. On the page of the book mentioned in note 1 in this section, five designs of Hepplewhite are given of such frame-works, with differing curves, which he called "sweeps for field bed tops." In these two bedsteads the foot–posts resemble those on No. 1053, having a vase under the swelling portion, but without fluting or reeding on any part. The legs are square and tapering, without spade feet. About 1785–1800.

No. 1059 is a field bedstead having upon the centre of the top an eight–sided ornamental piece which is supported by the four "sweeps" attached to the posts. These "sweeps" do not run parallel to the head–board, but to the centre. The design of these by Hepplewhite appears with those mentioned in the pre-ceding paragraph, but without the piece at the top. The curved head–board is very high, and is without ornament. The four posts are all plain, with the corners cut off, or chamfered, a treatment which is referred to in the comment on No. 1049. The legs are fluted and terminate in spade feet. It is said that this bedstead was made in one of the English islands in the West Indies. About 1785–1800.

Field bedsteads in the Sheraton style are shown in Nos. 1064 and 1065 in the next section.

---

4. An inlaid bedstead similar in some respects to this is shown in the book entitled "Southern Antiques," by Mr. Paul H. Burroughs, published in 1931. On page 183 of his book it is said that the bedstead is in the Hepplewhite style, and that many such bedsteads have been found in South Carolina, most of them with the posts cut off.

5. In the "Drawing book" of Sheraton is a bedstead, somewhat similar in shape, which he calls a "camp" bedstead. It is made with hinges, and folds up.

1052 (UPPER) MRS. THOMAS J. LINDSAY.   1053 (LOWER) MRS. MILES WHITE, JR.

1054 (Upper) Mrs. Wilbur W. Hubbard.   1055 (Lower) Mr. John C. Toland.

1056 (UPPER) MR. JOHN C. TOLAND.   1057 (LOWER) MR. W. W. LANAHAN.

1058 (Upper) Mrs. John S. Gibbs, Jr.   1059 (Lower) Mrs. Miles White, Jr.

589

Section 136. Sheraton style bedsteads.—As mentioned at the beginning of the previous section, the classification of the American bedsteads shown in this chapter as being in the style of Sheraton is mainly based upon the round and tapering legs which are characteristic of the American pieces made in that style; and it is stated that certain details, such as inlay, carving and other matters are not convincing in deciding whether a bedstead is in the style of Sheraton or of Hepplewhite, because the same details were used by the cabinet makers of both schools. It is possible that some of the bedsteads here shown may not be properly placed, but as a practical method of treating a doubtful subject the classification based upon the legs is reasonably accurate and easily understood.

The bedsteads shown in this section were followed by those in which the Empire style was predominant.

In No. 1060 the legs are not only round and tapering, but are also ornamented by reeding which is characteristic of the Sheraton style but is not very often seen on the legs of bedsteads. The upper part of each of the four posts is reeded, and under the reeding are carved leaves. Vase–shaped forms are below, carved with festoons and leaves. The head–board is scrolled, with an urn between the inner ends, as in Nos. 1050 and 1063. About 1795–1810.

No. 1061 is in almost the same design as the Hepplewhite style bedstead No. 1053, which is the property of the same owner. In each bedstead the head–board is similar, the head–posts are plain, the foot–posts are reeded, and below is another reeded portion; but the legs are different, those in No. 1053 being square, with block feet, and those in No. 1061 being round and tapered, placing the piece in the Sheraton style. The furnishings are attractive, especially the valances upon which verses and proverbs appear, as on the well–known bedstead in the Jail Museum at York, Maine. The words in the right hand corner of the valance are suggestive of the maxims of Benjamin Franklin: "When we have not what we like we must like what we have"—advice which may be good for some owners, but is bad for amateur collectors of antiques. The interesting bell pull on the wall will be noticed. About 1795–1810.

In No. 1062 all four posts are reeded, under the reeding are vase–shaped forms carved with graceful drapery, and the head–board is scrolled and carved. In these features there is a close resemblance to the Hepplewhite style bedstead No. 1052; but this piece has round and tapered legs, differing from the Hepplewhite style which has square legs, often with spade feet. Here also we see a cornice above the valance. About 1795–1810.

No. 1063 has a head–board which is perhaps too high, with a scrolled top with rosettes on the inside ends, between which is an urn. All four posts are reeded and under each is a carved vase–shaped form. The corners of the columns are "chamfered," as in No. 1049 and others, making them eight–sided; and the legs are round and tapered. The coverlet has probably attained the age of one hundred years, having the date "1831" under an eagle and the words "E pluribus unum," indicating that the patriotic spirit of earlier years was still in full force in the maker's household. About 1795–1810.

1060 (Upper) Mrs. J. Hall Pleasants.   1061 (Lower) Mrs. Miles White, Jr.

1062 (UPPER) MR. & MRS. EDWARD H. MCKEON.   1063 (LOWER) MR. EDGAR G. MILLER, JR.

1064 (UPPER) MR. J. RAMSEY SPEER.   1065 (LOWER) MR. & MRS. HENRY LAY DUER.

In No. 1064 we again see an inlaid bedstead, the others being Nos. 1056 and 1057 in the Hepplewhite style. This piece is a "field" bedstead in a different form from those in Nos. 1058 and 1059. The lines of inlay are seen on the double–arch head–board, on the front and side rails and on the foot–board, the latter board appearing here for the first time. Here also we see for the first time ornamental urns at the top of the posts; all of these posts are round and plain. The legs are reversed forms of those previously seen, the swelling part being below; legs of this kind, resembling ten–pins, are also seen on the corner chairs Nos. 429 and 435. About 1795–1815.

No. 1065 is another "field" bedstead in the Sheraton style, having round and tapering legs. The foot–posts are reeded in part and below the reeding is a vase–shaped portion which is carved with leaves. The head–posts are round and plain. Remarks upon field bedsteads are in the comments on No. 1058. About 1795–1815.

It is sometimes said, as mentioned in section 133, note 4, D, that what we know as "twin beds" were not made until recently; but the idea was developed by Sheraton in his design of a "summer bed" shown in No. 1066. This is in fact two bedsteads under one canopy, substituting an arch for two inside foot–posts. The explanation by Sheraton is copied in the note.[1] The architectural arch and

1066. SUMMER BED

1.   This drawing appears in the third edition of Sheraton's "Drawing Book," 1802, plate 41. page 314, and in "Chippendale, Sheraton and Hepplewhite furniture designs," arranged by J. M. Bell. page 114. The explanation by Sheraton is as follows: "Summer Bed. These beds are intended for a nobleman or gentleman and his lady to sleep in separately in hot weather. . . The passage up the middle, which is about twenty–two inches in width, gives room for the circulation of air and likewise affords an easy access to the servants when they make the beds. The passage gives opportunity for curtains to enclose each compartment, if necessary on account of any sudden change of weather. It makes the

columns will be noticed, and also the legs and feet resembling some of those previously designed by Hepplewhite, shown in illustration No. 1048.

Section 137. Empire style bedsteads.—As with other articles of furniture, the high–post bedsteads in the Empire style were often characterized by large size and great weight, especially in the latter years of the Empire period. In the earlier years, about 1800–1820, the Empire features were not very objectionable, although they included large spiral reedings on the posts, coarsely carved leaves and pineapples, and certain other features of less importance. About 1820 the high–post bedstead with its tester and drapery began to go out of style and the low–post type, without drapery, came into fashion. This type often had a somewhat high head–board, the front surface of which was ornamented with panels, as in some of the bureaus, sideboards, and other pieces of the period.[1]

About 1830–1840 the style again changed, following that of the French Empire. The low posts were not used, the head–board and foot–board became curved and almost all of the carving seen on previous pieces was omitted. This was the period of the "sleigh" bed, so named because of the resemblance to a type of sleigh. At about the same period, or later in the Victorian style, bedsteads with "ring" or "spool" ornamentation were made, and the head–board and foot-board were open frames as in Nos. 1074 and 1075. In another type, at the head and foot of small bedsteads or cots, there were very short posts connected by a rail as in No. 1077; this type is sometimes mistakenly called a day–bed.[2]

The dates mentioned in connection with these Empire style bedsteads are merely approximate, and doubtless many pieces of the various types were made before or after the dates given. Moreover, there were many bedsteads made with variations from the designs above mentioned.

Almost all these bedsteads of the better class were of fine mahogany, although sometimes of maple; but ordinary and later pieces were generally made of cherry or other local woods.

No. 1067, a maple bedstead, might be regarded as in the Sheraton style but for the high head–board with its rectangular panels and the ringed horizontal bar at its top, which indicate that it was made in the Empire period. Other bars may be seen on the backs of Empire style sofas, as in Nos. 587–589; and similar panels are shown on the pieces referred to in note 1. The posts and legs, however, are in the Sheraton style, resembling in form those in No. 1065, but

(NOTE 1, *continued*)

whole considerably more ornamental, uniform and light. The first idea of this bed was communicated to me by Mr. Thompson, groom of the household furniture to the Duke of York."

A pair of bedsteads with a single canopy and a passage between them, somewhat in the style of this "summer bed," is shown in "The Antiquarian," May, 1925, page 27.

1. Panels may be seen in the bureau No. 751; in the sideboard No. 1009 and others; and in the desks, No. 835 and others. In section 21 the Empire style is considered and somewhat different dates are given.

2. Day–beds are shown in section 65.

without reeding or carving. Upon the principle, mentioned in section 6 at note 4, that when features of different styles or periods appear on articles of furniture, the latest feature determines the date, this bedstead is regarded as being in the Empire style. About 1800–1820.

No. 1068 is of a type said to be chiefly found in the South. The posts are all large and heavy, with the carved vase–shaped portion and the swelling shaft at a higher position than in preceding pieces; and under them the posts are eight–sided, with cut off, or chamfered, corners. The head–board is paneled and at its top are two small carved horizontal bars, under each of which is a carved festoon; a similar treatment is on the low–post bedstead No. 1071. As in the previous piece there is a reminder of the Sheraton style in the round and tapering legs. About 1810–1820.

In No. 1069 the carved spiral twist or reeding on the four similar posts and the panels on the head–board, indicate the Empire style. The legs are copied from the Hepplewhite style, being tapered and ending in spade feet. The head–board is furnished with scrolls between whose ends is an urn, as in No. 1060. About 1810–1820.

No. 1070 is a large and very elaborate bedstead. The cornice is crowded with intricate carvings. Below the valance each of the four posts has a heavy spiral reeding, a round section cut criss–cross, an acanthus leaf design and a square block with each of its surfaces carved; then there is a ring portion, and below are the legs which have no ornamentation except the round covers for the bolts which hold the frame together; lastly are the round parts of the legs, somewhat similar to those in the Sheraton style. The paneled head–board has two scrolls, between which is a horizontal bar with the ends curving downward and inward, as in the Empire sofas Nos. 587–589. This piece is in the Empire style of about 1810–1820.

Many other high–post bedsteads in the Empire style might be shown, with numerous variations in details, but the four here illustrated include the most distinctive features, except the pineapple designs which appear in the next piece.

No. 1071 is a low–post bedstead made of mahogany. This type, as mentioned above, became the fashion when the high–post bedsteads went out of style. In this piece the head–board is in about the same design as that in the larger bedstead No. 1068, having at the top a horizontal carved bar under which is a carved festoon. At the top of each of the four posts is a carved pineapple, the emblem of hospitality, and under these are round plain blocks, below which are ringed and reeded designs, each post ending in round and tapering legs. Many bedsteads of this kind were made with foot–boards. In plain pieces the wood was often cherry or maple, especially in New England. A miniature bedstead of this type is seen in No. 1086. About 1820–1830.

No. 1072 is a finely veneered mahogany bedstead in the French Empire style which was popular in our country for some years after about 1820, and was called a "sleigh" bed. The heavy character of this piece is seen in the lower portion, and especially in the large feet. The paneled head–board rolls over in a form some-

1067 (Upper) Mrs. Daniel Miller.   1068 (Lower) Bishop & Mrs. Edw. T. Helfenstein.

597

1069 (Upper) Miss Mary S. Schenck.   1070 (Lower) Mr. & Mrs. Wm. M. Ellicott.

598

1071 (Upper) Mrs. Maurice F.   1072 (Centre) Mr. & Mrs. James   1073 (Lower) Miss Ethel Knight.
    Rodgers.   Carey, Jr.

what resembling that in the "roll over" sofas of the period, as in the Madame Recamier sofa No. 586; the foot–board, of the same height as the head–board, has a more pronounced roll inward. The molding above the base, running from the head to the foot, is in a design which became popular on various articles at about this time, and for making which it is said that a machine was invented about 1840. Some bedsteads of this kind contained drawers in the base and at the ends; and in most cases the foot–board was in about the same shape as the head–board. About 1830–1840.

In No. 1073 both the head–board and foot–board have somewhat of a roll-over shape. Wooden covers for the bolts which hold the frame together are faintly seen. Many bedsteads of the same general type were made, some more ornate. The round and tapering legs indicate the influence of the Sheraton style as in No. 1062 and others. Probably about 1810–1820.

In Nos. 1074 and 1075 we take leave of bedsteads with solid head–boards and foot–boards in the manner of the two preceding pieces and we see later ones made with open and "turned"[3] work in about the same manner as in the cradle No. 1082. These bedsteads were made in great numbers about the middle of the last century. In No. 1074 the "turnings" of the thin vertical bars are in a series of vase–shaped forms with rings, and the other turnings are in the form of spools or knobs separated by rings. The legs are round and have knob feet. About 1840–1850.

In No. 1075 the head–piece and foot–piece are each turned in knob or spool forms and the upright posts and the legs have the ring form. The tops of the posts are turned in both of these forms. About 1840–1850.

Nos. 1076 and 1077 are small bedsteads, or perhaps cots. In No. 1076 the curve of the head–piece and foot–piece resembles that on the bedstead No. 1073; but instead of having a solid head–board it has an open framework, as in the previous two pieces. About 1820–1830.

No. 1077 has a simple form of "turned" head–piece and foot–piece and the legs are in a similar design. It resembles in some respects a settee without a back such as is shown in illustration No. 527. About 1820–1830.

No. 1078 is a "trundle–bed," which means a child's or servant's bed, generally moving on casters, and low enough to go under a higher bed, where it stays during the day and at night is brought out for use. The word "truckle–bed"[4] has the same meaning. Around the rails are the knobs[5] or pegs to which strong cords or ropes were laced, making a support for a mattress, somewhat similar to the support given

3. "Turning" is defined in connection with the arms and legs of chairs in section 35.

4. This word and the kind of bed are of English usage. In the "Merry Wives of Windsor," published in 1602, Act 4, scene 5, the host of the "Garter Inn" is asked where Sir John Falstaff may be found in the inn and he jokingly answers, pointing to a room. "There's his chamber, his house, his castle, his standing bed and truckle–bed," the latter being for Sir John's imaginary servant.

5. These knobs were often inserted in a rectangular cut in the inner side of the rails in such a manner that they did not extend above the side rails; examples are in Mr. Lockwood's "Colonial Furniture," volume 2, figure 808 and another on page 334.

1074 (Upper) Mrs. John S. Gibbs, Jr.　　1075 (Next to Upper) Mr. & Mrs. C. E. McLane.
1076 (Next to Lower) Mrs. John S. Gibbs, Jr.　　1077 (Lower) Mrs. John S. Gibbs, Jr.

by the webbing in a sofa or chair; and in some cases the cord supported a piece of canvas upon which the mattress was placed. The same method was used in the high–post beds, but is better understood in this piece in which we see the knobs. The wire support is of course recent. The simple turnings of the posts indicate an early but uncertain date. A similar trundle–bed in the Robert E. Lee home at Arlington is shown in "Antiques," January, 1935, page 27.

Section 138. Cradles; bed steps.—Three cradles and one crib are illustrated in this section. The word "cradle," as here used, implies that the piece has rockers or that it swings in some manner; a "crib" stands on legs and does not rock or swing. Two kinds of cradles were made, one with rockers and the other suspended between upright posts and swinging above the floor. Cradles of the first kind are by far the most numerous, being less expensive for the parents and probably safer for the child.[1]

The cradles with rockers cannot be dated with any certainty as they were apparently made during a long period of years, perhaps during the whole of the eighteenth century and later; the "suspended" kind was apparently made in the time of Sheraton about 1810 and later, as mentioned in the comment on No. 1080 and note 2.

No. 1079 is of the first type, with rockers and a wax occupant. The head of the cradle has wings at the sides and an arched hood to give protection against drafts. The sides of the wings are cut in curves and an opening for a hand is on each of the sides. Almost all of the cradles of this kind are similar in form, the chief difference being in the ornamental features, such as the shaping of the ends. A miniature cradle of this kind without a hood is shown in No. 1085.

1.   In Mr. Edward Wenham's "Collector's Guide," pages 246–247, fifteen examples of cradles are shown, thirteen of which are on rockers; dates are not assigned to any of them. Some cradles were made in the "Windsor chair" style, that is, with spindles on the sides instead of solid wood.

An almost sacrilegious use is sometimes made of these old cradles, and is even suggested by one writer, that is, as a box to hold firewood. Any use of an article of antique furniture for a purpose other than that intended is an unpleasant perversion. Another disagreeable sight is a table made from a discarded square piano with its heavy legs, entirely unsuited for a table; and close to the border line is the fitting of oriental vases with electric lamps.

Two very old and interesting cradles are shown in Mr. Lockwood's "Colonial Furniture," volume 2, figures 799 and 800. The first is made of oak and is thought to date about 1600. In shape it is not very different from later pieces, but it has spindles similar to those on the Brewster chair No. 25 and with turnings of the period. The second is a wicker cradle which came from Holland—perhaps one of the "Mayflower" collection, as to which see section 11, note 1, G. The first piece is also shown in Mr. Wallace Nutting's "Furniture Treasury," volume 1, figure 1564, where it is said that the tradition is that Samuel Fuller, one of the "Mayflower" passengers, brought it with him; and in a painting in Pilgrim Hall, at Plymouth, Massachusetts, this cradle appears as it was being put aboard the ship—sufficient proof of its identity and of the truth of the story! But Mr. Nutting, somewhat dubious of the importation by Samuel Fuller, remarks that it appears that Fuller was not married at the time and "he would scarcely have brought the cradle unless he had been a man of very great faith, even for a Pilgrim. Furthermore, the side panels and the lid of the hood are of American pine"; and that Fuller "mended his ways and took a wife after reaching Plymouth."

1078 (Upper) Dr. James Bordley, Jr.

1079 (Centre) Mr. & Mrs. Lennox Birckhead.   1080 (Centre) Mr. J. Ramsey Speer.

1081 (Lower) Chase House, Annapolis.   1082 (Lower) Mr. & Mrs. Wm. M. Ellicott.

No. 1080 is a cradle of the second kind, suspended in the manner of a swing between round upright posts which are connected at the top by a curved bar or stretcher. In order to avoid the danger of overturning sideways the base is made with trestle feet, as in the tables Nos. 1300–1302. The head has wings and a hood as in the previous piece. This form of cradle follows the principle of a design of Sheraton published in 1812.[2]

No. 1081 is also a cradle with rockers, but with a later and different type of bedstead, having four posts with a tester. Around the sides are railings, one of which, as in other cradles of this kind, is removable in order to dress the bedstead easily. The long legs below are round and tapering in the Sheraton manner, and the posts above are similar to some of the vase–shaped portions of the posts seen in the previous sections of this chapter. This cradle was probably made about 1810–1820.

No. 1082 is a crib, having no rockers, and is shown open, one side railing being removed. The legs and posts are "turned" in about the same knob or spool form as in the horizontal parts of the head–piece and foot–piece in the bedstead No. 1075; these and also the "finials" on the top of the posts indicate that the two pieces were made at about the same period. The upright bars are turned in spiral form. About 1840–1850.

No. 1083 is an open frame "bed steps" in the Sheraton style as shown by the round and tapering legs. Bed steps were used because a pile of three or four feather beds[3] was so high that it was difficult to climb into them. About 1800–1820.

No. 1084 is a different type of bed steps, following a design of Sheraton[4] in which he combined several purposes in one article. This type of furniture was popular in his time, especially in the bed room, as mentioned in note 3 in section 133. Here the lid and the drawers are opened in order to show the uses other than that of bed steps; when the lid is up, a washstand appears with a round cup for a piece of soap; and the open drawer may be for shoes. The brass handles are in the oval form used on drawers of the period, as on bureaus and other pieces; the upper handle is ornamental only, making a "sham"[5] drawer. The legs are in the characteristic round and tapering form. About 1810–1820.

2.   The design appears on page 187 of "Chippendale, Sheraton and Hepplewhite furniture designs" arranged by Mr. J. M. Bell.

3.   In "Furniture of the Olden Time," by Miss Frances Clary Morse, page 73, a quotation is made from a description of "cording" a bedstead and making it ready for occupancy, as follows: "When the bedstead was duly corded . . then a straw bed, in a case of brown home–made linen, was first placed over these cords, and upon this were piled feather beds to the number of three or four, and more if this was the spare–room bed"; and Miss Morse remarks that the height of the top of one of those feather beds from the floor was so great that steps were required to mount it.

4.   A design suggestive of No. 1084 is in the book "Chippendale, Sheraton and Hepplewhite furniture designs," arranged by J. M. Bell, page 90.

5.   As to "sham" parts see note 5 in section 163.

1083 (UPPER LEFT) DR. JAMES BORDLEY, JR.
1085 (LOWER LEFT) MRS. FRANCIS T. REDWOOD.

1084 (UPPER RIGHT) CHASE HOUSE, ANNAPOLIS.
1086 (LOWER RIGHT) MRS. FRANCIS T. REDWOOD.

Nos. 1085 and 1086 are miniature pieces made for children's toys. The first is a cradle resembling No. 1079, but without a hood. The sides and ends are shaped in curves, and the rockers are larger in proportion and more curved than in the full–sized pieces. No. 1086 is a cunning little bedstead resembling No. 1071 with its carved horizontal bars across the head–board and foot–board; and the posts and legs also are similar to those of No. 1071, although not ornamented with exactly the same carving; and on the tops of the posts are urns instead of pine-apples. About 1820–1830.

Chapter XVII

MIRRORS; SCONCES; DRESSING GLASSES

Section 139. General remarks.—The story of antique "mirrors," or "looking-glasses,"[1] in our country begins about the year 1700. It is thought that at that date the glass was imported and continued to be imported until after the Colonies became States; but that many frames[2] for the glasses were made here, especially those of a plain character, from about 1710.

1. A "Looking-glass" is a descriptive word, meaning a piece of glass coated on the back with a preparation and showing images by reflection; especially a glass into which one may look and see his image. This word was used in the inventories of the estates of deceased persons in the eighteenth century in our country.

The word "Mirror" is broader in meaning than "Looking-glass." A mirror is any polished surface, whether of metal or glass, used to reflect objects. Metal mirrors have been used from remote antiquity, and are now used in some of the Asiatic countries, and also in our country for some purposes.

As all of the mirrors shown in this chapter are of glass, and as those of the eighteenth century were called "looking-glasses," the latter term is perhaps more suitable in a book on antique furniture; but the word "mirror" is shorter and its exact meaning cannot be misunderstood. Mr. Lockwood uses the word "looking-glass"; Mr. Cescinsky uses "mirror."

Convex and girandole mirrors and sconces are defined in section 150.

2. The terms "looking-glass" and "mirror" are commonly used to mean both the glass and the frame which holds it; but in considering the various styles, the frame is the important feature.

Many advertisements of looking-glasses are found in the American newspapers after about 1750.

John Elliott of Philadelphia evidently found that "advertising pays," as he continued his advertisements from about 1756 to 1776. In one published in 1763 he stated that he "will undertake to cure any English looking-glass that shows the face either too long or too broad or any other way distorted."

The Elliotts and their mirrors are also referred to in this volume in notes on pages 611, 622, 629, 632 and 686.

(*Note 2 continued on page 608.*)

The amount of the English "luxury tax" was according to the size of the mirror and thus influenced the size of the glass used and the designs of the frames. It is said that the high cost[3] of large glasses was the reason for so many of the mirrors in the Queen Anne style being in two sections, thus using small pieces, as will be seen in section 141. For the same reason, in the time of Chippendale and Robert Adam, the large mirrors were made in several sections, the joints between the parts being concealed by decorative moldings.

The beveling of the glasses in the old mirrors was a difficult operation, usually done while the glass was in a molten condition. The angle of these bevels was very slight, often barely felt by the fingers, and seldom sufficient to create the prismatic colors seen in the modern beveled edges when rays of the sun strike them. This beveling is also referred to in section 44, paragraph No. 2.

An interesting matter in connection with mirrors is the long continuance in style, or the revival, of certain types. It is hard to realize that fretwork mirrors, shown in section 143, began to be made about 1720 and continued in style until after 1800; and that gilded mantel mirrors, shown in section 149, were made from about 1740 to 1830. Moreover, all of these types are now constantly reproduced, which shows their continued popularity.

Many of the fine English mirrors with carved and gilt frames were copied in our country so exactly that it is said to be often difficult to distinguish between the English and the American pieces, especially when on the English pieces a carved American eagle was used, a decorative detail said to have been popular in England[4] about 1780 to 1790. One detail, however, is said to be noticed, namely, that in the English mirrors the board at the back is of a size to fit inside the frame, very close to the glass, but in the American pieces the backboard was generally

(Note 2, *continued from page 607.*)

In 1784 James Reynolds of Philadelphia advertised that he had "just imported and to be sold at his looking–glass store, The Golden Boy, near the Bunch of Grapes Tavern, in Third Street, a great variety of English, French and Dutch Looking Glasses."

The above quotations are taken from "The Arts and Crafts in Philadelphia, Maryland and South Carolina, 1721–1785," published by the Walpole Society, 1929, pages 196 and 197.

A comprehensive label of Thomas Natt, of Philadelphia, is quoted in section 152, note 6.

3. The cost of manufacture until near the end of the eighteenth century was high. Mr. Cescinsky mentions that in a bill of Chippendale for certain large mirrors made by him the carved and gilded frames were priced at thirty–eight pounds and the glasses at three hundred pounds. Plain transparent glass was proportionately costly. In the case of prints the glass must have been more costly than the print itself. Nearly all of those which were framed and covered with glass had the broad margins cut down; and it is only the prints which were published in a book or kept in a portfolio which have survived to our day with their margins intact; Cescinsky and Hunter, "English and American Furniture," page 255; Cescinsky, "English Furniture of the eighteenth century," volume 1, pages 227–232.

Notwithstanding the high cost of glass it seems that the famous "Mistress Nell Gwynn," 1650–1687, had one of her rooms completely paneled with mirrors which served as decorations for the room and also enabled her to see herself from all points of view.

4. As stated by Mr. F. S. Robinson in his "English Furniture," page 306. See also section 142, note 11.

larger than the opening of the frame and was nailed to the back, giving a space between the backboard and the glass, a method which tended to protect the back of the glass.[5]

It is said by Mr. Cescinsky that of the entire range of English furniture of the eighteenth century the carved mirror frames of the Chippendale period are the most easily faked, usually in so skilful a manner that it requires expert examination by one having actual workshop experience with the methods used in the period.[6]

Old handmade glass may often be recognized by its thinness as compared with modern glass; and also by its irregularities and its slightly wavy appearance, differing in this respect from the modern glass. A piece of modern glass is generally thicker and heavier than an old piece of equal size. This weight sometimes causes the old frames of mirrors fitted with new heavy glass to break at the lower points where the parts are glued together.

Mirrors intended to be hung on a wall are of two types, one being merely called "mirrors" and the other being known as "pier mirrors." This classification does not include round convex mirrors or "girandole mirrors," as these are not mirrors in which one's image may be well seen, but are merely decorative, as shown in section 150. "Pier" mirrors are so called because they were intended to be hung on a "pier," an architectural word which means the portion of a wall which is between two windows or two doors; and they were also used over tables standing at a wall. These pier mirrors were generally very large, often as much as six or eight feet high, but in other respects they were not noticeably different from other wall mirrors. Other types of mirrors, not to be hung on a wall, include mantel mirrors, which are seen in section 149, and dressing glasses, which are shown in section 152.

In mirrors in which any of the wood of the frame is exposed, that is, not gilded or otherwise covered, the wood is generally the same as that of other furniture of the period in which the mirror was made. Thus in the mirrors in the walnut age of the Queen Anne style the wood is walnut, and in the mahogany

---

5.   This is remarked by Mr. Cescinsky in "English and American Furniture," page 256.

The antique mirrors found in American homes include some which were made in France, so often the leader in styles, and others made in Italy, where the finest early glass was made and whose workmen were brought to England to work in the Vauxhall works. It is difficult for the amateur, and for the writer, to determine whether a particular mirror is of English or other make. See the note to the mantel mirror No. 1231 which was finally found to be of French make. The distinctive features of style which are seen in various other articles of furniture made in different European countries are not always apparent in mirrors, probably because the makers in one country copied the styles of those in other countries.

6.   This is stated by Mr. Cescinsky in "English Furniture," volume 2, page 341.

A similar remark may be made in regard to American mirrors of almost all periods and styles. Small pieces of old wood, taken from old articles of no value, may be used in the frame; new gilding may be "aged" sufficiently to give an appearance of having been "regilded" many years ago, instead of recently. Original glass is not always expected by purchasers; and indeed new glass may be desired by those who prefer to have a "restored" glass rather than an original one which does not reflect perfectly. See also note 1 in section 143.

age of the period of Chippendale and later it is usually mahogany.[7] The kind of wood is mentioned in the sections treating of the mirrors of the various periods and styles. When the wood was gilded or painted or lacquered, pine was commonly used.

Section 140. Early types of mirrors.—The earliest mirrors found in our country, some dating back even prior to the year 1700, were imported, and are now few in number and are seldom seen outside of museums. Examples are shown in illustrations Nos. 1087 and 1088. In these mirrors the main feature is the square or rectangular frame with a curved top.

1087 (Left) Mr. L. V. Lockwood.   1088 (Right) Anonymous.

In the first type, shown in No. 1087, the frame is made of olive wood and is almost square. The top is in the form of sections of circles. The frame is decorated with inlaid designs of curves and flowers and on the top are inlaid birds which are not clearly seen in the engraving. About 1690–1700.

In the next type, shown in No. 1088, the frame is made of walnut. In this mirror the shape of the frame is similar to that in the previous piece, but the top is in the form of a semi–circle and is elaborately cut in curves with a flower in the centre. About 1700–1710.

These two illustrations are taken by permission of Mr. L. V. Lockwood from his "Colonial Furniture," volume 1, figures 310 and 312.

7. See "Oak and Walnut" and "Mahogany," sections 28 and 29.

Section 141. Queen Anne style mirrors.—The style of Queen Anne, as seen in mirrors, was a favorite one in our country for a long period after the end of her reign, (1702–1714), probably even as late as about 1765,[1] in the middle of the period of the Chippendale style; and this without material changes in its principal features.

These mirrors are most easily recognized by the design of the upper portion of the frame, not including a "cresting" often seen over the top. This design consists of curves at the top of the glass which extend downward on the sides until they reach the straight portion of the sides. Moreover the glass[2] is usually in two parts, both of which are generally beveled. The upper part of the glass is cut in a manner to follow the curved lines of the frame; this upper glass overlaps the lower one, without any molding to conceal the overlapping. An ornamental design of some kind, such as leaves, was often cut on the upper glass. The lower glass was rectangular. A "cresting" over the top of the frame was often used, cut in curved designs, as are the fretwork[3] mirrors shown in section 143. In some cases there was fretwork at the bottom also. All of these features will be seen in the illustrations.

The wood is almost always walnut, solid or veneered on the frame, the cresting being of the same wood but not veneered.

Examining the illustrations, we see four mirrors, Nos. 1089–1092, which are said to be of the period of about 1710–1725. These have the glass in two sections, the upper one decorated with cut–in designs.

In No. 1089 the high cresting, cut in various curves, seems to derive its design from a mirror such as No. 1088 in the previous section. Such crestings are made of thin wood which is liable to warp and break. The frame is veneered in walnut. The top of the upper portion of the frame itself is in the curve of a half circle, below which are two "cyma" curves, which are described and illustrated in section 23. The glass is in two sections, the upper one being beveled and

1. This date is thought to be definitely established by labels found on mirrors of this style made by John Elliott of Philadelphia, the labels being of a kind which were used by him at the date mentioned. See on this subject note 3 in section 143.

2. The glass in these mirrors is not often all original. The first English glass of good quality was made in the time of Charles the Second, about 1662, at a glass factory established by the Duke of Buckingham near Vauxhall, which is now a part of London. In some cases the claim is made that the glasses are original Vauxhall pieces, a claim which should be received with caution.

3. The use of fretwork on the upper and lower parts of mirror frames is so much a characteristic of a large group of pieces that they are made the subject of a separate section, No. 143, entitled "Fretwork mirrors," and it may be thought that some of the mirrors shown in this section with fretwork designs should appear in that section; but such mirrors here shown are so definitely in the Queen Anne style, (except perhaps No. 1098), that it seems proper that they should appear in this section.

In some early mirrors of the Queen Anne style the cresting was made separate from the frame and was detachable from it; but in later pieces, from about 1725, the cresting was made as a part of the frame.

In some mirrors of the period the back of the frame extends upwards in a solid piece for an inch or two above the curved portion at the top, as though the piece had not been completely finished. This may have been to hold a cresting.

decorated with cut–in designs; the lower section is new. This mirror is about forty–two inches high. About 1710–1725.

No. 1090 is very similar to the previous one except that there is no cresting, which may have been broken off, or perhaps the piece was made without one. The bevel of the edge of the upper glass is clearly seen. The formal flower design is cut in. The lower glass is also beveled. In this mirror, as in the previous one, the wood is veneered walnut. About 1710–1725.

In No. 1091 the cresting is somewhat smaller than in No. 1089 and the fretwork is less elaborate. Here the molding on the inside of the frame is in a form which is used on several other mirrors shown in this section. The upper glass is shaped in the same curves as the frame around it and is decorated with a design. This and the two preceding mirrors are somewhat more than three feet high. About 1720–1735.

In No. 1092 the character of the cresting again changes, being ornamented with gilded edges and a gilded and concave medallion with a design of a shell. The curves of the upper portion of the frame differ somewhat from those in the previous pieces. The upper glass is ornamented with a cut–in design of fanciful foliage. The entire inside edge of the frame is gilded. This mirror is almost five feet high. About 1725–1735.

In the next group, Nos. 1093–1098, are six other mirrors, four of them with the glass in two parts.

No. 1093 is a tall and narrow mirror, its height being almost five feet. In the centre of the cresting is a pierced and gilded design and on the top are some of the many curves seen on the fretwork mirrors in section 143. Around the upper glass the frame is in a series of short curves. About 1725–1750.

No. 1094 is very similar to the previous one, but without the gilded design in the cresting and with slightly different curves in the upper portion. This also is a tall and narrow mirror. On the back is a label of John Elliott[4] of Philadelphia, in English and German, the label being of the kind which was used by him between the years 1762 and 1767. The date is thus about 1765 if the label indicates that Elliott was the maker, not merely the repairer of a previously made mirror. The style is that of about 1730–1740.

In No. 1095 the frame is lacquered, or japanned, a kind of decoration which is explained in section 31, and is ornamented with gilding. There is no cresting on the top, which is arched but not in the same manner as in Nos. 1089 and 1090. The height is four feet. About 1710–1725.

No. 1096 is a smaller mirror, twenty–eight inches high and twelve inches wide. The curved cresting is plain in design. Both the upper and lower sections are beveled. Although without elegance, this mirror is a pleasing piece. About 1750–1760.

<hr/>

4.   See note 3 in section 143 in regard to Elliott mirrors.

1089 (UPPER) ANONYMOUS.   1090 (UPPER) MR. JOHN S. MCDANIEL.
1091 (LOWER) ANONYMOUS.   1092 (LOWER) ANONYMOUS.

1093 (UPPER) MRS. HOWARD SILL.
1096 (LOWER) ANONYMOUS.

1094 (UPPER) MRS. ARTHUR HALE.
1097 (LOWER) ANONYMOUS.

1095 (UPPER) MR. JOHN S.
        MCDANIEL.
1098 (LOWER) ANONYMOUS.

1099 (Upper) Dr. James Bordley, Jr.   1100 (Upper) Dr. James Bordley, Jr.
1101 (Lower) Mrs. Miles White, Jr.   1102 (Lower) Anonymous.

No. 1097 is still smaller, being only twenty inches high, so small that one piece of glass was used instead of two. Here the walnut veneer of the frame is made and applied in numerous small pieces, a method called "cross–banding," because the grain of the veneer is cross–wise. From the appearance of the mirror it would seem that the veneer was badly cracked; there may be some cracks, but the openings are mainly caused by the shrinking of the pieces of veneer. The form of the frame approaches a rectangular shape, only the upper inner corners being curved. The edges of the glass are beveled. About 1750–1760.

No. 1098 is also small, the height being twenty–five inches. The frame is rectangular, having no curves at any point; even the moldings around the glass are not curved at the upper inner corners, differing from those in the preceding pieces. The mirror is probably not strictly in the Queen Anne style but may be a later and simplified form of that type.[5] About 1740–1760.

Nos. 1099 and 1100 are of a different type, being wider in proportion to their height than the preceding mirrors, and having very ornamental crestings.

In No. 1099 the cresting is cut in a group of ornamental designs. In the upper part of the walnut frame six curved and three small and straight portions may be counted, the curves being of the cyma type, which is shown in section 23. The lower portion is plain, as also in the next mirror. About 1725–1750.

In No. 1100 the cresting is low and the forms include flowers and leaves. At the bottom of the cresting will be seen four "C" curves, the outer ones being elongated; these curves were much favored by Chippendale, and many will be seen in the mirrors in the Chippendale style in the next section, as in No. 1103 and others. The top of the frame is almost straight, but on each side are the usual curves extending down to the top of the lower glass. About 1725–1750.

In the next two mirrors, Nos. 1101 and 1102, the frame around the upper part of the glass is not curved in the manner of most of the preceding pieces, being rectangular except at the two upper inner corners, which are curved.[6] This general form of frame was followed in a simplified way in many fretwork pieces shown in section 143. Mirrors of this type are said by Mr. Lockwood to represent the best work of the Queen Anne period. They were generally gilded and were of fine proportions.

In No. 1101 the top has two scrolls in the manner seen in several mirrors in the Chippendale period shown in the next section. Between the scrolls is an ornamental figure called a "cartouche,"[7] and the inner ends of the scrolls terminate

5. A mirror of this kind is illustrated, and is discussed by the editor, in "Antiques," January, 1924, page 11, and the date is regarded as stated above; also in the issue of September, 1924, pages 131–132, where it is said that the label on the mirror was probably that of a repairer, not of the maker.

6. Mirror frames entirely rectangular in form were also made in the Queen Anne period. Examples are shown in Mr. Cescinsky's "English Furniture," volume 1, figures 238, 249 and others.

7. This word "cartouche" is defined in connection with highboys in section 87, note 5, as "a carved ornament of fanciful form. It has no similarity in meaning to a cartouche of the Egyptian kings."

in rosettes and vertical leaves. At the upper corners are other scrolls which are duplicated at the bottom of the frame. On the base are two vacant spaces where candle brackets were perhaps attached by nails. In the centre of the base is a carved shell. Almost the entire surface of the frame and cresting is covered with ornamental designs of leaves. About 1725–1750.

No. 1102 is of the same type as No. 1101. The scrolls at the top, the cartouche in the centre, the scrolls at the four outer corners, the two curved upper inner corners and the shell at the bottom are all somewhat similar to those in the preceding piece. In addition, there is a string of flowers on each side. This mirror is copied from Mr. Lockwood's "Colonial Furniture," volume 1, figure 325. About 1725–1750.

A similarity of form will be noticed between some of the mirrors in the dressing glasses of the Queen Anne period, such as Nos. 1255–1258 in this chapter, and some of the wall mirrors of about the same period illustrated in this section.

Section 142. Mirrors in the Chippendale period.

—Very few mirrors strictly in the *style* of Chippendale, that is, in a style which Chippendale originated or developed, were made in our country; but many mirrors made in the *period* of Chippendale, which in our country was from about 1755–1785, are commonly called by the name of Chippendale, meaning the "Chippendale period," although in some cases certain features in these mirrors may be in the style of Queen Anne.

For convenience of discussion we consider first the mirrors Nos. 1103–1106 made in the general style which Chippendale exhibited in his book the "Director,"[1] published in 1754; next we see a group, Nos. 1107–1112, made in the Chippendale period, but with certain features of the Queen Anne style; these are followed by several others, Nos. 1113–1120, of different types; and in a separate section, No. 143, are the fretwork mirrors which originated in the reign of Queen Anne, 1702–1714, and continued to be popular in our country throughout the Chippendale period and later, and are sometimes called by his name. It is difficult, if not impossible, to fix with certainty the dates of all of these mirrors and some of the dates here given are merely approximate and perhaps conflicting.

In the first group of mirrors, Nos. 1103–1106, in which the Chippendale[2] style is shown, the principal features are that the entire wooden front framework is carved and gilded; the lines of the frame are in a variety of curves, in which a favorite curve somewhat in the form of the letter "C" is almost always seen;[3] and

1. This book is mentioned in "The Chippendale style," section 15.

2. Mirrors in the "Chippendale style" were made by several prominent cabinet makers whose names are mentioned in the books. A number of designs by these men and others are shown in the book "English Furniture, Woodwork and Decoration," by Mr. T. A. Strange.

   Many of these elaborate pieces were "pier" mirrors, which are referred to in section 139, near the end; see also "pier" tables which are mentioned in section 174 entitled "Miscellaneous tables."

3. The presence of these "C" curves on an article of antique English furniture is generally an indication of the Chippendale period, but they were occasionally used both before and after the Chippendale period. Moreover, they were revived in the Victorian period, as shown in the bureau No. 768. This curve follows the French designs.

around a large glass are often a number of small and separate glasses whose junctions are concealed by wooden partitions. Some of these mirrors are highly ornamented by carved designs of birds, leaves, flowers, animals, Chinese subjects or fanciful forms, such as "dripping water," and to them the term "rococo"[4] is generally applied. Elaborate mirrors of this type were probably not made in our country, but a few of a plainer kind were made here and some fine ones were imported from England, where they remained in vogue for a number of years after other articles of Chippendale style furniture had gone out of fashion. The dates of those shown here are about 1755–1790.

Pine wood was generally used for these mirrors as well as for other articles which were entirely covered with gilding, a treatment which is mentioned in section 34.

No. 1103 is a somewhat plain example. The entire frame and ornamental additions are made of wood, which is gilded. Around the large glass in the centre are small glasses, the junctions between them being concealed by the framework. The "C" curves above referred to are clearly seen; the large one on the left of the frame is in the natural position, facing the right; the other large one, on the right, faces the left. Below each of these large C curves is a smaller curve of the same type, and at the bottom are two other small ones; and above the large curves are ten others, some not very distinct. The popularity of these decorative curves is indicated in this mirror. The ornament at the top seems to be an American eagle on a rectangular platform, holding in its claws a shield and several arrows, which may be compared with the inlaid eagles on the much later desks Nos. 803 and 805. This patriotic ornament, not harmonious either in design or date with the mirror itself, must have been substituted for an earlier design. An urn with festoons of drapery is on each side. An oval mirror, No. 1241, with brackets for candles attached, has probably been in the same house with this mirror for much longer than a century. About 1770–1780.

No. 1104 is another mirror in which there is an inner frame enclosing a large glass, around which are smaller panels of glass surrounded by an outer frame carved in leaf designs. This form has a very light and graceful appearance. At the top is a scroll on each side, between which is a small glass, and below are glass panels enclosed by carved partitions. On the sides are other glass panels and at the base are three others, the central one having C curves; other curves of the same kind may be seen in several places. About 1765–1775.

4. This word "rococo" is defined in connection with "Philadelphia style" lowboys in section 92, note 2, as follows: "Generally a meaningless, though often a very rich, assemblage of fantastic scrolls and crimped conventional shell work, wrought into irregular and indescribable forms."

   Large mantel mirrors and small wall mirrors of very elaborate "rococo" character, in the Chippendale style, are shown in the English books. None of these were made in our country, but a few were imported. They are not illustrated here.

   A mantel mirror in the Chippendale style is shown in No. 1228 in section 149, and elaborate ones are shown in Mr. Lockwood's "Colonial Furniture," volume 1, figures 336–337.

   A fine wall mirror in the Chippendale style is one of the series of "Little-known Masterpieces" in "Antiques," February, 1923.

1103 (Upper) Chase House—Annapolis.
1104 (Upper) Anonymous.
1105 (Lower) Mrs. Miles White, Jr.
1106 (Lower) Mrs. Miles White, Jr.

No. 1105 is another handsome and elaborate mirror in the rococo style of Chippendale. At the top is a Chinese seated figure, apparently Buddha. The painting on the semi–circular glass represents a country scene, with two Chinese figures, a bridge, some flowers and a large bird; the curved portion of the frame around this glass is in six C curves. The mirror glass is rectangular, except that the corners are in C curves. Strings of leaves and flowers are on the sides on which are also large elongated C curves. At least twenty–nine C curves may be counted on this mirror. About 1755–1770.

No. 1106 is another good example of rococo work. There is only one glass and this is in a rectangular frame on the sides of which are finely carved designs of fruits and flowers. At the top and bottom are fanciful carvings. Nineteen C curves may be seen. About 1755–1770.

The next group of mirrors in the Chippendale period, Nos. 1107–1112, are distinguished by a "scroll pediment"[5] at the top. Mirrors of this type are not shown in the "Director," the book of designs by Chippendale, but they were made in the Chippendale period and are commonly called by his name in our country, but in England are often known merely by the name "Georgian."[6] In addition to the pediment these mirrors are distinguished by having some parts gilded and other parts not gilded.[7] A gilded molding extends around the sides and the bottom, with right–angle corners near the top and a lower line connecting them. The base is cut in several curves, among which the cyma[8] curve is always present. On each side there is generally a string of leaves or fruits or flowers. The wood

5. The word "pediment" is an architectural term which, in connection with mirrors and other articles of furniture, means an ornamental feature above a horizontal band or cornice. In the mirrors in this group it consists chiefly of two curved pieces, or scrolls, whose inner ends generally terminate in rosettes; and between the scrolls is an ornament, generally a bird. This ornamental form is seen with variations on other pieces, such as the highboy No. 666, the secretary–bookcase No. 858; see also the mirrors Nos. 1159–1161, and the Index under the word "Pediment."

6. In England, mirrors of this type were made from about 1740, and are called "Georgian," an indefinite term, as explained in section 14, note 2. The four "Georges" reigned from 1714 to 1830.

Mirrors Nos. 1107–1112 are often called "Martha Washington" or "Constitution" mirrors in our country. There seems to be no sufficient reason to justify either of the names.

It is said that the name "Martha Washington" was given to the mirror from the fact that one of this type belonging to Martha Washington was in Mount Vernon, a reason which would make the name apply as well to other mirrors in that residence. The word "Constitution" is often supposed to refer to the United States ship "Constitution," (Old Ironsides), whose victory over the British ship "Guerriere" in the war of 1812 caused its name to be a familiar and patriotic word; but the name is a manifest misnomer when applied to a style of mirror made in the previous century. The word cannot properly apply to the "Constitution of the United States," because there is no connection between the Constitution and a mirror, and also because the Constitution went into effect in 1789, some years after the mirror became the fashion.

7. The word "parcel–gilt" is often applied to mirrors which are partly gilded. Shakespeare used the word in "King Henry the Fourth," part 2, act 2, scene 1, line 78, where the hostess said to Sir John Falstaff, "Thou didst swear to me upon a parcel–gilt goblet . . to marry me." The use of the word at the present time seems somewhat pedantic.

8. The "cyma curve" is explained and illustrated in section 23.

1107 (UPPER) MR. ALBERT G. TOWERS.   1108 (UPPER) MR. ALBERT G. TOWERS.
1109 (LOWER) MR. C. EDWARD SNYDER.   1110 (LOWER) DR. M. A. ABRAMS.

is either walnut or mahogany. Mirrors of this type were apparently made in America from about 1760 to near the end of the century.[9]

In No. 1107 we see the characteristic features mentioned above and also other details. At the top are two gilded scrolls, somewhat taller than usual, at the inner ends of which are rosettes from which leaves are hanging. Between the scrolls is a gilded "cartouche."[10] Below the gilded band under the scrolls is a gilded molding with right–angle corners, the inner ends of which are connected by a lower line. The base projects beyond the side lines and is cut in a series of curves. On the sides are carved strings of fruits and leaves. The glass is surrounded by the gilded sides of the frame which is cut in a series of double cyma curves with curved corners similar to those seen in the mirrors Nos. 1139–1141 and in the secretary–bookcases Nos. 849, 898 and 900. About 1750–1775.

No. 1108, also, has a cartouche between the scrolls which terminate in rosettes and leaves. On the sides are carved draperies ending in tassels. The glass is rectangular and the base has projecting ends and is cut in a series of curves. About 1750–1775.

In No. 1109 we see, instead of a cartouche, a pheasant in a defiant attitude, one of the birds which were favorite ornaments of many mirrors of this and later periods, either between the scrolls or in openings cut in the fretwork of the mirrors shown in the next section; birds also appear on some of the girandole mirrors illustrated in section 150. It is said that the pheasants, usually having a long tail, were copied from Chinese designs, not from the European type. Some of the birds are very fanciful and are unknown to ornithologists. They were used as far back as about 1715 on the English mirrors.[11] On the sides of this mirror are carved leaves. About 1760–1775.

No. 1110 also has a pheasant at the top between the scrolls. The frame differs from the previous ones in that there is no carving on the sides, and the moldings at the ends of the base form pointed projections with the moldings on the sides. The moldings on the base turn inward and upward over the surface, as also in No. 1115. The frame is curved at the upper inner corners as in the mirrors Nos. 1101–1102 in the Queen Anne Style and in some of the fretwork type. About 1750–1775.

Nos. 1111 and 1112 are tall and handsome mirrors which were no doubt made to hang on the "piers" between windows or doors, and are therefore known as "pier mirrors," as mentioned in the next to the last paragraph of section 139.

9.   Several of this type have the label of John Elliott, of Philadelphia, the label being in the style used by him about 1760. See note 3 in section 143.

10.   The word "cartouche" is referred to in note 7 in the previous section.

11.   As mentioned in section 139 at note 4, it is said that many English mirrors of about the period of 1780 to 1790 used the American eagle. In Mr. Lockwood's "Colonial Furniture," volume 1, figure 333, a mirror is illustrated with a bird which he states has an eagle's head and a pheasant's tail. The French form of eagle may be seen on some pieces of French furniture, especially those in the Empire style. Even the "phœnix," the mythological sacred bird of antiquity which rose from its own ashes every five hundred years, is supposed to be represented on some mirrors; the Japanese "phœnix" is a long-tailed domestic fowl, not likely to be meant when the word is used. Birds are also referred to in section 37.

1111 (Left) Mr. & Mrs. Bayard Turnbull. 1112 (Right) Mrs. Miles White, Jr.

Illustrations of similar mirrors are in Mr. Lockwood's "Colonial Furniture," volume 1, page 392.

In No. 1111 the general design is about the same as in the preceding four mirrors, having gilded scrolls at the top, gilded moldings at the top and base and around the sides and the glass. The framework at the top of the glass, however, is in the curved style characteristic of the Queen Anne style mirrors shown in the previous section. Between the scrolls at the top is a basket with flowers, a decorative feature which is said to have come from Chinese designs and is seen in the English Queen Anne style pieces as well as in later ones. On the sides are long strings of flowers and leaves. About 1750.

No. 1112 is similar in some respects to No. 1110 but is different in general appearance, and is of greater height. The upper part of the glass is not curved in the manner of the preceding mirror. The curves of the sides at the base make projections, and the bird resting upon leaves is of the usual type. This piece has strings of leaves and fruits on the sides. About 1750.

Nos. 1113–1116 are four mirrors which have not architectural pediments but are somewhat similar to the preceding mirrors having those pediments.

In No. 1113, at the top, are gilded scrolls whose inner ends are ornamented with rosettes and leaves. Between the scrolls is a "cartouche," resembling that in No. 1107, which is referred to in the comment on that piece. The frame around the glass is curved at the top in the manner seen in some of the Queen Anne style mirrors. Gilded moldings are around the glass, the sides and the curved base, the latter being in the style of the six previous pieces. The projections at the sides near the base are somewhat similar to those in Nos. 1110 and 1111. We miss, however, the strings of flowers on the sides. About 1750.

In No. 1114 the gilded scrolls at the top terminate without rosettes, and between them is a cartouche, as in the previous mirror. The frame around the glass is curved at the upper corners as in some of the Queen Anne style pieces. The fretwork at the bottom is not gilded. On the sides are designs of drapery, carved as in No. 1108. A gilded ornament is applied on the base. About 1760.

In No. 1115 we again see a bird, probably a pheasant, on a pedestal between the gilded scrolls, and on each side of the pedestal are other gilded forms. Four C curves are on each side of the upper portion of the frame and below them are strings of leaves and flowers. The inner edge of the frame is cut in a series of cyma curves as in No. 1107, projections are on the sides near the base as in Nos. 1110 and 1112, and four gilded moldings extend upward from the bottom, similar to two in No. 1110, between which are three moldings in C curves. About 1770.

No. 1116 is regarded as a modified form of the mirrors having a pediment, such as Nos. 1107–1112, the central part of the gilded band below the scrolls being omitted, and there being no molding with right angle corners. Between the gilded scrolls is a pedestal upon which there is a gilded vase. On the edges of the fretwork portions on the sides of the top, and at the base, indistinct lines are cut into the wood, making incisions called "incised" lines, which are often gilded. Similar incised lines, gilded, will also be seen in some of the fretwork mirrors in the next section, as in Nos. 1139–1141 and others. On the sides are strings of gilded flowers and leaves. Mirrors of this kind are said to be of a transition character, linking the Chippendale with the later styles of Adam, Hepplewhite and Sheraton. The cresting, however, may be a substitute.[12] About 1770.

No. 1117 is another of the mirrors with a broken pediment. In the centre is a gilded "cartouche" in a fanciful design. At the inner ends of the scrolls are rosettes with leaves hanging from their centres. The wide molding around the inner frame is gilded and has curved corners. We miss, however, the gilded moldings on the sides and the base. The wood is walnut. About 1750–1775.

---

12.   Incorrect restorations are frequently found on mirrors. An eagle may be substituted for a broken pheasant; a new finial may be on the pedestal; a glass may be obviously modern. Accidents are inevitable in the course of a century or more, especially in mirrors. In this chapter, and in other chapters of this book, minor imperfections are not always mentioned.

1113 (UPPER) DR. JAMES BORDLEY, JR.
1115 (LOWER) MR. EDGAR G. MILLER, JR.

1114 (UPPER) DR. J. HALL PLEASANTS.
1116 (LOWER) DR. JAMES BORDLEY, JR.

The next three mirrors, Nos. 1118–1120, are probably not of American make, but are shown here as interesting pieces.

No. 1118 is fully gilded and is well supplied with rococo designs. It may be compared with No. 1106. The C curves are spread over the entire frame, at least thirty being visible upon close inspection, those at the inner and outer corners of the frame being especially conspicuous. Several other decorative designs may also be seen. About 1760.

No. 1119 is also gilded at all points. At the top is a bird of somewhat uncertain pedigree standing on a platform. At the upper corners are curved designs somewhat resembling the letter "S," and C curves are seen at the inner upper corners of the frame. At the sides are forms of various kinds and at the lower corners are large C curves. These rococo decorations are of a fanciful and meaningless character, as mentioned in note 4 in this section. About 1750.

No. 1120 should perhaps appear in section 141 with other mirrors in the Queen Anne style, the upper part of the frame being curved in the manner of that style. The cresting and the base are ornamented with scrolls and other rococo designs among which numerous C curves may be seen. About 1740–1750.

This section on "Mirrors in the Chippendale period" is now at an end. The dates are not as accurate as those in the later styles of Hepplewhite and Sheraton. As mentioned at note 6 in this section, many English mirrors are attributed merely to the long period known in England as the "Georgian period," 1714–1830, or to the "Early Georgian" or other indefinite part of the period; see also section 14, note 2.

Section 143. Fretwork mirrors.—In this section are mirrors in which both the top and the base are cut in fretwork, because of which they are called "fretwork mirrors." Certain other mirrors have fretwork designs only at the top, such as the early one No. 1088, and others of this type were made in the Queen Anne style, such as Nos. 1089 and 1093; other mirrors have fretwork designs only at the bottom, such as Nos. 1159–1161 in the Hepplewhite style. These mirrors which have fretwork at either the top or the bottom, but not at both, may be regarded as being in the style, for example, of Queen Anne or of Hepplewhite, the fretwork not always being the principal features; but in those which have fretwork at both the top and the bottom the fretwork is generally the main feature.

The fretwork mirrors here shown are commonly said to be in the Chippendale style, although they were not mentioned in Chippendale's book, the "Director," nor were any ever made by him so far as is known; and it is not likely that Chippendale would have associated his name with any article so plain as a "fretwork mirror," which in his time had been in common use for many years. They were, however, made throughout the Chippendale period and this fact seems to be the reason for the use of his name in connection with them.

1117 (Upper) Metropolitan Museum of
    Art.
1119 (Lower) Miss Helen H. Carey.

1118 (Upper) Mr. C. Edward Snyder.
1120 (Lower) Mr. John C. Toland.

An interesting point in connection with these fretwork mirrors is that they were made with but little change for almost a century. The second one here shown, No. 1122, is English and is dated by Mr. Cescinsky at about 1715 to 1725, many years before the time of Chippendale, as mentioned in the comments on that piece; and it is known that such mirrors were made in our country as late as about 1800. During this period there were at times some minor changes in the designs, but none of any very distinctive nature. The result of this long continued sameness of style is that it is difficult or impossible to fix a date of manufacture for many of the pieces unless we have the aid of labels of recognizable date, or other documentary evidence, or moldings or other features used only at certain periods.[1]

In these mirrors, next to the glass, there is almost always a small gilded molding; and sometimes there is in the top or base a round and carved decorative design, often representing a shell. A very popular ornament was a carved and gilded bird, either a pheasant or an eagle, in an opening in the top, often apparently in the act of flying through the hole; and occasionally there is a gilded bird, perhaps made of composition, applied on the surface of the top. The frames are generally of walnut or mahogany, often veneered upon pine or other suitable wood.

Most of these mirrors were made from about 1750 to 1800, a period which included all of the Chippendale, Adam and Hepplewhite periods, and a part of the Sheraton period. As mentioned above, it is not possible to determine the exact dates of manufacture of the various mirrors, for the reason that their styles continued in vogue for such a long period. One distinctive detail, however, is the curve of the upper inner corners of the frame, this being characteristic of the Queen Anne style, as seen in section 141; but in our country these curved corners were used for perhaps fifty years after the Queen Anne style passed out of fashion.

From the large number of available photographs of fretwork mirrors, often differing merely in their size and curves, only twelve, Nos. 1121–1132, are shown in the first group, in which the upper inner corners of the frames are curved; in the six mirrors in the second group, Nos. 1133–1138, all the corners are rectangular. These groupings have no special significance and do not establish a date with certainty.

Beginning with No. 1121 we see a mirror which is definitely in the Queen Anne style, as shown by the two glasses, upper and lower, and by the curves of the frame around the upper glass, both of which features appear in the mirrors in the Queen Anne style in section 141. In the opening in the centre of the cresting

1. Another result is that it is difficult for the writer to avoid repetition in the comments, as the features are so similar. In the selection of illustrations the aim is to show some of the most pleasing forms of fretwork. These mirrors, especially those made in the latter half of the eighteenth century, are perhaps more often found than any other single article of antique furniture except chairs.

It may be mentioned that many of these mirrors are very easily and frequently faked. A model to copy, a few pieces of old wood, some tools and a modern glass, (the old (?) one said to have been broken), are all that is needed. See also note 6 in section 139.

is a form said to represent a shell. The scrolls in the cresting and at the sides of the top are duplicated on the base, but in a reversed position. The wood is walnut and the date is about 1725.

No. 1122 is an English fretwork mirror which is said by Mr. Cescinsky[2] to be a good type of the ordinary frames which were made in great numbers in England from about 1715–1725. In this mirror are the principal features seen in the fretwork mirrors from these dates to about 1800, when the style passed out of fashion in our country. The cresting at the top with the fretwork extensions at the sides, and the base with its extensions, are cut in scrolls and other forms which may be seen, with some variations, in many later pieces. No special names have been given to all of these various fretwork forms, and in fact it would be almost impossible to find such names for all of the great variety of curves. The gilded design in the centre of the top, and the oval one at the base, are ornaments which are not essential parts of the mirror and are not found in the great majority of pieces. The upper inner corners of the frame are curved. The wood is mahogany. About 1725.

In No. 1123 there is a round carved shell at the top. The curves of the inner upper corners will again be noticed. As is usual, the design of the fretwork at the bottom differs from that at the top and the cresting is somewhat larger than the base. About 1740–1750.

In No. 1124 there is a round opening at the top in which there is a gilded form of a shell resembling that in No. 1121. The carved scrolls at the four outer corners of the frame are very delicate and liable to breakage. About 1740–1760.

In No. 1125 the fretwork is simpler in design, but of the same general character. There are no decorative features. The outlines of the fretwork at the top and base resemble those in No. 1131. On this mirror is a label of John Elliott, of Philadelphia, who is the subject of the note.[3] About 1760–1770.

2. In his "English Furniture," volume 1, at figure 250, which is here copied with his permission.

3. Somewhat lengthy mention may be made of the numerous mirrors of John Elliott of Philadelphia because of his advertisements in the newspapers and his labels on many fretwork mirrors. It is said that he came from England to Philadelphia in 1753 and was in business in that city until about 1776, when he retired. The business was carried on by his son John Elliott, Jr., who in 1804 was joined in business by his two sons who continued it until 1809 under the name of "John Elliott and Sons."

These Elliotts placed their labels on very many of the mirrors which they handled. At least three different types of labels were used by the first John Elliott, in both English and Pennsylvania German, the latter apparently because of the large number of German people who had settled in the neighborhood of Philadelphia; these "Pennsylvania Dutch" are referred to in the chapter on "Chests," section 78, note 1. The first type of label mentioned his store "in" Chestnut Street, where, as appears from his advertisements, he was located from 1753 to 1761; the second type of label mentioned his store "in" Walnut Street, where he was from 1762 to 1767; the third type was apparently used from 1768 to 1776.

In 1756 the first advertisement of John Elliott, "cabinet maker," appeared. It called attention to "a neat assortment of looking glasses, viz., piers, sconces and dressing glasses" which he imported from London. His advertisements generally displayed a dressing–glass of the type of

(Note continued on page 632.)

1121 (UPPER) MR. L. V. LOCKWOOD.
1124 (LOWER) DR. JAMES BORDLEY, JR.

1122 (UPPER) ANONYMOUS.
1125 (LOWER) MR. ALBERT G. TOWERS.

1123 (UPPER) FAMILY OF THOMAS CRADOCK.
1126 (LOWER) DR. JAMES BORDLEY, JR.

1127 (Upper) Mr. Edgar G. Miller, Jr.

1130 (Lower) Mr. & Mrs. Carroll Van Ness.

1128 (Upper) Mrs. Wm. M. Roberts.

1131 (Lower) Dr. M. A. Abrams.

1129 (Upper) Mrs. Wm. DeFord.

1132 (Lower) Mr. J. F. H. Maginn.

In No. 1126 the moldings around the glass are well seen in the engraving The top and base are somewhat larger than usual and are without any decoration. About 1760–1770.

No. 1127 is a large mirror, forty–four inches high and twenty–eight inches wide at the widest point. The sides are ornamented with vertical carved and gilded applied pieces. The carving of the fretwork is more delicate and the design is more intricate than in most of the mirrors of this type. The beveled edge of the new glass may be seen. About 1760–1770.

No. 1128 has a favorite form of cresting, often seen in mirrors of the period, with variations, and there are delicate bits of carving at several points on both the top and the base, with small scrolls at four points on the sides. About 1760–1770.

Nos. 1129–1132, the four other mirrors in the group of twelve having curved inner upper corners, are decorated with birds, three of which have long tails probably indicating their membership in the pheasant family. These birds were carved from wood and then gilded. There is no particular significance in this form of decoration, except that the mirrors of this kind in which birds were used were generally of the period of about 1780–1800. The similarity of these mirrors makes unnecessary a detailed comment on each piece.

In No. 1129 the fretwork is delicately made. The tail and wings of the pheasant here, as in the two following mirrors, extend well over the surface of the cresting upon which it is applied. About 1780–1800.

No. 1130 is a similar piece, with delicate fretwork. On the upper part of the sides are two attachments, not visible in the illustration, by which the mirror was hung upon the wall. About 1780–1800.

(NOTE 3, *continued from page 629.*)

No. 1259; see the note to this dressing glass. He also advertised that he repaired frames and resilvered glasses.

The mirror No. 1094 in section 141, in the Queen Anne style, bears the second type of label, 1762 to 1767, indicating a later use of the Queen Anne style than would be expected. In the period of about 1755 to 1785 the fashionable style of mirror was that of Chippendale, shown in section 142; but the Elliott fretwork mirrors were plain and inexpensive and naturally continued to be made for those who did not wish to buy the more elegant pieces. The fretwork mirrors were made in practically the same design by the members of the Elliott family from about 1753 to 1809, a long period which exceeds the periods of the styles of Chippendale, Adam, Hepplewhite and some years of the style of Sheraton.

The label of John Elliott, Jr., was apparently used by him between about 1784–1803. It mentions "Looking–glasses in neat mahogany frames of American manufacture." The firm of "John Elliott & Sons," 1804 to 1809, also used a label.

It should be borne in mind that the label may indicate either that Elliott, or his successors, made the mirror, or that they repaired it or that they sold it as an importer or dealer. The label cannot always be relied on as fixing the date of manufacture. See on this point the remarks in section 6 at note 10.

The historical matters stated in this note are taken mainly from the "Pennsylvania Museum Bulletin" of April, 1924. See also an article in "Antiques," September, 1924, pages 131–132, and previous articles there cited.

In No. 1131 the fretwork is less delicate, but the mirror was formerly more decorative, having a pheasant at the top and in the base a circular opening with a gilded ornament as in the dressing glass No. 1275. The fretwork at the top is similar to that in No. 1125. About 1780–1800.

No. 1132 is of a different type, having a scroll top with an eagle in the centre, by reason of which the fretwork at the top is confined to the corners. This piece combines features of the usual fretwork mirror with the scrolled and ornamental top of the mirrors in the Hepplewhite style shown in section 145 as Nos. 1159–1161. About 1785–1800.

In the next group, Nos. 1133–1138, the upper inner corners of the frame are rectangular, not harmonizing with the curves of the cresting so well as do the curved corners; and other features will also be noticed.

In No. 1133 the fretwork cresting is higher and the base is deeper than in previous pieces. At the top of the cresting a gilded eagle is applied on the surface. The form of the molding around the glass is well seen. About 1780–1800.

No. 1134 also has a high cresting and a deep base, neither of which are decorated. The design of the cresting may be a variation of the popular design in No. 1128. About 1780–1800.

No. 1135 is also a popular form. It has an oval opening in the cresting in which are five gilded leaves, and also several cut–in, or "incised," carvings on the top and base. About 1780–1800.

No. 1136 differs from other fretwork mirrors already seen, having a gilded string of flowers and leaves on each side and an applied pheasant on the cresting in the popular form of Nos. 1128 and 1134. About 1780–1800.

No. 1137 also has gilded flowers and leaves on the sides. The cresting is in the form of two scrolls between which is a pedestal supporting a pheasant. About 1770–1790.

No. 1138 may be compared with No. 1132, having scrolls at the top with a pedestal between them. The ornament which was on the pedestal is missing, but a gilded eagle is applied under the pedestal. Near the top are small pieces of fretwork, and at the bottom the fretwork is cut in an unusual manner. About 1790–1800.

In the last group of fretwork mirrors, Nos. 1139–1144, several features will be noticed. One is that the gilded inner edges of the frames are generally in a series of "cyma" curves, (as to which see section 23), resembling those on the mirror No. 1107 and on the doors of several secretary–bookcases mentioned in the comment on that mirror; another feature is that several of these mirrors are ornamented with gilded designs "cut in" the wood, or "incised"; the third is that all but one have strings of carved flowers and leaves on the sides; and the fourth feature is the pheasant which was the favorite bird for ornament.

1133 (UPPER) DR. JAMES BORDLEY, JR.
1136 (LOWER) MRS. MAURICE F. RODGERS.

1134 (UPPER) MRS. MAURICE F. RODGERS.
1137 (LOWER) ANONYMOUS.

1135 (UPPER) MR. E. G. MILLER, JR.
1138 (LOWER) MR. & MRS. EDW. H. McKEON.

1139 (UPPER) ANONYMOUS.
1142 (LOWER) MR. C. EDWARD SNY-
        DER.

1140 (UPPER) ANONYMOUS.
1143 (LOWER) MRS. MILES WHITE,
        JR.

1141 (UPPER) MISS MARY DORSEY
        DAVIS.
1144 (LOWER) MRS. W. W. HUBBARD.

In No. 1139 the top has two gilded scrolls and a pedestal upon which is a gilded pheasant, and under these is an "incised" gilded decoration of dainty sprays of flowers which are repeated on the base. The four inner corners are in the form closely resembling a "C" curve, and two small distinct curves of this kind are on the sides of the gilded central portion of the base. This mirror is about two feet in height. The wood is walnut and the date is about 1780–1790.

No. 1140 is similar to the previous one, but is less elegant in the incised decorations. Two "C" curves are on each of the scrolls at the top, and two are in the decoration of the centre of the base. This mirror is about four feet high. The wood is mahogany veneered on pine. About 1780–1790.

No. 1141 is more clearly in the form of a fretwork mirror, especially at the top, where there is a round opening within which is an eagle with open wings. Incised decorations of leaves are at the top and on the base. The design of the fretwork at the bottom is plain. About 1780–1790.

In No. 1142 there is a gilded design in the round opening in the cresting, and gilded sprays of incised flowers are on the cresting and the base. The inner edges of the frame of this mirror are not in cyma curves; but the upper inner corners are in a curved form resembling those seen in Nos. 1122–1132. About 1780–1800.

In No. 1143 the top is finely cut and is ornamented with a gilded pheasant in a round opening. On the base are small sprays of leaves. Here there are no strings of leaves and flowers. About 1780–1790.

In No. 1144 there are no incised decorations, but gilded leaves are applied on the top and a gilded shell on the base. The inner edge of the frame is in the form of modified cyma curves. The form of the upper fretwork resembles the popular one seen on No. 1128. About 1780–1790.

This concludes the group of mirrors which have fretwork at both the top and bottom. Others with fretwork at the bottom only will be seen in section 145, which treats of mirrors in the Hepplewhite style.

Section 144. Adam style mirrors.—As mentioned in section 16, entitled "The Adam style," it is not usual for books on American antique furniture to consider the Adam style at any length, because furniture in that style was apparently not made in our country. But although mirrors in the Adam style may not have been made here to any extent, we see in the next section certain features of that style in our American mirrors made in the style of Hepplewhite who followed the designs of Adam in many respects. Moreover the English mirrors in the Adam style are so handsome that the reader will be interested in seeing a few illustrations of them.[1]

1. It has been said that the Brothers Adam will "always be gratefully remembered for the mirror frames they designed, even though all their other work were forgotten"; quoted from "The Practical Book of Period Furniture," by Eberlein and McClure, page 196.

In section 16, above cited, two mirrors, one rectangular and one oval, designed by Robert Adam, are seen in the full page illustration No. 4, containing six articles in the Adam style. The designs of these two mirrors are typical of the style and differ from all others previously made in England or America. In the illustrations in this section several other examples of rectangular and oval mirrors are presented.

The distinctive features of the mirrors in the Adam style are that various parts of the frames are generally of a more delicate design than those of the preceding styles of Chippendale or Queen Anne; over the entire surface they usually are carved, especially with fluting, and gilded; they are generally decorated with strings of flowers, either straight or in festoons; and are also frequently ornamented with a classic urn or other classic designs.

Many of the graceful festoons and wreaths on the mirrors were too delicate to be made of wood, and were made of a plaster composition which was applied on wire and became very hard and could be gilded or painted.[2] The charm of the Adam mirrors is largely based upon these decorations and the harmony of design between them and the frame.[3]

Turning to the six examples of the Adam style in illustration No. 4 in section 16, we see two mirrors in that style, not numbered. The *upper* one is a large rectangular mirror of simple design. At the top is an urn in classic style, containing fruits, and on the sides of the urn are branches with leaves, in graceful curves. Mr. Cescinsky mentions that these ornaments at the top could not be used without the aid of wired composition. The sides of the frame are fluted. The *lower* mirror is oval, and is regarded as being of fine design and workmanship. The leaves and the strings of flowers are of composition, "carved wood being impossible with such delicacy of treatment." At the top, over the urn, is a classic form known as an "anthemion," or honeysuckle, which was a favorite decoration for many years. It is well seen on the chairs Nos. 178 and 179 in the Chippendale style, and on the settees Nos. 522 and 523; see also note 48 in section 51, and the Index. Under the urn are festoons of drapery suspended from

2. This composition, sometimes referred to as "compo," a substitute for carved wood, was developed in Italy. It was introduced into England by Robert Adam, and was a necessity in much of the work designed by him. The strings and festoons of flowers and leaves on mirrors, often not attached to the frame except at their extremities, could not be successfully made of wood. In some mirrors and other articles both carving and composition were used; for example, carved and gilded wooden urns or other ornaments were at the top or bottom and composition strings of flowers were on the sides. Composition work of this kind is known as "filigree." The composition is sometimes called "gesso," which is an Italian word meaning "plaster" or "chalk." The word "filigree" is also defined in note 2 in section 145.

Pine wood was generally used for such portions of the frame as were to be gilded or carved.

3. As mentioned in section 16, when the Brothers Adam designed a house they also designed the furniture in order that it might be in harmony with the style of decoration of the house; and as many of the houses had lofty ceilings, many mirrors were made very high, one "pier mirror," (see section 139), shown by Mr. Cescinsky in his "English Furniture," volume 3, figure 73, being ten feet high. These pier mirrors matched the decorative scheme of the table or mantel over which they were hung. The mantel mirrors also were often very large.

a horizontal bar, a detail which will also be seen in the Adam style sconces Nos. 1250 and 1251. About 1770.

In the next four illustrations, Nos. 1145–1148, the mirrors are rectangular, and in Nos. 1149–1151 they are oval; all except Nos. 1148 and 1151 are copied from Mr. Cescinsky's "English Furniture," volume 3, chapter 4, with his permission.

In No. 1145, at the top, is an urn from which three festoons of flowers hang, and on the sides are strings of the same flowers. At the base is a ram's head with curled horns, and here also are festoons of flowers. The rectangular frame is ornamented by horizontal flutings in groups which are divided by round applied rosettes. About 1770.

No. 1146 is an unusual type,[4] having an inner glass surrounded by ten smaller ones, all rectangular, the joints between them being concealed by moldings, as in the Chippendale style mirror No. 1103 and others. Here also we see an urn at the top, under which, in a half–circle, is another form of anthemion, or honeysuckle. Festoons and strings of flowers, made of composition and not attached to the sides, ornament the top and sides. About 1770.

No. 1147 is a tall mirror, similar to No. 1145 in having the frame decorated with horizontal flutings and rosettes. In the oval panel at the top is a plaque of Wedgwood ware and above is an anthemion, or honeysuckle, ornament. The two mythological griffins,[5] part lion and part bird, are a characteristic detail of the Adam style. About 1775.

No. 1148 is a large and handsome mirror. At the top is an urn under which is a finely carved oval design. The leaves and flowers and scrolls combine to make a graceful decoration. At the sides are strings of flowers, not attached to the sides, and at the bottom are festoons of drapery. This form of mirror seems to have been the model for several of the drawings of Hepplewhite shown in illustration No. 1152. This mirror and two sconces, one of which, No. 1250, is shown in section 150, form a charming "mirror set by the Adam Brothers" which is the property of the Pennsylvania Museum of Art, through whose courtesy these objects are illustrated here. About 1775.

---

4. A mirror of this type, but without any ornamentation outside of the frame, is illustrated in "Antiques," February, 1929, page 126, and is said to have been brought by Thomas Jefferson to Monticello from France.

5. These griffins are also seen on the top of the Hepplewhite mirror No. 7 in illustration No. 1152, and in the wall mirror No. 1221 and the mantel mirror No. 1229. See also the Index.

The following quotation in regard to griffins is copied from page 425 of the "Accompaniment" to Sheraton's "Drawing Book" which is mentioned in section 18: "The griffin is another fabulous being, existing only in the vain imaginations of the ancient heathen poets. . . They represented it partly an eagle, and partly a lion, that is, the lower part of it. They supposed it to watch over golden mines and hid treasures. It was consecrated to the sun, whose chariot was drawn by a number of them. And these, if you please, may be introduced into subjects intended to represent covetousness; or they may be placed over cabinets where treasure is kept."

1145 (Upper) Anonymous.
1147 (Lower) Anonymous.

1146 (Upper) Anonymous.
1148 (Lower) Penna. Museum of Art, Phila.

Four oval mirrors are interesting. The first is the lower one shown in illustration No. 4 in section 16, referred to in the early part of this section; that mirror and the three on this page illustrate Mr. Cescinsky's remark that "Robert Adam's oval hanging mirrors are among his happiest" works. In these mirrors the frames, as usual, are of wood and the ornaments are of composition.

In No. 1149 the top is ornamented with an "anthemion," or "honeysuckle," design under which is a small rectangular painted panel, and at the bottom is another similar anthemion design under which is still another one in a reversed position. On the top, bottom and sides are gilded leaves and flowers. About 1775.

1149 (LEFT) ANONYMOUS.   1150 (CENTRE) ANONYMOUS.   1151 (RIGHT) MRS. JOHN S. GIBBS, JR.

At the top of No. 1150 is an urn with small openings and in a form which was copied in part by Hepplewhite in some of his drawings shown in No. 1152. Here the curved strings of flowers, made of composition, extend down from the urn almost to the bottom, supported on the sides at several places. At the bottom are leaves and ribbons. About 1770.

No. 1151 is a charming oval mirror in which strings of flowers, rising from the urn, fall in graceful curves to the sides of the frame where they are almost met by other flowers which extend to the bottom and are supported by an oval plaque. The urn is in an uncommon design and at the very top are three flowers. About 1775.

In the next section are drawings and mirrors in the Hepplewhite style in which the style of Adam is frequently followed, with variations.

Section 145. Hepplewhite style mirrors.—In illustration No. 1152 are designs of eight mirrors, copied from Hepplewhite's "Guide" which is mentioned in section 17; in these designs the influence of the Adam style in the work of Hepplewhite is clearly shown.[1] The rectangular form is similar; and the scrolls at the top, the festoons and the strings of drapery, leaves and flowers are all gilded on "composition," as in the mirrors in the Adam style which we have seen in the previous section. In certain of these Hepplewhite designs we see other features characteristic of the Adam pieces; thus in the design 2 the inner glass and

1152—Designs of mirrors in Hepplewhite's "Guide."

1. This illustration is an arrangement of Hepplewhite's designs, by Mr. T. A. Strange, in his "English Furniture," etc., page 277. Designs 6 and 10 are of sconces, as to which see section 150.

These eight designs of mirrors are dated "September 1, 1787," in Hepplewhite's "Guide." In the third edition, published in 1794, they are on plates 116, 117 and 118. The designs of the two sconces 6 and 10 are on plates 113 and 115. The designs of the mirrors appear also on pages 250 and 252 of the book "Chippendale, Sheraton and Hepplewhite" by J. M. Bell.

In reference to these designs it is said by Mr. Strange, pages 275–277, that "the influence of the classic taste is here distinctly discernible. Some of these designs might be taken to be by the Brothers Adam, so light and tasty are they."

It is suggested that the preceding section No. 144 on the "Adam style mirrors" be examined in connection with this section.

the smaller glasses surrounding it are similar to those in the Adam mirror No. 1146; in design 5 at the top is an oval panel and in design 7 are two griffins, all of which are seen on the Adam mirror No. 1147; and other resemblances, such as the frequent use of urns at the top, will be noticed.

Illustrations Nos. 1153–1158 show examples of this Hepplewhite style, or, as it may be called, the Adam–Hepplewhite school or period. It is said that mirrors of this type were made in our country from about 1785–1800. Because of the character of their ornamentation they are sometimes called "filigree"[2] mirrors, a term which is equally applicable to some of the mirrors in the Adam style.

No. 1153 is a pleasing mirror in the Hepplewhite style. At the top are ears of wheat in an urn from which festoons of leaves and flowers extend downward. On the top of the frame are spiral scrolls supporting the festoons and at the base are other floral forms. The rectangular frame is gilded and is decorated with lines of beading. It is said that a number of mirrors of this kind have been found in the neighborhood of New York City. The similarity of the cresting of this mirror to that on the one marked 1 in No. 1152 will be noticed. About 1790–1800.

No. 1154 is a very similar mirror although the urn is of a different type, and the spiral scrolls are smaller, and perhaps even more pleasing, than those in the preceding piece. Here also the frame is decorated with lines of beading and at the base are festoons of leaves and flowers with a central ornament. About 1790–1800.

In No. 1155 the elaborate cresting consists of an urn or vase with fluted sides, containing flowers, from which festoons and strings of leaves and flowers extend over the sides. At the base are other festoons. The edges of the frame are in a wavy design. About 1790–1800.

No. 1156 is a less elegant mirror than the three mentioned above. The frame is plainer and the strings of leaves falling on the sides are not as delicate. The cresting is formed of spiral scrolls and a vase in which are flowers. The frame is hollowed out and has rosettes at the corners. About 1790–1805.

No. 1157 is an example of a type of gilt mirrors which were popular about 1790, showing agricultural products, such as fruits, in cornucopias which were emblems of plenty. Here there are three spiral cornucopias, two with fruits, ribbons and strings of flowers. The frame has lines of beading and spiral columns, with rosettes at the corners. About 1790–1815.

No. 1158 is a small mirror of less elegant design. At the top is a platform upon which is an urn, and from the urn festoons of leaves extend over the sides which are ornamented with applied forms, as are also the corners. At the base

2. This word is defined as ornamental work consisting of gold, silver, or sometimes copper, wire formed into delicate traceries of scrolls, network or the like; or any kind of ornamental openwork similar to filigree. In a figurative sense the word means anything very delicate, light and fanciful, especially anything too delicately formed to be serviceable; Century Dictionary. See note 2 in section 144.

1153 (UPPER) ANONYMOUS. 1154 (UPPER) ANONYMOUS. 1155 (UPPER) ANONYMOUS.
1156 (LOWER) MR. E. G. MILLER, 1157 (LOWER) MRS. MAURICE F. ROD- 1158 (LOWER) MR. E. G. MILLER, JR.
JR. GERS.

643

are other festoons of leaves caught up at the ends and centre. This mirror may perhaps be considered as following the style of Adam more closely than that of Hepplewhite. About 1785–1800.

Another type of mirror is shown in Nos. 1159–1161. In each of these are two gilded scrolls on a pediment[3] top and between the scrolls is an urn; and gilded leaves and flowers are on the sides. The large surfaces are not gilded and the base is generally cut in fretwork designs. Such pieces are commonly said to be in the Hepplewhite style, although there are no mirrors with fretwork in his

1159 (Left) Mr. & Mrs. Geo. Ship-   1160 (Centre) Metropolitan Mu-   1161 (Right) Anonymous.
    ley.   seum.

"Guide"; but they were apparently made in the years in which the Hepplewhite style was in vogue in our country. These mirrors are generally made of mahogany veneered on pine. As in other pieces of the kind, the flowers and other such decorations are very fragile, especially those in the urn, and few of the mirrors are in their original condition. The American cabinet makers evidently did not feel themselves bound to confine their designs to any one style either in form or decoration; in some of these mirrors they introduced patriotic features, such as an inlaid oval with the American eagle.

3. Pediment tops with scrolls are also seen in the mirrors Nos. 1107–1112 and are described in note 5 in section 142. See also the Index under the word "Pediment."

No. 1159 is a large and handsome mirror in which the features above mentioned, and others, are seen. In the urn are ears of wheat, and below the urn is an inlaid oval in which there is an inlaid American eagle. Directly below the eagle is a group of six inlaid vertical bars,[4] and two other groups are at the ends but are not well seen in the engraving. The eagle and the bars are also seen in the Hepplewhite style sideboard No. 955, which belongs to the same owners. Inlaid eagles are referred to in section 33. About 1790–1800.

In No. 1160 the height of the mirror in proportion to its width is somewhat greater than usual, and perhaps on this account a panel is placed above the glass. On this panel a scene on the seashore is painted and there are a number of small lines which represent waves. In an inlaid oval there is an eagle with a shield, over which is an inlaid group of eighteen stars.[5] About 1790–1805.

No. 1161 is similar to the two previous mirrors in most respects, but the urn is of a different type. Three groups of six inlaid vertical bars, not well seen, are similar to those in No. 1159. There is a gilded molding around the frame and within the molding is a line of inlay, giving a pleasing appearance. About 1790–1805.

Section 146. Mirrors in the Sheraton period.—Although Sheraton did not exhibit any mirrors in his "Drawing–Book," (mentioned in section 18), his name has been attached to a large number of mirrors having certain characteristics, and the term "Sheraton style" is commonly, but loosely, used in referring to them. Moreover, it is often not entirely clear whether certain mirrors of this kind should be classified under the name of "Sheraton style" or under the name of the succeeding "Empire style." In these circumstances, it seems best to consider the mirrors shown in this section as being in the "Sheraton *period*," about 1795 to 1820 in the case of mirrors, rather than in the "Sheraton *style*," thus regarding them as having been made in a certain period instead of in an uncertain style.[1]

4. These decorative bars are shown on the left of the centre of the Shearer sideboard "A" in illustration No. 949; also in the mirror No. 1161.

5. These eighteen stars may not have been intended to represent the number of States in the Union at the time the mirror was made, but if they were so intended they indicate the date to be after the admission of the eighteenth State, Louisiana, in 1812, and before the admission of the nineteenth State, Indiana, in 1816, a date which seems to be later than would be supposed from the style of the mirror.

Similar indications of dates are on the desks Nos. 803 and 805, and on the mirrors Nos. 1168, 1173 and 1196. See the Index under the word "Stars."

This mirror is in the Metropolitan Museum of Art and is shown as No. 147 in "The Homes of our Ancestors," by Halsey and Tower, on page 183 of which book it is said that "the superb gilt and mahogany mirror, figure 147, has the eagle with its clustering stars inlaid beneath the pediment. The painting of the glass panel is characteristic of some Baltimore maker."

1. Of course all of the mirrors made in the Sheraton "period" were not made in the Sheraton "style." Some mirrors in the true Chippendale style continued to be made until about 1800, and some in the Hepplewhite style were made as late as 1810, or even later if the stars in No. 1160 are relied on. But in the period of about 1795–1820, the fashionable style was that of Sheraton. Moreover in

A great number of the mirrors of the Sheraton period have a cornice[2] under which acorns or balls are attached, with columns on the sides, and with two panels, the upper one of glass or wood and decorated, the lower one of clear glass as in No. 1165. Other types of mirrors were made in which certain features of the Sheraton style appear, as in mantel mirrors and dressing glasses; these types are shown in later sections of this chapter.

To us, who are proud of our country's history, the most interesting mirrors of the Sheraton period are those which are decorated with paintings of a patriotic character, especially those portraying the naval battles of the war of 1812–1815, and the ships which contributed to the victorious result. In those days of our young republic, when the national spirit was highly aroused, these mirrors, with scenes of the victory of the "Constitution" over the "Guerriere," or with views of our ships, or with the American eagle as an emblem of sovereignty, or with our flag and its stars and stripes, were exceedingly popular; and with mirrors of this type we begin the Sheraton period, although they are among the latest in date.

In the first group, Nos. 1162–1167, the scenes are of our naval victories in the war of 1812 and of some of the ships which won them. On some of the mirrors

(NOTE 1, continued)

this period many pieces were made in the American Empire style. There was overlapping both forward and backward.

A well illustrated article entitled "Tabernacle Mirrors" by Alice Van Leer Carrick is in "Antiques," July, 1922, pages 11–15. See also section 147, note 2.

2. A. The cornice, meaning the projection at the top, and the columns are architectural features, and mirrors of this kind are sometimes called "architectural mirrors." The word "tabernacle" has also been applied to them because of a supposed resemblance to a tabernacle in the architectural sense, meaning a canopy or projection. Fortunately these terms need not be used unless one wishes to speak in a technical manner.

B. Several frequently used words of an architectural character may be defined in order that they may be clearly understood. They are necessarily used here to some extent in order that the mirrors may be properly described. In several books and many articles it is assumed that the reader knows their proper meaning. The definitions are based upon the Century Dictionary.

C. A "column" or "pillar" in mirrors, as in architecture and in common usage, is an upright piece, cylindrical or slightly tapering, which generally serves as a support to something resting on its top. In mirrors the columns appear to support the part which is above them, but actually they are merely ornamental. They are "applied" on the frame of the mirror.

D. A "capital" is the uppermost part of a column, or pillar or pilaster, the latter being a flat column. In classical architecture the different columns, such as the Doric, Ionic and Corinthian, had their respective appropriate capitals. A capital is indispensable at the top of a column. In mirrors it may be carved or rounded or plain.

E. A "cornice" is a projection which extends beyond the line of the part to which it is affixed; for example, the cornice of a house. In mirrors it is the top which projects forward beyond the line of the lower parts of the mirror. Cornices are seen in almost all of the mirrors of the Sheraton period, and under them acorns or balls are generally attached.

F. "Pendent," sometimes spelled "pendant," means "hanging." In architecture it means a hanging ornament. In mirrors it is used to indicate the hanging strings of flowers or leaves, such as those on the mirrors of the Adam style and Hepplewhite styles; or to the gilded balls hanging from the cornice in the mirrors in the Sheraton and Empire styles. Pendent balls are first seen here on No. 1163 and pendent acorns in No. 1167.

the names of the ships are given. The artists who painted the scenes naturally drew on their imaginations in many details. Each of the gilded frames is different in some features which are mentioned in the comments. The illustrations are too small to present clear pictures of the paintings of the ships.

In No. 1162 the painting shows two war-ships in action, supposed to be the "Constitution" and "Guerriere," on August 19, 1812; the ships are very close together, as are all of the ships in the battle scenes. Here the painter adorned with mountains the scene of battle which was in the Atlantic ocean, far from land; or perhaps the ships are not those they are supposed to be. The gilded frame has an elaborate molding on the cornice, and, with the double columns on each side, presents more of an architectural appearance than is shown in some other mirrors. The border around the painting is in three colors. This mirror is about four feet high. About 1815–1820.

In No. 1163 the words "Constitution and Java" are in the border below the painting, which represents another victory of the American ship, on December 29, 1812. Here the border is decorated with foliage and a shield. Under the cornice are the familiar gilded balls. The ends are hollowed out in a semi-circular form in which are moldings in a spiral form. This mirror is about three feet high. About 1815–1820.

In No. 1164 the words "Enterprise and Boxer" in the border are not well seen in the engraving. The victory of the "Enterprise" was won on September 5, 1813. The frame is similar to that in the preceding mirror, except that instead of the balls under the cornice there is a molding in the same spiral form as on the sides. The border is ornamented with blue and gold foliage. The height is about three feet. About 1815–1820.

In No. 1165 the words "Perry's Victory" on the border refer to the battle of Lake Erie on September 10, 1813, in which our Commander Oliver Hazard Perry announced his victory in the memorable words "We have met the enemy and they are ours." The ends and bottom are hollowed out and are decorated with a beading. The border is in blue and gold and the height is about three feet. About 1815–1820.

No. 1166 is a handsome mirror with double columns on each side, with gilded balls between them and also at the bottom and under the cornice. The painting shows the "Constitution" and several other craft in the lower bay of New York, on a white panel decorated with leaves. This is a tall "pier" glass of fine workmanship. About 1815–1820.

No. 1167 has two types of double columns which meet at the top of the glass, as also appears in No. 1192 and others. Large gilded acorns are under the cornice and gilded balls are below them. Under these balls are several applied decorative moldings. The name of the warship is not given, but it may be assumed that it is the "Constitution." About 1815–1820.

1162 (Upper) Anonymous.
1165 (Lower) Anonymous.

1163 (Upper) Anonymous.
1166 (Lower) Metropolitan Museum of Art.

1164 (Upper) Anonymous.
1167 (Lower) Anonymous.

1168 (Upper) Metropolitan Museum.
1171 (Lower) Anonymous.

1169 (Upper) Anonymous.
1172 (Lower) Anonymous.

1170 (Upper) Metropolitan Museum.
1173 (Lower) Metropolitan Museum.

In the next group of six illustrations, Nos. 1168–1173, we see other patriotic mirrors of the Sheraton period. Each of these mirrors exhibits the national spirit of the new republic without special reference to the war of 1812; and, as in the previous group, the frames are all different, each one showing some particular feature of interest.

In No. 1168 the top is of the architectural "broken pediment" type, and upon the pedestal is an American eagle and below are festoons of leaves. Broken pediments of this kind are also seen in other articles such as the secretary–bookcase No. 851; but here the seventeen stars[3] in the oval indicate a date between the years 1803 and 1812. The decorations in the oval represent the growing commerce of the country; and above is the word "Liberty." On the frame the fluted columns, the horizontal lines of beaded molding and the other decorative work unite in producing a handsome and interesting mirror. About 1804–1812.

In Nos. 1169–1173 the patriotic spirit is shown by the memorials to Washington and by the paintings of the American eagles or flags.

No. 1169 is in honor of Washington, whose portrait appears in the glass panel, with two memorial urns under weeping willow trees. The columns at the sides are hollowed out and in each is a spiral molding. Under the cornice are thirteen gilded balls, perhaps referring to the thirteen original States. About 1800–1820.

No. 1170 is also in memory of Washington, whose name is on the base of the memorial urn which is kept green by the flowers springing from it. On each side of the urn are flags. The frame is plain, but under the cornice is an unusual type of ornamental molding which may be well seen with a magnifying glass. About 1800–1810.

In No. 1171 are the familiar gilded balls, under which are applied decorations of baskets of flowers. In the white painted panel is an oval within which is the American eagle. Around the oval are flags and warlike emblems. On each side of the panel is a large acanthus leaf on a curved form which supports the cornice, and is known as a "corbel," which is illustrated and explained in connection with the mantel mirror No. 1231. Below are two columns on each side. The height is about four and one–half feet. About 1815–1820.

In No. 1172, also, there are two columns on each side, and between them are gilded balls, which are also seen under the cornice and on the base as in No. 1166. On the white painted glass is an oval containing an eagle with a shield, and surrounded on three sides by festoons of flowers. This mirror is four feet high. About 1815–1820.

No. 1173 is a plain but interesting mirror. The frame is unusual in having a small panel at the base, decorated with gilded designs. In the upper panel is an American eagle holding in its beak a streamer containing the patriotic words

---

3.   See the comments on Nos. 1160 and 1196. Note particularly the references to the dating of furniture by means of the number of stars used in the decoration.

1174 (Upper) Mrs. John S. Gibbs, Jr.
1176 (Lower) Mr. J. Gilman D'Arcy Paul.

1175 (Upper) Anonymous.
1177 (Lower) Anonymous.

"E Pluribus Unum." Around the eagle are sixteen stars, none of which are conspicuous and some of which have become almost invisible. These sixteen stars probably indicate that the mirror was made at a time when there were sixteen States in the Union; if so, this mirror was made between the year 1796, when the sixteenth State, Tennessee, was admitted to the Union, and 1803, when the seventeenth State, Ohio, was admitted. Other mirrors with stars are Nos. 1160 and 1196. See also the two desks, Nos. 803 and 805, with similar star and eagle decorations. About 1800.

Passing from the mirrors with patriotic features, we now examine other mirrors which are shown in groups for ease of comparison. Although there may be some uncertainty as to dates, all of these mirrors are regarded as having been made within the period of about 1795 to 1820.

Nos. 1174–1177 are wide in proportion to their height, and on each side are two separated columns within which is a narrow glass panel generally of the same height as the central glass. These mirrors may be English.

No. 1174 was perhaps intended for a mantel, its width being about thirty-three inches and its height about forty-three inches. At the top are three paintings on glass, the middle one showing a country landscape. Under the cornice are small gilded balls. On each side are long glass mirrors between the fluted columns. About 1790–1800.

No. 1175 is of a similar design, but not so wide as the preceding mirror. The three panels at the top and the two long panels at the side are fully decorated with gilt floral designs.[4] Above the four columns, the divisions separating the three panels are ornamented with applied flowers; and below the columns are applied rosettes. About 1800–1810.

In No. 1176 the two long glass panels at the sides extend from the cornice to the base and are decorated with gilt grapevines on a dark background. There is also a panel at the top, adorned with floral festoons, and one at the base with grapevines, both on a white background. Around the central glass is a reeded border which is stained black in imitation of ebony, as are the circular borders around many of the convex glasses and girandole mirrors shown in section 150. About 1800–1810.

No. 1177 is interesting although similar in general form to the three preceding mirrors of this type. Between the slender columns on each side is a glass panel painted in gilt with leaves twining around a third column. At the top is a panel decorated with a ship, a bridge and rocks upon which there are trees. About 1800–1810.

---

4. The French word "églomisé" is sometimes used in describing glass panels painted in gilt. An eighteenth century French designer, named "Glomi," used a certain method of decorating a glass object, such as a looking glass, with a gold leaf painting. His work was much admired and the word "églomisé," in which his name appears, was invented in 1825 to indicate his method. See "Nouveau Larousse Illustré," volume 4, page 80. Several mirrors with gold leaf paintings are shown in this section.

In Nos. 1178–1181 the panels are decorated with delicately painted and graceful designs of flowers.

No. 1178 has the familiar gilded balls under the cornice, below which is a line of applied oval decorations. In the panel are flowers under which is a festoon of drapery and tassels. On each end of the panel is a front view of a "corbel" supporting the cornice, as explained in note 2 in the comment on No. 1231. About 1800–1820.

No. 1179 is a tall mirror, forty–eight inches high, with a panel in which there is an urn from which several large gilded flowers arise, and a multitude of other leaves and flowers are in unsupported positions. The columns here extend to the top of the panel. On the back of the frame are the remains of a label bearing the name "Barnard Cermenati," of Newburyport, whose work was mentioned in "Antiques," October, 1922, page 153, and September, 1925, page 139. About 1800–1806.

In No. 1180 the panel is white and the decorations are a group of flowers gracefully springing from flower–pots in the lower corners. In the centre is another floral design. Here also the columns extend to the top. About 1800–1820.

In No. 1181 there is a white panel in which are bunches of grapes and leaves in festoons suspended from rosettes. Around the edges of the panel are delicate traceries, not well seen in the illustration, and under the cornice are seven applied rosettes. At the bottom are two brass knobs supporting the mirror, such as are referred to in section 151. About 1800–1820.

In Nos. 1182 and 1183 the upper panels are ornamented with another type of decoration. In No. 1182 the upper panel is fully covered with decorative designs which are not very well seen in the engraving. In the centre is a small landscape and on each side is a round star–like painting of brilliant color. The other portions of the panel are filled with gilded designs of graceful form. About 1800–1820.

In No. 1183 the painting of a castle in the centre of the panel suggests that the mirror is of English make. On each side of the castle scene is a painting with a dark background. The frame is large and is covered with ornamental work, such as the beaded moldings in several places and the acanthus leaves on the "corbel" supporting the cornice as in No. 1178. About 1800–1820.

In the next group, Nos. 1184–1187, are four mirrors in which a lattice–work design is used in the panel. This design, with variations, appears also in the backs of several chairs in the Sheraton style shown in Nos. 234, 269 and 270. It is also seen in a vertical position on the doors of secretary–bookcases, as in Nos. 852 and 854. Two fine mantel mirrors with lattice–work are shown as Nos. 1231 and 1232.

In No. 1184 the panel is of wood and the lattice–work design is applied, and resembles a series of diamond–shaped forms. The reeded columns extend upward to the same height as the glass. Under the cornice is a row of small gilded balls. About 1800–1820.

1178 (UPPER) MR. & MRS. WM. D. POULTNEY.
1181 (LOWER) MRS. JOHN S. GIBBS, JR.

1179 (UPPER) MR. E. G. MILLER, JR.
1182 (LOWER) ANONYMOUS.

1180 (UPPER) MRS. JOHN S. GIBBS, JR.
1183 (LOWER) ANONYMOUS.

1184 (Upper) Mr. J. Gilman D'Arcy Paul.   1185 (Upper) Mr. Edgar G. Miller, Jr.
1186 (Lower) Anonymous.   1187 (Lower) Mrs. Arthur Hale.

In No. 1185 the lattice–work is painted on a glass panel and encloses an oval in which a landscape appears. The frame is decorated with rosettes at the four corners and with three horizontal lines of beaded molding. The columns extend upward beyond the glass and around them are four gilded bands. The cornice projects forward very slightly. About 1800–1820.

No. 1186 is a handsome mirror with a large eagle at the top holding in its beak two festoons of chains and balls which are supported at the ends by urns or ewers. The eagle stands upon a small wooden panel under which is the glass panel decorated with lattice–work. The urns, the festoons and the small wooden panel suggest the Adam style. In the centre of the panel is an oval with a landscape. As in the previous mirror, the cornice projects forward very slightly. About 1800–1820.

No. 1187 has not only a panel with applied lattice–work at the top, but also a glass panel below it with a gilded urn from which gilded flowers extend horizontally in somewhat the same manner as those in No. 1179. On each side are two columns, as in No. 1162, around which there are three horizontal bands. About 1800–1820.

The next four mirrors, Nos. 1188–1191, have in the panel at the top a type of decoration, known as "low relief," or "bas–relief," which projects slightly above the surface of the panel and is made of composition and applied on the panel.[5] Designs of fruits, flowers, shells, stars, leaves and cornucopias[6] are seen on mirrors of this type. These mirrors may be dated at about 1800–1820; but "relief" work is also seen in mirrors of a later date in the American Empire style.

In No. 1188 the panel is decorated with three festoons of drapery, and other forms are suspended and are also on the ends of the panel, all doubtless being survivals of the Adam and Hepplewhite styles of festoons seen in the two previous sections. About 1800–1820.

In No. 1189 the panel is decorated with flowers, and under the cornice are the familiar gilded balls. Horizontal bands are around the clustered columns. About 1800–1820.

In No. 1190, on the panel, is a figure of an angel, as stated in Mr. Lockwood's "Colonial Furniture," figure 384, and also a festoon of flowers and leaves. The columns extend from the base almost to the cornice. About 1800–1820.

In No. 1191 are bunches of grapes on vines in a graceful design. The columns taper gradually to the top and at the base are reeded vase–like forms. Under the cornice is a row of ornamental figures. About 1800–1820.

---

5. The word "relief," as used in this connection, is defined as "the projection of a figure or feature from the ground or plane on which it is formed. 'Relief' is, in general, of three kinds: high relief, low relief, (or bas–relief), and middle relief. The distinction lies in the degree of projection." Otherwise stated, "low relief," or "bas–relief," is "a form of relief in which the figures or other objects represented project very slightly from the ground." Century Dictionary.

A design in "relief" which is constantly seen, but seldom noticed, is that of words or figures on a coin.

6. A cornucopia design is in No. 1196 in this section. See also No. 1220 in section 148 and for other cornucopias see the Index.

1188 (Upper) Mr. E. G. Miller, Jr.   1189 (Upper) Mr. E. G. Miller, Jr.   1190 (Upper)   Metropolitan Mu-
1191 (Lower) Anonymous.   1192 (Lower) Mrs. F. G. Boyce, Jr.   seum.
                                                                         1193 (Lower)   Metropolitan Mu-
                                                                                seum.

Other illustrations of mirrors in the Sheraton period, Nos. 1192–1199, are of several different types, each type showing some characteristic of the period.

No. 1192 is a fully decorated mirror. Acorns are under the cornice, and below the acorns are four applied rosettes and a festoon of drapery, below which is a painted glass panel with a festoon of flowers. At each side of the panel are two short columns, below which are spiral columns extending to the base, as also in No. 1167. About 1800–1810.

No. 1193 is a handsome mirror which shows features of the Adam and Hepplewhite styles in the three urns, the small panel under the centre urn and the festoons of leaves, such as are seen in No. 1152; in other respects it resembles in general design some of the mirrors of the Sheraton period shown above. In the upper panel is a painting representing "Liberty" and a ship in the background typifying commerce; in this respect it may be compared with No. 1168. About 1800–1810.

In No. 1194 there is a suggestion of the lattice–work seen in the panels of Nos. 1184–1187, but the design is not fully carried out, as there is a painting of a house in the centre, and between the arms of the cross–pieces are painted leaves. At the top are two lines of molding and at the upper corners are rosettes. About 1800–1810.

No. 1195 is a mahogany mirror and has no gilding. The reeded columns are slender and delicate. In the glass panel is a painting of Mt. Vernon with its eight columns and the Potomac river in the background. About 1810–1820.

No. 1196 is of a different type. The large upper and recessed panel, instead of being made of glass, is of wood. On the panel is an applied spray of leaves and a graceful cornucopia with fruits. The sides are wide and flat and the top is carved. On the sides and the base are fifteen stars which perhaps represent the number of States in the Union at the time the mirror was made, and indicate the date to be between 1792, when the fifteenth State, Kentucky, was admitted into the Union, and 1796, when the sixteenth State, Tennessee, was admitted; see the mirrors Nos. 1160 and 1173, with the comments in notes and text. This mirror has been gilded. If the so–called stars are correctly understood, the date was about 1795; but they may be rosettes and of a later date.

No. 1197 is a plain mirror of a somewhat similar type, and doubtless is a later form of the previous piece. It has a curved cresting, and is of mahogany and without decoration. The sides are wide, and are flat except at the edges where there are slender reeded columns. About 1810–1820.

In No. 1198 there are no columns on the sides or elsewhere. Over the large panel is a band of light wood and the panel is decorated with inlay, and other lines of inlay are at the base. Four rosettes are at the corners of the glass. Mirrors of the type of this and the preceding one seem to be plain and later variations of those shown in Mr. Lockwood's "Colonial Furniture," figures 370 and 371. About 1815–1825.

1194 (Upper) Mr. E. G. Miller, Jr.   1195 (Upper) Mr. & Mrs. James   1196 (Upper) Mr. C. W. L. John-
1197 (Lower) Mr. E. G. Miller, Jr.   Carey, Jr.   son.
                                       1198 (Lower) Mr. E. G. Miller, Jr.   1199 (Lower) Lock. Col. Fur., Fig.
                                                                                385.

659

In No. 1199 the spiral columns taper towards the upper ends and are of a somewhat heavy type. Under the cornice are acorns, below which are two classical figures, and between them is a large applied shell. At the bottom the columns terminate in reeded forms. This mirror may perhaps be regarded as in the American Empire style because of the heavy columns. About 1820–1825.

Illustrations of many similar mirrors of the Sheraton period would be shown if space permitted; but those here presented are examples of the principal types. In later sections, treating of mantel mirrors and others, are additional illustrations of the fashion of the period.

Section 147. Empire style mirrors.—In mirrors of the Empire style,[1] some of the same features are found as in other articles of furniture in that style, the principal one being the use of larger and heavier parts than in the previous styles and periods. In mirrors this is particularly seen in the columns, which are often larger in size and less elegant in design than those in the Sheraton period. The delicate reeding on the columns of the earlier pieces disappeared and the columns were frequently covered with somewhat coarse carvings of leaves, spirals or rings. In some cases there was a combination of gilded and black portions on the same column.

The cornice and columns which were used so generally in the Sheraton period, giving an architectural[2] appearance to the frame, were sometimes omitted and the frame thus lost the dignity and completeness of the earlier pieces. The mirrors, however, in many cases continued to be made in two sections, the upper one usually containing a painting or an applied decoration; but in the mirrors in which the cornice and columns were omitted there was generally only one section. All of these features will be seen in the illustrations, which are comparatively few in number because there is much sameness in the designs of the mirrors in the Empire style.

Mirrors of this type are not generally considered to any extent in the books, as they are not fine antiques, either in age or appearance. The dates of those shown here are from about 1815 to 1830, overlapping the Sheraton period, which, in mirrors, was in vogue from about 1795 to 1820, as mentioned in the previous section.

1. As to the Empire style, see section 21. The term "Empire" style is commonly used to mean the "American Empire" style, as distinguished from the English and French Empire styles.

2. As to this, see note 2, A in the previous section. An Empire style mirror without a cornice and columns is sometimes called "non–architectural" because their absence deprived the mirror of its architectural features and appearance.

Several mantel mirrors which well illustrate the Empire style are shown in section 149. Note especially Nos. 1235, 1236, and 1237.

Each of the Empire mirrors Nos. 1200–1203 has a projecting cornice and columns, as most of those in the Sheraton period have, and the mirror is therefore regarded as being architectural in design. In Nos. 1204–1206 there are no projecting cornices and the mirrors are known as non–architectural.[3]

In No. 1200 the cornice is rounded at the ends, giving a somewhat heavy appearance to the top. Under the cornice are acorns, below which are some fanciful designs of applied work. The upper glass panel represents a country scene with a man on a prancing horse. The columns are the principal indication of the Empire style, being carved in rings and lacking the elegance of the reeded or fluted ones of the Sheraton period. The partition covering the junction of the upper and lower glasses is also ringed. About 1820–1830.

In No. 1201 the gilded columns are carved in a spiral or twist in the centre, with a vase–shaped top and bottom, and at the base is a carved horizontal piece. In the panel is a painting of a New York church and other buildings, over which are two urns and a shell. Four rosettes are at the corners. About 1825–1830.

In No. 1202 the cornice is reeded on the edges and the centre is in a curved form. Each column is decorated with coarsely carved acanthus leaf designs between which are ringed portions. Brass rosettes are at the four corners, as in the previous piece. About 1810–1815.

No. 1203 is in a popular form, the columns having a series of three gilded and ringed sections between which are two sections which are "ebonized," meaning that they are stained black to imitate ebony. The glass panel has a painting of what is supposed to be a Chinese building. Note the heavier effect of columns and cornice, as compared with the grace and delicacy of the Sheraton mirrors illustrated on the preceding pages. The painting is within a stenciled border. In this mirror and the two following ones the columns are similar. About 1810–1820.

In Nos. 1204–1206 there are no projecting cornices, but the columns are present. Nos. 1203–1205 have the same type of columns, but their appearance is much changed by other features.

In No. 1204, except for the absence of a cornice, the general design of the frame resembles that of the previous piece. The columns are partly ringed and gilded and partly black, the black portions being reeded. Around the glass is a reeded black border which is enclosed within a gilded one. On the glass panel is a painting of a naval battle, presumably of the war of 1812–1815. About 1815–1820.

No. 1205 is another in which the columns are partly ringed and gilded and partly black. Four rosettes are at the corners. This is a smaller and plainer piece than the two preceding ones, having no painting at the top nor other ornamental features. About 1820–1830.

3. In "Antiques," July, 1926, pages 31–35, several similar mirrors in the Empire style are illustrated, with comments.

1200 (UPPER) MR. & MRS. GEO.
SHIPLEY.
1203 (LOWER) ANONYMOUS.

1201 (UPPER) ANONYMOUS.
1204 (LOWER) ANONYMOUS.

1202 (UPPER) ANONYMOUS.
1205 (LOWER) ANONYMOUS.

1206 (LEFT) ANONYMOUS.   1207 (CENTRE) MR. & MRS. WM. A.   1208 (RIGHT) ANONYMOUS.
                                              DIXON.

No. 1206 has a frame of a different type. The columns and the top and bottom are wholly gilded and are ornamented with applied designs. In the panel is a painting of a landscape. Around the panel and the glass are gilded borders. About 1820–1830.

Great numbers of Empire mirrors of the types shown in this section, and other similar types, are to be seen in shops and private houses.

No. 1207 is a mirror of light wood, with a concave frame on the edges of which is a plain molding. Around the glass is a border stained to represent ebony. Although without decoration by gilding or otherwise this mirror is an attractive one and is especially so over a bureau in a room furnished in maple. About 1820–1830.

No. 1208 is a very familiar type in black and gilt. Around the frame and also around the glass is a border of gilt, and between these borders the mahogany is in a concave form. The bright lines at the upper right corner appear to be gilt, but in fact are merely reflections of light. A large mirror of this type may be used either vertically, as over a bureau, or horizontally, as on a mantel or in a hallway. About 1820–1830.

Section 148. Other wall mirrors.—In this section are presented several mirrors of different styles or periods. Some of these pieces might have been placed in previous sections, but they are of special characters which make it difficult to classify them as being in a particular style.

In Nos. 1209–1212 we see a type of mirror which in certain respects resembles some of the fretwork mirrors shown in section 143, but in other respects is very different. The fretwork is on the top and the base, but not on the sides which are straight and not ornamented. The special feature is that the cresting is very high and was decorated with a carved, gilded and applied design which in many cases has disappeared; and the base was decorated in the same manner. Almost all of these mirrors are less than three feet in height. It is said that mirrors of this type are not uncommon and that they were made prior to 1750, and with some changes were again made as late as about 1770 to 1800, perhaps by way of reviving an old style.

No. 1209 seems to be an early example of this type. The cresting is very high and is cut in a series of "C" curves, which were a favorite form of decoration in the time of Chippendale and even earlier, as mentioned in section 142, in note 3. A gilt ornament was no doubt on the cresting, but is now missing, which is natural in view of the warping of the thin wood of which the cresting is made; on the base is a new gilded decoration in the style of the period. About 1750–1760.

No. 1210 is a curiosity. It is on a larger scale than the others on the page and at first sight it appears to have no similarity to the preceding mirror or the next one; but in fact it seems to be a similar piece which has lost its high cresting, and is hung upside down, with the base at the top. The writer purchased this piece some years ago thinking it was a mirror of the same type as No. 1098, in the Queen Anne style, and he now keeps it (and several other articles) as a warning. It is "cross–banded," which is explained in the comment on No. 1097. The date is supposed to be about 1750–1760.

No. 1211 is probably in a somewhat later style than No. 1209. The cresting is in another design and there are no "C" curves. The applied gilded decorations are probably new; that on the base is much the same as in No. 1209. About 1770.

No. 1212 is a later development of the style of Nos. 1209 and 1211, with a tall cresting; but instead of the fretwork on the cresting of those two mirrors, in this one the edges of the cresting are ornamented with graceful molded and gilded designs of scrolls and leaves, and in the centre of the top is a pheasant. At the four corners of the frame rosettes are applied upon the square blocks. About 1785–1795.

No. 1213 is another type which was popular at about the same time as the preceding one. Here the top is in a different form from any previously seen, consisting of a wide central platform upon which are gilded leaves and flowers, and two smaller platforms, with gilded leaves, at the ends. Below the top are lines of molding around the edges and the glass, and four rosettes upon blocks. There are no curved lines in the frame of the mirror except the two concave curves at the top. All of the moldings, blocks, rosettes and feet, and all of the gilded ornaments at the top, are applied, and almost all are of composition. About 1785–1800.

In No. 1214 the top is in an unusual form, having a "broken" effect as in No. 1168, but with concave curves at each side. The ornament which doubtless was in the centre is missing. Below are festoons such as those seen on the mirrors in the Adam and Hepplewhite styles; and on the curved base is a gilded design. The glass is beveled and around it is a gilded molding. About 1785–1800.

1209 (Upper) Mr. E. G. Miller, Jr. 1210 (Upper) Mr. E. G. Miller, Jr. 1211 (Upper) Anonymous.
1212 (Lower) Lockwood's Col.   1213 (Lower) Anonymous.   1214 (Lower) Mrs. E. N. Dunham.
    Furn., Fig. 365.

665

The next two mirrors, Nos. 1215 and 1216, are known as "Bilbao" mirrors. This name is said to be given to mirrors of this type because they were brought to the seaport towns of New England in ships coming from the town of Bilbao in Spain, not far from the French border. The frames of these mirrors are made of pieces of marble of various colors, cemented or glued on wood; or perhaps of a synthetic marble made in Italy. Around the glass are gilt moldings. Because of the heavy marble of the frame and the delicacy of the scroll work at the top these mirrors are seldom found entirely in their original condition. From the decorations at the top it seems probable that the designs were suggested by those of Adam or Hepplewhite, shown in sections 144 and 145.

No. 1215 is a handsome mirror of the Bilbao type. At the top are two large scrolls with leaves and flowers and between the scrolls in an oval frame is a painting of a woman standing alone in an open landscape. At the ends of the top of the frame are urns. The tapering columns are in two parts, and are seen to be formed of a number of small pieces of marble. At the bottom are feet as in No. 1212. Around the frame, and also around the glass, are gilded moldings. About 1780–1800.

In No. 1216 the top is ornamented with gilded designs of flowers and leaves in scrolls, between which there is a vase with flowers, resting on a platform. Under these is a semi–circular marble arch enclosing a glass. This glass and the rectangular one below are bordered with gilded moldings. The rounded columns at the sides are slender and tapering and rest upon rectangular bases. About 1780–1800.

No. 1217 is a handsome gilded mirror with a cornice which does not project in the usual manner. At the top is a row of leaves under which are flowers arranged in the form of a double cyma curve, as to which see section 23. Around the top and sides of the frame and the mirror are lines of beaded moldings. On each of the reeded columns are six bands and at the four corners are blocks upon which are rosettes. This mirror should perhaps have been shown in section 146 which is on the Sheraton period. About 1800–1810.

No. 1218 is a "courting" mirror, of which a considerable number have been found in New England near the seaport towns, such as Salem. Mr. Lockwood, in his "Colonial Furniture," volume 1, page 328, states that his examination of a large number has convinced him that the original ones were brought to our country from China, for the reasons that the frame is not in any European style, the wood is the same as that used in certain Chinese picture frames, and strips of Chinese paper have been found in the backs. It seems that these mirrors were copied in England and America, as indicated by the use of walnut wood, often with a wide convex molding on the frame. In the illustration of this courting mirror we see the shallow box in which it is supposed to have come from China; the cover of the box is missing. All around the cresting and the frame are wooden moldings between which are pieces of glass crudely painted with unfamiliar flowers and leaves. In the cresting are flowers painted on glass. The height is about sixteen inches. The date is thought to be about 1800–1810.

1215 (Upper) Metropolitan Museum.
1218 (Lower) Anonymous.

1216 (Upper) Mr. Albert G. Towers.
1219 (Lower) Anonymous.

1217 (Upper) Mr. & Mrs. Bayard Turnbull.
1220 (Lower) Mr. Geo. Bradford Simmons.

667

No. 1219 is an interesting mirror with unusual designs. In the pointed crest-ing are three sunken panels, one oval and two arched, with inlaid shells; and a white carving in bone representing the rising sun, or perhaps a shell, is in the centre. The sides and other parts of the frame are flat and wide as in Nos. 1197 and 1198. At the top of the glass is a row of interlaced semi–circular and Gothic arches, and other openwork is at the base. A line of inlaid molding is around the glass. This mirror was perhaps made about 1800. Its origin is not known.

No. 1220 is an oval mirror in which the frame is formed of two cornucopias which are joined at the top and bottom. The mouths of the cornucopias are seen to be filled with fruits and vegetables, and are connected with each other by strings of flowers upon which an American eagle stands with outspread wings.[1] About 1790–1800.

In No. 1221 the two applied griffins in the panel at the top are a character-istic detail of the Adam style, as mentioned in the comment on the Adam style mirror No. 1147, note 5. They are also seen in No. 7 in the Hepplewhite designs in No. 1152; and with a wreath between them they appear on the mantel mirror No. 1229. In the panel at the base is a leaf design and on the top, sides and base are other leaf figures, with four rosettes at the corners. About 1800–1810.

In No. 1222, a somewhat large rectangular mirror, the top is decorated with leaves and flowers and in the centre is a small rectangular glass panel with painted flowers. As in No. 1217, the cornice does not project. The columns are reeded and the base is ornamented with moldings. This mirror may be compared with the upper mirror in the Adam style, in illustration No. 4 in section 16. About 1800.

No. 1223 is an oval mirror in which the frame, except for its shape, resembles the round convex mirrors and girandole mirrors shown in section 150. Upon a pedestal at the top is an eagle and on each side and at the bottom are leaves. Around the glass is a reeded band of wood stained black to resemble ebony, beyond which are more than fifty gilded balls such as are in the convex and girandole mirrors. About 1800.

No. 1224 is an English mirror in an oval frame which is very similar to the preceding one, but is more highly decorated. At the top is a gilded basket with flowers and with garlands of flowers hanging down on the sides. At the base are gilded oak leaves extending up the sides. The ebonized wood around the glass is not reeded. This is a well proportioned and pleasing piece. About 1800–1810.

No. 1225 is an oval Victorian mirror with a frame carved in designs which faintly recall the "rococo" ornamentation seen in the Chippendale style mirrors Nos. 1118–1120 and there mentioned in the comments. At the top are fruits and on the sides are bunches of grapes, except for which, and the oval glass, the mirror might be mistaken for one in the Chippendale period. Several "C" scrolls with

1. A fine mirror of this type is shown in the frontispiece of "Antiques," October, 1929. Others are in Mr. Lockwood's "Colonial Furniture," volume 1, pages 324 and 396.

1221 (UPPER) MR. & MRS. GEO. SHIPLEY.
1224 (LOWER) ANONYMOUS.

1222 (UPPER) MRS. M. F. RODGERS.
1225 (LOWER) ANONYMOUS.

1223 (UPPER) MR. ALBERT G. TOWERS.
1226 (LOWER) ANONYMOUS.

one end terminating in leaves will be noticed. A form of "C" scrolls also appears in the next mirror and in the Victorian bureau No. 768, indicating a revival of the design. About 1840–1850.

No. 1226 is also an oval Victorian mirror in which there are "C" scrolls at the top and the bottom. The outer portion of the frame is pierced with many round openings, and on the inner and outer edges of each space between these openings are four "C" scrolls, almost too numerous to count and too small to be well seen without a magnifying glass; but even with its superabundance of "C" scrolls this mirror could not be mistaken for one of the Chippendale period. A spiral molding is within the outer portion of the frame. About 1830–1840.

Section 149. Mantel mirrors.—Although there are a few mantel mirrors in our country in the styles of Queen Anne and Chippendale they are seldom seen, and therefore we present only one example of each style.

No. 1227 is regarded as being in the Queen Anne style. The base extends in curves at the ends as in Nos. 1107–1113, and on the blank spaces at the ends two candle holders were probably placed. The ends and the glass are surrounded with carved and gilded moldings. The glass is beveled and is in one piece instead of in three parts as in most of the other mantel mirrors shown here. This mirror is also shown in Mr. Lockwood's "Colonial Furniture," volume 1, page 390. About 1730–1750.

No. 1228, in the Chippendale style,[1] is an ornate and fully gilded mirror in three parts, on which we see several of the popular "C" curves of the Chippendale period which are referred to in connection with Nos. 1103–1106. The moldings at the base extend in curves beyond the ends. At the top are two squirrels and under the arch in the centre is a swan. In the left section of the glass is a painting of a man in Chinese costume with white sleeves and a fan; in the right section is a Chinese woman; and in both sections are painted trees. The four upright columns are finely designed and executed. About 1760–1770.

The other mantel mirrors shown in this section are all of a later date than the foregoing ones.

Although No. 1229, with its columns and cornice, is in the style of Sheraton, it has also an indication of the styles of Adam and Hepplewhite in the applied griffins on a raised panel under the cornice. These imaginary creatures are seen in the Adam style mirror No. 1147, in the Hepplewhite figure 7 in No. 1152, in the card table No. 1516 and the wall mirror No. 1221. The griffins hold between them a wreath of laurel, an emblem of victory or distinction. They are described in note 5 in section 144. On each side is a glass panel painted with festoons of

1. Two handsome gilded mantel mirrors in the Chippendale rococo style are shown in Mr. Lockwood's "Colonial Furniture," volume 1, figures 336 and 337. Mirrors of this kind were apparently not made in our country, but a few were imported from England. In recent years reproductions have been made and are very effective in the proper setting, but are generally regarded as having too fanciful decorations for rooms furnished in the styles of our antique furniture.

1227 (Upper) Hammond-Harwood House.   1228 (Next to Upper) Mrs. John S.
1229 (Next to Lower) Mrs. Reginald W. Petre.   Gibbs, Jr.
                                   1230 (Lower) Mrs. Maurice F. Rodgers.

leaves suspended from a horizontal bar, in the centre of which is a portrait; this design also may be a derivation from the Adam style. This mirror is finely decorated at all points. About 1800–1820.

In No. 1230 the laurel wreaths under the cornice are of about the same type as the wreath held by the griffins in the preceding piece. In the centre is a raised panel with an oval design of flowers. Around the three sections of the glass and on the partitions between them are moldings of the same design as in the preceding mirror; and the lyre–shaped ornaments above the two columns on the ends are also the same in each piece. These similarities suggest that the two mirrors were probably designed or made by the same person. About 1800–1820.

No. 1231 is a well known mantel mirror in the Peirce–Nichols house in Salem, Massachusetts, and belongs to the Essex Institute, through whose courtesy the photograph appears. The purpose of showing on the right a side view of the "corbel" on a larger scale is stated in the note.[2] Under the reeded edge of the cornice and the numerous gilded balls is an applied composition lattice–work in two parts between which is a panel with two festoons of drapery. Under these is a panel with applied composition designs of trumpets at the ends and two branches of leaves in the centre. Three bands are on each of the four columns. The date has been the subject of an interesting difference of opinion, as mentioned in the note.[3]

2.   The shape of the curved pieces with a carved leaf, over the two columns at the ends, appearing to support the parts above, is not well seen in the photograph, which was taken from the front, and in order to get a better view a photograph taken from the side is shown. This piece is seen on mirrors, mantels and some other articles. It is known by the architectural name "corbel" and is defined as a projection from the vertical face of a wall, supporting a part above. In furniture it is also known as a "bracket" or "console." As viewed from the side it is almost in the shape of a cyma curve, as to which see section 23. Other examples are in the mirrors Nos. 1171, 1178 and 1183. The presence of a "corbel" does not seem to indicate any definite date for the object on which it appears.

A pleasing illustration of the mirror is in "Antiques," February, 1931, page 119, in an article by Mr. Fiske Kimball, entitled "Furniture carvings by Samuel McIntire."

3.   Four opinions as to the date have appeared in well known publications. There is a local tradition that the mirror was bought in 1783 at the time the house was built.

One writer stated that the mirror was probably bought "some few years after the house had been built, for the mirror is in the style which was popular about 1790."

Another writer regarded the mirror as a "war's–end mirror"; the "branches of leaves are the palms of heroic martyrdom"; the trumpets are those of fame. The Revolutionary War having ended, the mirror was probably made shortly thereafter, "between the closing of the war in 1781 and the signing of the treaty of peace in 1783."

A third writer terms the mirror a "McIntire glass," (as to McIntire see the chapter on "Sofas," section 72, notes 5 and 6), and considers that it was "probably made for its present position about 1790."

The fourth writer mentions a tradition that the mirror was "made to fit the panel over the mantel" in a room built in 1783, and accepts that date as the date of the mirror.

Happily for all concerned, all being wrong, it has since been made clear by definite information that the mirror was made in Paris in 1801 as a wedding present for a daughter of the Peirce family. After this disclosure one of the writers remarked that the moral is that in fixing dates of antiques "it is well to distrust all evidence save that of style and of provable contemporary document"; as to which see also section 6 entitled "Dating antique furniture."

1231 (Upper) Essex Institute, Salem.
1232 (Lower) Mrs. Homer Eaton Keyes.

No. 1232 is a handsome mantel mirror with two reeded columns at each end, resting upon blocks which are ornamented with two rosettes. Under the cornice are gilded balls and below these is an applied lattice–work which extends across the entire front and is decorated at each intersecting point with a rosette. As in the preceding piece, the edge of the cornice is reeded. This mirror is forty–eight inches high and fifty–five inches long. About 1790–1800.

No. 1233 has four columns, each consisting of a cluster of three upright wooden rods connected by bands and resting on small gilded balls standing on blocks with rosettes; similar rosettes are above the tops of the columns. Under the cornice is a concave surface, below which in the centre are interlaced strings of leaves. There are no gilded balls or acorns. On the base are two lines of molding and another is under the concave surface above mentioned. About 1800–1810.

In No. 1234 the distinctive feature is that the two columns at the ends are not in a rounded form, but have flat surfaces which are ornamented with bands and raised designs; and similar flat horizontal forms are under the cornice and at the base. The three glasses are not as high in proportion to their width as are those in the other mantel mirrors shown here. About 1810–1820.

No. 1235, in the Empire style, has no gilded balls or panel under the cornice, but the space is occupied by a horizontal half–round piece which is partly gilded and partly stained black to represent ebony; and the same method of decoration is used on the two vertical columns at the ends. Two gilded columns divide the glass into sections. This black and gold decoration is similar to that seen in the wall mirrors Nos. 1203–1205. About 1810–1820.

No. 1236, also in the Empire style, has gilded rings under the cornice and on the columns at the ends, parts of which are carved in designs which may represent pineapples. At the two lower corners are bunches of grapes and leaves and at the upper corners are rosettes over which are acorns. The columns dividing the glass are in an unusual design. The top, bottom and ends are hollowed out, as in Nos. 1163 and 1164. About 1810–1820.

In No. 1237, in the Empire style, groups of rings are on the top and ends and between the rings are fanciful designs, and at the bottom and on the four corners are other decorations.[4] The columns dividing the glass into three sections are also ornamented and around the glass is a decorative border. There are no gilded balls on this mirror. About 1810–1820.

In No. 1238 we see indications of the influence of the Adam style in the festoons and oval rosettes in the upper portion, and also in the panel in the centre with figures in the manner of Wedgwood. The border around the glass and the columns dividing the glass into three sections are reeded and stained black in imitation of ebony, as in the wall mirror No. 1176 and in the convex mirrors and girandole mirrors shown in the next section. This is probably a Victorian revival of previous styles, but might easily be mistaken for an earlier mirror. The date is said to be about 1850–1860.

---

4.   A similar mantel mirror is shown in "Antiques," July, 1926, page 31, where fourteen mirrors of the period of about 1780–1840 are illustrated, with brief comments.

1233 (UPPER) MISS HARRIETT R. CHEW.   1234 (NEXT TO UPPER) MISS HELEN H. CAREY.
1235 (NEXT TO LOWER) MRS. WM. M. ROBERTS.   1236 (LOWER) MR. & MRS. BAYARD TURNBULL.

1237 (Upper) Mr. Edgar G. Miller, Jr.
1238 (Lower) Anonymous.

Section 150. Convex mirrors; girandole mirrors; sconces.—The term "convex mirror" is sufficiently descriptive to require no explanation other than that it is generally a round mirror in which the glass is convex, not flat; but the meanings of the words "girandole" and "sconce" are somewhat indefinite.

In the dictionaries it is said in substance that a "girandole" is a bracket to hold candles or other lights. It may be a branched candlestick to be used on a table or mantel; or it may be a wall bracket with receptacles for candles, somewhat resembling in form a gas bracket or an electric light bracket. A "girandole," in its proper sense, is complete without a mirror,[1] but it and a mirror are often combined in one piece. In our country a round convex mirror in a gilt frame with brackets for candles is often called a "girandole"; but a more expressive term is "girandole mirror," that is, a round mirror, with girandoles in the sense of candle brackets; and this term is therefore used in this book.

A "sconce," in its proper meaning, is said to be a wall bracket, or group of brackets, holding candles or lights, without a mirror; but although a mirror is not necessarily a part of a sconce, a sconce is often fitted with a flat mirror. Sconces with and without flat mirrors are shown in Nos. 1248–1253.

By way of summary of these definitions it may be said that a girandole mirror is generally round and convex, with candle brackets attached; and a sconce is a wall bracket for candles and may or may not have a mirror attached.

The frames of the convex mirrors and of the girandole mirrors are gilded and are very similar in construction. The round convex glass is usually surrounded by a border which is stained black to imitate ebony, and is fully reeded. Around this border is a molding which is either hollowed out in concave form, in which case the concave portion is generally ornamented with gilded balls, or in convex form. In a few mirrors, not illustrated here, the glass is concave, not convex. Because of their convex or concave form, the glasses always give a distorted reflection; if the glass is convex, the image of the reflected scene becomes a miniature; but if the glass is concave, the image is enlarged. These pieces were made in pairs and were used for decorative purposes, as they could not be used as "looking" glasses. Perhaps some of these mirrors were made in our country, but most of them seem to be of English or French make.

1. To call a mirror which has no lighting arrangements a "girandole" is a misuse of the word because its primary meaning is connected with lighting, not with mirrors.

Flat mirrors in the Chippendale style were sometimes fitted with candle brackets; No. 1241 is an example.

In the Macquoid and Edwards "Dictionary of English Furniture," volume 3, page 57, under the heading "sconces and wall-lights" it is said that "a variety of lighting arrangements are included in th's heading, the terms used to define them having a somewhat vague" meaning.

The word "girandole" is not used in the same sense by all of the English or American writers. In "Antique Furniture," by Mr. F. W. Burgess, page 369, it is said that the term is often misapplied. It is here also said that "when coal gas superseded candles, (about 1820), girandoles were discarded, and many were broken up and the metal work melted; but a goodly number survived and are now welcome additions to twentieth century furnishings, especially as they are so well adapted to the new (electric) methods of lighting." This book is an English one.

The ornamental features are of various kinds and quality. At the top the favorite feature was the American eagle as understood by foreign designers, often standing on a pedestal of rocks, from which there is in some cases a "dripping water effect," imitating a design used in the time of Chippendale, as mentioned in the third paragraph of section 142. A dolphin, or sea–horse, was also a popular figure, and baskets of fruit or flowers were sometimes used. On the sides and base there were other decorations, generally of leaves or shells or both, made of composition or of composition on wood.

These convex mirrors and girandole mirrors are all dated from about 1800 to 1820.

Nos. 1239 and 1240 are convex mirrors, not girandole mirrors, as they have no candle brackets. In No. 1239 the round frame is hollowed out and is ornamented with numerous gilded balls. On the top is an eagle with outstretched wings standing on a pedestal of rocks, as also in No. 1245, and on each side are leaves carved in scrolls. At the base are other carved leaves, between which is a gilded shell. The glass is surrounded with a border stained black. About 1800–1820.

In No. 1240 there is a vase at the top filled with fruits and grain, and on each side of the vase are leaves. On the sides are other leaves and at the base are others. In this mirror the surface of the round frame is hollowed out in concave form, but there are no gilded balls within it. The reeded black border around the glass is well seen. About 1800–1820.

No. 1241 is a mirror with attached brackets for candles. The large central glass is oval and flat, not convex, and is surrounded by small glasses, the joints between them being concealed by moldings, resembling in this respect the Chippendale style mirror No. 1103. At the top is an urn from which hang branches with leaves and fruit. At the base are carved and gilded leaves and flowers and in the centre are two brackets for candles; here also, but not well seen, are several "C" curves which were a favorite form of decoration before, during and even after the time of Chippendale, as mentioned in note 3 in section 142. This mirror and the mirror No. 1103 are believed to have been for much over a century in the Chase House, in Annapolis, which was built in 1771. About 1770–1775.

The next six illustrations, Nos. 1242–1247, are girandole mirrors, that is, round convex mirrors with girandoles, meaning brackets for candles.

No. 1242 is ornamented at the top by two dolphins facing each other and provided with very flexible tails; these dolphins may be compared with those on the card table No. 1556. The surface of the frame is hollowed out and numerous gilded balls are attached to it. The usual black and reeded border surrounds the glass. The base is ornamented with leaves and ribbons. Three candle brackets are attached to each side, not to the bottom as in the previous piece. About 1800–1820.

1239 (Upper) Mr. J. F. H. Maginn.   1240 (Upper) Anonymous.
1241 (Lower) Chase House, Annapolis.   1242 (Lower) Mr. Arthur E. Cole.

No. 1243 is a fully ornamented girandole mirror. At the top is a vase in which there are leaves and a shell–shaped design. On the upper part of the sides are bunches of fruits and flowers. The gilded molding around the glass is a half–round one and is divided into four parts by rings and other designs. About 1800–1820.

In No. 1244 there are no leaves or other designs around the frame, nor any gilded balls. At the top an eagle is upon a pedestal and from its beak two chains hang in festoons and extend down to the brackets on the sides. Lines of ornamental molding are on the inner and outer edges of the gilded frame. As the receptacles for candles are well shown here it may be mentioned that the round brass piece made to hold a candle is known as a "bobèche," a French word meaning the "socket of a candlestick." The glass saucers catch the candle drippings. It is often imagined that the saucers and the glass "drops" are of the highly esteemed old Waterford glass. About 1800–1820.

No. 1245 is a fully ornamented girandole mirror. At the top is an eagle on a pedestal of rocks, as in the convex mirror No. 1239. The sides and lower parts have leaves, and a shell is on the base. The frame is hollowed out and gilded balls are attached to it; and surrounding the balls is an ornamental molding. About 1800–1820.

In No. 1246 an unusual feature is that on each side there is an attachment to which the brackets holding the candles are fixed. Over the spiral design of the attachment is a small figure apparently representing a pineapple. An eagle on a platform is at the top and within the frame there is a very large number of gilded balls. About 1800–1820.

No. 1247 also has an eagle at the top and on each side and on the base are gilded leaves. Here the brackets extend further in front of the glass than in the other girandole mirrors, giving a more brilliant diffusion of light. About 1800–1820.

Six sconces are shown in Nos. 1248–1253. The first two of these, Nos. 1248–1249, are examples of sconces in the proper meaning of the word as stated at the beginning of this section, namely, wall brackets for candles, without a mirror attached. The other four sconces, Nos. 1250–1253, are fitted with flat mirrors, not convex or concave. Two of these mirrors, however, Nos. 1250 and 1253, are evidently not intended to be used as "looking glasses," the reflecting glasses being so fully decorated that they are useless for that purpose. All these sconces are effective for lighting purposes and several of them are very graceful and delicate articles, so delicate, in fact, that restorations have no doubt been necessary from time to time. These sconces are regarded as of English origin. They are not often seen in our country, but are so interesting that space must be given to them.

1243 (Upper) Col. Washington Bowie, Jr.   1244 (Upper) Miss Eleanor S. Cohen.
1245 (Lower) Hammond-Harwood House.   1246 (Lower) Mr. & Mrs. B. Turnbull.
                                              1247 (Lower) Mr. J. G. D'A. Paul.

No. 1248 is one of a pair of sconces with spears which suggest the ancient Roman "fasces," a word revived in the "fascism" of Mussolini's Italy. An eagle is on a rock and below is a horizontal bar under which two candle brackets are attached and also two festoons of flowers. About 1775–1800.

In No. 1249 the main features are similar in character to those in the preceding piece. Here are three spears, an eagle on the top of a column, and sus-

1248 (Left) Metropolitan Mu-   1249 (Centre) Mrs. John S. Gibbs,   1250 (Right) Pennsylvania Mu-
    seum of Art.   Jr.   seum of Art.

pended tassels. The candle brackets, however, are in a different position from the previous ones and are larger and more graceful. On these brackets are glass saucers from which glass drops are suspended. About 1775–1800.

No. 1250 will be recognized at once by those who have examined section 144 as being in the Adam style. The urn with flowers at the top, the flowers falling in graceful lines, the oval in which there are small glasses surrounding a small oval with a classical dancing girl, the horizontal platform from which the candle brackets are suspended, the fluted vase–shaped base with flowers below—all these are in the style of Robert Adam. A pair of these sconces are side pieces of the fine Adam mirror No. 1148. About 1775.

No. 1251 is somewhat similar in form to the preceding sconce. Above the urn in the upper portion are vertical leaves from which long strings of flowers extend down to the base of the oval glass which is supported upon a horizontal bar. At the ends of this bar are small urns and in the centre are two curved candle brackets. Below are festoons of flowers. About 1775–1790.

No. 1252 is also in the style of Adam as is shown by the urn at the top, under which is a vase-shaped form from the sides of which strings of leaves fall gracefully over the sides of the round mirror below. At the base are two brackets for

1251 (Left) Mr. A. G. Towers.   1252 (Centre) Metropolitan Mu-   1253 (Right) Mrs. John S. Gibbs,
                                         seum of Art.   Jr.

candles, and furnished with glass saucers from which glass drops are suspended as in No. 1249. About 1775–1790.

No. 1253 answers to the definition of a sconce, having candle brackets, and in this case also a mirror.[2] This is of a different type from the preceding sconces and recalls certain other mirrors in having a Chinese scene, as in the same owner's mantel mirror No. 1228, and a base projecting beyond the side lines as in No. 1112 and others. Drapery is suspended, as on a bedstead, from the domed top and on the sides. This piece is small and is one of a pair. About 1760–1770.

2. Two designs by Hepplewhite of very delicate sconces without mirrors are Nos. 6 and 10 in illustration No. 1152.

An illustrated article entitled "Eighteenth Century Lighting Devices," by Mr. R. W. Symonds, is in "Antiques," October, 1932, pages 139–142, in which several sconces are shown.

Section 151. Knobs for mirrors.—In the latter part of the eighteenth century and in the early part of the nineteenth it was the fashion to support mirrors on two small round or oval knobs, with a screw at the back, which were put in the wall at such a height as would cause the mirrors to tilt forward somewhat and thus give a downward reflection. The faces of these knobs were generally made either of enamel in a brass frame, or wholly of pressed brass, and were decorated with a variety of patriotic or other subjects; among these were portraits of American statesmen, naval or military commanders, ladies in the costumes of the times, views of land and sea, ships of war, thirteen or more stars and weeping willow trees in graveyards. The most desirable knobs were known as "Battersea"[1] enamel knobs, from the place of their original manufacture in a section of London; but many knobs made elsewhere in resemblance of them appropriated their name.[2]

In illustration No. 1254 three examples of enamel knobs are given. The first is a portrait marked "Com. Perry," the second "Gen. Washington" and the

1254—ANONYMOUS.

third is a sea scene with a lighthouse and also a dwelling which is alarmingly near the waves.[3]

1. A descriptive and illustrated article entitled "Battersea Enamel Knobs," by Miss Christine Adams, is in "Antiques," August, 1922, pages 73–75. See also the same magazine of November, 1931, page 289, figures 9 and 10; also July, 1929, page 29.

When used on fretwork mirrors, the knobs were placed in the curves of the base; on mirrors with columns they were probably under the columns, but they appear to better advantage if placed nearer the centre of the base.

2. The Battersea factory was in operation from 1750 to 1756, when it became bankrupt.

The word "Battersea" now indicates merely the type of knob; no reliance should be put on the word with respect to age or origin. Moreover many small enamel articles, such as tea caddies, cups or plates which were apparently not made in the factory, are now offered as Battersea enamel pieces.

These knobs are about two inches in diameter. Larger sized brass knobs, made after about 1800, were used to hold window curtains in place.

3. His victorious battle of Lake Erie on September 10, 1813, made Commander Oliver Hazard Perry a national hero. He died in 1819. A mirror with the words "Perry's Victory" is shown in No. 1165.

A large number of mirror knobs are shown in Mr. Wallace Nutting's "Furniture Treasury," Nos. 3564–3602.

Section 152. Dressing glasses.—From the reign of Queen Anne, (1702–1714), until about a century later, dressing glasses[1] were a favorite form of mirror for the dressing room. They were intended to stand on the top of dressing tables or chests of drawers and were made in many shapes; but all of them have the same general character, being small mirrors swinging between two upright posts which were attached to a box–like group of small drawers in which toilet requisites could be placed. In some of the early pieces there were also writing compartments, as in Nos. 1255 and 1256.

In these dressing glasses the lower part with drawers, sometimes called the "box," is as important a feature as the glass, and both parts follow the styles of the periods in which they were made. Thus we see the styles of the Queen Anne, (seldom Chippendale), Hepplewhite, Sheraton and Empire periods; and the reader who has examined the preceding mirrors shown in this chapter will see in these small mirrors some of the styles which were seen in the larger ones; and in the "box" portion some of the same curved fronts, inlay, veneering and, in some cases, handles and feet,[2] will be seen as in the bureaus of the respective periods. These similarities are referred to in the comments. The wood also was the same as that of other furniture of the same period, walnut being generally used in the earlier pieces and mahogany in those after about 1750; but a particular kind of wood was not restricted to any definite period.

No. 1255 and 1256 are dressing glasses which not only have two or three drawers, but also a desk compartment.

In No. 1255 the Queen Anne style will be recognized in the shape of the mirror frame, which resembles those in Nos. 1095 and 1099. The upright supports are "turned" in a round form and rest on feet which resemble the trestle feet seen on the tables Nos. 1300–1302; these feet hold the mirror more firmly in place than those used in some of the later pieces. The open lid of the desk portion is supported by small "pulls" such as those on the desk No. 777; and below the desk is a drawer. The ball feet seem to be small forms of those on the desk referred to. About 1725–1750.

No. 1256 was probably made in Holland or in England with some of the Dutch features and styles. The Queen Anne style appears in the cresting on the top of the mirror, somewhat similar to that in the mirror No. 1100; the glass, however, is rectangular at the inner upper corners. The upright supports of the mirror resemble in form the side supports of the backs of many of the Queen Anne style chairs, such as Nos. 58–63 and others. The curved front of the lower portion resembles in some respects the front of the Chippendale style "bombé" bureau

---

1. In the English books these glasses are called "toilet glasses." In our country they are sometimes called "shaving stands," a term which is unsuitable, as it limits their usefulness to masculine purposes. The words "dressing glasses" seem to be appropriate.

2. The handles and feet of these pieces were necessarily very small, in fact were miniatures, and were very frequently broken, and when this occurred new handles or feet in a later style were often substituted. Handles, knobs and feet of the various styles are shown in sections 39, 40 and 25, respectively.

No. 724. The corners of the framework are cut in a wide form of chamfering, as to which see the bureaus Nos. 713 and 714. This piece is made of walnut and is about thirty–three inches high and twenty–two inches wide. About 1730–1750.

No. 1257 also shows features of the Queen Anne style, the upper portion of the frame of the mirror being in a series of curves as in the Queen Anne style mirrors Nos. 1093 and 1094. Here the uprights supporting the mirror are straight and rectangular and are held in position by being inserted in holes in the top of the "box." A distinctive feature of the box in this and the next two dressing glasses is the shape of the three small drawers which form the front of the piece and curve inwardly from the bottom. About 1735–1760.

No. 1258 seems to follow the Queen Anne style, which is indicated by the inward curve of the fronts of the drawers, and by the curves of the mirror frame at the upper inner corners, as in the Queen Anne mirrors Nos. 1101–1102 and in the fretwork mirrors in the same style, Nos. 1121–1126; but, as mentioned in section 143, mirrors with these curved inner corners were made for many years, apparently from about 1730 to the end of the century.[3] The finials, the ornaments which were at the top of the uprights, are missing. The tiny brass handles and the miniature bracket feet will be noticed. Perhaps about 1750–1785.

In No. 1259 the frame of the mirror is entirely rectangular and at the top is a fretwork cresting of somewhat the same plain character as in the Queen Anne style mirror No. 1098 which continued to be made until after 1800. Here the drawers are in the same inward curve as in the previous two pieces. The original brass handles are missing. About 1750–1785.

At this point another mirror of about the same period should appear, but it was mislaid for some time and is now shown as No. 1275, the last in this chapter.

The next ten dressing glasses, Nos. 1260–1269, are in the styles of Hepplewhite and Sheraton. It might be possible to determine which of these pieces are in the Hepplewhite style and which are in the style of Sheraton, as in the consideration of sideboards in section 127; but as similar dressing glasses were made by many cabinet makers working in the two styles at about the same time, it seems better to consider them all as being in the "Hepplewhite–Sheraton period" and thus avoid possible errors in making distinctions of little real importance.[4]

In these dressing glasses the mirrors are either shield–shaped, oval or rectangular in form, and the front of the "box," or lower section, is either serpentine,

3. John Elliott, of Philadelphia, who is referred to at length in note 3 in section 143, advertised in the local newspapers from 1756 to 1776, showing rough sketches of dressing glasses of the type above; but none of the mirrors are in exactly the shape with which we are familiar. Advertisements do not, however, always establish the date of manufacture; even now we may see in the country newspapers advertisements of auction sales showing illustrations of furniture made in the Victorian style of the Centennial year 1876.

4. In Mr. Strange's "English Furniture," etc., page 273, twenty drawings are shown of the "Hepplewhite and Sheraton period toilet glasses," and in Mr. Cescinsky's "English Furniture," volume 3, figure 301, eight types of "toilet mirrors of the Sheraton period" are illustrated.

1255 (Upper) Dr. James Bordley, Jr. 1256 (Upper) Mrs. Miles White, Jr.
1257 (Lower) Mr. John C. Toland. 1258 (Lower) Mr. E. G. Miller, Jr. 1259 (Lower) Dr. James Bordley, Jr.

bow–shaped or straight. The lower section usually has three small drawers, often inlaid with rectangular or curved designs. Several of the comments on these pieces mention resemblances to features found in bureaus and other pieces of the period. The wood is mahogany and the dates are from about 1785–1810.

In No. 1260 the mirror is in the shape of a shield, with a serpentine top which was seen in so many chairs in the Hepplewhite style, such as Nos. 200–208. The front of the lower section is also in a serpentine curve. There are three drawers, the central one of which is larger than the end ones, as usual in these

1260 (Upper) Mr. John C. Toland.   1261 (Upper) Lock. Col. Fur., Fig.   1262 (Upper) Mr. & Mrs. H. L.
1263 (Lower) Mr. E. G. Miller, Jr.   400.   Duer.
                                       1264 (Lower) Mr. Arthur E. Cole.   1265 (Lower) Mr. Arthur E. Cole.

pieces. The feet are small, flat and round. The wooden knobs are probably sub-stitutes for the original brass ones. A dressing glass of this type is commonly regarded as in the Hepplewhite style on account of its shield shape, but is not placed by the English writers mentioned in note 4 exclusively in that style but merely in the "Hepplewhite–Sheraton period." About 1790–1810.

In No. 1261 the mirror is also in the form of a shield, with a top which is not serpentine but is in two concave curves which meet in the centre. The fronts of the two drawers in the lower section are also in concave curves. The feet are of the bracket type and the knobs are small brass ones. This type is shown by Mr. Cescinsky as one of the Sheraton period. About 1790–1810.

In No. 1262 the mirror is oval. Ivory rosettes are at the top and near the bottom of the uprights holding the mirror. In the lower section the three drawers, with lines of inlay on the edges, are in a serpentine form. This dressing glass would look well on the serpentine front bureau No. 729. The feet are in a bracket form and the handles are of brass. About 1790–1810.

In No. 1263 the oval mirror is in a position requiring the lower section to be somewhat wider than that in the preceding piece. The lower section is plain and is in a shape which would match fairly well with the bow–shaped bureau No. 738. The round knobs are of brass and the feet are of the bracket type.[5] About 1790–1810.

In No. 1264 the mirror is rectangular, the top and bottom shorter than the sides, and is supported by rectangular uprights. The frame of the mirror and also the uprights have lines of inlay. Conforming with the shape of the mirror, the top and bottom of the end drawers are shorter than the sides. The front is serpentine in form and is ornamented with lines of inlay. Tiny brass knobs are on the drawers. About 1790–1810.

In No. 1265, also, the mirror is rectangular, and the top and bottom are wider than the sides, with rectangular uprights. The lower section is flat at the ends, between which it is bowed. The ends are ornamented with inlay and the three drawers have lines of inlay on the edges, with glass knobs. The feet are of the ball type. About 1790–1810.

In No. 1266 the uprights are "turned" in a plain design, but the mirror and the lower section are decorated with inlay. The inlay on the finely veneered fronts of the three drawers is in the form of parallel lines with rounded ends as in the bureaus Nos. 737 and 738, a design apparently first shown by Shearer, on a sideboard, as mentioned and illustrated in section 127 and note 6. Small brass knobs are on the drawers. About 1790–1810.

No. 1267 has uprights which are more elaborately "turned" than in the preceding piece. The front is slightly bowed. Here there are two drawers, finely veneered, on which are large brass knobs. A label on this dressing glass bears the name of Thomas Natt, of Philadelphia.[6] About 1790–1810.

5. The spaces between the sides of the frame of the dressing glass and the upright posts were caused by warping of the posts. An attempt to bring the posts closer together by tightening the screws resulted in one of the posts breaking under the strain. After the broken parts of the post were glued together, the spaces between the mirror frame and the posts were filled with washers, and sufficiently tight contact was thus obtained to hold the mirror in any position without putting too much strain on the posts. This cabinet–work detail may be useful to some owners.

6. His label is as follows, mentioning a variety of mirrors, domestic and imported: "Thomas Natt, Looking glass manufacturer, printseller, and importer of British Plate Glass, Mirrors, etc. No. 164, Market Street, three doors above Fourth, on the south side, Philadelphia. Constantly on hand an extensive and elegant assortment of fancy framed looking glasses, gilt mantel and pier glasses, mahogany and curled maple do., toilettes, sconces, swings, etc., etc.—Tablet, stained pillar, and fluted framed looking glasses in great variety. . . Plain, fancy and ornamental gilding and resilvering. . . On hand, looking glass plates, prints and mirrors of superior quality and late importations."

See also note 3 in this section in regard to the advertisements of John Elliott.

No. 1268 is an English dressing glass and is of a different type, having no drawers. The oval frame is supported by uprights which are similar in form to those in No. 1262, but rest upon feet of the trestle type. The lower framework is held together by a curved bar. This kind of dressing glass is not often seen in our country, but is illustrated in the English books referred to in note 4 in this section. The form is about the same as that of the usual type of "horse" or "cheval" glasses [7] of the period. About 1790–1810.

1266 (Upper) Sheppard & E. P. Hospital.
1269 (Lower) Metropolitan Museum.
1267 (Upper) Mr. & Mrs. Wm. A. Dixon.
1270 (Lower) Dr. James Bordley, Jr.
1268 (Upper) Anonymous.
1271 (Lower) Mr. E. G. Miller, Jr.

7. This is copied from figure 301 in volume 3 of "English Furniture of the Eighteenth Century," by permission of Mr. Cescinsky.

In Sheraton's "Drawing Book," (as to which see section 18), third edition, 1802, page 383, the large dressing glasses which stood on the floor and in which one's whole figure could be reflected, were called "horse–dressing glasses." The word "horse," as the first part of a compound word, indicated a large or coarse thing of its kind, as in the words "horse–chestnut," "horse–play," etc. The word "horse–dressing glass" was used to distinguish the large dressing glass from the small ones, such as those in our illustrations. The French word for a horse, "cheval," was later substituted for the English word and the large piece became known as a "cheval glass," meaning a "large dressing glass." "Dressing glasses" were thus in two types, one of which, now commonly called merely a "dressing glass," was small and was meant to stand on a bureau or lowboy or table; the other, the "cheval glass," was large and was meant to stand on the floor, as above stated. This large "cheval glass," first made in the time of Queen Anne, again became the fashion in the Sheraton period when the cost of glass had fallen greatly from its high prices in previous years.

No. 1269 is in the style of Sheraton, as will be seen by comparing the lower section of the dressing glass with some of the upper part of the Sheraton style sideboard No. 1002. There are two drawers at the ends above the level of the central portion, with two deep drawers below, and a long drawer in the centre, under which is an arch. Four brass handles with a ring in a lion's mouth are on the three lower drawers, and the feet are of the brass claw type; both of these brasses are seen on pieces in the latter part of the Sheraton period and on several tables and chairs made by Duncan Phyfe. The uprights are reeded, with brass balls at the top and brass knobs at the sides for holding the mirror in any position. About 1800–1820.

No. 1270 is an unusual piece in both the upper and lower sections. The plain rectangular mirror frame, with slightly curved inner corners at the top, is supported by two large and deeply grooved uprights of a kind apparently not seen in other American dressing glasses, but which resemble designs in English books. Feet with somewhat similar grooving are in the tripod table No. 1589. The lower section has four projecting round columns, not reeded or fluted, but apparently for ornament. The feet are of the flat type as in No. 1260. The central drawer is recessed and below it the "apron" is cut in cyma curves. Perhaps about 1820–1830.

No. 1271 is also an unusual and peculiar piece. The oval mirror is supported by uprights which have scrolls both at the top and bottom. In the lower section there is a round projecting column at each end, in this respect resembling the previous piece to some extent. Under the columns are ball feet. There are three drawers, the fronts of which are "blocked" in part. The two outer drawers are concave and the central one is serpentine. The wood is walnut. Perhaps about 1800–1810.

The next three dressing glasses, Nos. 1272–1274, are in the Empire style.[8]

In No. 1272 the upper section, with its rectangular mirror and its "turned" supporting uprights, is not materially different from several others in this section. The lower section, however, departs from the curved form of front and

(NOTE 7, *continued*)

Cheval glasses were occasionally made in our country in the Sheraton period, and until about 1830, but original ones are now seldom seen. One made by Duncan Phyfe is shown in "Furniture Masterpieces of Duncan Phyfe," by Mr. C. O. Cornelius, plate 51. One in the Empire style is in Miss Morse's "Furniture of the Olden Time," No. 389. One of the earliest English pieces is shown in Mr. Cescinsky's "English Furniture," volume 1, figure 185, dated about 1720; another is in Mr. Nutting's "Furniture Treasury," No. 3201. All of these cheval glasses have the same type of feet as in No. 1268 above.

Designs of large fire screens, not mirrors, made in the style of the cheval glasses, are called "horse screens" by Chippendale in his "Director," as to which book see section 15. The same term was used by Hepplewhite and Sheraton in their books.

8. During the period of the Empire style the mirrors began to be attached to the tops of bureaus and thereafter dressing glasses ceased to be made. See the bureaus Nos. 764–768.

Another form of dressing glass made especially for shaving purposes was popular about 1840 and for some years thereafter. It consisted of a round or rectangular swinging mirror attached to the top of a small box of drawers made to hold shaving requisites, the box being supported by a

(*Note 8 continued on page 692.*)

presents a straight one with three drawers which have small glass knobs. The four small round columns at the front indicate the Empire style, as in the bureaus Nos. 763–766. About 1830.

In No. 1273 the Empire style appears in the rounded front of the single drawer, as in the bureau No. 765 in that style. The frame more nearly approaches a square form than in previous dressing glasses. The feet are of the ball type. The handles are of an earlier design. About 1830–1840.

No. 1274 recalls the bureaus Nos. 765–766 in having the supports of the mirror in carved scrolls which if closer together and furnished with strings would

1272 (UPPER) MR. E. G. MILLER, JR.   1273 (UPPER) MISS ELISABETH H. BARTLETT.
1274 (LOWER) MR. JOHN C. TOLAND.   1275 (LOWER) MR. ARTHUR E. COLE.

resemble a lyre. In the straight front are three drawers with circular wooden knobs. The feet here are of the ball type as in the preceding piece. About 1830–1840.

No. 1275 should have appeared in connection with No. 1259, but was mislaid. The cresting is cut in fretwork and was adorned with a leaf or other carving in a circular opening. The lower section has three curved drawers, the central part being in a serpentine form. The upper inner corners are rectangular, as in Nos. 1133–1134 and others. The wood is mahogany. About 1750–1780.

(NOTE 8, *continued from page 691*.)

single column about four or five feet high under which were feet. These shaving stands were unstable and unsightly, in spite of spiral turnings and fanciful feet. The height of the mirror was made adjustable to the requirements of the user.

CHAPTER XVIII

TABLES AND STANDS

Also ADVICE TO AMATEUR COLLECTORS

Section 153. In general.—The table[1] is one of the indispensable articles of domestic furniture and has been in use from remote times in all civilized countries. It was a familiar object in every household at the period when our country was settled, but only a few of the early American examples have survived to the present time.[2] The earliest one now known, dating from about 1650, shown as

1. The word "table" is defined as "an article of furniture consisting of a flat top, (the table proper), of wood, stone or other solid material resting on legs or on a pillar with or without connecting frame–work"; Century Dictionary. In England the word "table" has a somewhat broader usage than without; for example, what we call a flat–top desk is there called a "writing table." See also note 1 in section 173.

2. Mr. Lockwood in his "Colonial Furniture," volume 2, page 167, states that "more early tables have survived than early chairs. The reason is perfectly obvious, as the former were intended to hold dead weight and the chairs were put to the strain of live weight."

No. 1276 in the next section, was called a "table board and frame," the "board"[3] being the flat top and the "frame" being the lower part which supports the top.

Few articles of furniture have been made in as many forms as tables, for the reason that tables have been made for so many different purposes, each purpose requiring a special type. Thus we have dining tables, tea tables, serving tables, dressing tables, card tables, sewing tables and others. One term, more frequently used in England than in our country, is "occasional" table, meaning a small movable table suitable for various purposes[4]—an indefinite word which is not often used when a more descriptive one can be found.

In tables a distinctive feature, and one which generally determines the style, is the leg. The principal forms are the cabriole leg with Dutch, or club, feet of the Queen Anne style; the cabriole leg with ball and claw feet, and the straight and square leg, both of the Chippendale style; the straight leg of the Adam style; the straight, square and tapering leg of the Hepplewhite style; the curved leg or the straight, round and tapering leg of the Sheraton style; and several other less important kinds of legs. These types, with certain variations, are easily recognized in our American tables.

The other distinctive feature of tables is, of course, the top. This varies in design and size from the large tops of the long dining tables, such as No. 1317, to the tiny round tops of certain tripod candle stands, such as No. 1398, all of which will appear in the illustrations.[5]

As seen in the list of sections, this chapter is divided into twenty-three sections, one of which, No. 161, is on the subject of stands.

Section 154. Several early types.—In this section we examine certain tables of different types which were in vogue at various times from the date of the earliest American pieces, about 1650. The illustrations do not include two well–known kinds of early tables which, because of their importance, are treated separately in the next two sections, namely gate–leg tables and butterfly tables; but those which are shown here comprise about all of the types which the amateur collector is likely to find very interesting.

3. This word "board" in connection with a table continues in use with us in several expressions. Thus there is a "board of directors," figuratively called a "board" because the directors sit around one; and in the expression "board and lodging" we use the word "board" as meaning food, which is served on a board. The word "table" is also used in a figurative sense, meaning that which is placed upon a table for refreshment; Century Dictionary.

4. In "A Glossary of English Furniture," by Penderel–Brodhurst and Layton, page 115, an "occasional table" is defined as "a small light portable table, used for ladies' work, flowers, ornaments and a variety of other purposes. The shape and adornment of tables of this character are infinitely various." In "American Furniture" by Mr. E. S. Holloway, page 85, occasional tables are referred to as being "for any purpose to which at the moment they might be convenient."

When used in reference to a chair the word "occasional" means an odd chair, not forming part of a set; Century Dictionary.

5. In this chapter three hundred and twenty-seven illustrations of tables and stands are presented, a number in one chapter exceeded only by the four hundred and eighty–two illustrations of chairs.

For many persons these early tables, as well as other articles of the period, have a certain charm and interest on account of their age, their simplicity and their association with the founders of our country; but to many other persons they are not very attractive. This diversity of opinion applies especially to the small and plain tables which are often called "tavern" tables.[1] Moreover, wholly genuine tables of the early period are not often seen outside of museums, and are seldom obtainable by the amateur collector. Plain and small tables recently and skillfully made from old parts of other articles are not easily distinguishable from genuine antique ones.

In the note brief mention is made of several early types which are not illustrated here.[2]

No. 1276 is a well–known table, referred to in the previous section, owned by the Metropolitan Museum of Art through whose courtesy the illustration appears. It is said by Mr. Lockwood, in his "Colonial Furniture in America," to be the oldest American table known. A table of this type, used as a dining table, was known as a "table board and frame" and is described in those words in inventories of the estates of deceased persons. The table is in fact an oak frame upon which a removable pine board was placed. Here the board is about twelve feet long

1. These "tavern" tables are now less popular among collectors than they were a few years ago. See note 4 in this section.

A valuable work on early American furniture is Mr. Wallace Nutting's "Furniture of the Pilgrim Century," Revised Edition, 1924, with more than fifteen hundred illustrations.

2. A. A "chair table" is an ungainly combination of the two articles composing its name. A large table top, either round or rectangular, was attached to a large low back chair in such a manner that the top could lie horizontally over the chair and be used as a table, or could be raised vertically so that the chair could be used. A drawer was under the seat of the chair. When not used in the centre of a room as a table it could be placed against the wall, saving space. A chair table with a long rectangular table top is in the "seventeenth century room" of the Metropolitan Museum of Art. Several are shown and explained in Mr. Nutting's "Furniture of the Pilgrim Century," Revised Edition, pages 450–453. See also paragraph 3 in note 6 in section 46, and figures 439–441 in Mr. Lockwood's "Colonial Furniture." About 1640–1700.

B. A "hutch table" is similar in construction to a chair table, but, instead of a chair, there is a "hutch," meaning a box on two legs, to which the top is attached. Several are shown in the books mentioned in the preceding paragraph. About 1700.

C. Small tables or lowboys with a slate top set into the frame are known as "slate–top" tables or lowboys. Around the slate is a wooden border a few inches wide which is finely made and decorated. It is thought that the slate was intended to hold hot dishes which would injure a wooden top. Marble tops were used for the same purpose on the sideboard tables Nos. 1305 and 1306. Mr. Lockwood, in his "Colonial Furniture," volume 1, page 73, states that in his opinion these slate–tops were made in Holland, where Delft tiles were similarly used; see also his volume 2, figures 705, 706. About 1700.

D. "Drawing tables" were rectangular tables which could be enlarged. One method was by "drawing" out leaves which were placed in the ends and "were supported by wooden braces which drew out from the frame and held the ends firmly on a level with the table." This type of table is illustrated in Mr. Lockwood's "Colonial Furniture," volume 2, figure 675. Another type of "drawing tables" is known as "architects' tables," illustrated in Nos. 1635–1637.

E. Several tables called by Mr. Wallace Nutting "communion tables" and others known as "refectory tables" are shown in his "Furniture of the Pilgrim Century," Revised Edition; see the Index to his book.

and only two feet wide, the diners sitting on one side only. The frame consists of three "trestles," the word "trestle" in connection with a table meaning an upright supporting piece, or leg, at each end, and sometimes also in the middle, as here. These three trestles are held in position by a horizontal bar which passes through them. The feet are known as trestle feet, a type necessary to keep the uprights firmly in position. Because of the trestles, tables of this kind are called "trestle" tables.[3] About 1650.

No. 1277 is a much more substantial table, having massive legs connected by heavy stretchers. Perhaps originally the piece had feet of a small rounded type. There are two paneled drawers with wooden knobs. The top is of maple and extends considerably beyond the frame at both ends; the frame seems to be of oak. A number of tables of this general form, but often with ornamental features, have been found, and are regarded as being either communion tables, parlor tables, dining or kitchen tables, the latter because of the drawers which were often of different sizes in one table. This piece is about five feet long. About 1700–1720.

No. 1278 is an early English dining table which is shown here as an example of an important type in the development of tables. This piece is in the Metropolitan Museum of Art, through whose courtesy it is illustrated here. The conspicuous feature is the form of the six legs with their massive carved "bulbs," similar to those seen on the bedsteads of the period, which are not illustrated in this book. Tables and bedsteads of this kind have not been found in our country and it is probable that none were imported because of their cost and the difficulty of transporting objects of such large size. About 1650.

Passing on to the small tables we see in No. 1279 a table with spiral or twisted legs and stretchers. The spiral feature was one of the earliest types of ornamentation and was very often used. It is seen, for example, in the gate–leg table No. 1291 to which a note on the subject is appended; the purpose of the references is stated in section 1, pages 9–10. The number and arrangement of

3.   A.   Another "table board and frame" is shown in Mr. Nutting's "Furniture of the Pilgrim Century," Revised Edition, No. 673. On page 465 he states that recently a number of trestle–board tables have been found which were made about 1800 by the Shakers. Recently tables of the same general character have been imported from Sweden. An illustrated article on these Swedish tables and other articles is in "Antiques," July, 1932, page 16. Two other New England tables are shown in the same magazine, July, 1927, page 30.

B.   An interesting matter is mentioned by Mr. Nutting in his book on pages 454, 459–460. He states that it was the custom after meals to remove the trestle dining table from the centre to the side of the room so as to have more open space; and that later when gate–leg tables were used as dining tables the custom continued, letting down the leaves and placing the table by the wall. "We remember one ancient and huge kitchen where only two members of the family were left. Invariably the dining table was closed and pushed to the wall after every meal, leaving a great empty space of no possible benefit. Our grandmothers would as soon have thought of leaving the dishes unwashed as of leaving the table" in the centre of the room.

C.   As is seen in the illustration, the trestle feet are merely blocks of wood attached to the trestle legs and extending out at right angles to the top. Similar forms of trestle feet are in Nos. 1300–1302. Other forms, apparently adapted from trestle feet, were used in the late Sheraton, Empire and Victorian periods, as in table No. 1632.

1276 (Upper) Metropolitan Museum of Art.   1277 (Centre) Mr. John S. McDaniel.
1278 (Lower) Metropolitan Museum of Art.

the stretchers will be noticed. Stretchers turned in the form of balls or knobs are also seen on tables of this period, as in No. 1282. About 1650–1700.

No. 1280 has four plain and heavy stretchers, suitable for rough usage. The legs are turned in vase–shaped forms with rings between them. The feet are not rounded as they are in most of the tables of this type. This piece and several others following are of the kind often called "tavern"[4] or "tap–room" tables, indefinite terms which should be avoided. The term "small turned–leg tables," is perhaps sufficiently descriptive if understood not to include butterfly tables and small gate–leg tables. About 1700–1725.

No. 1281 has a round top and the legs slant outward, or, as the term is, they are "raked" or "splayed," as in the Windsor chairs shown in illustration No. 440. The turnings of the legs are in the vase–and–ring style and the stretchers are heavy and plain. About 1700–1725.

In No. 1282 the top is rectangular and the legs are turned in a slender form with rings above and below. The stretchers, as mentioned in section 26, note 4, form an "H" and are known as "H stretchers," and are "turned" in the ball, or knob, pattern. The round brass handle of the drawer is of a much later type. About 1700–1725.

No. 1283 has slender and graceful stretchers instead of plain and heavy ones; and the legs also are slender, as in the preceding piece. The upper portion contains a drawer, and the "skirt" is in a form which suggests that of the highboy No. 651 and the lowboy No. 679. About 1700–1720.

In No. 1284 the legs are turned in the "inverted cup" pattern, as in the highboys Nos. 632–634, and the lowboys Nos. 669–671. The cross–stretchers are turned in a vase–and–ring design. The brass escutcheons and drop handles of the period will also be noticed. About 1700–1720.

4. A. The term "tavern table" has been applied to various kinds of small tables of the period from about 1675 onwards. Because of their small size, compared with gate–leg and other tables, they were easily movable and on this account were much used in the public rooms of taverns; and their small size was equally suitable for use in kitchens and other rooms. They were either square, rectangular, octagonal, oval or round, and generally had an overhanging top. One or more of the feet is often replaced with a new one of incorrect design.

B. It is not possible to divide the tables of this general character into exact classes according to their probable usage; but it is likely that the large tables were for dining purposes, the next in size for taverns and general household use and a still smaller size for use as a "stand"; but the difference between a small table and a "stand" is in many cases uncertain at this early period as well as in the time of Hepplewhite and Sheraton; see the first paragraphs in section 173.

C. A "half–moon" table is illustrated in "Antiques," March, 1922, page 113, as a "Little Known Masterpiece." This almost round table is in two parts of nearly equal size and when the table is not in use one part is turned upside down and placed within the other part. About 1725.

D. In a "sawbuck" table the board may be supported by a horizontal bar as in the table No. 1276. The ends of the bar rest upon an X–shaped support or rack of the kind seen in a "sawbuck" or "sawhorse" which is used for holding wood when being cut by a wood–saw; Century Dictionary. In "Antiques," February, 1935, page 63, is an illustrated article on a sawbuck table now in Dartmouth College. Illustrations of similar tables are Nos. 804 and 810 in Mr. Wallace Nutting's "Furniture Treasury." See also illustrations of three "X–trestle" tables in "Antiques," November, 1926, page 358.

1279 (Upper) Metropolitan Museum of Art.
1281 (Centre) Mrs. John S. Gibbs, Jr.
1283 (Lower) Hammond-Harwood House.

1280 (Upper) Dr. James Bordley, Jr.
1282 (Centre) Anonymous.
1284 (Lower) Hammond-Harwood House.

The next five tables, Nos. 1285–1289, are in the Queen Anne style, as to which see section 14, and have Dutch, or club, feet, and are not strictly in the "early types," as they are all of the eighteenth century. On each of the preceding small tables we have seen stretchers, which, as stated in section 26, were frequently used in our country in the Queen Anne period, but not in England until they were revived in the time of Chippendale. The wood of these tables in the Queen Anne style is generally walnut or maple.

No. 1285 has "raked" legs as in No. 1281. These legs are pleasing in form and terminate in Dutch, or club, feet such as are seen on chairs, highboys and other articles in the Queen Anne style. About 1730–1750.

In No. 1286 the "skirt" is cut in arches and curves as in highboys of the period, such as No. 637. The legs are straight, not raked or cabriole in form; similar legs are on No. 1288 and on the large table No. 1308, and are referred to in note 2, A in section 25. The feet are of the Dutch type with a ball under each foot. About 1730–1750.

No. 1287 is a three–legged, or tripod, table. As in the preceding piece, the skirt is cut in curves, here in the shape of two cyma curves, as to which see section 23. The legs are raked, and end in the same type of feet as in the two preceding tables. About 1730–1750.

No. 1288 is a walnut rectangular table with a full overhang at each end and with a drawer in the centre. The legs, two of which in the engraving have an erroneous appearance of being raked, are straight and terminate in Dutch feet, under which are high "shoes" which may be compared with those in No. 1286. About 1730–1750.

No. 1289 is a smaller table than the preceding one, with legs which become round as they extend downward and terminate in the usual Dutch feet. Three arches are cut in the skirt under the drawers in the manner of those on some of the lowboys in the Queen Anne style, as in No. 686. About 1730–1750.

In No. 1290 the legs are slightly curved and are attached to the skirt above its base. The brass ring handle in the drawer is of a later period than the other parts of the table. The balls in the ball and claw feet are more nearly spherical than in many other tables. About 1725–1750.

In connection with some of the plain and originally inexpensive tables shown in this section it should be particularly noted that the dates here given are merely the approximate dates at which the styles were in fashion; and that tables in these styles continued to be made, especially in the smaller towns, for many years after the styles passed out in the large cities. The study of the subject makes it possible to know the approximate dates when most of the furniture styles *began* to be fashionable, but it is not possible to fix the date at which articles in a particular style were no longer made. This subject is also mentioned in connection with "dates," in paragraph 2 of the text in section 6.

1285 (UPPER) MR. ALBERT G. TOWERS.
1287 (CENTRE) MR. ALBERT G. TOWERS.
1289 (LOWER) MR. J. F. H. MAGINN.

1286 (UPPER) MR. J. F. H. MAGINN.
1288 (CENTRE) COLL. OF MRS. J. STABLER.
1290 (LOWER) DR. JAMES BORDLEY, JR.

Section 155. Gate–leg and folding tables.—Both of these tables are varieties of drop–leaf tables. In a gate–leg table the legs which support the leaves resemble gates somewhat in appearance and swing out in the manner of gates. A folding table is similar in having a swinging gate, but the gate operates in a different manner, which is better understood by examining the illustrations Nos. 1300–1302 than by reading a printed explanation.

Gate–leg tables were the favorite tables in our country from about 1650 until the change in style in the Queen Anne period,[1] about 1720, when they were

1. A. It is said that in America gate–leg tables continued to be made until about 1750, or later in the country districts. They originated in the Jacobean period, as to which see section 12.

B. After more than two centuries it is difficult to be certain of the dates of tables of such similar character. Mr. Lockwood, in his "Colonial Furniture," refers to most of the gate–leg tables shown by him as being in the style of the last quarter of the seventeenth century, which was 1675–1700. Concerning dates see also section 6.

C. It is said that tables on the gate–leg principle again became popular in England about 1750 to 1775 and later, with legs and stretchers of a very light character. In "Old English Furniture," by Mr. G. Owen Wheeler, London, 1924, pages 570–574, these "spindle" or "spider–leg" tables are illustrated and are dated 1775–1795. An example is in Mr. Wallace Nutting's "Furniture Treasury," No. 967, and in "Furniture of the Olden Time" by Miss Morse, No. 239. See also "Antiques," December, 1934, page 220.

D. The wood used in gate–leg tables was generally maple in New England, but sometimes walnut; further South, walnut was almost always used; but other woods are occasionally found.

E. The top of the table is the part most likely to be damaged by usage. In pointing out the danger of asserting that a table has its original top, Mr. Wallace Nutting, in his "Furniture of the Pilgrim Century," Revised Edition, page 460, states that "there is no possible method of proving such an assertion"; but that "ancient table tops, however, are often found and are adaptable to ancient table frames, especially in the case of the tavern table with its one piece top." Many gate–leg tables have tops which are not the original ones.

F. The leaves are attached by hinges to the stationary top in several methods which are difficult to make clear without using technical words which are avoided in this book so far as possible. These methods to some extent indicate the period in which the table was made, although of course any cabinet maker could at any time use any method known to him. By the more usual method the hinges are not visible. See the comment on No. 1297.

G. The feet on almost all of the gate–leg tables are rounded, and, if original, are usually worn or injured. A few tables have "Spanish" feet, a type which may be seen on other pieces of the period of about 1690–1710, as on the lowboy No. 674, and the chairs Nos. 39–41. See also illustration No. 11.

H. The stretchers are usually "turned," the vase–and–ring design being most frequently seen; but in some tables the stretchers are plain and straight, indicating, it is said, that the piece is of Southern origin.

I. In large tables there may be a drawer at each end, but in smaller ones there is but one drawer which is about two–thirds of the length of the table.

J. Gate–leg tables vary greatly in size, ranging in width with the leaves open from about seventy–eight inches to about thirty–six inches. The medium sized ones are most often found. The very large ones and the very small ones are more desirable because of their comparative rarity.

K. Several gate–leg tables have been found with four gates, two on each side, with two feet on each gate, that is, eight feet on the four gates and four on the frame, making twelve feet in all. The usual number of gates is two, with one foot on each gate. In No. 1292 there are eight feet in all.

L. Reproductions of these gate–leg tables have recently had a large sale. A prominent department store advertised reproductions of forty–nine different examples of genuine gate–leg tables. Whether an original or an exact reproduction, a gate–leg table is a desirable article of furniture.

to a great extent superseded by drop–leaf tables in which the leaves were supported by movable legs without the gate features, as in the tables shown in section 162. Anticipating somewhat, it may be said here that later, in some drop–leaf tables, legs were not used as supports and the leaves were supported by movable brackets as in the Pembroke, library and sofa tables shown in sections 163–165. On card tables and some others, however, movable legs continued to be used.

The usual form of a gate–leg table has a top attached to a somewhat narrow frame and the frame rests upon two legs at each end. On each side of the frame are the gate–legs which support the leaves, as above mentioned. The leaves were generally semi–oval in form, but in some cases they were rectangular; and if in the latter form, two or more tables could be connected, and thus make one large table. A large gate–leg table was generally used as a dining table, and was no doubt satisfactory for that purpose, except that it "condemned at least some of those seated around it to acute discomfort owing to the multiplicity" of the legs.

In these tables the principal features are the size, the character of the turnings, the number of feet and the plainness or elegance of the tables in general appearance; in other respects they are very similar and call for little comment.

No. 1291 is a small gate–leg table of an early type as is indicated by the form of the spiral[2] turnings of the legs. The stretchers are all plain, not turned, and are heavy and strong. As mentioned in note 1, H, it is said that stretchers of this plain character often denote a Southern origin. Here the inner legs of the gates do not extend to the floor and have no feet, so that there are only six legs with feet. About 1650–1680.

No. 1292 is a larger table in which the inner legs of the gates extend to the floor so that there are eight legs with feet. The stretchers of the gates and of the front and back of the central portion are turned in a vase–and–ring form; but at the ends of the side stretchers of the central portion are other turnings. About 1675–1700.

In No. 1293 the turnings of the legs are very similar to those in the preceding table, being of the vase–and–ring type; but the turnings of the stretchers are of a somewhat heavier form. Here also there are only six feet. A drawer is in the front and the skirt under the drawer is cut in two cyma curves. About 1675–1700.

2. The spiral type of turning, or carving, on legs, stretchers and other parts was used in different forms and in widely separated periods. In the gate–leg table here shown, about 1650–1680, and in the table No. 1279, the legs are in an early form which is easily distinguished from the later type. The spiral turning is seen on the pedestal of the tripod stand or table No. 1394, in the Chippendale style, about 1760–1780, on which the turning is more delicate. On the legs of the so-called serving table No. 1446, in the Sheraton style, about 1810–1820, the turning is somewhat heavier. In the table No. 1450, about 1815–1830, the turnings have become less elegant and are characteristic of the Empire period, in which they were very popular. The slight and somewhat arbitrary difference between the spiral turnings of the late Sheraton style and those of the Empire style is that the latter are generally heavier and coarser than the former. Other examples are in the dressing table No. 1472, the card table No. 1538 and the sewing tables Nos. 1575 and 1588. Spiral turnings are also seen on the bedposts Nos. 1069 and 1070 and the sideboards Nos. 1015 and 1016. The term "twist" is sometimes used in the sense of "spiral turning." See also the Index under the word "Spiral."

1291 (UPPER) DR. JAMES BORDLEY, JR.
1293 (CENTRE) MR. J. F. H. MAGINN.
1295 (LOWER) DR. JAMES BORDLEY, JR.

1292 (UPPER) MR. & MRS. J. MARSH MATTHEWS.
1294 (CENTRE) MRS. MILES WHITE, JR.
1296 (LOWER) MR. & MRS. CHARLES E. ELLICOTT.

1297 (UPPER) MRS. MILES WHITE, JR.
1299 (CENTRE) MRS. JOHN S. GIBBS, JR.
1301 (LOWER) MR. J. F. H. MAGINN.

1298 (UPPER) MR. EDGAR G. MILLER, JR.
1300 (CENTRE) LOCKWOOD COL. FURN., FIG. 689.
1302 (LOWER) MRS. MILES WHITE, JR.

No. 1294 also has plain stretchers except on the front and back where they are turned. The turnings of all of the legs are in a form resembling somewhat the turnings on the six–legged highboy No. 632 in the William and Mary style. About 1675–1700.

No. 1295 is another small table, resembling No. 1291 except in the leg turnings which are in the form of an elongated vase. The stretchers are plain and there are six legs with feet. About 1675–1700.

No. 1296 is a large table. The turnings on the side stretchers of the central portion are of two kinds; those in the centre are of the vase–and–ring type and those at the ends are in a ring form. On the six outer legs the turnings are of the vase–and–ring type with a ball foot below. The drawer of this table is seen on the left. About 1675–1700.

In No. 1297 the turnings of the front and back legs are in a form which is said to be found mainly in the South. The design of the stretchers in the gates is a pleasing variation from the vase–and–ring form. The legs of the gates are turned in a different manner from those of the front and back. The usual method of connecting the edges of the leaves to the edges of the top appears near the drawer; the hinges underneath are not visible, whether the leaves are up or down. See note 1, F in this section. About 1675–1700.

No. 1298 is a plainer gate–leg table than the others shown here and is small. The turnings of the legs are said to be in a Southern manner. The stretchers are all plain. The height is about twenty–seven inches, the length thirty–four inches and the width when open is thirty–seven inches. About 1675–1700.

No. 1299 may be regarded as a gate–leg table of an unusual kind. The framework on the left is triangular, with a half–round stationary top. The half–round drop–leaf on the right is attached by hinges to the top and is supported by the gate. The triangular portion has a stationary gate–like support in the front, and under the top is a drawer. The legs are turned and the stretchers are plain. Probably about 1725.

The next three illustrations, Nos. 1300–1302, are of folding gate–leg tables in which one part of the table folds into the other part, as will be seen in the examples. This folding and easily movable table is sometimes called a "tuckaway" gate–leg table.

No. 1300 is a form of folding table which shows a close relationship to the form of the gate–leg tables. Here, however, there is only one leg at each end, instead of the usual two, to support the top; and when the two gate–legs are folded in, the leaves drop down and the table would easily fall over except for the wide base stretcher with trestle feet. About 1675–1700.

In No. 1301 the usual two gates on the sides are made as one gate which swings as a whole on a pivot where there is a pointed ornament, and supports the top. There is no wide base stretcher such as is seen in the preceding piece, but the trestle feet prevent the table from falling. About 1675–1700.

No. 1302 is very similar to the preceding piece in construction, and is noticeable for the turned legs and stretchers and for the support by the double gate by which the leaves are held in a horizontal position. The legs at the ends are supported by trestle feet as in the previous pieces. About 1675-1700.

In addition to the types shown here there are simple folding tables which have a single gate on one side only; others with two gates swinging from the sides of the frame; others, of much later date, with folding legs and tilting top; others with a rectangular top; and others with various details of no special importance.

Section 156. Butterfly tables.—These tables, as well as those shown in the two preceding sections, are early tables, but are of such a different character and of such interest at present that they are considered in this separate section.

The butterfly table is doubtless an American development from the gate-leg tables. It acquired its modern name from the supposed resemblance of its brackets, or supports, which hold up the leaves, to the wings of butterflies. At the lower part of the table these brackets are attached to the side stretchers and above they are attached to the framework. With these two connections the brackets may be swung out to support the leaves.[1] A butterfly table is in fact a drop-leaf table in which the leaves are supported by a wing bracket and not by a gate-leg as in the tables shown in the previous section, nor by the usual kind of movable leg seen in the drop-leaf tables in section 162, nor by a small bracket as in the Pembroke tables shown in section 163 and in other tables. A necessary feature in true butter-

1. The tops of these tables were generally made of maple or cherry; the other parts were of various woods. There is usually a drawer, the bottom of which is wider than the top, because the sides slant in the same manner as the legs. On the drawer a small wooden knob was used. The stretchers are generally plain and straight, but "turned" ones are also found. The tops when opened are usually either oval or rectangular. The feet are of the small ball-foot kind, but there are variations of this pattern. Hinges of the type known as "butterfly" hinges, shown in section 42, are not named from butterfly tables, although they have been found in these tables. Butterfly tables are small, the height ranging from about twenty-five to twenty-seven inches.

A butterfly table with four wings, two on each side, is illustrated and discussed in "Antiques," August, 1924, frontispiece. The table is much larger than those with two wings, being three feet wide and five feet and six inches long.

The subject of butterfly tables suggests the matter of fakes. As with other furniture pieces, a counterfeit may be so well made by a skilful forger that only an equally skilful critic, familiar with all details by actual experience, can detect the fraud. In this book "Knowing, collecting and restoring early American antique furniture," 1930, page 152, Mr. Henry Hammond Taylor explains the methods of the faker; and Mr. Wallace Nutting in his "Furniture of the Pilgrim Century," Revised Edition, page 566, gives a warning to collectors and states that "it is a favorite trick of furniture forgers to place a butterfly top on the splayed-leg frame of a small tavern table." The high prices brought by genuine butterfly tables in fair condition make successful faking a very profitable operation.

Butterfly tables are seldom found in good condition, and a certain amount of restoration or replacement seems to be expected. For example, a replacement of one of the leaves may be regarded by a seller as only a slight defect. Just what restorations or replacements should be tolerated by a purchaser is a matter of individual opinion and taste. See "Restorations," section 10 and notes. An article entitled "New Wings for an Old Butterfly," in "Antiques," February, 1927, page 112, illustrates a table before and after restoration.

In "The Antiquarian," April, 1931, page 40, is a fully illustrated article, by Mr. Walter A. Dyer, entitled "Butterflies," meaning "Butterfly tables."

Butterfly tables are referred to as one of the few exclusively American tables on page 28, section 8.

fly tables is the slant outwards, or "splay," or "rake," of the legs, the top of the frame being narrower than the lower part; if the legs were exactly vertical, the wings, or brackets, would not be workable. These tables have been found in Connecticut and other States of New England; they are not known in England. They are all dated at about 1700–1725.

In No. 1303 we see the characteristic features of butterfly tables. The top is oval, the brackets supporting the leaves are cut in the form regarded as resembling the wings of a butterfly, the legs are slanting, and the stretchers are plain and straight. The usual and only ornamental effect is in the turnings of the legs. The small ball feet will also be noticed. About 1700–1725.

1303 Mrs. John S. Gibbs, Jr.   1304 Anonymous.

No. 1304 is very similar in its general appearance, but the wings are larger and in a more rounded pattern and are thus more conspicuous. The drawer is unusually deep, extending back to the end of the frame. The knob on the drawer should be a small wooden one. This table is somewhat larger than usual, being twenty–seven inches in height and about forty–two inches in length when the wings are opened, as in the illustration. About 1700–1725.

Section 157. Sideboard tables; dining tables.—The "sideboard table" is the ancestor of the modern sideboard as stated in the chapter on sideboards, where it is also said, in section 126, that these tables are not readily distinguishable from certain other tables.[1] The sideboard table was used in dining rooms as a serving table and was generally placed against the wall; but it is not to be regarded as merely a "side" table as we now use that term and as illustrated in section 166 Sideboard tables were apparently not made after the modern sideboard was developed.

In England these sideboard tables were often very elaborate, and frequently had tops of marble which would not be injured by hot dishes. In the time of

1. Section 166, entitled "Side tables; serving and hunters'," may be examined in connection with this section.

Chippendale they reached their highest point of workmanship and design; and the designs of Robert Adam were also of much elegance.[2] Few, if any, sideboard tables of such excellence were made in our country and in fact not many sideboard tables of any kind seem to have survived; only three are illustrated here,[3] two of which, Nos. 1305 and 1307, appear through the courtesy of Mr. L. V. Lockwood.

No. 1305 is a walnut sideboard table with a white marble top. The legs and the Dutch, or club, feet place the table in the Queen Anne style. The legs are straight, not in the cabriole form. These straight legs with Dutch feet, said to be found chiefly in Rhode Island, are also shown in No. 1308 and are referred to in No. 1286 and in note 2, A in section 25. The tops of the legs are rounded. About 1720–1750.

No. 1306 is a mahogany sideboard table whose legs and feet indicate it to be in the Chippendale style; and the shaggy claw feet seem to place its origin in Philadelphia. The top is white marble. The skirt is cut in cyma curves and the knees are carved with leaves. This table is not a large piece, being twenty–nine inches high and four feet long. About 1750–1760.

No. 1307 is also in the Chippendale style, having the straight rectangular legs which are seen on so many of his chairs and other articles. The top is of wood. The brackets at the intersection of the legs and the "skirt" are a feature of the Chippendale style. This is a higher table than the previous ones. About 1760–1770.

Passing to the "dining tables," it is said that few tables in the Queen Anne or Chippendale style can be identified as dining tables exclusively. All which appear to be dining tables have drop–leaves, but may have been used in other rooms than the dining room. As mentioned in the third paragraph of section 155, gate–leg tables were often used as dining tables. It is said that there are no designs of dining tables in any of the books of the cabinet makers in the time of Chippendale. In Mr. Lockwood's "Colonial Furniture" are illustrations of several tables which he regards as dining tables of the two periods mentioned, and Nos. 1309 and 1310 are copied here.[4]

No. 1308 is a large walnut table in the Queen Anne style, about nine feet long and five feet wide across the open leaves. The eight legs are straight, a form of leg said to be found chiefly in Rhode Island, as mentioned in the comment on No. 1305. It is said that this table has always been in Southern Maryland until recently, and others with similar legs have been seen by the writer in Williamsburg, Virginia. The feet are of the Dutch, or club, type. The joints between the leaves and the central part of the top are faintly seen in the engraving. It is probable that this table was not made for a dining table; see "Antiques," July, 1933, page 12. About 1725–1740.

2. An Adam style sideboard table, with pedestals and urns on the side, is No. 948, A, in the chapter on sideboards.

3. These two are figures 197 and 201 in Mr. Lockwood's "Colonial Furniture," volume 1.

4. No. 719 in the second volume of Mr. Lockwood's "Colonial Furniture" is our No. 1309 and our No. 1310 is on his page 328.

No. 1309 is regarded as a walnut dining table, with a rectangular top and six cabriole legs having ball and claw feet. The outer four of these legs swing out and support the leaves and the two in the centre are stationary. About 1725–1750.

In No. 1310 the mahogany and the ornamental carving indicate the Chippendale style. As in the preceding table, there are on each side two legs which swing out and support the leaves, and the four legs under the frame, in the centre, are stationary. One of the two drawers is seen, under which is a carving and there is also carving on the knees of the legs. About 1760–1770.

We now examine the dining tables in the Hepplewhite style. These tables are chiefly found in the South, especially in Maryland. They are almost all of the same general character, having two rounded end parts which may be connected, thus forming a rounded or oval table, and frequently having one or more separate rectangular sections which may be placed within the end parts, thus forming a longer table. In some cases, as in No. 1313, a rectangular leaf is attached to one or both of the end parts, by means of which the table may be made longer without using a separate section. All of these dining tables are of mahogany.

The inlaid decorations of these tables are very pleasing. The places where decoration may be used are on the surface under the top, called the "skirt" or "apron" or "frieze," and on the legs, and at these places the inlaid forms of the Hepplewhite–Sheraton period are seen. The chief differences in the appearance of the tables here shown are in these decorations and the number of legs. Some of the dining tables in this style are without decoration of any kind, but the very plain ones are not shown here. The legs are square, straight and tapered as on the sideboards and card tables in the Hepplewhite style. About 1785–1800.

In No. 1311 only the two ends are used, making an almost round table. On each of these ends are four legs and some of these eight legs are perhaps too close together for the comfort of those seated at them, and in this respect the table may rival the gate–leg tables referred to at the end of the third paragraph of section 155. Under the top, on the "skirt," are inlaid designs of parallel lines with rounded ends, a form which has been previously referred to several times, as in note 6 in section 127 of the chapter on sideboards. The legs are tapered in the Hepplewhite manner and some are inlaid on more than one of the surfaces. Bands of satinwood are near the feet, which are supplied with casters. About 1785–1800.

No. 1312 is a wide table from which some of the inner leaves have been removed for the purpose of this illustration. It is supported by ten legs which terminate in brass feet with casters. The long inlaid oval in front, with corresponding ones at other places, the small ovals above the legs, the strings of flowers inlaid on the legs and the satinwood bands all contribute to the decorative design of this table. About 1785–1800.

In No. 1313 each of the ends has a drop–leaf so that the table may be enlarged by the use of one or both leaves which may be supported by one or both

1305 (Upper) Lockwood Col. Furn., Fig. 197.   1306 (Upper) Anonymous.
1307 (Centre) Lockwood Col. Furn., Fig. 201.   1308 (Centre) Georgetown University.
1309 (Lower) Lockwood Col. Furn., Fig. 719.   1310 (Lower) Mr. L. V. Lockwood.

of two legs which swing. Under the top are rectangular inlaid forms and oval medallions and on the eight legs are inlaid strings of flowers. Here also, as in No. 1311, the tapering legs are inlaid on more than one of the surfaces. About 1785–1800.

No. 1314 is a two–part table with an oval top, formed by having a central leaf between the two rounded ends. There are eight square and tapered legs, which are inlaid with lines on the front; and other inlaid forms are seen under the top. This table is fifty–three inches wide and six feet long. About 1790–1800.

No. 1315 is shown with the two ends forming almost a round table and with a fifth leg supporting the centre. With only five legs in all, there can be no discomfort to those seated at the table. As in many other pieces the inlay is pleasing, resembling No. 1311 in that respect. About 1785–1800.

In No. 1316 we see one end of a dining table to which a large rectangular leaf is attached. In this form it is not suitable for dining purposes but may serve well as a side table by removing the leaf. A feature of the table is the inlaid coat of arms of the Bosley family, of Maryland, one of which was the original possessor of the table and was an ancestor of the present owner. About 1785–1800.

No. 1317 is a three part table with sixteen legs. Each of the two ends with their drop leaves is supported by six legs and the central section has four legs. The edge of the top has lines of inlay and the outer legs are ornamented with an inlaid design. Under the top at the ends are oval medallions and three vertical lines of inlay of the same type as the six lines in the sideboard No. 955 and several other pieces. This dining table is almost fourteen feet long and its width is four feet. About 1785–1800.

In No. 1318 the ends are semi–circular, or nearly so. Fourteen legs support the ends and the extensions. The legs are rectangular and some are grooved, a form of ornamentation used in the Chippendale style and followed in that of Hepplewhite; other examples of grooving are in the Pembroke tables Nos. 1405 and 1409. About 1785–1800.

The next dining tables, Nos. 1319–1327 are in the Sheraton style. The principal features distinguishing the dining tables in this style from those in the Hepplewhite style are that the legs, if they are straight, are round and generally reeded; that in many cases the legs are not straight but curved, and support a platform or pedestal; and that inlay was not used, but carving was often used on the curved legs and on other parts. All of the tables are of mahogany, as in the Hepplewhite style.

No. 1319 is a dining table of the same general shape as the preceding one in the Hepplewhite style, but with rounded corners and twelve reeded legs. The edge of the top is also reeded. About 1810–1820.

Comparing No. 1320 with No. 1313 in the Hepplewhite style, we see that from each a drop–leaf hangs; and in each the legs are straight and tapering. In No. 1320, however, there is no inlay, the legs are round and reeded and the feet end in brass sockets fitted with casters. The edge of the top is also reeded. There are ten legs, two of which are swinging legs which hold up the leaves. The table

1311 (UPPER) MRS. C. P. ROGOW.
1313 (CENTRE) ANONYMOUS.
1315 (LOWER) MRS. A. ADGATE DUER.

1312 (UPPER) MR. J. G. D'ARCY PAUL.
1314 (CENTRE) ANONYMOUS.
1316 (LOWER) MR. GEORGE W. EVANS, JR.

1317 (Upper) Anonymous.   1318 (Next to Top) Dr. James Bordley, Jr.
1319 (Next to Lower) Mrs. Miles White, Jr.
1320 (Lower) Mr. J. Ramsey Speer.   1321 (Lower) Mrs. Wm. M. Roberts.

1322 (Upper) Dr. Jas. Bordley, Jr.   1323 (Next to Top) Anonymous.
        1324 (Next to Lower) Met. Mus. of Art.
1325 (Lower) Met. Mus. of Art.   1326 (Lower) Met. Mus. of Art.

is four feet wide and when a separate section and all the additional leaves which belong to it are in place it is fourteen feet long and has sixteen legs. The reeding on this table is of finer character than in some later pieces. About 1800–1815.

No. 1321 is of the same type but of somewhat later construction, as is shown by the less delicate reedings which project further outward. Here also are ten legs. In this and the preceding table there is a ring under the reeding on each leg and below the ring the leg continues in the round and tapering form seen on other articles of the Sheraton style, as in the chairs Nos. 276 and 277. About 1810–1820.

Six other dining tables, Nos. 1322–1327, have curved legs. Some of these tables have two or more pedestals and others have a platform on which are vertical columns supporting the top.

Nos. 1322 and 1323 are examples of the first kind, with two or more pedestals supporting the top. These follow the designs of the English examples of the Sheraton period and are said to have a great advantage in giving "free play to the sitter's knees," an agreeable feature not possessed by many other dining tables of earlier periods, "and on account of this virtue the patterns are sought after in America."[5] These tables were made with either three legs, in the tripod form, or with four legs, and in some pieces both types were used.

No. 1322 is composed of three parts. The top of each part is supported by a round "turned" pedestal which rests upon finely reeded concave legs sloping downward and outward. The legs terminate in brass cups with casters. There are three legs on each of the end sections and four legs on the central section, the latter being for extra stability. About 1800–1815.

No. 1323 is a two–part table. The central portion of the top is an extension leaf[6] supported by two swinging brackets which open from the pedestals. The edges of the top are reeded and on each pedestal is a reeded form of a vase. The legs are carved with acanthus leaves on the upper portion, below which they are reeded. This piece is in the style of Sheraton, and its ornamental reeding and carving suggest the workmanship of Duncan Phyfe. About 1810–1825.

The next three illustrations, Nos. 1324–1326, are of two dining tables made by Duncan Phyfe, which are now in the Metropolitan Museum of Art, through whose courtesy they are shown here. Nos. 1325 and 1326 are views of the same table.[7] These tables follow the Sheraton style which was in fashion during the

5. As remarked by the English writer Mr. G. Owen Wheeler in his "Old English Furniture," third edition, pages 576–578, where an illustration is given of a Sheraton style dining table with two pedestals, each with three legs. See also a remark quoted in section 155, paragraph 3, in connection with gate–leg tables.

6. The device by which tables may be extended and reduced in length by a telescopic arrangement immediately under the top was invented in 1800 by Robert Gillow, one of the celebrated firm of cabinet makers in London commonly called "Gillows." This was in the Sheraton period.

7. The book "Furniture Masterpieces of Duncan Phyfe," by Mr. Charles Over Cornelius, published for the Metropolitan Museum of Art by Doubleday, Page & Company, 1922, contains fifty–six illustrations, including Nos. 1325 and 1326 here shown, which are on plate 39.

period of Phyfe's best work, about 1800–1820, and have some of the embellishments and fine workmanship which have made his furniture famous. They are, however, regarded as in the Sheraton style, not in a "Duncan Phyfe style," for the reasons mentioned in sections 20 and 171. In these tables the features are the platforms supported by the four curved legs, and the four columns which rest upon the platform and hold the top. A similar platform is seen on the table No. 1640.

No. 1324 is a long table consisting of two end tables and one central one. The top of each part is supported by four carved columns. The delicate carving on the columns and on the upper part of the legs, not well seen in a small engraving, is a decorative feature used by Phyfe. The form of the legs is not one of the best of the Phyfe designs. About 1800–1820.

Nos. 1325 and 1326 are two illustrations of another dining table by Phyfe, the first showing a side view and the second showing an end view. Here there are two platforms with carved columns and carved and curved legs which terminate in brass feet finished with casters. The graceful proportions of this table, especially when seen from the end as in No. 1326, and its decorative elegance, are much admired. About 1800–1820.

Table No. 1327 is of an unusual type and would be better understood if it had been photographed in the same position as the similar table No. 770 in volume 2 of Mr. Lockwood's "Colonial Furniture."[8] At each of the two ends is a group of three legs, two of which extend sideways as in No. 1326; the third leg is attached to the other two at a right angle. The groups may be turned inward as in the illustration, or outward if desired. Above the legs are inverted lyre–shaped supports to which the top is attached. About 1800–1820.

The next four dining tables, Nos. 1328–1331, are in the Empire style, which will be recognized by the heavily built pedestals which are used instead of the lighter and more graceful ones seen above, and also, in some places, by the animals' claw feet and other somewhat inelegant carvings.

In No. 1328 each of the heavy pedestals is supported by four legs which are not well seen and in form resemble those in No. 1322, with which this dining table may be compared. The top is partly supported by four swinging brackets About 1815–1830.

In No. 1329 only the two ends of the table are shown. Here also are massive pedestals carved mainly with leaves. The heavy reeded legs end in animals' claw feet, and coarse leaf carvings are on the "skirt." About 1820–1830.

In No. 1330 the heavy pedestals are ornamented with a series of rings. The legs are in a form used in the Empire period; the upper portion of the legs is carved in a plain design and the lower portion is reeded. About 1820–1830.

No. 1331 is one end of an elaborately ornamented dining table which is now used as a side table. As in the previous Empire style pieces, we see the massive

8. An illustration of a similar dining table, with a comment, is in "Antiques," January, 1932, page 32.

1327 (Upper) Mr. C. W. L. Johnson.

1329 (Centre) Coll. of Late Mrs. J. Stabler.

1331 (Lower) Est. of Mrs. J. H. Whiteley.

1328 (Upper) Mr. J. L. G. Lee.

1330 (Centre) Mrs. F. G. Boyce, Jr.

1332 (Lower) Mrs. Joseph Whyte.

1333 (UPPER) MR. & MRS. M. P. MORFIT.   1334 (UPPER) MR. JOHN C. TOLAND.
1335 (CENTRE) ANONYMOUS.   1336 (CENTRE) ANONYMOUS.
1337 (LOWER) MRS. S. JOHNSON POE.   1338 (LOWER) MISS HELEN H. CAREY.

carved pedestal under which is a heavy platform carved on the top. The grotesque legs are carved to represent those of animals. About 1820–1830.

No. 1332 is a dining table in the late Empire style. It is not shown here as an antique in the strict sense of the word, but as an example of the last development of style before the Victorian style became the fashion. The heavy legs, "scrolled" in form, and the heavy base, very close to the feet of a sitter, are characteristic of the period in which massive size and great weight were the predominant features. The two columns in the centre were probably made to support an extension leaf. About 1835–1840.

Section 158. Rectangular tea tables.—Small tables made especially for tea service, and hence known as tea tables, were in two forms. In one form the table has four legs and a top which is rectangular, or nearly so, and in the other form there are three legs, making a tripod, and generally a round top. These tables were very popular for many years from about 1725, but in the time of Hepplewhite and Sheraton they were almost superseded for tea service by the Pembroke tables, such as some of those shown in section 163.

The rectangular tables may be recognized as tea tables by their small size and especially by having in most cases a rim,[1] or raised edge, which projects above the level of the top to prevent the cups and saucers and other articles from slipping off, and gives to the top the appearance of a tray.[2] Under the top in the earlier tables, such as Nos. 1333–1335, there is a plain surface three or four inches deep; in the three later tables, Nos. 1336–1338, about that much space was often taken by a drawer.

No. 1333 is a rectangular tea table in the Queen Anne style with cabriole legs terminating in pointed Dutch, or club, feet, a type of foot which is shown as figure 12 in illustration No. 11. A rim, or raised edge, is around the top and below is a plain surface under which is a small skirt which "flares," or slants, outward. About 1735–1750.

No. 1334 is also in the Queen Anne style, with cabriole legs ending in round Dutch, or club, feet with "shoes" underneath. Here the skirt is conspicuous and its flare is clearly seen. The knees at the top of the legs are carved in a shell pattern, and the fact that all four knees are carved, and not those on the front only, shows that the table was meant to be seen from all sides. About 1735–1750.

In No. 1335 the skirt is cut in a series of double cyma curves, as to which see section 23. The legs are long, slender and graceful and terminate in Dutch, or club, feet. This table is about twenty–eight inches high. About 1735–1750.

---

1. It is said that counterfeits of these tables are made by adding a rim to an old rectangular table with a plain top.

2. Tea trays were fitted with a rim for the same purpose.

Eleven tea tables with four legs are shown in Mr. Lockwood's "Colonial Furniture," figures 729–739, dating from about 1725 to 1770.

The three–legged, or tripod, tea tables are considered in the text and notes in section 159. These charming and convenient tables have long been popular favorites with furniture designers as well as buyers, and many of them rank as minor masterpieces of the cabinet maker's art. Nests of tables, used for tea, are shown in section 174, Nos. 1623–1625.

No. 1336 is a mahogany tea table which became celebrated because it brought at auction the highest price ever paid for an American table.[3] It is in the Chippendale style, as shown by the legs and the ball and claw feet. The rim is cut in the same shape as that of the skirt, which is a modified form of the "block" work shown in the chapter on "Block–front furniture," sections 118–119. The skirt is deep and is not ornamented by carving; but the upper part of the legs is finely carved with leaves. The legs are angular, not round. The date is known to be 1763.

Nos. 1337 and 1338 are in a somewhat different form, each having an unusual kind of rim and also having a wide drawer.

No. 1337 has cabriole legs and Dutch, or club, feet. The corners of the rim project somewhat upward and outward in a curved form. A drawer in tea tables is not often seen, but is occasionally found. The handles on the drawers are of a later period. Perhaps about 1750–1775.

In No. 1338 the rim is somewhat higher than in the preceding piece and resembles the rim of the tripod table shown in No. 1389. The corners of the rim project upward and outward as in the preceding table. The drawer is concave in the upper portion and convex in the lower portion. The escutcheon and handles are in the Chippendale style. Perhaps about 1750–1775.

Section 159. Tripod tables.—This section includes almost all kinds of three-legged tables except the pie–crust tables and the tripod candle stands, the latter of which are merely a certain type of small tripod tables. For convenience the pie–crust tables and the candle stands are considered in separate sections, Nos. 160 and 161.

The tripod[1] form, generally regarded as popularized in England by Chippendale, became fashionable in that country about 1755, and shortly after that

---

3. This tea table was sold at auction for $29,000. It is apparently the one referred to in certain correspondence of John Goddard, cabinet maker, of Newport, Rhode Island, in 1763, who is mentioned in section 114, note 3. It was in the collection of the late Philip Flayderman, of Boston, and was sold in January, 1930, at the American Art Association Anderson Galleries from whose catalogue the above engraving and information are copied.

Our large metropolitan newspapers often report the prices paid for important antiques in their regular news or special columns.

1. A. The word "tripod" as an adjective means "having three feet or legs"; as a noun it means "any object having three feet or legs as a three–legged stool"; Century Dictionary.

B. In "English and American Furniture," by Cescinsky and Hunter, page 212, Mr. Cescinsky writes that "a definite idea is embodied in the tripod form. A table or other article supported on four legs will rock on an uneven floor; one with three only, (a tripod), will rest firmly anywhere." On the plainer type of tripod tables there is no carving and the pedestal is "turned" in a simple form. It is said that these pedestals are often "glorified" by carving them. Mr. Cescinsky mentions on page 214 that in England, by reason of this modern embellishment, the tables without carving are diminishing in number and the supply of ornate ones is increasing.

The words "pedestal," "pillar," "column" and perhaps other words have been used by writers as synonymous in descriptions, as in Mr. Lockwood's Colonial Furniture, page 213, and in "Furniture Masterpieces of Duncan Phyfe," by Mr. C. O. Cornelius, plate 27, and others.

(*Note 1 is continued on page 722.*)

date it became popular in our country. In the Chippendale period it was used for the legs of small round tables, candle stands, pole screens, wig stands and several other articles. In the Hepplewhite–Sheraton period, and later, it served the same purposes and was also used for the pedestals of dining tables and for certain other tables shown in this book. The tables in this section are arranged mainly according to their style and shape, not according to the purposes for which we may think the tables were to be used, because many tables were used for several purposes.

The tripod table is in three parts, the top, the pedestal and the three feet or legs which give the table its name. The top is generally made to tilt, frequently to revolve but often is stationary.

The principal differences in tripod tables of the same type are in their size and shape, the presence or absence of carving or inlay, and the character of the wood and workmanship. These tables were all made in the mahogany period and most of them were of that wood, although some may be of walnut, cherry or other woods. So many tripod tables are owned in private houses that it seems desirable to present a considerable number of them.[2]

The round tops of tripod tables may be divided into five types, known as plain tops, tray tops, (also called "dish" tops), pie-crust tops, plate tops and gallery tops. Almost all of the gallery top type are regarded as of English make and only one is shown here, No. 1343, which is octagonal. These names are fairly descriptive of the tops, as will be seen in the illustrations, and need not be explained here. In addition to the round tops there were also tops in other forms— square, oval and octagonal.

The sizes of these tables varied greatly. The large ones were generally for afternoon tea, with ample space for cups and saucers as well as for the kettle and other accessories.[3] Perhaps the smallest tables were those for holding candles,

(NOTE 1, *continued*)

    C.   The legs of many tripod tables are braced together with pieces of iron screwed into them on the under side where they join the pedestal. The purpose of this is to prevent the legs from breaking away from the pedestal, which would occur if the strain on them from the weight of the upper part and of any objects placed on the top was too great.

    D.   The shrinkage of the tops of round tables as an indication of age is referred to in connection with pie–crust tables in section 160, note 1, E.

    E.   A revival of fashion in England in about 1875–1885 led to the reproduction of tripod tables with fretted galleries in the style of No. 1343. In Mr. Cescinsky's "English Furniture," volume 2, page 209, it is said that there was no intention to deceive in making these reproductions, "the rage for the collection of antique furniture having hardly begun at this period"; but "it is frequently by no means easy to detect them from the originals." In order to strengthen the open frets, they were "laminated," that is, made up of three layers of veneer, the grain of the centre layer being placed at right angles to the grain of the other two layers.

    2.   Most of the tripod tables shown here are small and are fairly well seen in the small engravings. The writer thinks that the reader will prefer to have a large number of small but clear illustrations rather than a less number of large illustrations. Many of the tables are very similar.

    3.   In "English and American Furniture," by Cescinsky and Hunter, pages 222–224, Mr. Cescinsky makes some interesting remarks on "purpose–made furniture," such as tables made for card–playing and others made for afternoon tea. He mentions that "an accompanying piece was the urn

known as "candle stands." Between these large and small tables there were many of intermediate sizes which were useful for tea or candles or ornaments or any objects of small size. These medium sized tables are by far the most numerous, and it is often difficult or impossible to determine whether such a piece is a table or a stand; in fact, between a small tea table and a candle stand of the same character there is often no real difference. Section 161 on tripod candle stands and section 160 on pie–crust tables should be examined in connection with the present section.

The first group of tripod tables here shown, Nos. 1339–1344, has a type of foot often used on these tables, known as a "snake" or "snake head" foot, which is more clearly shown in figure 20 in illustration No. 11 in section 25. The principal difference in these tables is in the design of the top and of the pedestal supporting it. All have small tops averaging about sixteen inches in diameter. They are regarded as being in the Chippendale style.

No. 1339 has a rim around the top, giving to the top a resemblance to a tray, or dish, and hence is known as a "tray top," or "dish top," table. The tapering pedestal, although long and without any ornamental "turnings," except at the base, gives a graceful appearance to the table. The legs are in the usual form and terminate in snake feet. About 1760–1790.

No. 1340, also, has a tray top. A vase–shaped "turning" is on the lower part of the pedestal. About 1760–1790.

No. 1341 has a plain top, meaning one without ornamentation by a rim or otherwise. Under the top is an attachment, sometimes called a "birdcage," by which the top may be tilted or revolved or both, a device which is more fully illustrated in connection with the tripod table No. 1373. About 1760–1790.

No. 1342 is another tray top table, more ornamental than the previous ones, the pedestal being fluted and turned. The legs are pointed, not rounded, on the upper side. The height is twenty–two inches. About 1760–1790.

In No. 1343 the top is octagonal in shape and is ornamented with a fretwork "gallery" around the edge. The presence of a gallery is generally regarded as

(NOTE 3, *continued*)

table made to support the silver or plated hot water urns of the period. The water was heated before being placed in these urns and kept to a high temperature" by a certain device. "The secret of making tea with water absolutely boiling was unknown at this date (the Chippendale period) and is far from being general in America at the present day." An American urn stand is shown in "Antiques," April, 1930, page 330. An old saying is apropos here: "Except the kettle boiling be, filling the tea pot spoils the tea."

In "Antique Furniture," page 348, by Mr. F. W. Burgess, an English writer, it is said that tripod tea tables and coffee tables with cabriole legs were made from about 1760 when the fashion for drinking tea began and there were no tables for holding the fine china that was made for the new beverage. These tables were so useful for the purpose that long after the cabriole leg passed out of style in chairs and other furniture it remained in vogue in the tripod tea tables. Tripod tables with cabriole legs had, however, been made before the tea drinking fashion began, and were used as candle stands. Some of the little tripods were no doubt intended as stands for ornaments.

Urn stands and other varieties of small tables were used in connection with tea tables.

indicating that the table is an English one, which is probably the case with this table as it was inherited with other furniture known to be English. A gallery of this type is called a "spindle" gallery because it is made with small spindles. A note on tables with fretwork galleries is numbered 1, E in this section. About 1760–1790.

In No. 1344 the top is tilted upward in order to show clearly its design. The round inner portion is composed of eight wedge–shaped pieces whose points unite at the centre somewhat in the manner of No. 1370. A circle of inlay separates the central portion from the outer one. The fine grain and color do not appear well in the engraving. About 1760–1790.

In the next group, Nos. 1345–1350, the cabriole legs and the ball and claw feet place the tripod tables in the full Chippendale style. Here also the tops average about sixteen inches in diameter.

No. 1345 has a plain round top under which is a "birdcage" attachment by which the top may be revolved and tilted, as in No. 1373. The pedestal is turned in a vase form. About 1760–1790.

No. 1346 has a tray top, and the pedestal is turned in a plain column under which is an enlarged turning known as a "bulb," which is also seen on No. 1347 and others. About 1760–1790.

No. 1347 is also a tray top table and has a "birdcage" as in No. 1373, under which is a pedestal having a form somewhat similar to that in the preceding table. About 1760–1790.

No. 1348 is an English table which is in the same ownership as No. 1343. The rim is finely carved and there is also carving on the pedestal. In the legs there is an opening which gives a lighter appearance to them. About 1760–1790.

No. 1349 appears with the top up, showing the rim to some extent. The pedestal is turned in a vase design under which is a bulb. The claws holding the balls are conspicuous, as in No. 1346. About 1760–1790.

No. 1350 is more ornate than the other tables in this group. Under the tray top is a "birdcage," below which the pedestal is turned for a few inches and then carved. The legs are carved with leaves. About 1760–1790.

The next eleven tables, Nos. 1351–1361 are in the Sheraton style. Here the cabriole legs seen above are superseded by other types of curved legs, the curves being either convex, as in most of the tables, or concave. The tops are without rims and in a variety of forms, and the pedestals are in various designs. Tripod tables were apparently not made with straight tapering legs which are features of the Hepplewhite style.

No. 1351, shown with the top up, is a pleasing tripod table with an oval top, in the centre of which is an inlaid American eagle with a shield and arrows, but without the stars supposed to indicate the number of States in the Union as on the desks Nos. 803 and 805. A line of inlay is near the edge. The pedestal is turned in a manner resembling Nos. 1340 and 1354. About 1800–1810.

1339 (Upper) Mr. & Mrs. B. Turn-
      Bull.
1342 (Centre) Miss M. C. Painter.
1345 (Lower) Mrs. T. J. Packard.

1340 (Upper) Mrs. Howard Sill.
1343 (Centre) Mr. & Mrs. E. H.
      McKeon.
1346 (Lower) Mr. & Mrs. B. Turn-
      Bull.

1341 (Upper) Mrs. A. Morris
      Carey.
1344 (Centre) Mr. & Mrs. Wm. M.
      Ellicott.
1347 (Lower) Mrs. Jos. Whyte.

No. 1352 is more ornamental than many others, the top having a border of light wood, and an inlaid centrepiece which is in the same eight–sided form as the top itself. Bands of inlay are on the lower part of the legs. The convex form of legs of this and other tables is shown in Sheraton's "Drawing Book," plate 54 and others. The pedestal is turned with rings. About 1800–1810.

No. 1353, also shown with the top up, has a top with the corners cut in curves. The pedestal is turned in a vase and ring design. About 1800–1810.

No. 1354 has a plain top under which is a "birdcage" device as in several other pieces. The turning on the pedestal is a vase as in No. 1351 and others. Lines of inlay are on the legs. About 1800.

In No. 1355 the top, at the corners, is cut in curves. The pedestal has a vase pattern with other designs. About 1800–1810.

No. 1356 is a curly maple table which was photographed with a leaf screen and a candle stick which, however, do not indicate that the table is a candle stand. The top is round and the pedestal has a vase design. About 1800–1810.

No. 1357 has an octagonal top which is grooved on the edges. The turned pedestal has a vase over which is a plain column. The legs seem to be somewhat heavy for the other parts. About 1800–1810.

No. 1358 is a curly maple table with a top cut in a concave curve on each side and a convex curve at each corner. The pedestal is turned in a vase pattern with a plain section above. About 1800–1810.

No. 1359 has a top somewhat similar to that of No. 1355. The lower part of the pedestal is turned in a vase form and is reeded, an ornamental treatment which will be seen in No. 1367 and other tables of the finer sort. About 1800–1810.

In No. 1360 the curved legs are more nearly upright than in the previous tables, giving an appearance of greater height. The top is octagonal and has a line of inlay near the edge. About 1800–1810.

In No. 1361 also the top is octagonal. The pedestal has a heavy reeding, similar to that on the legs of the dining table No. 1321. The base of the pedestal is larger than in the preceding pieces. The legs are concave and heavily reeded, terminating in brass feet. About 1810–1820.

No. 1362 is in the early Empire style, as is indicated by the heavy base of the pedestal and the carved portion having the familiar pineapple design of the period, often seen, for example, on the posts of bedsteads, as on No. 1071. The top is rounded at the corners. About 1815–1830.

Nos. 1363–1365 are unusual tables. The first two are of the Sheraton period, but the third is earlier in date.

In No. 1363 the square top of light wood is decorated with delicate flowers in the centre, inlaid fans at the corners and inlaid lines around the sides. The upper portions of the legs are convex and are carved with leaves. The feet are grooved in the same manner as the bottoms of the supports on the dressing glass No. 1270. Probably about 1815–1820.

1348 (UPPER) MR. & MRS.
    E. H. McKEON.
1351 (CENTRE) HAMMOND-HAR-
    WOOD HOUSE.
1354 (LOWER) MRS. MILES
    WHITE, JR.

1349 (UPPER) MRS. PAUL H.
    MILLER.
1352 (CENTRE) MR. E. G. MILLER,
    JR.
1355 (LOWER) MISS M. C. PAINTER.

1350 (UPPER) ANONYMOUS.
1353 (CENTRE) MRS. T. J.
    LINDSAY.
1356 (LOWER) MR. & MRS.
    W. A. DIXON.

In No. 1364 the feature is the group of three slender turned columns, instead of one pedestal, supporting the top and resting upon a small platform. The columns may be compared with those on the Sheraton style card table No. 1550. The legs are carved at the top, and terminate in brass feet.[4] About 1820.

In No. 1365 there is the same kind of legs and snake feet as Nos. 1339–1344. At the position occupied in some other tables by pedestals or columns, supporting the top, there is a cabinet with a door upon which a shell is carved. This cabinet closely resembles in form the central compartments seen in so many desks in the Chippendale style, such as Nos. 791–794 and others. The square top has doubtless been substituted for an original round one.[5] About 1760–1780.

The next two tripod tables, Nos. 1366–1367, are examples of fine workmanship and elegant design.

No. 1366 is a side table, not a card table, as it has no folding top. The top has three curves in the so-called "clover–leaf" design which is seen also in the Sheraton style card tables Nos. 1548 and 1549. The upper portion of the pedestal is fluted and below is a vase carved with leaves. The upper parts of the concave legs are carved with leaves, under which are reedings. The brass feet are in the form of animals' claws, and have casters. About 1810–1820.

No. 1367 is a similar table made by Duncan Phyfe and now in the Metropolitan Museum of Art. The top is reeded on the edges and is in a series of curves. The upper portion of the pedestal is in a plain design, below which is a reeded vase. The concave legs are reeded and terminate in brass feet and casters. About 1810–1820.

In No. 1368 the rectangular top is plain on one side and on the other side is a board for chess and other games.[6] The drawer below is for the accessories of the games. The top is supported by a vertical sliding bar which holds the board at a desired height. The delicate reeding of the pedestal and of the concave legs will be noticed. About 1810–1820.

The next three tripod tables, Nos. 1369–1371, are in the Empire style, which is recognized by the heavy pedestals and the kind of platforms and feet.

In No. 1369 the base of the pedestal is fully but coarsely carved with leaves and other objects, and rests upon a large and heavy triangular platform with concave sides. The feet are carved and end in animals' paws. About 1820–1830.

In No. 1370 the finely veneered top is in twelve wedge–shaped parts which extend to a brass circle in the centre, a method which is also used in No. 1344. A carved form of vase is at the lower end of the pedestal, under which is a base in the form of a dish. The platform is of the same type as that in the preceding table. The feet are brass, in a scroll design. About 1820–1830.

4.   In "Antiques" May, 1927, pages 364–365, two tables are shown which have four slender and fluted columns supporting large round tops.

5.   In "Antiques," November, 1923, pages 224–225, is an article illustrating three tables of this type having large round tilting tops and larger compartments than the one here shown.

6.   An article entitled "Backgammon tables of the Eighteenth Century," by Mr. Robert Tasker Evans, with many illustrations, is in "The Antiquarian," March, 1931, pages 33–37. The article of Mr. Evans is also referred to in section 169, note 2. The tables are not in the tripod form.

1357 (Upper) Md. Soc. Col. Dames. 1358 (Upper) Mrs. J. S. Gibbs, Jr. 1359 (Upper) Mrs. F. T. Redwood.
1360 (Centre) Mr. & Mrs. M. P. 1361 (Centre) Dr. H. J. Berkley. 1362 (Centre) Dr. M. A. Abrams.
  Morfit. 1364 (Lower) Anonymous. 1365 (Lower) Mr. Morris Whit-
1363 (Lower) Mrs. F. P. Garvan. ridge.

1366 (UPPER) MR. & MRS. BAYARD TURNBULL.
1368 (CENTRE) MR. EDGAR G. MILLER, JR.
1370 (LOWER) MR. EDGAR G. MILLER, JR.

1367 (UPPER) ANONYMOUS.
1369 (CENTRE) MISS HELEN H. CAREY.
1371 (LOWER) JUDGE F. N. PARKE.

730

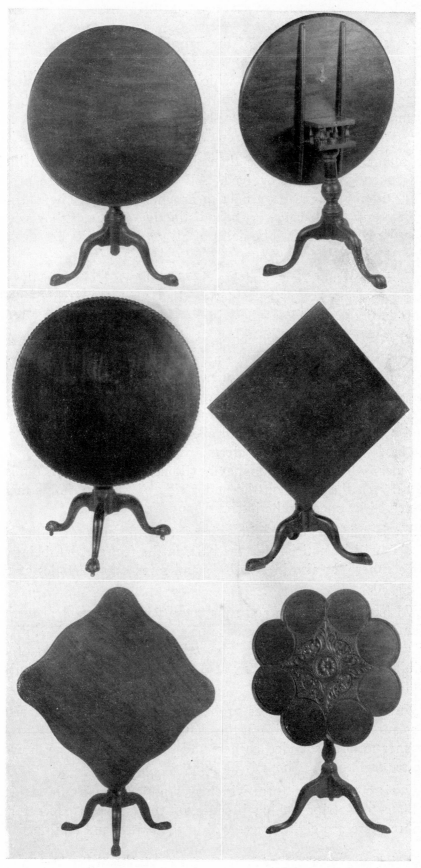

1372 (Upper) Mrs. I. R. Trimble.
1374 (Centre) Coll. of Mrs. J. Stabler.
1376 (Lower) Md. Society of Colonial
        Dames.

1373 (Upper) Mrs. I. R. Trimble.
1375 (Centre) Chase House,
        Annapolis.
1377 (Lower) Anonymous.

No. 1371 shows the last type of the Empire style. The pedestal has lost its former shape and seems to represent a four–sided vase. The platform is round and is supported by three scroll feet which are in about the same shape as those on the sewing table No. 1580, which is illustrated on page 809, and belongs to the same late Empire period. About 1830–1840.

With No. 1372 we begin another type of tripod tables. Almost all of these have large round tops, often more than three feet in diameter, which may be tilted and frequently may be revolved. All of these tables were probably used as tea tables, although some have no rim around the top. The pie–crust tables belong to this group, but because of their distinctive character they are considered separately in the next section. The dates of all of these tables are probably about 1760–1780.

No. 1372 is the front view, and No. 1373 is the rear view, of the same table. The top has a rim and hence the table is called a tray–top table. The legs and snake feet are in the same style as those in Nos. 1339–1344. About 1760–1780.

In No. 1373 we see the construction of the "birdcage" by which the top may be tilted or revolved or both. First we notice the two long pieces of wood, called "cleats," which are screwed on the under side of the top and tend to prevent it from warping. The base of the "birdcage" consists of a square piece of wood resting on the round pedestal which extends loosely through a round opening in the base and permits it to revolve; and over the base are four small posts which connect the base with its top. The cleats are connected with the top of the base by pivots by means of which the top may be tilted. When the table top is down, the latch, seen between the cleats on the under side of the top, holds the top down until it is released by opening the latch. About 1760–1780.

No. 1374 is a tripod table with a large top, the edge of which is cut in a rope design. It will be noticed that the balls in the feet are flat, being only about one–half of a sphere, as also in No. 1378 and some other articles of the period. About 1770–1780.

No. 1375 has a large plain and square top which is attached to the pedestal in a position which gives an appearance of greater height and width than if its sides were upright and horizontal. This table and other articles of the period are on exhibition in the Chase House, at Annapolis; the house was built in 1770–1771. About 1770–1780.

No. 1376 has a top which was probably made of two boards instead of the usual one, as appears from a joint in the centre. The form is that of a square top cut in a manner to have rounded corners and serpentine sides, with cyma curves, as to which see section 23. About 1770–1780.

No. 1377 is a table in a form which was popular in England. It has been called a "plate–top" tripod table because of the curved spaces for plates or saucers.[7] Here there are eight spaces within the raised and scalloped rim and in

7. Tables of this type are illustrated in Mr. Lockwood's "Colonial Furniture," volume 2, figure 752, and in Mr. Cescinsky's "English Furniture," volume 2, figure 211.

the centre are elaborately carved leaves and figures. The legs are carved and the "snake" feet are of the same type as those seen in Nos. 1339–1341. Tables with a similar form of top, but without the eight spaces or the central carving, have been called "scalloped" tables and by other partially descriptive terms. This table is doubtless of English make. It has been regarded as an original table of the period, but the owner is of the opinion that the eight spaces and the carving in the centre are "glorifications" of later date than the date of its arrival in Charleston, South Carolina, where it was found. About 1760–1780.

Section 160. Pie–crust tables.—These are the most highly esteemed of the tripod tables. In their general form they follow the tables Nos. 1372–1374, having a large circular top made of a single piece of wood, usually mahogany; the top always tilts and generally revolves; and there is a pedestal which rests upon three wide–spreading cabriole legs with feet of the "snake," or the ball and claw, type, the latter generally birds' claws. The distinctive ornamental feature is that the raised edge of the top, instead of being plain, as in other tables, is carved in a series of curves which are supposed to resemble the edge of the crust of a pie.[1]

Mr. Lockwood, in his "Colonial Furniture," volume 2, page 213, mentions that the type of edge most frequently used consists of a combination of only three different curves which are repeated around the entire raised edge; and he points out that if these three curves vary in their relative sizes on different tables the tops have a different appearance, although they have the same curves. This feature

1. A. The pie–crust table is a development from the plain tripod tables, such as No. 1372, with the edge cut in curves and generally with carving on the pedestal, legs and feet.

B. The word "pie–crust," as applied to these tables, originated in England. The pie which is honored by the use of the form of its edge as an ornamental feature of these tables, was probably an English cold veal pie. Our American cabinet makers followed the design of the English pie–crust table, but our cooks fortunately abandoned the English cold veal pie.

C. Mr. Cescinsky, in "English and American Furniture," pages 213–214, states that the word pie–crust "expresses nothing in particular, and is copied, perhaps, from the small silver trays—'waiters' as they are styled—of the period."

D. The high prices brought by these tables have led to much faking. A table with a plain top may be furnished with an applied edge cut in a pie–crust form. The wood of a plain top may be cut down in a manner to produce a raised rim, in which case the original thickness of the wood will be noticeably reduced. Plain pedestals and legs have been "glorified" by recent carving; see the previous section, note 1, B, and also No. 1377. These faking tricks may be discovered by an expert cabinet maker who knows the details of the making of antique furniture, but will seldom be noticed by an amateur.

E. The round top of any table will surely shrink *across* the grain, not *with* the grain, and the length across the grain will therefore be less than with the grain. If the top of an alleged antique pie–crust table is in a perfect circle, it is probably a fake. If a round top has been recently made of old wood which has already shrunk all it can, the top may be a perfect circle and the substitution may be apparent. In the small pie–crust table No. 1379, the shrinkage is three–eighths of an inch as mentioned in the comment.

F. An article entitled "A study of American Pie–crust Tables," by Mr. Wm. M. Hornor, Jr., is in the "International Studio," June, 1931, pages 38–40.

will be referred to in the comments. In some of the tables other forms of edges are seen, all of a character adapted to the round shape of the top.

In addition to the ornamental pie–crust edge, these tables are often decorated with fine carving on the pedestal and on the legs and feet. A flattened ball, or "bulb," on the lower part of the pedestal, as shown in No. 1388, is said to be an indication of the workmanship of Philadelphia, where the finest American pie–crust pieces were made. Only a few pie–crust tables were made in New England. These tables are all of the Chippendale period.

In all fine tripod tables much of the charm comes from the harmony of size between the top and the legs. This is particularly true in the case of pie–crust tables, which being elegant in workmanship require elegance in design. In all cases the size and diameter of the top should be in proper proportion to the spread of the legs. A table with a small top should not have wide–spreading legs, and vice versa. The eye of the trained observer, accustomed to the best, will discriminate between the perfect and the merely good.

In pie–crust tables the chief differences are in the combination of curves on the edge, the number of repetitions of that combination, the carving on the pedestal and legs, and the kind of feet. As the edge is the distinctive feature, the tables are shown with their tops up, hiding almost all of the pedestal; but in order that a fine pedestal may be seen in some detail, one is shown without the top in No. 1388. In Nos. 1378–1381 the same design on the edge appears six or more times on each table. This design was apparently the favorite one.

In No. 1378, at the centre of the top, we see a short projection which appears to be straight, but which is generally slightly curved, as it is a curve of the circumference of the round board from which the top was made. To the right of this circumference curve is a small half–round curve; next to the right is a long serpentine curve, to the right of which is another half–round curve. These four curves constitute one section of the pie–crust design of this table. This section appears eight times on the edge of the table. On the pedestal a carved bulb will be seen, and the legs are also carved, terminating in flat ball and claw feet. About 1760–1780.

In No. 1379 also there are eight sections on the edge, and the curves are the same as in the preceding table and are of almost the same relative size. Here the feet are in the snake form, as in Nos. 1339–1344 in the previous section. The top of this small table measures twenty–four inches with the grain and three–eighths of an inch less across the grain, probably indicating the shrinkage referred to in note 1, E. About 1760–1780.

In No. 1380 the relative sizes of the same three curves vary somewhat from those in the two preceding pieces, and the actual sizes of the curved parts are so much smaller that ten sections are required to fill the edge. The pedestal has a carved vase at its base and other carving is on the legs. The feet are in a ball and claw form. The top of this table is twenty–six inches in diameter. About 1760–1780.

1378 (UPPER) DR. JAS. BORDLEY, JR.
1380 (CENTRE) MR. & MRS. H. L. DUER.
1382 (LOWER) MR. JOHN C. TOLAND.

1379 (UPPER) MR. EDGAR G. MILLER, JR.
1381 (CENTRE) DR. M. A. ABRAMS.
1383 (LOWER) MR. & MRS. J. MARSH MATTHEWS.

No. 1381 has the same three curves, appearing six times; but the relative sizes of the curves are somewhat different, the lengths of the circumference curves and the serpentine curves being greater than in the preceding pieces. The upper portion of the leg is carved and the snake feet are also carved. Here there are six sections on the edge. About 1760–1780.

In No. 1382 we notice a variation from the preceding tables, there being no serpentine curves. The circumference curve and the two half–round portions are used twelve times. The legs are carved at the top, terminating in a kind of animals' feet. About 1760–1780.

In No. 1383 also there are no serpentine curves. The circumference curve is small, and it and the two half–round portions each appear twenty times on the edge. The base of the pedestal is carved, as are also the upper portions of the legs, and the feet are of the ball and claw pattern. About 1760–1780.

No. 1384 is another table which has only two kinds of curves, the circumference curve and the half–round one. This form is used eighteen times. The base of the pedestal is ringed. The legs are carved on the upper portion and the feet are of the ball and claw type. About 1760–1780.

No. 1385 has a different kind of rim. The circumference curve is at the top as usual, next to which on each side is a half–round, and then a double cyma curve and then another half–round. This section appears eight times. A carved form is at the base of the pedestal and carving is also on the legs which terminate in ball and claw feet. About 1760–1780.

In No. 1386 the carving on the top changes the appearance of the table, which has almost the same three curves in each section as No. 1378. Two of these curves, the circumference curve, which is not exactly at the top here, and the serpentine curve, are decorated with carving; the other curve, the half–round, is plain. Each section here appears eight times. The legs are carved and the feet are of the snake type. About 1760–1780.

No. 1387 is also a handsomely decorated table, not exactly of the pie–crust type, but resembling the type in some respects. Here the edge is cut in nine "C" curves, (as to which see the mirror No. 1103 and the comment), nine shells and eighteen other curves. The pedestal and legs are decorated with carving. About 1760–1780.

No. 1388 shows the pedestal and feet of a fine pie–crust table on a larger scale than in the preceding pieces in order that the carving may be more clearly seen. Under the "birdcage" is a fluted column, below which is a carved "flattened" ball or "bulb" which, as mentioned above, is said to be a clear indication of Philadelphia workmanship. The legs are carved and end in ball and claw feet. The carving is of a high quality, but cannot be fully appreciated in a small engraving. It may be mentioned that in all cases where there is carving, it is the "quality" which determines whether or not it adds to or detracts from the elegance of the piece.

In No. 1389 the top is not cut in the usual "pie–crust" form, but may be regarded as being a variation of that type of table. The rim is carved in a series of

1384 (UPPER) MR. S. JOHNSON POE.
1386 (CENTRE) MR. & MRS. E. H. MCKEON.
1388 (LOWER) METROPOLITAN MUSEUM OF
    ART.

1385 (UPPER) MRS. ALEXANDER ARM-
    STRONG.
1387 (CENTRE) MRS. MAURICE F.
    RODGERS.
1389 (LOWER) DR. JAS. BORDLEY, JR.

double cyma curves, (as to which see section 23), which rise above the edge of the table, and between these curves are half–round prominences. There are certain points of resemblance between this top and that of the rectangular tea table No. 1338. The pedestal is fluted above and a vase below is carved. The legs are carved and the feet are of a claw type. About 1750–1775.

Section 161. Tripod candle stands.—The term "tripod candle stand" is often somewhat loosely applied to almost any tripod table with a small top; but in correct usage the term only applies to tripod tables which, because of their small tops or other distinctive features, were apparently made for holding a candlestick rather than for general household purposes. A tripod table with a top of medium size could serve for holding a candlestick as well as one with a small top, but in this section the tripod tables illustrated were probably made only for the purpose of holding candlesticks, because the tops are too small for the service of tea or for other domestic uses, except perhaps for a flower pot or a vase of flowers.[1]

A large number of plain candle stands in a variety of forms were made in our country throughout the eighteenth century. It is said that they come under the class of "folk furniture,"[2] and not many have sufficient merit in design or workmanship to be illustrated here. Three examples of the better sort are shown, Nos. 1390–1392.

No. 1390 is regarded as the oldest of the first three. It is said that candle stands of this type were first made about 1700, and continued to be made for very many years thereafter. The top is sixteen inches square, resting on a turned pedestal which is supported by a cross base. The height is about twenty–six inches. This is in the style of 1700, but may have been made much later.

1. A. Tall candle stands, called "torchères," in pairs and ranging in height from about three feet to five feet, were made in England in the time of Chippendale, who published several designs of them in his "Director," as to which book see section 15. A few of these tall candle stands have been found, especially in some of the southern States. Several are shown in Mr. Wallace Nutting's "Furniture Treasury," Nos. 1322–1328. See Nos. 1397 and 1398 in this volume.

B. These pieces are called "candle stands," not "candle tables." As to the distinction between a "table" and a "stand," see the remarks at the beginning of section 173.

C. In section 169 two card tables Nos. 1478 and 1479 have flat places at the corners for holding candles. These candle places were seldom constructed in card tables after the movable and more convenient candle stands came into fashion.

D. An article entitled "Rare Windsor Candlestands," by Mr. Clarence W. Brazer, is in "Antiques," October, 1924, pages 190–194, with ten illustrations. These pieces have a large or small round top resting on three "turned" legs which, as also the stretchers, resemble those seen on certain Windsor chairs. They are plain, but are interesting on account of their use of the Windsor chair designs.

2. As remarked by Mr. Wallace Nutting in his "Furniture Treasury," volume 1, at No. 1336. Mr. Nutting shows candle stands of this general character in his illustrations Nos. 1318–1393. At No. 1364 he remarks: "The variety of these wooden stands is endless. The author saw in one shop twelve different patterns, all of them new, all purporting to be old. Good patterns were rare and the demand always finds itself met by a certain sort of supply."

As to the word "pedestal" and others see the last note on page 721.

1390 (UPPER) MRS. FRANCIS P.
      GARVAN.
1393 (CENTRE) MR. & MRS.
      H. L. DUER.
1396 (LOWER) COLL. OF LATE
      MRS. J. STABLER.

1391 (UPPER) MRS. FRANCIS P.
      GARVAN.
1394 (CENTRE) MRS. J. S. GIBBS,
      JR.
1397 (LOWER) ANONYMOUS.

1392 (UPPER) HAMMOND–
      HARWOOD HOUSE.
1395 (CENTRE) MRS. HOWARD
      SILL.
1398 (LOWER) ANONYMOUS.

No. 1391 has a round top, eleven inches in diameter, with a raised edge. The turnings of the column are more ornamental than those in the preceding piece. The column rests upon a round platform which is supported by three slanting, or "raked," legs, sometimes called "peg legs." The height is twenty–five inches. Perhaps about 1750–1775.

No. 1392 is often called a screw candle stand, because the round stand intended for candlesticks screws up and down on the pole, thus regulating the height. In this piece there is also an arm which holds two candles. Candle stands of this type were generally about three feet or more high, but were also made in a small form to be placed on a table or elsewhere. About 1725–1750.

Nos. 1393–1398 are candle stands of later date and finer quality.

No. 1393 has a small round tray top supported by a column of which the lower part is ornamented with a ring and vase design. The legs and the snake feet are similar to those of the tripod tables Nos. 1339–1344 in section 159. About 1760–1790.

No. 1394 is a small candle stand, or perhaps a tea kettle stand, only twenty–two inches high. The top is octagonal and has an upright rim. The upper portion of the column is carved in a spiral pattern, as to which see note 2 in section 155. The legs and feet resemble those in the preceding piece. About 1760–1790.

In No. 1395 the top is cut in a series of curves and is supported by a tapering column which has a turned vase at the base. The legs and feet are of the same type as in the tripod tables No. 1345–1350. About 1760–1790.

No. 1396 is a small table with a top in the tray form. The lower part of the column is in the shape of an elongated vase with rings. The legs and feet are of a later period than the other parts and are probably about 1820.

No. 1397 is a tall candle stand, thirty–six inches high. The top is about nine and one–half inches in diameter and has a raised edge. The legs end in ball and claw feet. This and the next piece are examples of "torchères," referred to in note 1, A in this section. About 1760–1780.

No. 1398 is another tall candle stand which differs from the preceding one mainly in the form of the column which is here turned in a series of graceful forms. The top is very small and the feet are of the ball and claw type. About 1760–1780.

Section 162. Certain drop–leaf tables.—The descriptive term "drop–leaf" applies of course to any table having leaves which drop; but certain kinds of drop–leaf tables, in which the drop–leaf is an essential but not the distinctive feature, are known by special names, such as gate–leg tables, butterfly tables, Pembroke tables, library tables, sofa tables and corner tables. Moreover many tables with drop–leaves were used for a special purpose from which they acquire their names, such as dining tables.[1] All of these special kinds of tables are shown in other sections, leaving for this section only a few drop–leaf tables having drop–leaves as their distinctive feature and having a utility value for almost any purpose for which a plain table is desired.

The leaves of these drop–leaf tables, like those of the gate–leg tables, were so made as to hang down on hinges from the sides of the central section when not in use, and when up they were held in position by legs which swing out. When both leaves were extended, the top of the table was sometimes round but usually oval, or rectangular.[2]

The points of difference in the form of these drop–leaf tables are the size and shape of the top, the type of legs, the kind of feet and the treatment of the ends of the central portion. In these features the styles of the Queen Anne period and the Chippendale period will be noticed. Drop–leaf tables of the type here shown passed out of fashion in the time of Hepplewhite and Sheraton.

No. 1399 is an oval drop–leaf table with six legs instead of the usual four. The centre section has four fixed legs and the other two legs swing out and support the leaves. This six–legged type is regarded as more elegant than the type with four legs. The Queen Anne style is indicated by the cabriole legs, here graceful and delicate, and by the Dutch, or club, feet. The end of the central section is cut in a double cyma curve, as to which see section 23. About 1740–1760.

In No. 1400 the leaves are rectangular and their inner edges are made in such a manner that the hinges are not seen, as referred to in note 2, and as in the gate–leg table No. 1297. There are four legs in the cabriole form and the feet are in the Dutch, or club, style with a large "shoe" or "cushion," even larger than those on some of the highboys, such as No. 636; see note 10 in section 85. The end of the centre section is cut in a semi–circular form. About 1740–1760.

No. 1401 is a somewhat smaller drop–leaf table in which the leaves are cut in pleasing curves in about the same design as in the Pembroke tables Nos. 1406–1408 in the next section. The cabriole legs terminate in Dutch three–pointed feet such as are seen on the lowboy No. 692; see figure 11 in illustration No. 11. The end of the centre section is cut in arched curves. About 1740–1760.

1. Many drop–leaf tables were used as dining tables and several of these were shown in section 157. In some cases it may be possible to distinguish those tables from drop–leaf tables which were not intended for dining purposes, but it is difficult to see any clear distinction between them. The larger ones were doubtless used for dining purposes. Gate–leg tables were also much used as dining tables; see section 155. Drop–leaf tables with square or rectangular tops could be coupled together and thus form one long table.

2. In his "English Furniture," volume 2, page 32, Mr. Cescinsky mentions that in England these drop–leaf tables were orginally nearly always rectangular, but later the tops were generally cut to an oval form which was more convenient for the purpose of a dining or centre table.

    The tops or leaves of these tables are frequently missing or in bad condition so that a restoration is necessary. In section 155 on gate–leg tables, note 1, E, are remarks as to the difficulty of determining whether a top is original or otherwise. The hinges connecting the leaves with the central section of the top were of the same type as those of the gate–leg tables, and the usual form of joint was so made as to conceal the hinges, as is well seen in No. 1400; see also note I, F, in section 155.

    The wood is generally either walnut or mahogany.

No. 1402 is a round drop–leaf table with four almost straight legs ending in Dutch, or club, feet. The two side legs are swung out to support the two leaves. This is a·small table about two feet high and with a diameter of twenty–nine inches across the top. The end of the central section is cut in a double cyma curve. The wood is mahogany. About 1740–1760.

No. 1403 has cabriole legs and ball and claw feet. The leaves are rectangular as in No. 1400 and may be connected with another similar table if a larger one is desired. The appearance of a single table of this kind is not as attractive as that of a table with oval or other curved leaves. About 1740–1760.

No. 1404 is an oval top table, with ball and claw feet as in the preceding piece. The upper part of each leg, called the "knee," is carved. The proportions of the leaves seem to be well adapted to the size and shape of the piece. About 1740–1760.

Section 163. Pembroke tables.—The small and attractive drop–leaf tables were apparently first made in the time of Chippendale, but the name "Pembroke" was given at a somewhat later period.[1] Their distinctive feature is that the drop–leaves are short and when open are supported by brackets which swing out under the leaves, instead of by swinging legs such as are seen in previous types of drop–leaf tables. They were popular during the Chippendale, Hepplewhite and Sheraton periods, extending from about 1760 to 1820.

The tables were made with tops of various forms. In the Chippendale period the tops were often in a square shape, but their leaves were as often in a serpentine form. In the Hepplewhite and Sheraton periods the tops are generally in an oval shape, but in some cases the leaves have other curved forms. There is generally one drawer. These tables are finished on all sides, as usual with tables which are meant to stand in the centre of a room, where all parts may be seen. They were often used as tea tables in our country in the Hepplewhite and Sheraton periods, superseding the tripod tables of the Chippendale style.

Nos. 1405–1408 are in the Chippendale style; Nos. 1409–1411 are in a transition[2] form, having features of both the Chippendale and the Hepplewhite styles; Nos. 1412–1414 are in the Hepplewhite style, and Nos. 1415 and 1416 are in the Sheraton style.

In No. 1405 the square legs are grooved in the manner seen in many chairs and other pieces of the Chippendale period. The inner edges of the legs are cut off somewhat, making the legs irregularly shaped and providing flat surfaces for

1. Tables of this type were called "breakfast" tables by Chippendale in his "Directory." In Hepplewhite's "Guide," they are called "Pembroke" tables, and it is said that they "are the most useful of this species of furniture"; and elaborate inlaid designs of them are given. In the "Maryland Gazette," April 10, 1786, John Rutter, a cabinet maker of Baltimore, advertised "Pembroke tables." In Sheraton's "Drawing Book," it is said on page 337 of the edition of 1802 that "the use of this piece is for a gentleman or lady to breakfast on."

2. As to "transition" pieces, see the chapter on chairs, section 51, notes 17 and 43.

1399 (Upper) Mr. Albert G. Towers.   1400 (Upper) Mr. Albert G. Towers.
1401 (Centre) Mrs. Thos. J. Lindsay.   1402 (Centre) Anonymous.
1403 (Lower) Mrs. Arthur Hale.   1404 (Lower) Lockwood Col. Furn., Fig. 724.

the insertion of stretchers. The leaves are short and rectangular. Under the drawer is a molding in the form known as "godroon."[3] About 1760–1780.

No. 1406 is more ornate, the leaves being serpentine on the sides with rounded corners and concave ends. The stretchers are flat, pierced and crossed,[4] and at their intersection is a platform upon which a vase of flowers or other objects could be placed. As in the preceding table the inner edges of the grooved legs are cut off, making flat surfaces in which the stretchers are inserted. About 1760–1780.

No. 1407 has similar leaves and grooved legs. This is a somewhat plain form of the preceding tables, having no decoration or ornamental stretchers. About 1760–1780.

In No. 1408 the leaves are rounded at the corners, and have two concave curves on their sides and one on their ends. The front and back of the top of the central section are also cut in concave curves. The cross–stretchers are vertical and are in an openwork design. About 1760–1780.

Nos. 1409–1411, as mentioned, are transition tables, having features of both the Chippendale and the Hepplewhite styles. In No. 1409 the Chippendale style predominates, the table having square and grooved legs, four carved brackets at the junctions of the legs and the skirt, and convex and concave leaves. The features of the Hepplewhite style are the veneered drawer with inlay and the slight tapering of the legs on the inside, none of which details were used in the Chippendale style. The illustration is taken from the front, and in the rear we see that the table is finished wih a similar veneered drawer front, but no drawer; this is called in England a "sham" drawer. In our country the less descriptive words "blind" or "dummy" are used, not implying, however, an intention to deceive.[5] About 1780–1790.

No. 1410 is a table resembling No. 1406 in having crossed stretchers and also in general form, but it has no ornamental features. The Hepplewhite style is seen in the tapering of the legs. About 1780–1790.

No. 1411 is a transition table in which the features of the Hepplewhite style are more noticeable than those of the style of Chippendale. The principal Chippendale feature is seen in the form of the leaves, which have a serpentine curve

3. This word, sometimes erroneously spelled "gadroon," is derived from the French word "godron," meaning ruffle or plait. As used here it means a curved ruffle or fluted ornament, of great variety in form, straight, concave or convex, used as a carved decoration on tables, chairs and other articles of furniture.

4. The stretchers on these tables are crossed and are known as "cross–stretchers," "X" stretchers or "saltire" stretchers, the latter word meaning the same as "saltier," that is, in the form of a St. Andrew's cross, which is X-shaped. See section 26, note 4.

5. In England, in the latter part of the eighteenth century, "sham" drawers, doors and some other parts were much used, the method being called "shamming." The purpose was to have a proper decorative balance and its use was regarded as a legitimate treatment.

Other examples are on the sideboard No. 953 and others, where two shallow drawers are apparently seen although there is merely one cupboard; on the highboy Nos. 646–647 where three apparently separate drawers are in reality one; on the Sheraton style desk No. 838 where there seem to be drawers at the ends; and on No. 1650 where one door appears to be four drawers. See "Shamming" in the Index.

1405 (Upper) Mrs. W. D. Steuart.　　　　1406 (Upper) Dr. Jas. Bordley, Jr.
1407 (Centre) Mr. J. G. Whitely.　　　　1408 (Centre) Col. Mrs. J. Stabler.
1409 (Lower) Mr. Edgar G. Miller, Jr.　　1410 (Lower) Mrs. M. S. Hartshorne.

on the sides and corners and a concave curve on the front, as in No. 1406 and others. The Hepplewhite features are the square tapering legs with spade feet, and the inlay on the legs, leaves and front. About 1780–1790.

Many pleasing Pembroke tables were made in the Hepplewhite style. The principal characteristics are the square legs, generally tapering on the inner sides, the spade feet, the oval form of the top and the abundance of inlay.

No. 1412 is wholly in the Hepplewhite style and is finely ornamented with inlay. The tapering legs are decorated with inlaid strings of flowers and over the legs are inlaid oval medallions with American eagles, without stars. A wide border of inlay is between the medallions. The top being oval, the front of the central section of the top is curved. The brackets which swing out and support the leaves are seen here. About 1785–1800.

No. 1413 is a handsome oval table, decorated with a fine inlay of flowers on the legs, and with a band of inlay near the bottom. The inlay on the drawer and the top will be noticed, and also the medallions on the front and side, the latter being partly visible even when the leaves are down. The height of this table is twenty–eight inches and the length when open is forty inches, which are about the usual dimensions of these tables. About 1785–1800.

No. 1414 is similar in form to the preceding table, but the inlaid decoration is less attractive. Above the legs are diamond–shaped designs in inlay. The small visible spaces on the sides of the frame are decorated with fan designs. Perhaps the inlaid fans were used in order to cover the vacancy caused by the short leaves, or perhaps the leaves were made short in order not to hide the inlaid fans. Here the height is thirty inches and the length when open is thirty–five inches. About 1785–1800.

No. 1415 is a Pembroke table in the Sheraton style, which is recognized by the familiar round and reeded tapering legs with "turned" feet. There is no inlay, but the leaves are rounded and are of a light wood, making a pleasing decorative contrast with the mahogany. About 1795–1810.

No. 1416 is a plain table, also in the Sheraton style. The front of the table is veneered and there are small veneered panels over the legs. The upper portion of the legs is turned in a ring form. About 1795–1810.

Section 164. Library tables.—Perhaps because there is no better name which can well be applied to them, the term "library tables" seems to be suitable for the drop–leaf tables shown in this section. In some cases these tables have been called "breakfast tables,"[1] a term which implies the use of the table for a single purpose. The presence of drawers seems to indicate that the tables were not intended to be used for meals.

1. Other names given to these tables are "drop–leaf tables" and "centre tables." These terms apply equally well to several other kinds of tables and are too indefinite.

In "English and American Furniture," by Cescinsky and Hunter, pages 212–213, Mr. Cescinsky, referring to certain tripod tables of moderate size, states that they "are usually termed 'breakfast tables' on the principle that guests do not, as a rule, stay over night, and a smaller table

1411 (Upper) Mrs. John S. Gibbs, Jr.
1413 (Centre) Anonymous.
1415 (Lower) Mrs. Edwin B. Niver.

1412 (Upper) Mrs. Wm. M. Roberts.
1414 (Centre) Anonymous.
1416 (Lower) Mr. Edgar G. Miller, Jr.

The upper portion of these tables, that is, the top, the brackets and the frame and drawer, resembles in form and construction that of the Pembroke tables seen in the previous section; but often the lower portion, instead of having the four legs of the Pembroke tables, has one or more pedestals resting upon four curved legs, similar to those seen on some of the dining tables of the period, such as Nos. 1322–1326. These library tables are larger than the Pembroke tables shown in the preceding section, and are finished on all sides for use in the centre of a room, where all parts may be seen.

Tables of this type were chiefly made in the Sheraton period and style, about the year 1800, and they continued to be made in the early part of the Empire period. The wood is mahogany, generally of fine quality.

In No. 1417 the top of the central section is rectangular and the two drop–leaves are cut in a favorite pattern. The edge of the top is reeded. The drawer should be furnished with a "lion's–head and ring" handle or a brass knob, as in Nos. 1418 and 1419. A small drop or "pendant" hangs from each corner of the centre section, a detail seen on many of these library tables. The upper part of the pedestal is in the form of a vase carved with acanthus leaves, and the base is also carved. The four concave and wide–spread legs are tapered and are ornamented above with carved acanthus leaves and below with reeding, terminating in brass paw feet and casters. The height of tables of this type is generally about twenty–nine inches and the length when open about fifty inches. About 1810–1820.

No. 1418 is regarded as having been made by Duncan Phyfe in his late period, and is partly in the Empire style.[2] The upper portion is similar to that of the preceding table, except that the edge of the top is not reeded. The drawer is furnished with a brass "lion's–head and ring" handle of the period. Instead of a single pedestal seen in the preceding table, there are four carved columns which rest upon a heavy platform. This platform has concave sides, and is supported by heavy carved legs placed under it and terminating in large animals' paw feet; these features indicate the Empire style. Other somewhat similar columns and platforms are seen in the dining tables Nos. 1324–1326, the table No. 1640 and also in No. 1421. About 1815–1825.

No. 1419 is less ornate than the two preceding tables. The upper portion is in about the same form, but with somewhat longer drop–leaves than in No. 1417.

(NOTE 1, continued)

only is required in the morning than on the night before"; and he pleasantly continues: "It may be useful here to cite Earl Balfour's definition of a bore as 'one who, invited to tea, stays to dinner.' Presumably the tea–invited who remains to breakfast is a super–bore; certainly he may be a nuisance, which is much the same thing."

    A table of a different type, called a library table, but without drop–leaves, was made by Duncan Phyfe. The table was finely made, but was apparently not popular. It is shown as No. 1644 in section 174. In England it is called a "Canterbury" table.

    Three other tables which perhaps should be called "library tables" are shown in section 174, Nos. 1638–1640. They may have been made either for a library or a drawing room.

    2. The Empire style in the furniture of Duncan Phyfe is mentioned in section 20.

1417 (UPPER) MISS ELEANOR S. COHEN.
1419 (CENTRE) MR. EDGAR G. MILLER, JR.
1421 (LOWER) DR. M. A. ABRAMS.

1418 (UPPER) MR. HOWARD MANSFIELD.
1420 (CENTRE) MR. F. HIGHLANDS BURNS.
1422 (LOWER) DR. M. A. ABRAMS.

The panel on each side of the drawer, the pendants under the panels, and the brass knob, will be noticed. The single pedestal has a spiral turning on a vase form. The legs are grooved. About 1810–1820.

No. 1420 is recognized as having features of the late Sheraton and early Empire styles by its less delicately reeded legs and its larger and heavier pedestal. The upper portion is similar in form to that of the preceding tables. The top is reeded all around, as in No. 1417. The drop handle on the drawer is not of the period. The brass animals' claw feet are furnished with casters, as was usual at the time. About 1815–1825.

No. 1421 is somewhat similar in form to No. 1418, but may be regarded as being in the Sheraton style. The upper portion is supported by four small and slender columns, called "colonnettes," which rest upon a platform. Other slender columns are in the tripod table No. 1364 and in No. 1424. This platform is supported by four reeded legs. The corners of the leaves are cut off, making the top different in form from the others. The round brass handles on the drawer drop from the top. About 1810–1820.

No. 1422 is different in some respects. The upper portion is supported by two large upright "standards" which rest upon the parallel legs and are connected by two horizontal bars or stretchers. At the ends of these bars are applied rosettes. The fine reeding on the legs is too delicate to be well seen, and the reeding is continued on the brass feet, a method which is mentioned in the comments on the sewing tables Nos. 1574 and 1589. About 1815–1825.

Section 165. Sofa tables.—The principal features of a sofa table such as No. 1423, compared with a library table such as No. 1421, are that the front of the sofa table has two drawers and is therefore wider, and that the legs, being further apart, require a stretcher. Nos. 1423 and 1424 are very graceful and elegant tables; Nos. 1425 and 1426 are of different types in later styles. It is said that in England these sofa tables are generally placed in front of a sofa where they are convenient for the use of persons sitting on the sofa, especially for ladies with needle–work and tea; in our country, however, they are often placed behind the sofa,[1] or in the centre of the room or in the hall or elsewhere, and are used for any purpose desired. Being seen from all sides they are generally finished on all sides. They were first made in the Sheraton period, about the year 1800, and continued in fashion until the end of the Empire period, about 1840.

No. 1423 is a handsome sofa table made by Duncan Phyfe in the Sheraton style, and now owned by the Metropolitan Museum of Art. The edge of the top is reeded and the drop–leaves are supported by brackets. The two drawers are bordered with a light veneer and are furnished with brass knobs. At the ends are graceful carved and reeded lyres which support the upper portion and rest

1. It is said that the sofa table was often placed behind the sofa, for two reasons, that is, to hide the back of the sofa when the latter was in the centre of the room, and to hold a lamp to furnish light to one sitting on the sofa.

1423 (Upper) Metropolitan Museum of Art.
1425 (Lower) Lockwood Col. Furn., Fig. 797.

1424 (Upper) Metropolitan Museum of Art.
1426 (Lower) Mr. & Mrs. Wm. A. Dixon.

upon concave legs which are carved and reeded and are connected by a stretcher. The fine workmanship and design of this table and the next one are examples of the skill of Phyfe at his best period. About 1805–1815.

No. 1424 is also by Duncan Phyfe in the Sheraton style, and is equally fine.[2] The leaves are bordered with a light veneer, as in the preceding table, but the veneer is not well seen in the engraving. Each end is supported by two small columns, or "colonnettes," under which are carved and reeded legs. The two delicate stretchers are reeded in the centre. About 1805–1815.

No. 1425 illustrates the decline of the sofa table from the style of Sheraton as interpreted by Phyfe to the style of the late Empire period. Here the lyre supports have no delicacy, the heavy stretcher is a shelf with lyre–shaped ends, and the feet are of the coarse animals' claw pattern seen in so many pieces of the period. About 1825–1835.

No. 1426 is probably a Victorian sofa table, with certain features more pleasing than those in the preceding Empire style. At this period there was a revival and mixture of many earlier forms as in the bureaus Nos. 767 and 768. Above the trestle are small moldings in an arched form. There is one large drawer with a curved front and three heavy upright supports on each end, but no stretchers. The mahogany veneer is of fine quality. About 1840.

Section 166. Side tables; serving and hunters' tables.—Almost all of the tables shown in previous sections may be called "centre tables," that is, tables which are intended to be placed in the centre or open spaces of a room or at least not against a wall, and are therefore finished on all four sides. "Side tables" are intended to stand against a wall and are not finished on the rear; these are shown in the present section and in later ones.[1] The side tables in this section are to be distinguished from the "sideboard" tables shown in section 157. The tables shown

---

2. In his "Furniture Masterpieces of Duncan Phyfe," page 77, Mr. Charles Over Cornelius remarks that these two sofa tables are "superb examples of absolutely finished workmanship."

1. Several side tables of a special character, and known by special names, are shown in other sections. A tripod side table is No. 1366. Card tables may be used as side tables when the folding leaf is down. The ends of dining tables in the Hepplewhite and Sheraton styles are sometimes used as side tables. Pier and console tables are also side tables; see section 174, Nos. 1647, 1648.

In the full page illustration of furniture in the Adam style, No. 4 in section 16, two side tables are illustrated in order to show some of the important features of that style, although such furniture was seldom if ever made in our country for the reasons mentioned in that section.

In the rectangular table at the upper left corner the skirt is fluted and in the centre is a panel with festoons of drapery tied with tassels, and at the ends are oval applied rosettes. The legs are straight, square and tapering, a form which was followed by Hepplewhite and to some extent by Sheraton.

In the half–round, or semi–circular, table the skirt is ornamented with a series of festoons of drapery, the legs are fluted, at the tops of the legs are applied rosettes and the feet are of the spade type. The top of the table is decorated with paintings.

These features were copied by later cabinet makers, but the original designs are those of Robert Adam. The illustrations are from Mr. Cescinsky's "English Furniture," volume 3, figures 14 and 18, and appear here through his courtesy. Both of these tables were about 1765–1780.

here were made for various purposes and therefore differ considerably in height and length and in other respects. The wood is usually mahogany.

First we see four side tables, Nos. 1427–1430, in the Chippendale style.

No. 1427 is a handsomely carved side table in the Chippendale style. On the "skirt," under the top, the carvings are in a variety of designs and on the upper part of the legs are carved leaves which at their ends take the shape of "C" curves. The legs are in the cabriole form and terminate in ball and claw feet, the ball being somewhat flattened. This table is thirty–one inches high and forty–two inches long. About 1760–1780.

No. 1428 is a plain table in the same style. Here the legs are square and straight, as in so many of the Chippendale style chairs and tables, and terminate in block feet, a type from which the spade feet were later developed by Adam and Hepplewhite. The upper portion is without ornament except that small brackets in a "C" form are at the junction of the legs and the skirt. About 1760–1780.

No. 1429 has a feature of the Adam style, that is, the "fluting" of the skirt, a decorative form explained in section 41. This feature is seen on the two tables shown on the page of Adam style furniture, illustration No. 4, mentioned in note 1. The Chippendale style appears in the brackets and in the square and straight grooved legs with the inner edges of the legs cut off, as in the Pembroke table No. 1405 and others. The height is thirty–eight inches and the length forty–four inches. About 1770–1780.

No. 1430 is said to be the most elaborate American side table now known. It is called the "Cadwalader" table from the name of the family in Philadelphia for which it was made. It is mainly in the French, rather than the English, style, and was originally gilded and had a marble top. This table is fully carved with "C" curves, such as those on the mirrors Nos. 1103–1106 and others, and with leaves and fanciful designs; and it has "French" feet such as those on the chairs Nos. 116 and 117, although the "shoes" or "cushions" under the feet are of English usage. It is of a special character, and although interesting, is not of importance to the amateur in the study of American styles. See also section 174 in connection with pier tables. About 1770.

In the next group of side tables, Nos. 1431–1436, several resemble a card table of the Hepplewhite style, but they do not have a folding leaf supported by a swinging leg which are seen on card tables. Because of their moderate size, these tables were probably suitable for general household purposes. It will be noticed that none of these tables have a drawer, mainly on account of the curved shape of the frames.

No. 1431 is a half–round or semi–circular side table, in the Hepplewhite style, sometimes erroneously referred to as a "pier table," or "console table," as to which see section 174 and Nos. 1647–1648. The skirt is inlaid with rectangular forms and panels and the tapering legs are decorated with inlaid flowers, such as those seen on the Hepplewhite style dining tables in section 157 and the sideboards in section 128. Because of the semi–circular form, the two front legs present two sides to the front view, as also in the next table, but here only one of the sides is decorated. About 1785–1800.

1427 (Upper) Hammond–Harwood House.
1429 (Lower) Hammond–Harwood House.

1428 (Upper) Mrs. Howard Sill.
1430 (Lower) Metropolitan Museum of Art.

1431 (Upper) Mr. H. Oliver Thompson. 1432 (Upper) Mr. & Mrs. E. L. R. Smith.
1433 (Centre) Anonymous. 1434 (Centre) Miss Elisabeth H. Bartlett.
1435 (Lower) Mr. John Ridgely, Jr. 1436 (Lower) Hammond–Harwood House.

No. 1432 is also a half–round side table, painted white with graceful decorations. The festoons of flowers on the skirt, the oval medallions and the strings of leaves on the legs follow designs of Robert Adam which were copied by Hepplewhite. The curved stretchers are in a "dome" form used in the period; a somewhat similar design appears in the small table No. 1602. See also the companion chair No. 295 which has a similar decoration. About 1775–1790.

No. 1433 is another side table in the Hepplewhite style. The skirt is veneered with panels of finely grained and colored wood, the central panel enclosing an oval one. The legs have lines of inlay and are tapered to a smaller end than usual, almost pointed, a method occasionally seen, as in the card tables Nos. 1506–1507 and others. The top is in the same form as in the card tables Nos. 1505–1508. About 1785–1800.

No. 1434, in the Hepplewhite style, is also finely ornamented on the skirt with three small panels in front and with several rectangular forms enclosing other inlaid forms in which the corners are cut in a concave shape. Below the lines of inlay on the legs are strings of flowers. About 1785–1800.

No. 1435 is in the Sheraton style, as appears from the round and tapering legs which project forward from the line of the framework, a method seen in the bureaus and sideboards of that style and in the card tables Nos. 1521, 1522 and others. This is a painted table, with a landscape on the eight–sided panel in the centre of the skirt. The legs at the upper ends are decorated with a leaf design and below are inlaid with vertical lines of light wood, an ornamental feature also seen in the Baltimore tables Nos. 1436, 1441, 1442 and 1462. About 1800–1810.

No. 1436, also, is in the Sheraton style, as shown by the legs and the use of carving upon them. Under the almost half–round top the skirt is decorated with a series of applied arches under which are inlaid leaf designs. At the upper ends of the four legs are carved vases supporting the top, and below these vases the legs are carved for a short distance and are ornamented with vertical lines of inlay as in the preceding table. The height of this table is about thirty–five inches, and the length is about fifty–four inches. About 1800.

Side tables such as Nos. 1437–1442 are often called "serving tables," that is, primarily, tables used in the dining room for the service of meals; but their variety and fine character of their design, workmanship and materials seem to indicate that they were also used for other purposes. The presence of marble tops on the last two of this group may mark them as serving tables; but the others are so elegant that their place would seem to be in the best room of the house. The height of these tables is in most cases about thirty–eight inches or a little more.

No. 1437, a half–round satinwood side table, has a very pleasing appearance. As in Nos. 1431 and 1432, each of the two front legs, following the semi–circular line of the framework, exposes two sides to the view, and here these two sides are decorated with strings of flowers. Bands of dark wood are near the bottom, making an effective contrast with the light colored satinwood. This table is thirty–eight inches high. About 1800.

1437 (UPPER) MR. ARTHUR E. COLE.　　1438 (UPPER) MR. ARTHUR E. COLE.
1439 (CENTRE) MR. & MRS. H. L. DUER.　1440 (CENTRE) MR. J. F. H. MAGINN.
1441 (LOWER) MR. CHAS. MORRIS HOWARD.　1442 (LOWER) ANONYMOUS.

No. 1438, in the Hepplewhite style, has a serpentine front, and on the skirt are two large and one small rectangular inlaid panels. Decorative rectangular panels of this type will also be seen on Nos. 1441, 1442 and other pieces. The legs have lines of inlay and strings of flowers, with bands of light wood near the bottom. This table is thirty–seven inches high. About 1800.

No. 1439, in the Hepplewhite style, is of unusual distinction, having six legs on each of which is a wide inlay of satinwood extending more than half the length of the leg. This satinwood inlay is in turn inlaid with strings of darker wood terminating in tassels, and below the wide inlay are inlaid strings of flowers. A somewhat similar highly decorative treatment, said to be peculiar to Baltimore, will be seen in the Hepplewhite style card tables Nos. 1487–1490, and is referred to in the comments on those pieces. The skirt is ornamented with rectangular forms and in the centre is a panel of darker wood. Card tables with five or six legs are Nos. 1493–1497. About 1800.

In No. 1440 the front is in the form which, in sideboards, indicates the Hepplewhite style, that is, the ends are concave, not convex, as stated in section 128. On the front are three diamond–shaped inlaid designs in satinwood and on each of the tapering front legs are four small inlaid diamond–shaped designs in dark wood enclosed in inlaid forms. The front of No. 1495 is similar in shape. About 1800.

No. 1441 is in the Sheraton style for reasons mentioned in the comment on No. 1435. Here the marble top, cut in curves in the form of the woodwork, indicates that the table was probably intended as a serving table upon which hot dishes could be placed without injury. The legs are ornamented with inlaid vertical lines as in No. 1435 and others. The front skirt is painted in panels, the one in the centre enclosing a painting of musical instruments and the other two containing designs of painted leaves and flowers, which are repeated on the ends of the table. This is one of the "Baltimore Sheraton style painted" tables, another example of which is next shown. In this connection reference may be made to the Baltimore painted chairs Nos. 290 and 291. About 1800.

No. 1442, also, has a marble top, shaped in curves to fit the woodwork. The skirt is veneered with fine mahogany and in the centre is a glass panel decorated with a classic scene painted in gilt and blue. Particular interest attaches to the slender legs which are about the same as those in the corner table No. 1462; these two tables were probably made by the same Baltimore cabinet maker, at present not certainly known. The legs are said to be ornamented with inlaid lines as in the preceding table. The shelf is cut in the same general curves as the top and is attached to small square and decorated blocks. This serving, or mixing, table is thirty–seven inches high. About 1800.

The next eight tables, Nos. 1443–1450, also known as "serving tables," are somewhat different from the preceding ones in this section; and it is uncertain whether the term "serving table" should be applied to all of them.

No. 1443 is a small illustration of a large and high table in the Sheraton style as appears from the convex ends of the top which distinguish the sideboards

1443 (Upper) Metropolitan Museum of Art.
1445 (Lower) Anonymous.

1444 (Upper) Anonymous.
1446 (Lower) Mr. & Mrs. Wm. A. Dixon.

in that style from those of the Hepplewhite style, the latter having concave ends; spade feet[2] were used in both styles. There are six tapering legs; the two central front ones are inlaid with lines and flowers on three sides. The six stretchers are concave. The three drawers are inlaid with panels of dark wood. About 1800–1810.

Nos. 1444 and 1445, in the Sheraton style, were probably made by Duncan Phyfe, and have been called "serving tables."[3] They are not as high as the preceding piece.

In No. 1444 there is one wide drawer and below is a concave shelf. The round legs project forward from the line of the front as in the card tables Nos. 1533 and 1534 and others, and are finely reeded from the top to the brass feet, except below the drawer and at the square blocks to which the shelf is attached. The handles are of the "lion's head and ring" type, which was a favorite with Phyfe. About 1800–1810.

No. 1445 is of the same general type, but differs from the preceding table in having three drawers, two small ones above a wide one, and in not having a shelf. The fronts of the drawers are finely veneered with a darker mahogany than that of the other framework. The delicacy and fine proportions of these two serving tables will be noticed. Their projecting and reeded legs follow the form of other pieces in the best Sheraton style, as in the card tables mentioned in the comment on the preceding piece. About 1800–1810.

No. 1446 is a somewhat later form of the same type of serving tables as the two preceding ones. Here we have the projecting legs and a shelf as in No. 1444, and three drawers as in No. 1445. The legs are in spiral forms, as to which see section 155, note 2; and other differing details will be noticed. The handles are of an unusual pattern. About 1810–1820.

The serving tables Nos. 1447–1449 are in the late Sheraton style and No. 1450 is in the Empire style.

No. 1447 is thirty-seven inches high, not counting the back board, and has thick tapering legs with coarse reeding, over which is a carved ring and vase. At the two ends of the skirt are panels with applied carvings. About 1815–1825.

No. 1448 is a small table with a marble top. On the skirt are two small panels at the ends and a larger one in the centre. The legs, with carved tops, are heavily reeded as on the preceding table. Under the legs are square plain blocks and ball feet, as in the sideboard No. 1014 and other pieces; see also figure 3 in illustration No. 11. About 1815–1825.

No. 1449 is a large serving table with six heavily reeded legs. The top has a low back board which extends over the ends. There are two small end drawers and a large one in the centre with brass lion-and-ring handles. About 1815–1825.

2.   See section 127 as to spade feet and also figure 17 in illustration No. 11.

      This table seems to be an American adaptation of a design in plate 4, dated 1793, in the Appendix to Sheraton's "Drawing Book," as to which see section 18; almost the same table appears in some of the English books.

3.   As in "Furniture Masterpieces of Duncan Phyfe," by Mr. Charles Over Cornelius, plates 48 and 50. Very similar tables have been called "dressing tables" by other writers.

1447 (UPPER) MR. JOHN C. TOLAND.
1449 (LOWER) MR. W. W. LANAHAN.

1448 (UPPER) MISS HELEN H. CAREY.
1450 (LOWER) MRS. I. R. TRIMBLE.

No. 1450 has a marble top, under which the skirt is decorated with fanciful carvings on the panels at the ends and still more fanciful carvings on the panel in the centre, showing scrolls and leaves. At the tops of the legs are vase–shaped forms carved with leaves and in a reversed position, as in No. 1472. The heavy spiral twists on the legs are such as were used in the early years of the Empire style, as on the posts of the bedsteads Nos. 1069–1070, which are mentioned in note 2 in section 155. The feet seem to have been removed. About 1815–1830.

The next six side tables, Nos. 1451–1456, are the so-called "hunters' tables," or "hunting tables" or "hunting boards." On these long and high tables, found chiefly in the South,[4] liquid and other refreshments were served before and after the hunt. The tables illustrated here are all in Maryland homes, where some of them have been for several generations. They are about thirty–seven to forty–two inches high by about five to six feet long. The first five tables, Nos. 1451–1455, are in the Hepplewhite style, with graceful serpentine fronts, and are very similar, the principal difference between them being in the inlaid ornamentation; the sixth example, No. 1456, is in the Sheraton style. All are made of mahogany and are of about the same date.

No. 1451 is more fully decorated than the other hunters' tables, almost the entire skirt being covered by rectangular inlaid panels. The legs have the usual strings of flowers used on tables in the Hepplewhite style and above the legs are other inlaid designs. In this table is clearly seen a feature of the Hepplewhite style, used also to some extent in the Sheraton style, that is, the tapering of the legs is made only on the inner side, not on both sides as generally in the Adam style; hence the outside of the leg is exactly vertical. This is also seen in the next piece. About 1800.

In No. 1452 the skirt is veneered with finely figured mahogany. Here also the skirt and the ends are decorated with oval medallions, and lines of inlay are on the legs. The serpentine form of the front is well seen in this engraving. About 1800.

No. 1453 is six feet long and about thirty–seven inches high, and the top at its widest point in the centre of the serpentine form is about two feet in depth. At each end a drawer is shown open. The inlay consists of lines on the edge of the top and on the skirt and legs. About 1800.

No. 1454 is forty–two inches high and sixty inches long. Its height, the shallow skirt and the long, slender and tapering legs give an unusual appearance to this "hunters' table." The inlay consists of three oval medallions on the skirt and the ends, and strings of flowers and bands on the legs. About 1800.

4.   Tables of the same or similar name were used in several of the Southern States, especially in South Carolina. Those tables, however, were of a different type from those shown here, being of small size, with cupboards or drawers, and with few or no decorative features, appearing in fact to be small sideboards. Several illustrations of this type of tables are in "Antiques," November, 1927, pages 378–379, and August, 1931, pages 83–85. Georgia "huntboards" are illustrated and discussed in the issue of September, 1932, page 105.

In "Southern Antiques," by Mr. Paul H. Burroughs, 1931, pages 61–67, a number of pieces regarded as "hunting boards" are illustrated. Most of these bear little or no resemblance to the handsome pieces shown in this section.

1451 (Upper) Mr. W. W. Lanahan.   1452 (Upper) Mr. Albert G. Towers.
1453 (Centre) Mr. & Mrs. J. M. Matthews.   1454 (Centre) Mr. & Mrs. H. L. Duer.
1455 (Lower) Mrs. Miles White, Jr.   1456 (Lower) Mr. & Mrs. Geo. Ward.

In No. 1455 the serpentine form is well seen. The two oval medallions above the legs are inlaid with American eagles, and inlaid strings of flowers are on both the front and rear legs. The height is thirty–eight inches and the length is about sixty–eight inches. The tapering legs terminate in spade feet. About 1800.

No. 1456 is in the Sheraton style as appears from the convex, not concave, ends, and also by the carving over the legs, which was not used on the tables in the Hepplewhite style. Square tapering legs with spade feet, such as those here, were used in both styles, as shown in section 128 in the chapter on sideboards. The brackets at the intersections of the skirt and the legs will be noticed. Two round ebony knobs, with ivory centres, are on the drawer; there are no drawers in the ends. This table is thirty–eight inches high and sixty–six inches long and is of mahogany. It may be English, but it has been in our country in the family of the present owners for several generations. About 1800.

Section 167. Corner tables.—The usual type of corner tables has a triangular frame with four legs, of which three are stationary and one swings out and supports a drop–leaf when it is raised. The stationary top over the frame, and also the drop–leaf, are triangular and of the same size, so that when the drop–leaf is up, the top is square; but when the drop–leaf is down, as in the first three illustrations, the top is triangular and the table may be placed in a corner of a room. This feature gives the table its name of "corner table," although whether square or triangular the table may well be used in other parts of a room. Nos. 1457–1459 are examples of this type. Many of them are small and plain. Other types are shown in Nos. 1460–1462.

In No. 1457 the drop–leaf is down and the table may be placed in a corner with the drop–leaf facing the centre of the room. The movable leg which swings out and supports the drop–leaf is the next to the last on the left. This table is in the Queen Anne style, as indicated by the shape of the legs and also by the feet which are in a modified form of the Dutch, or club, feet. About 1750–1760.

In No. 1458, in which also the drop–leaf is down, we see a similar corner table from another point of view. The sides, which were not visible in the preceding illustration, are seen here to be finished suitably for the centre of a room. The Queen Anne style is apparent from the legs and the Dutch, or club, feet which are protected by "shoes," as in the card table No. 1477 and others. About 1750–1770.

No. 1459 is a very small table. The square and straight legs are in the Chippendale style, as are so many on the chairs in that style, such as Nos. 98–100 and others. The inner corners of the legs are cut off, as in the Pembroke table No. 1405, making flat surfaces which here are not intended to hold stretchers. About 1760–1780.

The next three tables, which are without leaves, are more strictly "corner tables," because they can be well used only in a corner. In each table the frame has a curved front and four or more stationary legs. In appearance these tables are more attractive than those of the preceding type.

1457 (Upper) Mr. John C. Toland.
1459 (Centre) Mr. John S. McDaniel.
1461 (Lower) Mrs. Jas. W. Wilson.

1458 (Upper) Mrs. Miles White, Jr.
1460 (Centre) Mrs. Wilbur W. Hubbard.
1462 (Lower) Miss Eleanor S. Cohen.

No. 1460 is an example of a corner table with a curved front. This piece is in the Chippendale style, as appears from the straight and square rear leg and the three front legs which have a peculiar cabriole form and ball and claw feet. The skirt is cut in two sections of double cyma curves, as to which see section 23. Small corner tables of similar shape were also made in the Hepplewhite style. They are typical of the emphasis placed on convenience as well as beauty by the designers of that day. About 1760–1780.

No. 1461 also was made to stand in a curved corner of a room. It is rounded in the rear, where it is supported by two legs. The front is serpentine and is well ornamented. The skirt has a border of inlay and the tapering legs with spade feet are decorated with strings of flowers over which are small inlaid panels, not clearly seen. This table is in the Hepplewhite style and its date is probably about 1790–1800.

No. 1462, said to have been made in Baltimore, is a corner table of an unusual type. The skirt is concave at the ends and is straight in the centre. The ends are inlaid with a design of parallel lines with rounded ends such as are mentioned in section 127, note 6. The glass panel in the central straight portion is painted with patriotic designs similar to those on the mirrors in Nos. 1171 and 1172. The upper portion of the legs is ornamented with inlaid lines in the same manner as on the serving table No. 1442; the lower portion of the legs is in dark wood. The short columns over the legs are painted with the same design of leaves as in No. 1442 and the feet are the same in both tables. The stretchers are "domed," as in Nos. 1432 and 1602, and at their junction there is a carved vase. A very similar table is owned by Dr. James Bordley, Jr., of Baltimore. About 1800.

Section 168. Dressing tables.

—In his chapter on "Chests of Drawers" Mr. Lockwood applies the term "dressing tables" to the low chests of drawers which we know as "lowboys,"[1] the term "dressing tables" being historically correct and also descriptive of their utility, whereas the term "lowboy" is merely a popular one. But as the word "lowboy" is in general use in our country, the dressing tables of that type are considered in this book separately in chapter 10, sections 88–92.

In addition to lowboys there was another kind of dressing tables, known as "knee–hole" dressing tables.[2] These knee–hole dressing tables are very similar in

1. "Colonial Furniture," volume 1, figure 55 and many others. See also the remarks in the present book on lowboys as dressing tables, section 119.

2. In Mr. Lockwood's book, volume 1, several articles of this type are illustrated; figures 113 and 123 are termed "knee–hole dressing table"; figure 253, a very similar piece, is termed a "knee–hole desk," because the top drawer has writing arrangements; figure 295 is termed a "knee–hole writing table" for the reason that it has a lid which falls over and rests upon pulls as in our secretary desks Nos. 800, 801 and others.

When a dressing table of this kind was used for the purposes of the toilet, a movable dressing glass such as one of Nos. 1255–1259 was generally placed on the top. See also the comment on No. 1468.

Mr. Lockwood states, page 114, that knee–hole tables were never popular in our country and that few were found "until the time of their revival in the block–front type in the third quarter of the eighteenth century"; as to which see section 119 in the present book.

1463 (Upper) Mrs. John S. Gibbs, Jr.   1464 (Upper) Dr. Jas. Bordley, Jr.
1465 (Lower) Dr. Jas. Bordley, Jr.   1466 (Lower) Chase House, Annapolis.

form to the knee–hole desk No. 832 and are also similar to the block–front knee–hole desks Nos. 904–907. Indeed these knee–hole dressing tables and the knee–hole desks are so similar that it may be difficult to distinguish easily the one from the other. This will be noticed by comparing the first four dressing tables with the knee–hole desk No. 832. Moreover, the knee–hole dressing tables were used as desks and the desks were used as dressing tables, each being suitable for both correspondence and the arts of the toilet. It is therefore possible that some of the knee–hole tables here presented as dressing tables may have been known and used as desks at the time they were made.

The four knee–hole dressing tables here shown are very similar in character. The wood is generally walnut or mahogany. It is suggested that section 119 in the chapter on "block–front furniture" be examined in connection with these dressing tables, and also the knee–hole desk No. 832 in the chapter on desks.

No. 1463 has one long drawer with an early type of handle such as No. 9 in illustration No. 13. The central portion below is called the "recessed portion," made to accommodate the knees of a person sitting at the table, but not wide enough to be comfortable. On each side of this recessed portion are three drawers, graduated in depth, which are provided with locks, and at the rear is a large plain door within which is a cupboard. The feet are of the straight bracket type and are cut in curves. About 1760–1780.

No. 1464 is similar to the preceding dressing table, differing in some details. The door of the cupboard in the recessed portion is paneled in the arched form seen on the doors of many secretary–bookcases, such as Nos. 841 and 845; the skirt under the door is cut in a double cyma curve, as to which see section 23; the feet are of the straight bracket type cut in a modified form of a cyma curve; and the skirt at the top of the recessed portion, which is often the front of a small drawer, is cut in a series of cyma curves. About 1760–1780.

In No. 1465 the variations from the preceding dressing table consist of the plain door of the cupboard in the recessed portion, the plain skirt over that portion, and, more especially, the form of the two feet which are of the "ogee" bracket type, as to which see figure 9 in illustration No. 11. The absence of the two feet at the inner ends of the bottom drawers gives the front a somewhat unfinished and vacant appearance, as also in the sideboard No. 994 and the dressing tables Nos. 1467 and 1468. About 1760–1780.

No. 1466 is in the Chase House, at Annapolis, where it has probably been ever since the house was built in 1770–1771. Under the top is a slide which pulls out, and below is the usual long drawer, with handles in an open–work pattern. On each side there is a closed cupboard instead of drawers, and at the rear of the recessed portion there is the usual plain cupboard. The feet are of the straight bracket type, cut in cyma curves. About 1760–1780.

No. 1467 is a dressing table in the Hepplewhite style, resembling a small sideboard in some respects, such as No. 994. There is one long drawer in the centre and under it is a large arch which doubtless enables a person to sit comfortably at the table with his knees under it. On each side of the arch are three small drawers. The legs are slightly tapered. Tables similar to this were also made in the Sheraton style, but with reeded legs. About 1790–1800.

No. 1468 is also in the Hepplewhite style, and is somewhat higher than the preceding piece. Here the small arch in the centre is for ornamental purposes, as it is of no service to one sitting at the table. Under the long drawer are two short ones at the ends and a small shallow one in the centre. Dressing glasses such as Nos. 1260–1263, shown in section 152 in the chapter on mirrors, were no doubt used on these two dressing tables. See note 2 in this section. About 1790–1800.

Nos. 1469 and 1470 are very different in appearance from the preceding two dressing tables in the Hepplewhite style, but they have about the same form of arched framework and drawers, evidently following the Hepplewhite and Sheraton styles in that respect. Under the framework, however, the parts are of the early Empire style, well made and with fine mahogany veneer. In both of these pieces the lyres are an important feature, as are also the heavy platforms and the feet with animals' paws. About 1810–1830.

In No. 1469 the framework, as mentioned, resembles to some extent that of Nos. 1467 and 1468, having a long drawer under which are two small drawers. The finely grained mahogany veneer and the oval brass handles hanging from the top of the plate will be noticed. The rear supports are wide and plain. The use of carved lyres as front supports for a dressing table is an unusual application of that favorite ornamental feature.[3] About 1820–1830.

In No. 1470, also, the framework is somewhat similar in form to Nos. 1467 and 1468, with one long and two small drawers, here with brass "lion–and–ring" handles. The rear supports are in the same form as in the preceding piece; the four front legs are round columns with brass caps at the top and bottom, similar in form to the columns on the Empire style table No. 1653 and the bureau No. 764. The feet are of the animals' paw type, with scrolls on the sides. The fact that the mirror is a structural part of this piece, not removable, may perhaps constitute the piece a bureau in the modern sense. It is interesting to examine this dressing table in connection with the bureaus Nos. 753–756. About 1820–1830.

No. 1471 is a plain dressing table in the late Sheraton style, the legs being heavily reeded as in the serving table No. 1449. Above the top are three drawers similar to those on the Sheraton style bureau No. 759, and over these is a back–board. Under the top is a slide which pulls out and below this is a long drawer. Wooden knobs of graduated size are on the drawers, the smaller knobs being on the smaller drawers. About 1810–1820.

No. 1472 is in the Empire style, as shown by the heavy spiral, or rope, legs, with a carved vase in a reversed position, as in the serving table No. 1450. On the top are two small drawers with a third drawer above them, and above the latter is a back–board in the same design as the tops of the fretwork mirrors No. 1128 and others. Large knobs are on the large drawer and smaller ones on the others. About 1820–1830.

3.   Compare the card tables Nos. 1539–1542 in which the supports are lyres; also the sewing tables Nos. 1566–1571. A note on lyres is in section 171, note 7.

1467 (Upper) Mr. & Mrs. H. L. Duer.   1468 (Upper) Dr. Jas. Bordley, Jr.
1469 (Centre) Dr. J. Hall Pleasants.   1470 (Centre) Mr. & Mrs. E. H. McKeon.
1471 (Lower) Mrs. P. L. C. Fischer.   1472 (Lower) Md. Soc. Colonial Dames.

1473 (Upper) Mr. & Mrs. E. G. Gibson.   1474 (Upper) Mr. & Mrs. H. L. Duer.
1475 (Lower) Mr. W. W. Lanahan.   1476 (Lower) Mr. Herbert T. Tiffany.

The four dressing tables, Nos. 1473–1476, are of the type commonly called "Beau Brummell" dressing tables, a name given to them at one time in honor of the famous English leader of fashion.[4] They are fitted with mirrors, and their small drawers are for cosmetics and other aids to beauty, and also for the implements of the toilet.

No. 1473 is a "Beau Brummell" dressing table in the Hepplewhite–Sheraton period, following designs in the books of both Hepplewhite and Sheraton.[5] The two folding half–tops, opening sideways, are held in place by hinges and when in this position the attached mirror may be raised as in the illustration. On each side of the mirror are compartments for toilet accessories. Below are three drawers under which is a slide which pulls out. About 1800.

No. 1474 is a similar dressing table of the same period. The mirror may be lowered into a space in the back, vertically. This arrangement requires a deeper frame than that in the previous example, and the additional space is occupied by cupboards and a drawer, on which are lines of inlay. These ingenious tables show that the emphasis on convenience is not entirely a contemporary product. About 1800.

No. 1475 is a dressing table resembling in form No. 1467, except that here there is a rectangular opening in front instead of an arch. The central portion of the top opens upward and on the top is an inlay of flowers and rectangular forms. The inlay on the front of the five drawers is in the same design as that in the lowboy No. 685. The legs, tapered on the inside, and the surfaces above, are grooved. About 1790–1800.

No. 1476 has a top in one piece, on the inner side of which is a large mirror which in the illustration reflects a marble surface upon which toilet accessories may be placed. When the top is down the table resembles the preceding piece in outline. The three drawers are bordered with brass moldings and the round and tapering legs have brass caps at the tops. This seems to be French. About 1800–1810.

4.   Beau Brummell, 1778–1840, had a varied career, rising to the height of public interest, later sinking to the depths of poverty and ending his days in a charitable asylum. From his early years he paid great attention to his dress. At Eton and Oxford he was known as a wit and a good story–teller, and was found so amusing by the Prince of Wales that the Prince became his patron and gave him a commission in his own regiment. In 1798 he inherited a considerable fortune. "His social success was instant and complete, his repartees were the talk of the town. . . Though he always dressed well, he was no mere fop. Lord Byron is credited with the remark that there was nothing remarkable about his dress, except 'a certain exquisite propriety.' For a time Brummell's sway was undisputed. But eventually gambling and extravagance exhausted his fortune, while his tongue proved too sharp for his royal patron." In 1816 he fled to France to avoid his English creditors. Later his French creditors had him imprisoned for a time. He and his predecessor "Beau Nash," (1674–1762) were bachelors. "Beau Nash" was the master of ceremonies at Bath, the celebrated English watering place. This information is condensed from the Encyclopædia Britannica.

It should be recalled that the word "Beau" as applied to Brummell and Nash does not mean a man who is attentive to a lady; the meaning is "one who is very neat and particular about his dress, and fond of ornaments and jewelry; a fop; a dandy; now most often said of a man of middle age or older"; Century Dictionary.

5.   In the "Guide" of Hepplewhite and the Appendix to Sheraton's "Drawing–Book" are drawings of dressing tables almost the same in form as those here shown, including the mirror, slide and tapering legs, but decorated with a different style of inlay.

Section 169. Card tables; Queen Anne and Chippendale styles.—In England throughout the eighteenth century "the rage for play and for high stakes was a characteristic and fashionable vice," as remarked by Mr. Cescinsky,[1] particularly during the latter part of the period. "Card tables were indispensable articles of furniture in the drawing room and the salon, from six to twelve of a kind being no unusual number in one house among the wealthy" aristocracy of that period; and they seem to have been almost equally popular in America. The shapes of the card tables of the Queen Anne, Chippendale, Hepplewhite and Sheraton styles were about the same, but the details of their ornamentation, the forms of the legs and feet, and some minor features, were very different. In this section we see several card tables in the Queen Anne and Chippendale styles. The tops of the tables made in these two styles were often covered with cloth; but this was generally not used on the later tables in the styles of Hepplewhite and Sheraton, the folding top being finished so that it would look well when opened against a wall.

Nos. 1477–1480 are shown with the folding tops raised, in order that the shape and conveniences for play may be well seen. On each table one of the rear legs swings out and supports the folding top.

No. 1477 is in the Queen Anne style, as appears from the cabriole legs and the Dutch, or club, feet, which here are protected by "shoes" as in many other pieces, such as the corner table No. 1458. The four rectangular corners are enlarged in order to provide spaces for candlesticks. The four oval shaped cups, or wells, sunk below the surface, are to hold money or chips. There is no front drawer in this table. The skirt and the legs are plain. On the two rectangular plates are inscriptions as to the former ownership. About 1750–1770.

1.   A.   In "English Furniture," volume 2, page 164.

B.   In "The Homes of our Ancestors," by Halsey and Tower, page 112, it is said that "after supper, which was usually served at nine o'clock, it was time for some other form of amusement. Cards were a favorite pastime and certainly not a vice. In Washington's account book there are frequent entries of winnings or losings, without any apparent thought of the right or wrong of gambling. . . Indeed cards were even more necessary in colonial times than they are today, for books were scarcely written to entertain, even if the light for reading in the evening had been better."

C.   The distinctive feature of card tables is that the top is in two equal parts, one of which folds over upon the other. One part of the top is permanently "fixed" to the frame–work, and the other is attached to the fixed one at the rear ends, by hinges, in such a manner that it may fold over on the fixed part, or may stand upright if leaning against a wall, or may fall back horizontally, in the latter case the two parts making one top. In this latter position the folding part is supported by one or more swinging legs, in the manner shown in the drop–leaf tables in previous sections. Occasionally the whole top may revolve, the front moving to the sides. In some cases there are two folding tops, as in No. 1478. In certain fine English tables the back legs do not swing, but are attached to an extension under the frame and may be drawn backward to support the folding top in somewhat the manner mentioned in the comment on the card table No. 1642.

D.   A card table and a side table may be of about the same size, design and ornamentation, the chief difference being that the card table has a second top which folds over, as above stated, giving the appearance of a top with a double thickness, whereas a side table has only one top. Compare the top of the side table No. 1433 in the Hepplewhite style and that of the card table No. 1506 in the same style.

E.   The most elaborate American card table in the Chippendale style is that known as the "Cadwalader *card* table" which is illustrated in "Antiques," January, 1930, page 22. The "Cadwalader *side* table" is illustrated in this book in section 166, No. 1430.

No. 1478, in the Chippendale style, is a combined card and backgammon[2] table, known as a "triple–top" table, having one fixed and two folding tops. The enlarged rectangular corners of the fixed top and of the first folding one are slightly sunken for candlesticks, and there are four cups, as in the preceding table. The lower surface of the second folding top and the upper surface of the first folding one are inlaid in forms for backgammon. The skirt is molded in a "godroon"[3] design, the knees of the legs are carved in a shell design and the feet are of the ball and claw type. About 1760–1780.

In No. 1479, also in the Chippendale style, the enlarged corners of the fixed top are round, instead of rectangular as in the preceding pieces, and are slightly sunken. The folding top also is round at the corners, following the form of the frame. The legs are carved at the knees and terminate in ball and claw feet. This table has been in the possession of the present Maryland family, and on the same land, since about 1760. Here also there is a drawer in the skirt. About 1750–1770.

No. 1480 is a plain type of card table in the Chippendale style. The edge of the top is in a series of serpentine curves, and has a rim to prevent the chips from sliding off. The legs terminate in small ball and claw feet. There is one drawer in the front and a smaller one on the side, and under the front drawer is a carved ornamental design. This is probably a Dutch table. About 1760–1780.

Nos. 1481–1486 are shown with the folding tops down. Some of these tables have the same form of top as in the preceding examples, and in others the tops are rectangular.

No. 1481 is in the Queen Anne style and has the same type of plain legs with Dutch, or club, feet with a "shoe" as in No. 1477. The edges of the tops are carved in an unusual design and the corners are enlarged and rounded as in the two preceding tables. A drawer is in the skirt. About 1750–1770.

No. 1482 and the following card tables in this section are in the Chippendale style. This table resembles Nos. 1477 and 1478 in having enlarged rectangular corners for candlesticks. The skirt is plain but the upper portion of the legs, the "knees," are carved in a large leaf design. The feet are of the ball and claw type. About 1760–1780.

In No. 1483 the front of the top is in a serpentine curve and the corners are rectangular but are not enlarged sufficiently to hold candlesticks; this may indicate that the candlesticks were to be placed on candlestands, because when candlestands came into use the places on the card tables for candlesticks were no longer made. The edges of the top are carved with flowers and leaves. The base of the skirt and the edges of the front legs are carved in tiny beads. The legs are straight and square and are grooved, as on many chairs and tables of the Chippendale style. About 1760–1780.

2.　An article entitled "Backgammon tables of the Eighteenth Century," by Mr. Robert Tasker Evans, with many illustrations, is in "The Antiquarian," March, 1931, pages 33–37. Some of the tables have also boards for chess and other games.

　　A chess–board table in the Sheraton style is shown in No. 1368.

3.　This word is defined in section 119, note 3.

1477 (UPPER) MD. HISTORICAL SOCIETY.
1479 (LOWER) FAMILY OF THOS. CRADOCK.

1478 (UPPER) MR. JOHN C. TOLAND.
1480 (LOWER) COL. OF MRS. JORDAN STABLER.

No. 1484 resembles No. 1479 in having round corners on the top and ball and claw feet. Here also the front is serpentine, and the bottom of the skirt is ornamented with "godroon" carving as in No. 1478. The knees, also, are carved. In this and the two preceding tables there is no drawer. About 1760–1780.

No. 1485 has a rectangular top. Under the drawer the skirt is cut in a series of cyma and other curves. The legs are plain and terminate in ball and claw feet. About 1760–1780.

No. 1486 is similar to the preceding card table in having a rectangular top and plain legs with ball and claw feet. Under the drawer and on the ends the skirt is carved in the "godroon" form. About 1760–1780.

Section 170. Card tables; Hepplewhite style.—The fine card tables in the styles of Hepplewhite and Sheraton are so pleasing in form and decoration that it is difficult to decide in one's mind which are the most attractive; but if we are guided by the opinions of our ancestors as indicated by the number of pieces which have survived, the palm must be awarded to those in the style of Hepplewhite. All of the Hepplewhite style tables were probably made before any decadence in furniture styles took place, whereas the tables in the late style of Sheraton gradually became somewhat coarse under the influence of the Empire style, as will be seen in the next section.

Of the large number of card tables in the Hepplewhite style[1] available for illustration in this book, the limited space allows only thirty–four examples to be shown, which have been selected chiefly because of their elegant appearance. All have certain characteristic features which the reader has already seen in the Hepplewhite style sideboards, dining tables, Pembroke tables, side tables and dressing tables. These features are mainly the straight and tapered legs sometimes ending in spade feet, and the inlaid ornamentation.

The tables illustrated here are arranged according to their special and conspicuous features, rather than by their supposed dates, in order that those of similar appearance may be easily compared. Thus in the first group, of six tables, Nos. 1487–1492, the noticeable features are the decorative treatment of the legs of the first four and the shape of the tops of all; in the second group, Nos. 1493–1498, all the tables have five or more legs; and other groups have certain special features. This arrangement has no importance other than that of convenience, and is not altogether satisfactory. The last ten tables, Nos. 1511–1520, are shown with the folding tops up, in order that the shapes of the tops may be clearly seen. The height of these card tables, sometimes made in pairs, is about twenty–nine or thirty inches. The wood is almost always mahogany, often inlaid with maple or satinwood. They are all of the period of about 1785 to 1800, or a little later.

1. In Hepplewhite's "Guide," as to which see section 17, only two designs of card tables are shown. In the edition of 1804 these are on plate 60. Both have straight and tapered legs and spade feet. The American cabinet makers used the general style of the drawers of Chippendale, Hepplewhite and Sheraton but often added or omitted details as they or their customers desired.

The distinctive feature of card tables is stated in note 1, C in the preceding section.

1481 (Upper) Mr. John C. Toland.
1483 (Centre) Mr. John C. Toland.
1485 (Lower) Mrs. Wilbur W. Hubbard.

1482 (Upper) Mr. Arthur E. Cole.
1484 (Centre) Mr. John C. Toland.
1486 (Lower) Mr. John C. Toland.

Nos. 1487–1490, four handsome tables in the first group of six, were doubtless made in Baltimore, as they have apparently been found only in or near that city. Each of these four tables is highly decorated in much the same style, which also appears in the serving table No. 1439. All of the six tables have the same form of top, the corners of which are rounded, a better illustration of which appears in No. 1511, in which the top is up, showing the corners and the straight front between them.

No. 1487 has the usual Hepplewhite style square and tapered legs, one of which swings out and supports the folding part of the top. The corners of this top are rounded, as mentioned. The sections of the skirt are banded with a light wood, and between them are inlaid oval medallions with leaves. The most notable feature is that the legs have a wide inlay of light wood for about half of their length and this inlay is itself inlaid with strings of flowers of a darker color. Further below is an inlaid string ending with a tassel. This table has been referred to by a learned critic as a "Baltimore card table that offers the most brilliant treatment of veneers and inlays of any American item" known to him and as "exemplifying the Southern taste for richness of ornament and restraint of line." About 1790–1800.

In No. 1488 the frame is in the same shape as in the preceding piece, and the wide inlay on the legs, and the oval medallions above them, are similar. The skirt is inlaid with forms which have concave corners as in the next table; and the edge of the skirt is bordered with inlay. The illustrations of this and the three other tables of this character cannot do justice to their elegance. About 1790–1800.

No. 1489 is even more fully decorated than the others in this group. The wide inlay of light wood on the legs extends almost to the bands of similar wood near the bottom. The skirt in front is ornamented with two large inlaid ovals, between which is an inlaid design with concave corners as in the preceding table. Over the legs are medallions and on the curved portion of the skirt are other inlaid designs. The inlaid lines on the edges of the fixed and the folding top will be noticed and also the bright bands of inlay within the line of the top. About 1790–1800.

In No. 1490 the long inlay on the legs tapers gradually to a point. Above the front legs are inlaid oval medallions. The tapering of the legs on the inside is noticeable, as in many other tables in the Hepplewhite style. About 1790–1800.

In Nos. 1491 and 1492 the top is in the same form as in the preceding tables, but there is not the same ornamental treatment of the legs. In No. 1491 the edges of the top are veneered with a light wood which is also used around the panels in the skirt and the ends, and also on the small panels above the legs. Each of the four legs is decorated with inlaid lines and strings of flowers. About 1790–1800.

No. 1492 is ornamented with inlaid lines on the edges of the top. On the skirt are long parallel lines of inlay with rounded ends, as also in No. 1499, a design which is referred to in section 127, note 6, and section 96, note 1, C; and on the edge is a delicate border of light wood. In the small ovals above the legs are inlaid urns, and on all the legs are decorations similar to those in the preceding table. About 1790–1800,

1487 (Upper) Mr. & Mrs. B. Turnbull.   1488 (Upper) Mr. John C. Toland.
1489 (Centre) Mr. A. E. Cole.   1490 (Centre) Dr. George E. Hardy.
1491 (Lower) Mr. Arthur E. Cole.   1492 (Lower) Mrs. Edward Shoemaker.

In the next group of six tables, Nos. 1493–1498, each of the tables has five or six legs four of which are stationary and the other one or two swing out and support the folding lid. The side table No. 1439, also, has six legs, and several card tables in the Sheraton style have more than four, such as Nos. 1527 and 1535. The use of more than four legs is not confined to any particular type of card table in the Hepplewhite style and seems to have no significance except as a variation from the usual form. Other than the number of legs, the principal differences in these six tables are in the inlay and the shapes. About 1790–1800.

No. 1493, with six legs, is shown with the folding lid in use, supported by the two swinging legs in the rear. The top is eight-sided as shown here, and six-sided, including the back, when the folding top lies on the "fixed" one. The edges of the two front legs face the front, thus presenting two inlaid sides to the view. The inlaid forms on the skirt are rectangular, with the exception of the diamond-shaped panel in light wood, and the inlaid oval medallions at the corners. About 1790–1800.

In No. 1494, with five legs, the corners of the top are in the same rounded form as those in the tables Nos. 1487–1492 and 1511; between the corners the top is straight. The skirt is ornamented with a series of rectangular inlaid forms, and the legs have interlacing lines of inlay. About 1790–1800.

No. 1495 has five legs all of which are ornamented with inlaid flowers. The ends are concave, between which the front is straight, as in the serving table No. 1440. On the skirt are rectangular inlaid forms and on the lower edge is a band of inlay. About 1790–1800.

In No. 1496 the top is rounded at the front corners; this form of top appears also in the Sheraton style card table No. 1531 and others. Above the two front legs are rectangular panels, and in the centre of the skirt is an inlaid panel of light wood in which there is an inlaid centre of dark wood. Here also are five legs. About 1790–1800.

No. 1497, also with five legs, has a bowed or swell front, in this respect resembling No. 1519. The skirt is ornamented with inlays of dark and light wood. The two large dark inlaid panels have the same form as in No. 1488, with corners in a concave form; and between these panels is a third one, with an oval design in light wood. The legs are tapered to an unusual degree. About 1790–1800.

No. 1498 is a round card table which might be mistaken for a round dining table, such as No. 1315. In the illustration the folding top is supported by the leg in the rear which swings back when not needed. About 1790–1800.

The next group is of six card tables, Nos. 1499–1504, which are round when open and half-round when the folding top rests upon the fixed one. As in the two preceding groups, the principal difference between these tables is in the ornamentation. In these tables the two front legs, being attached to a curved skirt, are in a position which shows two sides.

1493 (UPPER) HAMMOND–HARWOOD HOUSE.
1495 (CENTRE) MR. & MRS. RALPH ROBINSON.
1497 (LOWER) MR. ALBERT G. TOWERS.

1494 (UPPER) MR. J. F. H. MAGINN.
1496 (CENTRE) MISS ELISABETH H. BARTLETT.
1498 (LOWER) MRS. C. E. HENDERSON.

In No. 1499 the edges of the top are veneered with a light wood, as in No. 1491. On the skirt are three long parallel forms of inlay in light wood with rounded ends, as are also seen and referred to in No. 1492, and two small panels of the same wood are over the legs. About 1790–1800.

In No. 1500 the skirt is ornamented with long ovals in dark wood, between which are two small panels with designs in light wood on a dark background. The legs have lines of inlay and strings of flowers. About 1790–1800.

No. 1501 is more fully decorated, having in the skirt inlaid forms with concave corners, between which are two ovals with figures of an eagle clutching a snake. On the front legs are inlaid designs, apparently of flowers. About 1790–1800.

In No. 1502 the front and ends have inlaid horizontal strings of flowers tied in the centre and at each end. In the panels over the front legs are inlaid shells under which, on the legs, are other shell designs. About 1790–1800.

No. 1503 is shown with the half-round folding top in a vertical position as though it were leaning against a wall. The top is bordered with a light wood which is also seen on the panels in the skirt. Oval medallions are over the front legs, and all the four legs are inlaid with strings of flowers. About 1790–1800.

No. 1504 is shown from the rear in order to see the inlaid semi–circle which is at the rear of the folding top. When this folding top is resting flat upon the fixed top, and the table is closely in front of a low mirror, the folding top, with its inlaid semi-circle, is reflected and makes a complete circle. This reflection is also mentioned in connection with pier tables in section 174, note 1. When the folding top falls back upon the swinging leg, the inlaid semi–circle is on the under side and is not visible. About 1790–1800.

In the next four tables, Nos. 1505–1508, the top is in a different form from those seen above. The front is curved in a bow, or swell, form, and the ends are in cyma curves, as to which see section 23. The shape of the top is more clearly seen in No. 1512. When the folding top is in use, the fixed and folding tops together form curves on the sides.

No. 1505 is shown from the side in order that the end may be well seen. All the legs are inlaid with strings of flowers on two sides, and over the legs are oval medallions with inlaid leaves and flowers. The skirt has inlaid rectangular panels with wide borders. The cyma curve of the ends will be noticed. About 1790–1800.

No. 1506 is in the same form with more abundant decoration. The skirt has five panels, the one in the centre enclosing an oval which is veneered with dark wood; and four small panels are over the legs which terminate in pointed feet. About 1790–1800.

No. 1507 is similar to the preceding table, especially in having five panels on the skirt and in having pointed feet. The oval in the central panel is veneered with light wood with a finely figured grain, and the other panels on the front and ends are also of fine wood. About 1790–1800.

1499 (UPPER) MR. C. EDWARD SNYDER.
1501 (CENTRE) MRS. J. P. PLEASANTS.
1503 (LOWER) MRS. S. S. BUZBY.

1500 (UPPER) MRS. C. P. ROGOW.
1502 (CENTRE) MR. & MRS. JAS. CAREY, JR
1504 (LOWER) MISS HELEN H. CAREY.

No. 1508 has an unusual type of bright inlay on the edge of the skirt and on the small panels over the legs; and on the skirt are rectangular designs in line inlay. On the legs are the usual flowers. About 1790–1800.

Nos. 1509 and 1510 are similar in having rounded ends with a concave centre, a form of which is also seen in No. 1514, in which the top is up. This type of card table was apparently not very often made, perhaps because the concave front was not so well adapted to sit at as the straight or convex fronts. A similar card table in the Sheraton style with reeded legs is seen as No. 1527.

In No. 1509 the skirt has inlaid designs of parallel lines with rounded ends, within each of which is another inlaid design of parallel lines with pointed ends. Medallions of inlaid leaves and flowers are over the legs which end in tapered feet. About 1790–1800.

In No. 1510, which belongs to the same owner as the preceding table, the lines of inlay on the skirt may be seen but are difficult to describe. Over the legs are small panels of light wood within which are diamond–shaped panels of dark wood. About 1790–1800.

The remaining ten illustrations of card tables in the Hepplewhite style, Nos. 1511–1520, were taken with the folding tops up in order that their shapes might be well seen. The fixed top and the folding top of a card table are of course exactly of the same shape and size.

Nos. 1511 and 1512 are handsome card tables belonging to the same owner. They are similar in having in the centre of the skirt an inlaid American eagle with a shield, above which are eighteen stars. These stars may represent the number of States in the Union at the time the tables were made,[2] and if so the date would be between the year 1812, in which the eighteenth State, Louisiana, was admitted to the Union, and the year 1816, in which the nineteenth State, Indiana, was admitted. This date seems to be late for the Hepplewhite style. Other similar features are the inlaid urns in medallions over the front legs, and the almost pointed feet.

In No. 1511 the top is in the same shape as in Nos. 1487–1492 and 1494, having rounded ends and a straight front. The skirt has brilliant mahogany veneer, matched.[3] The inlaid eagle and stars are referred to in the preceding paragraph. Lines of inlay are on the front legs, but not on the rear ones. The legs taper sharply at the bottom. Assuming that the date is indicated by the number of stars, it is about 1812–1816.

In No. 1512 the top is in the same shape as in Nos. 1505–1508, the ends being in curves and the front being in a bow, or swell, form. The panels on the front and the ends are of curly maple. Delicate lines of inlay are on the front legs. The finely grained mahogany of the folding top will be noticed. About 1812–1816.

2.   Other articles of which the dates are shown in this manner are the desks Nos. 803 and 805, and the mirrors Nos. 1160, 1173, and 1196, with explanatory notes. See note 5, section 145; also the Index, under the word "Stars."

3.   This word "matched," as used here, is explained in section 32, note 2. Other examples are in Nos. 1610 and 1616.

1505 (Upper) Mr. Herbert T. Tiffany. 1506 (Upper) Hammond–Harwood House.
1507 (Centre) Mr. J. Gilman D'Arcy Paul. 1508 (Centre) Mr. & Mrs. J. M. Matthews.
1509 (Lower) Mrs. I. R. Trimble. 1510 (Lower) Mrs. I. R. Trimble.

In Nos. 1513 and 1514 the tops are almost in the same form as in Nos. 1509 and 1510, having a concave portion in the centre, making the front recessed. On the skirt of No. 1513 are inlaid forms with concave corners, and strings of flowers are on the legs, over which are small inlaid panels with leaves and flowers. About 1790–1800.

In No. 1514 the recessed concave portion of the top is larger than in the preceding table. On the skirt are inlaid forms with concave corners, a small similar form enclosing a six–pointed star, and oval medallions over the legs. The usual strings of flowers are on the front legs and on these and the rear ones are lines of inlay. The legs are unusually delicate, ending almost in points. About 1790–1800.

In No. 1515 the top is in the so–called "clover–leaf" pattern, which consists here of five sections of circles of different sizes. This form, and also the three–curve one, was a favorite of Duncan Phyfe and appears on the Sheraton style card table No. 1535. The line of the top follows that of the frame, making an interesting shape, although probably not a convenient one for the card players. The skirt is ornamented with inlay and the usual medallions and flowers are on the legs. About 1790–1800.

In No. 1516 the top resembles somewhat that in Nos. 1487–1492 and 1494, having curved corners; here, however, the centre of the front is not straight but is in a graceful serpentine curve. A band of satinwood surrounds the under side of the folding lid and the top of the fixed one. On the skirt are four rectangular panels with satinwood borders. In the centre of the skirt is an inlaid griffin, said to be chained.[4] The tops are covered with green baize. About 1790–1800.

No. 1517 has another form of top, with rounded ends and a serpentine curve in the centre. The edges of both the fixed and the folding tops have lines of inlay. In the centre of the skirt is a panel of curly maple and on each side are other inlaid designs. About 1790–1800.

In No. 1518 the top is very similar in form to that of the preceding table. A pleasing feature is that the edges of the folding and fixed tops are finely reeded. On the skirt are rectangular inlaid forms, and the rear and front legs are ornamented with inlay. About 1790–1800.

In No. 1519 the top is in the same form as that of No. 1497, having a bowed, or swell, front. The front part of the skirt is in three sections, the centre one of which encloses an oval of dark and light wood. Here the tapering legs extend into pointed feet. About 1790–1800.

No. 1520 is an ordinary Hepplewhite style card table in a rectangular form, but of a somewhat agreeable appearance. This table, with little inlay, seems plain

---

4.   A design of a similar character, with the griffin holding a string of flowers, appears on plate 56 in the 1802 edition of Sheraton's "Drawing Book," (as to which see section 18), between pages 352 and 353, where it is termed an "Ornament for a frieze or tablet." Figures of griffins are also seen on the mantel mirror No. 1229 and on other articles referred to in the comments on that mirror; and see also the Index and the Sheraton style card table No. 1553 and note 11 in section 171.

1511 (Upper) Mrs. Francis P. Garvan.   1512 (Upper) Mrs. Francis P. Garvan.
1513 (Centre) Mr. Morris Whitridge.   1514 (Centre) Col. of Mrs. Jordan
1515 (Lower) Mrs. A. Morris Carey.   Stabler.
                             1516 (Lower) Mrs. Francis P. Garvan.

in comparison with the previous pieces with their abundant inlay, curved tops and decorated skirts. Here there are three drawers, with oval brass handles of the period. About 1790–1800.

Section 171. Card tables; Sheraton and Empire styles.—In this section are thirty–six illustrations of card tables, many of which are in the early and finer style of Sheraton;[1] others are of the later and less desirable type which also bears his name, and a few are in the still later Empire style.

Many of the card tables in the Sheraton style differ from those in the Hepplewhite style chiefly in having round and reeded tapering legs instead of the square, inlaid and tapering legs of the Hepplewhite style; several tables will be seen in which this is the only noticeable difference.

The style of Sheraton was the fashionable one in our country from about 1795 to 1815, or later, as mentioned in section 18, and it was in this period that Duncan Phyfe made his best furniture and became the leading cabinet maker in New York. It was natural, of course, that Phyfe should work in that style in those years, and that his card tables and other articles of furniture should be made in that style. We may regret that Phyfe did not often use the Hepplewhite style also, but the fact that he did not do so is an indication that his work was done at a time when that style was not the most fashionable one. The main features of his card tables are in the Sheraton style, to which Phyfe added various embellishments of carving and other details which contributed to the elegance of his furniture. His work seems to have been copied by other cabinet makers, but not with all of his details. We may repeat what has been stated in substance in other sections, namely, there was and is no "Duncan Phyfe style" of furniture[2] in the sense that there was a Hepplewhite style or a Sheraton style.

The height of these card tables, as of those in the Hepplewhite style, is about twenty–nine inches, and the wood is almost always solid or veneered mahogany, often veneered also with maple or satinwood. The dates are from 1795 to 1825.

The straight and reeded legs of the card tables in the Sheraton style are very similar to the legs on several other articles made in that style; this will be seen, for example, in the illustrations of the dining tables Nos. 1319–1321 and the sideboard No. 996. Some of the legs project beyond the line of the frame, as in the Sheraton style bureau No. 745 and others, and in the sideboard No. 992 and others. In the first group, Nos. 1521–1538, the legs are attached directly to the frame of the table, as in the Hepplewhite style tables, not to a lyre or platform or pedestal as in others in this section.

---

1.   Two designs of card tables are shown on plate 11 in the Appendix to Sheraton's "Drawing Book," edition of 1802, as to which see section 18. On the plate are the words "Published by T. Sheraton, April 30, 1793." One of these designs, with projecting legs, is evidently the model for tables in the form of No. 1521. The other design has not apparently been exactly copied by the American cabinet makers.

The distinctive feature of card tables is stated in note 1, C in section 169.

2.   See "The Duncan Phyfe furniture," section 20, and "The American Directory style," section 19.

1517 (Upper) Mr. Edgar G. Miller, Jr.
1519 (Lower) Anonymous.

1518 (Upper) Rt. Rev. & Mrs. E. T. Helfenstein.
1520 (Lower) Dr. Jas. Bordley, Jr.

In No. 1521 the skirt and top are in a bowed, or swell, shape except a small straight portion at each end. The skirt is finely veneered with a light wood which extends over the rounded corners to the back. The tapered legs are reeded and at the bottom are "turned" feet, as to which see section 35. The projection of the legs beyond the line of the frame will be noticed. Card tables of this type are said to be of New England origin. About 1800–1815.

In No. 1522 the top and the skirt are in a serpentine curve. In the centre of the skirt is a large oval of veneered light wood. Here also, as in the preceding table, the front corners are rounded, below which are carved rings over the projecting reeded and tapered legs which end in turned feet. About 1800–1815.

In No. 1523 the top is bowed, or swelled, with rectangular corners. The front of the skirt has three panels of finely figured veneer and at each end is a small panel over the leg. The fixed and the folding top are each ornamented with two lines of inlay. The form of the top of this table resembles that of the Hepplewhite style card table No. 1519. About 1800–1815.

No. 1524 has the same shape of top as the Hepplewhite style tables Nos 1505–1508, the front being curved in a bow, or swell, form. The shape of this kind of top is clearly seen in the Hepplewhite style table No. 1512, which it resembles also in having on the skirt four panels of satinwood, and between the front ones is a panel of dark wood enclosing an inlaid oval. About 1800–1815.

No. 1525 is similar in shape to No. 1522, having a serpentine front with rounded corners. Here the veneer on the front is carried around the corners and on the ends as in No. 1521. The legs are in a different form from the usual one, being without reeding but turned with several rings. About 1800–1815.

No. 1526 resembles somewhat No. 1493 in the Hepplewhite style, having a top which is six–sided, including the back, when the folding top lies upon the fixed top, and becomes eight–sided when it is supported by a swinging leg. The four legs are ornamented with somewhat heavy reeding which indicates a later date than that in the preceding examples. About 1810–1820.

No. 1527 resembles the Hepplewhite style card tables Nos. 1509–1510, which belong to the same owner, in having a top and skirt with rounded ends and a concave centre in the manner of No. 1514. The edges are finely reeded and also the five legs, but are not distinct in the engraving. In this piece and in several others, especially those of Duncan Phyfe, there is no decoration with inlay of different colors; the fine effects are secured by the harmonious proportions, the quality of the mahogany, either solid or veneer, and the elegance of the carving. About 1800–1815.

No. 1528, with a form resembling that of the preceding table, is fully and finely decorated with paintings of a character similar to those on the chairs Nos. 290 and 291. In the concave portion of the skirt is an eight–sided panel with a painting of a large building, and on the ends are similar panels with paintings of musical instruments. The edges of the top are painted in the same style as the borders of the rectangular panels. The legs, instead of being reeded, are inlaid

1521 (Upper) Mr. Edgar G. Miller, Jr.   1522 (Upper) Mr. Edgar G. Miller, Jr.
1523 (Centre) Hammond-Harwood House.   1524 (Centre) Mr. Arthur E. Cole.
1525 (Lower) Hammond-Harwood House.   1526 (Lower) Mr. & Mrs. H. L. Duer.

in the same manner as in the Baltimore corner table No. 1462 and the serving tables Nos. 1441 and 1442. This table was made by Robert Fisher,[3] a Baltimore cabinet maker. About 1800–1815.

No. 1529 has about the same form and workmanship as certain tables known to have been made by Duncan Phyfe, but in the absence of definite proof it cannot be said to be a product of his shop. The skirt is veneered with mahogany, and four small panels are above the legs, which terminate in round brass feet. The fifth leg is the inner one on the rear left. About 1800–1815.

No. 1530 is known to be a product of Duncan Phyfe. With the folding top down, the top is six–sided, including the back, and is eight–sided when it is in use. The skirt is ornamented in the centre with a panel carved with a festoon of drapery, and over the legs with smaller panels. The upper portions of the curved legs are carved with acanthus leaves, below which the legs are plain and terminate in animals' claw feet—a combination which has not been admired by all collectors.[4] About 1815–1825.

No. 1531 is in the form of a card table although its width of forty–four inches is greater than usual. The edges of the tops are grooved and the folding top when in use is supported by a swinging leg in the usual manner. The legs are ringed at the top, and below are reeded in the heavy form which is seen in other pieces in the late Sheraton style, such as the dining table No. 1321. In form this table resembles No. 1496 in the Hepplewhite style, having rounded corners and straight front and ends. About 1810–1820.

No. 1532 is in the Empire style, as indicated by the kind of carving on the legs and the skirt; the feet, however, are of the Sheraton type. Instead of being ornamented with reeding, the legs are carved with large leaves which twine around them. Above the legs are small panels carved with leaves, and in the centre of the skirt is a panel in which there is a carved eagle with outspread wings. The form of the top is very similar to that in the preceding table. About 1810–1820.

The next six card tables in the Sheraton style, Nos. 1533–1538, are shown with their folding tops up in order that the shapes may be well seen, as with several tables in the Hepplewhite style in the previous section. The fixed tops are of course exactly the same in shape as the folding tops.

---

3.   Robert Fisher has been identified by labels on furniture and by the city directories as a cabinet maker of Baltimore. He used paintings on several pieces known to have been made by him, such as the "fancy" chair No. 291, the settee No. 516 and the window seat No. 536, all of which are now the property of the same owner. Fisher's name appears in the Baltimore City directories from 1800 to 1812 as a chairmaker. He is mentioned in section 20, note 1, in connection with Lachlan Phyfe.

4.   By one experienced writer this design has been called "highly dramatic and stimulating"; by another it is regarded as an example of the beginning of the decline of Phyfe's style. But all agree that the table is of the finest material and workmanship. Similar combinations were used by Phyfe on some of his chairs, not illustrated in this book.

1527 (Upper) Mrs. I. R. Trimble.
1528 (Upper) Mrs. Miles White, Jr.
1529 (Centre) Miss Margaret C. Painter.
1530 (Centre) Mrs. Francis P. Garvan.
1531 (Lower) Mrs. Rignal W. Baldwin.
1532 (Lower) Mr. J. Ramsay Speer.

No. 1533 is a handsome table which in form resembles No. 1521, having a skirt which is bowed or swelled in the centre, but with straight ends, and also with rounded corners and reeded, tapering and turned legs projecting beyond the lines of the frame. On the edges of the fixed and folding tops are small bands of inlay in a "checker" pattern, that is, having small blocks of wood of alternate dark and light color, as on a checker board. The oval and rectangular panels are veneered with satinwood. The folding top appears less shapely in the upright position; it may be compared with the top of the table in the Chippendale style with rounded corners, No. 1479. About 1800–1815.

In No. 1534 the curves of the folding top are somewhat more graceful than in the preceding table, although the corners are not pleasing when seen in a vertical position. The skirt is similar to that in No. 1524, having four veneered panels of satinwood, with an inlaid oval in the mahogany central panel. As in the preceding table, there are ringed columns over the legs. About 1800–1815.

In No. 1535 the top is in the so–called "clover–leaf" pattern, with five curves, similar to those in No. 1547 and in the Hepplewhite style card table No. 1515. This table follows a design of Duncan Phyfe in having no inlay, relying upon the fine proportions of the piece, with carving in some instances. The five legs are finely reeded and terminate in round brass feet, differing in these respects from the Hepplewhite table. About 1800–1815.

In No. 1536 the centre of the top is recessed in a serpentine curve, which is more graceful than that in the Hepplewhite style table No. 1514. There is no decorative inlay, but the edges of the tops, the legs and the small panels over them are finely reeded. About 1800–1815.

In No. 1537 the top is in the same form as that in No. 1534 and the edges are finely reeded; but the reeding of the legs, and of the columns above them, as well as the carving of leaves between, are of a less elegant character, indicating the change from the early to the later Sheraton style. About 1810–1820.

No. 1538 has a clover–leaf design of three curves. The legs are carved in the heavy spiral form which was much used in the Empire period, and the table must be regarded as having features of the Empire style and therefore as of that period.[5] About 1820–1830.

The next group of card tables in the Sheraton style, Nos. 1539–1546, are known as "lyre" card tables because the top is supported by two lyres, or lyre–shaped pieces, which are called the "standards"[6] of the table. The lyre form was

5. This is in accordance with the principle that the date of the latest feature determines the date of the piece, as mentioned in section 6.

6. The word "standard" as applied to tables means the upright part which supports the frame and top of the table. In these lyre card tables the lyres are the standards.

1533 (Upper) Anonymous.
1535 (Centre) Mrs. M. S. Hartshorne.
1537 (Lower) Mr. S. Johnson Poe.
1534 (Upper) Anonymous.
1536 (Centre) Dr. M. A. Abrams.
1538 (Lower) Mrs. A. Morris Carey.

a favorite of Sheraton[7] and was copied by Duncan Phyfe[8] in his furniture in the Sheraton style, as in the chair No. 326, the sofa No. 574 and the sofa table No. 1423. In these card tables and others the top revolves to a position in which the folding portion when open is supported by the frame, as shown in No. 1541. The strings on the lyre are almost always made of brass, but sometimes whalebone was used. The eight illustrations exhibit the gradual change from the delicate forms of the early Sheraton style to the heavy form of the late Empire period. The lyre sewing tables, Nos. 1566–1571, may be examined in connection with these card tables.

No. 1539 is a fine example of lyre card tables and was probably made by Duncan Phyfe. The slanting position in which the photograph was taken gives to the carved panel in the skirt the appearance of not being in the centre. The lyres and the legs are carved with acanthus leaves and the platform on which the lyres rest is fluted. The four legs are attached to the platform and are in concave curves and end in brass claw feet with casters, as in the Sheraton style dining table No. 1326 and the library table No. 1421. This table, like No. 1493 in the Hepplewhite style and No. 1526 in the Sheraton style, has eight sides when the folding top is in use and six sides when the folding top lies upon the fixed one. Very few of these tables have been found. About 1810–1815.

No. 1540 is known to be by Duncan Phyfe. Here the two lyres are "crossed," not parallel as in the preceding table, and the strings are attached to crossed bars at the top. In some tables of this type the strings are omitted and an ornamental pineapple is placed at the base. The arms of the lyres are carved with acanthus leaves and a small rope design. The platform is plain, but the legs have a carved rope design similar to that on the arms. The concave legs are wide–spreading as in the preceding piece, but are not quite as long. About 1810–1815.

No. 1541 is shown with the top open and turned around. As with No. 1539, this table was photographed in a slanting position, causing the joint between the fixed and folding top to appear off the centre. Instead of two lyres with strings, there is only one, the other standard being a solid piece of wood in the lyre shape,

7. In Sheraton's "Drawing Book," (as to which see section 18), edition of 1802, in its Appendix, plate 13, a fire screen is shown with an elaborate lyre on the screen portion; on plate 26, dated September, 1793, is a "ladies work table" with lyre standards at the ends; on plate 29 a lyre is at the top of the case of a grandfather clock; and on plate 36, dated August, 1792, it is in a chair back. On plate 4 of the "Accompaniment" to the "Drawing Book," dated November, 1793, a lyre is in a painted panel on a wall; in plate 9, January, 1794, it is on the top of a table leg; on plate 12, February, 1794, it is on a window cornice. See also the chair No. 13 in the full page illustration No. 234. Other examples might be cited, showing the frequent use of the lyre as a decorative feature in the book of Sheraton which is known to have been used, but not precisely followed, by the American cabinet makers of the period. Our cabinet makers also derived their designs from the English furniture which they imported. See the paragraph entitled "The lyre as an ornament" in section 44.

8. The idea that the lyre form in furniture was introduced by Phyfe, or that almost any article of furniture with a lyre was in the manner of Phyfe, instead of Sheraton, is of course erroneous.

In a letter written in 1794 by an English visitor, before Phyfe had become a prominent cabinet maker, reference is made to the English chairs in a Philadelphia drawing room with "the backs in form of a lyre." This appears in an article by Mr. William M. Hornor, Jr., in the "International Studio," March, 1931, page 47.

1539 (Upper) Dr. Jas. Bordley, Jr.   1540 (Upper) Mrs. Francis P. Garvan.
1541 (Lower) Dr. M. A. Abrams.   1542 (Lower) Dr. J. Hall Pleasants.

as also in Nos. 1566 and 1567. This less elegant treatment, not as expensive as the other, was sometimes extended to both lyres, as in No. 1543. The legs are in the form of cyma curves, as to which see section 23, and are grooved, terminating in brass claw feet. About 1815–1820.

In No. 1542 two parallel lyres with strings support the frame above. The front of the skirt is ornamented with a brass design and with two panels of figured maple, all of which are repeated on the platform below. On the arms of the lyre and at its base are other brass ornaments. The concave legs are in a different form from those seen on previous card tables, being rectangular and without carving as also in the tables Nos. 1568 and 1586. The use of the metal mounts and the form of the table place it in the early Empire style, which is here seen at its best.[9] About 1810–1820.

No. 1543 has a curved top which is supported by two solid standards in the lyre form. At the upper ends of the standards are two small applied rosettes and two larger ones are near the base. The legs are in the form of cyma curves, and are grooved, as in the table No. 1541. About 1810–1820.

Nos. 1544–1546 are in the Empire style, the first two being in an early form of that style and the third in the last form.

In No. 1544 the two parallel lyre standards are in the graceful form of the earlier tables, and have strings as in No. 1539; but the awkward legs, placed under the heavy platform, not attached to the sides, are coarsely carved and end in the claw feet seen on other pieces of the period, illustrating an important departure from the Sheraton style. About 1820–1830.

No. 1545 is a rendition in the Empire style of the Sheraton style card table No. 1540, with "crossed" lyres which here have only two strings each. The lyre-shaped standards are without ornamentation and rest upon a large and heavy platform. As in the preceding table, the legs, which are placed under the plat-form, are coarsely carved, here with an unusual type of feet. About 1815–1825.

In No. 1546 we see one of the last forms of the Empire style card tables, from which the charm of the Sheraton style has wholly disappeared. The moldings on the skirt and on the base suggest the Victorian style. The top is supported by one lyre-shaped standard, of massive proportions and without strings, which rests upon a large and heavy base with an applied molding. Under the base are scroll feet.[10] The top is in a serpentine form with rounded corners. In spite of its form this table must be admired for its fine mahogany, both solid and veneered. We also notice the four applied rosettes on the lyre, as in No. 1543. About 1830–1840.

Each of the three fine Sheraton style card tables, Nos. 1547–1549, have a pedestal and three legs. These tables are without inlay.

9.   See section 38 entitled "Applied decorations; mounts."

10.   In connection with this table, the two tables flanking the fireplace in Illustration No. 6 (page 62) will make an interesting comparison.

1543 (Upper) Mr. Blanchard Randall.
1545 (Lower) Mr. & Mrs. E. H. McKeon.

1544 (Upper) Mr. John C. Toland.
1546 (Lower) Mrs. G. Frank Baily.

In No. 1547 we recognize the five–curve clover–leaf top which appears also on the table No. 1515 in the Hepplewhite style and on No. 1535 in the Sheraton style. This table was made by Duncan Phyfe, who is said to have been the only cabinet maker who made a card table without a skirt, as here. The top is bordered with veneer, is covered with baize and is supported by a pedestal with a reeded vase similar to those on the tripod tables Nos. 1366 and 1367. The concave legs are carved above with acanthus leaves, below which they are reeded, terminating in brass claw feet. About 1810–1820.

No. 1548, also by Phyfe, has a three–curve clover–leaf top, and a veneered skirt. The pedestal has a vase–shaped portion, below which is a round carved portion. The legs are carved with acanthus leaves which extend almost to the brass feet. In this table, as explained in the comment on the next one, the side legs may be made to swing back and thus give greater stability. About 1810–1820.

No. 1549 is a somewhat plainer table of the same type as the two preceding ones. The top is in a three–curve clover–leaf form and the edges are reeded. The pedestal is in the shape of a large vase and the legs are in the form of cyma curves. On the base of the skirt are small carved panels under which are drops. An interesting feature of this and the two preceding tables is that in the rear of the frame there are two brackets which swing out and support the folding top when it is opened flat, and the movement of these brackets, by an ingenious mechanism, moves the two side legs backwards and thus gives the table a firmer support. About 1810–1820.

In No. 1550, also, the top is in a three–curve form as in the two preceding pieces. The supports are four slender columns, or colonnettes, which are reeded at the top, with rings and acanthus leaves below. These columns may be compared with those on the tripod table No. 1364. Under the columns is a small platform from which four concave legs extend, ornamented with acanthus leaves and reeding. About 1810–1820.

The next four card tables, Nos. 1551–1554, have features of the late Sheraton style; the last two, Nos. 1555–1556, are in the Empire style.

In No. 1551 the top has rounded front corners resembling those in the next table and in No. 1531. The edges of the top are reeded, as are also the concave legs, but not finely. The pedestal has a vase–shaped portion which is reeded, below which is a ringed design. About 1800–1820.

In No. 1552 the top is in the same form as in the preceding table, with reeded edges. The skirt is made of a light wood and is ornamented with inlaid panels of dark wood, an example of contrasting colors which was a favorite decorative feature. The pedestal is ringed and is in a vase shape. The legs are convex and reeded above and are concave below, somewhat in the form on the dining table No. 1330 and the tripod table No. 1363. On the corners of the platform are four small applied horizontal and cylindrical forms which are also seen in No. 1646 and are mentioned in the comment on the sewing table No. 1568. About 1810–1820

1547 (UPPER) ANONYMOUS.   1548 (UPPER) MRS. FRANCIS P. GARVAN.
1549 (LOWER) ANONYMOUS.   1550 (LOWER) MR. ALBERT G. TOWERS.

No. 1553 is one of a type of rectangular and painted card tables which have been found in Maryland and Virginia. This table presents an interesting study of several features, as stated in the note.[11] About 1820–1830.

No. 1554, also a painted card table, is similar in general form to the preceding table, except that the legs are of the concave type and the round and ringed pedestal is without a vase. The skirt is decorated at each end with a wreath enclosing a star, and in the centre with a sword and a wreath, as in the chair No. 329 belonging to the same owner. At the base of the pedestal is another "anthemion," or honeysuckle, design, mentioned in note 11. About 1820–1830.

No. 1555 is in the early Empire style, as shown by the character of the carving and the rounded skirt which latter resembles in form the rounded fronts of the drawers in the sewing tables Nos. 1578–1580. The top is six–sided when closed, as here, and eight–sided when open. The pedestal is carved in three sections. The legs are carved on the upper surface with acanthus leaves and on the sides down to the feet with small lines supposed to represent the hair[12] on the legs which here terminate in animals' claw feet. About 1820–1830.

No. 1556, a card table with a folding top, is a monstrosity in the Empire style. The tops revolve, and rest on the skirt when they are open as in No. 1541. Two fierce–looking creatures of the ocean serve as legs and supports of the top; these represent dolphins[13] which in England at certain periods were favorite decorative features on tables and were also seen on girandole mirrors, as in No. 1242. Under the legs are platforms connected by a horizontal carved stretcher supported by animals' claw feet, making a kind of trestle base in a form such as appears on some of the early tables, as Nos. 1300–1302. The time and skill spent on the carving on this card table were worthy of a better style, especially on the carving of the scales, of the shells under the skirt, and of the leaves over the feet, the latter being also seen in No. 1577. About 1820–1830.

11.   The skirt is decorated with small griffins and large floral designs as in the Adam style mirror No. 1147, the Hepplewhite style card table No. 1516, the Sheraton style mantel mirror No. 1229, and the Empire style chair No. 328. The pedestal is round, with rings and a vase which is painted with leaves. These leaves seem to be a form of the "palmette," a small palm leaf, which appears on the knees of the chair No. 342 and on other pieces of the period. The horizontal legs include "corbel" forms illustrated in connection with the French mantel mirror No. 1231 and the French stable No. 1656.

On the base of the pedestal is a Grecian "anthemion," or honeysuckle, a design which is mentioned in note 48 in section 51. It is also an important architectural decoration of the cornice and other exterior parts of the new "Enoch Pratt Free Library" of Baltimore, which was opened in January, 1933. The designs at the ends of the skirt consist of wings, arrows and another object.

The vertical feet are in the general form used in several designs by Sheraton in his "Drawing Book," and copied by Duncan Phyfe on a sewing table shown in plate 33 in "Furniture Masterpieces of Duncan Phyfe" by Mr. Charles Over Cornelius; simpler forms are on the Sheraton style sewing table No. 1594.

12.   It is said in reference to a certain dog's–foot design used by Duncan Phyfe that "the hair on the leg is suggested by small, irregular, curved grooves"; by Mr. Charles Over Cornelius in his "Masterpieces of Duncan Phyfe," page 54.

13.   Dolphins on sofas are in No. 585 and in Mr. Lockwood's "Colonial Furniture," volume 2, figures 667 and 669. See also note 5 in section 174 in the present book.

1551 (UPPER) MR. C. EDWARD SNYDER.
1553 (CENTRE) MR. ALEXANDER BROWN.
1555 (LOWER) MR. DANIEL R. RANDALL.

1552 (UPPER) MRS. EDWIN B. NIVER.
1554 (CENTRE) MR. & MRS. J. M. HARRIS.
1556 (LOWER) ANONYMOUS.

Section 172. Sewing tables.—Perhaps no other minor articles of antique furniture have survived in such numbers as the small tables, and of these the most important are the sewing tables, or "work tables" as they are often called in the books. This is doubtless because the sewing tables sustained almost no weight and were used only by gentlewomen.[1]

These sewing tables were made to some extent in the Hepplewhite style,[2] but the great majority of them were in the Sheraton and Empire styles. Certain kinds of sewing tables were made in each of these three styles; and in order that a comparison may be easily made of the tables of the same kind, but of different styles, the illustrations are given in groups. One group is of the so–called "Martha Washington" tables, which were made in the Hepplewhite,. Sheraton and Empire styles; another group is that in which the upper portion is supported by lyres; and similarly with other kinds.

The wood of these tables is almost always mahogany, often finely veneered in parts with maple or satinwood; the height is generally about twenty–eight to thirty–one inches; the dates range from about 1800 to as late as 1840.

Nos. 1557–1565, and also No. 1566 in the next group, are sewing tables of the type commonly called "Martha Washington," a name based upon the tradition that the lady used one of this kind of sewing table at Mt. Vernon, as also the "Martha Washington" chair No. 419. This type of table was apparently not copied from England. The distinctive feature is that the upper portion is in an oval form, or nearly so, having rounded or angular ends which serve as boxes. The tops are either in one piece which lifts up from the rear, or are in three parts, the central one of which does not lift up, and two others, over the boxes at the ends, which do lift up. The upper portion is supported either by a pedestal or by four legs, or by lyre standards. These tables seldom have a silk bag. In all cases the interior is fitted with arrangements for sewing accessories, and in some cases with a mirror or a writing board.

No. 1557, in the Sheraton style, is a sewing table of elegant appearance and fine wood and workmanship. The top, reeded on the edges, is in one piece and

1. A silk bag, generally used as a screen to hide a wooden box inside, but sometimes used merely as a bag without a box, will be seen on many sewing tables. This bag could not be expected to survive the usage of a century or more, and hence a modern bag has often been substituted for the original one, or both the bag and the box have been removed; in the latter case some of the tables may not be easily distinguishable from certain other small tables with drawers, such as some of those shown in the next chapter.

2. In Hepplewhite's "Guide," (as to which see section 17), there are no designs of sewing tables, but the cabinet makers working in the Hepplewhite style had no difficulty in adapting that style to the requirements of a sewing table, as in the Martha Washington table No. 1559. There are no designs of these tables in Chippendale's book.

In the "Appendix" to Sheraton's "Drawing Book," (as to which see section 18), page 403, plate 26, dated September, 1793, are two designs of "work tables" which have not been exactly followed by our cabinet makers. The silk bags were ornamented with drapery.

The illustrations in this section are small, as the writer thinks that the reader will prefer a large number of small, but clear, illustrations, rather than a smaller number of larger ones, as remarked in connection with several other articles.

1557 (UPPER) MR. H. T. TIFFANY. 1558 (UPPER) MRS. WM. M. 1559 (UPPER) MR. A. McLANAHAN.
1560 (CENTRE) MR. & MRS. JAS.   ROBERTS.   1562 (CENTRE) ANONYMOUS.
      CAREY, JR.   1561 (CENTRE) MR. A. G. TOWERS. 1565 (LOWER) MR. & MRS. W. M.
1563 (LOWER) MR. B. RANDALL.   1564 (LOWER) MR. A. G. TOWERS.   ELLICOTT.

lifts up from the rear. Under the top is a wide veneered band of finely grained light wood, below which the entire frame is in delicate "tambour" work, such as is seen on the desks Nos. 815–824 in the Sheraton style. The plain pedestal is vase–shaped, the four concave legs are veneered on the upper surface with the same light wood as used on the wide band under the top, and the feet are brass, with casters. Under the single drawer is a compartment which opens from the side. A duplicate of this table descended from the same ancestor to Miss Mary Leigh Brown, of Baltimore. About 1800–1810.

In No. 1558, also in the Sheraton style, the top is in three parts, the central one and the two end ones. There are three drawers, each with replaced handles, and the usual two end boxes which are in one continuous curve, not in several sections as in the next table and others. The pedestal is in a vase–shaped and reeded form and the concave legs, also reeded, terminate in animals' wooden claw feet. About 1800–1810.

No. 1559 is in the Hepplewhite style, as indicated by the tapering and inlaid legs, and the use of several inlaid designs on the central portion. Here the ends of the sewing table are not in one continuous curve, but are each in seven sections, which is an easier form of construction. There are two large drawers and two small square ones, all of which are veneered with dark wood. Between the two small drawers there is a small arch, as also in the small table No. 1608. About 1790–1810.

No. 1560, a plain sewing table, is in the Sheraton style, as shown by the round, "turned" and tapering legs. The ends are in a continuous curve and there are three drawers with round wooden knobs. The legs are in about the same form as in the next table. About 1800–1810.

No. 1561 is one of a pair of sewing tables of curly maple. The ends are in five sections of the type of those in No. 1559. The three drawers have glass knobs. The round legs have an unusual turning near the bottom, and end in round feet. About 1800–1810.

No. 1562 is even more clearly in the Sheraton style, having reeded legs, above which are reeded panels. The edge of the top is also reeded. The three drawers have small glass knobs. The ends are in a continuous curve. About 1800–1810.

In No. 1563 the top is in one piece which lifts up from the rear as in No. 1557. There is a drawer at the base with a brass lion–and–ring handle, above which is a large panel which does not open. The keyhole at the top is for a lock for the top. The legs are reeded, as are also the panels above. The ends are in a series of sections and are furnished with brass handles. About 1800–1810.

In No. 1564, also, the top is in one piece. It is in the Hepplewhite style, with inlay on the skirt and on the square and tapered legs. Below the skirt the frame is covered with silk in four sections. The ends are in a continuous curve. This sewing table is of a somewhat unusual type. About 1800-1810.

In No. 1565 the top is similar in form to several of the preceding pieces, being in three parts. The pedestal and the base, however, are of a later form than in the preceding tables. The reeding of the pedestal is of a heavy type of the late

Sheraton style and the platform upon which it rests is in a triangular form seen on other tables in the Empire period, such as Nos. 1369, 1592 and others. About 1820–1830.

Nos. 1566–1570, in the Sheraton style, have lyres or lyre-shaped pieces as supports, or standards, upon which the upper portion rests. They may be compared with the lyre card tables Nos. 1539–1546.

No. 1566 is a so-called Martha Washington sewing table with two lyre standards, one being a lyre with strings and the other a solid piece in the lyre shape, as also in the next table and in the Sheraton style card table No. 1541. The top is in three parts and the ends are in several sections as in No. 1559 and others. In the centre are one shallow and one deep drawer, on each side of which is a reeded panel with a drop ornament. The front of the lyre with strings is carved with leaves as are the upper portions of the concave legs. About 1800–1810.

In No. 1567 the lower portion is almost the same as in the preceding piece. The upper portion is of a different type, being rectangular, with reeded and projecting columns at the four corners, a favorite form in the Sheraton style as will be seen from other tables below. Three horizontal bands of lighter wood form a contrast with the color of the drawers. The handles are of the lion–and–ring pattern. About 1800–1810.

No. 1568 has two parallel lyres resting upon a platform which is supported by concave legs, as in the Sheraton style card table No. 1542. At the top of the legs, as also on the card tables Nos. 1542 and 1552, and more clearly in No. 1646, are small horizontal cylindrical forms, a frequent ornamental detail of the period. The upper portion is in about the same form as in the preceding table, with projecting columns which are ringed instead of reeded. Brass knobs are on the two drawers. About 1800–1810.

No. 1569 resembles the preceding piece in the form of the upper portion. The two drawers are inlaid and banded with light wood and the projecting columns are turned in a ring–and–spool design. The two lyres are in a less attractive form than the others. The legs are concave, in a form sometimes called a "C" curve, resembling the curves of that name much used in the Chippendale period, as mentioned in the comment on the mirror No. 1103 and others. About 1810–1820.

No. 1570 has at the corners large and plain round projecting columns instead of reeded or ringed ones, and the entire fronts of the two drawers are veneered in a light wood, making a pronounced contrast in color. The legs are reeded, but not delicately, and are somewhat heavy for a table of the size, as is also the platform upon which the lyres rest; these features and the corner columns indicate a change towards the Empire style. About 1815–1825.

No. 1571 is a lyre sewing table constructed in a form to hold a bag. Here the two lyres, with their ends towards the front, are attached to a heavy Empire style platform, and support a deep box with a lid. Below the box is a shallow drawer, under which is a frame which holds the silk bag and may be pulled outward. Excepting the two lyres and the bag, this table shows no features of the Sheraton style, and is therefore regarded as being in the Empire style, in which the lyre continued to be popular as an ornamental detail. About 1825–1835.

1566 (Upper) Dr. M. A. Abrams. 1567 (Upper) Mr. W. W. Lanahan. 1568 (Upper) Dr. Wm. P. E. Wyse.
1569 (Lower) Mr. B. C. Howard. 1570 (Lower) Mr. H. T. Tiffany. 1571 (Lower) Mr. & Mrs. J. Carey, Jr.

1572 (Upper) Mr. A. G. Towers. 1573 (Upper) Mr. C. E. Snyder. 1574 (Upper) Mr. H. O. Thompson.
1575 (Centre) Mrs. John Stokes. 1576 (Centre) Mr. J. C. Toland. 1577 (Centre) Miss E. M. Miller.
1578 (Lower) Miss Mary K. Hink- 1579 (Lower) Mr. S. Johnson Poe. 1580 (Lower) Mrs. R. W. Baldwin.
ley.

In the next group of nine tables, Nos. 1572–1580, the upper portions are rectangular and are supported by a pedestal, in which respect these tables are similar in their general form, and illustrate both the Sheraton and the Empire styles. The first three may be regarded as in the late Sheraton style; the other six, Nos. 1575–1580, show the change from the early to the late Empire style. Rectangular upper portions supported by pedestals are also seen in other groups in this chapter.

No. 1572 is of mahogany and bird's–eye maple. The two small upper drawers and the large one below form a pleasing contrast in color to the dark pedestal and legs, in which respect it may be compared with the small table No. 1606 in the next section. The legs are concave and end in a "C" curve, as in No. 1569. About 1810–1820.

In No. 1573 the upper portion is ornamented with broad bands of curly maple around the two drawers, upon which are large cut glass knobs. At the corners are round columns with turned rings, and drops below. The lower portion has carving upon the vase–shaped pedestal, the round platform and the upper part of the legs, below which they are grooved, ending in brass claw feet. About 1810–1820.

In No. 1574 the columns at the corners are turned in rings and other forms. The pedestal is reeded above and carved below. The legs have a higher curve than usual and are carved with leaves at the top and reeded below. The reeding on the legs does not stop at the feet but continues into them, a method referred to in the comments on Nos. 1422 and 1589. This method was also used by Duncan Phyfe on card tables. About 1810–1820.

No. 1575 has ringed columns at the corners. The oval brass handles upon the two drawers are of an earlier style than the table. The pedestal has the spiral carvings which were a feature of the Empire style, and the concave legs are grooved and end in brass feet. About 1810–1820.

No. 1576, also in the Empire style, has a straight upper drawer overhanging in part the two curved lower ones. The top is in two equal parts, or lids, which are on hinges on the sides. Near the top of each side is a small and not well seen "pull" which when drawn out may support the lids when open, in the manner of Nos. 1473–1474. The small columns at the corners are fully carved, as are also the lower part of the pedestal and the grotesque legs which are attached to the bottom of the platform and end in animal's claw feet. About 1820–1830.

In No. 1577, in the Empire style, the upper portion is ornamented with four painted designs, the two on the drawers being on a dark background. The panels within the lines of inlay on these drawers project forward slightly as the top does in No. 1591. The knobs are of wood. The carved pedestal is in a vase–shaped design and rests upon a large platform with concave sides. The legs are carved and are attached to the bottom of the platform, as in the preceding table. Over each of the feet is a leaf which projects forward in the manner of those in No. 1556. About 1820–1830.

No. 1578, in the Empire style, has two rounded drawers in the upper portion and ringed columns at the corners. The pedestal is carved in the central portion and on the base. As in the preceding piece the platform has concave sides. The winged legs and the animal's claw feet are under the platform. About 1820–1830.

In No. 1579 the rounded overhanging upper drawer is prominent; the two small columns at the corners, one of the last surviving features of the late Sheraton style, become smaller; the former round and carved pedestal gives way to a heavy and plain one; the platform of the Empire style continues, and the Empire style scroll feet supersede the carved ones. About 1830–1840.

No. 1580 is wholly in the late Empire style. The columns at the corners have disappeared; the pedestal is plain and has another shape. Scrolled feet of this type are only seen on the furniture of the late Empire period, as in the tripod table No. 1371 and others. A study of the tables on this page will show clearly the trend away from the late Empire, toward the over-elaboration and awkwardness of the Victorian. The drop–leaves on the sides of the upper portion, when raised, are supported by small brackets, as in No. 1576. About 1840.

In the next group, Nos. 1581–1592, are twelve sewing tables, each with a silk bag which generally conceals a box for sewing materials. In most of the tables of this type the bag and box are attached to a slide, under the drawers, which pulls out and gives access to the interior, as shown in No. 1595. In some cases, as in No. 1564, silk coverings are placed in sections between the legs around the entire frame. Each of these tables is in a different design.

No. 1581 is a curly maple sewing table in the Hepplewhite style, the legs being square and tapered. There is one drawer, below which is a slide which pulls out and to which the bag is attached. About 1790–1810.

No. 1582, also, is in the Hepplewhite style, in a form not often seen in American pieces. The oval top is in one piece and opens from the rear as in the "Martha Washington" table No. 1557 and others. The slender tapering legs are square, curving outward at the lower end, as in one of Hepplewhite's designs, and are braced by cross–stretchers with a shelf, as also in No. 1600 in the next section. About 1790–1810.

No. 1583, also in the Hepplewhite style, has an eight–sided top which is decorated with inlay. The legs are square and tapered, with a slight curve at the bottom, and are attached to the centre of the corner sections. About 1790–1800.

No. 1584, in curly maple, is in the Sheraton style, as indicated by the legs which are square and reeded above the stretchers and round below them. The top is eight–sided, with brass handles at the ends. About 1800–1810.

No. 1585, also of fine maple, is in the Sheraton style, having the same familiar projecting, rounded and tapered legs as the tables Nos. 1521, 1533 and others. There are two drawers with brass lion–and–ring handles. About 1800–1810.

In No. 1586 the edges of the top and its two drop–leaves are grooved, and the four supporting columns and the stretcher are reeded. Under the two drawers with glass knobs is the slide with the bag attached. The two reeded columns at each end rest upon the two connected concave legs; this trestle method may also be seen on the table No. 1644 and others. About 1800–1810.

1581 (UPPER) MR. & MRS. H. L. DUER.
1584 (CENTRE) MRS. JOHN S. GIBBS, JR.
1587 (LOWER) ANONYMOUS.

1582 (UPPER) MRS. A. ARMSTRONG.
1585 (CENTRE) MRS. P. H. MILLER.
1588 (LOWER) MRS. E. N. DUNHAM.

1583 (UPPER) HAMMOND–HARWOOD HOUSE.
1586 (CENTRE) ANONYMOUS.
1589 (LOWER) MRS. E. N. DUNHAM.

1590 (UPPER) MR. W. W. LANAHAN.   1591 (UPPER) MRS. J. S. GIBBS, JR.   1592 (UPPER) MISS H. H. CAREY.
1593 (LOWER)   HAMMOND–HARWOOD   1594 (LOWER) MR. B. RANDALL.   1595 (LOWER) MRS. F. G. BOYCE, JR.
   HOUSE.

No. 1587 is a finely decorated mahogany table in about the same form as No. 1585. The edges of the top are reeded, and the columns over the reeded legs are carved, probably by Samuel McIntire,[3] with pineapples and leaves. One of the two drawers is for writing and underneath is the pull–out frame to which the bag is attached. About 1800–1810.

In No. 1588 the twist of the legs is a change from the Sheraton to the Empire style. The other parts of the sewing table, however, with the drawers, slide and wooden knobs, follow the designs of preceding pieces in the Sheraton style. About 1815–1825.

No. 1589 more fully shows the Empire style. The fronts of the three drawers are rounded, the supporting columns are round and plain, the platform with concave sides is large and heavy and the feet are in the shape of scrolls; some of these features resemble those in Nos. 1579 and 1580. The feet are not connected with legs, but are reeded as though their reeding were a continuation of reeding on legs, a method seen in Nos. 1422 and 1574. About 1820–1840.

Nos. 1590–1592 are three unusual sewing tables on which there are bags. In the first two of these tables the upper portion rests upon a form of "curule"[4] support, and in the third the support is of a somewhat similar character. They are in the late Sheraton or early Empire style, and are of about the same date.

In No. 1590 the two drawers are bordered on the edges with maple, as is also the slide below, to which the silk bag is attached. The supports have a short pedestal which rests upon a small platform to which concave legs are attached. These legs are plain and terminate in brass animals' claw feet. About 1810–1820.

In No. 1591 the top opens from the rear and has a raised panel in the centre in about the same form as on the drawers of No. 1577. Small round columns are at the four corners, as in No. 1578. The concave pedestal rests upon a heavy platform with concave sides as in Nos. 1577–1580 and others. The feet are reeded. About 1810–1820.

In No. 1592, which is shown on a more reduced scale, the upper portion is square and when the top is open, as here, it is held in position by a metal support. The bag and box are within four curved arms which rest upon a small round platform which is supported by a short, reeded and gilded pedestal. The lower platform is triangular and under it the brass feet are attached. About 1810–1820.

No. 1593 resembles a sewing table from which a bag has been removed. The top is in the shape of a Martha Washington table, but is not as deep as others of

3. The fine carving on this sewing table is now regarded as being the work of Samuel McIntire of Salem, Massachusetts. Careful investigation has shown that McIntire was not a cabinet maker, but that he was a skillful carver in addition to being an architect. The subject is more fully mentioned in section 72, notes 5 and 6. See also "Antiques," December, 1933, page 218.

4. As to the "curule" form see the comment on chair No. 490 and see also the Index under "Curule."

A sewing table of this type is illustrated in an advertisement of Beach and Loveland, cabinet makers, on August 22, 1820, in a newspaper of Northampton, Mass.; and two somewhat similar tables are shown in Mr. Wallace Nutting's "Furniture Treasury," Nos. 1009 and 1187.

that type shown in Nos. 1557–1565, having only two shallow drawers, with small boxes at the ends. The long and slender legs are very delicately reeded in the Sheraton style. About 1800–1810.

No. 1594 is an unusual sewing table having a round top with a raised rim, as on the tripod tray–top tables Nos. 1339, 1350 and others. Under the top is a round box with a drawer. The pedestal is long and plain, and rests upon three legs in the form of cyma curves, as to which see section 23. The feet are somewhat in the shape of those on No. 1553. About 1815–1825.

No. 1595 is presented here in order to show the slide to which the bag and box of many of these sewing tables were attached. Here the slide, without the bag and box, is pulled out a short distance. If the slide were not seen, it might be difficult to decide from the photograph whether this table is a sewing table or merely a small table or stand. This piece is in the Hepplewhite style and has cross–stretchers with a small shelf in the centre as in No. 1582. About 1790–1800.

Section 173. Other small tables.—In this section are illustrations of twenty–seven small tables, some of which may apparently be called either "tables" or "stands." These words in connection with furniture appear to have almost the same meaning in some cases; thus the terms "sewing table" and "sewing stand" seem to be equally appropriate.[1] On the other hand, the word "candle–stand," not "candle–table," is used when speaking of a small table made to hold a candle-stick. According to the dictionaries a "stand" is a small table, and the word "table" thus includes the small table called a "stand."[2] Whether certain of the small tables shown in this section should be called "tables" or "stands" may be a question of individual choice, and not worthy of debate; but it is clear that the small tables shown in section 161 should be called "stands."

Another question is whether some of the small tables are "sewing tables" or merely "tables." In some cases the interior fittings or other evidence, not visible in the illustrations, may show that a table was made as a sewing table; and even

---

1. As mentioned in section 153, note 1, the word "table" in the Century Dictionary is defined as "an article of furniture consisting of a flat top (the table proper) of wood, stone or other solid material, resting on legs or on a pillar; .. as a dining–table, writing–table, work–table," etc. A stand is defined as "a table, set of shelves or the like, upon which articles may be placed .. specifically, a small light table, such as is moved easily from place to place."

Mr. Lockwood, in his "Colonial Furniture," applies the word "stand" to small tables made to hold candlesticks and to one small oval table like No. 1599.

Mr. Cornelius, in his "Masterpieces of Duncan Phyfe" does not use the words "sewing table," preferring "sewing stand."

Mr. Nutting, in his "Furniture Treasury," at No. 1214, remarks: "The reader will be lenient with us in the matter of classification (of certain tables and stands). . . The greatest difficulty seems to occur with stands. . . The division must . . be arbitrarily made."

2. In "The Dictionary of English Furniture" by Macquoid and Edwards, volume 3, page 140, it is said that "the term 'stand,' used in a very comprehensive sense, implies almost any kind of support, either forming a distinct object, as a candle stand, or in connection with another piece of furniture, as a stand for a cabinet. . . The many purposes to which they could be applied preclude an exhaustive classification."

if a table was not made as a sewing table, it may have acquired that name from long usage as such a table. Judging from their appearance, however, almost all of the small tables shown in this section may be regarded merely as small tables suitable for any domestic purposes. If intended to be seen on all sides, a table is always finished on all sides.

These tables are arranged in the Hepplewhite, Sheraton and Empire styles; they are generally of mahogany or maple; and their dates range from about 1790 to 1840.

Nos. 1596–1604 form a group of nine small tables in the Hepplewhite style. As in other tables in that style, the legs are square and tapering, in some cases slightly curved at the lower end. Some of these tables may have been made as sewing tables. Only brief comments are made, as the general features are familiar to the reader who has examined other tables in the Hepplewhite style.

No. 1596 has a rectangular top whose edges are lined with inlay. The single drawer is banded with inlay, as also is the bottom of the skirt. The slender legs are inlaid with the usual lines and strings of flowers and near the lower ends are inlaid bands. About 1790–1810.

No. 1597 is unusual in having three drawers with inlaid edges, on each side of which is a long inlaid panel. The tapering of the legs is on the inside as usual. About 1790–1810.

No. 1598 is an oval table with a top which lifts up from the rear as in the next table and in the oval sewing table No. 1557. The two wide drawers are bordered with inlay, and similar inlaid decorations are on the sides and back. The four legs are inlaid on more than one side. About 1790–1810.

No. 1599 also is oval and is shown with the top partly raised. The skirt is ornamented with parallel lines of inlay with rounded ends, a design which is seen also in No. 1492 and is referred to more fully in section 127, note 6, and in section 96, note 1, C. The legs are slender and graceful and over them are inlaid satinwood panels. About 1790–1800.

No. 1600 is decorated with an inlaid border on the skirt. The legs are slightly curved at the lower end as in one of Hepplewhite's designs and as in the sewing table No. 1582. The crossed stretchers form a small shelf. About 1790–1810.

No. 1601 is a different form of table. The top is provided with two small drop–leaves which, when open, are supported by brackets, and form serpentine curves on all sides, with rounded corners, as is also seen in the Pembroke table No. 1406. There is one drawer and below is a shelf with a rim which is cut in a series of curves or scallops. There is no inlay on this table. See also No. 1610. About 1790–1810.

No. 1602 has a rectangular top with edges lined with inlay, as is also the edge of the skirt. The legs are ornamented with the usual inlay. The crossed stretchers are of the type called "domed" because of the dome–like shape, as in Nos. 1432 and 1462. About 1790–1810.

1596 (Upper) Mr. & Mrs. R. Robinson.
1599 (Centre) Mr. A. E. Cole.
1602 (Lower) Mr. & Mrs. J. Carey, Jr.

1597 (Upper) Mr. J. S. McDaniel.
1600 (Centre) Mr. B. Randall.
1603 (Lower) Mrs. Miles White, Jr.

1598 (Upper) Mr. & Mrs. B. Turnbull.
1601 (Centre) Mrs. M. White, Jr.
1604 (Lower) Mr. A. G. Towers.

In No. 1603 the top and the drawers are recessed in concave curves, as in the Hepplewhite style card table No. 1514. The two drawers have oval handles of the period. As in No. 1601 there is no inlay. The height is about twenty-four inches. About 1790–1810.

No. 1604 is a rectangular table, plain in shape but pleasing in appearance and unusual in having inlay on curly maple. Small panels of darker wood are inlaid on the upper portions of the legs, and below these panels are lines of inlay with an inlaid flower suspended in the centre. About 1790–1810.

The next group of small tables, Nos. 1605–1613, are in the Sheraton style, as appears from the round and tapered legs, some of which are reeded, and the "turned" feet. Several of these tables, as in the previous group in the Hepplewhite style, may perhaps be regarded as sewing tables.

No. 1605 is of curly maple. The corners are cut out and the projecting columns above the legs are inserted in the recess. The round and tapered legs end in small ball feet. In the centre of the drawer is a panel of darker wood. About 1800–1820.

No. 1606 is of curly maple and mahogany. Above and on the sides of the two drawers are panels of the lighter wood; the legs below are of mahogany. The oval handles will also be noticed. About 1800–1820.

No. 1607, also chiefly of maple, differs from the preceding table in having the legs of the light wood and the panels above of dark wood. The two drawers have glass knobs. About 1800–1820.

In No. 1608 the front resembles the central portion of the "Martha Washington" sewing table No. 1559, having two wide drawers above two small square ones, with a small arch in the centre. Two drop–leaves are on the sides. The knob on the upper drawer is missing. The round and tapering legs, and the panels above, are reeded. The feet are larger at the lower end than above, a form occasionally seen, resembling a vase as also in No. 1620 and in the corner chairs Nos. 429 and 435. About 1800–1820.

No. 1609 is a plain table, distinctly in the Sheraton style as shown by the round legs, here not so gracefully tapering as in some other cases, but ending in small round feet. About 1800–1820.

No. 1610 has the characteristic projecting legs of the Sheraton style, with rings on the upper portion, as in No. 1521 and others, but without reeding. The tapering begins below the shelf, which has a raised rim cut in curves, or scalloped, as in the Hepplewhite style table No. 1601 which has also drop leaves. The two drawers have finely grained and "matched"[3] mahogany veneer, with brass ring handles. About 1800–1820.

No. 1611 is a table with drop leaves. The edges of the top and the leaves are reeded, as are also the tapering legs, and the two drawers have glass knobs. About 1800–1820.

---

3. This method is explained in section 32, note 2.

1605 (Upper)   Hammond–Harwood House.

1608 (Centre)   Miss H. R. Chew.

1611 (Lower)   Miss E. S. Cohen.

1606 (Upper)   Rev. & Mrs. A. C. Powell.

1609 (Centre)   Mr. & Mrs. W. A. Dixon.

1612 (Lower)   Mr. & Mrs. R. L. Cary.

1607 (Upper)   Mr. & Mrs. W. A. Dixon.

1610 (Centre)   Miss E. S. Cohen.

1613 (Lower)   Mrs. J. V. Wagner.

In No. 1612 the top is bowed, or swelled, following the form of the two drawers, resembling the front of a bureau. The edges of the top are reeded, and also the legs. About 1800–1820.

In No. 1613 we again see the legs projecting beyond the corners of the frame of the table, and finely reeded above and below. The legs do not extend above the top, but in the tables Nos. 1615–1617 they seem to extend slightly above perhaps by an applied ornament. About 1800–1820.

The next seven tables, Nos. 1614–1620, resemble in general form the Sheraton style tables here shown and might be regarded as being in the late Sheraton style; but they also exhibit certain features of the still later Empire style and therefore should be called by that name, for the reason mentioned in section 6 at note 4. These features are chiefly seen in the legs, leaves, spiral twists, rings or other forms, all of which compare somewhat unfavorably with the previous features in elegance of carving and design. Nos. 1621 and 1622 are in the early Victorian style for the reasons mentioned in the comments.

In No. 1614 the legs are carved with large acanthus leaves and above them are other leaves carved somewhat coarsely. The two large drawers are fitted with glass knobs. About 1810–1825.

In No. 1615 the corners are cut out and the projecting legs are placed in the recess and extend slightly above the top, as also in the next two tables. The legs have thick rings above and a large spiral form below. The fronts of the two drawers are of finely grained and "matched" mahogany veneer, as in No. 1610. The handles are of later date. About 1815–1825.

No. 1616 is a similar table in which the legs have become heavy and ungraceful and the carving is not delicate. The feet may have been partly cut off. The front of the drawers is finely veneered and "matched" and the legs extend above the top, as in the preceding table. About 1815–1830.

No. 1617 presents a different form of ornamentation of the legs, consisting of turnings of spools, rings and vases, with ball feet. The rings have the appearance of horizontal reedings. The drawers are veneered with curly maple and have wooden knobs. About 1815–1830.

No. 1618 has three drawers with finely veneered fronts and large glass knobs. The legs are elaborately turned with more than twenty rings in the central portion. A plain shelf is supported on square blocks. About 1815–1830.

In No. 1619 the legs are carved in a design which is suggestive of a pineapple, the emblem of hospitality. The shelf is cut in a double cyma curve. The upper portion, like that in the preceding table, is in a plain design. About 1815–1830.

In No. 1620 there is an upper rounded drawer as in the Empire style sewing table No. 1579 and others; the entire front of this top drawer is of curly maple, making a very strong contrast with the mahogany. On the legs are carved square blocks of the type seen on the bed–post No. 1070. Below these blocks are large carved acanthus leaves. The feet are in the form seen in No. 1608. About 1825–1835.

1614 (UPPER) MRS. M. F. RODGERS.
1617 (CENTRE) MRS. E. N. DUN-
HAM.
1620 (LOWER) MRS. C. E. HENDER-
SON.

1615 (UPPER) MR. M. WHITRIDGE.
1618 (CENTRE) MRS. JOS. WHYTE.
1621 (LOWER) MISS H. H. CAREY.

1616 (UPPER) MRS. E. N. DUNHAM.
1619 (CENTRE) MRS. F. G. BOYCE,
JR.
1622 (LOWER) MR. & MRS. J. CAREY,
JR.

Nos. 1621 and 1622, although having legs with the Empire style turnings called "spool" or "ring," are regarded as of the Victorian era because of the moldings around the drawers. It is said that moldings of this type, resembling somewhat those on the table No. 1632, were made by a machine which was invented after 1840. A marble top is on No. 1622. About 1840–1860.

Section 174. Miscellaneous tables.—In this last section on tables are illustrations of several types which differ in form and purpose from those seen in the preceding sections.

In the first group are three nests of tables, Nos. 1623–1625. This type of tables may have been originated by Sheraton, who published a design of them in his "Drawing Book," as to which see section 18, and who called them "quartetto" tables because they were made in nests of four. They are small and light, are made in different sizes in order that the smaller ones may be enclosed within the largest, require but little room and are easily separated. They were used mainly as tea or coffee tables.

No. 1623 is shown with a front view. Each table has a stretcher which is concave when seen from the front. These tables are lacquered and are ornamented on the ends and the front with floral and other designs. The top is supported by standards in the form of lyres without strings, which rest upon an arched base with concave legs and claw feet. Perhaps about 1820–1830.

No. 1624 is a very similar table, shown from the side in order to have a clear view of the pleasing decorations. The form of the standards is seen here to better advantage than in the preceding illustration. The lacquer and the style of decoration suggest that these two nests of tables were made in China or at least in the Chinese manner. Perhaps about 1820–1830.

No. 1625 is a plainer nest of tables with slender legs supporting the top. In the illustration some of the legs are so close together in the line of vision that they are not seen as separate legs. Three of the stretchers are missing. In England legs of this type are called "spindle legs" or "spider legs," which are referred to in note 1, C, in section 155. About 1800–1810.

Nos. 1626–1628 are three "drum" tables which have acquired their name from the resemblance of the form of their upper portions to the form of a drum. They were popular in England at about the beginning of the nineteenth century, and most of those found here are of English origin. The distinctive features are the single pedestal, the round upper portion, which in some cases revolved, and the skirt of sufficient depth to contain one or two rows of drawers. Because of the round form of the upper portion the drawers could not be of the usual rectangular shape. Parts of the skirt were often paneled to imitate drawers and were furnished with handles, making "sham" drawers, a term which is referred to in the comment on the Pembroke table No. 1409. The wood was mahogany in almost all cases.

No. 1626, in the Sheraton style, has a revolving top with drawers which are lined with mahogany and maple. The pedestal is carved in a so–called pineapple

1623 (Upper) Miss H. H. Carey.   1624 (Upper) Mrs. J. S. Gibbs, Jr.   1625 (Upper) Dr. H. M. Fitzhugh.
1626 (Lower) Anonymous   1627 (Lower) Col. Mrs. J. Stabler.   1628 (Lower) Mrs. R. W. Petre.

pattern and the four concave legs are reeded, and terminate in brass claw feet. The diameter of this table is about twenty-four inches and the height about thirty-one inches. About 1810–1820.

No. 1627 has a deeper skirt containing two drawers, one above tne other. The pedestal is vase–shaped and reeded, and carved on the base. The legs are carved on the upper portion and reeded below, and terminate in animals' claw feet. The lower portion resembles that of the Sheraton style sewing table No. 1573 and others. About 1810–1820.

No. 1628 may be regarded as being in the Empire style as is shown by the form of the legs and the carving, which is of a somewhat coarse character. This table may be compared with the French Empire style table No. 1656. On each side of the drawer in the centre is a "sham" drawer. The legs and feet may be compared with those on the sewing table No. 1576 and others. About 1820–1830.

Nos. 1629–1633 are oval tables which were meant to stand in the centre of a room, but apparently not for any special purpose. The first three and the fifth are in the Hepplewhite style, are graceful in form and pleasing in decoration, and although similar in appearance are all worthy of examination. The wood is mahogany.

No. 1629 is the largest in size and has more than the usual overhang at the ends. The skirt is inlaid with rectangular forms and with small panels over the legs which have the usual lines of inlay, strings of flowers, and bands near the lower ends. Lines of inlay are also on the edges of the top and on the bottom of the skirt. About 1790–1800.

No. 1630 is a very small table and is similar in form to the small table No. 1599, in which latter, however, the top opens from the rear, whereas in this table the top does not open and there is a drawer. The inlay here is on the skirt and the legs. About 1790–1800.

No. 1631 is less in size than No. 1629, but is not a small table, being forty–seven inches long and thirty–three inches wide. The inlay on the skirt consists of lines on the base and oval panels over the legs, and on the legs are the usual lines and flowers. About 1790–1800.

No. 1632 is a small oval table, far removed in style and date from the preceding three pieces in the period of Hepplewhite. Here the Victorian style, as to which see section 22, is seen in the moldings around the edge of the top and the skirt, somewhat similar to the moldings on the small table No. 1621; and also the style is seen in the "trestle" form of the feet. About 1840–1850.

No. 1633, in the Hepplewhite style, approaches a circular form, the length of the table being less in proportion to the width than in Nos. 1629 and 1631. The inlaid ornamentation on the legs resembles somewhat that on the two preceding tables. About 1790–1800.

In No. 1634 the top is six–sided as in the sewing tables Nos. 1583 and 1584. The pedestal is triangular and concave, as is also the too small tripod base which

1629 (Upper) Rev. & Mrs. A. C. Powell.   1630 (Upper) Estate of Mrs. J. H. Whiteley.
1631 (Centre) Bishop Edward T. Helfenstein.   1632 (Centre) Miss Mary S. Schenck.
1633 (Lower) Dr. Henry J. Berkley.   1634 (Lower) Mr. Herbert T. Tiffany.

in part resembles that in the sewing table No. 1565. The paintings on the skirt and the base will be noticed. This table seems to have indications of both the Empire and the Victorian styles, but may be French. About 1840–1850.

The next group, Nos. 1635–1637, is known as "architects'" tables or "drawing" tables, the former name being preferable. Architects' tables were made in the styles of Chippendale, Hepplewhite and Sheraton. They are fitted with various devices, such as an adjustable and hinged top which may be raised and sloped, and with compartments for drawing implements and materials used by architects. The wood of these tables is mahogany.

No. 1635 is an English architects' table and is in the Chippendale style, as is shown by the plain square legs, the brackets at the junctions of the legs and the skirt, and the fretwork of the skirt. The top may be raised to any angle desired or may be laid flat on the frame. About 1760–1780.

No. 1636 is in the Hepplewhite style, as is indicated by the tapering of the straight and square legs. Here also the top is attached to a movable frame in such a manner that it may be held at any angle. The leaves are in a serpentine form and are supported by brackets, giving to this table, when the top also is flat, the appearance of a Pembroke table such as those in section 163. This table was probably made in the West Indies. About 1785–1800.

No. 1637 is in the Sheraton style, as is shown by the round, reeded and tapering legs, of which there are five. The top, here in a vertical position, may be folded back upon the fifth leg, which is the inner one of the two close together in the rear right. The sloping board, covered with baize, may be adjusted as desired. About 1800–1810.

No. 1638–1640 should perhaps have appeared in section 164 with the library tables, but they differ from the latter in having one large top without drop leaves or drawers. In these tables there are devices under the top by which the latter may be easily removed or tilted to an upright position, as otherwise the large tops would prevent their passage through a door of the usual size. These tables are not often seen. They are in the Sheraton style, are made of mahogany and are of about the same date.

No. 1638 has a plain round pedestal, supported by concave legs which are carved with acanthus leaves on the upper portion and are reeded below, terminating in brass feet and casters. About 1800–1820.

In No. 1639 the edge of the top is reeded, and two of the sides are in a serpentine form, the other two sides being straight with rounded corners. The vase–shaped pedestal and the curved legs are reeded. The form of the legs is much the same as that in the small tripod tables Nos. 1354–1356. This table is of South Carolina origin. About 1800–1820.

No. 1640 is a larger table, fifty–five inches in length and forty inches in width. Four spiral and carved columns support the top and rest upon a platform below, as in the dining tables Nos. 1324–1326. The concave legs are reeded and end in brass feet and casters. About 1800–1820.

1635 (UPPER) MR. & MRS. HENRY L. DUER.   1636 (UPPER) MR. AUSTIN MCLANAHAN.
1637 (CENTRE) ANONYMOUS.   1638 (CENTRE) MR. C. EDWARD SNYDER.
1639 (LOWER) MR. BENJAMIN H. READ.   1640 (LOWER) MR. EDGAR G. MILLER, JR.

Nos. 1641–1646 form a group which is truly "miscellaneous," each table being of a different type from the others in the group and in most cases different from any others illustrated in this chapter.

No. 1641, at first sight, resembles a corner table such as those shown in section 167; but it is evident that it would not fit in a corner because the back is straight. The semi–circular folding lid turns back and in that position, making a round table, is supported by one of the rear legs which swings out. If the fixed top be lifted a compartment within the skirt is seen, furnished with a lock. The legs are round and almost straight, ending in Dutch, or club, feet and shoes, resembling the legs in the table No. 1308 and others. The upper ends of the legs continue round to the top. About 1740–1760.

No. 1642 also at first glance resembles a corner table, but the rear line of the top is straight and could not be placed in a corner. It is in reality a card table in which the folding top may be folded back, making the table square. The particular feature is that the central rear leg, which supports the folding top when it is open, does not swing out, but pulls out from the back like a desk pull which is pulled out to support the lid. This method is referred to in section 169, note 1, C. About 1800–1810.

No. 1643 is a well–known table belonging to the Metropolitan Museum of Art. It is called a "mixing" table because the two compartments with knobs are for bottles and the flat surface under the curved tambour top is of marble. This covered table is generally shown with the tambour top up in order to show the table open, but here the tambour top is down, because the chief interest is in the design as a whole. The elegant satinwood inlay on the tapering legs resembles the inlay on the Baltimore card tables Nos. 1487–1490. This table is in the Hepplewhite style, with some features suggesting the Sheraton style especially the ornamental features. About 1800–1810.

It is said that No. 1644, also the property of the same Museum, was made by Duncan Phyfe and called a "library" table. In England it would be called a "Canterbury" table, meaning a small table with drawer and shelves. It is referred to in section 164 on library tables, note 1. The upper portion has a large drawer, with lion–and–ring handles, and is supported at each end by two carved columns which rest upon trestle feet similar in form to those in the sofa table No. 1424 and others. The two shelves have reeded edges. About 1800–1810.

No. 1645 is called a "book" table because when both drop–leaves are down it is in the shape of a book with a narrow back above and leaves below. The two large drop–leaves are attached to a round horizontal piece about four inches in diameter which is the only "top" of the table when the leaves are down. Under each leaf are two swinging brackets which support the leaf when raised. A solid pedestal in a lyre form supports the upper portion and rests upon a platform with four short legs. The Empire style will be recognized in the pedestal, the carving and the legs. About 1825–1835.

No. 1646 is a table in the late Empire style. The large curved drawer is finely veneered and the corners of the skirt are rounded as in the bureau No. 768

1641 (Upper) Mr. & Mrs. Richard L. Cary.
1643 (Centre) Metropolitan Museum of Art.
1645 (Lower) Mrs. J. P. Pleasants.

1642 (Upper) Mr. & Mrs. Edward H. McKeon.
1644 (Centre) Metropolitan Museum of Art.
1646 (Lower) Mr. H. Oliver Thompson.

and the bookcase No. 875. The pedestal is very large and heavy. In this illustration are shown clearly two cylindrical forms, reeded at the ends, near the lower end of the pedestal, which are of the same character as those shown on a smaller scale on the card tables Nos. 1542 and 1552. The feet are of the trestle type and the newly developing heaviness in furniture design was clearly evident in this pre–Victorian table.

Mention should be made of "pier tables"[1] and "console tables." As stated in reference to "pier mirrors," in section 139, near the end, the word "pier" is an architectural one meaning a wall space between two windows; and it was the fashion throughout the eighteenth century to place a "pier table" against the wall in a "pier," with a "pier glass" behind it, the pier table and the pier glass together producing a handsome effect. Large and highly ornamental pier tables were designed by Robert Adam, and in the books of Hepplewhite[2] and Sheraton[3] are elaborate drawings for these tables in their respective styles, often to be painted on the top. Some of these designs show semi–circular tables and others almost rectangular ones.

In our country the use of pier tables and pier mirrors in combination between windows was of course not as general as in England;[4] but in many cases, no doubt, side tables were placed under mirrors and were called "pier tables"; but such tables do not often appear to be of any special elegance nor made particularly for use under a mirror.

Many side tables have been referred to in books and magazine articles as pier tables on the supposition that they were made or used as such tables. The finest American example now known is said to be the Philadelphia–made side table known as the "Cadwalader table" which is illustrated as a "side" table in No. 1430; and perhaps some of the other side tables may have been made or used as pier tables, including the Empire style tables Nos. 1651–1653 in this section. The presence of a marble top should not of itself be regarded as indicating a pier table, because a marble top was often used, for example, on serving tables, as in Nos. 1441 and 1442. The English pier tables were taller than card tables, being about thirty-eight inches in height, and should not be confused with console

1. A pier table is defined in the Century Dictionary as "an ornamental table intended to stand between two windows. . . It is often combined with a pier–glass and the glass is sometimes carried down below the top of the table and between its uprights." Mr. Cescinsky in "English and American Furniture," glossary, page 295, defines a pier glass as "a wall mirror hanging between windows, usually above a semi–circular or pier table." These mirrors were often very tall and extended below the top of the table, in which case the top of the table was reflected in the mirror. If the table was semi–circular, it and its reflection produced the appearance of a round table. See the comment on the card table No. 1504.

2. In Hepplewhite's "Guide," (as to which see section 17), third edition, page 12, it is said that "pier tables are made to fit the pier and rise level with or above the dado of the room."

3. In the Appendix to Sheraton's "Drawing Book," (as to which see section 18), plate 4, page 371, it is said "as pier tables are merely for ornament under a glass, they are generally made very light, and the style of finishing them is rich and elegant. Sometimes the tops are solid marble, but most commonly veneered in rich satinwood."

4. In Mr. Lockwood's "Colonial Furniture," volume 2, a marble top table is illustrated, page 224, which resembles to some extent the table mentioned in the text above, and it is said that "a few specimens are found in this country."

1647 (UPPER) MISS HELEN H. CAREY.   1648 (UPPER) MRS. W. D. STEUART.
1649 (CENTRE) MRS. ARTHUR HALE.   1650 (CENTRE) MRS. WM. DEFORD.
1651 (LOWER) MR. & MRS. CHARLES H. WYATT.   1652 (LOWER) MISS MARY LEIGH BROWN.

tables.[5] This is a point even the advanced collector has been known to overlook.

The next three tables, Nos. 1647–1649, are in the French Empire style, which is shown by the rounded front of the skirt, the round columns serving as legs, the heavy shelves, and the large animals' brass or gilded claw feet—the latter being the only objectionable feature of these dignified and well proportioned pieces These tables are side tables, made to stand against a wall, either in a room or in a hallway, as are the side tables in section 166. The wood is mahogany.

No. 1647 is a case where the Empire style is seen in all parts of the table—the rounded skirt, the large round columns, the large claw feet and the somewhat coarse carving. About 1810–1830.

No. 1648 is very similar to the preceding table, except that it has a heavy recessed platform or shelf and a marble top. In the Empire period many tables were made with marble tops and their presence does not indicate that the table was made as a serving table or as a pier table. The columns taper upwards and terminate in scrolls with carved and gilded leaves. About 1810–1830.

In No. 1649, also with a marble top, the two rounded columns have brass caps on the upper ends and smaller ones on the base. A shelf, with brackets under the ends, is set back from the line of the front, and a mirror is at the rear in a wooden frame. About 1810–1830.

Nos. 1650–1652 are also French tables of a type which was popular in our country in the early part of the nineteenth century. These tables are made of fine mahogany. The first two are decorated with brass designs, and the third is painted on the top as well as on the lower portion.

No. 1650 is a round table with a top supported by four pairs of round columns which rest upon a heavy platform with concave sides. Each of the four feet is in the form of the Egyptian sphinx, a favorite design following the conquest of Egypt by Napoleon in 1798, an interesting feature of which is referred to in section 64, note 1. About 1810–1820.

No. 1651 is an elaborate table, in much the same general form as No. 1649. The upper portion is supported by two large white marble columns, with brass capitals, resting upon a concave platform, or shelf, under which are large brass decorations of scrolls and flowers. The feet, also, are of brass. In the rear is a large mirror with a small one on each side. About 1810–1820.

5. In the Century Dictionary the term "console table" is defined as "a table which, instead of straight or nearly straight legs, has consoles or legs so curved as to resemble them, and is therefore usually set against the wall from which it appears to project as a sort of bracket." Mr. Cescinsky in "English and American Furniture," page 196, refers to tables of "the console type where the framing of the top is supported on front legs only, being secured at the back" to a wall. The same meaning is given in Macquoid and Edwards' "Dictionary of English Furniture," volume 3, page 254, in the Encyclopædia Britannica and in Murray's Dictionary.

The reader may have noticed a tendency in this book to be over–particular in regard to the exact meaning of various words; but the writer thinks that this caution may be helpful in avoiding confusion of thought and a misunderstanding of the subject. For example, we should surely know the exact difference between a "pier table" and a "console table," as established by the authorities on the English language. Calling a semi–circular table with four legs a "console table," as is often done, is obviously erroneous, although it may be a common usage.

In No. 1652 the round top is fully decorated with paintings, those in the centre being surrounded by a circle of flowers. On other parts, especially in the base, are several forms and designs which have been seen on other pieces, such as the card table No. 1553. The designs on these two tables include the favorite Grecian "anthemion," or honeysuckle, which appears on the centre of the base of the pedestal, and also the several forms resembling "corbels" which we have seen in illustration No. 1231. This table may be compared with No. 1628, a drum table. About 1810–1820.

Section 175. Advice to amateur collectors.—In almost all books on antique furniture the writers have thought it necessary, or at least proper, to give to the reader a chapter of well–meaning advice on how not to make mistakes in the purchase of articles said to be antique[1] and how to take care[2] of them if they are purchased. It is hoped that in the purchase of articles offered for sale as genuine antiques the readers of this book may be assisted by the advice in this section. The advice is plainly expressed and for convenience of reference the paragraphs are numbered.

The items of advice here presented to the amateur collector are meant as suggestions of some things to do and some things not to do in the fascinating pursuit of antique furniture. These items are all taken from serious books or magazine articles or from personal experiences of the writer and others.

1. Read all you can about the article in which you are specially interested at the time. No one can appreciate an article of antique furniture or realize what

1. In Mr. Nobili's "The gentle art of faking," pages 172–175, is a story of an Italian dealer and his skill in evading the Italian law which forbids the exportation of works of art from Italy without permission of the authorities and the payment of a tax. The dealer entered the Export Office with several antique bas–reliefs of a noted artist and handed his documents to the inspector, who examined the bas–reliefs and stated that being antiques they could not be exported. The dealer then scraped a piece of plaster from the apparently antique back of one of the pieces and showed that the plaster was new and was stamped with the name of a prominent Italian factory. The dealer said that the pieces were to go to America and that the smart Americans were fooled in believing they were getting antiques. The inspector then approved the shipment and did not discover that all the other bas–reliefs were genuine old antiques.

In the English books the subject of fakes and faking is plainly discussed and fakers are called fakers; in the American books, magazines and newspapers there seems to be some hesitation in calling a spade a spade. No American book has been published on "The Gentle Art of Faking Furniture," which is the title of a book by Mr. Cescinsky; nor has the book of Mr. Nobili, entitled "The Gentle Art of Faking" been widely circulated.

In the third volume of Mr. Wallace Nutting's "Furniture Treasury," the subject of "Pitfalls for the collector" occupies pages 262–272; and on pages 127–135 "The Art of Collecting" and "Method of Collecting" are considered.

2. As to the care of antique furniture, referring both to cabinet work and to the use of polishes or other preparations, the best printed advice is "Do not try to do the work yourself," unless you are experienced in such work; this refers to all kinds of decoration including gilding and painting; but if you prefer to try to repair or restore any of your antique furniture without trained help, consult the book referred to in section 10, note 1, entitled "Knowing, collecting and restoring early American furniture," by Mr. Henry Hammond Taylor, published in 1930 by J. B. Lippincott Company, Philadelphia. This book may assist you but will not make you a cabinet maker.

is fine and valuable and what is not, unless he knows something of the principal furniture periods and styles. Read this book, which is intended to give the information in a pleasing way; but if you do not find the subject interesting as here presented, get the smaller book entitled "Furniture of the Olden Time" by Miss Frances Clary Morse and read it.

2. Get fixed in your mind's eye, by examining the illustrations, the characteristic features of one or two articles, such as chairs or tables, during each of the furniture periods. When these features are once learned, you will never forget them and will be able to recognize them in other articles of the same periods.

3. Besides book learning, study real antiques in the homes of friends and acquaintances, and in museums and other collections. Almost every one who owns antiques, especially if they are family pieces, is glad to show them to others who are really interested.

4. Collect American furniture only, as advised in section 8 of this book. To put it the other way—do not collect foreign furniture; first, because we are Americans, and we naturally are more concerned in American things; second, because fine American furniture is as fine as European in many respects, although generally not so elaborate; third, because foreign furniture brought to America for sale here is often likely to be faked; fourth, because the value of American antique furniture will probably increase in value as the years pass by, whereas European furniture has a more settled standard of price and may not rise in value so readily. Alleged antique furniture has been imported in great quantities from England and is offered in many shops, but real and fine American antiques are not plentiful.

5. Buy things in the rough rather than in a new condition. If repairs or restorations are necessary, have them made by your own cabinet maker, if he is experienced in working on antique furniture. If you buy things that have been skilfully restored and refinished for the purpose of sale, it is almost impossible for an amateur to know what parts of the article are original and what are new. This is especially true of gilded looking glasses. If you buy things in the rough you will have the satisfaction of seeing exactly what you pay for.

6. If you think of buying a piece of furniture which is not in the rough, always ask the owner, whether he is a dealer or not, what repairs and restorations have been made, and whether they were made by him or by some one else.

7. Examine in a bright light the inside and underside, as well as the outside, of anything you wish to buy. If the article is genuine, the owner will not object to the closest scrutiny. Moreover, it is well to carry with you a magnifying glass.

8. If you are a little doubtful about an article which is offered to you as a genuine antique, but you decide to buy it, you should require the seller to give you a written guarantee that it is genuine. The following form is legally binding when written on the bill and signed by the seller when the price is paid: "Received payment in full for the above article and for my guarantee, which I hereby give, that the said article is a genuine antique throughout, and if it is not, I will refund the purchase money on demand and return of the article."

9. Before buying an article about which you have serious doubt, have it examined for you by some one who is really an expert, preferably a cabinet maker

or dealer of high standing and long experience with antique furniture. His fee may be trifling in comparison with the benefit to you.

10. If you have a number of articles of considerable value, whether acquired by inheritance or purchase, get an appraisement of them by two well informed persons, either dealers or appraisers. This is for fire insurance purposes and for possible use in the settlement of your estate. The appraisers' fees may be money well spent. Some of your things may have increased in value and others may have declined.

11. Do not buy a piece of antique furniture for yourself unless you have use for it in your home or elsewhere. Antique furniture should be bought for use or for its artistic interest, or both. Moreover, do not buy things which are too large for your rooms, for example, a bookcase which almost touches the ceiling. Also do not buy things which are not in themselves attractive. Mere age does not generally make articles of furniture attractive. Antique furniture which was crude and ugly when made is still crude and ugly now, and ought not to be in the home, although perhaps allowable in a museum in order to show changes of styles.

12. Do not buy any article of antique furniture unless its style is that of one of the recognized periods of American cabinet making. The history of furniture has been minutely studied and the styles are well known and are illustrated in many books. Articles in any of the antique styles, and made within the period, are valuable even though they are in a transition state; articles not made in one of such styles are not worth collecting. They may be desirable in a great museum, but not in your home. The amateur collector should confine himself to the established styles and periods; otherwise he will find himself possessed of a lot of junk.

13. Do not esteem "rarity" too highly. If the shape of a chair is unusual, the chair may be rare, but it does not follow that it is valuable. It may have been merely an experiment, an oddity; or it may have been made on the order of a customer who had a queer fancy. One may say "I never saw a chair like that in all my experience; it is a very rare piece." It may indeed be rare, but the reason for its rarity may be because few persons wanted chairs like that and there was little sale for them, and therefore only a few were made. Of course if Chippendale himself had made the chair it would be valuable, because anything that Chippendale made would now be valuable; but if not made by a well-known cabinet maker, the chair, in spite of its rarity, would be an almost worthless freak. It is well said that the rarity now desired is that of quality, not of kind.

14. Do not buy an alleged article of antique furniture that is offered at a low price compared with the price elsewhere, unless you are very sure of what you will get. Dealers generally know what real antiques are worth and a very low price may be an indication that something is wrong.

15. Do not be influenced by lively bidding at an auction sale. The owner of the article may have his agent bidding against you, running it up. At some auction sales the articles are chiefly those of dealers or other owners who cannot get rid of them in their shops or homes.

16. Unless there is a positive advertisement or statement by the auctioneer that an article is a genuine antique the purchaser has no redress if it should turn out

to be a fake. The Latin legal phrase "Caveat emptor" controls, meaning "let the purchaser beware."

17. Do not pay as much for a veneered mahogany article as for a solid mahogany one. Veneer was and is made in thin strips which are sold by the yard. A veneered mahogany article may have a brilliant color, and show a fine grain, but its value never was, and is not now, equal to one made of the solid wood. You may know a veneered table by looking at the under side; if the wood and grain underneath is different from that on the surface, the surface is probably veneered. See section 32 as to veneer.

18. Do not make a new piece of furniture out of parts of one of a different kind nor change one piece into another. We sometimes find the heavy legs and other parts of a piano supporting a table; or a washstand converted into a telephone stand or a bedside table. A vase may no doubt be properly fitted with lighting appliances, or a necklace may be made into a bracelet; but we cannot make a decent new article of furniture out of an old one of a different kind. Any new article created in this manner is unworthy of a place in the home of a collector of fine antiques.

19. Do not paint an article of antique furniture if it was made without paint. The natural color of the wood may have been lost but an experienced cabinet maker will know what to do.

20. If you are fully satisfied with the antiquity of a certain article and it suits you exactly, buy it, as you may never find another. But if you are in doubt as to the desirability of the article, decide against it and you will not be obliged to explain to your visitors why you bought it. A dealer may buy such pieces without hesitation because he will probably have other customers who are not so well informed.

Query. In many books and magazines the writers relate with glee their purchases from ignorant country people at a small fraction of the real values. If a collector is offered a chair for five dollars which he knows to be worth fifty, what is the honorable thing for him to do? Legally he need not pay the owner more than the owner asks, nor need he tell the owner that it is worth more—but how can any collector of antiques be proud of taking advantage of the ignorance of some poor old man or woman? One writer mentions that having discovered in a farm building the ball and claw feet of a chair protruding from the top of a wood pile, he almost lost his balance in his efforts to get it; and states that "with the duplicity learned in years of collecting" he concealed his emotions until the chair had been secured.

INDEX

References are to pages unless otherwise specified

References are to pages unless otherwise specified

References are to pages unless otherwise specified

References are to pages unless otherwise specified

References are to pages unless otherwise specified

References are to pages unless otherwise specified

References are to pages unless otherwise specified

References are to pages unless otherwise specified

References are to pages unless otherwise specified

References are to pages unless otherwise specified

References are to pages unless otherwise specified

References are to pages unless otherwise specified

References are to pages unless otherwise specified

References are to pages unless otherwise specified

References are to pages unless otherwise specified

References are to pages unless otherwise specified